RHS GARDEN FINDER 2007-2008

EDITOR: CHARLES QUEST-RITSON

THINK BOOKS

THINK
BOOKS

A Think Book

First published in Great Britain in 2007 by
Think Publishing
The Pall Mall Deposit
124-128 Barlby Road, London W10 6BL
www.think-books.com

Published in association with
Royal Horticultural Society
80 Vincent Square, London SW1P 2PE
www.rhs.org.uk

Distributed in the United States and Canada by:
Sterling Publishing Co., Inc.
387 Park Avenue South, New York, NY 10016-8810

Managing Editors: Emma Jones and Simon Maughan
Sub Editors: Rica Dearman and Marion Thompson
Designer: Lou Millward
Picture Research by Tania Adams

Maps produced by JP Map Graphics

A CIP catalogue record for this book is available from the British Library.

ISBN-10: 1-84525-018-4
ISBN-13: 978-1-84525-018-8

Printed and bound in Italy by Printer Trento.

Main cover image: Anna Halm Schudel / Flowerphotos.com
Additional images: Front cover, left to right: Toddington Manor, Sissinghurst, Lydney Park.
Back cover, from top: Ventnor, Felley Priory, Cawdor Castle, East Lambrook, Birr Castle.
Spine: Dalemain.

CONTENTS

KEY TO SYMBOLS

Parking available	Dogs permitted
Toilet facilities	Access for the disabled
Plants for sale	Gift Shop
Restaurant	Light refreshments

RHS, THE UK'S LEADING GARDENING CHARITY

The RHS believes that horticulture and gardening enrich people's lives. We are committed to bringing the personal and social benefits of growing plants to a diverse audience of all ages, to enhance understanding and appreciation of cultivated plants, and to provide contact with the natural world.

We believe that good practice in horticulture and gardening in both private and public spaces is a vital component of healthy sustainable communities and the creation of long-term environmental improvements.

The RHS has four gardens around the UK: Wisley in Surrey, Hyde Hall in Essex, Rosemoor in Devon and Harlow Carr in North Yorkshire, as well as over 100 partner gardens. It runs some of the best flower shows in the world and is a world leader in horticultural science and libraries. The RHS runs education and outreach programmes across the UK to help people realise their potential.

Its charitable activities include:

- Helping over 600,000 children a year through hands-on opportunities for children to grow plants and learn about the natural environment
- Encouraging sustainable horticulture and environmental care
- Promoting biodiversity and creating wildlife habitats at its gardens

- Providing expert gardening advice
- Running the RHS Award of Garden Merit scheme to help gardeners choose plants that perform well
- Undertaking scientific research into issues affecting gardeners
- Educating and training gardeners of all levels and experience
- Maintaining the Lindley Library, the finest horticultural library in the world

The RHS relies heavily on donations and sponsorship to help enhance people's lives through gardening. For every pound received from its members' subscriptions, the charity needs to raise more than twice as much again to fund its charitable work.

While the charity receives some income from garden operations, flower shows, shops and plant centres, support from donors and sponsors is vital to its mission to bring the benefits of gardening to all.

INDEX OF GARDENS FREE TO MEMBERS OF THE RHS

For gardens that are open to RHS members at selected times of year only in your county, please visit www.rhs.org.uk/rhsgardenfinder/gardenfinder.asp

INTRODUCTION

The Gardens

Welcome to the new edition of the *RHS Garden Finder 2007–2008*. This is a companion volume to the *RHS Plant Finder*. The *RHS Plant Finder* tells you where to find the right nurseries for plants: the *RHS Garden Finder 2007–2008* will tell you where to see the same plants growing in gardens that are open to the public. We list nearly 100 new gardens and, for the first time, have colour photographs throughout the book.

The aim of this book is to supply sufficient detail to enable readers to decide if and when to plan a visit. The list is not exhaustive. It offers a selection of the different types of garden that are open to the public: ancient and modern, large and small, public and private. We welcome suggestions for additions, deletions or alterations to entries (please email us at questritson@aol.com). All major gardens which are open regularly are listed as a matter of course. These include many gardens of the National Trust and the National Trust for Scotland as well as botanic and public gardens and those attached to stately homes. But many gardens do not open to visitors regularly: the National Gardens Scheme lists over 3,000. In this book you will find a selection of these gardens which open only once a year or by appointment: if a good garden is seldom open, it is all the more important to know when the opportunity to see it will arise. This book also concentrates upon gardens with plants: some of the great historic gardens of the 18th century have comparatively brief descriptions, because their landscapes are rather short on horticultural content. The same is true of modern gardens that are over-designed and under-planted; we have omitted some whose standards of maintenance are poor. On the other hand, some of the best gardens are those which have large 'living collections' of plants for teaching purposes – botanic gardens, and those attached to horticultural colleges. They may be weak on history and design, but they are often among the most interesting for plant-lovers to visit.

Members of the RHS enjoy free entry to many gardens throughout the British Isles. Some are free throughout the year: others for only a month or so. It is important that members should note carefully when they may expect free entry and when they may not. In most gardens the privilege applies only to members of the RHS, not to any guests who accompany them. Nevertheless, it is an impressive list and a major benefit of membership. The list has grown considerably in recent years, and the Society hopes to expand it yet further.

The Nurseries

Because this book is plant-led, it also includes about 80 leading nurseries. Almost all have a demonstration garden attached to them, just as most gardens have a nursery or plant stall. This is a recent development – it started about 25 years ago – but is now quite normal: visitors to a nursery like to see plants growing in a garden before making their purchases, and visitors to a garden like the opportunity to buy some of the plants they have seen there. It would not be right to exclude the inspirational series of model gardens at Barnsdale in Leicestershire or the National Garden Exhibition Centre in Co. Wicklow just because they are attached to a commercial enterprise that sells plants. And nurseries like Mallet Court in Somerset, The Vernon Geranium Nursery in Surrey and

Kathleen Muncaster Fuchsias in Lincolnshire are fascinating to visitors who are interested in plants.

How to use this book

Gardens are listed by county or region (for Scotland), and then alphabetically by name. The order is England, Scotland, Wales, Channel Islands, Northern Ireland and the Republic of Ireland. In general, we have stuck to the familiar 1974 counties of England and Wales and to the Scottish regional divisions. There are three exceptions: the county of Avon has been redistributed between Gloucestershire and Somerset, Cleveland has been included with North Yorkshire, and Humberside has been split between Lincolnshire and the East Riding of Yorkshire. We have also divided Hereford & Worcester into its two component parts again. We have been careful to ensure, so far as possible, that gardens are listed in the county or region in which they actually lie, which is not always the county or region their postal addresses suggest, or where their owners believe themselves to live. Thus the Savill Garden lies in Surrey, even though most of Windsor Great Park is in Berkshire, and the gardens at Burford House near Tenbury Wells are neither in Herefordshire nor in Worcestershire, but across the border in Shropshire. To find out about a specific garden, turn to the index at the back: it should take you straight to the page you need.

Practical details

Our source for practical information about directions, opening times, admission charges, parking, lavatories, disabled facilities and refreshments has been the owners or their staff, backed up by our own enquiries where appropriate. The accuracy of these details is not guaranteed, but is believed to be correct at the time of going to press. We rely to a great extent on information that has been submitted to us by third parties. Not everyone who was approached has replied – or replied in time – and this explains some gaps. We very much regret having to drop a number of important gardens that have failed to reply to our requests for a 2007 update. A paperless version of the book is online as part of the Royal Horticultural Society's website (www.rhs.org.uk) and updates will be made as and when they are available. Inclusion in this book or on the society's website, or exclusion from either of them, should not be construed as a recommendation or condemnation. And, though this book carries the Royal Horticultural Society's endorsement, its comments and opinions are the editor's, and his alone.

Contacting gardens

In order to assist readers with special needs, or those hoping to arrange a group visit by special appointment, we list the telephone and fax numbers to which enquiries should be directed. In many cases this is the private telephone line of the owners: readers are urged to respect their privacy. If telephone and fax numbers have been omitted, this is because the owners prefer to receive such requests by letter.

Websites

Almost all gardens and nurseries regularly open to the public have dedicated internet sites. Many are beautifully designed and extremely informative. They help to attract visitors, especially groups from gardening clubs and tour operators, and they are worth consulting before you set out to make a visit to check that the information in this guide has not changed. Please remember that website addresses sometimes change for no obvious reason. We have checked all the hundreds in this book during the late autumn of 2006 and have only included those which are up and running and seem to us to offer useful information. Many websites are of excellent quality: some of the nursery sites permit online ordering. Others exist only as registered names: we have omitted them.

Visiting times

Many gardens are attached to other attractions – most typically, a house, which is also open to the public. The visiting times we have given relate only to the garden. Please remember that most gardens have a last admission time. Typically it will be 30 or 45 minutes before they close, but it can be much longer. Remember, too, that a pre-booked group can often make a visit at a time or season when the garden is not open to individual visitors.

Prices

As with times, so with prices. The admission prices we have given relate only to the garden. If the house or some other attraction is open at the same time, a supplement may be payable. Some owners insist on you buying a full ticket (notably the Tussauds Group at Alton Towers and Warwick Castle and the National Trust at Clandon Park), though most are more reasonable. It is true that some gardens may seem rather expensive but, generally speaking, the market rules of supply and demand apply and you get what you pay for. And it should be said that for every garden that is over-priced there are 10 inspirational plantsman's gardens, run by their owners on a strictly non-commercial basis, where you can be certain of wonderful flowers, good design and a genuine welcome.

Many gardens offer special rates to groups and, if details are not given, it may be worth asking whether a reduction is available and what minimum number is acceptable. Please remember, however, that not all gardens permit parties: popular gardens that already suffer from wear and tear may not welcome increased visitor numbers. Special rates for families are sometimes available, especially at larger gardens attached to stately homes, where the garden is only one of many entertainments offered to the visitor. There are endless permutations on the numbers of adults and/or children that constitute a 'family' and the age at which a child becomes an adult and has to pay the full entry price. Season tickets are sometimes available, and good value for people who live near a large garden or stately home.

Entrance fees vary, and a few owners have told us that they may increase fees in the middle of the season. Some have a high season for a month or so – like Exbury in Hampshire and Leonardslee in West Sussex in spring. Others have a special day of the week or open days for charity when the entrance fee is higher. A few owners had not yet fixed their 2007 times or admission charges by the time we went to press and we have therefore indicated that the times or prices quoted are for 2006. All entrance fees are, in any event, liable to be changed: visitors would do well to take more money than they think they will need. Some gardens have honesty boxes, and it is also important to take lots of change, so that you are not forced to choose between paying too much and paying too little.

A number of National Trust properties have asked us to mention that their entrance fee includes a voluntary donation, typically of around 10%. Visitors can, however, choose to pay the standard admission price which is displayed at the property and in its brochures, guidebooks and website. Readers are strongly recommended to join the National Trust in any event: members are usually admitted free and its portfolio of blue chip gardens is so comprehensive that no garden tour is complete without a visit to one or more of its properties.

Facilities

This guide uses a variety of symbols to show whether a garden has such facilities as public conveniences or plants for sale. We have indicated whether parking is available: this may be at the garden itself or on a public road very close to it. Parking may be at some distance from the house. At Saltram, in Devon, it is 500 yards away, and this is by no means exceptional. You can however expect better parking facilities at a popular property which offers a wide range of entertainments than at a small plantsman's garden in a country lane.

It is often a condition of admission that no photograph taken within the garden may be sold or used for public reproduction without the consent of the property owner. Some forbid photography altogether. Corporate owners like the National Trust or English Heritage do not welcome dogs at their properties, except guide dogs. Some restrict dogs to particular areas of a property, like the car park, or the woods and parkland rather than the garden proper. Private owners are generally better disposed, though visitors should remember to keep their dogs on leads. A few owners – like the Howards at Castle Howard – go out of their way to say that dogs are actually welcome, but not all have shaded areas for parking.

Disabled visitors

We have generally indicated which gardens are suitable for disabled people, though it is important to stress that access may only be partial. Often an area around the house or entrance is accessible for people in wheelchairs, but the more remote parts of the garden are quite unsuitable. It is best to ring before your visit to check. The same is true of other disabled facilities. We have not specified the nature of those facilities, but in most cases it includes lavatories and ramps that are suitable for the wheelchair-bound. It is best to enquire in advance of a visit if particular items of special equipment are required. The National Trust is especially good at adapting its properties to accommodate the needs of disabled visitors.

Size of gardens

We have asked owners to indicate the size of their garden and the number of people who work in it. Taken together, these two statistics help to suggest how intensively a garden is worked and how long you need to allow for your visit. The number of gardeners must be interpreted flexibly. Some owners have told us how many paid gardeners they employ: others have included their own contributions and based their figure on how much time they and their family give to the garden.

The NCCPG

Four common abbreviations are used freely throughout the text: RHS for the Royal Horticultural Society, NGS for the National Gardens Scheme, SGS for Scotland's Gardens Scheme, and NCCPG for the National Council for the Conservation of Plants and Gardens. We have noted the NCCPG National Collections that are held at the gardens and nurseries we list, and we have supplied a separate index of them towards the end of the book. Not all genera are the subject of a National Collection: there are still some horticulturally important groups of plants that have not yet been seriously collected and studied under the auspices of the NCCPG. Other genera have been split into a number of different collections. This is particularly necessary in the case of such a large genus as *Rhododendron* or those, like *Euphorbia*, that require a great variety of growing conditions. Moreover, the NCCPG has wisely introduced a system of duplicate collections to insure against the risks that face every collection of rare plants. The need to maintain duplicate collections and split large genera explains why certain names occur several times in the list of National Collections towards the end of the book. The list of National Collections on the NCCPG website (www.nccpg.com) is updated fairly regularly.

Champion trees

For most gardens, we give a brief list of features. These include general information like 'good collection of trees' and more specific facts like 'tallest *Quercus cerris* in the UK'. Occasionally we have added some features that are not strictly plants, but do add enormously to the character of a garden. Information about outsize trees is taken principally from the records kept by that excellent organisation the Tree Register of the British Isles (see www.tree register.org). There are two ways of measuring trees: height and girth. Sometimes the tallest specimen will also have the thickest trunk – but not always. Both the tallest and the biggest can claim to be the champion tree, and we have sometimes made this distinction when noting record-breakers in gardens. Tree measurements can never be fully up to date: some records have not been verified since the great gales of 1987 and 1990.

2006

Many garden owners regarded 2006 as a fairly good year for visitors and are hopeful for 2007. This is especially true for owners who advertise widely and can offer other attractions, in addition to visiting their gardens. There is no doubt, however, that garden visiting is meeting stiff competition for visitors' time and money; a few owners of some of our most distinguished gardens told us that their visitor numbers were markedly down in 2006. Some owners are extending their open season – several now open only when the snowdrops are in flower – while others cram the calendar with events of every kind, which rather change the nature of a visit for garden-lovers. For many such gardens the cost of employing extra staff to offer refreshments, and maintain plant sales and gift shops is uneconomic. Even with these facilities, which members of the public expect and should increase their spending, a large garden needs at least 40,000 visitors a year to remain profitably open throughout the season.

Events

In addition to its Free Access gardens, the Royal Horticultural Society runs lectures at a number of nurseries and garden centres, most of which are listed in this book, with a note of how to find out further details. The Society's own *Members' Handbook 2007* and website (www.rhs.org.uk) give full details of these and of the many lectures, demonstrations, workshops, garden walks and other events held at RHS Partner Colleges.

Acknowledgements

The editor is very grateful to the many people who have helped in the compilation of this work. First and foremost he thanks all the garden owners, nurseries, horticulturists, colleges, societies and everyone else who has responded to his requests for information. He is greatly indebted to them, and regrets that it is not always possible to give each the personal attention that is their due. Particular thanks go to the staff in the regional offices of the National Trust. Special thanks are also due to Ian Buckley, Brent Elliott, Ali Higgs, Geoff Hodge, Caroline Houlden, Simon Maughan and our colleagues at Think Publishing. Finally, thanks are due for their endeavours to Brigid and Madeline Quest-Ritson and Christopher and Katharine Blair.

Charles Quest-Ritson, Editor
The RHS Garden Finder, PO Box 673, Salisbury, Wiltshire SP3 4BU
questritson@aol.com

GARDENS TO VISIT

ENGLAND

Gardens and gardening are English interests. England has always taken the lead in horticultural matters within the British Isles, and gardening is one of our most important cultural, artistic and scientific exports. Amateur gardening is probably at its strongest as a national pursuit in the south-east of the country, where more than half the Royal Horticultural Society's members live. But there are good gardens of every kind open to the public in every part of the country. In fact they are also fairly evenly distributed throughout England, except perhaps for the East Midlands, which has fewer good gardens than its rich agriculture might suggest. Within England there are differences of garden emphasis and style between regions. Alpine gardening has many followers in the North of England; Cornish gardens tend to be rhododendron woodland gardens; the smart designers tend to practise in and around London. Gardens and garden making depend as much upon social and economic circumstances as upon soil and climate.

A word about the grading of historic gardens is needed. During the 1980s, English Heritage's predecessors compiled a register of gardens and parks of special historic interest. There are three gradings, each of which assesses the historic layout, features and architectural ornaments. Grade I parks and gardens are 'of exceptional interest'; Grade II* parks and gardens are 'of great quality'; Grade II parks and gardens are 'of special interest'. The register is in 46 parts, one for each of the 1974 English counties, and copies are available from English Heritage. The information they contain about the individual gardens is very comprehensive. It covers the site, area, dates and designers of key surviving elements, surviving features of the garden or park, and other interesting aspects such as historic associations.

The starting point for visiting gardens must be the National Gardens Scheme's list of gardens of England and Wales open to the public, now officially entitled *The Yellow Book*, its nickname for many years past. *The Yellow Book* is a bestseller. Its sales immediately after publication in mid-February exceed 5,000 copies per week, three times the success rate of its nearest rival among bestselling paperback reference books. It is wonderfully comprehensive and totally undiscriminating. The owners write their own garden entries, with the result that a really good garden may come across as self-deprecatingly boring, while an exciting description can often lead to disappointment. Beware of self-publicists: you can usually spot the hype. *The Yellow Book* lists over 3,500 gardens, including 450 new ones for 2007; it is the single most important guide to visiting gardens in England and Wales and, at £7.99, the least expensive.

BEDFORDSHIRE

Both the Grade I gardens in Bedfordshire – Woburn Abbey and Wrest Park – are open to the public. Few of its other important gardens remain open to visitors, though every garden visitor should seek out the gloriously eccentric Swiss Garden (Grade II*). The headquarters of the Royal Society for the Protection of Birds, The Lodge at Sandy, is also rated as a Grade II garden and open daily throughout the year. Shuttleworth College at Old Warden is now a RHS Partner College, but Bedfordshire is otherwise horticulturally underdeveloped. It is not over-endowed with arboreta, though Woburn has a fine collection of trees: there are a number of record-breakers there, as well as at Swiss Garden, Toddington Manor and Wrest Park. Surprisingly few private gardens open for the National Gardens Scheme and the county has no National Collections. There are few nurseries, too: best known is Blom's Bulbs at Melchbourne, close to the border with Northamptonshire, but it is not open to visitors. One para-horticultural curiosity worth seeing is the 'Tree Cathedral' near Whipsnade Zoo.

THE MANOR HOUSE

Church Road, Stevington, Bedford MK43 7QB

Tel 01234 822064
www.kathybrownsgarden.homestead.com
Location 5 miles north-west of Bedford, off A428
Opening hours 10.30am to 3pm, 10 and 11 February; 2pm to 6pm, 27 May, 24 June (NGS) and 29 July; groups at other times by appointment
Admission fee Adults £4 (£3.50 in February); children free

This is a very interesting newish garden – the owners moved here in 1991 and have designed and planted it with a sense of style that is contemporary rather than nostalgic. Kathy Brown is a garden writer and cookery writer, and these interests have overlapped in such titles as *The Edible Flower Garden* (1999). But she has also written books about container gardening, bulbs and cottage gardening – all of which have to some extent been worked out in the garden here. She is very good on structure: the French garden is an essay in formal design. It starts right outside the house, with a terrace that has a *gâteau* of tiles and stone at its centre: box cones and gravelled parterres lead down to a circular fountain. Planting is another of her skills: the containers are exuberantly filled with all kinds of unconventional material including long-term succulents and other exotics. Elsewhere are masses of bulbs, some for winter and spring and many for summer display. Ninety late-flowering clematis extend the season alongside rambling and climbing roses. Grasses, stems, bark and bulbs give interest throughout the winter months. Gazebos, pergolas, a parterre leading to a wildflower meadow with a prairie planting of grasses at the centre, a cottage garden and a wisteria walk are among the many other features. The latest designs are a grass garden inspired by Barbara Hepworth's *Green Caves* and a topiary garden derived from Mark Rothko's abstract expressionism. Hokusai, Kandinsky and Mondrian are other influences that have been responsible for new features. Definitely a garden to see now and return to in future, as it develops.

good modern design; bulbs; old roses; clematis; wildflower meadow; containers; succulents; grasses; cream teas; soup in winter

Owned by Simon and Kathy Brown
Number of gardeners owners only
Size 1.8ha (4½ acres)

SWISS GARDEN

Old Warden, Biggleswade SG18 9EA

Tel 01767 627927
www.shuttleworth.org
Location 1½ miles west of Biggleswade

Opening hours 10am to 5pm (4pm from November to March) daily, all year; closed Christmas week
Admission fee Adults £5; concessions £4; children free

The Swiss Cottage in the Swiss Garden was built in the 1820s for Lord Ongley – the guidebooks call it 'an outstanding example of the Swiss picturesque' – but most of the rustic, Gothic, landscape garden we see today was largely developed by the Shuttleworth family in the 1870s. It is a remarkable relic: a picturesque pleasure ground of winding paths and sinuous waterways, little cast-iron bridges and romantic huts, Pulhamite rockwork and thatched curiosities, quaint kiosks and soaring ironwork arches, gullies and ferneries, vast conifers and cheerful rhododendrons, and an early grotto glasshouse (note the small panes of glass) planted as a fernery. In short – most enjoyable to visit.
picturesque landscape; rhododendrons; Pulhamite grotto; fernery; Swiss Cottage; publications and visitor centre; restaurant at nearby Shuttleworth Collection

Owned by The Shuttleworth Trust
Number of gardeners 2
Size 3.6ha (9 acres)
English Heritage Grade II*

TODDINGTON MANOR
Toddington LU5 6HJ

Tel 01525 872576 **Fax** 01525 874555
www.toddingtonmanor.co.uk
Location M1, Jct 12; first right in village; house just past 30mph sign
Opening hours 11am to 5pm, 28 May (plus 10 other gardens in village); pre-booked group visits welcome from June to mid-July
Admission fee Adults £3.50; children free

This garden is now in its prime, and has been made by the owners since 1979 around some magnificent old trees. It has some excellent features, notably a lime avenue which leads into a cherry walk, and a wonderfully high standard of maintenance. The walled garden has long beds of delphiniums and peonies and a fine garden of herbs (culinary, medicinal and insect-repelling),

The gardens at Toddington Manor

while the double herbaceous border has been extended and is now 100m (328ft) long and 6m (20ft) wide. There is also a good modern rose garden of white and yellow floribundas interplanted with philadelphus. Further away from the house are a wild garden and three small ponds.
woodland walks; roses (mainly old-fashioned); herbs; mature conifers; good herbaceous borders; largest *Tilia* 'Petiolaris' in the British Isles; refreshments for groups

Owned by Sir Neville and Lady Bowman-Shaw
Number of gardeners 1 full-time and 4 part-time
Size 2.4ha (6 acres), plus 8ha (20 acres) of woodland

WOBURN ABBEY
Woburn MK17 9WA

Tel 01525 290333 **Fax** 01525 290271
www.woburnabbey.co.uk
Location 1½ miles from Woburn on A4012
Opening hours 10am to 4pm, daily, 24 March to 2 October
Admission fee Park: £3 per car

Woburn may not have the reputation of being a gardener's garden, but Humphry Repton, who designed the park, considered it one of his finest

Woburn Abbey

achievements. The deer park is home to 10 different types of deer: one is the muntjac deer from China, some of which escaped during World War II and have spread through much of England. Nearer the house are a pinetum and a quercetum (a collection of oaks), cedars, redwoods, huge swamp cypresses and such rarities as mature specimens of the hardy 'rubber tree' *Eucommia ulmoides* and *Acer triflorum*. Elsewhere are lily ponds, fritillaries, wild orchids and masses of naturalised *Narcissus* – more than 100 daffodil cultivars. The private gardens are simple and formal, mainly 19th-century and Italianate, but they include a circular hornbeam maze with a Chinese pavilion at its centre, herbaceous borders, a rose garden, a camellia house, and lots of good statues.
mature conifers; fine collection of trees; deer park; tallest *Zelkova sinica* (17m; 56ft) in the British Isles; shop; lunches and teas

Owned by The Duke of Bedford
Number of gardeners 6
Size 16.8ha (42 acres)
English Heritage Grade I

WREST PARK
Silsoe MK45 4HS

Tel 01525 860152 (weekends)
www.english-heritage.org.uk
Location 3/4 mile east of Silsoe
Opening hours 10am to 6pm (5pm in October), Saturdays and Sundays, April to October
Admission fee Adults £4.50; concessions £3.40; children £2.30; families £11.30

The 'English Versailles' is dominated by a graceful long canal which runs down to the classical domed pavilion built by Thomas Archer in 1710. Capability Brown came here later, but worked around the earlier design. The house came later still, in the 1830s. Many historic garden buildings have survived, some from as far back as the 1730s and others from the 19th century, including the orangery, the Mithraic altar, the bowling-green house and the Chinese temple and bridge. In the walled garden and around the house are a rose garden, bedding displays and glasshouses. In the park are handsome specimen trees, including a fine example of the purple-leaved birch (*Betula pendula* 'Purpurea').
grand parterres; long vistas; largest pink chestnut (*Aesculus* x *carnea*) in the British Isles; gift shop; light refreshments

Owned by English Heritage
Size 36ha (90 acres)
English Heritage Grade I

Autumn at Woburn Abbey

BERKSHIRE

Even in its attenuated post-1974 shape, Berkshire is well provided with good gardens. Few of its great historic gardens and landscapes are open to the public, though Berkshire's only Grade I landscape, Windsor Great Park, is of course open all the time, while Inkpen House and Lutyens's masterpiece Folly Farm (both Grade II*) open for the National Gardens Scheme. There are good specimen trees in Windsor Great Park and the grounds of Eton College. Nurseries are less common than garden centres: Henry Street Garden Centre at Arborfield is one of the more individual ones, with a special line in roses. Berkshire has comparatively few National Collections, though the Crown Estates have no fewer than nine of them at the Savill Gardens and Valley Gardens, just over the border into Surrey.

ENGLEFIELD HOUSE

Englefield, Theale, Reading RG7 5EN

Tel 0118 930 2221 **Fax** 0118 930 3226
Location On A340, 1 mile from M4, Jct 12
Opening hours 10am to 6pm, Mondays, all year, plus Tuesdays to Thursdays from 1 April to 1 November
Admission fee Adults £3; children free

P ♿

The garden at Englefield descends dramatically from the hill above the house through open woodland where mature native trees mix with Victorian conifers. The underplanting was begun in 1936 with advice from Wallace & Barr and has continued ever since. Here are collections of camellias, rhododendrons, eucryphias, acers, magnolias, cornus, davidias, azaleas (many of them the nearly extinct Ghent varieties) and other unusual trees and shrubs. A grotto has lately been built at the top of the stream, lined with a mosaic of pine cones. There are drifts of daffodils and other spring and summer bulbs and wonderful autumn colour. Grey stone balustrades and wide staircases, built in 1860, enclose the lower terraces where there are formal plantings, mixed borders, roses, topiary, wide lawns, water features and small enclosed areas (some lately paved and pebbled).
A children's garden with hidden jets of water from four small statues is fun for younger visitors. A walled kitchen garden has recently been restored to produce many varieties of fruit, vegetables, herbs and flowers. The garden is enclosed by a deer park, with magnificent views over the lake and surrounding countryside.

woodland garden; roses (mainly old-fashioned); rhododendrons and azaleas; daffodils; good herbaceous borders; deer park

Owned by Sir William and Lady Benyon
Number of gardeners 3
Size 3.6ha (9 acres)
English Heritage Grade II

FOXGROVE

Skinners Green, Enborne, Newbury RG14 6RE

Tel 01635 40554
Location On western edge of Skinners Green
Opening hours 10am to 4pm, 16 February for snowdrops; groups welcome by appointment
Admission fee Adults £2; children free

P 🚻 ❁

Foxgrove is a plantsman's garden, linked to Louise Peters' nursery next door: Audrey Vockins is her aunt. Bulbs, alpines and herbaceous plants are Audrey's great interest. The hellebores, crocuses and snowdrops give a great display in early spring. There are good shrubs (including more than 50 daphnes), roses and handsome small trees, too. Louise's nursery (a RHS Partner Nursery) is open from 10am to 5pm from Wednesday to Sunday, but closed in August. It carries an interesting range of hardy and cottage garden plants, including several new *Saxifraga* cultivars from the Czech Republic. Its speciality is snowdrops, which

are sold by mail order 'in the green'. Other specialities – worth visiting the nursery to see – are hellebores, grasses and penstemons, and some newly-planted herbaceous borders.
snowdrops; good herbaceous borders; primulas; spring bulbs; cyclamen and colchicums in autumn; bluebells; bank garden; tea and cakes

Owned by Miss Audrey Vockins
Size 0.8ha (2 acres)

FROGMORE GARDENS
The Home Park, Windsor Castle,
Windsor SL4 2JG

Tel 020 7766 7305 **Fax** 020 7930 9625
www.royalcollection.org.uk
Location Via the Long Walk from Park Street, Windsor
Opening hours 10am to 5.30pm (last admission 4pm), 15 to 17 May and 25 to 27 August
Admission fee £4 in May (garden only; no reductions); adults £6; OAPs £5; children £4 in August (includes house)

Frogmore was for many years a royal residence: most of the house dates from the reign of George III. The grounds were first laid out in 1793, when the lake was excavated and the spoil used to create a series of mounds and banks. The many garden buildings include a gothic temple, an Indian kiosk, a tea house, the Duchess of Kent's mausoleum and the Royal Mausoleum where Queen Victoria and Prince Albert lie. Nearby,

Frogmore's Indian kiosk

Frogmore Gardens

but closed to visitors, is a cemetery where many members of the royal family have been interred since the middle of the 19th century. During the 1920s and 1930s, the gardens were extensively developed by the planting of ornamental trees and shrubs, underplanted by bulbs. The May openings are less expensive than the August ones, because the price for the latter includes a visit to the house. The house may also be visited in May, but there is a separate charge for it then.
historic landscape and buildings

Owned by HM The Queen
Number of gardeners 5
Size 14ha (35 acres)
English Heritage Grade II*

THE LIVING RAINFOREST
Hampstead Norreys, Thatcham RG18 0TN

Tel 01635 202444 **Fax** 01635 202440
www.livingrainforest.org
Location Signed from M4, Jct 13; from A34 southbound, follow signs to East Ilsey, then Hampstead Norreys
Opening hours 10am to 5.15pm, daily, all year; closed 25 and 26 December
Admission fee Adults £6; concessions £5.40; children £4.20 (prices under review)

The Living Rainforest consists of two large landscaped glasshouses, computer-set to create two different rainforest climates. Each has a thickly planted collection of exotic plants of every kind,

THE HARRIS GARDEN

University of Reading, Plant Science Laboratories, Whiteknights, Reading RG6 6AS

Tel 0118 378 8070 **Fax** 0118 378 8160
www.friendsoftheharrisgarden.co.uk
Location On A327, 1 mile south-east of Reading
Opening hours 2pm to 6pm, 15 April, 13 May, 10 June, 8 July, 12 August, 9 September and 14 October (closes at 5pm)
Admission fee Adults £3; children free

The Harris Garden was begun as recently as 1988, though it occupies what was once part of a famous landscape garden created by the 4th Duke of Marlborough (while still Marquess of Blandford) between 1798 and 1817. The idea was to develop a garden as an adjunct to the teaching of horticulture, landscape and botany by the School of Plant Sciences at the University. It is very much a gardener's garden, full of horticultural interest. Annuals, for example, are grown both in traditional drifts of individual plants, and in experimental mixtures. There is a 'jungle garden' of plants grown solely for spectacular subtropical effects. The winter garden concentrates upon plants whose flowers, bark or form give particular pleasure in the dark months of the year. The orchard is not a fruit garden, but a collection of ornamental crab apples underplanted with wildflowers and bulbs which flower from January to early June. There is a large heather garden, where plants are in turn interplanted with dwarf conifers; it is designed to lead naturally to a wildflower meadow. The walled garden has been developed as a traditional kitchen garden, with fruit trained on the walls, vegetables, herbs and flowers. The formal gardens include an area where Gertrude Jekyll's famous flower border at Munstead Wood has been reproduced to illustrate her ideas on colour planting – Richard Bisgrove is the great expert on Jekyll's planting style and one of the team behind the Harris Garden. But there is much more to see, including the woodland garden, a golden garden, a cherry bowl (flowering cherries around a circular clearing with bulbs which flower at the same time), a stream and pond garden, an autumn foliage bed and a splendid mixed border nearly 130m (427ft) long.

subtropical plants; roses (mainly old-fashioned); plantsman's collection of plants; herbs; plants under glass; good herbaceous borders; fine collection of trees; Mediterranean shrubs; hardy annuals; heathers; primula dell; water garden; teas

Owned by The University of Reading
Number of gardeners 2
Size 5ha (12 1/2 acres)
NCCPG National Collections *Iris* (species)

many of them rare or endangered. There is a particularly fine and near-comprehensive collection of tropical aroids, including the epiphytic *Anthurium warocqueanum* from Colombia and the terrestrial *A. watermaliense* from Costa Rica. The flowering plants are wonderful in winter when the tropical orchids flower, and in spring when the jade vine (*Strongylodon macrobotrys*) flowers for several months – it has even set seed here. Later, in the summer, *Victoria amazonica* becomes one of the great attractions when it fills one of the pools. But the Living Rainforest is fascinating whatever the season or the weather outside, and there are free-ranging lizards, butterflies and birds, too.
tropical plants from the Amazon basin and around the world; gift shop; refreshments

Owned by The Living Rainforest
Number of gardeners 2
Size 1,860 sq m (20,000 sq ft) under glass

MARINERS

Mariners Lane, Bradfield RG7 6HU

Tel 0118 974 5226
Location Take road north-east from South End, first left into Mariners Lane, garden on left at bottom
Opening hours 2pm to 6pm, 17 June; and by appointment between 28 June and 15 July
Admission fee Adults £3; children free

Though full of interesting plants, Mariners opens only when the old-fashioned roses are at their peak. Climbers, species and shrub roses are richly underplanted with clematis and herbaceous plants and the wildflower meadow across the river is full of colour.
refreshments for groups by arrangement

Owned by Anthony and Fenja Anderson
Number of gardeners some part-time help
Size 1ha (2½ acres) including wildflower meadow

OLD RECTORY

Burghfield RG30 3TH

Tel 0118 983 3200
Location Right at Hatch Gate Inn and first entrance on right
Opening hours 2pm to 6pm, 6 August; for NGS
Admission fee Adults £2.50; children free; groups £3

This highly acclaimed garden was designed by Ralph Merton and planted by Esther Merton, a first-rate plantswoman who knew exactly what she wanted to achieve. She had a very good eye for plants, and collected them herself all over the world, as well as exchanging gifts with her gardening friends throughout Britain. Her legacy includes wonderful roses, lush summer pots, quantities of spring bulbs (some of them rare), tiny alpines and unusual hellebores – all of them extremely well grown. The *tour de force* is a double herbaceous border where plants build up their impact through repetition, backed by yew hedges which get taller towards the end, to cheat the perspective. It leads to a pool framed by dense plantings of strong foliage – ferns, hostas, maples. But the planting continues, and recent additions include a new Mediterranean border and a 'heritage kitchen garden' for growing vegetables from the HDRA Heritage Seed Library.
snowdrops; rock garden; plantsman's collection of plants; good late herbaceous borders; stone troughs; exotic displays in tubs; hellebores; lilies; teas

Owned by AR Merton
Number of gardeners 2
Size 1.8ha (4½ acres)

OLD RECTORY
Farnborough, Wantage OX12 8NX

Tel 01488 638298 **Fax** 01488 638091
Location In Farnborough village, opposite church
Opening hours 2pm to 5.30pm, 22 April, 13 May and 24 June; and by written appointment (£5, which includes tea, coffee and cakes, in aid of Farnborough Church)
Admission fee Adults £2.50; for NGS

This excellent garden has been made by the owners on a high, cold, windy site since 1965. Lots of hedges and thick planting were the keys to survival, but the effect now is of shelter and luxuriance. There are splendid double herbaceous borders, clever colour plantings, a collection of clematis, a kitchen garden, a *boule* garden and an expanding arboretum (191 trees so far).
roses (mainly old-fashioned and climbers); good herbaceous borders

Owned by Mr and Mrs Michael Todhunter
Number of gardeners 1/2
Size 2.4ha (6 acres)

WALTHAM PLACE
Church Hill, White Waltham SL6 3JH

Tel 01628 825517 **Fax** 01608 825045
www.walthamplace.com
Location 3 miles south-west of Maidenhead
Opening hours 10am to 4pm, Wednesdays, May to September; groups welcome on Tuesdays and Thursdays; plus guided tours on Fridays at 11am and 2pm
Admission fee Adults £3.50; children £1

tea room

Owned by Mr and Mrs Nicholas Oppenheimer
Number of gardeners 7
Size 16ha (40 acres)

WELFORD PARK
Welford, Newbury RG20 8HU

Tel 01488 608691 **Fax** 01468 608853
www.welfordpark.co.uk
Location On south-west edge of Welford village
Opening hours 11am to 4pm, daily, except Monday and Friday, 30 January to 4 March; Monday to Saturday, 4 June to 6 July, except 16 June; and by arrangement at other times
Admission fee Adults £4; concessions £3

Welford means snowdrops – acres and acres of them, as well as aconites and other early-flowering bulbs. It offers one of the most rewarding winter displays in the south of England. But the rest of the garden is now being restored, and there are some fine new plantings around the handsome house.
tea room

Owned by Mr and Mrs James Puxley
Number of gardeners 2 1/2, plus owners
Size 10ha (25 acres)

BUCKINGHAMSHIRE

Buckinghamshire is wonderfully stocked with large estates and grand, historic gardens. All three Grade I landscapes – Cliveden, Stowe and West Wycombe Park – are regularly open to the public, as are the two Rothschild gardens at Ascott and Waddesdon. These estates also have many fine trees. The National Gardens Scheme is active in the county, and lists over 90 gardens to visit, often in village clusters. Dorneywood Garden at Burnham is particularly worth seeing on its all-too-rare openings for the National Gardens Scheme. There are, however, comparatively few National Collections in the county.

ASCOTT
Wing, Leighton Buzzard LU7 0PS

Tel 01296 688242 **Fax** 01296 681904
www.nationaltrust.org.uk
Location 1/2 mile east of Wing
Opening hours House and garden: 2pm to 6pm, Tuesday to Sunday, 27 March to 29 April and 31 July to 14 September; Tuesday to Thursday, 1 May to 25 July. Garden only: 7 May and 27 August for NGS
Admission fee Garden only: adults £4; children £2

Ascott is an opulent late-Victorian extravaganza. It was largely planned by Leopold de Rothschild and planted with trees and shrubs supplied by the famous Chelsea nurseryman Sir Harry Veitch. The Dutch garden, the Madeira walk, the Venus garden and the topiary sundial date from this period (c.1880-1920) and include two fountains by Thomas Waldo Story. The topiary sundial is famous: its Roman numerals are planted in box and the gnomon at the centre is made of golden yew grafted onto green Irish yew. The motto – in Latin – reads 'Light and shade by turn, but love always'. Much in these old gardens has been restored, remade and replanted in recent years. The bedding in the Dutch garden changes its plants and colours twice a year. The 'long walk' to the lily pond now has a serpentine shape created by beech hedges and the old fern garden has been replanted as a box parterre and is now known as the sunken garden. And there is a 'planet topiary garden', built to resemble the astrological symbols of the 12 planets and showing their position in the sky at the very moment Sir Evelyn and Lady de Rothschild were each born. But there are fine old trees, and new plantings, too, including a young collection of modern magnolias and groups of *Davidia involucrata*, *Aesculus indica* and *Juglans nigra*, and good spring bulbs.

woodland garden; topiary; mature conifers; good herbaceous borders; spring bulbs; Dutch garden; tallest *Cedrus atlantica* 'Aurea' in the British Isles

Owned by The National Trust
English Heritage Grade II*

BLOSSOMS
Cobblers Hill, Great Missenden HP16 9PW

Tel/fax 01494 863140
Location 2 1/2 miles north-west of Great Missenden by Rignall Road, signed Butlers Cross, to Kings Lane about 1 mile on right, then to top of Cobblers Hill; right at yellow stone marker and right after 50 yards
Opening hours By appointment only
Admission fee £2.50 for NGS

The origins of this fascinating plantsman's garden go back to 1925 when a previous owner started to plant up a four-acre field and an acre of beech wood filled with bluebells. Dr and Mrs Hytten have lived here since 1975 and have benefited from the substantial windbreaks planted in the 1920s and 1930s. Having once been open – there is still a fine view of the Misbourne Valley – Blossoms is essentially a woodland garden now, with an established apple orchard and some lusty specimen trees including a liquidambar and a fern-leaved beech *Fagus sylvatica* 'Aspleniifolia'. The Hyttens have thickened up the woodland themselves and

made good collections of maples, eucalyptus and willows, together with some more unusual trees, such as *Tetradium daniellii*, *Davidia* and *Metasequoia*. Add on a herbaceous border, shrub borders (including some interesting new shade-lovers), a scree garden, a rock garden, a rare collection of herbaceous plants, a cutting garden, a number of very large climbing roses, a small lake, smaller ponds, patios and statues (mostly woodcarvings) – and the scale and variety of the owners' achievement will be apparent. The owners say that spring and autumn are the best seasons, but like all good plantsman's gardens there is lots of interest throughout the year.
a plantsman's collection of good plants; woodland walks; trees, ponds and wooden sculptures; rock garden; good herbaceous borders; teas by arrangement

Owned by Dr and Mrs Frank Hytten
Number of gardeners owners only
Size 2ha (5 acres)

CHENIES MANOR
Chenies WD3 6ER

Tel/fax 01494 762888
www.cheniesmanorhouse.co.uk
Location Centre of Chenies village
Opening hours 2pm to 5pm, Wednesdays, Thursdays and Bank Holiday Mondays, April to October; plant and garden fair 10am to 5pm, 15 July (£5)
Admission fee Gardens only £4

The richly planted gardens at Chenies Manor are full of variety but designed to complement the Elizabethan house. Their most spectacular period is spring – April and early May – when 300 different cultivars of tulip come into flower in and around the sunken garden, modelled on Hampton Court. All come from Bloms and all are clearly labelled: each is grown in groups of 10 to 50 bulbs and offers a wonderful opportunity to learn about tulips. Later comes the summer bedding, interspersed with herbaceous plantings – red dahlias with white forms of *Campanula latiloba*, for example – and spectacular herbaceous salvias. And there are colour borders everywhere: a very easy but effective one mixes *Alchemilla mollis* with catmint and *Sisyrinchium striatum*. Add in a

The sunken garden at Chenies Manor

physic garden for herbs, a grass labyrinth, a yew maze, a kitchen garden, and some beautiful old lawns and yew hedges, and you have a garden of great harmony.
bulbs; topiary; herbs; fruit; physic garden; award-winning maze; tea, coffee, home-made cakes

Owned by Mrs A MacLeod Matthews
Number of gardeners 1, plus family and volunteers
Size 1.8ha (4 1/2 acres)
English Heritage Grade II*

CLIVEDEN
Taplow, Maidenhead SL6 0JA

Tel 01628 605069 **Fax** 01628 669461
www.nationaltrust.org.uk
Location 2 miles north of Taplow, M4 Jct 7
Opening hours 11am to 6pm (4pm from 29 October), daily, 14 March to 23 December
Admission fee Grounds: adults £7.50; children £3.70; families £18.70. Woodlands: adults £3; children £1.50; families £7.50

Cliveden is a vast (and very important) landscape garden, filled with whatever money could buy: balustrading from the Villa Borghese in Rome, the dramatic 'Fountain of Love' and a huge parterre below the house. The best of all is the Arcadian ilex wood. Allow lots of time to visit this garden of wonders.
woodland garden; snowdrops; roses (mainly modern); fruit; good herbaceous borders; bluebells; good autumn colour; tallest *Juglans cinerea* (24m; 79ft) in the British Isles; meals

Owned by The National Trust
Number of gardeners 9
Size 64ha (160 acres)
NCCPG National Collections *Catalpa*
English Heritage Grade I

HARTWELL HOUSE
Oxford Road, Aylesbury HP17 8NL

Tel 01296 747444 **Fax** 01296 747450
www.hartwell-house.com
Location 2 miles from Aylesbury, on A418 towards Oxford
Opening hours For guests of the hotel
Admission fee Free to patrons

The gardens at Hartwell House were laid out early in the 18th century, in the formal style. When they were landscaped by Richard Woods (a follower of Capability Brown), most of the garden buildings were retained, in particular a Gothic tower and pavilion by James Gibbs. The modern gardens are especially fine in springtime, with hosts of snowdrops, daffodils, winter aconites, primroses and anemones. In the orchard old varieties of apples are grown, while the walls of the former kitchen garden support apricot, peach, pear and plum trees – the same cultivars as were originally planted in 1868. Flowers for the house and fresh herbs and vegetables for the kitchen are grown in Hartwell's gardens. 2005 saw the reopening of the restored Sir William Lee folly bridge and Ladies' Walk. Most restoration is planned for this year, notably the Lady Elizabeth Lee garden. There will be one RHS Special Event at Hartwell House in 2007, on Wednesday 13 June; details from 020 7821 3408.
hotel, restaurant and spa

Owned by Historic House Hotels Ltd
Number of gardeners 3
Size 36ha (90 acres)
English Heritage Grade II*

HUGHENDEN MANOR
High Wycombe HP14 4LA

Tel 01494 755573 **Fax** 01494 474284
www.nationaltrust.org.uk
Location 1 1/2 miles north of High Wycombe
Opening hours 11am to 5pm, Wednesday to Sunday plus Bank Holidays, 3 March to 28 October; plus noon to 4pm on 1, 2, 8, 9, 15 and 16 December
Admission fee Garden only: adults £2.60; children £1.90. Park and woodland: free

Hughenden is not a great garden, but interesting for its association with Disraeli. The garden was made by his wife in the 1860s and has a classic gardenesque planting of specimen trees on the North Lawn and a more Italianate design on the southern side. The National Trust has restored it, using photographs taken in 1881, so that the parterres are once again planted with Victorian annuals and bedding. Work has now begun on restoring the walled garden, and tours to inspect progress are available at 11am on Fridays.
good herbaceous borders; 61 old apple varieties; rolling parkland; formal Victorian parterres with bright bedding out as in Disraeli's day; National Trust shop; stableyard restaurant

Owned by The National Trust
English Heritage Grade II

THE MANOR HOUSE
Bledlow, Princes Risborough HP27 9PB

Tel 020 7584 4243 **Fax** 020 7823 1476
Location Off B4009
Opening hours 2pm to 6pm, 6 May and 17 June for NGS; and by appointment
Admission fee £4.50

This is one of the greatest gardens of our times: beautifully planted and well maintained, it has all been made on thin chalk soil since 1969. There are four parts: first, the garden 'proper' round the house, enclosed by hedges of beech, hornbeam or yew. Best is the armillary garden, an exercise in topiary with the sphere at its centre, surrounded by four cubes of yew, smaller hedges and labels of box. Next comes the walled garden with a gazebo in the centre whose eight trellised posts are planted with rambling roses. The central grass walk is lined with apple trees trained as spheres around a wire globe: they rise from parterre boxes of teucrium, each planted with a different

herb – sage, chives, Greek oregano and so on. The third part of the garden is quite different – 21/2 acres of sculpture garden, started in 1991 and already remarkably mature. The land has been contoured to maximise the movement of the surface, and give contrasts of height and depth. Its fluid modern design is a great foil to the formal gardens around the house. The presiding spirit is a life-size gorilla by Michael Cooper. The fourth part of the garden is different again – four acres of water garden, started in 1979 on the site of three old watercress beds. The 13 springs which issue from its sides are the headwaters of the River Lyde, a tributary of the Thames. The steep valley sides are thickly planted with shrubs and herbaceous plants. A wooden walkway, Japanese in style, takes you round the edge of the lakes at the bottom. The muddy banks are planted with candelabra primroses, gunneras, hostas and astilbes. Unlike the rest of the garden, this part is open daily (and free) from dawn to dusk.
good herbaceous borders; sculptures; new water feature by William Pye

Owned by Lord and Lady Carrington
Number of gardeners 3
Size 3.6ha (9 acres)

STOWE LANDSCAPE GARDENS

Stowe, Buckingham MK18 5EH

Tel 01280 822850 **Fax** 01280 822437
www.nationaltrust.org.uk
Location 3 miles north-west of Buckingham
Opening hours 10.30am to 5.30pm (last admissions 4pm); Wednesday to Sunday and Bank Holiday Mondays, 1 March to 4 November; 10.30am to 4pm, Saturdays and Sundays, 10 November to 24 February 2008; closed 26 May and for some of the Christmas period; garden may close in bad weather
Admission fee Adults £6.50; children £3.20; families £16.30

This mega-landscape is considered by some the most important in the history of gardens. William Kent designed the Temple of Venus (1731), the Shell Bridge (1733) and the highly original Temple of British Worthies (1734), which has statues of Alfred the Great, the Black Prince, Queen Elizabeth, John Milton and 12 further historic persons – Stowe was a highly fashionable garden with a strong political message. Capability Brown laid out the Grecian Valley in the 1740s: it was while he was head gardener at Stowe that he developed his skill in simplifying formal gardens and creating the distinctive curves and contours which we now recognise as an essential feature of the English landscape garden. The National Trust has undertaken extensive restoration and renovation since it took over in 1989. Go if you have not been already, and go again if you have. Stomp round slowly, and contemplate the history and symbolism of each feature. Read the National Trust's excellent guide and then go round again, this year, next year, every year, and commune with the *genius loci*.
tallest *Fraxinus angustifolia* var *lentiscifolia* (24m; 79ft) and largest x *Crataemespilus grandiflora* (9m; 30ft) in the British Isles; National Trust shop; tea room

Owned by The National Trust
English Heritage Grade I

TURN END

Townside, Haddenham, Aylesbury HP17 8BG

Tel 01844 291383 (291817 evenings and weekends)
Location Turn at Rising Sun in Haddenham, then 300 yards on left; park in street
Opening hours Groups of 10+ by appointment; for NGS: 2pm to 5pm, 7 May
Admission fee £2.50 on 7 May; groups by agreement

Peter Aldington was once a young architect, much influenced by Le Corbusier and James Stirling. In 1963 he and his wife bought this plot and built their house – a modern architectural classic, much photographed, cited, visited and copied (and now listed). Aldington believed that his job as an architect was to make connections and create forms which enclosed spaces for people to use and enjoy. He then set out to apply the same principles to his garden, drawing upon his love of textures and materials to design and plant it.
The garden, like the house, became one of the most acclaimed to be made in the latter half of the 20th century. Over the years Aldington was

Waddesdon Manor

able to increase its size by small additions. It still covers less than one acre, but never was space so ingeniously used to create an illusion of size. A brilliant series of enclosed gardens, sunken or raised, sunny or shady, each different and yet harmonious, contrasts with lawns, borders and glades. The story is told in *A Garden & Three Houses* by Jane Brown (Garden Art Press, 1999); the Aldingtons still have a few copies for sale.
brilliant design - a series of spaces; rock garden; a plantsman's collection of plants; ferns; grasses; teas on 7 May

Owned by Mr and Mrs Peter Aldington
Number of gardeners 1
Size 0.4ha (1 acre)

WADDESDON MANOR
Aylesbury HP18 0JH

Tel 01296 653226 **Fax** 01296 653212
www.waddesdon.org.uk
Location A41 Bicester and Aylesbury; 20 miles from Oxford
Opening hours 10am to 5pm, Saturdays and Sundays, 6 January to 18 March; Wednesday to Sunday and Bank Holiday Mondays, 21 March to 23 December
Admission fee Grounds only: adults £5.50; children £2.75; RHS members free in March, September and October

The garden at Waddesdon was laid out in the 1870s and 1880s for Baron Ferdinand de Rothschild by the French landscape designer Elie Lainé. This involved levelling the crown of a hill, planting it with mature trees and creating the drives, banks and formal gardens which were essential to the design. The result is one of the finest Victorian gardens in Britain, which has been meticulously restored since 1990 by Lord Rothschild, working in conjunction with the National Trust. A long drive winds through splendid rolling parkland with spacious views over the vale; the baron intended it to be the most impressive approach in England. Near the house are a valley of dicksonias, a Pulhamite rock garden, a rococo aviary, a circular rose garden enclosed by an iron fence and wonderful statues everywhere. But nothing matches the splendour of the formal gardens in front of the house – extravagant, opulent, spectacular displays of intricate colour, horticultural excellence and family wealth.
daffodils; good herbaceous borders; magnificent bedding; spring walk with 80,000 crocuses; gift and wine shop; tea room; restaurant

Owned by The National Trust
Number of gardeners 8 full-time, 2 part-time, plus interns and students
Size 66ha (165 acres)
English Heritage Grade II*

WEST WYCOMBE PARK
West Wycombe HP14 3AJ

Tel 01494 513569/755573
www.nationaltrust.org.uk
Location West end of West Wycombe on A40
Opening hours 2pm to 6pm, Sunday to Thursday, April to August
Admission fee Adults £3; children £1.50

This park, with a lake in the shape of a swan, was made by Sir Francis Dashwood between 1735 and 1782, in a rococo style that was modified by later generations. It has been well restored and embellished by modern additions, including three modern eye-catchers designed by Quinlan Terry.

Owned by The National Trust
English Heritage Grade I

CAMBRIDGESHIRE

Cambridgeshire has a good number of historic gardens. Though only Wimpole Hall is rated as Grade I, there is a great cluster of Grade II* and Grade II landscapes in Cambridge itself: these include the University Botanic Garden and the following colleges: Christ's, Emmanuel, King's, Queen's, St John's and Trinity (including Trinity Hall). The Backs are also rated Grade I – and one of the few places in the country where the strange but beautiful parasite *Lathraea clandestina* has naturalised (RHS Garden Wisley is another). The University Botanic Garden has by far the most exciting and comprehensive collection of plants in the county, especially for those trees that grow particularly well in the dry climate: many are the tallest of their kind in the British Isles. The National Gardens Scheme is well supported in Cambridgeshire, and has quite a number of villages where several smaller gardens open together. In Cambridge itself, several colleges open for the National Gardens Scheme, including Clare, Emmanuel, King's and Trinity. The county is thinly supplied by nurseries and garden centres, but Monksilver Nursery is a magnet for keen plantsmen and of international importance as a source of rare plants. Cambridgeshire has its fair share of National Collections – here again the lead is set by the University Botanic Garden with no fewer than nine National Collections from *Alchemilla* to *Tulipa*.

ABBOTS RIPTON HALL

Abbots Ripton PE28 2PQ

Tel 01487 773555 **Fax** 01487 773545
Location Off B1090
Opening hours 2pm to 5pm, 20 May, 17 June, 1 and 15 July and 5 August for various local charities; groups of 12+ by appointment at other times
Admission fee Adults £3; children (under 16) £2
Owned by Lord De Ramsey
Number of gardeners 2, plus 1 part-time
Size 3.2ha (8 acres)
English Heritage Grade II

Ⓟ 🚻 ♿ ✺

Humphrey Waterfield, Lanning Roper and Jim Russell all worked here, and few garden owners have had as many gardening friends as Lord De Ramsey's parents, who made and remade this garden over more than 50 years. The result is a garden of stylish individuality – as witness the Gothic trellis work and the bobbles of yellow philadelphus – but also of great unity. The present Lady De Ramsey has retained the unity of style while replanting many of the borders. In early summer it can fairly claim to be the most beautiful garden in England.

irises; grey border; Chinese bridge; trellis work; splendid herbaceous borders; tallest *Pyrus pyraster* (12m; 39ft) in the British Isles; new arboretum of rare oaks; teas

ANGLESEY ABBEY

Lode CB5 9EJ

Tel 01223 810080 **Fax** 01223 810088
www.angleseyabbey.org
Location Off B1102, signed from A14
Opening hours 10.30am to 5.30pm (last admissions 4.30pm), Wednesday to Sunday and Bank Holiday Mondays, 21 March to 28 October; plus Tuesdays in local school holidays. Winter Garden: Wednesday to Sunday, 3 January to 19 March and 31 October to 23 December, then from 28 December to 29 February 2008
Admission fee Gardens: adults £4.95, but £4.40 in winter

Ⓟ 🚻 ♿ ✺

Though not begun until 1926, the grounds at Anglesey already deserve to be famous, for they are the grandest made in England during the 20th century. Majestic avenues and 14ha (35 acres) of fine turf are the stuff of them: visit Anglesey when the horse-chestnuts are out and tulips glow among

Abbots Ripton Hall

cowslips in the wildflower meadows. Large formal gardens, carved out of the flat site by yew hedges, house the 1st Lord Fairhaven's collection of classical and renaissance sculpture. The winter garden bursts with snowdrops and aconites, coloured stems and glistening evergreens. Then there are smaller gardens, said to be more intimate, where thousands of dahlias and hyacinths hit the eye: glorious or vainglorious, Anglesey has no match.
snowdrops; good herbaceous borders; landscaping on the grandest scale; long avenues of trees; dahlias; cyclamen; good autumn colour; winter walk; National Trust shop; licensed restaurant and picnic area

Owned by The National Trust
Number of gardeners 6
Size 39ha (98 acres)
English Heritage Grade II*

CHIPPENHAM PARK
Chippenham, Ely CB7 5PT

Tel/fax: 01638 721991
Location 5 miles north-east of Newmarket
Opening hours 11am to 5pm, 1 April, 17 June and 7 October; groups of 20+ by arrangement
Admission fee Adults £4

There is much to see at Chippenham. The formal canal dates from the 1690s and survived the landscaping by William Emes in the 1780s. The modern gardens are very floriferous – masses of daffodils in spring, roses and eremurus in summer and borders that carry the colour through until autumn leaves take over. The Crawleys usually invite 20-25 nurserymen to sell plants when they open the garden for the NGS.
refreshments

Owned by Anne Crawley
Number of gardeners 3 1/2
Size 6ha (15 acres)

CAMBRIDGE UNVERSITY BOTANIC GARDEN

Bateman Street, Cambridge CB2 1JF

Tel 01223 336265 **Fax** 01223 336278
www.botanic.cam.ac.uk
Location Entrance on Bateman Street, 1 mile south of city centre and 5 mins from railway station
Opening hours 10am to 4pm in winter (5pm in spring and autumn, 6pm in summer), daily, except 24 December to 2 January
Admission fee Adults £3; OAPs £2.50; children free

This exceptionally attractive botanic garden is essential visiting for any garden-lover who does not already know it. It has so many good and interesting features that you could spend all day here and not be bored. Cambridge's is also one of the most beautiful and best-maintained botanic gardens in the country. The limestone rock garden, newly interpreted, is one of its major attractions, where the plantings are arranged geographically. It overlooks the small lake whose surface is covered by water lilies. Late spring is the time to see the nearby woodland garden. Here are fine tree specimens, including *Dipteronia sinensis*, *Tetracentron sinense* and the hardy pawpaw *Asimina triloba*, and a dawn redwood (*Metasequoia glyptostroboides*) grown from the original introduction of seed into the UK in 1948. Along the sides of the little stream which runs through the wood are candelabra primulas, astilbes, irises and a bed of the giant horsetail *Equisetum telmateia*. Late spring is also the time to see the horse-chestnuts in flower, the Persian lilacs and the National Collections of shrubby *Lonicera* and *Ribes*. The garden has a very good collection of peony species, which are in some places interplanted with its hardy geraniums. Perhaps one reason why the garden is so attractive is that its National Collections are of supreme horticultural value. The garden also maintains two acres of (mainly herbaceous) systematic beds, a feature which was created by the first curator Andrew Murray in 1845. It contains some 1,600 species, belonging to 98 families and growing in 157 beds; it is historically important and beautiful in its design. A more modern addition is the genetic garden, whose scientific purpose is to demonstrate the natural effects of genes on plant morphology. Everywhere, too, are wonderful trees: was there ever a tree more beautiful than the type specimen of *Quercus* 'Warburgii'? The winter garden, planted in 1978, is the best in England, and draws on stems, leaves, bark and flowers to create its unique beauty. The superb series of linked glasshouses, currently being restored and replanted, are a blessed sanctuary to horticulturally smart undergraduates during the cold months of an East Anglian winter, but every aspect of the garden's existence is educationally aware and it goes out of its way to attract and interest schoolchildren, too.

good herbaceous borders; important rock garden; species roses; dry garden; genetics garden; British wild plants; winter garden; tallest *Catalpa* x *erubescens* 'Purpurea' (11m; 36ft) in the British Isles (and 21 other record trees); shop in summer months; light refreshments

Owned by The University of Cambridge
Number of gardeners 18
Size 16ha (40 acres)
NCCPG National Collections *Alchemilla*; *Bergenia* (species and primary hybrids); *Fritillaria* (European species); *Geranium* (species and primary hybrids); *Lonicera* (shrubby species and primary hybrids); *Ribes* (species and primary hybrids); *Ruscus*; *Saxifraga* (European species); *Tulipa* (species and primary hybrids)
English Heritage Grade II*

CLARE COLLEGE FELLOWS' GARDEN

Clare College, Trinity Lane, Cambridge CB2 1TL

Tel 01223 333200 **Fax** 01223 333219
www.clare.cam.ac.uk
Location Enter from Clare Old Court off Trinity Lane, or from Queens Road
Opening hours 10.30am to 4.30pm, daily, April to September
Admission fee £2.50

♿

Two acres of views and vistas, walks and Hidcote-style enclosures filled with exquisite spring bulbs, spectacular hot-colour borders dating from the 1950s and herbaceous borders. The Fellows' Garden was largely laid out from 1947 onwards by Professor Nevill Willmer, who died in 2001 aged 98. The features include a pond garden, a scent garden, a new Victorian-style subtropical garden and fine examples of taxodiums, metasequoias and *Tilia* 'Petiolaris'. Willmer was extremely skilful in his manipulation of perspective and colour. Elizabeth Banks Associates have recently set out a 10-year plan to restore some of the original features which have been lost over the years.

Owned by The Master and Fellows
Number of gardeners 2
Size 0.8ha (2 acres)
English Heritage Grade II*

CROSSING HOUSE GARDEN

Meldreth Road, Shepreth, Royston SG8 6PS

Tel 01763 261071
Location 8 miles south of Cambridge off A10
Opening hours Dawn to dusk, daily, all year; park on road; no coaches
Admission fee Free

One of the wonders of modern gardening, the Crossing House celebrates the achievements of its makers since 1959, on an unpropitious site right beside the main railway line to Cambridge. Box-edged beds separated by granite paths contain thousands and thousands of different plants, densely planted in the cottage style. Shrubs, herbaceous plants, alpines and bulbs are planted in the same beds to maximise the effect at all seasons. Peat beds, arches, topiary, a pool and raised beds are some of the features which add variety to the most intensely and intensively planted small garden in England. And every few minutes a London express whizzes past.
plantsman's collection of plants

Owned by Mr and Mrs DG Fuller and Mr J Marlar
Number of gardeners owners only
Size 0.1ha (1/2 acre)

DOCWRA'S MANOR

Shepreth, Royston SG8 6PS

Tel 01763 261473/261557/260235
www.docwrasmanorgarden.co.uk
Location Off A10 to Shepreth, 5 miles north-east of Royston
Opening hours 10am to 4pm, Wednesdays and Fridays, all year; 2pm to 5pm, first Sunday of month, April to October; for NGS: 20 May; and by appointment
Admission fee Adults £4; children free

(P) ♿

This is very much a plantsman's garden, whose lush profusion defies the dry, cold, alkaline site. Docwra's Manor is a series of small gardens – walled, wild, paved and so on – each brimming with interesting plants and good combinations. There is a sense of abundance, whatever the season. Interesting seedlings are encouraged and nurtured. Everything you see has been made by Mrs Raven since she and her late husband bought the house in 1954. Do read John Raven's charming and erudite *The Botanist's Garden*, available from Mrs Raven by post for £10 and one of the classics of 20th-century garden writing.
plantsman's collection of plants; good herbaceous borders; Mediterranean plants; teas for NGS opening

Owned by Mrs John Raven
Number of gardeners 1
Size 1ha (21/2 acres)

ELGOOD'S BREWERY & GARDENS

North Brink, Wisbech PE13 1LN

Tel 01945 583160 **Fax** 01945 587711
www.elgoods-brewery.co.uk
Location On western edge of Wisbech, near Peckover House
Opening hours 11.30am to 4.30pm, Tuesday to Thursday, May to September
Admission fee Adults £3; OAPs and children £2.50

Behind this traditional family brewery is a walled enclosure where a pretty modern garden has been made around some trees. There are herbaceous borders, a rock garden, a large pond and a herb garden, all attractively planted and well maintained. The trees include a ginkgo, a walnut, a mulberry, a liriodendron and a variegated sycamore, all about 200 years old. Beyond the walled garden is a maze.
gift shop; licensed bar; café

Owned by Elgood & Sons Ltd
Number of gardeners 3
Size 1.6ha (4 acres)

ELSWORTH HERBS

Avenue Farm Cottage, 31 Smith Street, Elsworth, Cambridge CB3 8HY

Tel/fax 01954 267414
Location Smith Street runs through the middle of Elsworth; the garden is towards the western end
Opening hours By appointment
Admission fee Free

This is an excellent example of a small boutique nursery attached to a National Collection – in this case two of them, *Artemisia* and *Nerium oleander*. Its range is wide – over 50 oleanders, for example, which is twice as many as anyone else – but the owners do not carry large stocks, so they are happy to propagate to order. The list of *Artemisia* species is quite unique – a triumph of plantsmanship.

Owned by Dr JD and JM Twibell
Number of gardeners owners only
Size 0.3ha (¾ acre)
NCCPG National Collections *Artemisia*; *Nerium oleander*

ELTON HALL

Peterborough PE8 6SH

Tel 01832 280468 **Fax** 01832 280584
Location A605, 8 miles west of Peterborough
Opening hours 2pm to 5pm, Wednesdays, June to August; also Thursdays and Sundays in July and August, 27 and 28 May and 27 August; parties by appointment
Admission fee Garden only: adults £5; children free; RHS members free from May to July

The house is a castellated extravaganza. The Victorian and Edwardian gardens have been energetically restored in recent years which makes Elton highly visitable. The high spots are the parterre, the sunken garden, the millennium orangery and the new rose garden designed by Xa Tollemache. Best in June and July.
roses (mainly old-fashioned); good herbaceous borders; fine collection of trees; handsome hedges; good colour plantings; plant centre on-site; tea room

Owned by Sir William Proby Bt
Number of gardeners 2½
Size 10.3ha (26 acres)
English Heritage Grade II*

HARDWICKE HOUSE

High Ditch Road, Fen Ditton, Cambridge CB5 8TF

Tel 01223 292246
Location ½ mile east of village
Opening hours By appointment only
Admission fee Adults £3; children 50p

This is an excellent plantsman's garden with an emphasis on herbaceous plants, roses and bulbs. The owner has a particular interest in Asia Minor, as witness an area devoted to Turkish plants and bulbs. The aquilegias are good, too.
plantsman's collection of plants; good herbaceous borders; bulbs

Owned by John Drake
Number of gardeners owner only
Size 0.8ha (2 acres)
NCCPG National Collections *Aquilegia*

THE MANOR, HEMINGFORD GREY

Hemingford Grey, Huntingdon PE28 9BN

Tel 01480 463134 **Fax** 01480 465026
www.greenknowe.co.uk
Location In centre of village; park in High street and walk down to river; signed left on towpath
Opening hours 11am to 5pm (or dusk, if earlier), daily, all year
Admission fee Adults £2; children free

The owner's mother was Lucy Boston, the author of the *Green Knowe* books, who set her stories in the garden she made around the house, built in 1160 and said to be the oldest in England. The yew topiary has grown into a splendid variety of shapes and sizes, and there is a good collection of old-fashioned roses and bearded irises dating from the 1950s. A period piece of great charm.
old roses; irises; topiary; gift shop; refreshments by arrangement for groups

Owned by Diana Boston
Number of gardeners 2 part-time
Size 1.4ha (3 1/2 acres)

MONKSILVER NURSERY

Oakington Road, Cottenham CB24 8TW

Tel 01954 251555 **Fax** 01223 502887
Location North of Cambridge, between Oakington and Cottenham
Opening hours 10am to 4pm, Friday to Saturday, March to June, and October; special open day 11am to 4 pm, 23 September
Admission fee Free

This remarkable nursery is deservedly fashionable and now has an excellent display area. Monksilver specialises in finding and rescuing very rare plants. They say that their areas of speciality include *Anthemis*, *Arum*, *Astrantia*, *Aster*, bulbs, *Euphorbia*, ferns, *Galanthus*, grasses and sedges, *Hemerocallis* species, herbaceous perennials, *Lamium*, *Lathyrus*, *Monarda*, Pink Sheet plants ('pink sheets' are NCCPG search lists), *Pulmonaria*, *Ranunculus ficaria*, *Sedum*, *Solidago*, *Vinca*, rare shrubs and trees, variegated and wild collected plants. But the truth is that they list hundreds of other plants which are equally interesting. Many nurseries claim to have 'rare and unusual' plants: in the case of Monksilver, the boast is consistently true. A fifth of the catalogue changes each year.

Owned by Alan Leslie and Joe Sharman

NETHERHALL MANOR

Tanners Lane, Soham, Ely CB7 5AB

Tel 01353 720269
Location In middle of Soham, turn right off the main road into Tanners Lane
Opening hours 2pm to 5pm, 1 April, 6 May, 5 and 12 August
Admission fee Adults £2

This is an unusual garden, worth seeing for its individual collections of genera and plant groups which offer something of interest at every season. Many came from Timothy Clark's great-grandmother, who was a herbalist. The hellebores are good in spring and include many seedlings given by Helen Ballard. Elsewhere are the seldom-seen *Helleborus* 'Günther Jürgl' (one of the first of the upright-facing, double cultivars), *H.* 'Circe' (long thought to be extinct, but saved by Nancy Lindsay) and a small collection of Eric Smith's selections, including *H.* 'Sirius' which Timothy Clark considers still the best yellow. Other goodies include: *Primula auricula* 'Duke of Edinburgh'; the double-flowered sweet rocket *Hesperis matronalis* 'Flore Pleno', which was reintroduced from meristems collected in this garden; *Fritillaria imperialis* 'Foremost'; *Hyacinthus* 'Prince Albert Victor'; and the collection of 19th-century *Pelargonium* cultivars, including 'Turtle's Surprise' and 'Sophie Dumaresque'. Calceolarias, heliotropes and florists' tulips are other specialities (look out for *T.* 'Cardinal Manning', 'Lincolnshire' and 'Bacchus', all *extremely* rare). Some of the garden's progeny are now finding their way into the *RHS Plant Finder*, including *Heliotropium arborescens* 'Netherhall White' and *Chrysanthemum* 'Netherhall Moonlight'. The one-acre garden is immaculately maintained – its lawns are completely weedless – and includes a neat, organic, kitchen garden area.
a great plantsman's garden; hyacinths; Victorian pelargoniums; florists' tulips; teas in aid of charity

Owned by Timothy Clark
Number of gardeners 1 part-time
Size 0.4ha (1 acre)

PECKOVER HOUSE & GARDEN
North Brink, Wisbech PE13 1JR

Tel/fax 01945 583463
www.peckoverhouse.co.uk
Location Signed from Wisbech
Opening hours noon to 5pm, Tuesdays, Wednesdays, Saturdays and Sundays, 2 May to 5 November; plus weekends only from 25 March to 30 April, Good Friday and Bank Holiday Mondays; and Mondays from 31 July to 1 September; 29 and 30 June for Wisbech Rose Fair
Admission fee Adults £3

Peckover is an exceptionally fine example of a walled town garden, dating principally from the 19th century, complete with monkey puzzle, fernery and spotted laurel shrubberies. It has good herbaceous borders, Victorian bedding schemes, over 70 different roses, summerhouses and pool gardens. Three of the orange trees in the conservatory are 300 years old.
Victorian shrubberies; orangery; fernery; good bedding; herbaceous borders; gift shop; restaurant

Owned by The National Trust
Number of gardeners 1 1/2
Size 0.8ha (2 acres)
English Heritage Grade II

WIMPOLE HALL
Arrington, Royston SG8 0BW

Tel 01223 206000 **Fax** 01223 207838
www.wimpole.org
Location 8 miles south-west of Cambridge on A603
Opening hours 10.30am to 5pm, daily, except Thursdays and Fridays (but open Good Friday), 17 March to 31 October; open on Thursdays from 21 July to 30 August, 11am to 4pm; daily, except Thursdays and Fridays, 3 to 14 March and 3 November to 23 December; park open all year
Admission fee Garden: adults £3.30; children £1.75; park: free

Wimpole is an important classical 18th-century landscape where Bridgeman, Brown and Repton have all left their mark. It has a fine 19th-century collection of trees in and around the park, and grand Victorian parterres, where 72 flowerbeds are arranged as eight Union Jack patterns and brightly arrayed with 24,000 bedding plants. There is a lot of new horticultural interest in the old two-acre kitchen garden, where fruit and vegetables are grown on a big scale to supply the National Trust restaurant, and flowers are grown for traditional decoration. An improving garden.
woodland garden; daffodils; Chinese bridge; parterre; traditional greenhouses in walled garden; National Trust shop; restaurant and tea room

Owned by The National Trust
Number of gardeners 3
NCCPG National Collections *Juglans*
English Heritage Grade I

CHESHIRE

Cheshire has a fair number of important historic landscapes, including Adlington Hall, Arley Hall, Eaton Hall, Lyme Park and Tatton Park, but none is important enough to be accorded Grade I status by English Heritage. Nevertheless, Cheshire has a good reputation for gardens and gardening: it is a prosperous county, with sandy soils and plenty of rainfall. This makes it a good area for nurseries and garden centres; probably the best known are Bridgemere Nurseries and Stapeley Water Gardens, both at Bridgemere, where the International Water Lily Society also has its base. Collinwood Nurseries at Mottram St Andrew is one of the leading growers of chrysanthemums, with an exceptionally comprehensive list of cultivars. Other specialist nurseries are Caddick's Clematis Nursery at Thelwall and the two rose nurseries C & K Jones at Tarvin and Fryer's Roses at Knutsford. The National Gardens Scheme lists a fair number of middle-sized gardens: azaleas and rhododendrons are particularly popular. Reaseheath College near Nantwich is a RHS Partner College.

ADLINGTON HALL

Macclesfield SK10 4LF

Tel 01625 829206 **Fax** 01625 828756
www.adlingtonhall.com
Location 5 miles north of Macclesfield off A523
Opening hours 2pm to 5pm, Sunday to Wednesday, August (but closed 19 August); at other times by prior appointment on weekdays for groups of 20 or more
Admission fee Adults £6; children £3; groups (20+) £5.50

It is good to see this important historic garden regularly open to the public again, and to know that the owner is adding her own improvements in another part of the estate. These include a maturing maze, a rose garden, a parterre and the 'Father Tiber' water garden. Many of the historical features have been restored: some are still awaiting their turn. One of the oldest is an avenue of yews planted in 1660. An ancient avenue of lime trees, planted in 1688 to celebrate the accession of William and Mary, leads to a woodland wilderness with follies. These include a shell cottage (1750s), a temple to Diana, a Chinese bridge and a hermitage.
historic landscape; ancient lime avenue; woodland garden; tea room

Owned by Mrs CJC Legh
Number of gardeners 4
English Heritage Grade II*

ARLEY HALL

Great Budworth, Northwich CW9 6NA

Tel 01565 777353 **Fax** 01565 777465
www.arleyhallandgardens.com
Location 5 miles west of Knutsford
Opening hours 11am to 5pm, Tuesday to Sunday and Bank Holidays, April to September; plus weekends in October
Admission fee Adults £5; OAPs £4.50; children £2; RHS members free, except during special events

Arley has pleached limes, red *Primula florindae*, clipped ilex cylinders (10m – 33ft – high), pretty shrub roses and a magnificent collection of rhododendrons, azaleas and rare trees and shrubs. But its claim to fame is the double herbaceous border, backed and buttressed by yew hedges, perhaps the oldest and certainly still one of the best in England. The arboretum has been built by Lord Ashbrook over the last 30 years and is underplanted with rhododendrons, azaleas and flowering shrubs. Last year (2006) over 6,000 spring bulbs have been planted in the woodland walk by staff and Friends of Arley. There will be one RHS Special Event at Arley Hall in 2007, on 5 July; details from 020 7821 3408.
topiary; avenues; two walled gardens; roses (mainly old-fashioned); good herbaceous borders; HHA/Christie's Garden of the Year in 1987; shop; nursery; lunches and light refreshments

Arley Hall

Owned by Viscount Ashbrook
Number of gardeners 5
Size 7.2ha (18 acres)
English Heritage Grade II*

BLUEBELL COTTAGE GARDENS & LODGE LANE NURSERY

Lodge Lane, Dutton, Warrington WA4 4HP

Tel 01928 713718
www.lodgelanenursery.co.uk
Location Turn off A533 midway between Runcorn and Northwich
Opening hours Nursery: 10am to 5pm, Tuesday to Sunday and Bank Holidays, mid-March to mid-September. Garden: 10am to 5pm, Friday to Sunday and Bank Holidays, May to August
Admission fee Adults £3; children free; RHS members free; nursery free at all times

Lodge Lane Nursery sells more than 2,000 different herbaceous plants: it is particularly strong on penstemons, but there are big collections of achilleas, alliums, asters, campanulas, digitalis, euphorbias, geraniums, nepeta, salvias and ornamental grasses, too. Bluebell Cottage Gardens are the nursery's show gardens, well worth a visit in their own right. The gardens have been developed as a series of smaller gardens within the garden. Each has a different theme: among them are the herb garden, the yellow garden, the 'healing' garden and the scree bed. Large island beds are used to display herbaceous plants: the owners believe that there is nothing to beat them for colour (and sheer garden value) from early to late summer. The wildflower meadow has three acres of native flowers among the grasses, including perennial cornflowers, scabious, yarrows, red clover and meadow cranesbill. At the far side of the meadow are three more acres of native woodland, carpeted with bluebells in May. Two RHS Special Events will take place at Bluebell Cottage Gardens during 2007: details from 020 7821 3408.
wildflower meadow; 3,000 different plants

Owned by Jack and Anne Stewart
Number of gardeners 4 part-time
Size 0.6ha (1 1/2 acres), plus meadow and woodland

BRIDGEMERE GARDEN WORLD

Bridgemere, Nantwich CW5 7QB

Tel 01270 521100 **Fax** 01270 520215
Location M6, Jct 15 and 16, follow signs
Opening hours 9am to 7pm (6pm in winter), daily, all year, except 25 and 26 December
Admission fee Free

More than 20 immaculate show gardens in different styles are the attraction of Bridgemere. They are intended to give you ideas on design and planting for your own garden. There is a very wide range of interesting plants for sale, too – Bridgemere propagates its own stock. A new arboretum opens in 2007, and the narrow-gauge railway which takes you there is already in place. Definitely worth a visit, whatever the season.
woodland garden; roses (ancient and modern); rock garden; plantsman's collection of plants; herbs; plants under glass; fruit; good herbaceous borders; several shops, as well as the famous garden centre; restaurant and coffee shop

Owned by J Ravenscroft
Number of gardeners 3
Size 2.4ha (6 acres)

CAPESTHORNE HALL

Siddington, Macclesfield SK11 9JY

Tel 01625 861221 **Fax** 01625 861619
www.capesthorne.com
Location A34, 3 miles south of Alderley Edge
Opening hours Noon to 5pm, Mondays, Sundays and Bank Holidays, April to October
Admission fee Adults £4; OAPs £3; children £2

There are lots of interesting things to see at Capesthorne Hall, provided you are prepared to explore the grounds and find them. Fine trees are certainly a feature: the Victorian arboretum contains some very vigorous wellingtonias and chestnuts, supplemented by recent plantings over the last 50 years. Vernon Russell-Smith designed the formal lakeside gardens in the 1960s: mixed borders of shrub roses and herbaceous plants. Along the rhododendron walk is a splendid

mixture of hardy hybrids interspersed with *Rhododendron ponticum* and the sweet-scented *Rhododendron luteum*. They flourish under a canopy of tall English oaks and wild cherries. Here, too, are two cork trees, *Quercus suber*. By the time you have discovered the rose arbour, the avenue of American hawthorns, the ice house and the golden glade (planted to commemorate the golden wedding of Sir Walter and Lady Bromley-Davenport in 1983), you will have some measure of just how much the garden has to offer.
woodland garden; fine collection of trees; historic park; tea room

Owned by WA Bromley-Davenport
Number of gardeners 2

CHOLMONDELEY CASTLE GARDENS
Malpas SY14 8AH

Tel 01829 720383 **Fax** 01829 720877
Location Off A49 Tarporley to Whitchurch road
Opening hours 11.30am to 5pm, Wednesdays, Thursdays, Sundays and Bank Holidays, April to September
Admission fee Adults £4; children £2; reduced rates for groups; RHS Members free in June

The gardens below this handsome early 19th-century castle set in rolling parkland have been redeveloped since the 1960s with horticultural advice from Jim Russell. New this year (2007) is a water garden around a restored ruin and a memorial mosaic designed by Maggie Howarth. The modern plantings have been well integrated into the classical landscape and have added an entirely new horticultural dimension. The exquisite temple garden, curling the whole way around a small lake, is breathtakingly beautiful. Highly recommended.
woodland garden; rock garden; good herbaceous borders; fine collection of trees; azaleas and rhododendrons; gift shop; tea room; light lunches and home-made teas

Owned by The Marchioness of Cholmondeley
English Heritage Grade II

DORFOLD HALL
Nantwich CW5 8LD

Tel 01270 625245 **Fax** 01270 628723
Location 1 mile west of Nantwich on A534
Opening hours 2pm to 5pm, Tuesdays and Bank Holiday Mondays, April to October; also 2pm to 5.30pm on 20 May for NGS
Admission fee House and gardens: adults £5; children £3; NGS day: adults £5; children £2.50

William Andrews Nesfield designed the formal approach but the main reason for visiting the gardens at Dorfold Hall is the new woodland garden of rhododendrons and other shrubs, leading down to a stream where *Primula pulverulenta* has naturalised in its thousands. Recent additions include summer herbaceous borders and an orchard walk. Do not miss the incredible hulk of an ancient Spanish chestnut in the stable yard.
spring woodland garden; camellias; magnolias; rhododendrons and azaleas; daffodils and bluebells; good summer herbaceous borders

Owned by RC Roundell
Number of gardeners 2
Size 7.2ha (18 acres)
English Heritage Grade II

DUNGE VALLEY HIDDEN GARDENS
Windgather Rocks, Kettleshulme, High Peak SK23 7RF

Tel/fax 01663 733787
www.dungevalley.co.uk
Location 1 mile south of Kettleshulme village: follow brown tourist signs and turn down a minor road towards Goyt Valley
Opening hours 10.30m to 5pm, Thursday to Sunday, March to August; plus Tuesdays and Wednesdays in May; open on Bank Holiday Mondays
Admission fee Adults £3; children £1

These hidden gardens 300m (984ft) up in the Pennines are a surprise and a delight: few are so high, and fewer still so full of colour. It is not only the number of plants which gives such pleasure,

but the surprise of finding so many that one might suppose too tender – embothriums, desfontainias and mahonias, for example. But there are also fine rhododendrons, old-fashioned roses and flowering borders in an almost Himalayan setting. The nursery has one of the largest selections of rhododendrons for sale in northern England.
rhododendrons and azaleas; roses; hardy trees and shrubs; tea room; lunches and light refreshments

Owned by David and Elizabeth Ketley
Number of gardeners 2
Size 2.6ha (7 acres)

GRANADA ARBORETUM
Jodrell Bank, Macclesfield SK11 9DL

Tel 01477 571339 **Fax** 01477 571695
www.jb.man.ac.uk/viscen
Location On A535 between Holmes Chapel and Chelford
Opening hours 10.30am to 4.30pm, daily, mid-March to 29 October; 10.30am to 3pm, Tuesday to Friday, November to mid-March; 11am to 4pm on Saturdays and Sundays during Cheshire school holidays
Admission fee Adults £1.50; children £1

The Granada Arboretum at Jodrell Bank was founded by Sir Bernard Lovell in 1971 with funding from the Granada Foundation. The arboretum specialises in alders, birches, crab apples, maples and *Sorbus*. Long straight rides lead spaciously into the distance. The plantings are young and vigorous, the groupings imaginative. A radio telescope dominates: an awesome presence.
shop; café

Owned by Manchester University
Number of gardeners 2
Size 14ha (35 acres)
NCCPG National Collections *Malus*; *Sorbus*

HARE HILL GARDEN
Garden Lodge, Over Alderley, Macclesfield SK10 4QB

Tel 01625 584412 **Fax** 01625 587555
www.nationaltrust.org.uk
Location Between Alderley Edge and Prestbury
Opening hours 10am to 5pm, Wednesdays, Thursdays, Saturdays, Sundays and Bank Holiday Mondays, 31 March to 1 November; open daily from 7 May to 1 June for rhododendrons and azaleas
Admission fee Adults £3.20; children £1.50; parking £1.80 (refunded on admission)

Hare Hill is a woodland garden, thickly planted with trees and underplanted with rhododendrons, azaleas and shrubs by Jim Russell in the 1960s. In the middle is a walled garden which has been developed as a flower garden with a pergola, arbour and tender plants against the walls. Planting continues with new cultivars. Perhaps best in May, there are still some rhododendrons to flower with the roses in July.
woodland garden; rock garden; plantsman's collection of plants; good herbaceous borders

Owned by The National Trust
Number of gardeners 1½
Size 4ha (10 acres)

LITTLE MORETON HALL
Congleton CW12 4SD

Tel 01260 272018 **Fax** 01260 292802
www.nationaltrust.org.uk
Location 4 miles south of Congleton on A34
Opening hours 11.30am to 5pm (or dusk, if earlier – 4pm until 25 March), Wednesday to Sunday and Bank Holiday Mondays, 3 March to 4 November; 11.30am to 4pm, Saturdays and Sundays, 10 November to 16 December
Admission fee Adults £6; children £3; families £14; parking £5 (refunded on admission)

Little Moreton Hall is the handsomest timber-framed house in England – an icon of domestic Tudor architecture. When the National Trust asked Graham Stuart Thomas to design and plant a suitable period garden, he specified box-edged borders with yew topiary and gravel infilling – and very fine they are. too. A speciality has been made of old varieties of fruit, vegetables and herbs around the knot garden. Peaceful, charming and orderly.
herbs; fruit; good herbaceous borders; shop; licensed restaurant – lunches, coffee, teas

Owned by The National Trust
Number of gardeners 1
Size 0.4ha (1 acre)
English Heritage Grade I

LYME PARK
Disley SK12 2NX

Tel 01663 762023 **Fax** 01663 765035
www.nationaltrust.org.uk
Location 6½ miles south-east of Stockport on A6, just west of Disley
Opening hours 11am to 5pm, daily, 25 March to 31 October; noon to 3pm, Saturdays and Sundays, 4 to 24 March and 4 November to 16 December
Admission fee Garden only: adults £3.80; children £2.20; £4.60 for car (National Trust members free)

There is much of horticultural interest at Lyme, as well as the razzmatazz of a country park: traditional bedding out, two enormous camellias in the conservatory, and a Jekyll-type herbaceous border by Graham Stuart Thomas where the colours run from orange to deepest purple. Best of all is the sunken Dutch garden whose looping box and ivy parterres contain the most extravagant bedding displays. The National Trust has now assumed full control of the garden and restored the structure in line with the original Lewis Wyatt design. Lyme Park featured as Pemberley in the BBC's *Pride & Prejudice*.
roses (mainly old-fashioned); good herbaceous borders; spring bulbs; bedding out; orangery by Wyatt; Dutch garden; shop; restaurant and coffee shop (April to October)

Owned by The National Trust
Number of gardeners 4
Size 6.7ha (17 acres)
English Heritage Grade II*

MELLORS GARDEN
Hough Hole House, Rainow, Macclesfield SK10 5UW

Tel 01625 573251 **Fax** 01625 572389
Location In Sugar Lane
Opening hours 2pm to 5pm, 28 May and 27 August; and by appointment
Admission fee £1.50

This remarkable small garden was laid out in the 19th century as an allegory of Christian's journey in *Pilgrim's Progress* and originally planted only with plants that are mentioned in the Bible. Features represent such places as the Wall of Salvation, the Cave of the Holy Sepulchre, Vanity Fayre, the Dark River, the Delectable Mountains, Doubting Castle and the Celestial City. A spiritual and historical experience more than a horticultural one.
refreshments by arrangement

Owned by Mr and Mrs A Rigby
Size 0.8ha (2 acres)

MOUNT PLEASANT GARDENS
Yeld Lane, Kelsall CW6 0TB

Tel 01829 751592
www.mountpleasantgardens.co.uk
Location North-west of Kelsall and just north of A54
Opening hours Noon to 5pm, Wednesdays, Saturdays and Sundays, May to September
Admission fee Adults £3; children free; RHS members free

This young garden, started in 1994 and well-known for its sculptures, makes very good use of evergreens to provide density and bulk as other plants grow up. Rhododendrons and azaleas give a fine show in late spring, as does the laburnum tunnel. Elsewhere are two ponds, a stumpery, herbaceous plantings and a wildflower meadow.
tea and cakes

Owned by Dave Darlington and Louise Worthington
Number of gardeners 2
Size 4ha (10 acres)

NORTON PRIORY MUSEUM & GARDENS
Tudor Road, Runcorn WA7 1SX

Tel 01928 569895 **Fax** 01928 589743
www.nortonpriory.org
Location Well signed locally
Opening hours Noon to 5pm (6pm at weekends and Bank Holidays), daily, March to October
Admission fee Adults £4.95; OAPs £3.50; families £12.75

NESS BOTANIC GARDENS

Neston CH64 4AY

Tel 0151 353 0123 **Fax** 0151 353 1004
www.nessgardens.org.uk
Location Signed off A540, Chester to Hoylake
Opening hours 9.30am to 4.30pm (5pm from February to October), daily, all year; closed 25 December
Admission fee Adults £5.50; concessions £5; children £2.50. Adults £3.70 from November to January

Ness was the creation of a Liverpool cotton merchant, Arthur Bulley, who laid out the garden in 1898 and started to plant it with new species from abroad. He was particularly interested in Himalayan and Chinese plants: he believed that many could become established in cultivation in Britain and he therefore sponsored such plant collectors as George Forrest and Frank Kingdon-Ward. It is to Bulley that we owe such plants as *Gentiana sino-ornata* and *Pieris formosa* var. *forrestii*, and it was at Ness that many Chinese plants were first grown in Europe – notably the candelabra primulas. Ness was presented to the University of Liverpool by Bulley's daughter in 1948 and has continued to develop as a public amenity, a tourist attraction and a teaching garden, while still retaining the 'feel' of a private garden. It is beautifully laid out in a sequence of incidents: both its design and

plantings have continued to improve year by year. The main features are as follows: a laburnum arch; a herb garden; a rhododendron border (long and deep) underplanted with many lilies; an excellent heather garden; sandstone terraces where tender plants like *Ribes speciosum* flourish; a rock garden with an enormous range of different environments, south-facing and north-facing, limestone and sandstone, sunny, shaded and damp; a water garden; a camellia collection; an arboretum; a *Sorbus* collection, recently recognised by the NCCPG as a National Collection; herbaceous borders; and glasshouses with arid displays including the crown of thorns (*Euphorbia milii*). As with all botanic gardens, there is no end of things to see whatever the season, and your visit can be as short or as long as it suits. In practice, however, Ness is one of those gardens where you tend to spend much longer than you intended. The Friends of Ness are very active and the website, too, is very comprehensive.
roses (mainly old-fashioned); mature conifers; fine collection of trees; 30m (98ft) laburnum arch; camellia walk; notable collections of *Sorbus*, *Betula*, *Salix* and *Cotoneaster*, tallest *Alnus cremastogyne* (3.3m; 11ft) in the British Isles; gift shop; plant nursery; café

Owned by The University of Liverpool
Number of gardeners 11
Size 26ha (65 acres)
English Heritage Grade II

The old walled garden at Norton Priory has a new layout modelled on 18th-century precedents. A cottage garden border, a medicinal herb garden (featured on BBC2's *Hidden Gardens* in 2006) and an orchard rub shoulders with colour borders, kitchen gardens and a scented garden. Beyond are 16 acres of woodland garden with Georgian summerhouses and glades by the stream.
roses (ancient and modern); rock garden; herbs; fruit; good herbaceous borders; current holder of Sandford Award; garden produce shop; refreshments at museum

Owned by Norton Priory Museum Trust (Halton Borough Council)
Number of gardeners 2
Size 15ha (38 acres)
NCCPG National Collections *Cydonia oblonga*

PEOVER HALL

Over Peover, Knutsford WA16 9HW

Tel 01565 830395 **Fax** 01565 830241
Location 3 miles south of Knutsford
Opening hours 2pm to 5pm, Mondays and Thursdays, April to October; and for NGS
Admission fee Adults £3; children £2

First a classic 18th-century parkland, then an Edwardian overlay of formal gardens, yew hedges and brick paths. Peover has modern plantings, too – borders in colour combinations, a herb garden, and a rhododendron dell in the woods.
topiary; roses (mainly old-fashioned); herbs; walled garden; landscaped park; rhododendrons; tea room (Mondays only)

Owned by R Brooks Ltd
Number of gardeners 3
Size 6.4ha (16 acres)
English Heritage Grade II

THE QUINTA

Swettenham Village, Congleton CW12 2LD

Tel 01477 537698 (answering machine)
www.tattongardensociety.co.uk

Location Access through the Swettenham Arms garden
Opening hours 9am to dusk, daily, all year, except 25 December; for NGS: 7 May and 10 September
Admission fee Adults £2.50; RHS members free

The Quinta Arboretum was created by Sir Bernard Lovell, originator of the Jodrell Bank Radio Telescope, and is now owned by the Tatton Garden Society, of which he is president. The garden features more than 10,000 trees and shrubs (2,000 taxa), with a 5ha (12 acres) wild wood (owned by Cheshire Wildlife Trust), flower-rich meadows and beautiful views over the valley of the River Dane. The Royal Botanic Garden Edinburgh has sponsored a collection of endangered conifers. Also of merit are collections of *Quercus* species and *Hebe* cultivars, each with 90+ taxa.
nice young arboretum; wildflowers; woodland garden

Owned by Tatton Garden Society
Size 11ha (28 acres)
NCCPG National Collections *Fraxinus*; *Pinus*

REASEHEATH COLLEGE
Nantwich CW5 6DF

Tel 01270 625131 **Fax** 01270 625665
www.reaseheath.ac.uk
Location 1 mile north of Nantwich on A51
Opening hours 2pm to 5pm, 16 and 24 May. College open day 11am to 5pm, 13 May; guided tours for groups at other times
Admission fee Donation to NGS

Reaseheath has been thoroughly replanted recently: there is an enormous amount to enjoy and learn here. Highlights include a woodland garden, a model fruit garden, a lake, a gravel garden, good bedding on the formal terraces and splendid mixed borders.
woodland garden; rhododendrons and azaleas; good herbaceous borders; fine collection of trees; heather garden; formal bedding; Reaseheath Garden Centre, open daily, all year; shop and coffee lounge

Owned by Reaseheath College
Number of gardeners 2
Size 12ha (30 acres)

RODE HALL
Church Lane, Scholar Green,
Stoke on Trent ST7 3QP

Tel 01270 882961 **Fax** 01270 882962
www.rodehall.co.uk
Location 5 miles south-west of Congleton between A34 and A50
Opening hours 2pm to 5pm, Tuesday to Thursday and Bank Holiday Mondays, 1 April to 30 September; plus noon to 4pm, daily except Mondays, 1 to 28 February, for snowdrops
Admission fee Garden only: adults £3; OAPs £2.50; RHS members free

Stand on the terraces at Rode Hall and take in the prospect: William Andrews Nesfield's 1860s rose garden and Humphry Repton's landscape beyond. The 'pool' is nearly a mile long and 150 yards (137m) wide. But horticulture is also here in abundance: take the boathouse walk past the old stew pond (pretty marginals and a waterfall) to the wildflower garden (terraced rock garden – early 19th century – *very* early for this sort of garden) where snowdrops, sarcococcas, hellebores (lots), ferns, primroses and soldanellas flourish in the lee of rhododendrons. Note the splendid Loderi crosses, which smell of sugared almonds and extend the flowering season into early June. Admire Professor Pratt's scented azaleas (would that more people knew and grew them) and note how the plantings of rhododendron species are being extended into the adjacent Old Wood. Inspect the new Italian garden that is being developed in the ruins of the old Tenants' Hall. Then visit the walled kitchen garden (about two acres) and see the rows of decorative vegetables set between cornflowers, poppies, marigolds and flowers for drying. Espaliered fruit trees cover the walls between 4m (13ft) abutilons: Cheshire has a mild climate. Look inside the greenhouses and see the many geraniums with scented leaves. And ponder the industry of the head gardener, Kelvin Archer, who grows over 40 cultivars of gooseberry here and holds the world record for the largest gooseberry fruit.
woodland garden; topiary; snowdrops; roses (mainly old-fashioned); fruit; mature conifers; ice house; rhododendrons; grotto; laburnum walk; fully functional two-acre walled kitchen garden; garden produce; cream teas; light lunches in February

Owned by Sir Richard Baker Wilbraham
Number of gardeners 2
Size 2.4ha (6 acres)
English Heritage Grade II

STAPELEY WATER GARDENS
London Road, Stapeley, Nantwich CW5 7LH

Tel 01270 623868 **Fax** 01270 624919
www.stapeleywg.com
Location A51, 1 mile south of Nantwich
Opening hours Water Garden and Garden Centre: 9am (10am on Sundays) to 6pm (5pm in winter, 4pm on Sundays and 8pm on summer Wednesdays), daily, all year, except Easter Sunday and Christmas Day. The Palms Tropical Oasis: 10am to 6pm (5pm in winter), daily, all year, except Christmas Day
Admission fee The Palms Tropical Oasis: Adults £4.45; OAPs £3.95; children £2.60

Part entertainment, part nursery and part display garden, the Palms Tropical Oasis is worth a visit in its own right. A long rectangular pool in the Moorish style is flanked by tall palms, strelitzias and other showy tropical flowers. The display gardens outside are fascinating all through the year, especially the water gardens where all the water lilies grow.
plants under glass; collection of hardy water lilies; *Victoria regia*, the giant water lily; major nursery and garden centre; cafeteria and terrace restaurant

Owned by Stapeley Water Gardens Ltd
NCCPG National Collections *Nymphaea*

STONYFORD COTTAGE
Stonyford Lane, Oakmere, Northwich CW8 2TF

Tel 01606 888128
Location 2 miles west of Cuddington; take Norley Road off A556
Opening hours 1.30pm to 5pm, Tuesday to Sunday and Bank Holiday Mondays, 2 April to 5 October; for NGS: 10 June
Admission fee Adults £3

Water plants are the speciality of this small garden; they are thickly planted around a large pool and in the bog garden, especially irises and candelabra primulas, hostas and mimulus. But there is also a dry, sheltered corner planted with some surprising Mediterranean and tender plants.
small specialist nursery; cream teas on NGS day

Owned by Mr and Mrs A Overland
Number of gardeners 1
Size 0.2ha (1/2 acre)

TATTON PARK
Knutsford WA16 6QN

Tel 01625 534400 **Fax** 01625 534403
www.tattonpark.org.uk
Location Off M6, Jct 19 and M56, Jct 7 – well signed
Opening hours 10am to 6pm, Tuesday to Sunday and Bank Holiday Mondays, all year, but open 11am to 4pm from 1 October to 14 March 2008
Admission fee Adults £3.50; children £2; RHS members free; cars £4.20

Humphry Repton laid out the parkland at Tatton. Sir Joseph Paxton designed both the formal Italian garden and the exquisite fernery, claimed as the finest in the UK. Later came a Japanese garden (restored for the Japanese Festival in 2001) and Shinto temple (1910), such follies as the African hut, and the mass plantings of rhododendrons and azaleas. The pineapple house in the walled garden has just been restored and opens for the first time this year (2007). Tatton Park is wonderfully well organised for visitors, and gets better every year. Be prepared for a long and absorbing visit. The RHS Flower Show at Tatton Park will take place from 18 to 23 July 2007 (tickets from 0870 906 3811).
good herbaceous borders; fine collection of trees; rhododendrons & azaleas in May; biggest *Quercus schochiana* in the British Isles; current holder of Sandford Award; Europa Nostra award for restored orangery and fernery; shop (closed Mondays); restaurant (closed Mondays in winter)

Owned by The National Trust (managed by Cheshire County Council)
Number of gardeners 13
Size 20ha (50 acres)
NCCPG National Collections *Adiantum*
English Heritage Grade II*

CORNWALL

Many of the great historic gardens of Cornwall are also the most interesting horticulturally. Mount Edgcumbe and Tresco are both rated Grade I gardens of national importance, while Caerhays Castle, Lanhydrock, Tregrehan and Trewithen are Grade II* and Antony, Carclew, Chyverton, Cotehele, Glendurgan, Heligan, Lamellen, Pencarrow, Penjerrick, St Michael's Mount, Trebah, Trelissick and Trengwainton are all Grade II. It is a proud list, unmatched by any other county, and evidence of how the big estates have always dominated the gardening scene in Cornwall. The county still has its own horticultural organisation, the Cornwall Garden Society: its spring show is a showcase for camellias and rhododendrons. About 80 gardens open every year for the Cornwall Festival of Spring Gardens which runs from mid-March to the end of May: details from the Cornwall Tourist Board on 01872 322900. Cornish gardens are usually best in spring when the rhododendrons, azaleas, camellias and magnolias are at their peak and the days are lengthening. Almost all the gardens have fine collections of trees, too: those at Trebah, Tregrehan and Trewithen are particularly noted for the age and size of their specimens, while the woodlands of Caerhays contain an exceptional number of well-grown rarities. A new type of Cornish garden has, however, been emerging over the last 25 years, where the owners have taken advantage of the climate to grow a very wide range of newer plants: Pine Lodge, Lamorran and Bosvigo are good examples and will doubtless be followed by others. The county's National Collections reflect the opportunities which the mild climate makes possible: among them are *Escallonia* at Duchy College, *Azara* at Trelissick, *Grevillea* at Pine Lodge and *Acacia* at Tresco. Finest of all is the National Collection of *Dahlia* at Varfell Farm at Long Rock, just off the A30, where some 2,000 species and cultivars can be seen by prior appointment (further details from dahlias@wgltd.co.uk). Cornish nurseries cater well for the local market; best known is Burncoose & South Down Nurseries, a regular winner of Gold Medals for its spectacular displays of flowering trees and shrubs at RHS shows throughout the year.

ANTONY

Torpoint PL11 2QA

Tel 01752 812191 **Fax** 01752 815724
www.nationaltrust.org.uk
Location 5 miles west of Plymouth; 2 miles north-west of Torpoint
Opening hours 1.30pm to 5.30pm, Tuesday to Thursday and Bank Holiday Mondays, 3 April to 31 October; plus Sundays from June to August
Admission fee Adults £3; children £1.50; combined ticket with Antony Woodland Garden: adults £4.80; children £2.40

Antony has been a historic and important garden for centuries – and every generation has left its mark. Its classic late 18th-century landscape is superb, though there is considerable debate as to whether Humphry Repton designed it or the Pole-Carews (as they were then called) listened to Repton's advice but followed little of it. The yew walk with its lead statues of a shepherd and his shepherdess and the huge Burmese temple bell, flanked by stone lanterns, date from the 19th century. Much of the horticultural interest was created by Sir John Carew Pole in the middle of the 20th century – masses of bulbs, the lime tree avenues, over 600 early *Hemerocallis* hybrids from the USA, a 9.2m (30ft) loquat tree (*Eriobotrya japonica*) against the house, the vast cork oak (*Quercus suber* –another record-breaker), the venerable old 'Black Walnut'

(*Juglans nigra*) on the main lawn and the beautiful spring-flowering *Magnolia denudata*. The position is superb – an elevated promontory above the Tamar estuary, just across Plymouth Sound from Devon. Sir Richard and Lady Carew Pole, who now live at Antony, have continued to intensify and extend this plantsman's garden: more spring-flowering trees and shrubs have been planted, alongside the creation of gardens for summer and autumn interest. The Summer Garden is particularly effective: hybrid musk roses are underplanted with lilies, irises, phlox and peonies and its walls are covered in clematis, climbing roses, lemon-scented verbena and *Cytisus battandieri*. But there is much to see at every season – the magnolia walk in spring, the knot garden, the terraces in high summer with giant catmint (*Nepeta* 'Six Hills Giant') mingling with the floribunda rose 'Iceberg' and free-standing fig trees *Ficus carica* 'White Marseilles' in autumn. And it is a large garden, so you need to allow a lot of time to do it justice.

mature conifers; good herbaceous borders; magnolias; yew hedges; tallest Japanese loquat *Eriobotrya japonica* (9.2m; 30ft) in the British Isles (and two other tree records); National Trust shop; tea room

Owned by The National Trust
Number of gardeners 3, plus 2 trainees
Size 14ha (35 acres)
NCCPG National Collections *Hemerocallis*
English Heritage Grade II

ANTONY WOODLAND GARDEN

Antony House, Torpoint PL11 2QA

Tel 01752 812191 **Fax** 01752 815724
Location 5 miles west of Plymouth; 2 miles north-west of Torpoint
Opening hours 11am to 5.30pm, daily, except Mondays and Fridays (but open on Bank Holidays), 1 March to 31 October
Admission fee Adults £4; accompanied children free

P 👪

This is the 'Cornish' part of the grounds at Antony, still controlled by the Carew Pole family rather than the National Trust. It is a garden of considerable botanical interest divided into two main areas. First comes the Wilderness, a wooded area to the north-west of the house which runs down to the banks of the River Lynher. Three vistas frame the house from the river: Humphry Repton's influence is apparent here. The Wilderness has been planted with trees and shrubs like Japanese maples, a tunnel of *Camellia* x *williamsii* 'Donation' and *Camellia japonica* 'Lady de Saumarez', *Magnolia obovata*, rhododendron species and hybrids including the strongly scented 'Loderi' and *R griffithianum*. There is a conifer dell with giant redwoods *Sequoiadendron giganteum*, *Cryptomeria japonica* and *Taxus baccata* 'Dovastoniana' and three ponds cascading down a valley to the salt pans and the Bath House pond. The second area is Westdown, where the planting consists mainly of camellias of considerable variety (including the National Collection of *Camellia japonica*) interspersed with Asiatic magnolias and rhododendron species, thriving in the deep valley. The magnolias include specimens of 'Charles Raffill', *M dawsoniana*, and *M campbellii* subsp. *mollicomata* 'Lanarth'. The two areas are joined by the Garden Field where ornamental trees have been underplanted with flowering shrubs and daffodils. A path through deep-scented shrubs and birches completes the link along the river's edge. The Carew Poles have also commissioned several pieces of contemporary sculpture for the garden and the wider estate.

woodland garden; plantsman's collection of plants; mature conifers; camellias; magnolias; rhododendrons and azaleas; tea room as for Antony (qv)

Owned by The Carew Pole Garden Trust
Number of gardeners 1
Size 26ha (65 acres)
NCCPG National Collections *Camellia japonica*

THE BARBARA HEPWORTH MUSEUM & SCULPTURE GARDEN

2 Barnoon Hill, St Ives TR26 1AD

Tel 01736 796226 **Fax** 01736 794480
www.tate.org.uk/stives/hepworth
Location In town centre
Opening hours 10am to 5.20pm, daily, March to October; 10am to 4.20pm, Tuesday to Sunday, November to March; last admissions 30 mins before closing; closed 24 to 26 December

Admission fee Adults £4.75; concessions £2.75; free to over-60s and under-18s

Dame Barbara Hepworth's studio and garden have been run by the Tate Gallery since 1980. Hepworth died in 1975, and asked (in her will) that Trewyn studios and the subtropical garden should become a permanent setting to exhibit her works. Visiting them gives you a remarkable insight into one of the 20th century's most important sculptors and the garden which was an essential part of her creative process.
shop

Owned by Tate Gallery and Hepworth Estate
Number of gardeners 2
Size 0.2ha (1/2 acre)
English Heritage Grade II

BOCONNOC

Lostwithiel PL22 0RG

Tel 01208 872507 **Fax** 01208 873836
www.boconnocenterprises.co.uk
Location 3 miles east of Lostwithiel
Opening hours 2pm to 5.30pm, 15, 22 and 29 April, and 6, 13, 20 and 27 May; and by arrangement for groups
Admission fee Adults £4.50

Boconnoc House has a historic landscape, laid out by Thomas Pitt, 1st Lord Camelford, who also erected the Obelisk in 1771, and incorporating a much older deer park. There is much planned by way of restoration shortly, but the main horticultural interest lies in the woodlands, thick with bluebells and planted with rhododendrons, azaleas and camellias; some date back to the 1850s. In the pinetum, also undergoing restoration, is a fine collection of conifers, many of them collected by William Lobb.
cream teas

Owned by Anthony Fortescue
Number of gardeners 2
Size 12ha (30 acres)
English Heritage Grade II*

BONYTHON

Cury Cross Lanes, Helston TR12 7BA

Tel 01326 240550 **Fax:** 01326 240478
www.bonythonmanor.co.uk
Location 1/2 mile east of A3083 at Cross Lanes
Opening hours 10am to 4.30pm, Tuesday to Friday, April to September
Admission fee Adults £5; children £2

Bonython's gardens have been revived and greatly improved since Sue Nathan took over in 1999. The woodlands have been cleared to reveal extensive plantings of rhododendrons and azaleas, and wild bluebells and ramsons. An avenue of hydrangeas has been added for summer and autumn colour. The walled garden is outstanding for its herbaceous borders, colour themed in blue, purple white and yellow. Agapanthus, salvias, roses, clematis, honeysuckle and three large eucryphias also ensure that Bonython is not just another Cornish spring garden. A new gravel border by the lake is planted with colourful late-summer beauties, like amaranthus, dahlias and cannas. Elsewhere are restios, proteas and tree ferns.
refreshments

Owned by Mr and Mrs Richard Nathan
Number of gardeners 2
Size 8ha (20 acres)

BOSAHAN

Manaccan, Helston TR12 6JL

Tel 01326 231351 **Fax** 01326 231497
www.gardensofcornwall.com
Location Off Manaccan to St Anthony road, or uphill from Treath and first left
Opening hours 11m to 4.30pm, Monday to Friday, 19 March to 17 September, but closed on all Bank Holidays; open day: 1pm to 5pm on 6 May
Admission fee Adults £4; OAPs £3; disabled £2; children £2

Bosahan dates from the 19th century but is being restored and revived. An atmospheric valley of large tree ferns, rhododendrons,

magnolias, azaleas, palms, conifers, camellias and southern hemisphere plants leads down to the Helford River. Down by the large pond are good plantings of bog plants and marginals. Bosahan is said to have been one of the inspirations for Daphne du Maurier's novel *Rebecca*. The views are stupendous.
subtropical trees; rhododendrons

Owned by Mr and Mrs RJ Graham-Vivian
Number of gardeners 1
Size 4ha (10 acres)

BOSVIGO
Bosvigo Lane, Truro TR1 3NH

Tel/fax 01872 275774
www.bosvigo.com
Location Turn off A390 at Highertown, just west of Sainsbury's roundabout, then down Dobbs Lane by Aldi sign and 500 yards on left
Opening hours 11am to 6pm, Thursdays and Fridays, 3 March to 30 September
Admission fee Adults £4; children (5-15) £1

Not a typical Cornish garden, the emphasis at Bosvigo is upon herbaceous plants, chosen for their individual qualities and planted in fine colour combinations. The woodland garden is more traditional, and underplanted with snowdrops, hellebores, wood anemones, erythroniums and epimediums, but the rest of the garden is at its best in summer and keeps well into the autumn. Over the last 25 years or so, Wendy and Michael Perry have created a series of small walled or hedged garden 'rooms' around the mainly Georgian house. Each has its own colour theme: the walled garden heaves with polite blues, mauves and pinks while another is mainly of gold and white. Reds and oranges co-exist in a 'hot' garden which, according to Patrick Taylor in the *Daily Telegraph*, 'will blow your socks off'. Many of the plants are rare, and some are sold in the small specialist nursery.
woodland garden; plantsman's collection of plants; good herbaceous borders; unusual perennials; Victorian conservatory; colour borders; excellent small herbaceous nursery

Owned by Wendy and Michael Perry
Number of gardeners owners only
Size 0.8ha (2 acres)

BURNCOOSE GARDENS & NURSERIES
Gwennap, Redruth TR16 6BJ

Tel 01209 860316 **Fax** 01209 860011
www.burncoose.co.uk
Location Directly on A393 Redruth to Falmouth road between villages of Lanner and Ponsanooth
Opening hours 8.30am (11am on Sundays) to 5pm, daily, except 25 December, all year
Admission fee Gardens: adults £2; children free. Nursery: free

Burncoose Nurseries specialise in rare and unusual plants: they list over 3,500 different ones – mainly ornamental trees and shrubs – which makes them one of the best for sheer choice in all Europe. Their real specialities are camellias, rhododendrons, magnolias and conservatory plants. Burncoose has won 20 gold medals at the last 25 Chelsea Flower Shows and numerous gold medals at Hampton Court, Tatton Park and other shows. The garden is a woodland garden, carpeted with bluebells, primroses, snowdrops and wild violets in spring. Two monkey puzzles *Araucaria araucana* are over 30m (100ft) high and a *Eucryphia* x *nymansensis* reaches 13m (40ft). Most of the ornamental plants have been planted since 1900 and the older ones have been matched in recent years by substantial additions. There will be two RHS Special Events at Burncoose Nurseries in 2007; details from 020 7821 3408 or 0845 612 1253.
woodland garden; rhododendrons and azaleas; plantsman's collection of plants; camellias; bluebells; magnolias; rare trees and shrubs; important nursery (major RHS gold medal winner); teas and light refreshments

Owned by Charles Williams
Number of gardeners 1
Size 12ha (30 acres)

CAERHAYS CASTLE GARDENS

Gorran, St Austell PL26 6LY

Tel 01872 501310 **Fax** 01872 501870
www.caerhays.co.uk
Location Between Mevagissey and Portloe
Opening hours 10am to 5pm, daily, 12 February to 3 June
Admission fee Adults £5.50; children (5-16) £2.50; RHS members free from 13 February to 12 March

Caerhays has belonged to the Williams family since 1853, but it was not until the young JC Williams took over the estate in the 1890s that they began to develop the gardens. It seems that the original inspiration came from a RHS daffodil conference: it sparked JCW's lifelong interest in hybridising. By 1903 he was sponsoring EH Wilson's collections in China and this was followed by a partnership with George Forrest. Of the many plants that these expeditions introduced, Caerhays is best known for its magnolias, but JCW is also remembered as a great hybridiser of rhododendrons and camellias. *Camellia* x *williamsii* was named for him: some of the original plants still flourish at Caerhays, including 'JC Williams', 'Mary Christian' and 'Saint Ewe'. The present owner, and his son Charles Williams, have been no less involved in conserving and improving the remarkable plant collections at Caerhays. They make a point of trying to accommodate rare and unusual plants, whose cultural requirements take precedence over the niceties of garden design. And the Williams are still involved in wide-scale plantings – especially since the garden suffered serious damage in the 1990 great gale. Magnolias remain a major interest and almost all the new forms and cultivars coming out of Australia, USA and New Zealand have been added to the garden and have grown away well. One of the joys of Caerhays is to stumble upon magnificent old specimens deep in its 100 acres of woodland. Among the many rare trees are fine specimens of *Laurus azorica*, *Lithocarpus cleistocarpus*, *Lithocarpus henryi*; magnolias like M. *delavayi*, M. *nitida*, M. *robusta* and M. *salicifolia*; and such oaks as *Quercus acuta*, Q. *crassifolia*, Q. *glauca*, Q. *ilicifolia*, Q. *lamellosa*, Q. *lanata*, Q. *lodicosa*, Q. *oxyodon* and Q. *phillyreoides*. Almost all these species are known to few of us: this litany of names is a measure of the importance of Caerhays. There is much to discover, so you should allow plenty of time. And see the website – very informative. There will be six RHS Special Events at Caerhays in 2007; details from 020 7821 3408.

woodland garden; plantsman's collection of plants; mature conifers; fine collection of trees; camellias; magnolias; rhododendrons; tallest specimen of *Emmenopterys henryi* (17m; 56ft) in the British Isles, and 37 other record-breaking trees (including eight *Acer* species); gift shop; tea room and beach shop/ café in car park

Owned by FJ Williams CBE
Number of gardeners 4
Size 24ha (60 acres)
NCCPG National Collections *Magnolia*
English Heritage Grade II*

CARCLEW GARDENS
Perran-ar-Worthal, Truro TR3 7PB

Tel 07747 111477
Location A39 east at Perran-ar-Worthal; 1 mile to garden
Opening hours 2pm to 5.30pm, for NGS and other charities; and at any time by written appointment
Admission fee Adults £3.50; children 50p

Ⓟ

Carclew's garden first opened to the public in 1927 and has continued to do so for charity every year since then. It was once the greatest rhododendron garden in the South West: some of the oldest rhododendrons were grown from Sir Joseph Hooker's Himalayan collections nearly 150 years ago. The many fine trees include a large gingko and a form of *Quercus* x *hispanica* which is *not* 'Lucombeana'. The Chopes have been busy replanting and restoring the garden: the waterfall has recently been repaired.
woodland garden; roses (mainly modern); rhododendrons; tallest *Pseudolarix amabilis* (23m; 75ft) in the British Isles

Owned by The Chope family
Number of gardeners 1
English Heritage Grade II

CARWINION
Mawnan Smith, Falmouth TR11 5JA

Tel 01326 250258 **Fax** 01326 250903
www.carwinion.com
Location From Mawnan Smith, turn left at Red Lion, 500 yards up hill on right
Opening hours 10am to 5.30pm, daily, or by appointment, all year
Admission fee Adults £4; OAPs £3.50; children free

Ⓟ

Twelve acres of Cornish jungle, exotically thick with vast rhododendrons, camellias, *Trachycarpus fortunei*, drimys, gunneras, lysichitons, ferns, hellebores and the largest collection of bamboos in the South West.
woodland garden; subtropical plants; mature conifers; nearly 200 different bamboos; gunneras; bluebells; teas in summer

Owned by Anthony Rogers
Number of gardeners 1
Size 4.8ha (12 acres)

CHYVERTON
Zelah, Truro TR4 9HD

Tel 01872 540324 **Fax** 01872 540648
Location 1 mile south-west of Zelah on A30
Opening hours By appointment from March to May, magnoliaphiles at any time by appointment
Admission fee Adults £6; children (under 16) free; visits are personally conducted

Ⓟ

Chyverton started out as a Georgian landscape garden. Later owners planted a pinetum in the 1830s and the first rhododendrons in 1890. The horticultural plantings have, however, been very much extended since the 1920s, initially with some advice from Sir Harold Hillier (his first ever advisory visit), but latterly by the owners themselves. Nigel Holman is a distinguished plantsman: Hugh Johnson calls his garden 'a magic jungle'. Magnolias are a particular interest: there are over 150 cultivars and several Chyverton seedlings now bear cultivar names. Many other established plants have also been grown from seed, including plants collected by Nigel Holman in China. But there is much more to interest the plantsman. A lanky red-stemmed hedge of *Luma apiculata* below the house is outstanding. The planting continues – no sprays or trimmed edges – and is now accompanied by the placement of statues in suitable sites.
woodland garden; plantsman's collection of plants; mature conifers; magnolias, including four record-breakers; nothofagus; tallest *Rhododendron* 'Cornish Red' (16m; 52ft) in the British isles

Owned by Nigel Holman
Number of gardeners 1
Size 50ha (125 acres)
English Heritage Grade II

Cotehele

COTEHELE

St Dominick, Saltash PL12 6TA

Tel 01579 351346 **Fax** 01579 351222
www.nationaltrust.org.uk
Location 14 miles from Plymouth via Saltash
Opening hours 10.30am to dusk, daily, all year
Admission fee Adults £5; children £2.50

Cotehele's garden is laid out on Victorian terraces below the house. Frost drops away, so the garden can boast such tender plants as *Jasminum mesnyi*, *Tibouchina urvilleana* and *Beschorneria yuccoides*. Below is a dense woodland valley, a jungle of camellias, rhododendrons, fuchsias, azaleas, crinodendrons and magnolias, all kept damp by a small stream. The National Trust has undertaken much gentle restoration and renewal in recent years. The plants of *Schizophragma integrifolia* against the walls of the outhouses are very impressive when they flower in late summer.
woodland garden; topiary; roses (mainly modern); daffodils; fine collection of trees; palms; ferns; pretty dovecote; National Trust gift shop; restaurant (mid-March to October)

Owned by The National Trust
Number of gardeners 3, plus 2 students
Size 5.6ha (14 acres)
English Heritage Grade II

THE EDEN PROJECT

Bodelva, St Austell PL24 2SG

Tel01726 811911 **Fax** 01726 811912
www.edenproject.com
Location Signed from A30, A390 and A391
Opening hours 10am to 6pm (closes at 4.30pm from November to March; last admissions 1½ hours before closing), daily, all year, except 24 and 25 December
Admission fee Adults £14; OAPs £10; children £5; families £35

The promoters of this imaginative project hope to provide visitors with an understanding of the world of plants, and their importance to human welfare. The area under glass is described as being the size of 30 football pitches. One of the gigantic conservatories – all made in a disused clay pit near St Austell – is landscaped as a rainforest. The others represent Mediterranean, South African and Californian climate zones. Staples like cocoa, coffee, bananas and rubber are grown alongside plants used in paper, wine, scent and brewing. Outside are collections of camellias, lavender, sunflowers and hemp, and one million spring bulbs. There is plenty of hype, too, but visitors all speak enthusiastically of the experience.
giant glasshouses; exotic plants; gift shop; several cafés and restaurants

Owned by The Eden Trust
Number of gardeners 30, plus support staff
Size 14.7ha (37 acres)

GLENDURGAN

Mawnan Smith, Falmouth TR11 5JZ

Tel 01326 250906 **Fax** 01872 865808
www.nationaltrust.org.uk
Location 1 mile west of Mawnan Smith, close to Trebah
Opening hours 10.30am to 5.30pm (last admissions 4.30pm), Tuesday to Saturday, and Bank Holiday Mondays, 10 February to 3 November; closed Good Friday
Admission fee Adults £5.20; children £2.60

Glendurgan is a steep, subtropical valley garden on the Helford River with a good collection of old rhododendrons and camellias. It also boasts an extraordinary 1830s maze of clipped cherry laurel, recently restored and best seen from the new viewing platform above. Indeed, the whole garden is almost best when viewed from the top, but the temptation to wander down and into it is irresistible.
woodland garden; subtropical plants; mature conifers; laurel maze; wildflowers; huge tulip tree; tallest *Eucryphia lucida* (13m; 42.6ft) in the British Isles; small shop; tea room

Owned by The National Trust
Number of gardeners 3, plus 1 trainee
Size 14ha (35 acres)
English Heritage Grade II

The Lost Gardens of Heligan

HEADLAND
Polruan-by-Fowey PL23 1PW

Tel 01726 870243
www.headlandgarden.co.uk
Location Find Polruan: go to bottom of Fore Street, along West Street, left up Battery Lane to end
Opening hours 2pm to 6pm, Thursdays, May to August
Admission fee Adults £2.50; children £1

A cliff garden with 500 steps, the sea on three sides and a sandy beach, Headland is a lesson in what will tolerate salt-laden winds: eucalyptus, acacias, foxgloves and junipers, but especially cacti and succulents – agaves, aloes, echeverias, sedums, lampranthus and crassulas. The design and the variety of the planting make it seem much larger than it really is and there are many stone seats tucked in between the rocky outcrops.
cacti and succulents; salt-spray resistant plants; cream teas in garden

Owned by Jean Hill
Size 0.5ha (1 1/4 acres)

HELIGAN GARDENS
Pentewan, St Austell PL26 6EN

Tel 01726 845100 **Fax** 01726 845101
www.heligan.com
Location St Austell to Mevagissey Road, follow brown tourist signs
Opening hours 10am to 6pm (5pm from November to February), daily, all year except 24 and 25 December
Admission fee Adults £8.50; OAPs £7.50; children £5

Heligan calls itself 'The Lost Gardens of Heligan', but its 200 acres have been spectacularly rescued since 1990 from a jungle of neglect. The owners emphasise that it is 'definitely not just another pretty garden', but best described as a whole series of gardens within a garden. Its productive kitchen gardens – there are five walled gardens – are of particular interest: they contain over 300 cultivars of fruits, herbs and vegetables, some of them no longer commercially available – there is a strong emphasis on heritage varieties. Many of the working buildings are once again carrying out their original functions – fruit stores, tool and potting sheds, pineapple pits, peach, vine and melon houses, manure-heated frames and the bachelor gardeners' bothies. Elsewhere is an Italian garden, a sundial garden, a New Zealand garden, and the alpine ravine. The 22-acre lost 'jungle' valley has a collection of Tasmanian tree ferns that is claimed to be the largest in England, as well as 60 bamboo cultivars and a recent extension planted with agaves and proteas. The background to all this modern activity is a 19th-century plantsman's jungle, with conifers, palms, camellias, tree ferns and rhododendrons dating from the Hooker expeditions of 1849-50. The enthusiasm of the restorers is infectious and their achievements are already substantial, but the gardens can get very crowded.
woodland garden; subtropical plants; rock garden; rhododendrons and azaleas; beautiful ferny gully; splendid kitchen garden; farm shop; licensed restaurant; tea rooms

Owned by Heligan Gardens Ltd
Number of gardeners 25
Size 80ha (200 acres)
English Heritage Grade II

KEN CARO
Bicton, Liskeard PL14 5RF

Tel 01579 362446
Location Signed from A390, midway between Callington and Liskeard
Opening hours 10am to 6pm, daily, 25 February to 30 September
Admission fee Adults £4.50; children £1

Ken Caro was started in 1970 as two acres of intensely-planted formal gardens, and extended in 1993 by taking in a further two acres whose design is rather more free-flowing and modern. It is very much a plantsman's garden with good herbaceous plants and shrubs, not at all a traditional Cornish garden. All-round colour is important: the owners are flower arrangers – look for architectural plants and original combinations. The planting is bold, and never bitty, unlike some plantsmen's gardens and

everything is maintained to a very high standard. The views of the surrounding countryside are stupendous. But the garden is approached along narrow lanes, only for the brave.
plantsman's collection of plants; mature conifers; good herbaceous borders; tea/coffee

Owned by Mr and Mrs KR Willcock
Number of gardeners 2
Size 1.8ha (41/2 acres)

LAMORRAN HOUSE
Upper Castle Road, St Mawes TR2 5BZ

Tel 01326 270800 **Fax** 01326 270801
www.lamorrangardens.co.uk
Location 1/2 mile from village centre
Opening hours 10am to 5pm, Wednesdays and Fridays, April to September
Admission fee Adults £5.50; children free; groups £5

(P) ♠ 👫

The garden at Lamorran has been almost entirely made since 1980, on a steep site above Falmouth Bay. It is tightly designed in the Italian style, but also full of unusual plants – an English Mediterranean garden in Cornwall, say the owners, or a mainland Tresco, though it is closest to the great English garden at La Mortola on the Italian Riviera. Their latest ventures are a new walled garden and a bank planted with cacti and succulents. They have also greatly increased the number of cyatheas in the garden. But tender rhododendrons from Asia are yet another interest, and plants from Australia, too. The collection of unusual plants is simply amazing: very adventurous. The planting is guided by a desire to experiment with hardiness and tempered by the aesthetic demands of the whole garden. So the garden is not a *botanic* collection, but an extremely good *horticultural* one, and the plants are chosen and placed for their decorative merit and their contribution to the whole.
subtropical plants; plantsman's collection of plants matched to a firm design; good herbaceous borders; fine collection of trees; extensive plantings of Australian and South African plants; over 25 different palms

Owned by Mr and Mrs Robert Dudley-Cooke
Number of gardeners 2
Size 1.8ha (41/2 acres)

LANHYDROCK
Bodmin PL30 5AD

Tel 01208 265950 **Fax** 01208 265959
www.nationaltrust.org.uk
Location 21/2 miles south-east of Bodmin

Opening hours 10am to 6pm (dusk, if sooner), daily, all year
Admission fee Garden: adults £5.30; children £2.65

Lanhydrock is a grand mansion, mainly 19th century, with one of the best formal gardens in Cornwall – clipped yews, box parterres and bedding out, as well as large herbaceous borders. The woodlands behind are impressive for their size and colourful rhododendrons in spring. But it is the magnolias which impress the visitor most: 140 different species and cultivars.
woodland garden; topiary; good herbaceous borders; bluebells; Victorian parterres; spring bulbs; National Trust shop; restaurant

Owned by The National Trust
Number of gardeners 5
Size 12.3ha (31 acres)
English Heritage Grade II*

MARSH VILLA GARDENS
St Andrew's Road, Par PL24 2LU

Tel 01726 815920
Location Turn left off A390 at traffic lights in St Blazey; 1st left, then 800 yards on left
Opening hours 11am to 6pm, Sunday to Wednesday, April to October
Admission fee Adults £3.50; disabled £3; children £1.50

The rich alluvial soil and mild climate gives very good growth in this attractive modern garden. The owners started making it in 1988, planting herbaceous and mixed borders among the network of small waterways that drain the marshes. The design is fluid, with several large island beds, and much attention is given to the effects created by different colours and shapes. Despite being so close to the sea, there are few really tender plants, but *Cornus capitata* makes a good display in June.
coffee and teas

Owned by Judith Stephens
Number of gardeners 1
Size 1.2ha (3 acres)

MOUNT EDGCUMBE GARDENS
Cremyll, Torpoint PL10 1HZ

Tel 01752 822236 **Fax** 01752 822199
www.mountedgcumbe.gov.uk
Location At end of B3247 in south-east Cornwall, or by ferry from Plymouth
Opening hours Formal gardens and park: dawn to dusk, daily, all year. House and Earl's Garden: 11am to 4.30pm, Sunday to Thursday, April to September; guided tours for groups by appointment
Admission fee Formal gardens and park: free. House and Earl's Garden: adults £4.50; OAPs £3.50; children £2.25

A long, stately grass drive runs down from the house to Plymouth Sound, through oak woods interplanted with large ornamental trees. The formal gardens are right down on the waterside, protected by a clipped ilex hedge 10m (33ft) high. There are no less than 10 acres of gardens here, including an Italian garden (made in the 1790s), a French garden (Regency), a modern American garden, a New Zealand garden complete with geyser, a Jubilee garden, the 18th-century Thomson's Seat, an orangery with newly

Mount Edgcumbe's geyser

acquired orange trees, and the fern dell with ivies and tree ferns. The two-acre Earl's Garden has a 400-year-old lime tree and a Victorian shell seat among the herbaceous borders, summerhouses and statues. Allow plenty of time to do justice to these majestic pleasure gardens.
subtropical plants; plants under glass; daffodils; good herbaceous borders; fine collection of trees; summer bedding; deer park; formal gardens; fern dell; genuine Victorian rose garden; tallest cork oak *Quercus suber* (26m; 85ft) in the British Isles; gift and book shops; tea room; restaurant in orangery

Owned by Cornwall County Council and Plymouth City Council
Number of gardeners 4
Size 4ha (10 acres), plus 320ha (800-acre) park
NCCPG National Collections *Camellia*
English Heritage Grade I

PENCARROW
Washaway, Bodmin PL30 3AG

Tel 01208 841369 **Fax** 01208 841722
www.pencarrow.co.uk
Location 4 miles north-west of Bodmin, signed off A389 at Washaway
Opening hours 9.30am to 5.30pm, daily, 1 March to 31 October; for NGS: 19 April
Admission fee Adults £4; children £1; groups welcome by appointment (discounts and guided tours usually available)

The mile-long drive at Pencarrow leads to an avenue of rhododendrons and rare conifers before you eventually come to the pretty Anglo-Palladian house. On one side are the outlines of an Italian garden, complete with fountain, laid out in the 1830s, and next to it a great granite rock garden where vast jagged boulders from Bodmin Moor lie strewn among the trees and shrubs. Pencarrow is famous for its conifers: an ancestor planted one of every known variety in the mid-19th century and the survivors are so venerable that the great Alan Mitchell wrote a guide to them. The monkey puzzle *Araucaria araucana* acquired its nickname when a visitor to Pencarrow, Charles Austen, remarked to his host, after some thought, 'that tree would puzzle a monkey'. Since about 1970 the owners have steadily retrieved the garden from the state of dereliction in which it was left at the end of World War II and added a further 200 or so conifers. Recent plantings have involved the addition of over 700 of the best modern rhododendrons, 70 camellias and many other broadleaved trees and shrubs. It is good to see the fortunes of such a distinguished garden revived.
important collection of mature conifers; Italian garden; rhododendrons; camellias; great granite Victorian rock garden; blue hydrangeas; ice house; monkey puzzle avenue; craft shop; light lunches; cream teas

Owned by The Trustees of the Molesworth-St Aubyn Family
Number of gardeners 3
Size 20ha (50 acres)
English Heritage Grade II

PENJERRICK
Budock Water, Falmouth TR11 5ED

Tel 01872 870105
www.penjerrickgarden.co.uk
Location 3 miles south-west of Falmouth, entrance at junction of lanes opposite Penmorvah Manor Hotel
Opening hours 1.30pm to 4.30pm, Wednesdays, Fridays and Sundays, March to September
Admission fee Adults £2.50; children £1

The garden at Penjerrick was begun by the Fox family in the mid-19th century. It is a great plantsman's garden, famous in particular for its Barclayi and Penjerrick hybrid rhododendrons. Some of the original plants still survive in the peaceful woodland garden, thick with exotics: tender plants thrive in the lush, sheltered valley. The garden is recovering well from a period of neglect: it sums up all that was best about private Cornish gardens 100 years ago. Take your gumboots, and prepare for a fascinating walk.
woodland garden; rhododendrons; camellias; tree ferns; ponds and bamboos

Owned by Mrs Rachel Morin
Number of gardeners 1/2
Size 4ha (10 acres)
English Heritage Grade II

PINE LODGE GARDENS & NURSERY
Holmbush, St Austell PL25 3RQ

Tel 01726 73500 **Fax** 01726 77370
www.pine-lodge.co.uk
Location East of St Austell between Holmbush and Tregrehan
Opening hours 10am to 6pm, daily, all year, except 24 to 26 December
Admission fee Adults £5.50; children £3

This modern 30-acre garden is quite unlike the typical Cornish garden. It has several distinct styles and contains over 6,000 different plants, all of which are labelled. In addition to the rhododendrons, magnolias and camellias so familiar in Cornish gardens there are Mediterranean and southern-hemisphere plants grown for year-round interest, herbaceous borders, a fernery, a formal garden, a Japanese garden, a woodland walk and shrubberies. The water features include a large wildlife pond, an ornamental pond, a lake with breeding black swans and an island, and marsh gardens. Trees are a particular interest: Pine Lodge has an acer glade, a young four-acre pinetum, and an arboretum. The wildflower meadow has over 7,000 bulbs and flowers. The pace of the garden's development is very exciting and the owners' appetite for new plants grows stronger every year.
woodland garden; good herbaceous borders; Japanese garden; good water features; lots of interesting plants; garden nursery with plants from wild-collected seed; tea room

Owned by Mr and Mrs Raymond Clemo
Number of gardeners 4
Size 12ha (30 acres)
NCCPG National Collections *Grevillea*

PINSLA GARDEN & NURSERY
Cardinham, Bodmin PL30 4AY

Tel 01208 821339
www.pinslagarden.net
Location Follow brown tourist signs from Cardinham village
Opening hours 10am to 6pm, daily, March to October
Admission fee Adults £2.50; children free; nursery free

Winding paths, granite boulders, unusual textures and a stone circle in the meadow: these, and the sculptures are some of the garden features designed to 'arouse your emotions and feed your soul' at Pinsla. But there are also fine herbaceous borders, naturalistic plantings, shade-plantings and alpine beds – and a nursery with a good choice of herbaceous and alpine plants, ferns, bamboos and succulents.
good nursery; teas

Owned by Mark and Claire Woodbine
Number of gardeners 1½
Size 0.6ha (1½ acres)

ROSELAND HOUSE
Chacewater, Truro TR4 8QB

Tel: 01872 560451
www.roselandhouse.co.uk
Location At east end of main street in Chacewater, 4 miles west of Truro
Opening hours 1pm to 6pm, Tuesdays and Wednesdays, April to September
Admission fee Adults £2.50; children free

This is the show garden attached to a small nursery. The main speciality is clematis, but the garden exhibits a very wide selection of interesting plants, especially rare climbers and shrubs for maritime climates.
nursery; teas and home-made cakes

Owned by Mr and Mrs Charles Pridham
Size 0.4ha (1 acre)
NCCPG National Collections *Lapageria*; *Clematis viticella* cvs.

ST MICHAEL'S MOUNT
Marazion TR17 0EF

Tel 01736 710507/710265 **Fax** 01736 719930
www.stmichaelsmount.co.uk and www.nationaltrust.org
Location Boat or causeway from Marazion
Opening hours Garden: 10.30am to 5.30pm, Monday to Friday (weather and tide permitting), May and June; Thursdays and Fridays only, July to October
Admission fee Adults £3; children £1

St Michael's Mount is a triumph for man's ingenuity in the face of Atlantic gales, salt spray and bare rock – with sand for garden soil. Careful experiment over the generations has enabled the owners to plant a remarkable garden of plants which resist the elements: *Luma apiculata*, Rugosa roses, correas, nerines, Hottentot figs and naturalised agapanthus. On the north side, a sparse wood of sycamores and pines gives protection to camellias, azaleas and hydrangeas. Nigel Nicolson called it 'the largest and loveliest rock garden in England'. There is nothing rare about the plants: the wonder is that they grow at all.

subtropical plants; natural rock garden; wild narcissus; naturalised kniphofias and agapanthus; shop; café; restaurant

Owned by James St Aubyn and The National Trust
Number of gardeners 4
Size 4ha (10 acres)
English Heritage Grade II

TREBAH GARDEN TRUST

Mawnan Smith, Falmouth TR11 5JZ

Tel: 01326 252200 **Fax:** 01326 250781
www.trebahgarden.co.uk
Location 4 miles south-west of Falmouth, signed from Treliever roundabout at A39/A394 junction, through Mawnan Smith to garden
Opening hours 10.30am to 5pm (last admission), daily, all year
Admission fee Adults £6.50; OAPs £6; children £2 (under 5 free); half price from November to mid-February; RHS members free from November to March

Trebah has been vigorously restored and improved since the Hibberts bought it in 1980. The view from the top is magical: a beautiful, secret, wooded valley which runs right down to the Helford estuary. A new Monet-style bridge provides a focal point at the bottom. A stream cascades over waterfalls, through two acres of blue and white hydrangeas, and spills out over the beach. Vast trees, natural and exotic, line the steep sides, while the central point is held by a group of elegant tall palms. Glades of huge subtropical tree ferns mingle with giant gunneras, puyas and echiums, while along the sides and overhead is the rolling canopy of 100-year-old rhododendrons. A paradise for plantsmen, Trebah is also popular with children, whose curiosity is aroused by trails, quizzes and educational games. It is a garden for all people and for all seasons – open every day of the year.

woodland garden; subtropical plants; plantsman's collection of plants; fine collection of trees; massed hydrangeas; lilies and candelabra primulas; extensive new plantings of palms and succulents at the top of the garden; tallest hardy palm *Trachycarpus fortunei* (15m; 49ft) in the British Isles and three other tree records; plants for sale; café; shop

Owned by The Trebah Garden Trust
Number of gardeners 4, plus volunteers and students
Size 10ha (25 acres)
English Heritage Grade II

TREGREHAN

Par PL24 2SJ

Tel 01726 812438 **Fax** 01726 814389
www.tregrehan.org
Location 1 mile west of St Blazey on A390
Opening hours 10.30am to 5pm, Wednesday to Sunday, plus Bank Holiday Mondays, mid-March to May; 2pm to 5pm, Wednesdays, June to August
Admission fee Adults £4; children free

An old Cornish garden whose 20 acres of woodland date back 200 years and include a fine range of Victorian conservatories, tall conifers and vast, venerable rhododendrons. Tregrehan is best known for the camellias bred there by the late Gillian Carlyon, especially 'Jenefer Carlyon' which won her the Cory Cup from the RHS. But Tom Hudson's collections in warm temperate regions have also made a big impact on the garden which, under his guidance, has become an important living genebank of known-source plants. His recently planted South-East Asia garden is open only to groups, by prior appointment.

woodland garden; camellias; pinetum; walled garden; sunken garden; phytogeographic planting; teas

Trebah Garden Trust

Owned by TC Hudson
Number of gardeners 2
Size 8ha (20 acres)
English Heritage Grade II*

TRELISSICK GARDEN
Feock, Truro TR3 6QL

Tel 01872 862090 **Fax** 01872 865808
www.nationaltrust.org.uk
Location Take A39 off main Truro to Falmouth road; or summer ferry from Falmouth, St Mawes and Truro
Opening hours 10.30am to 5.30pm, daily, 10 February to 28 October; 11am to 4pm, daily, 29 October to 23 December; 11am to 4pm, 27 to 31 December, and 2 January to 9 February 2008
Admission fee Adults £5.80; children £2.90

Once famous as 'the fruit garden of Cornwall' – there is a newly planted (2003) Cornish apple orchard – and still maintained by the National Trust, Trelissick is particularly colourful in August and September when the hydrangeas are in full flower. There are over 100 cultivars, some in a special walk. But venerable conifers and tender plants are also features: *Erythrina crista-galli*, cannas and hedychiums are among the many good things that overwinter outside, not to mention daffodils, rhododendrons and camellias in spring.
woodland garden; plantsman's collection of plants; mature conifers; aromatic plant garden; fig garden; hydrangeas; tallest tree fern *Dicksonia antarctica* (6m; 19.7ft) in the British Isles; National Trust shop; refreshments

Owned by The National Trust
Number of gardeners 4
Size 10ha (25 acres)
NCCPG National Collections *Azara*; *Photinia*
English Heritage Grade II

TRENGWAINTON GARDEN
Madron, Penzance TR20 8RZ

Tel 01736 363148 **Fax** 01736 367762
www.nationaltrust.org.uk
Location 2 miles north-west of Penzance, 1/2 mile west of Heamoor
Opening hours 10am to 5pm (5.30pm from April to September), Sunday to Thursday and Good Friday, 11 February to 4 November
Admission fee Adults £5.20; children £2.60

Trengwainton has one of the best collections of tender plants on the Cornish mainland, all thanks to the Bolitho family who started planting seriously only in 1925. Much came from original seed from such collectors as Kingdon Ward: some rhododendrons flowered here for the first time in the British Isles, among them *R. maccabeanum*, *R. elliottii* and *R. taggianum*. The plants in many Cornish gardens are past their best. Not so at Trengwainton, where many are in their prime. It is a garden to wander through slowly, giving yourself as much time as you need to enjoy its riches. Tree ferns, echiums, magnolias, camellias and olearias line the drive – the long, narrow garden is little more than the driveway and its flanks. At the top you emerge from the woodland and cross a lawn towards a 100m (328ft) terrace that runs between two latticed summerhouses, edged with agapanthus. Broad views down to the sea open out – a brilliant contrast to the thickly wooded garden.
woodland garden; subtropical plants; roses (mainly old-fashioned); lilies; acacias; *Myosotidium hortensia*; tree ferns; tallest *Xanthoceras sorbifolium* (7m; 23ft) in the British Isles (and two record trees); National Trust shop; tea room

Owned by The National Trust
Number of gardeners 4
English Heritage Grade II

TRERICE
Kestle Mill, Newquay TR8 4PG

Tel 01637 875404 **Fax** 01637 879300
www.nationaltrust.org.uk
Location 3 miles south-east of Newquay, turn right off A3058 at Kestle Mill
Opening hours 10.30am to 5pm, daily, except Saturdays, 18 March to 4 November
Admission fee Adults £2.20; children £1.10

A perfect West Country manor house with pretty Dutch gables, Trerice is unusual among Cornish

Trengwainton

gardens. It is small and comparatively formal: the design and herbaceous plantings are its best points. It is not surrounded by swirling rhododendron woodland. There is a perfect harmony between the Elizabethan architecture and the gardens. Somewhat anomalously, it boasts the largest collection of mid-Victorian to current-day lawn mowers in the country. They are both interesting and fun to visit.
colour borders; good collection of apple trees; lawn mower museum; National Trust shop; restaurant

Owned by The National Trust
Number of gardeners 1
Size 5.6ha (14 acres)

TRESCO ABBEY
Isles of Scilly TR24 0PU

Tel/fax 01720 424105
www.tresco.co.uk
Location Direct helicopter flight from Penzance, or boat from St Mary's
Opening hours 10am to 4pm, daily, all year
Admission fee Adults £9; children free (under review)

The subtropical gardens on Tresco are unique in the British Isles. They were first designed and planted by Augustus Smith in 1834: his successors have been equally passionate in their search for tender plants that will grow outside on Tresco's south-facing terraces as nowhere else in Britain. The collection is especially strong in plants from South Africa, Australia and New Zealand but, even though any account of Tresco reads like a list of plants, it is still very much an ornamental garden which strives for horticultural effect. The oldest specimens include Canary Island palms, a large number of aeoniums from both the Canary Islands and Madeira, agaves from America and puyas from Chile. Since the great gale of 1990, the gardens have been extensively replanted, with hundreds of exotic plants from Kew, all protected by extensive new shelter belts. No matter what time of the year, there is always a lot of colour and much of interest: proteas and acacias in winter; the shrubby foxglove (*Isoplexis sceptrum*); mesembryanthemums and agapanthus in summer. There is also a shady area where tree ferns and *Musschia wollastonii* flourish. Many people come here year after year to admire the displays of plants which cannot be seen elsewhere in Britain. The standards of maintenance are exemplary. The heliport has now been moved further away from the garden, which improves the visitor's enjoyment enormously.
subtropical plants; plantsman's collection of plants; mature conifers; cacti; succulents; South African, Australian and New Zealand plants; tallest *Luma apiculata* (20m; 65.6ft), *Metrosideros excelsa* (20m) and *Cordyline australis* (15m; 49ft) in the British Isles; gift shop; licensed café

Owned by Robert Dorrien Smith
Number of gardeners 5, plus 3 students
Size 6.7ha (17 acres)
NCCPG National Collections *Acacia*
English Heritage Grade I

TREVARNO GARDENS & NATIONAL MUSEUM OF GARDENING
Helston TR13 0RU

Tel 01326 574274 **Fax** 01326 574282
www.trevarno.co.uk
Location 3 miles west of Helston, signed from the junction of A394 and B3302
Opening hours 10.30am to 5pm, daily, all year, except 25 and 26 December
Admission fee Adults £5.75; OAPs £4.95; children £2.10; RHS members free

P

Trevarno is an interesting project – an old estate which has been restored and developed since 1997 and which promises to become one of the great gardens of Cornwall again. The old woodland gardens have been cleared, the lake dredged, the 19th-century Italian garden restored and the fountain conservatory refurnished. Work continues: there are plans for a series of stylishly themed gardens dedicated to the flora of different parts of the world. Meanwhile the National Museum of Gardening has a vast collection of old garden tools and horticultural equipment of every sort; it alone is worth a long journey to see.
garden restoration; museum of gardening; shop; refreshments

Owned by M Sagin
Number of gardeners 4
Size 12ha (30 acres)

TREWIDDEN GARDENS
Penzance TR20 8TT

Tel 01736 363021 **Fax** 01736 368142
Location Off A30, 2 miles west of Penzance
Opening hours 10.30am to 4.30pm, Wednesday to Sunday, and Bank Holiday Mondays, 4 February to 30 September
Admission fee Adults £4.50; children free

The gardens at Trewidden have only been regularly open to the public since 2002, and there is much to see. It is essentially a springtime garden, perhaps at its best towards the end of March, but there is plenty of colour and interest in every season – which is why the garden is now open right through to October. The camellia collection is one of the largest (300+ cvs.) while the tree fern dell claims to have more dicksonias than any other garden in the northern hemisphere, some of them 150+ years old. Rare specimens include a venerable jelly palm *Butia capitata*, Chilean nut trees *Gevuina avellana* and the garden's own magnolia 'Trewidden Belle'.
broadest *Metasequoia glyptostroboides* in the UK; unusual plants for sale; light refreshments

Owned by Alverne Bolitho
Number of gardeners 2
Size 4.8ha (12 acres)

TREWITHEN
Grampound Road, Truro TR2 4DD

Tel 01726 883647 **Fax** 01726 882301
www.trewithengardens.co.uk
Location A390 between Probus and Grampound
Opening hours 10am to 4.30pm, Monday to Saturday (and Sundays from March to May), March to September
Admission fee Adults £5; children £1; adults £4.50 (and RHS members free) from July to September

Trewithen's setting is magnificent. Instead of the steep terraces of most Cornish gardens, there is a spacious flat lawn that stretches for 200 yards into the distance, with gentle banks of rhododendrons, magnolias and rare shrubs on all sides. It sets the tone for the garden's grandeur, which was largely the work of George Johnstone in the early years of the 20th century. Johnstone was a great plantsman. He subscribed to plant-hunting expeditions, such as those of Frank Kingdon Ward. Note how he used laurel hedges to divide up the woodland and give structure to the garden. He also had an eye for placing plants to advantage. As a breeder, he gave us *Rhododendron* 'Alison Johnstone', *Ceanothus arboreus* 'Trewithen Blue' and *Camellia saluensis* 'Trewithen White'. The Michelin Guide gives Trewithen its top award of three stars – *vaut le voyage*!
woodland garden; rhododendrons and azaleas; plantsman's collection of plants; camellias; good herbaceous borders; fine collection of trees; magnolias; quarry garden; cyclamen tallest *Magnolia campbellii* subsp. *mollicomata* (19m; 62ft) in the British Isles and 16 more record-breaking tree species; excellent nursery and garden shop; tea room with light refreshments

Owned by AMJ Galsworthy
Number of gardeners 4
Size 12ha (30 acres)
English Heritage Grade II*

TREWOOFE HOUSE
Lamorna, Penzance TR19 6PA

Tel/fax 01736 810269
Location Signed from B3315, 3 miles south-west of Penzance
Opening hours 2pm to 5pm, Sundays, May to July; plus Wednesdays in May and June; and by appointment
Admission fee Adults £2.50; Children free

The main feature of the garden at Trewoofe is a charming bog garden that lines the sides of an old mill leat. The candelabra primulas and irises are especially beautiful, which is why the garden does not open until most Cornish gardens are past their best. Elsewhere in the garden are myrtles and other tender plants – watsonias, hoherias, *Melianthus major* and much else.
water plants; subtropical plants; teas by arrangement for groups

Owned by Mrs HM Pigott
Number of gardeners owner, plus 2 part-time
Size 0.8ha (2 acres)

CUMBRIA

Cumbria came into being in 1974, an amalgam of the old counties of Cumberland, Westmorland and the northern part of Lancashire. Gardening in Cumbria is dominated by the Lake District: both Wordsworth's garden at Rydal Mount and Ruskin's at Brantwood are open to visitors. There are good historic gardens of the grander sort, too. Though few in number, almost all the most important are open to the public: Levens is rated Grade I, while Dalemain, Holker, Muncaster and Sizergh are all Grade II*. Cumbria's acid soils and the highest rainfall in England are very favourable to the growth of conifers: many of the older gardens have fine specimens of *Abies*, *Picea* and *Pinus*, while Muncaster also offers an extensive collection of *Nothofagus* species. The National Gardens Scheme is active in the county, and particularly successful in persuading garden-owners in and around the Lake District to open for charity. Cumbria has comparatively few nurseries, but the ones we list below are exceptionally good. The county has its fair share of National Collections, with clusters of genera at three of the larger gardens: *Halesia*, *Pterostyrax*, *Styrax*, *Sinojackia* and other *Styracaceae* at Holker; *Astilbe*, *Hydrangea* and *Polystichum* at Holehird; and *Asplenium scolopendrium*, *Cystopteris*, *Dryopteris*, and *Osmunda* at Sizergh. Cumbria Campus at Newton Rigg near Penrith is a RHS Partner College, with lectures, demonstrations and garden walks throughout the year. www.visitcumbria.com is a useful website.

ACORN BANK GARDEN

Acorn Bank, Temple Sowerby, Penrith CA10 1SP

Tel 01768 361893 **Fax** 01768 366824
www.nationaltrust.org.uk
Location North of Temple Sowerby, 6 miles east of Penrith on A66
Opening hours 10am to 5pm, Wednesday to Sunday, and Bank Holiday Mondays, 24 March to 28 October
Admission fee Adults £3.40; children £1.70

Acorn Bank claims to have the largest collection (250 cvs.) of culinary and medicinal plants in the North: it was redesigned and replanted in 2002-2003. The garden is especially worthwhile in spring when thousands and thousands of daffodils fill the woodland slopes, and the fruit trees flower in the old walled garden. Best of all is the huge quince tree in the herb garden, a wondrous sight in flower or fruit.

woodland garden; roses (mainly old-fashioned); herbs; fruit; good herbaceous borders; spring bulbs; woodland walk past mill; National Trust shop; tea room

Owned by The National Trust
Number of gardeners 1
Size 1ha (2 1/2 acres)

BRANTWOOD

Coniston LA21 8AD

Tel 01539 441396 **Fax** 01539 441263
www.brantwood.org.uk
Location East side of Coniston Water, 2 1/2 miles from Coniston, 4 miles from Hawkshead
Opening hours 11am to 5.30pm, daily, mid-March to mid-November; 11am to 4.30pm, Wednesday to Sunday rest of year
Admission fee Adults £4; children £1.20

This woodland garden was laid out by John Ruskin from 1871 to 1886, but somewhat altered and neglected after his death in 1900. Working with the natural materials of the site, Ruskin developed a series of experimental gardens within the ancient woodland and on the high moorland behind. When the Brantwood Trust began the

task of reclamation, it decided to restore the garden as it was in Ruskin's lifetime, and to expand it as a modern reinterpretation of his ideas – thereby continuing his work and addressing contemporary issues. The Victorian 'viewing terrace' has been restored, and Ruskin's 'zig-zaggy garden' is now looking young again. Ascending from the Purgatory of the car park, visitors reach Paradise through the levels inspired by Dante's *Divine Comedy*. Here, too, are a Ruskin-style collection of British herbs in a Gothic walk. The idea is to 'explore cultural history through human reaction to plants'. So Brantwood is a garden which offers thought-provoking ideas for everyone. Below Ruskin's 'living laboratory', exotic ornamental plantings frame wonderful views across Coniston Water. There is a regular passenger ferry service from Coniston Boatbuildings: the steam yacht *Gondola* also calls from May to October.
rhododendrons and azaleas; daffodils; bluebells; cottage garden; extensive native fern collection; bookshop and craft gallery; plants for sale; meals, light refreshments and drinks all day

Owned by The Brantwood Trust
Number of gardeners 2
Size 10ha (25 acres)

BROCKHOLE
The Lake District Visitor Centre, Brockhole, Windermere LA23 1LJ

Tel 01539 446601 **Fax** 01539 445555
www.lake-district.gov.uk
Location On A591, halfway between Windermere and Ambleside
Opening hours 10am to dusk, daily, all year
Admission fee Free; car park charge

Brockhole is a show garden of the Lake District authority. It owes its structure to the great Arts and Crafts designer Thomas Mawson, who laid out the terraces in 1898. There are plans to restore it further but, meanwhile, the garden has a splendid collection of plants. Many can flourish only because of the mild, lakeside microclimate – eucryphias, desfontaineas, *Cupressus cashmeriana* and *Crinodendron hookerianum*. But there are also rhododendrons, azaleas, magnolias, camellias, good herbaceous borders, shrub roses, a wildflower meadow and kitchen garden to explore. And daffodils – hosts of them.
Thomas Mawson design; temperate shrubs; gift shop; café

Owned by The Lake District National Park Authority
Number of gardeners 3
Size 12ha (30 acres)
English Heritage Grade II

COPT HOUSE GARDEN
Chapel Stile, Great Langdale, Ambleside LA22 9JR

Tel 01539 437685
Location 3 miles west of Ambleside on B5343
Opening hours Noon to 5pm, 23, 26 and 30 March, 6, 7, 13, 27 and 28 April, 11-13, 21 and 25-27 May, 6, 13 and 20 June; plus Wednesdays form 28 March to 18 June; the garden is also open at other times, at short notice; listen to the weekly pre-recorded message on 01539 437685.
Admission fee Adults £3; children free

This is a very fine plantsman's garden, made on acid soil, high in the fells. Structure comes from the large numbers of rhododendrons, azaleas, camellias, maples and rare shrubs, as well as beech trees and oaks. The underplantings – perennials, bulb and alpines – come from all over the world. Many are the fruits of plant-hinting expeditions over the years. The habitats and the range of plants are awesome – and so are the views of Langdale Pikes.

Owned by Professor RN Haszeldine FRS
Number of gardeners 1
Size 0.8 ha (2 acres)

DALEMAIN
Penrith CA11 0HB

Tel 017684 86450 **Fax** 017684 86223
www.dalemain.com
Location M6, Jct 40, A66, A592, between Penrith and Ullswater

Opening hours 10.30am to 5pm, Sunday to Thursday, 1 April to 29 October; 11am to 4pm, Sunday to Thursday, 4 February to 29 March and 29 October to mid-December; open daily 18 to 25 February and 21 to 28 October
Admission fee Gardens only: adults £4.50; children free; RHS members free in April and September and from 1 to 28 October; NGS days: 29 April and 2 September.

Dalemain has belonged to the Hasell family since 1679. The history of the garden starts, however, with a 16th-century terrace, of which very few remain anywhere in the British Isles. Then comes a kitchen garden with fruit trees planted 250 years ago, though the overall 'feel' of Dalemain is Edwardian. Most of the plantings are modern, including the formal knot garden and the long and richly planted herbaceous border which overlooks the park and the Lakeland Fells. The mixed borders and roses are dreamily English, particularly the Rose Walk, which boasts more than 100 old-fashioned roses. Nearby is the wild garden with drifts of meconopsis and martagon lilies in late spring, though it is fair to say that this is a garden which looks good at all seasons. *Gardening Which* puts it in the Top Ten gardens of northern Britain. Plants are well labelled and well grown.

woodland garden; roses (mainly old-fashioned); herbs; meconopsis; old flower and fruit varieties; good herbaceous and mixed borders; biggest *Abies cephalonica* in the British Isles; gift shop; morning coffee, light lunches, afternoon teas

Owned by Robert Hasell-McCosh
Number of gardeners 2
Size 2ha (5 acres)
English Heritage Grade II*

GRAYTHWAITE HALL

Ulverston, Hawkshead LA12 8BA

Tel 01539 531248 **Fax** 01539 530060
www.visitcumbria.com/sl/grayhall
Location Between Newby Bridge and Hawkshead
Opening hours 10am to 6pm, daily, April to August
Admission fee Adults £3; children £1

Graythwaite shows Thomas Mawson on home ground and at his best. Formal gardens in the Arts and Crafts style by the house drop down to

sweeping lawns; beyond the stream is a woodland of rhododendrons and azaleas. The yew topiary is good – some castellated and some with a mixture of green and gold cultivars.
topiary; roses (ancient and modern); rock garden; fine collection of trees

Owned by Myles Sandys
Number of gardeners 1
Size 4.8ha (12 acres)

HARTSIDE NURSERY GARDEN
Alston CA9 3BL

Tel/fax 01434 381372
www.hartsidenursery.co.uk
Location 1¼ mile south-west of Alston on A686 to Penrith
Opening hours 11.30am to 4.30pm, Monday to Friday; 12.30pm to 4pm, Saturdays, Sundays and Bank Holidays; 10 March to 31 October; other months by appointment
Admission fee Free

This high-level nursery (over 300m; 984ft) specialises in alpines, particularly in primulas (lots of interesting forms of *Primula gracilipes*, for example), autumn-flowering gentians, dwarf shrubs, conifers and hardy ferns: all are home-grown in the cold North Pennines. The display gardens are maintained in a relaxed style and worth a visit: there is lots to admire.

Owned by Neil and Sue Huntley

HOLEHIRD GARDENS
Lakeland Horticultural Society, Patterdale Road, Windermere LA23 1NP

Tel 01539 446008
www.holehirdgardens.org.uk
Location 1 mile north of Windermere town, off A592, signed to Patterdale and Kirkstone
Opening hours Dawn to dusk, daily, all year; wardens usually on hand to give advice from Easter to October; groups strictly by arrangement
Admission fee Free, but suggested donation of £3; children free

Holehird is a demonstration and trial garden, maintained entirely by members of the Lakeland Horticultural Society. The society's aim is to 'promote and develop the science, practice and art of horticulture, particularly with regard to the conditions prevailing in the Lake District'. In practice this means an exposed site with neutral to acid soil conditions in a cool, wet climate, but a superb setting. The gardens have recently been extended to about 10 acres. The old walled garden has splendid herbaceous borders and island beds. Elsewhere are an extensive rock and scree garden and an expansive area of woodland as well as the formal gardens in front of the mansion. The interesting thing for visitors is to see what flourishes: alpines, rhododendrons and azaleas, camellias, magnolias, heathers, bulbs (especially snowflakes, cyclamen and wild daffodils), gentians, hostas, meconopsis, ferns and much, much more at every time of the year. The flowering of the National Collection of astilbes in July and August coincides with the first hydrangeas, which then continue into October. Some of the oldest plantings date back to the original owners in the 19th century. There will be an RHS Special Event at Holehird Gardens in 2007; details from 020 7821 3408.
woodland garden; rock garden; herbs; plants under glass; heathers; roses; hostas; ferns; Victorian garden; walled garden; spring bulbs; rhododendrons and azaleas

Owned by The Lakeland Horticultural Society
Number of gardeners about 70 volunteers
Size 4ha (10 acres)
NCCPG National Collections *Astilbe*; *Hydrangea*; *Polystichum*

HOLKER HALL
Cark-in-Cartmel, Grange-over-Sands LA11 7PL

Tel 01539 558328 **Fax** 01539 558378
www.holker-hall.co.uk
Location M6, Jct 36; follow brown tourist signs
Opening hours 10.30am to 5.30pm (last admissions 5pm), Sunday to Friday, 1 April to 28 October
Admission fee Adults £5.95; OAPs and students £5.25; children £3; RHS members free except during special events

The 19th-century formal gardens below the house are scrumptiously planted as herbaceous borders, the first of many imaginative modern designs and plantings throughout this extensive garden. The woodland has foxgloves, rhododendrons and splendid trees: Sir Joseph Paxton supplied a monkey puzzle and Lord George Cavendish the cedars grown from seeds he brought back from the Holy Land. The Gulf Stream enables many exotic trees and shrubs to flourish and flower which might not otherwise be hardy in this northerly climate.
formal and woodland gardens; roses (ancient and modern); rhododendrons; fine limestone cascade and fountain; HHA/Christie's Garden of the Year in 1991; tallest *Ilex latifolia* (15m; 49ft) in the British Isles (and two other tree records); food hall; gift shop; café (licensed)

Owned by Lord Cavendish of Furness
Number of gardeners 6
Size 10ha (25 acres)
NCCPG National Collections *Styracaceae* (incl. *Halesia, Pterostyrax, Styrax, Sinojackia*)
English Heritage Grade II*

HUTTON-IN-THE-FOREST
Penrith CA11 9TH

Tel 01768 484449 **Fax** 01768 484571
www.hutton-in-the-forest.co.uk
Location 3 miles from Exit 41 of M6 on B5305, 6 miles north-west of Penrith
Opening hours 11am to 5pm, daily, except Saturdays, April to October; Specialist Plant & Food Fair: 20 May; charity open days: 3 June, 8 July and 19 August
Admission fee Gardens only: adults £3.50; children £1

The charm of Hutton-in-the-Forest derives from its many architectural, gardening and landscape styles which span 400 years but come together as a historic and romantic whole. The pale pink sandstone house is old, handsomely sited and built onto a medieval pele tower. Salvin refashioned it in the 19th century and Gilpin restored the terraces at about the same time: the fine topiary is a little later. Beyond the terraces is a woodland garden where large conifers are underplanted by billowing rhododendrons. A woodland walk with 65 different tree species surrounds the property. The walled garden, once a kitchen garden dating from the 1730s, is now the main flower garden: a double herbaceous border runs from end to end, backed by thick yew hedges. This is a very traditional garden of great serenity.
woodland walk; herbaceous borders in the walled garden; terraces with topiary; 17th-century dovecote; refreshments when house open

Owned by Lord and Lady Inglewood
Number of gardeners 1
Size 4.4ha (11 acres)
English Heritage Grade II

LARCH COTTAGE NURSERIES
Melkinthorpe, Penrith CA10 2DR

Tel 01931 712404 **Fax** 01931 712727
www.larchcottage.co.uk
Location 4 miles south of Penrith, just off A6
Opening hours 10am to 5.30pm (dusk in winter), daily, all year, except over Christmas
Admission fee Free

This nursery garden has one of the longest list of plants in the North of England, including many items which are not available from anyone else. The specialities include perennials, dwarf conifers, Japanese maples, roses, shrubs and ornamental grasses. Within the walls are a smart restaurant in the Tuscan style, Dalle de Verre stained glass and a neat Japanese-style garden. But the plants deserve a long visit to study.
Japanese garden; unusual plants; nursery; restaurant

Larch Cottage Nurseries

Owned by Peter Stott
Number of gardeners 8, plus seasonal staff
Size 2ha (5 acres)

LEVENS HALL
Kendal LA8 0PD

Tel 01539 560321 **Fax** 01539 560669
www.levenshall.co.uk
Location 5 miles south of Kendal on A6
Opening hours 10am to 5pm, Sunday to Thursday, 1 April to 11 October
Admission fee Adults £6.50; children £3.50

Levens means topiary: huge overgrown chunks of box and yew. Some is said to be left over from a simple formal parterre laid out in 1694 and supplemented by golden yews in the 19th century. Some is more recent – successive generations have been good about replacing plants and restoring the garden when necessary. The arbours and high yew hedges, some of them crenellated, are spangled with *Tropaeolum speciosum* and the parterres planted annually with 15,000 plants, which makes Levens one of the best places to study the expensive art of bedding out. Well maintained.
topiary; spring and summer bedding; new fountain garden; HHA/Christie's Garden of the Year in 1994; gift shop and plant centre; light lunches and teas

Owned by CH Bagot
Number of gardeners 5
Size 4ha (10 acres)
English Heritage Grade I

MUNCASTER CASTLE
Ravenglass CA18 1RQ

Tel 01229 717614 **Fax** 01229 717010
www.muncaster.co.uk
Location A595, 1 mile east of Ravenglass on west coast of Cumbria
Opening hours 10.30am to 6pm, daily, all year; closed January
Admission fee Adults £7; children £5; RHS members free from 1 July to 4 November

Visit Muncaster in May, when the rhododendrons are at their peak. Many are grown from the original seed introduced by such plant hunters as Forrest and Kingdon Ward in the 1920s and 1930s. Some have turned out to be the tallest of their kind in England. In the Victorian kitchen garden, recently renovated, is a traditional vegetable garden and a modern herb and physic garden. The castle was revamped by Salvin in the 1860s: stand on its wonderful long curved terrace (*very* long – half a mile) above the steep slopes and soak up the intensely romantic landscape of the Lakeland hills around. Ruskin called it 'the gateway to Paradise'. There will be an RHS Special Event at Muncaster in 2007; details from 020 7821 3408.
woodland garden; mature conifers; camellias; maples; masses of new plantings; bluebells; tallest *Nothofagus obliqua* (31m; 102ft) in the British Isles; two gift shops; snacks and full meals

Owned by Mrs PR Gordon-Duff-Pennington
Number of gardeners 4, plus some part-time help
Size 31ha (77 acres)
English Heritage Grade II*

RYDAL MOUNT
Ambleside LA22 9LU

Tel 01539 433002 **Fax** 01539 431738
www.rydalmount.co.uk
Location 1½ miles north of Ambleside on A591, turn up Rydal Hill
Opening hours 9.30am to 5pm, daily, March to October; 10am to 4pm, daily, except Tuesdays, February, November and December; closed January
Admission fee Adults £2.50; guided garden tours with poetry reading, by arrangement, £5.50

Levens Hall

The garden at Rydal Mount is kept as a memorial to William Wordsworth; recently rediscovered sketches confirm that it has scarcely changed since he lived here (1813-59). The poet believed that a garden should be informal in its design, harmonise with the country and keep its views open. Lake Windermere and Rydal Water are the backdrop; the gardens include fell-sided terraces, herbaceous borders, rock pools and an ancient Norse mound. The rhododendrons and bluebells are spectacular in season – and the daffodils.
daffodils; bluebells; trees; rhododendrons

Owned by Rydal Mount Trust (Wordsworth Family)
Number of gardeners 1
Size 1.6ha (4 acres)
English Heritage Grade II

SIZERGH CASTLE
Kendal LA8 8AE

Tel 01539 560951
www.nationaltrust.org.uk
Location 3 1/2 miles south of Kendal
Opening hours 11am to 5.30pm, Sunday to Thursday, 1 April to 28 October; plus some winter openings
Admission fee Garden only: adult £4.50; children £2.20

One of the best National Trust gardens, Sizergh has lots of interest from wild daffodils and alpines in spring to magnificent herbaceous borders in summer and hydrangeas and a hot half-hardy border in September – *Beschorneria yuccoides* and *Buddleja colvilei* – followed by a fine display of October colour from the Japanese maples. Best of all is the 1920s rock garden, made of local limestone, and home to an important (and beautiful) collection of ferns – over 200 hardy species and cultivars. Some of the 60 dwarf conifers have grown to a remarkable size.
good herbaceous borders; wildflower meadow; tender plants; National Trust shop; café

Owned by The National Trust
Number of gardeners 2
Size 6.4ha (16 acres)
NCCPG National Collections *Asplenium scolopendrium; Cystopteris; Dryopteris; Osmunda*
English Heritage Grade II*

WINDERWATH GARDENS
Winderwath, Temple Sowerby, Penrith CA10 2AG

Tel/fax 01768 88250
Location On A66, 5 miles east of Penrith
Opening hours 10am to 4pm, Monday to Friday, 10am to noon, Saturdays, March to October; for NGS: 1pm to 4 pm, 10 June
Admission fee Adults £3; children free

The structure of the garden at Winderwath dates back to about 1900; the wellingtonia, cut-leaf beech and cedar date from this time. The present owner has planted extensive herbaceous beds, alpines and Himalayan species.
plants for sale

Owned by Jane Pollock
Number of gardeners 2
Size 2ha (5 acres)

DERBYSHIRE

Derbyshire has no fewer than five historic gardens that are listed as Grade I: Chatsworth, Haddon, Hardwick, Kedleston and Melbourne. All are regularly open to the public. The National Gardens Scheme is very active in the county, with a good number of medium-sized and small gardens listed in the Yellow Book. Nevertheless, it is the larger gardens on old estates that offer the most horticultural interest. Much of Derbyshire is high and cold in winter, yet it also has some excellent nurseries and garden centres. Bluebell Nursery & Arboretum, right in the south of the county, has one of the most exciting collections of trees and shrubs in the British Isles. And Abbey Brook Cactus Nursery in Matlock has long been the UK's leading specialist nursery for cacti and succulents. Its six National Collections of *Conophytum*, *Echinopsis*, *Gymnocalycium*, *Haworthia*, *Lithops* and *Mammillaria* are unmatched by any other collection holder. Begonias and gladioli are popular in Derbyshire, and fine displays are often seen at local flower shows. Derby College at Broomfield Hall is a RHS Partner College with workshops and lectures throughout the year: details from 01332 836600.

ABBEY BROOK CACTUS NURSERY

Bakewell Road, Matlock DE4 2QJ

Tel 01629 580306 **Fax** 01629 558552
www.abbeybrookcacti.com
Location On A6, 2 miles north of Matlock
Opening hours 1pm to 4pm, Wednesday to Friday; 1pm to 5pm, Saturdays, Sundays and Bank Holiday Mondays; closed January, plus 25 and 26 December and occasional weekends - see website for details
Admission fee Free

Abbey Brook celebrated its golden anniversary last year (2006), and was featured twice on *BBC Gardeners' World*; the UK's leading cactus nursery was founded in 1956. It is now 90% wholesale and with 1,000,000 plants in stock, but the retail list is still remarkable – it offers over 2,000 cultivars and has at least the same number again among its stock plants. The nursery is worth a visit at any time of the year – so is the website, which offers a full-colour catalogue. Cactus buffs need no introduction to Abbey Brook, but the nursery is also extremely interesting for those whose gardening interests are quite different. It displays the wonder and beauty of these plants in such a way that you cannot help responding to them – and their extraordinary diversity. There are three special open weekends for the NCCPG in 2007: 17 and 18 March, 2 and 3 June, and 21 and 22 July.
restaurant/café

Owned by Brian Fearn
Number of gardeners 4
Size 0.15ha (0.4 acres) of glass
NCCPG National Collections *Conophytum; Echinopsis hybrids; Gymnocalycium; Haworthia; Lithops; Mammillaria*

BLUEBELL ARBORETUM & NURSERY

Annwell Lane, Smisby, Ashby-de-la-Zouch LE65 2TA

Tel/fax 01530 413700
www.bluebellnursery.co.uk
Location 400 yards south of Smisby Church; follow brown tourist signs to arboretum
Opening hours 9am to 5pm (4pm from November to February), Monday to Saturday, all year; 10.30am to 4.30pm, Sundays, March to October (NB closed on Sundays from November to February); closed on Easter Sunday and from 24 December to 4 January
Admission fee Adults £2.50; children free; RHS members free

Bluebell Arboretum & Nursery has been a stalwart supporter of RHS shows for some years now and has won many medals for its displays of rare trees and shrubs. The six-acre arboretum has expanded every year since it was first planted in 1992 and is already remarkably mature, but the owners are keen to emphasise that 'you should not expect to find a Westonbirt, Wisley or Wakehurst' yet. Nevertheless, it is a most interesting place to visit, with a fluid design and two ponds. The tallest trees are birches, alders and some tearaway balsam poplars from Sissinghurst, which have already reached 15m (49ft). Most visitors are intrigued by the many cultivars of dogwoods (*Cornus alternifolia* 'Argentea' is especially fine), maples (look out for *Acer tegmentosum*) and beech (*Fagus sylvestris*). Particular successes include *Morus alba* 'Pendula', *Juglans nigra* 'Laciniata' and *Magnolia* 'Vulcan'. Other highlights are fine specimens of *Quercus castaneifolia* 'Green Spire' and the very rare *Quercus rhysophylla* from Mexico, and the largest collection of deciduous hollies (*Ilex verticillata)* in Europe. The website allows online ordering: the nursery sells many more plants than those listed in its excellent catalogue. Three RHS Special Events will take place at Bluebell Arboretum & Nursery during 2007 (details from 020 7821 3408) and Roy Lancaster will conduct guided tours on 9 May (tickets from nursery).
fine collection of trees and shrubs; important tree and shrub nursery

Owned by Mr and Mrs Robert Vernon
Size 2ha (5 acres)

THE BURROWS GARDENS

Burrows Lane, Brailsford, Ashbourne DE6 3BU

Tel 01335 360745
www.burrowsgardens.com
Location Signed from A52
Opening hours 10.30am to 4.30pm, 6, 7, 20, 27 and 28 May, 3, 10, 17, 18 and 24 June, 1, 2, 8, 22 and 29 July, 5, 6, 12, 26 and 27 August, and 2, 9, 10 and 16 September
Admission fee Adults £3.50; children free

The Burrows has been spaciously designed, with a little help latterly from Katy Walker-Okeover and Julian Dowle. It has mostly been made since the owner took it over from his parents in 1985. The structure is firm and inviting: broad walks, straight avenues, statues, urns and lots of wrought ironwork (simple and well chosen). The features are many, including an Italian garden and a bog garden, while the plantings are always made for colour contrasts and harmonies, to take effect at different times of the year. There are a lot of good plants here, often rare and always well placed. And the planting of trees extends a long way into the surrounding fields, whether as woodlands, groups or individual park trees.
teas

Owned by Craig Dalton
Number of gardeners owner, plus 1/2
Size 2ha (5 acres), plus 1.2ha (3 acres) of trees

CALKE ABBEY

Ticknall DE73 7LE

Tel 01332 863822 **Fax** 01332 865272
www.nationaltrust.org.uk
Location 10 miles south of Derby on A514 in village of Ticknall
Opening hours 11am to 5pm, Saturday to Wednesday, 17 March to 28 October; daily from 5 July to 7 September
Admission fee Adults £5; children £2.50

The 'sleeping beauty' house is matched by a deliberate air of fading glory in its garden. In the walled garden is a fine collection of old garden buildings, including a peach house, orangery, stove house, ice house and recently restored backsheds. Old cultivars of fruit (especially apples) jostle with heritage vegetables. The flower garden is planted in the 19th-century 'patchwork' style and includes the only surviving Auricula Theatre, originally built to display the perfection of these beautiful 'florist's' plants. The traditional summer bedding is very well done. The drive runs along a magnificent avenue of ancient limes.
vegetables; fruit; good herbaceous borders; dahlias; good Victorian-style bedding; deer park; horse-chestnut trees; local varieties of apples and soft fruit; National Trust gift shop; licensed restaurant

CHATSWORTH

Bakewell DE45 1PP

Tel 01246 582204 **Fax** 01246 583536
www.chatsworth.org
Location 8 miles north of Matlock off B6012
Opening hours 11am (10.30am from June to August) to 6pm (last admissions 5pm), daily, 14 March to 23 December
Admission fee Adults £6.25; OAPs £4.75; children £2.75; family ticket £15

Chatsworth sits near the bottom of a high valley on the edge of the Peak District surrounded by over 1,000 acres of beautiful landscaped park – the work of Capability Brown. Into this naturalistic setting successive Dukes of Devonshire have inserted formal designs, flower gardens and magnificent garden buildings. Despite their piecemeal history, the gardens at Chatsworth all come together as a single ornament for the house. They have been open to the public for nearly 200 years. The glory days of Chatsworth's garden were the 1830s and 1840s when Sir Joseph Paxton and the 'bachelor Duke' built the Emperor fountain, the rock garden (huge boulders surrounded by conifers), the arboretum, the pinetum and the 'conservative wall', which was intended to keep the heat and ripen fruit trees. The present Dowager Duchess has been responsible for some stylish additions such as the serpentine hedges which lead from the Victorian ring pond to a bust of the 6th Duke. Perhaps the best-known features at Chatsworth today are the Great Cascade, built in about 1700 and unique in England, and the Canal, dug at the same time as a formal sheet of water to set off the southern façade of the house. But there is much of horticultural interest, too: a tulip tree avenue, the bamboo walk, Victorian yews of different hues, the rose garden, the cottage garden, the kitchen garden, a 'sensory' garden, the blue and white and the orange borders and record trees like *Pinus peuce*. Chatsworth has also long been famous for its camellias and glasshouse grapes, both of which have won many prizes at RHS shows. But perhaps the greatest joy of Chatsworth is the sense, which still pervades the entire estate, that it is a private garden in which every visitor feels like a welcome guest.

woodland garden; topiary; roses (mainly modern); rock garden; rhododendrons and azaleas; fine collection of trees; pinetum; maze; tulip tree avenue; millennium planting of 100 oaks in 50 different varieties; tallest *Pinus strobus* (42m; 138ft) in the British Isles; plants for sale in stable yard; licensed self-service restaurant

Owned by Chatsworth House Trust
Number of gardeners 21
Size 42ha (105 acres)
English Heritage Grade I

The Cascades at Chatsworth

Owned by The National Trust
Number of gardeners 3, plus 1 trainee
Size 2.2ha (6 acres) garden, plus 12ha (30 acres) pleasure grounds
English Heritage Grade II*

CASCADES

Clatter Way, Bonsall, Matlock DE4 2AH

Tel 01629 822813
www.cascadesgardens.com
Location Via Gellia from Cromford; left uphill at Bonsall; on right before village green
Opening hours 10am to 5pm, Wednesdays and Sundays, April to September
Admission fee Adults £3; children free

The garden at Cascades is wrung from a steep valley, enclosed by the rock face. A stream runs all along its length and there are good herbaceous plantings along its sides and around the lawns above. Elsewhere are roses, shrubs, young ornamental trees and a small nursery.
small nursery; tea and coffee

Owned by Alan and Elizabeth Clements
Number of gardeners owners, plus help in summer
Size 1.6ha (4 acres)

DAM FARM HOUSE

Ednaston, Ashbourne DE6 3BA

Tel 01335 360291
Location Turn off A52 to Bradley, opposite Ednaston Lane end
Opening hours Mondays, Tuesday and Fridays, April to October; and by arrangement (telephone or letter)
Admission fee Adults £3.50; children free

Mrs Player (born a Loder) has made this outstanding garden on a greenfield site since 1980. The design is firm, and the planting exuberant. Clipped hedges enclose a series of separate gardens which flow into each other, but in contrast to the firm design, the planting belongs to the cottage garden tradition. There is a formal garden by the house which ends in a delicate white wire gazebo. The borders are richly planted with the best of modern plants – *Cercis canadensis* 'Forest Pansy', for example, and *Viburnum sargentii* 'Onondaga'. Clematis are a favourite and there is a surprisingly large number of plants which one might suppose too tender for Derbyshire – cistus, ceanothus and penstemons. Recent additions include a number of magnolias and a collection of *Cornus kousa* and *C. florida* forms and hybrids. This garden is now in its prime: the trees are semi-mature and the plants have lost none of their youthful vigour. Rare plants abound and are always being added, but it is their treatment which makes the garden such an exciting place to visit and learn from: their planting, training and cultivation are a model for our times.
roses (mainly old-fashioned); fine collection of trees; scree garden; young arboretum

Owned by Mrs Jean Player
Number of gardeners part-time help
Size 1.2ha (3 acres)

ELVASTON CASTLE

Borrowash Road, Elvaston DE72 3EP

Tel 01332 571342 **Fax** 01332 758751
www.elvastoncastle.org.uk
Location 5 miles south-east of Derby; signed from A6 and A52
Opening hours Dawn to dusk (Old English Garden, 9am to 5pm, but 4pm in winter), daily, all year
Admission fee Gardens: free. Car park: £1 midweek, £1.50 weekends

This is a historic garden, famous for its spectacular lumpy, yew topiary. It has good rhododendrons in the park, and magnificent conifers. It was saved from oblivion by Derbyshire County Council some 25 years ago. The parterres were replaced and the walled garden replanted with fine double herbaceous borders, good seasonal bedding and dahlias, and renamed the Old English Garden.
topiary; roses (mainly old-fashioned); good herbaceous borders; gift shop; restaurant open all year 11am to 3.30pm, closed Mondays

Owned by Derbyshire County Council
Number of gardeners 6
English Heritage Grade II*

Haddon Hall

Haddon Hall

EYAM HALL

Eyam, Hope Valley S32 5QW

Tel 01433 631976 **Fax** 01433 631603
www.eyamhall.com
Location In the centre of Eyam, off A623
Opening hours Noon to 4pm; 8 to 12 April, 6, 7, 27 and 28 May; then Wednesdays, Thursdays, Sundays and Bank Holiday Monday from 2 July to 31 August
Admission fee Adults £2; concessions £1.50; children £1; families £5

Eyam Hall's gardens are a modern restoration project, based on 17th-century family records. The walled garden contains four distinct areas: a knot garden, kitchen garden, bowling green and lawn. The village is famous for its self-sacrifice at the time of the Great Plague in 1665.
snacks and light lunches

Owned by Robert Wright
Number of gardeners 1 1/2
Size 0.4ha (1 acre)

HADDON HALL

Bakewell DE45 1LA

Tel 01629 812855 **Fax** 01629 814379
www.haddonhall.co.uk
Location 1 1/2 miles south of Bakewell on A6
Opening hours Noon to 5pm (last admissions 4pm), daily, May to September, plus Saturday to Monday in April and October (Easter opening Friday to Tuesday); closed 30 June and 1 July
Admission fee House and garden: adults £8.50; OAPs £7.50; children £4.50; families £22

Haddon Hall is a substantial house which dates from 1370 to 1600. The gardens, however, are less than 100 years old, having been laid out by the 9th Duchess of Rutland in the 1910s and 1920s along the much older terraces. The Duchess planted formal features like yew trees to add to the structure, but her great passion was for roses, and it is for these most beautiful of flowers that the garden is now known. The collection is a good one and, though it lacks any real rarities, it is kept up to date by the addition of all the best repeat-flowering cultivars, which means that there is a good selection of modern roses among

the older ramblers and noisettes. The hybrid teas include the bright crimson 'Royal William' and pink 'Paul Shirville' and among the floribundas are yellow 'Arthur Bell' and the dark red 'The Times' rose. But shrub roses and wild rose species are also well represented. There are 60 different cultivars of delphinium in the herbaceous borders, which are supplemented by tender perennials and annuals, hardy and half-hardy. In June and July there is no more beautiful and romantic garden in England.
topiary; good herbaceous borders; roses of every kind; clematis; delphiniums; coffee, lunch, afternoon teas

Owned by Lord Edward Manners
Number of gardeners 2
English Heritage Grade I

HARDWICK HALL
Doe Lea, Chesterfield S44 5QJ

Tel 01246 850430 **Fax** 01246 858424
www.nationaltrust.org.uk
Location Signed from M1, Jct 29
Opening hours Gardens: 11am to 5.30pm, Wednesday to Sunday, 17 March to 28 October
Admission fee Garden only: adults £4.50; children £2.25; families £11.25

The formal gardens at Hardwick are of special interest to those with a sense of history: tall hedges of hornbeam and yew, spacious and simple. In the 'Elizabethan' (actually 1970s) herb garden, thyme and chamomile, lavender, laurel and rue are supplemented by seasonal bedding and dahlias. Elsewhere are old fruit trees, a nut garden, a mulberry avenue, old roses and modern borders in the Jekyll style.
good herbaceous borders; daffodils; fine hedges; mulberry walk; hollies; refreshments Wed/Thurs/Sat/Sun when Hall is open

Owned by The National Trust
Number of gardeners 3, plus volunteers
Size 3.6ha (9 acres)
English Heritage Grade I

HOPTON HALL
Hopton, Wirksworth, Matlock DE4 4DF

Tel/fax 01629 540923
Location Well signed in Hopton village
Opening hours 10am to 4pm, daily, 3 February to 4 March
Admission fee Adults £3.50; children free

The woods are covered by snowdrops in late winter – and aconites, too. Meanwhile, there is an ongoing programme to restore the formal gardens round the house.
snowdrops; light refreshments

Owned by Mr and Mrs William Brogden
Number of gardeners 2
Size 2ha (5 acres) woodland, and 1.6 ha (4 acres) formal gardens

KEDLESTON HALL
Derby DE22 5JH

Tel 01332 842191 **Fax** 01332 844059
www.nationaltrust.org.uk
Location 5 miles north-west of Derby, signed at A38/A52 roundabout
Opening hours 10am to 6pm, daily, 10 March to 31 October
Admission fee Park and garden only: adults £3.60; children £1.80

Kedleston is an important historic garden. The 18th-century landscaped park runs down to a long lake. The house is matched by a Robert Adam summerhouse in the circular garden: impressive and important. Lord Curzon moved it to its present position at the side of the lawns. The park has some splendid trees, most notably a fern-leaved beech (*Fagus sylvatica* 'Aspleniifolia').
roses (mainly modern); rhododendrons and azaleas; handsome Adam orangery; National Trust shop; lunches and teas

Owned by The National Trust
Number of gardeners 2½
Size 7ha (17½ acres)
English Heritage Grade I

LEA GARDENS

Lea, Matlock DE4 5GH

Tel 01629 534380 **Fax** 01629 534260
www.leagarden.co.uk
Location 3 miles south-east of Matlock
Opening hours 10am to 5.30pm, daily, 20 March to 30 June
Admission fee Adults £3.50; children 50p; season ticket £6; wheelchair-bound free

These rhododendron gardens were started in 1935 by John Marsden-Smedley who was so inspired by his visits to Bodnant and Exbury that he decided to plant his own rhododendron collection. He was then aged 68. By the time he died aged 92 in 1959, the garden contained some 350 cultivars of rhododendrons and azaleas. Since that time, it has belonged to the Tye family, who have continued to maintain and develop it. The standard of maintenance is extremely high and it is one of the most beautiful gardens to visit in season. Much is on a steep slope and some of the paths are narrow, but an energetic pusher should be able to negotiate a wheelchair around most of the garden: the principal areas are fairly open. There are large numbers of modern, low-growing rhododendron and azalea hybrids underplanted with naturalised bluebells. Little attempt has been made to segregate the colours, but the plants are graded for height, so you stand on a path and look at a mass of rhododendrons of every imaginable hue rising from knee level right back to huge giants far behind. There have been some interesting interplantings with other plants in recent years – ornamental trees, especially conifers, and herbaceous plants like gunneras, celmisias, *Dactylorhiza foliosa* and *Meconopsis betonicifolia*. It should also be said that the garden is extremely well organised for visitors to enjoy themselves.
rhododendrons and azaleas; tea and coffee shop; light lunches

Owned by Mr and Mrs J Tye
Number of gardeners 3
Size 1.8ha (4.5 acres)

MELBOURNE HALL & GARDENS

Melbourne DE73 8EN

Tel 01332 862502 **Fax** 01332 862263
www.melbournehall.com
Location 8 miles south of Derby
Opening hours 1.30pm to 5.30pm, Wednesdays, Saturdays, Sundays and Bank Holiday Mondays, April to September; plus 2pm to 4.30pm daily in August (but closed on the first three Mondays)
Admission fee Adults £3.50; OAPs £2.50

Melbourne is a near-perfect example of an early 18th-century garden, influenced by Le Nôtre. It was laid out in 1704 by the royal gardeners London and Wise. Terraces, circular *bassins*, palisades of limes, intersecting *allées*, lumpy old hedges and the famous yew tunnel will all fire the visitor's imagination. The lead statues (from Jan van Nost's foundry in Piccadilly in about 1710) are unique: so is the large urn known as the Four Seasons, which was originally cast for Queen Anne.
rococo design; turf terracing; grand avenues; shop; refreshments

Owned by Lord Ralph Kerr
Number of gardeners 2
English Heritage Grade I

POSTERN HOUSE GARDEN

Turnditch, Belper DE56 2LX

Tel 01773 550732
www.postern.co.uk
Location Turn right off A317, 1/2 mile east of Turnditch
Opening hours 2pm to 5.30pm, 10 and 15 June, 1 July, 5 August
Admission fee Adults £2.50; children free

This modern garden makes the most of its size, and manages to appear much larger than it really is. Small shrubs and trees give structure, while much of the summer colour comes from clematis and herbaceous plants, especially hostas and geraniums. Pots and other containers are widely used to intensify the interest.
tea and home-made cakes

Owned by Liz Ruby
Number of gardeners owner only
Size 0.15ha (one-third of an acre), plus paddock

RENISHAW HALL

Renishaw Park, Sheffield S21 3WB

Tel 01246 432310 **Fax** 01246 430760
www.sitwell.co.uk
Location 2½ miles from M1, Jct 30
Opening hours 10.30am to 4.30pm, Thursday to Sunday and Bank Holiday Mondays, 29 March to 30 September; daily from 26 April to 13 May, for the bluebells
Admission fee Adults £5; concessions £4.20; RHS members free

The gardens at Renishaw were laid out in around 1900 by Sir George Sitwell, grandfather of the present owner. Sir George was an expert on Italian gardens and his book *On the Making of Gardens* (1909) is a gardening classic. He applied the principles of Italian renaissance gardens to the garden he made at Renishaw: symmetry, proportion, scale and shadow. What we see today are yew hedges, pools, fountains, grass and statues – a garden which would not be out of place in Tuscany or the Veneto. The plantings are modern, mainly herbaceous, and colour-schemed, but kept within pastel shades to emphasise the line of the formal garden. The soft colours of old-fashioned roses are perfect: Renishaw has three separate rose gardens with over 1,000 roses. In the woodland garden and against the walls of the kitchen garden, tender plants thrive that seldom survive in Derbyshire – *Acacia dealbata*, *Cytisus battandieri* and fremontias. Renishaw is also worth visiting in the spring, when daffodils fill the lime avenue: they were first planted in 1680 on the advice of no lesser authority than John Evelyn. They are followed by the flowering of the bluebell wood with rhododendrons, camellias and magnolias. In the recently restored orangery, the National Collection of yuccas is displayed against an Arizona landscape.
Italian garden; yew walks and pyramids; clematis; woodland walks; roses (ancient and modern); good herbaceous borders; daffodils; café

Owned by Sir Reresby Sitwell
Number of gardeners 4
Size 2.8ha (7 acres) of formal gardens, plus woodlands
NCCPG National Collections *Yucca*
English Heritage Grade II*

DEVON

No county has such an abundance of good gardens and nurseries as Devon: Devonians maintain that it is the best place in the world for gardening with plants. Rich soils ('Devon acres') and high rainfall make for excellent growth, but the county's microclimates are immensely variable, from the cold, windswept uplands of Dartmoor to valleys along the southern coast that are virtually frost-free. The Royal Horticultural Society's West Country flagship at Rosemoor shows what can be done to develop a major horticultural garden in a very short span. And there is no private garden in England to match the lifetime achievements of the late Dr Smart at Marwood Hill, now well maintained by his nephew. Devon has some fine general nurseries and garden centres, like Hill House near Ashburton, but surely no county ever had such an abundance of specialist nurseries. Their specialities include hostas (Roger and Ann Bowden near Okehampton), violets (Devon Violet Nursery at Rattery), rare trees (Thornhayes Nursery near Cullompton) and penstemons (Shirley Reynolds at Seaton). Devon has 51 National Collection holders, more than any other county, including many tender genera like *Azara* and *Agapanthus*. There are comparatively few top-class historic gardens and – such as they are – they tend to date from the 19th century, like Bicton. Nevertheless, the history of Devon gardens is extremely well documented and the Devon Gardens Trust has a large and vigorous membership. Bicton, Killerton and Endsleigh have splendid collections of old trees: in Edwardian times the avenue of monkey puzzles (*Araucaria araucana*) at Bicton was one of the wonders of English horticulture. Bicton College of Agriculture is a RHS Partner College. The National Gardens Scheme also does exceptionally well in Devon, with more gardens open for its charities than anywhere else in the South West. Deep, narrow lanes and inadequate signage are problems for garden visitors. Nevertheless, Devon remains a county of horticultural superlatives.

ARLINGTON COURT

Arlington, Barnstaple EX31 4LP

Tel 01271 850296 **Fax** 01271 851108
www.nationaltrust.org.uk
Location 8 miles north of Barnstaple on A39
Opening hours 10.30am to 5pm, Sunday to Friday, 18 March to 28 October; plus 10.30am to 5pm, Saturdays, July and August
Admission fee Gardens only: adults £5.20, but £2.80 on Saturdays in July and August

Arlington offers mature parkland on a level site in front of a fine Georgian house. It has a pretty Victorian formal garden: herbaceous borders and basket beds on three grass terraces, around a handsome conservatory. In the walled garden, recently part-restored, 19th-century fruit and vegetables grow alongside local cultivars.

mature conifers; huge old rhododendrons; National Trust shop; tea room

Owned by The National Trust
Number of gardeners 2
Size 12ha (30 acres)
English Heritage Grade II

ANN & ROGER BOWDEN

Hostas, Sticklepath, Okehampton EX20 2NL

Tel 01837 840481
www.hostas-uk.com

Location Near Okehampton, in centre of Sticklepath, near turning signed 'Skaighi'
Opening hours By appointment only; garden open for NGS: 10.30am to 5pm, 28 and 29 April, 26 and 27 May, 30 June, 1, 28 and 29 July
Admission fee Adults £2; children free

Ann and Roger Bowden know everything there is to know about hostas: they are the UK's leading ambassadors for these useful and easy-to-grow beauties. They sell them from a handsome catalogue with excellent photographs. Prices are fair and range from £3 for basic species to £15 for the latest imported hybrids. But the choice is magnificent: some 400 different hostas, of which a large number are new or reintroduced. Their garden at Cleave House in Sticklepath (NB there are two Sticklepaths in Devon – this is the Okehampton one) has been developed over the last 30 years with mixed plantings for year-round interest. But the display beds for their National Collection of hostas are here, too – an incredible 1,000 cultivars.

Owned by Mr and Mrs Roger Bowden
Number of gardeners 1
Size 0.4ha (1 acre)
NCCPG National Collections *Hosta* (modern hybrids)

Bicton Park

BICTON PARK GARDENS
East Budleigh, Budleigh Salterton EX9 7BJ

Tel 01395 568465 **Fax** 01395 568374
www.bictongardens.co.uk
Location On B3178 between Budleigh Salterton and Newton Poppleford
Opening hours 10am to 6pm (5pm in winter), daily, except Christmas Day
Admission fee Adults £6.95; OAPs £5.95; children £5.95; dogs £1 (on leads at all times); RHS members free in January, February and November

There is lots to see at Bicton, including the Italian garden, American garden, Mediterranean garden, and stream garden, as well as the classical orangery, the (recently restored) hermitage, and the finest pre-Paxton palm house, built from 18,000 tiny panes of glass. The trees are important and impressive: they include 25 champions. There are collections of dwarf conifers, roses (ancient and modern) and ferns. Colour comes from fine camellias, magnolias, azaleas and rhododendrons. A rugged *Wisteria sinensis* is thought to be Britain's oldest at over 180 years. And there is a narrow-gauge railway to chug you through the pinetum and lakeside areas.
woodland garden; roses (ancient and modern); plantsman's collection of plants; plants under glass; mature conifers; good herbaceous borders; fine collection of trees; tallest Grecian fir *Abies cephalonica* (41m; 135ft) ever recorded in the British Isles; garden shop; restaurant

Owned by Simon and Valerie Lister
Number of gardeners 4
Size 25ha (63 acres)
English Heritage Grade I

BLACKPOOL GARDENS
Blackpool, Dartmouth TQ6 0RG

Tel 01803 770606 **Fax** 01803 770311
www.blackpoolsands.co.uk
Location On A379, 3 miles south of Dartmouth
Opening hours 10am to 4pm, daily, April to September
Admission fee Adults £2.50; children free

Blackpool Sands is a private beach – one of the best on the south Devon coast. Just above it, on the other side of the road, the Blackpool gardens rise steeply to a viewpoint known as the Captain's Seat. The Newman family have for over 100 years been planting this south-facing slope with tender exotic trees and shrubs. Among the most interesting are *Feijoa sellowiana* planted in 1909,

Buckland Abbey

and *Cordyline indivisa* (1934) and *Leptospermum lanigerum* (1932), but there is a wealth of callistemons, olearias, embothriums and pittosporums, too. It all seems a world away from the beach below.
subtropical trees and shrubs; shop; beach café

Owned by Sir Geoffrey Newman
Number of gardeners contract gardeners
Size 0.8ha (2 acres)

BUCKLAND ABBEY
Yelverton PL20 6EY

Tel 01822 853607 **Fax** 01822 855448
www.nationaltrust.org.uk
Location Signed from A386 at Yelverton
Opening hours 12.30pm to 5pm, Saturdays and Sundays, 17 February to 11 March; 10.30am to 5.30pm, Friday to Wednesday, 17 March to 4 November; 12.30pm to 5pm, Saturdays and Sundays, 10 November to 2 December; 11am to 5pm, Thursday to Sunday, 6 to 23 December
Admission fee Adults £3.90; children £1.90; free in winter

Originally a Cistercian abbey, then the house of Sir Francis Drake, the main interest for garden-lovers is the charming herb garden along the side of the Great Barn. It has over 50 different culinary and medicinal herbs though the outlines have softened since its box hedges succumbed to box blight. The new Elizabethan garden has topiary bushes, Tudor-style plantings and a flowery mead with a small orchard of old fruit cultivars.
herbs; current holder of Sandford Award; National Trust shop; refreshments

Owned by The National Trust
Number of gardeners 1 1/2
Size 1.2ha (3 acres)

BURROW FARM GARDENS
Dalwood, Axminster EX13 7ET

Tel 01404 831285 **Fax** 01404 831445
www.burrowfarmgardens.co.uk
Location Turn north off A35 at Taunton Cross; follow brown tourist signs for 1/2 mile
Opening hours 10am to 7pm, daily, April to September
Admission fee Adults £4; children 50p

Buckland Abbey

There are nearly 10 acres of plantsmanship at Burrow Farm Gardens, and long views over the sweeping hills. A formal pergola walk is lined with shrubs and climbing roses, while the woodland garden is underplanted with rhododendrons, azaleas and interesting herbaceous plants. The candelabra primulas have naturalised all through the bog garden. And the garden is still growing – both in its size and in the intensity of its planting. A recent addition was the rill garden, lined with luxuriantly colour-themed plantings of shrubs and unusual herbaceous plants.
plantsman's collection of plants; woodland garden; nursery; morning coffee, light lunches, teas

Owned by Mr and Mrs J Benger
Number of gardeners 2
Size 4ha (10 acres)

CASTLE DROGO
Drewsteignton EX6 6PB

Tel 01647 433306 **Fax** 01647 433186
www.nationaltrust.org.uk
Location Drewsteignton village: signs from A30 and A382
Opening hours 10.30am to 4.30pm, 3, 4, 10 and 11 March; 10.30am to 5.30pm, daily, 17 March to 28 October; 10.30am to 4.30pm, daily, 29 October to 4 November; 11am to 4pm, Friday to Sunday, 5 November to 23 December
Admission fee Adults £4.75; children £2.60

This is a major 1920s garden, made to match the last castle built in Britain – a granite vanity which was one of Lutyens's most remarkable works. The gardens, too, are grand and grandiose and, up on the edge of Dartmoor, the highest gardens owned by the National Trust. They are mainly within a large enclosed area, tightly hedged against the wind by thick, clipped yew. The design, by George Dillistone, is formal and terraced with granite steps and walls. Both the rose garden (planted with hybrid teas and floribundas) and the vast and vivid herbaceous borders are a contrast with the austere castle on its windy bluff. Weather-beaten, lichen-heavy Japanese cherries, rhododendrons and acers survive in the woodland spring garden on the slopes below.
woodland garden; roses (ancient and modern); rock garden; good herbaceous borders; National Trust shop; self-service tea rooms

Owned by The National Trust
Number of gardeners 21/2
Size 5ha (121/2 acres)
English Heritage Grade II*

CASTLE HILL
Filleigh, Barnstaple EX32 0RQ

Tel 01598 760336 ext 4
www.castlehilldevon.co.uk
Location 5 miles north-west of South Molton
Opening hours 11am to 5pm, daily, except Saturday, April to August
Admission fee Adults £4

Castle Hill is a seriously important historic landscape, with a triumphal arch on the horizon across the valley and a sham castle to the north. But the gardens around the house are full of interest. Xa Tollemache designed the millennium garden (herbaceous borders lined with lavender all along their length) and Giles Rayner installed a 'topiary' water sculpture. In the bluebell woods behind are magnolias, camellias, rhododendrons, azaleas and fine ornamental plantings.
water sculptures; woodland gardens; historic landscape; cream teas on Sundays and Bank Holiday Mondays

Owned by The Earl and Countess of Arran
Number of gardeners 3
Size 20ha (50 acres)
English Heritage Grade I

CLOVELLY COURT
Clovelly, Bideford EX39 5SZ

Tel 01237 431200 **Fax** 01237 431205
www.clovelly.co.uk
Location Signed in village; next to Parish Church of All Saints
Opening hours 10am to 4pm, daily, March to October
Admission fee Adults £1.50; children free; RHS members free in March and October

The main thing to see at Clovelly Court is the range of five Victorian fruit houses against the south-facing side of the walled kitchen garden. They even have their original manual levers. Peaches, nectarines and apricots are the main fruits under glass, but grapes, melons (in hammocks), cucumbers and citrus fruit are also grown. Apples and pears have been trained outside as espaliers, fans and cordons. The working kitchen garden is organically run and supplies local businesses. It is unusual to see 19th-century domestic industry on such a scale today – well worth a quick visit. And the setting of parkland and Bideford Bay is very fine.

Owned by The Hon John Rous
Number of gardeners 1, plus 3 part-time
Size 0.6ha (1½ acres)

COLETON FISHACRE GARDEN

Coleton, Kingswear, Dartmouth TQ6 0EQ

Tel 01803 752466 **Fax** 01803 753017
www.nationaltrust.org.uk
Location 3 miles from Kingswear off Lower-Ferry Road
Opening hours 10.30am to 5pm, Wednesday to Saturday and Bank Holiday Mondays, 17 March to 28 October; plus Mondays from 23 July to 20 August
Admission fee Adults £5.90; children £3

The Lutyens-style house at Coleton Fishacre was built by Oswald Milne for Sir Rupert and Lady Dorothy D'Oyly Carte in 1925. Rare bulbs flourish in the warm terraces which surround it. The woodland garden, thickly planted with rhododendrons, azaleas and camellias, spills down a secret valley to the sea. A stream runs down the valley, dammed to make small pools along the way, where damp-loving perennials luxuriate. Almost frost-free, the range and size of southern hemisphere trees and shrubs is astounding.

woodland garden; subtropical plants; plantsman's collection of plants; good herbaceous borders; rhododendrons; rare trees; tallest *Catalpa bungei* in the British Isles (and two other record trees); interesting new plantings in the 'Holiwell' area; visitor reception area and tea room

Owned by The National Trust
Number of gardeners 3
Size 10ha (25 acres)
English Heritage Grade II

DARTINGTON HALL

Dartington, Totnes TQ9 6EL

Tel/fax 01803 862367
www.dartingtonhall.org.uk
Location 2 miles north-west of Totnes
Opening hours Dawn to dusk, daily, all year; groups by prior appointment only; and for NGS
Admission fee Donation (£2 suggested)

Dartington is one of the best examples of grand mid-20th-century gardening in England: it was restored and improved with American money at a time when few Englishmen could afford to spend on such a scale. Some famous designers are associated with it: Beatrix Farrand designed the courtyard and influenced the woodland plantings. Percy Cane built the long staircase and opened up some of the long vistas. Henry Moore deposited a reclining woman. The scale is magnificent, and wholly appropriate to the house and landscape. The grassy 'tiltyard', planted with Irish yews known as the 'twelve apostles', is now considered iconic. The gardens are very well maintained and full of horticultural interest, but the detail is never allowed to obscure the greater scheme of it. Dartington also has fine mature trees and some interesting modern additions like the quietly contemplative Japanese garden.

woodland garden; topiary; magnolias; rhododendrons; camellias; dry-landscape Japanese garden; refreshments

Owned by Dartington Hall Trust
Number of gardeners 4
Size 11.1ha (28 acres)
English Heritage Grade II*

DOCTON MILL

Lymebridge, Hartland, Bideford EX39 6EA

Tel/fax 01237 441369
www.doctonmill.co.uk
Location Follow brown signs from A39

Opening hours 10am to 6pm, daily, March to October
Admission fee Adults £4; OAPs £3.75; children (under 16) £1; RHS members free on Saturdays

Docton has a working water mill, a natural bluebell woodland (into which shrubs like rhododendrons have been planted over the last 20 years), an old orchard, and several distinct areas of herbaceous and shrub plantings. The daffodils in spring are spectacular. The new owners have made many improvements. First they planted up a small field with magnolias (25 cultivars) and flowering shrubs. Then they built and filled a large new glasshouse. But there is also a fine bog garden (candelabra primulas in late spring) and a collection of old roses underplanted with herbaceous and ground-cover plants. And the emphasis now is upon planting for summer show, especially in July and August.
apple orchards; daffodils; some young magnolias; light refreshments and cream teas

Owned by Mr and Mrs J Borrett
Number of gardeners 3
Size 3.4ha (8½ acres)

Docton Mill

ESCOT
Ottery St Mary, Exeter EX11 1LU

Tel 01404 822188 **Fax** 01404 822903
www.escot-devon.co.uk
Location Signed from A30 at Fairmile
Opening hours 10am to 6pm (5pm from November to March), daily, all year; closed 25 and 26 December
Admission fee Adults £5.95; OAPs and children £4.50 (under threes free)

Escot is an elegant Regency house, with distant views to East Hill: Capability Brown advised on the prospect. The walled garden has a pretty collection of climbing roses, and a few old shrub roses, too. The woodlands around the house are full of good Victorian rhododendrons, a hardy fernery, some good 19th-century trees (holm oaks, purple beech, cedar and wellingtonias) and good new plantings. Great efforts have been made to make Escot fun for the young – not just animals, fish and birds, but also trails, a maze by Adrian Fisher, a collection of upside-down trees and a cork oak hung with bottles by Ivan Hicks. It is fairly wild and roughly maintained, and is not a place for sensitive horticulturists, but brilliant for children.
snowdrops; rhododendrons and azaleas; mature conifers; bluebells; water plants for sale; home-cooked lunches and cream teas

Owned by John-Michael Kennaway
Number of gardeners 1
Size 10ha (25 acres)

EXETER UNIVERSITY GARDENS
Exeter EX4 4PX

Tel 01392 263059 **Fax** 01392 264547
www.ex.ac.uk/admin/be/grounds1969
Location 1 mile north of city centre: gardens throughout main campus
Opening hours Dawn to dusk, daily, all year
Admission fee Free

From the horticultural point of view, Exeter has the most interesting university campus in England: the gardens are educational, attractive and important. At the centre are the gardens around Reed Hall, laid out by Veitch in the 1860s at the then phenomenal cost of £70,000. This explains the framework of splendid mature trees and shrubs which give such character to the whole site – especially conifers, rhododendrons, magnolias and hardy palm trees. Modern plantings have kept pace: there is a particularly fine collection of Australasian plants including acacias, callistemons and eucalyptus. Other tender plants that grow outside include *Albizia julibrissin*, cacti-like *Opuntia humifusa* and the beautiful parrot-bill plant (*Clianthus puniceus*) from New Zealand. The

The Garden House, Buckland Monachorum

THE GARDEN HOUSE

Buckland Monachorum, Yelverton PL20 7LQ

Tel 01822 854769 **Fax** 01822 855358
www.thegardenhouse.org.uk
Location Signed off A386 on Plymouth side of Yelverton
Opening hours 10.30am to 5pm, daily, March to October
Admission fee Adults £5.50; OAPs £5; children £2

The Garden House was first developed by the late Lionel Fortescue, a retired Eton 'beak', between 1945 and 1981. The setting is awesome: a ruined ecclesiastical site on the edge of Dartmoor, with stupendous views. Fortescue was responsible for much of the design and planting as we still see it in the walled garden. He was a great plantsman and insisted upon growing only the best forms and cultivars. He also believed that plants should be well fed and firmly controlled: they still flourish on the treatment and Fortescue's plantings have continued to fulfil their early promise. Over the 25 years between 1978 and 2003, the Garden House was improved in quite a different way under the guidance of the curator Keith Wiley. He developed six acres of interconnected gardens, each dedicated to a single theme. The design keeps the house as a distant focal point and makes good use of features in the countryside around, like the distant church tower in the village of Buckland Monachorum itself. The South African garden (set off by three very handsome *Cornus controversa* 'Variegata') is intended to replicate the spring flowering of the South African veldt: it is probably best in July and August. Nearby is the quarry garden where natural outcrops have been covered with such plants as rock roses and creeping thymes around a series of ponds fed by a waterfall. The cottage garden is a wildflower meadow where the native campions and ox-eye daisies are joined by such plants as *Alchemilla mollis* and astrantias. There is a maple glade underplanted with thousands of naturalised crocuses in March, followed by azaleas in April and May. And the autumn colour is spectacular. Elsewhere are a lime avenue, a spring garden, a herbaceous bed, a wisteria bridge and a bulb meadow. But this is a garden in an active state of evolution, full of new features and stimulation at every time of the year. In 2003, Keith Wiley handed over to the present head gardener Matt Bishop, who is an authority on snowdrops; there are snowdrop walks to see his collection in February.

plantsman's collection of plants; good herbaceous borders; alpine bank; flowering cherries; wisterias; a developing naturalistic extension with *Acer* glade, spring garden, quarry garden, wildflower meadow and South African garden; plant sales centre; tea room with light lunches

Owned by Fortescue Garden Trust
Number of gardeners 5
Size 4ha (10 acres)

gardeners also practise with great artistry the Victorian art of bedding out.
tender plants; heathers; summer bedding; conifers; rhododendrons

Owned by The University of Exeter
Number of gardeners 25
Size 100ha (250 acres)
NCCPG National Collections *Azara*

GIDLEIGH PARK HOTEL
Chagford TQ13 8HH

Tel 01647 432367 **Fax** 01647 432574
www.gidleigh.com
Location 20 miles west of Exeter; approach from Chagford: do NOT go to Gidleigh
Opening hours Guests of the hotel and restaurant only
Admission fee Free to hotel and restaurant clients

Gidleigh has 45 acres of woodland on the edge of Dartmoor. Many of the rhododendrons and conifers were planted in the 19th century and are wonderfully mature. Around the Tudorised house – now a top hotel – is a 1920s garden. Below is a fine 1930s water garden. The garden contains nothing very rare or special, but the position is stupendous and the sense of space, even grandeur, is enhanced by immaculate maintenance. The hotel and restaurant have received innumerable awards over many years. Finding it needs careful map-reading: in Chagford Square turn right at Lloyds Bank and, after 150 yards, take the first fork to the right and follow the lane for two miles to its end.
woodland garden; two-star Michelin restaurant

Owned by Andrew and Christina Brownsword
Number of gardeners 4
Size 18ha (45 acres)

GNOME RESERVE & WILD FLOWER GARDEN
West Putford, Bradworthy EX22 7XE

Tel 01409 241435
www.gnomereserve.co.uk
Location Between Bideford and Holsworthy, signed from A39, A386 and A388
Opening hours 10am to 6pm, daily, 21 March to 31 October
Admission fee Adults £2.75; OAPs £2.50; children £2.25

There are four reasons to visit this remarkable conservation centre which has been featured on television more than 60 times: first, the two-acre gnome reserve in a beech wood with a stream; second, the two-acre pixies' wildflower meadow, with 250 labelled species; third, the kiln where pottery gnomes and pixies are born; fourth, the museum of rare early gnomes. A large slice of gardening history is displayed in this garden and its museum, while the wildflower meadow is one of the best in the country.
wildflower meadow; large shop selling gnomes; home-made food

Owned by The Atkin Family
Number of gardeners 3
Size 1.6ha (4 acres)

GREENWAY
Greenway Road, Galmpton, Churston Ferrers TQ5 0ES

Tel 01803 842382 **Fax** 01803 661900
www.nationaltrust.org.uk
Location 6 miles east of Brixham, on the Dart estuary
Opening hours 10.30am to 5pm, Wednesday to Saturday, 7 March to 13 October
Admission fee Adults £5.20; children £2.60; but £4.40 and £2.20 for visitors arriving on foot, bike or public transport

Greenway is one of the National Trust's newest acquisitions, with a wonderful collection of subtropical exotica: among the best specimens are mimosas, myrtles, mahonias and puyas. The collection of camellias (over 200 different cultivars, most of them in the sensational camellia walk) is exceptional, and there are more than 50 different *Eucalyptus* species. All visitors intending to arrive by car must telephone 01803 842382 to book a parking space in advance; the morning of the day in question is usually all right. Visitors arriving without having booked a parking space will not be admitted. There are no parking spaces on the narrow country lanes leading to the property.

camellias; subtropical plants; eucalyptus; National Trust shop; café

Owned by The National Trust
Number of gardeners 3
Size 13ha (33 acres)

HARTLAND ABBEY

Hartland, Bideford EX39 6DT

Tel 01237 441234 **Fax** 01237 441264
www.hartlandabbey.com
Location 1 mile inland from Hartland Point
Opening hours 12.30pm to 5pm, daily, except Saturdays, April to September
Admission fee Adults £4.50; wheelchair users £2; children £1

The Stucleys have transformed the gardens since they took over Hartland in 1996. The gardens were originally laid out with advice from Gertrude Jekyll in a sheltered frost-free combe. A fine collection of camellias, hydrangeas, eucryphias and rhododendrons were added to the woodland gardens in the 1950s and 1960s. Recent restoration has revealed the Victorian fernery and the 'Baronet's Bog Garden', where gunneras, hostas, primulas, astilbes and arum lilies flourish. The walled gardens boast fine herbaceous borders and naturalised *Echium pininana*.
rhododendrons; gift shop; light lunches and cream teas

Owned by Sir Hugh Stucley Bt
Number of gardeners 1 1/2
Size 4.8ha (12 acres)

HEDDON HALL

Parracombe EX31 4QL

Tel/fax 01598 763541
www.heddonhallgardens.co.uk
Location In Parracombe Lane, in centre of Parracombe
Opening hours 2pm to 5.30pm, Wednesdays and Sundays, May to July; for snowdrops: noon to 4pm, Sundays, February; and for NGS
Admission fee Adults £4 (£3.50 in February); children free

The garden at Heddon Hall has been made since 1987: Carol Klein, Roy Lancaster and Penelope Hobhouse have all had a hand in it. The sheltered, wooded valley has a stream running through, with old stew ponds and a lush bog garden on the way. The magnolias, rhododendrons and camellias make a fine display in spring, preceded by snowdrops and hellebores, for which the garden is open in February. But many of the plants are rare and of interest to the plantsman. The walled garden has box hedges and fruit trees grown as cordons as well as flowers for cutting, herbs and vegetables. A young arboretum, planted in 1997, shows promise.
snowdrops; cream teas

Owned by Juliet and Fred de Falbe
Number of gardeners owners, plus 2 part-time
Size 1.6ha (4 acres)

HIGHER KNOWLE

Lustleigh, Newton Abbot TQ13 9SP

Tel 01647 277275
Location 3 miles north-west of Bovey Tracey; turn off A382 towards Lustleigh; after 1/4 mile left, then right; after 1/4 mile steep drive on left
Opening hours 11am to 6pm, Sundays and Bank Holiday Mondays, 18 March to 28 May
Admission fee Adults £2.50; children free

Higher Knowle was built by a pupil of Lutyens on a wooded slope on the south-eastern edge of Dartmoor: a stream flows down towards the Bovey valley – the views are stupendous. The first plantings date from the 1950s – mature azaleas and magnolias around the house. The present owners bought the property in 1966 and have since planted up the lower woodland area with camellias, modern hybrid magnolias and rhododendrons. Bluebells, primroses and huge boulders of natural granite add to its charm, especially in spring.

Owned by Mr and Mrs David Quicke
Number of gardeners owners only
Size 1.2ha (3 acres)

HILL HOUSE

Landscove, Ashburton, Newton Abbot TQ13 7LY

Tel 01803 762273 **Fax** 01803 762716
www.hillhousenursery.co.uk
Location Off A384, follow signs for Landscove
Opening hours 11am to 5pm, daily (including Bank Holidays), all year; closed 15 December to 9 January; groups and guided tours by prior arrangement
Admission fee Free

This Victorian Old Vicarage was made famous by Edward Hyams's *An Englishman's Garden* but for many years now it has been the centre of a distinguished plantsman's nursery. Family-owned and family-run, the three-acre nursery has an excellent range of unusual or 'hard-to-find' plants – a list of over 3,000 in all, most of them available at any one time. In the glasshouses are handsome large specimens, particularly of fuchsias and passion flowers. Most of the stock is raised in the nursery. Raymond Hubbard breeds plants: this is where *Nemesia* 'Bluebird' originated. He is also the breeder of *Dianthus* 'Old Mother Hubbard', *Crocosmia* 'Krakatoa', *Plectranthus argentatus* 'Hill House' and *P. ciliatus* 'Sasha'.
mature conifers; daffodils; cyclamen and snowdrops; herbaceous borders; pond garden; conservatory; nursery; tea room (home-made cakes) March to September

Owned by Raymond and Matthew Hubbard
Number of gardeners 2 part-time
Size 1.2ha (3 acres)

HOLBROOK GARDEN

Sampford Peverell, Tiverton EX16 7EN

Tel 01884 821164
www.holbrookgarden.com
Location 1 mile north-east of Sampford Peverell, left-hand side of road to Holcombe
Opening hours 9am to 5pm, Tuesday to Saturday, April to October
Admission fee Adults £3; children free; RHS members free

This is the garden attached to Sampford Shrubs, an excellent plantsman's nursery just off the M5, which spills over into the garden itself. It was started in the early 1980s and has a good structure of garden-worthy rhododendrons and ornamental trees – many of them unusual, including a 6m *Pittosporum tenuifolium* 'Silver Queen'. Daffodils and fritillaries have naturalised and there are interesting herbaceous plantings everywhere.
Part of the garden has been converted to a new-style jungle garden with bananas and foliage plants. Other parts are microhabitats, including a 'stone' garden and a damp summer meadow.
The plantings build up towards a crescendo of heleniums, grasses, kniphofias, agapanthus and perennial daisies in August and September.
The experiments continue: there is lots to learn and admire here. There will be two RHS Special Events at Holbrook Garden in 2007; details from 020 7821 3408.

Owned by Martin Hughes-Jones and Susan Proud
Size 0.8ha (2 acres)
NCCPG National Collections *Helenium*

KILLERTON

Broadclyst, Exeter EX5 3LE

Tel 01392 881345 **Fax** 01392 883112
www.nationaltrust.org.uk
Location West side of B3181, Exeter to Cullompton road
Opening hours 10.30am to dusk, daily, all year
Admission fee Adults £6.30; children £2.80; reduced rates in winter

Killerton is a historic giant among gardens. Its long connections with Veitch's Nursery have bequeathed it a great tree collection. These include innumerable record-breaking specimens, many from collectors' seed, though one's sense of awe may be a little spoilt by droning traffic on the M5.
snowdrops; rock garden; rhododendrons and azaleas; daffodils; fine collection of trees; bluebells; tallest *Ostrya carpinifolia* (22m; 72ft) in the British Isles (and eight further record trees); magnolias; drifts of *Crocus tommasinianus*; National Trust shop; small well-run plant centre; waitress-service restaurant and self-service tea room

Owned by The National Trust
Number of gardeners 5
Size 8.7ha (22 acres)
English Heritage Grade II*

KNIGHTSHAYES GARDEN
Tiverton EX16 7RG

Tel 01884 254665 **Fax** 01884 243050
www.nationaltrust.org.uk
Location Off A396 Tiverton to Bampton road
Opening hours 11am to 4pm, Saturday to Monday, 2 to 12 March; 11am to 5pm, daily, 17 March to 4 November
Admission fee Adults £5.90; children £3

Knightshayes is a garden in a wood – one of the best of its kind in the world. Much of the original canopy is here – notably some very fine oaks – but it is now supplemented by magnolias, birches, nothofagus and sorbus. The garden unveils as a series of walks and glades, with beautiful rhododendrons, camellias and rare shrubs underplanted by hellebores, erythroniums, foxgloves, cyclamen and bluebells. Closer to the house are the stately formal gardens, enclosed by immaculately clipped yew hedges. Here alpine treasures and small bulbs grow in raised beds. The old bowling lawn is filled by a vast circular pool and a single weeping pear, *Pyrus salicifolia* 'Pendula', which is pruned to thin out its canopy of branches. The walled garden, near the stables, is being restored and run organically. In the surrounding park is a very fine collection of trees, including several record-breakers. The Douglas firs are particularly impressive.
woodland garden; topiary; good herbaceous borders; hellebores; cyclamen; bulbs; peat beds; centenary planting of 100 trees along visitors' entrance; tallest *Quercus cerris* (40m; 131ft) in the British Isles; National Trust shop and plant centre; licensed restaurant

Owned by The National Trust
Number of gardeners 6
Size 20ha (50 acres)
English Heritage Grade II*

LUKESLAND
Harford, Ivybridge PL21 0JF

Tel 01752 691749/893390 **Fax** 01752 698751
www.lukesland.co.uk
Location 1½ miles north of Ivybridge on the Harford road
Opening hours 2pm to 6pm, Wednesdays, Sundays and Bank Holiday Mondays, 1 April to 17 June; 11am to 4pm, Wednesdays and Sundays, 14 October to 11 November; and by appointment
Admission fee Adults £4; children free; reduced rates for groups of 20+

Lukesland is a woodland garden in a stream-fed valley on the southern edge of Dartmoor: it offers the perfect conditions for growing rhododendrons, azaleas and many other flowering shrubs. The house and the earliest plantings date from the 1880s, but most of what we see now has been planted by the Howells since 1975. The family's policy is to try to regenerate poor or over-mature areas, so that the quality and display of plants are improved; during the 1990s, for example, they planted a good selection of late-flowering rhododendrons at the north end of the pinetum. Here, too, in 1992, they built a striking reverse suspension bridge, designed by the Scottish architect Sir James Dunbar-Nasmith. The many paths and bridges crossing the stream open up different views as you progress through the garden. The fine examples of rhododendron species include the large-leafed *R. sinogrande*, *R. maccabeanum*, *R. falconeri* and *R. arizelum*. The Exbury hybrids include 'Cornish Cross', 'Hawk Crest' and 'Jalisco'. Camellias make an impact in early spring, while other good shrubs include *Drimys lanceolata*, *Michelia doltsopa*, hoherias and eucryphias. Maples, taxodiums, cornus and sorbus give good autumn colour, as does the shelterbelt of mature beeches. There are some very fine specimen trees: *Ginkgo biloba* at 18m (59ft), *Davidia involucrata* var. *vilmoriniana* planted in 1936 and now a broad 17m (56ft) specimen, and a magnificent *Magnolia campbellii* planted at the same time and now 19m (62ft) high – its exceptionally wide girth makes it a champion tree.
small pinetum; rhododendrons and azaleas; stream, ponds and waterfalls; tea room

MARWOOD HILL GARDENS

Marwood, Barnstaple EX31 4EB

Tel/fax 01271 342528
www.marwoodhillgarden.co.uk
Location Signed from A361 Barnstaple to Braunton road; follow brown tourist signs or check our website for directions
Opening hours Gardens: 9.30am to 5.30pm, daily, March to October; plant sales and garden tea room: 11am to 5pm, daily, March to September; please contact office for other opening times and details of events
Admission fee Adults £4.50; children free; groups welcome (by prior booking)

Marwood Hill is a remarkable plantsman's garden, conceived on a grand scale and fast maturing, though it is still expanding along the long sheltered valley which gives such vigorous growth to its plants. It is a tribute to the energy, determination and sheer plantsmanship of the late Dr Smart, who died in 2002. Marwood Hill is exciting for its scale and variety: there is no better place in the South West to learn about plants of every kind, especially as all the plants are clearly labelled. It is moreover a garden of year-round interest. Late in the year, are *Galanthus reginae-olgae* flowers with the last of the *Cyclamen hederifolium*: these are followed in midwinter by many other snowdrops and *Cyclamen coum*. There is a wonderful collection of camellias at this season, too – some in the open, and others (huge bushes of Reticulata hybrids) under glass. Magnolias are numerous, including many of the Jury hybrids from New Zealand, the dark form of M. *campbellii* called 'Betty Jessel', M. *sprengeri* var. *diva*, M. *dawsoniana*, M. x *wieseneri* and the home-grown 'Marwood Spring'. Many are underplanted with drifts of narcissi. Come the spring, and the pergola draped with 12 different wisterias starts to flower (the colour is extended by interplanted clematis and climbing roses) and the walled garden begins to make an impact with ceanothus, *Clianthus puniceus* and the poppy bush (*Dendromecon rigida*). In early summer the bog garden comes into its own, starting with drifts of candelabra primulas and continuing with astilbes from the National Collection: in fact the bog garden is full of colour right through until autumn. Hydrangeas are another success story: a large number of cultivars is planted throughout the garden. As the soil is acid, the 'mopheads' come out in many shades of blue, alongside the cultivars of *Hydrangea paniculata* (Dr Smart considered 'Pink Diamond' one of the best) and *Hydrangea quercifolia* whose oak-shaped leaves change to brilliant colours in the autumn. Leaves and bark are important elements of the garden: Dr Smart planted the birches close to the eucalyptus so that the contrasts of bark can be enjoyed together – he planted large numbers of both *Betula* and *Eucalyptus* species. He also had a high regard for the seldom-seen *Amomyrtus lechleriana* in the walled garden.
And there is a fine collection of rhododendrons, including large plants of *R. maccabeanum*, *R. sinogrande*, *R. eximium*, *R. arizelum*, *R. arboreum* and *R.* 'Sir Charles Lemon'. There are additions and improvements every year: 2004 saw the start of a three-year project to plant up the hilltop with four acres of prairie garden – grasses, perennials and flower meadows among the eucalyptus.
a supreme example of a plantsman's collection; roses (mainly old-fashioned and climbers); rhododendrons and azaleas; plants under glass; daffodils; good herbaceous plants; fine collection of trees; alpine plants; birches; *Eucalyptus*; camellias; hebes; teas, March to October

Owned by Dr JA Snowdon
Number of gardeners 4
Size 8ha (20 acres)
NCCPG National Collections *Astilbe*; *Iris ensata*; *Tulbaghia*

Owned by Mr and Mrs John Howell
Number of gardeners family, plus part-time help
Size 9.6ha (24 acres)

MOTHECOMBE HOUSE

Holbeton, Plymouth PL8 1LA

Tel 01752 830444 **Fax** 01752 830500
Location 10 miles south-east of Plymouth, signed from A379
Opening hours 2pm to 5pm, 5 and 6 May
Admission fee Adults £3; children free

Mothecombe is a beautiful, unspoilt estate which surrounds the Erme estuary. The walled garden has fruit, vegetables and flower borders. In the orchard are spring bulbs, flowering shrubs, streams and a bog garden, as well as a large pond. The camellia walk leads through a mass of bluebells and down to the sandy shore.
nursery plant sales; teas

Owned by Mr and Mrs A Mildmay-White
Number of gardeners 2
Size 6ha (15 acres)

THE OLD GLEBE

Eggesford, Chulmleigh EX18 7QU

Tel/fax 01769 580632
Location South (and uphill) of Eggesford station for 0.7 miles, right into bridleway
Opening hours 2pm to 6pm, 19, 20, 27 and 28 May for NGS; all customers by appointment
Admission fee Adults £2.50 and children £1 on NGS days

This is a great rhododendron collection, well-known to the *cognoscenti*. Nigel Wright grows over 6,000 plants and 800 different cultivars, and his nursery sells over 200 of them. It is one of the best lists in the UK. The house is an old rectory, with fine lawns, mature trees, walled herbaceous borders, a bog garden and a small lake.
rhododendrons

Owned by Mr and Mrs Nigel Wright
Number of gardeners 3 part-time
Size 2.8ha (7 acres)

ORCHID PARADISE

Burnham Nurseries, Forches Cross, Newton Abbot TQ12 6PZ

Tel 01626 352233 **Fax** 01626 362167
www.orchids.uk.com
Location Follow brown tourist signs from A382 between Newton Abbot and Bovey Tracey
Opening hours 10am to 4pm, daily, except Christmas and New Year
Admission fee Adults £2; children free

The Rittershausens are famous for their orchids – their books, their expertise, their exhibits and the range of what they grow and sell. The display houses are open all year – a place of pilgrimage for beginners and experts alike, and a feast for the eyes whatever the weather outside.
orchids for sale; tea, coffee and light refreshments

Owned by Sara Rittershausen

OVERBECK'S MUSEUM & GARDEN

Sharpitor, Salcombe TQ8 8LW

Tel 01548 842893 **Fax** 01548 845020
www.nationaltrust.org.uk
Location 2 miles south of Salcombe
Opening hours 10am to 5.30pm (or dusk, if earlier), Sunday to Friday, all year; daily, 16 July to 2 September
Admission fee Adults £5.80; children £2.90

Overbeck's has a small, intensely planted, almost jungly garden, perched above the Salcombe estuary. The formal terraces (rather 1930s) are stuffed with interesting tender plants: *Musa basjoo*, phormiums, agapanthus, self-sown *Echium pininana* and every kind of South African daisy, all held together in a framework of hundreds of *Trachycarpus* palms.
subtropical plants; bluebells; palms; mimosas; cyclamen; *Magnolia campbellii*; National Trust shop; tea room

Owned by The National Trust
Number of gardeners 2
Size 2.4ha (6 acres)
English Heritage Grade II

PAIGNTON ZOO & BOTANICAL GARDENS
Totnes Road, Paignton TQ4 7EU

Tel 01803 697500 **Fax** 01803 523457
www.paigntonzoo.org.uk
Location On A385 Totnes road, 1 mile from Paignton
Opening hours 10am to 6pm (or dusk, if earlier), daily, all year; closed 25 December
Admission fee Adults £11.35; OAPs £9.35; children £7.60

Once a private garden devoted to blue-flowered and blue-leaved plants, this is now an inspiring combination of zoo, botanic collection, public park and holiday entertainment. Themed plant collections are one of its more recent features: among them are economic plants, medical plants, palm species and a Mediterranean climate garden. There are tropical, temperate and desert-plant glasshouses.

mature trees and shrubs; unusual exotics; glasshouses with tropical plants; shops; large self-service restaurant

Owned by Whitley Wildlife Conservation Trust
Number of gardeners 6
Size 30ha (75 acres)
NCCPG National Collections *Buddleja*

PLANT WORLD BOTANIC GARDENS
St Marychurch Road, Newton Abbot TQ12 4SE

Tel 01803 872939 **Fax** 01803 875018
www.plant-world-seeds.com
Location Follow brown tourist signs from Penn Inn roundabout at Newton Abbot, at end of A380 dual carriageway from Exeter
Opening hours 9.30am to 5pm, daily, April to September
Admission fee Adults £3; children free

This plantsman's nursery sells a selection of alpines, perennials and shrubs. There is an illustrated seed list with fresh material from the gardens and some interesting collected species. The National Collection of *Primula* extends only to the Cortusoides section of the genus, but the nursery used to collect the Capitatae and Farinosae, too, and it still grows many from those sections. The nursery also has a strong line in new

Plant World Botanic Gardens

strains of aquilegias and hardy geraniums. The mature four-acre gardens are planted out as special habitat zones representing the five continents. They burgeon with rare trees and shrubs: worth a long journey to visit in their own right – as are the views of Dartmoor and Lyme Bay.
many good plants; innovative design; new café

Owned by Ray Brown
Number of gardeners 3
Size 1.6ha (4 acres)
NCCPG National Collections *Primula* (Cortusoides section)

POWDERHAM CASTLE

Exeter EX6 8JQ

Tel 01626 890243 **Fax** 01626 890729
www.powderham.co.uk
Location Off A379 Dawlish to Exeter Road at Kenton
Opening hours 10am to 5.30pm, Sunday to Friday, 4 April to 28 October
Admission fee Adults £7.95; OAPs £7.50; children £5.95

Powderham is not a major garden, though it has some good trees – notably the cork oak (*Quercus suber*) and its Devon hybrid *Q.* x *hispanica* 'Lucombeana'. Nevertheless the 18th-century landscaped park is serenely English, the woodland garden is stupendous in March and there is a cheerful modern rose garden all along the front of the house. The greenhouses in the Victorian walled garden are now back in commission after recent restoration.
roses (mainly modern); good trees in park; plant centre; licensed restaurant

Owned by The Earl and Countess of Devon
Number of gardeners 3
Size 22ha (55 acres), including grounds
English Heritage Grade II

Tel 01805 624067 **Fax** 01805 624717
www.rhs.org.uk/rosemoor
Location 1 mile south of Great Torrington on A3124 (formerly B3220)
Opening hours 10am to 6pm (but 5pm October to March), daily, all year, except 25 December
Admission fee Adults £6; children £2; pre-booked groups (10+) £5; RHS members (plus one guest) free

The Royal Horticultural Society's garden at Rosemoor has proved a great success. When Lady Anne Palmer gave it to the Society in 1988, few people imagined that it would develop into such a major tourist attraction. The setting certainly helped – the Torridge valley is unusually wooded and sheltered – and Lady Anne's original garden was full of plants, but the achievement is largely due to the Society's good management and its original garden masterplan. Rosemoor is now an all-year garden, with a great variety of designs, styles, plants and plantings in both its formal 'rooms' and in the more natural parts. It is therefore a good place for ideas and inspiration at every season. The winter garden is designed to show what can be done to fill a garden with colour and interest during the colder months. The alpine display house provides colour and interest all the year round. Two major features for the summer and autumn months are the Queen Mother's rose garden, for modern roses, and its companion shrub rose garden containing over 200 cultivars. The two colour-themed formal gardens provide strong contrasts: the spiral garden has cool, soft, pastel colours while the square garden contains 'hot' plantings. The cottage and herb gardens are more informal, but separated by the *potager* with its decorative vegetable planting. The foliage garden is especially good, and repays careful study, while the model gardens demonstrate three contrasting design solutions for the average domestic plot. Other attractions include the stream and bog garden; the lake; large areas of parkland; and the arboretum. An enormous number of events, shows, workshops, lectures, demonstrations and gardens walks take place at Rosemoor all through the year. For details see the Society's website.
woodland garden; roses (ancient and modern); plantsman's collection of plants; stream and bog

RHS GARDEN ROSEMOOR

Great Torrington EX38 8PH

garden; foliage garden; colour-themed gardens; fruit and vegetable gardens; herb garden; cottage garden; several record trees; library; good range of books and gifts; plant centre; library; licensed restaurant; tea room

Owned by The Royal Horticultural Society
Number of gardeners 20, plus 40 volunteers
Size 26ha (65 acres)
NCCPG National Collections *Ilex*, *Cornus*

Rosemoor

ROWDEN GARDENS

Brentor, Tavistock PL19 0NG

Tel/fax 01822 810275
www.rowdengardens.com
Location 1 mile west of North Brentor
Opening hours By prior appointment at any time
Admission fee Adults £2; children free

Rowden Gardens is a nursery with a show garden attached. Its speciality is aquatic plants, and more than 3,000 different plants grow in the garden, which provides the propagating material for the nursery. As well as two National Collections, there is a good choice of water lilies and *Iris ensata* cultivars, many raised by the nursery. Its list of non-aquatic herbaceous plants now totals nearly 2,000 cultivars, with a particularly strong hand of grasses, ligularias, rheums and rodgersias. Rowden is also *the* place for marsh marigolds and water irises. From its National Collections it grows and offers for sale more species and cultivars than anyone else in Britain. The nursery prides itself on being an introducer of new plants.

Owned by John Carter
Number of gardeners 2
Size 0.4ha (1 acre)
NCCPG National Collections *Caltha*; *Iris* (*fulva, pseudacorus, versicolor, virginica* and *laevigata* cvs.)

SALTRAM

Plympton, Plymouth PL7 3UH

Tel 01752 333500 **Fax** 01752 336474
www.nationaltrust.org.uk
Location 2 miles west of Plympton
Opening hours 11am to 4.30pm (4pm from 29 October to 28 February 2008), Saturday to Thursday, plus Good Friday, all year
Admission fee Adults £4.20; children £2.10

Twenty acres of beautiful parkland, whose huge and ancient trees are underplanted with camellias and rhododendrons. Best in spring when the daffodils flower in hosts.
rhododendrons and azaleas; camellias; parkland; handsome orangery; lime avenue; 'melancholy' walk;

tallest *Acer palmatum* 'Osakazuki' (13m; 43ft) in the British Isles; National Trust shop; restaurant

Owned by The National Trust
Number of gardeners 3
Size 8ha (20 acres)
English Heritage Grade II*

SHERWOOD

Newton St Cyres, Exeter EX5 5BT

Tel 01392 851216 **Fax** 01392 851870
Location 2 miles south-west of Newton St Cyres, at the end of a signed road
Opening hours 2pm to 5pm, Sundays, all year
Admission fee Adults £3; children free

This is an important rhododendron and magnolia garden with much more than the collection of Knap Hill azaleas to see and enjoy. The magnolias are good, and there are handsome collections of buddlejas, berberis, cotoneasters, hydrangeas and maples which take the garden through, with late-summer flowering and fine autumn colour, to the end of the year. And the planting continues: a new area of epimediums and similar small woodlanders is developing fast.
rhododendrons; magnolias; good collection of ornamental shrubs

Owned by Sir John and Lady Quicke
Number of gardeners 1 1/2
Size 6ha (15 acres)
NCCPG National Collections *Berberis*; *Magnolia*; *Rhododendron* (Knap Hill azaleas)

TAPELEY PARK

Instow EX39 4NT

Tel 01271 342558/860897 **Fax** 01271 342371
www.tapeleypark.com
Location Off A39 between Barnstaple and Bideford
Opening hours 10am to 5pm, daily, except Saturdays, 26 March to 31 October
Admission fee Adults £4; OAPs £3.50; children £2.50; RHS members free from 8 Jun to 8 July

Tapeley is a substantial house (early Georgian, plus Palladian additions) with fine views along Devon's north coast. Its garden's reputation rests upon three broad, impressive, Italianate terraces, dating from the early 20th century. The lowest has a handsome summerhouse at one end which recalls the garden's Edwardian heyday. The beds are planted with such tender plants as mimosas, giant echiums, *Sophora tetraptera* and *Myrtus communis* subsp. *tarentina*. One has fuchsia hedges. Nearby is an ilex tunnel that could have sprung from the Boboli gardens in Florence. An enticing staircase lined with tall cordylines and trachycarpus palms leads up to a shell house (in need of restoration), an ice house and the working kitchen garden with a long curvilinear range of glasshouses. Here, too, is a vast patch of *Iris unguicularis*. Rhododendrons, vast conifers and wild ramsons fill the woodland garden. Elsewhere are a lake surrounded by extremely ancient *Thuya plicata* and a new organic permaculture garden. Every corner of Tapeley has masses of horticultural interest – and charm.
woodland garden; plants under glass; fruit; gift shop; licensed lunches and cream teas

Owned by NDCI Ltd
Number of gardeners 2
Size 20ha (50 acres)
English Heritage Grade II*

THORNHAYES NURSERY LTD

St Andrew's Wood, Dulford, Cullompton EX15 2DF

Tel 01884 266746 **Fax** 01884 266739
www.thornhayes-nursery.co.uk
Location 10 mins from M5, Jct 28
Opening hours 8am to 4.30pm, Monday to Friday, 9.30am to 2pm, Saturdays, September to April
Admission fee Free

This nursery (retail and wholesale) was founded in 1991 with the aim of growing one of the widest ranges of ornamental and fruit trees in the UK. The emphasis, then as now, was on disease-resistant species and cultivars that would flourish in the wet, western side of Britain. Highlights include *Fitzroya cupressoides*, *Betula* 'Conyngham'

and good collections of sorbus, pyrus and crataegus: dendrophiles should take a closer look. Hard-to-get West Country apples for cider, cooking and eating are another speciality: these include 'Chorister Boy', 'Peter Lock' and 'Royal Somerset' – a total of 250 cultivars. Thornhayes' apple displays are one of the highlights of RHS Garden Rosemoor's annual Apple Day. There will be two RHS Special Events at Thornhayes Nursery in 2007; details from 020 7821 3408.
rare ornamental trees; West Country apples

Owned by KD and PM Croucher
Size 13ha (33 acres)

UGBROOKE PARK
Chudleigh TQ13 0AD

Tel 01626 852179 **Fax** 01626 853322
www.ugbrooke.co.uk
Location Signed off A380
Opening hours 1pm to 5.30pm, Tuesday to Thursday, Sundays and Bank Holiday Monday, 9 July to 7 September; and by appointment for groups at other times
Admission fee Adults £3; children £2

Ugbrooke's main claim to fame is the beautiful landscaped park laid out by Capability Brown in about 1770 and utterly unspoilt since then. His ponds and lakes still make for one of the best walks in Devon. In the park are mature specimens of Spanish chestnut, Turkey oak, holm oak and that West Country speciality *Quercus* x *hispanica* 'Lucombeana'. The gardens have been taken in hand in recent years, and now offer much to enjoy, including a rose garden, a maze, a small fernery, a lavender-and-box parterre, a hydrangea walk and a Spanish garden. New for 2007 are herbaceous borders and a magnolia walk designed by Michael Hickson.
landscaped park; fine trees; attractive new gardens; tea room

Owned by Clifford Estate Company
Number of gardeners 3
Size 2 ha (5 acres), plus 40-ha (100-acre) park
English Heritage Grade II*

WINSFORD WALLED GARDEN
Winsford Lane, Halwill EX21 5XT

Tel 01409 221477
www.winsfordwalledgarden.com
Location Brown tourist signs from Halwill Junction
Opening hours 9.30am to 5.30pm, daily, May to October; and by appointment; some days are for the NGS
Admission fee Adults £4.50; children free

This excellent plantsman's garden has been entirely made since 1999, within the walls of an 1880s flower garden. The collection of plants is very impressive – over 3,000 different taxa – and many features are used for their display. The alpine house is especially interesting.
small nursery; teas and coffee

Owned by Aileen Birks
Number of gardeners 2
Size 0.4ha (1 acre)

DORSET

Both Dorset's Grade I gardens – Abbotsbury and Athelhampton – have plenty of horticultural interest to offer their visitors as well as their historic importance. Abbotsbury has an especially good collection of old trees, including several UK record-holders. Minterne and Forde, too, are good for specimen trees, while one of the tallest examples in the British Isles of the dawn redwood (*Metasequoia glyptostroboides*) is a twin-stemmed specimen more than 25m (82ft) high in Bournemouth's Central Park. Unfortunately we are unable to list the gardens at Stapehill Abbey this year, as the property was in the process of changing hands as we went to press and the new owner's intentions were not disclosed. Most of Dorset's leading nurseries are close to the coast – the chalk hinterland can be cold in winter – and there is a cluster of eminent nurseries on the sandy soils in the south-east of the county. The National Gardens Scheme is very well supported and lists well over 100 gardens – a remarkable number for such a small county. A semi-horticultural curiosity is the grass steps at Milton Abbey school. The NCCPG has a very active group in the county, but there are comparatively few National Collections – among them *Hoheria*, *Ceanothus* and *Penstemon* – all benefiting from the mild climate along the Dorset coast. Kingston Maurward is a RHS Partner College: the estate was first made famous by Sir Thomas Hanbury, who gave Wisley to the Royal Horticultural Society.

ABBOTSBURY SUB TROPICAL GARDENS

Abbotsbury, Weymouth DT3 4LA

Tel 01305 871387 **Fax** 01305 871902
www.abbotsbury-tourism.co.uk/gardens.html
Location On B3157 coast road, in village
Opening hours 10am to 6pm (dusk in winter), daily, all year; closed over Christmas and New Year
Admission fee Adults £8; OAPs £7.50; children £5; RHS members free from October to February

Abbotsbury is a woodland garden of splendid trees and shrubs of great rarity which has enjoyed a spectacular renaissance in recent years. A vast *Pterocarya fraxinifolia* greets you by the entrance, and sets the tone for this superlative woodland garden, where rare plants (especially trees and shrubs) are matched by exceptional rates of growth and a very high standard of maintenance. Even the native oak trees are exceptional for their height. Palms, eucalyptus, pittosporum, banana plants, camellias, large areas of gunneras and streams of libertias all grow lushly in the sheltered valley and romantic walled garden. Among the trees are many exceptionally large specimens of species that are normally too tender to grow even in southern England – including *Buxus balearica*, *Ilex fargesii*, *Photinia nussia*, *Picconia excelsa* and *Pittosporum crassifolium*. The valley of tree ferns is extremely impressive, too. Spring colour gives way to a subtropical summer display – cannas, tree ferns, kniphofias, dahlias and bright bedding. Watsonias and agapanthus seem to have naturalised. There has been a lot of good planting in recent years, including many new species introduced by such collectors as Roy Lancaster. This is a garden of outstanding beauty and very high plant interest. An excellent nursery makes for added value. There will be two RHS Special Events at Abbotsbury in 2007; details from 020 7821 3408.

fine collection of trees; magnolias; candelabra primulas; free-standing loquat *Eriobotrya japonica*; excellent collection of rare trees and shrubs; camellias; rhododendrons and azaleas; bluebells; subtropical rarities; tallest English oak *Quercus robur* (40m; 131ft) in the British Isles; five other record trees; shop; plant centre; restaurant

Abbotsbury Sub Tropical Gardens

Owned by Ilchester Estates
Number of gardeners 5
Size 8ha (20 acres)
NCCPG National Collections *Hoheria*
English Heritage Grade I

ATHELHAMPTON
Dorchester DT2 7LG

Tel 01305 848363 **Fax** 01305 848135
www.athelhampton.co.uk
Location 5 miles east of Dorchester, off A35 at Northbrook-Puddletown junction
Opening hours 10.30am to 5pm, Sunday to Thursday, March to October; 10.30am to dusk, Sundays, November to February
Admission fee House and garden £8.50

Inigo Thomas designed these compact, architectural gardens about 100 years ago as the perfect complement for the perfect manor house – an enfilade of formal, interlinked gardens. Sharply cut cones of yew, a long canal with water lilies, and rambling roses in early summer are some of the main features, alongside tulips, magnolias and clematis. A purple and white border leads down to a glowering statue of Queen Victoria. The garden does not excel in horticultural interest, but is a splendid example of Edwardian style, and its overall effect is most satisfying and harmonious.

gazebos; beautiful walls and hedges; topiary; winner of HHA/Christie's Garden of the Year Award 1997; two *Metasequoia glyptostroboides* from the original seed; shop; restaurant; refreshments

Owned by Patrick Cooke
Number of gardeners 3
Size 4ha (10 acres)
English Heritage Grade I

BENNETTS WATER GARDENS
Putton Lane, Chickerell, Weymouth DT3 4AF

Tel 01305 785150
www.waterlily.co.uk
Location 2 miles west of Weymouth, on B3157 link road

Athelhampton

Opening hours 10am to 5pm, daily, except Mondays and Saturdays, but open on Bank Holidays, April to September
Admission fee Adults £6.45; OAPs £5.95; children £3.95

Bennetts Water Gardens are the leading nursery in the South West for aquatic plants, especially water lilies. The peak flowering season is from early June to late August, which coincides with the tourist season. The gardens have been developed as a visitor attraction: thousands of water lilies and a 'Monet' bridge.
water lilies; tropical house; museum; tea room

Owned by JL and AJ Bennett
Number of gardeners 3
Size 2.4ha (6 acres)
NCCPG National Collections *Nymphaea*

CHETTLE HOUSE
Chettle, Blandford Forum DT11 8DB

Tel/fax 01258 830858
Location 6 miles north of Blandford, 1 mile west of A354
Opening hours 11am to 5pm, first Sunday of each month, Easter to October; groups by appointment
Admission fee Adults £4.50; children free

Chettle House is stunning – built by Thomas Archer in the 1710s and actually improved in the 1840s, it is full of beautiful architectural detail. The gardens are old and formal in structure, but have been re-planted in the English style since about 1970. A croquet lawn fringed by herbaceous plantings fills the foreground to the park, while the borders in the main garden surround a sunken lawn. The plantings are effective, and include a variegated liriodendron, a stauntonia growing over an old yew, a holboellia, a small rose garden, a fine display of *Campsis* in late summer, some 60 clematis cultivars and 23 cultivars of lonicera. A walnut tree planted in 1957 is already nearly 18m (60ft) high. This garden is the original home of the very pretty (and popular) *Campanula persicifolia* 'Chettle Charm' which is white with a blue edge. But the really inspirational thing about the garden is that it is all maintained by the husband and wife owners who inherited the estate in 2002 and devote themselves to the ongoing restoration of both house and garden.
fine borders; tea room

Owned by Peter and Fiona Bourke
Number of gardeners owners only
Size 1.6ha (4 acres)

CHIFFCHAFFS
Chaffeymoor, Bourton, Gillingham SP8 5BY

Tel 01747 840841
Location At Wincanton end of Bourton, off A303
Opening hours 2pm to 5pm, Wednesdays and Thursdays, March to October; plus 25 March, 8 and 22 April, 6, 20 and 27 May, 10 and 24 June, 15 July, 26 August and 9 and 23 September
Admission fee Adults £3; Children 50p; RHS members free

A pretty cottage, with an excellent small nursery attached, and just off the A303. Started in 1978, the garden has a flowing design, exploits a great variety of habitats and burgeons with good plants. Spring bulbs, herbaceous borders, shrub roses, lilies and clematis are among its key features. A bluebell-lined path leads to the woodland garden, which boasts a splendid collection of rhododendrons, drifts of daffodils and candelabra primulas, and yet more carpets of bluebells. It was originally a dank and scrubby alder copse – on a spring line – but the Potts have cleared it, drained it and planted ornamental trees and shrubs, with autumn colour in mind as much as spring flowers. Here are about a dozen cultivars of *Liquidambar styraciflua* and groups of *Disanthus cercidifolius*, as well as magnolias, meconopsis, maples and gunneras. The nursery is open at the same times as the garden.
woodland garden; plantsman's collection of plants, designed for all seasons; spring bulbs; dwarf rhododendrons; excellent nursery attached; refreshments for groups (15+), by appointment

Owned by Mr and Mrs KR Potts
Number of gardeners part-time help
Size 1.4ha (3½ acres), including woodland

COMPTON ACRES GARDENS

164 Canford Cliffs Road, Poole BH13 7ES

Tel 01202 700778 **Fax** 01202 707537
www.comptonacres.co.uk
Location Well signed locally, follow brown tourist signs
Opening hours 9am to 6pm (10am to 4pm in winter), daily, all year; closed 25 and 26 December
Admission fee Adults £6.95; OAPs £6.45; children £3.95; families £16; RHS members free

Very touristy, very Bournemouth and very 1920s, Compton Acres offers 10 totally unconnected but highly entertaining gardens, all in different styles but joined by tarmac paths. They include the Egyptian Court garden, the Spanish water garden, the Roman gardens and the Canadian woodland walk. Best are the Italian garden (where an Italian villa has recently been added) and the stupendous Japanese garden. The gardens are undergoing extensive renovation and replanting, and the views across Poole Harbour have been opened out again. The atmosphere is still fairly commercial, but the standards of maintenance are among the highest in any garden; no visitor could fail to be cheered up by the bravura of it all.
conifers; rock plants; modern roses; woodland walks; subtropical plantings; several shops; plant centre; tea room and light lunches

Owned by Bernard Merna
Number of gardeners 5
Size 4ha (10 acres)
English Heritage Grade II*

CRANBORNE MANOR

Cranborne, Wimborne BH21 5PP

Tel 01725 517248 **Fax** 01725 517862
www.cranborne.co.uk
Location 10 miles north of Wimborne on B3078
Opening hours 9am to 5pm, Wednesdays, March to September; and other dates occasionally
Admission fee Adults £4; concessions £3.50; children 50p; RHS members free on Wednesdays

Much of the garden at Cranborne is modern, laid out and planted by Lord Salisbury's mother in the 1960s and 1970s. The Jacobean-style features are designed to complement the old house, which dates principally from the early 1600s, and to remind us that the first gardener was John Tradescant the Elder. You enter the garden through a large (and excellent) garden centre, passing through a small walled kitchen garden where apple trees are trained as 5ft espaliers. Espaliered apples appear almost as a *Leitmotif* in many other places in the garden. Everywhere are neat yew hedges and a little topiary. There are no horticultural rarities, but bulbs and polyanthus in spring and a cyclamen bank in autumn, and everywhere a sense of spaciousness, order and age. The classic view is of the narrow cottage garden walk, backed by more apple trees, leading towards the pretty flint church. Cranborne also has some fine old trees, notably beeches, limes and a vast low-branching *Quercus ilex* close to the house. You exit along an attractive double border, with windows cut into the yew hedge on one side, and finally through a herb garden.
topiary; roses (mainly old-fashioned); good herbaceous borders; Jacobean mount; new lavender garden (22 cultivars); garden centre; tea room

Owned by Viscount Cranborne
Number of gardeners 2, plus seasonal help
Size 3.2ha (8 acres)
English Heritage Grade II*

DEAN'S COURT

Wimborne BH21 1EE

Tel 01202 882456
Location 2 mins walk from central Wimborne
Opening hours For NGS on 8 and 9 April, 6, 7, 27 and 28 May, 17 June, 26 and 27 August, 9 September; 2pm to 6pm on the Sundays and 10am to 6pm on the Mondays
Admission fee Adults £3.50; OAPs £2.50; children free

There are some very fine old trees in the lawns and wild gardens around Dean's Court, but the most interesting part is the mellow walled garden with its long serpentine wall. Here are fruit, flowers and vegetables, traditionally grown without artificial fertilisers, pesticides or herbicides. Behind and to the side of the house is a small formal herb garden.

monastery fishpond; good trees; organic cultivation; herb garden; old roses; cream teas

Owned by Sir Michael and Lady Hanham
Number of gardeners 4
Size 5.2ha (13 acres)

EDMONDSHAM HOUSE
Edmondsham, Wimborne BH21 5RE

Tel 01725 517207
Location Off B3081 between Cranborne and Verwood
Opening hours 2pm to 5pm, Wednesdays and Sundays, April to October
Admission fee Adults £2; children 50p

The walled garden (one of the walls is of cob construction) is maintained organically, with beautiful herbaceous borders – go at midsummer to see the many hardy geraniums, or in August for the vast patches of white crinums. It is intensively cultivated and brims with interesting vegetables and fruit houses. There are fine trees around the main lawns and masses of spring bulbs.
herbaceous borders; fine kitchen garden; herbs; old roses; old grass cockpit; spring bulbs; teas when house open in April and October

Owned by Mrs Julia E Smith
Number of gardeners 1, plus 3 part-time
Size 2.4ha (6 acres), plus 0.4-ha (1-acre) walled garden

FORDE ABBEY
Chard TA20 4LU

Tel 01460 221290
www.fordeabbey.co.uk
Location 4 miles south-east of Chard
Opening hours 10am to 4.30pm, daily, all year
Admission fee Adults £7; OAPs £6.50; children free; RHS members free from October to February

The gardens of Forde Abbey surround the 12th-century Cistercian Monastery, a rambling private home since 1650, part Jacobean and part Gothic. They extend over 30 informal acres, with plants of interest and beauty throughout the year, set off by ancient and mellowed stone walls. Trees survive from 1700, although much has been planted in recent years: rhododendrons, azaleas, acers, magnolias, irises, meconopsis and candelabra primulas. But there are also mature Victorian conifers (*Sequoia sempervirens* and *Calocedrus decurrens*), lakes, ponds, streams, cascades, bogs and such oddities as a beech house and the highest powered fountain in England.
good herbaceous borders; fine collection of trees; rock garden planted by Jack Drake; Ionic temple (Ham-stone); 17th-century vistas; bog garden; working kitchen garden; HHA/Christie's Garden of the Year in 1993; tallest *Cornus controversa* (16m; 52ft) in UK; gift shop; plant centre; tea room

Owned by The Trustees of the GD Roper settlement
Size 12ha (30 acres)
English Heritage Grade II*

CW GROVES & SON LTD
Nursery & Garden Centre, West Bay Road, Bridport DT6 4BA

Tel 01308 422654 **Fax** 01308 420888
www.grovesnurseries.co.uk
Location South of town centre, by river, next to the Crown roundabout on A35 Bridport bypass
Opening hours 8.30am to 5pm, Monday to Saturday; 10.30am to 4.30pm, Sundays

This modern, up-to-date garden centre (rose beds, Koi carp etc) also has a traditional nursery attached. Founded in 1866 by the present owner's great-great-grandfather, it specialises in Sweet Victorian Hardy and Parma Violets. These are available from the garden centre as well as by mail order and include a large number of rarities – best seen when they flower in February, March and April, when they are displayed in a solar dome.
old-fashioned violas; café with home cooking

Owned by Clive and Diana Groves
NCCPG National Collections *Viola odorata* (cvs.)

HILLTOP GARDEN

Woodville, Stour Provost SP8 5LY

Tel 01747 838512
www.hilltopgarden.co.uk
Location 1 mile east of Stour Provost
Opening hours For NGS: 2pm to 6pm, 22, 26 and 29 July, 2, 5, 9 and 12 August; group visits by arrangement
Admission fee Adults £2; children free

Hilltop has a cottagey garden to match its thatched cottage. The name explains its position, on a south-facing slope with wide views of the countryside. Though there is colour in every season, the garden reaches a climax in midsummer, when annuals flower alongside such perennials as phlox, asters and kniphofias. Dahlias turn the mix into a spectacular display.
nursery; home-made refreshments

Owned by Brian and Josse Emerson
Number of gardeners owners only
Size 0.2ha (1/2 acre)

KINGSTON LACY

Wimborne Minster BH21 4EA

Tel 01202 883402 **Fax** 01202 882402
www.nationaltrust.org.uk
Location 1 1/2 miles from Wimborne on B3082 to Blandford
Opening hours 10.30am to 6pm, daily, 24 March to 28 October; 10.30am to 4pm, Friday to Sunday; 2 November to 16 December; 10.30am to 4pm, Saturdays and Sundays, 2 February to 18 March 2007
Admission fee Adults £5; children £2.50

The magnificent home of the Bankes family sits among 250 acres of parkland, filled in all directions as far as the eye can see with single specimen trees of great spread – beech, oak and chestnut. Nearer the house are a newly restored Edwardian Japanese garden, a camellia walk, a lime avenue, and a cedar avenue planted piecemeal over the centuries to commemorate visits by everyone from the Duke of Wellington to the Kaiser. Next to the house is a pretty formal garden, first laid out in 1899 and still planted with the original scheme of pink begonias and purple heliotrope in summer. Nearby is a fern garden with 30 cultivars under a canopy of hollies, bay and yew: gravel paths run between

IVY COTTAGE

Aller Lane, Ansty, Dorchester DT2 7PX

Tel/fax 01258 880053
Location Midway between Blandford and Dorchester
Opening hours 11am to 5pm, Thursdays, May to September; groups welcome by appointment at other times; picnickers welcome
Admission fee Adults £3; children free

This cottage garden has been made (and immaculately maintained) by the present owners since the mid-1960s and is crammed with interesting things, particularly moisture-loving plants. Springs and streams, combined with greensand soil, multiply the possibilities – drifts of marsh marigolds, astilbes and candelabra primulas. Many are chosen with wildlife in mind, especially birds, butterflies and bees. The new garage roof garden is an interesting addition; it can be seen from steps nearby. The kitchen garden is good, too.
plantsman's collection of plants; good herbaceous borders; small kitchen garden

Owned by Anne and Alan Stevens
Number of gardeners owners only
Size 0.7ha (1 3/4 acres)

irregularly shaped raised beds planted with male ferns and hart's tongues. There is little of floral interest apart from snowdrops and daffodils in spring and some pretty roses near the stables restaurant – notably 'Bonica', 'Cardinal Hume' and 'Anna Zinkeisen' – in summer. There are also many handsome trees, including a cut-leaved beech and several Lebanon cedars. The garden ornaments are, however, exceptional: they include an Egyptian obelisk (Ptolemy VII) and some first-class 19th-century marbles from Italy.
snowdrops; mature conifers; Victorian fernery; Dutch parterre; huge cedars of Lebanon planted by visiting royalty; shop; licensed restaurant

Owned by The National Trust
Number of gardeners 4, plus 1 seasonal
Size 12ha (30 acres)
NCCPG National Collections *Anemone nemorosa*; *Convallaria*
English Heritage Grade II

KINGSTON MAURWARD GARDENS
Kingston Maurward College, Dorchester DT2 8PY

Tel 01305 215003 **Fax** 01305 250001
www.kmc.ac.uk/gardens
Location 1 mile east of Dorchester from A35: signed
Opening hours 10am to 5.30pm (or dusk, if earlier), daily, 3 January to 21 December
Admission fee Adults £5; children £3; families £15.50; RHS members free except during special events

Kingston Maurward belonged to the Hanbury family who owned La Mortola on the Riviera, and laid out the formal gardens here in the Arts & Crafts style (with an Italianate overlay) in the 1920s. The parkland is older – a rolling 18th-century landscape. Much of the present planting is modern, including the terraces below the Grecian temple where a great number of different penstemons and the National Collection of hardy salvias are displayed. The features are many, and include a croquet lawn, a double herbaceous border, a large number of yew-hedged garden rooms, some nice pieces of topiary, good magnolias in spring and an enclosed Japanese garden. Kingston Maurward also makes use of extensive summer bedding displays, which are unusually well done. Make time to go to the demonstration garden at the far end where a wide variety of plants is grown to display their horticultural possibilities – highly instructive.
cyclamen; autumn crocuses; fine borders; daffodils; topiary; parkland; cakes and drinks

Owned by Kingston Maurward College
Number of gardeners 6
Size 14ha (35 acres)
NCCPG National Collections *Penstemon*; *Salvia*
English Heritage Grade II*

KNOLL GARDENS
Stapehill Road, Wimborne BH21 7ND

Tel 01202 873931 **Fax** 01202 870842
www.knollgardens.co.uk
Location Brown tourist signs from A31
Opening hours 10am to 5pm (or dusk, if earlier), Wednesday to Sunday, all year, except 18 December to 31 January 2007
Admission fee Adults £4.50; OAPs £4; children £3; RHS members free

This garden was once an intimate and enclosed collection of tender exotics, many of them Australian trees and shrubs which now form the framework for extensive newer plantings. It was here, too, that the first owner, John May, bred the hybrid *Phygelius* x *rectus* 'African Queen'. The modern plantings have come together well and provide much to admire: this is a garden to interest the plantsman as much as the less horticulturally minded. The many different

Knoll Gardens

Kingston Maurward Gardens

areas, winding pathways, and constantly changing views give an impression of a much larger area than its four acres. The owners continue to develop the garden and its plant collections, particularly of hardy perennials and grasses – in which the adjoining nursery specialises. There is a fine open area of lawn at the bottom which gives onto the gravel garden. The garden is maintained to a high standard. Masterclasses and other events (including RHS Special Events – details from 020 7821 3408) are held throughout the year.
rock garden; mature conifers; good herbaceous borders; *Eucalyptus*; gravel garden; ornamental grasses; self-service refreshments

Owned by John and Janet Flude and Neil Lucas
Number of gardeners 2
Size 1.6ha (4 acres)
NCCPG National Collections *Ceanothus* (deciduous); *Pennisetum*; *Phygelius*

MAPPERTON GARDENS
Beaminster DT8 3NR

Tel 01308 862645 **Fax** 01308 863348
www.mapperton.com
Location 2 miles south-east of Beaminster
Opening hours 11am to 5pm, daily, except Saturdays, March to October
Admission fee Adults £4; children £2; RHS members free

Mapperton has spectacular hanging gardens that you see laid out in their entirety from the lawn beside the house. First comes an enchanting steep formal valley garden, running down from a pinnacled orangery to a handsome pool surrounded by Italianate terracing and gardens of clipped yew. Below are a 17th-century summerhouse, two canals and finally a long dell garden, with an excellent collection of spring-flowering trees and shrubs, some of them rare and many with good autumn colour.
terraced design; topiary; fine collection of trees; small gift shop; licensed café

Owned by The Earl and Countess of Sandwich
Number of gardeners 3
Size 5.6ha (14 acres)
English Heritage Grade II*

MINTERNE
Minterne Magna, Dorchester DT2 7AU

Tel 01300 341370 **Fax** 01300 341747
www.minterne.co.uk
Location On A352 Dorchester/Sherborne road, 2 miles north of Cerne Abbas
Opening hours 10am to 6pm, daily, March to October
Admission fee Adults £4; children free

A woodland garden, best in spring, and well integrated into the park around the handsome Edwardian house. The valley was landscaped in the 18th century with a series of small lakes and cascades. The oldest rhododendrons came from Hooker's collection, but the remarkable Lord Digby (grandfather of the present owner) supported Farrer, Forrest, Rock and Kingdon Ward, which makes Minterne one of the best Himalayan collections. The circular walk down a greensand valley to the woodland stream is ravishing: magnolias and Japanese cherries are underplanted with camellias and azaleas. The fine collection of trees includes exceptional specimens of *Corylus avellana* 'Heterophylla' and *Cercidiphyllum japonicum*, while the many handkerchief trees (*Davidia involucrata*) are sensational in late May.
cherries; cyclamen; *Lathraea clandestina*; rhododendrons and azaleas; fine woodland walks; tallest *Chamaecyparis pisifera* 'Filifera' (25m; 82ft) in the UK

Owned by The Hon Henry and Mrs Digby
Number of gardeners 3
Size 11.5ha (29 acres)
English Heritage Grade II

MORETON GARDENS
Moreton, Dorchester DT2 8RH

Tel 01929 405084
Location Signed in village
Opening hours 10am to 5pm, daily, April to October; 10am to 4pm, Wednesday to Sunday, November to March
Admission fee Adults £3.50; Children free

This modern show garden has a gravel and turf maze, a formal rose garden, a long herbaceous

Moreton Gardens

border, banks of azaleas, lots of crinums and a large pond whose edges are planted with gunneras and weeping willows. Relics of an older garden include a good *Magnolia grandiflora* and a magnificent London plane *Platanus* x *hispanica*.
garden centre; drinks

Owned by The Penny family
Number of gardeners 4 part-time
Size 1.4ha (31/2 acres)

SHERBORNE CASTLE

New Road, Sherborne DT9 5NR

Tel 01935 813182 **Fax** 01935 816727
www.sherbornecastle.com
Location 1/2 east of Sherborne, signed from A30 and A352
Opening hours 11am to 4.30pm (last admissions), daily except Mondays and Fridays, April to October
Admission fee Adults £4; children free

It is the setting that is the making of Sherborne Castle. The gardens are not significant, but Capability Brown's lake offers a wonderful baseline for views of the castle and there are some good trees in the park, notably ancient specimens of *Ginkgo biloba*, *Metasequoia glyptostroboides*, *Quercus ilex* (dating from the 1770s) and a cedar of Lebanon that is even older, probably planted in about 1730.
Capability Brown landscape; shop; garden centre next door; tea room

Owned by John Wingfield Digby
Number of gardeners 3
Size 12ha (30 acres)

SNAPE COTTAGE

Chaffeymoor, Bourton, Gillingham SP8 5BZ

Tel/fax 01747 840330 (evening)
www.snapestakes.com
Location At west end of Bourton, 1/4 mile up Chaffeymoor Hill
Opening hours 10.30am to 5pm, last two Sundays of each month, February to August; plus Thursdays from May to August
Admission fee Adults £2.50; children free

This atmospheric cottage garden is crammed with thousands of plants and organically managed to attract wildlife. It has masses to interest all visitors, and is especially inspirational to those who garden with plants in a small space. Plant specialities include hellebores, narcissi, pulmonarias, auriculas, geraniums, dianthus, irises and asters. The garden is full of interest at every month of the year but perhaps the most impressive collection is of snowdrops (*Galanthus* species and cultivars) – over 250 different ones. There is a special emphasis on plant history and the conservation of 'old' cultivars of every sort. A real plantsman's garden.
lots of plants for plantsmen; home-made teas

Owned by Mr and Mrs IS Whinfield
Number of gardeners 11/2
Size 0.2ha (1/2 acre)

SPRINGHEAD

Fontmell Magna, Shaftesbury SP7 0NU

Tel 01747 811853
Location Off A350 between Shaftesbury and Blandford Forum
Opening hours For NGS; and by appointment
Admission fee Adults £3.50; children free

The chalk valley alongside this old mill is planted with herbaceous and bog plants. Old beech trees and venerable magnolias add to the beauty. But it is the wildflowers and the setting that leave the strongest impression.
light lunches and teas

Owned by The Springhead Trust
Number of gardeners 2, plus volunteers
Size 2.4ha (6 acres)

TOAD HALL

The Cross, Shillingstone, Blandford Forum DT11 0SP

Tel 01258 861941
www.toadhalluk.co.uk
Location In middle of Shillingstone, signed on NGS days

STICKY WICKET

Buckland Newton, Dorchester DT2 7BY

Tel/fax 01300 345476
www.stickywicketgarden.co.uk
Location 11 miles from Dorchester and Sherborne
Opening hours 10.30am to 8pm, Thursdays and Fridays, June to September. For NGS: 2pm to 8pm on 17 June and 19 August; groups welcome by appointment at other times
Admission fee Adults £3.50; children £1.50

Sticky Wicket is a highly original garden and worth revisiting frequently. Pam Lewis, like her late husband Peter who did so much to build up this garden, is both a designer and a conservationist. Her devotion to ecology guides her garden-making: she understands the need to attract birds, insects and other wildlife. Yet it is also one of the most photographed and admired of modern gardens, because of the subtlety and integrity of Pam Lewis's colour combinations. She and her husband began the garden in 1987 but the plantings are constantly reworked, so that you find new compositions and combinations every year. Berrying trees and shrubs and those with interesting winter stems are supplemented by plants chosen for their scent, decoration and usefulness to wildlife. The planting is increasingly naturalistic and draws upon a choice of native British plants which are then integrated with garden ornamentals. There are four principal wildlife gardens: the Frog and Bird garden where ponds, bird baths, nesting boxes and feeders are thickly incorporated into the design, to attract wildlife close to the house where they can be seen; the beautiful Round Garden, whose colours move from pastel tints to richer hues and back again, but where the plants are chosen for the nectar and pollen they offer to insects; the White Garden, where ornamental grasses and flowers in loosely planted borders echo the grassy effect of the meadows beyond; and the half-acre wildflower meadow, started in 1997, sown with seed of local provenance and managed as a traditional hay meadow, at its most glamorous in June and July. Throughout the garden, information boards explain how Pam Lewis preaches and practises 'gardening in tune with Nature'. This is expanded in Pam Lewis's excellent books *Making Wildflower Meadows* [Frances Lincoln, 2003] and *Sticky Wicket: Gardening in Tune with Nature* [Frances Lincoln, 2005].

wide collection of interesting plants; strong ecological interest; many ornamental grasses; good colour associations; tea, coffee and home-made cakes

Owned by Pam Lewis
Size 1ha (2 1/2 acres)

Opening hours 2pm to 5pm, Thursdays, May to August; for NGS: 2pm to 6pm, 27 May and 26 August; groups by appointment
Admission fee Adults £2.50; children 50p

Elizabeth Arden is a horticulturist and designer, and her professional good sense is very much in evidence in this young garden, which is still developing and consolidating. Distinct themes define such features as the water garden, woodland walk and vegetable garden (all organic), even if the Italian garden has rather more English roses than Italian formality. There is lots to think about here – and the views of the surrounding hills are magnificent.

home-made teas on NGS days

Owned by Elizabeth Arden and Norman Rogerson
Number of gardeners owners only
Size 0.4ha (1 acre)

DURHAM

Durham is too often – and wrongly – considered a horticultural wasteland, though it is true that in the 1980s the Royal Horticultural Society had fewer members in Durham than any other English county – less than 100. Things have come a long way since then. English Heritage has drawn attention to the importance of historic landscapes like Raby Castle and the Bowes Museum, and there are now seven National Collections in the county. Horn's Garden Centre at Shotton Colliery has the National Collection of coleus (*Solenostemon* cvs.) and a large collection of *Streptocarpus* and pelargoniums, too. East Durham & Houghall College is a RHS Partner College.

BARNINGHAM PARK

Barningham, Richmond DL11 7DW

Tel 01833 621202 **Fax** 01833 621298
Location 10 miles north-west of Scotch Corner off A66
Opening hours Parties only, by appointment
Admission fee By arrangement

This late 18th-century landscape includes terraces, an old bowling green and a skating pond. Humphry Repton may have had a hand in it. Keen horticultural Milbanks got to work in the 1920s. They designed the splendid rock garden and diverted a stream to form cascades and pools through it. Unknown and perhaps underrated, if Barningham were in the Home Counties everyone would rave about it.
hillside rock garden with stream; good herbaceous borders; terraced gardens; rhododendrons; woodland walks

Owned by Sir Anthony Milbank Bt
Number of gardeners 1
Size 1.6ha (4 acres), plus 24ha (60 acres) of woodland

THE BOWES MUSEUM GARDEN & PARK

Barnard Castle DL12 8NP

Tel 01833 690606 **Fax** 01833 637163
www.thebowesmuseum.org.uk
Location In Barnard Castle town
Opening hours Dawn to dusk, daily, all year
Admission fee Free

The splendid Victorian park at the Bowes Museum is now maintained by the trustees as a public amenity. The formal gardens around the newly restored fountains are good – a vast oval parterre remade in the French style in 1982 – and mature trees pepper the park. Almost all were planted in the 1870s: some of the conifers are particularly fine. A tree trail highlights their splendour and diversity.
fine collection of trees; parterre; large monkey puzzle; gift shop; café

Owned by Trustees of The Bowes Museum
Number of gardeners 1
Size 8.7ha (22 acres)
English Heritage Grade II

CROOK HALL

Frankland Lane, Sidegate, Durham DH1 5SZ

Tel 0191 384 8028 **Fax** 0191 386 4521
www.crookhallgardens.co.uk
Location Close to city centre
Opening hours 11am to 5pm, 5 to 10 April; then daily, except Mondays and Tuesdays, 27 May to 9 September; plus Sundays and Bank Holidays in May
Admission fee Adults £4.50; concessions £4

Crook Hall is a gem of a cottage garden – very peaceful and beautiful. Ignore the trendy circular maze of cotoneaster near the entrance and make straight for the garden proper – a series of many small, enclosed gardens with narrow paths. None of the plants are rare, but the new owners have begun to make additions. Old shrubs and hedges

Eggleston Hall Gardens

give structure: new underplantings supplement established colonies of campanulas and Spanish bluebells. The Cathedral Garden takes inspiration from stained glass windows. The Silver Wedding Garden is a contrast of greys, greens and whites.
tea room; café

Owned by Keith and Maggie Bell
Number of gardeners 2
Size 1.6ha (4 acres)

EAST DURHAM & HOUGHALL COMMUNITY COLLEGE

Durham DH1 3SG

Tel 0191 375 4700 **Fax** 0191 386 0419
www.edhcc.ac.uk
Location Follow A177 from A1 to Durham
Opening hours 1.30pm to 4.30pm, daily, all year
Admission fee Gardens: free. World of Trees: adults £2

Houghall is a well-run teaching garden, originally attached to Durham's horticultural college. There is much to see here: a fine collection of trees now (2007) known as the 'World of Trees Arboretum', an interesting young pinetum, good displays of perennial plants and shrubs (one of the best in northern England), and a wildflower meadow for summer interest. Many trials are conducted here, for example on the hardiness of fuchsias: the garden staff say that 'if it grows at Houghall it will grow anywhere'.
roses (mainly modern); rock garden; heathers; hardy fuchsias; seasonal bedding; young pinetum and arboretum; shop; good plant centre; refreshments available

Owned by East Durham & Houghall Community College
Number of gardeners 11
NCCPG National Collections *Sorbus*

EGGLESTON HALL GARDENS

Eggleston, Barnard Castle DL12 0AG

Tel 01833 650115 **Fax** 01833 650971
www.egglestonhall.co.uk/gardens.html
Location Off B6278, south of Eggleston village
Opening hours 10am to 5pm, daily, all year; closed Christmas and New Year period
Admission fee Adults £1; children free

Eggleston Hall Gardens are attached to a popular nursery with a lot to interest keen plantsmen – the home of *Celmisia spectabilis* 'Eggleston Silver'. The gardens are informal but strongly designed to show off good garden plants: *Syringa emodi* 'Aureovariegata', epimediums, abutilons, variegated blackberries and much else besides. Good at all seasons, too.
refreshments

Owned by Gordon Long and Malcolm Hockham
Size 1.8ha (41/2 acres)

RABY CASTLE

Staindrop, Darlington DL2 3AH

Tel 01833 660202 **Fax** 01833 660169
www.rabycastle.com
Location On A688, 1 mile north of Staindrop
Opening hours 11am to 5.30pm, Sunday to Wednesday, May to September; plus Thursdays and Fridays in July and August, and Bank Holiday weekends (Saturday to Monday) from Easter to August
Admission fee Adults £4; concessions £3.50; children £2.50; RHS members free, except during special events

The 18th-century walled gardens at Raby Castle are set within a 80ha (200-acre) deer park in the heart of Teesdale. Designers such as Thomas White and James Paine have worked on these magnificent gardens, which incorporate herbaceous borders, shrub borders, yew hedges, a conservatory, formal rose gardens and informal heather and conifer gardens. The gardens were considerably altered during the 20th century but many of the original features remain, notably the two fine 200-year-old yew hedges and the ornamental pond that dominates the central garden.
deer park; walled garden; fine yew hedges; gift shop; café

Owned by Lord Barnard
Number of gardeners 31/2
Size 2ha (5 acres)
English Heritage Grade II*

UNIVERSITY OF DURHAM BOTANIC GARDEN

Hollingside Lane, Durham DH1 3TN

Tel 0191 374 5524 **Fax** 0191 374 7478
www.dur.ac.uk/botanic.garden
Location In south of City of Durham
Opening hours 10am to 5pm, daily, March to October; 11am to 4pm, daily, November to February; closed for two weeks over Christmas and New Year
Admission fee Adults £2; concessions £1.50; children £1 (under review)

There is much to enjoy and masses of interesting plants to see at the University of Durham Botanic Garden. The cactus house and tropical house each have good collections. The Alpine garden has great potential, and includes a 'dry' garden and an area for South African plants. Elsewhere are some surprisingly tender plants like phormiums and a hedge of griselinia in the collection of Antipodean plants. The 'North American arboretum' (very attractive) was planted in 1980 to copy natural associations. Gunneras flourish in the pond garden alongside *Primula pulverulenta*. A woodland garden dates from 1988, a wetland garden from 1989, and 1992 saw the opening of the 'Prince Bishop's Garden' with statues transferred from the Gateshead Garden Festival. Unfortunately, the garden suffers from under-funding; with a little more input, it could become a major tourist attraction.
good collection of plants; tea, coffee, cold drinks and snacks

Owned by The University of Durham
Number of gardeners 3, plus volunteers

ESSEX

Considering its proximity to London, where fortunes have for centuries been made, Essex has few famous historic gardens: Audley End is the pre-eminent exception, and is as important horticulturally as historically. It is the county's only Grade I garden. Few of the county's other historic gardens are open to the public. Essex's most famous gardener was Miss Ellen Willmott of Warley Place, Great Warley, but her house was demolished shortly after her death in 1934 and the garden (what remains of it) is now a nature reserve: arrangements to visit it may be made through Essex Wildlife Trust. It has one of Essex's few record trees, an *Umbellularia californica* 20m (72ft) high. Low rainfall and hot summers define Essex gardening: Beth Chatto has made a study of dry gardening at her nursery near Elmstead Market. Other nurseries of exceptional interest to keen plantsmen are Glen Chantry and Langthorns Plantery. The National Gardens Scheme has a fair number of gardens opening for the Yellow Book, most of them medium-sized and good for seeing plants. There are 11 National Collections in the county. Writtle College near Chelmsford is a RHS Partner College, with lectures and workshops on a wide range of hands-on topics throughout the year. The garden at Hyde Hall has proved a successful interesting acquisition for the Royal Horticultural Society and has been much improved by new design features and new plants.

AUDLEY END

Saffron Walden CB11 4JF

Tel 01799 522842/520052 **Fax** 01799 521276
www.english-heritage.org.uk
Location On B1383, 1 mile west of Saffron Walden
Opening hours 10am to 6pm, Wednesday to Sunday and Bank Holidays, April to September; 10am to 5pm, weekends only, March and October
Admission fee Gardens: adults £5; OAPs £3.80; children £2.50; families £12.50

Capability Brown landscaped the park in 1763 but work on rejuvenating the garden at Audley End started some years ago with the parterre garden behind the house towards the Temple of Concord. This dates from the 1830s and has 170 geometric flower beds crisply cut from the turf and planted with original varieties of perennials, bedding plants and annuals for spring and summer. Nearby are the Elysian garden, designed in the 1780s by Placido Columbani, and the Victorian pond garden in the 'picturesque' style, whose walls and pergola are clad with climbing shrubs and roses. Work continues: the kitchen garden is now run as a joint venture with Garden Organic as a working organic garden. It looks much as it would have done in late Victorian times with vegetables, fruit, herbs and flowers to supply the household. The cultivation is, of course, entirely organic. The vinehouse is one of the earliest and largest in the country, with vines over 200 years old.

bedding out; parterre; magnificent plane trees; organic kitchen garden; ancient trees; shop; restaurant and picnic site

Owned by English Heritage
Number of gardeners 9
Size 40ha (100 acres), including parkland
English Heritage Grade I

COUNTY PARK NURSERY

384 Wingletye Lane, Hornchurch RM11 3BU

Tel 01708 445205
www.countyparknursery.co.uk
Location 2½ miles from M25, Jct 29; off Wingletye Lane, in Essex Gardens, Hornchurch
Opening hours 10am to 5pm, daily, except Wednesdays, March to October; open in winter by appointment only; please telephone before visiting
Admission fee Free

BETH CHATTO GARDENS

Elmstead Market, Colchester CO7 7DB

Tel 01206 822007 **Fax** 01206 825933
www.bethchatto.co.uk
Location 7 miles east of Colchester
Opening hours 9am to 5pm, Monday to Saturday, March to October; 9am to 4pm, Monday to Friday, November to February
Admission fee Adults £4.50; children free; RHS members free (but not all the time)

This beautiful and instructive garden was begun in 1960 and uses a very wide range of plants, mostly species, chosen for their foliage and form as much as for their flowers. Beth Chatto's planting is based largely on ecological principles, following her late husband Andrew Chatto's lifetime research into the natural associations of garden plants. The original site was wasteland, unfit for farming and unfit for the planting of many conventional plants, especially cultivars. It had – and still has – three very different ecologies: areas of hungry sand and gravel, a clay-based spring-fed hollow, and elsewhere dry shade beneath ancient oaks. Beth Chatto has developed three contrasting types of planting, based on the principle of finding the right plant for the right place, and thus turning problem areas into advantages. Around the modest house, where the soil is thin and dry, Beth Chatto used plants mostly from the Mediterranean: cistus, broom, salvias, euphorbias, potentillas, verbascums, and the tree-like *Genista aetnensis* have come together on the warm sandy slopes. A short walk leads down to a water garden of remarkable luxuriance, made by damming the spring-fed ditch to create a series of ponds in the valley. The lush plantings are quite untypical of Essex, where rainfall averages 50cm a year. Here are gunneras, astilbes, lysichitons, hostas, phormiums, water irises and the ostrich fern *Matteuccia struthiopteris*. They have a continuous background, not too intrusive, of conifers, specimen trees and shrubs – but the emphasis throughout the garden is on the herbaceous plants for which the adjoining nursery is famous. A copse has been developed as a woodland garden and a canopy of young oaks underplanted with shade-lovers. Here, and in the long shady border above the water garden, are rich plantings of bulbs, woodlanders and groundcover – aconites, cyclamen, erythroniums and dicentras. The gravel garden was made in 1992 on the site of the old car park, where drought-resistant sun-lovers have been planted in a fluid sequence of island beds. Before planting, this 3/4 acre of yellow sand and gravel was 'improved' with the addition of home-made compost, to give the plants a good start. Since then, however, the area has not been irrigated in any way, despite periods of drought, since it is a horticultural experiment to see which plants will survive and maybe inspire visitors who have hosepipe bans. But garden-making is only one of Beth Chatto's gifts: her writings and nursery have made her famous. And the standard of maintenance is impeccable.
colour contrasts; gravel garden; luxuriant water gardens; woodland garden; big nursery adjacent to the garden; nursery; tea room

Owned by Beth Chatto
Number of gardeners 4, plus seasonal help
Size 2ha (5 acres)

Easton Lodge

This small nursery specialises in Antipodean plants, many of them grown from native seed and not available from any other nursery in the UK. There is no show garden to speak of, but every tiny corner seems covered in pots of unusual plants – some for display and others for sale. There are hebes and parahebes, as well as New Zealand *Clematis* species, *Coprosma* and other shrubs like leptospermums. They also have a long list of podocarpus cultivars, selected for their spreading habit and unusual leaf colours. Very interesting.
plants from New Zealand and Australia

Owned by Graham Hutchins
Size 0.2ha (1/2 acre)
NCCPG National Collections *Coprosma*

EASTON LODGE
Warwick House, Great Dunmow CM6 2BB

Tel/fax 01371 876979
www.eastonlodge.co.uk
Location Signed from A120 at Great Dunmow
Opening hours Noon to dusk, daily, February to early March (ring for exact dates) for snowdrops; then noon to 6pm, Friday to Sunday and Bank Holiday Mondays, Easter to October
Admission fee Adults £4.20; OAPs £3.80; children £1.70

The garden was laid out by Harold Peto in 1902 for the Countess of Warwick (Edward VII's 'darling Daisy'), fell into serious neglect, and has been wonderfully restored since 1993. Much remains to be done, as the owner is the first to admit, but the lime grove has now been cleared and the Peto shrubbery has been rejuvenated. Work has begun on re-paving the Italian garden. There is an exhibition of how the house was built and the gardens made. The roses are very beautiful in high summer.
cream teas in courtyard and tea room

Owned by Brian Creasey
Number of gardeners 2
Size 9.2ha (23 acres)
English Heritage Grade II

THE GIBBERD GARDEN
Marsh Lane, Gilden Way, Harlow CM17 0NA

Tel 01279 442112
www.thegibberdgarden.co.uk
Location Leave Harlow on B183; Marsh Lane is on left: follow brown tourist signs
Opening hours 2pm to 6pm, Wednesdays, Saturdays, Sundays and Bank Holidays, April to September
Admission fee Adults £4; concessions £2.50; children free

This was the private garden of Sir Frederick Gibberd, the master planner of Harlow New Town. It was designed as a series of distinct rooms, and filled with sculpture, pots and architectural salvage. It is one of the most important architectural gardens of the 20th century and has been restored with aid from the Heritage Lottery Fund. The moated castle has been dredged and repaired and the top lawns and beds have been replanted. There is an active Friends organisation (details from Gordon Whittle on 01279 434840) which hopes to create a small museum during the years to come.
good modern design; wild garden; lime avenue; 'Roman Temple' vistas; shop; light refreshments

Owned by Gibberd Garden Trust
Number of gardeners 2 part-time, plus volunteers
Size 2.8ha (7 acres)

GREEN ISLAND
Park Road, Ardleigh, Colchester CO7 7SP

Tel/fax 01206 230455
www.greenislandgardens.co.uk
Location Off B1029 from Ardleigh to Bromley; look out for brown tourist signs
Opening hours 10am to 5pm, Wednesdays, Thursdays and Sundays, March to 12 October; plus 25 March, 8 July and 4 October for NGS; plus 11 November, and then 17 February 2008
Admission fee Adults £3; children £1; groups and guided tours by appointment

This old garden was redesigned by a professional designer in 1997. It has a water garden, a pond, a bamboo dell, a Japanese garden, woodland gardens, a 'seaside' garden, and much else besides.

GLEN CHANTRY

Ishams Chase, Wickham Bishops, Witham CM8 3LG

Tel/fax 01621 891342
www.glenchantry.demon.co.uk
Location Turn off B1019 just south of A12 towards Benton Hall golf course and Wickham Bishops: immediately left after bridge and up track 1/2 mile
Opening hours 10am to 4pm, Fridays and Saturdays, 7 April to 2 September; and for NGS
Admission fee Adults £3.50; children 50p; RHS members free (not June and July)

This remarkable garden has been made from a bare hillside since 1976: the owners have an excellent eye for good plants and for how to use them. You enter past a very pretty new *potager* and through the immaculately tidy nursery, itself a plantsman's treasure house for herbaceous plants. Then you step down into the garden, filled with endless microhabitats, some exploiting the opportunities offered by dry, stony acid soil, and others defying it. Scree beds, peat beds, raised beds and an artificial stream are part of the story, but so is a winding pattern of ebbing and flowing island beds. Along the centre of these beds are trees and shrubs which screen the two faces from each other and make it possible to plant both sides of a path with the same colour. The owners also practise 'vertical planting', which means that season after season different displays are possible from the same patch: in one small area, for example, the spring-flowering fritillaries, erythroniums and corydalis are covered in summer by hostas, grasses and rushes. A new bed planted with a wide selection of grasses, interplanted with late-flowering perennials, is maturing well. Glen Chantry is a model of what devoted plantsmanship can achieve: educational, functional and beautiful all at once. There is one formal garden near the house, white and green in summer with 'Katharina Zeimet' and 'Iceberg' roses, campanulas, lilies, eryngiums, alliums and geraniums, but the rest of the garden is fluid, however disciplined may be the controlling hand. In fact, very little seeding around is allowed – perhaps a few plants of Martyn Rix's form of *Eryngium giganteum* 'Silver Ghost' – because the planting is intended to slow you down and stop you on your way, to admire individual plants. Besides, the standards of maintenance are immaculate. There will be two RHS Special Events at Glen Chantry in 2007; details from 020 7821 3408.
alpines; herbaceous plants; bulbs; special habitats; masses of fascinating plants for plantsmen; fine specialist nursery attached; light refreshments

Owned by Sue and Wol Staines
Number of gardeners owners only
Size 1ha (21/2 acres)

But the main attractions are the fluid design, which leads you along quite naturally, and the spacious island beds, planted with a large number of herbaceous plants and shrubs. Seldom does a designer's garden display so much plantsmanship.
modern design; good plants; new woodland garden (2005); nursery; teas on Sundays

Owned by Fiona Edmond
Number of gardeners 1 part-time
Size 8ha (20 acres)

LANGTHORNS PLANTERY
Little Canfield, Dunmow CM6 1TD

Tel 01371 872611 **Fax** 0871 661 4093
www.langthorns.com
Location Between Takeley and Great Dunmow, signed off A120
Opening hours 10am to 5pm, daily; closed Christmas to New Year
Admission fee Free

Langthorns Plantery is a go-ahead modern nursery with an eye for good plants. Though best known for their wide range of hardy herbaceous plants, the owners apply their discriminating taste to all their stock – alpines, shrubs, trees and climbers, especially clematis. The garden is worth a visit in its own right but is not always open, so check before you visit. There is a special weekend opening on 9 and 10 June 2007 when the TV garden celebrity Christine Walkden will be available to answer questions.

Owned by The Cannon family
Size 1.2ha (3 acres)

MARKS HALL
Coggeshall CO16 1TG

Tel 01376 563796 **Fax** 01376 563132
www.markshall.org.uk
Location Signed from A120 Coggeshall bypass
Opening hours 10.30am to 5pm, Tuesday to Sunday and Bank Holiday Mondays, April to October; Friday to Sunday, November to March
Admission fee Adults £3; children £1

Marks Hall is a historic estate whose gardens and park have recently been transformed into a major horticultural attraction. The older features include the vast Honywood Oak (thought to be about 700 years old), two lakes, a snowdrop wood called Robin's Grove, and the relics of an oak avenue nearly one mile long. In the walled garden is a remarkable sequence of smaller gardens, all different in style, but united by a winding hedge of pittosporum that turns into a stone wall, dipping and turning in abstract sweeps along the way. The colour plantings here are very well done. The young arboretum, started in 1999, is also worth a long journey to see. It is laid out geographically, with areas representing Europe, Japan, China, Asia and the Americas. Best of all is Gondwanaland (the old name for Australasia), where 200 eucalyptus and innumerable nothofagus are growing fast and tall.
herbaceous plants; eucalyptus; shop; light meals and refreshments

Owned by The Thomas Phillips Price Trust
Number of gardeners 4
Size 80ha (200 acres)

OLIVERS
Olivers Lane, Colchester CO2 0HJ

Tel 01206 330575 **Fax** 01206 330366
Location 3 miles south-west of Colchester between B1022 and B1026
Opening hours By appointment
Admission fee Adults £3; children free

Quite a modern garden, started in 1968 around three small lakes, with an eye-catching walk to one side leading down to a statue of Bacchus. Good plants and planting everywhere, from the parterres by the house to the woodland where roses and rhododendrons flourish. The main borders underwent a highly successful major redesign in 1998 and are looking very good now. This is the garden of enthusiastic and energetic owners: an inspiration.
roses (ancient and modern); bluebells; rhododendrons; fine borders; refreshments by arrangement

RHS GARDEN HYDE HALL

Buckhatch Lane, Rettendon, Chelmsford CM3 8ET

Tel 01245 400256 **Fax** 01245 402100
www.rhs.org.uk/gardens/hydehall
Location South-east of Chelmsford, signed from A130; exit for Rettendon turnpike, north through Rettendon village and follow brown tourist signs
Opening hours 10am to 6pm (5pm or dusk from October to March), daily, all year; closed 25 December
Admission fee Adults £5; children (6-16) £.501; pre-booked groups (10+) £3.50; RHS members (plus one guest) free

You can see Hyde Hall long before you reach the RHS garden. It sits on top of a hill, surrounded by trees like a villa in Tuscany. The approach is so full of dramatic promise that it comes as a surprise to learn that 50 years ago the house had only six trees and no garden. Dick and Helen Robinson started to convert the 24 acres of farmland into a garden in 1955 and gifted it to the RHS in 1993. Helen's first decision was to buy some 60 young trees at an auction sale in Wickford Market. She quickly became an enthusiastic plantsman. The sheltered woodland garden she made on the northern side is a triumph of cultivation and helped to create many microclimates: *Eriobotrya japonica*, *Eucalyptus urnigera* and *Pittosporum tenuifolium* are grown in the open, *Buddleja officinalis* and *Crinodendron patagua* against a wall of the yard and *Acca sellowiana* against the house. The garden that the RHS inherited had much to commend it: masses of naturalised spring bulbs, a rich collection of roses, the national collection of viburnums and a striking collection of crab apples (*Malus*). But it needed a lot of infrastructure to turn it into a garden that could welcome more than 100,000 visitors a year. The challenge was to convert an extensive private paradise into a garden designed and maintained on a scale that people could relate to at home. This involved improvements like reworking the long herbaceous border so that it had shelter hedges of yew and tongues of yew to divide the plantings into smaller bays. It also meant replacing the old with the new. The Robinsons had a particular passion for roses, but their collection was ancient and not in the best of health. The RHS employed Robin Williams to design a new rose garden with both modern and old-fashioned roses including climbers and ramblers. But complete novelties were also needed. Hyde Hall is in one of the driest areas of the British Isles, with an average annual rainfall of just 600mm (24in). The RHS designed and planted the extensive Dry Garden to demonstrate how a garden can be created without the need for artificial irrigation. It is a model of sustainability both for the region and for low rainfall areas in general. Large boulders and stone mulch give the impression of a natural rocky outcrop, similar to the natural environment of many of the chosen plants. The plants are tolerant of drought, exposure and high light levels and, above all, thoroughly garden-worthy. The Dry Garden has over 4,000 plants representing 730 different species and cultivars from around the world; many carry the RHS Award of Garden Merit (AGM). Further new gardens are now under way. A 1.5ha (4-acre) perennial wildflower meadow has developed well since it was first sown in 2001. The Millennium Avenue in the Malus Field (300m long and 20m wide – 984ft long and 66ft wide) has been planted with *Fraxinus excelsior* 'Westhof's Glorie' for short-term effect and *Quercus frainetto* 'Hungarian Crown' for 100 years hence. Woodlands have been planted in other parts of the estate – 25,000 trees so far – and, over the next few years, Hyde Hall will grow to 24ha (60 acres) or more.
plantsman's collection of plants; good herbaceous borders; spring bulbs; ponds; heathers; new dry garden of drought-tolerant plants; visitor centre; shop; garden library; plant centre; licensed restaurant serving hot and cold lunches; afternoon teas; tea/coffee

Owned by The Royal Horticultural Society
Number of gardeners 14, plus students
Size 9.6ha (24 acres)
NCCPG National Collections *Viburnum*

Owned by Mr and Mrs David Edwards
Number of gardeners 2 part-time
Size 2.2ha (6 acres), plus woodland

R & R SAGGERS

Waterloo House, High Street, Newport CB11 3PG

Tel 01799 540858 **Fax** 01799 542900
www.randrsaggers.co.uk
Location On B1383 in centre of village
Opening hours 10am to 5pm, Tuesday to Sunday and Bank Holidays, all year
Admission fee Free

This garden nursery has a wide and ever-changing stock of herbaceous plants, as well as shrubs, climbers, old-fashioned roses and trees. Many are grown from seed. The owners offer a plant-finding service. The garden is beautifully maintained and runs down to a stream.
unusual plants for sale

Owned by Roger and Roslyn Saggers
Number of gardeners 3 part-time

SALING HALL

Great Saling, Braintree CM7 5DT

Tel/fax 01371 850274
Location 2 miles north of B1256 (old A120), between Great Dunmow and Braintree, at Blake End
Opening hours 2pm to 5pm, Wednesdays, May, June and July; groups by appointment on weekdays; please apply in writing
Admission fee Adults £3 (for NGS); children free

A thinking man's garden, Saling also provokes thought in its visitors. The plantsmanship is impressive, particularly the choice and placing of trees and shrubs, some of them extremely rare. Few modern gardens are conceived on such a scale, or mix classical and Japanese elements so smoothly. The moods, and the lessons, are endless. Hugh Johnson was for many years *The Garden*'s Tradescant, and his monthly column a rare source of wisdom – now transferred to *Gardens Illustrated*.
17th-century walled garden with fruit trees and borders; oriental touches; fine standing stone; Temple of Pisces, moat and water gardens

Owned by Mr and Mrs Hugh Johnson
Number of gardeners 2
Size 5ha (12½ acres)
English Heritage Grade II

GLOUCESTERSHIRE

Gloucestershire is rich in nurseries and large important gardens. Six of its nine Grade I historic gardens (a remarkable number for one county) are regularly open to the public – Batsford Park, Frampton Court, Hidcote Manor, Sezincote, Stanway House and Westonbirt Arboretum – while a seventh, Stancombe Park, is open by appointment. Almost all the county's Grade II* gardens also welcome visitors, including Abbotswood, Berkeley Castle, Kiftsgate Court, Miserden Park, Painswick House, Rodmarton Manor, Sudeley Castle and Westbury Court. Most have important collections of plants as well as attractive design features. Indeed, almost all Gloucestershire's leading historic gardens have been highly graded precisely because of their horticultural attractions. Rich clay soils account for some of the popularity of gardening in Gloucestershire, though the inland, upland parts of the county can be very cold in winter. Among garden centres and nurseries, the Batsford Garden Centre has a very good general range and makes a speciality of ferns, while Hunt's Court is excellent for roses of every kind. A very large number of gardens open for the National Gardens Scheme though, slightly confusingly, the southern part of the county, which used to belong to Avon, is still separately organised: both continue to be very successful in persuading garden owners to open their gardens and visitors to visit them. Permission to visit HRH The Prince of Wales's garden at Highgrove House near Tetbury may be given to garden clubs and similar organisations. In addition to the world-famous Westonbirt Arboretum, there are important collections of trees at Highnam Court, Batsford Park and Tortworth Court. The NCCPG is active in Gloucestershire and accounts for a large number of National Collections.

ABBOTSWOOD

Stow-on-the-Wold, Cheltenham GL54 1LE

Tel 01451 830173
Location 1 mile west of Stow-on-the-Wold
Opening hours 1.30pm to 6pm, 1 and 29 April, 3 June, 1 July, 5 August and 9 September
Admission fee Adults £3; children free

Abbotswood is one of the most interesting gardens in the Cotswolds – very Lutyens, very photogenic – with handsome formal gardens in front of the house. A stream meanders through a magnificent rock garden set with alpine meadows, bogs and moraines, past dwarf azaleas, primulas, lysichitons, heaths and heathers until it disappears. There is also a small, densely planted arboretum, with some unusual cultivars dating from about 100 years ago, fascinating to browse around: it is being cleared and replanted. The two-acre kitchen garden is worth the long walk on the occasions when it, too, is open: it has a fruit house, indoor roses and some interesting new plantings. Indeed there are plans for new developments throughout Abbotswood.

interesting topiary; fine collection of trees, including conifers; magnolias; heather garden; good borders; roses; good for plants; teas

Owned by Dikler Farming Co
Number of gardeners 4
Size 8ha (20 acres)
English Heritage Grade II*

BARNSLEY HOUSE GARDEN

Barnsley, Cirencester GL7 5EE

Tel 01285 740000 **Fax** 01285 740900
www.barnsleyhouse.com
Location On B4425 in Barnsley village
Opening hours 11am to 5pm, 19 and 24 May, 7 June, 19 and 25 July and 6 September
Admission fee Adults £5

Rosemary Verey's famous garden was started in 1952 and more or less finished 25 years later. The bones were a pretty house (1697), an 18th-century wall ending in an original Gothic summerhouse and ha-ha, and some fine 19th-century trees. Her architect husband David helped with the design, and together they commissioned sculptures by Simon Verity for important focal points. The result was compact, neat, thickly planted, fairly labour-intensive – and very influential. Mrs Verey reflected the aspirations of many garden owners in the difficult post-war years, so that when people had more money to spend again in the 1970s and 1980s, Barnsley was available to teach and inspire. The scale is surprisingly intimate – one of the garden's strengths – and the small decorative *potager* spawned many imitations. Barnsley is interesting at all seasons, particularly in early spring when it seems to have much more colour than other people's gardens, and again at midsummer rose time and when the salvias and asters flower in autumn. But it is probably at its best – and certainly at its most photographed – in late spring when the little laburnum walk and the purple alliums underneath are in flower together. The house is now an exclusive country house hotel.
good borders; old roses; ornamental *potager*

Owned by Tim Haigh and Rupert Pendered
Number of gardeners 6
Size 2.2ha (5½ acres)

BATSFORD ARBORETUM
Moreton-in-Marsh GL56 9QB

Tel 01386 701441 **Fax** 01386 701829
www.batsarb.co.uk
Location Off A44 between Moreton-in-Marsh and Bourton-on-the-Hill
Opening hours 10am to 5pm, daily, all year; closed on Wednesdays in December and January
Admission fee Adults £6; OAPs £5; children £2; RHS members free except in October

Batsford has an openness which makes its hillside a joy to wander through, passing from one dendrological marvel to the next. Begun in the 1880s, the arboretum also has several oriental curiosities brought from Japan by Lord Redesdale – a large bronze Buddha and an oriental rest house for instance. But the arboretum is mainly the work of the late Lord Dulverton, who added a large number of new plantings between 1956 and 1992. These include nearly 100 different magnolia cultivars, a comprehensive collection of Japanese cherries, some very beautiful conifers, and excellent collections of such genera as *Acer*, *Betula* and *Sorbus*. Some are already record-breakers: all are in the prime of their life, well-grown and vigorous. The underplantings of spring bulbs are worth seeing, but visit Batsford at any season and you will find much to admire and enjoy.
mature conifers; fine collection of trees; maple glade; bluebells; aconites; snowdrops; tallest *Betula platyphylla* (19m; 62ft) in the British Isles (and 12 other tree records); shop; garden centre; light meals and refreshments

Owned by The Batsford Foundation
Number of gardeners 2
Size 22ha (55 acres)
NCCPG National Collections *Prunus* (sato-sakura group)
English Heritage Grade I

BERKELEY CASTLE
Berkeley GL13 9BQ

Tel 01453 810332 **Fax** 01453 512995
www.berkeley-castle.com
Location M5, Jct 13 or 14; along A38
Opening hours 11am to 4pm, Tuesday to Friday, April to September; plus 2pm to 5pm, Sundays, April to October; gardens open at weekends only with combined castle ticket
Admission fee Garden only: adults £4; children £2; garden and castle: adults £7.50; concessions £6; children £4.50

The grim battlements of Berkeley Castle are host to an extensive collection of tender plants. On three terraces are *Cestrum*, *Cistus* and *Rosa banksiae* among hundreds of plant varieties introduced by the owner's grandmother, a sister of Ellen Willmott. An Elizabethan-style bowling green and a water lily pond fit well into the overall scheme.
roses (mainly old-fashioned); plantsman's collection of plants; mature conifers; good herbaceous borders; shop at castle; light lunches and afternoon tea

Owned by RJG Berkeley
Number of gardeners 2
Size 2ha (5 acres)
English Heritage Grade II*

BOURTON HOUSE

Bourton-on-the-Hill, Moreton-in-Marsh GL56 9AE

Tel 01386 700754 **Fax** 01386 701081
www.bourtonhouse.com
Location On A44, 1½ miles west of Moreton-in-Marsh
Opening hours 10am to 5pm, Wednesday to Friday, 23 May to 31 August; plus 27 and 28 May and 25 and 27 August, and Thursdays and Fridays in September and October
Admission fee Adults £5.50; concessions £5; children free

First laid out by Lanning Roper in the 1960s, but consistently improved by the present owners, the gardens at Bourton House are both fashionable and a delight. They include a knot garden, a small *potager*, a raised pond, the topiary walk, trellis work, a croquet lawn, and borders bulging with good colour schemes. The standard of maintenance is exemplary.
topiary; good colour plantings, especially of herbaceous plants; lots of unusual and little-known plants; light lunches and home-made teas

Owned by Mr and Mrs Richard Paice
Number of gardeners 2, plus 2 part-time
Size 1.2ha (3 acres), plus 2.8ha (7-acre) arboretum
English Heritage Grade II

COLESBOURNE PARK

Colesbourne, Cheltenham GL53 9NP

www.snowdrop.org.uk
Location On A435, halfway between Cheltenham and Cirencester
Opening hours 1pm to dusk, Saturdays and Sundays, 3 February to 4 March; plus 15 and 16 September
Admission fee Adults £6

Colesbourne is probably the most famous snowdrop garden in England. It was begun 100 years ago by Henry John Elwes, after whom *Galanthus elwesii* is named, and now has some 250 different cultivars. The sheets of naturalised snowdrops have recently been supplemented by a garden of early spring flowering plants, notably hellebores. Elwes's arboretum is also worth seeing, especially when the gardens open in September: EA Bowles called him 'the prince of plant collectors'.
winter-flowering plants; teas

Owned by Mr and Mrs Henry Elwes
Number of gardeners 2
Size 4ha (10 acres)

DYRHAM PARK

Dyrham, Chippenham SN14 8ER

Tel 0117 937 2501 **Fax** 0117 937 1353
www.nationaltrust.org.uk
Location On A46, 8 miles north of Bath
Opening hours 11am to 5pm, Friday to Tuesday, 16 March to 28 October; noon to 4pm, Saturdays and Sundays, 3 November to 1 January 2008
Admission fee Adults £3.50; children £1.80

Dyrham is fascinating for garden historians, who can study the Kip plan and trace the lines of the 17th-century formal garden which Charles Harcourt Masters turned into classic English parkland. A major programme of development is planned for the garden, including a formal garden in the 18th-century style and a contemporary garden that is linked stylistically to the past.
good herbaceous borders; deer park; handsome orangery; shop; tea room

Owned by The National Trust
Number of gardeners 3
Size 3.2ha (8 acres), plus park
English Heritage Grade II*

EASTLEACH HOUSE

Eastleach Martin, Cirencester GL7 3NW

www.eastleachhouse.com
Location On edge of village, opposite church gates
Opening hours 2pm to 5pm, Fridays, June and July; and by appointment in writing for groups; for NGS on 6 May (teas in village hall)
Admission fee Adults £5; children free

Eastleach House is at the top of a steep slope, and the garden has been laid out to provide enclosure and protection, while not interfering with the magnificent views. Each area is treated differently, but the garden is brought together by bold plantings, including an avenue of limes, and by inspired plantsmanship. The rill garden is exceptionally pretty. There is colour at every season: in May from the iris borders, in June from rambling roses, in high summer from spectacular borders, and in autumn from late-flowering herbaceous plants and the small arboretum.
good design; rich plantings; wildflower meadow; good hedging and topiary; knot garden; herb garden

Owned by Mrs David Richards
Number of gardeners 3 part-time
Size 5.6ha (14 acres)

EMMAUS HOUSE

Clifton Hill, Clifton, Bristol BS8 1BN

Tel 0117 907 9950
www.emmaushouse.org.uk
Location On the corner of Clifton Hill and Hensman's Hill
Opening hours For NGS: 11am to 4.30pm, 3 June, 22 July and 2 September; and by appointment
Admission fee For NGS: adults £2.50

The gardens around Emmaus House are designed to support its function as a retreat house and conference centre. As it is close to a busy city, the emphasis is upon quiet and peace. The gardens include a formal herb garden, a Victorian courtyard garden and a Zen garden with water features and bamboos. They have won many prizes for their holistic design.
light lunches and teas

Owned by The Congregation of La Retraite
Number of gardeners 2
Size 0.6ha (1 1/2 acres)

ERNEST WILSON MEMORIAL GARDEN

High Street, Chipping Campden GL55 6AF

Tel 01386 841298
Location North end of main street
Opening hours 9am to dusk; daily, except Christmas day, all year
Admission fee Collection box for donations

A collection of plants all introduced by Ernest H Wilson, the greatest of European plant hunters in China: Chipping Campden was his birthplace. *Acer griseum*, *Clematis montana* var. *rubens* and the pocket-handkerchief tree (*Davidia involucrata*) are among his best-known introductions: all are represented here.
herbaceous borders; trees and shrubs

Owned by Chipping Campden Town Council
Number of gardeners 1
Size 0.1ha (1/4 acre)

FRAMPTON COURT

Frampton-on-Severn GL2 7EU

Tel 01452 740267/740698 **Fax** 01452 740698
www.framptoncourtestate.uk.com
Location Signed to Frampton-on-Severn from M5, Jct 13 (3 miles)
Opening hours By appointment all year
Admission fee House and garden £6; garden £3

This beautiful and mysterious garden has changed little since 1750. The Dutch water garden – a long rectangular pool – reflects the orangery of Strawberry Hill Gothic design. Nearby Frampton Manor, also owned by the Cliffords, may also be visited; it has a pretty walled garden with shrub roses.
gothic orangery; teas for pre-booked groups

Owned by PRH Clifford
Number of gardeners 1
Size 1.2ha (3 acres)
English Heritage Grade I

GOLDNEY HALL

Lower Clifton Hill, Clifton, Bristol BS8 1BH

Tel 0117 903 4873 **Fax** 0117 903 4877
www.goldneyhall.com
Location Top of Constitution Hill: entrance on Lower Clifton Hill
Opening hours 2pm to 6pm, 29 April; plus 20 May, 24 June and 5 August (see website for times)
Admission fee Adults £3; concessions £1.50

A Bristol merchant's extravagance, nearly 300 years ago. Ten acres in the middle of the city, with an elegant orangery, a Gothic folly tower and the gorgeous Goldney Grotto, which sparkles with crystalline rocks among the shells and follies.
plants under glass; good herbaceous borders; holm oak hedge; many varieties of fruit; the *Chronicles of Narnia* were filmed in the grotto; cream teas in the orangery

Owned by The University of Bristol
Number of gardeners 2
Size 4ha (10 acres)
English Heritage Grade II*

HIGHNAM COURT

Highnam, Gloucester GL2 8DP

Tel 01452 308251
Location Entrance on A40/A48 roundabout
Opening hours 11am to 5pm, first Sunday of the month, April to September
Admission fee Adults £4; children free

Little remains of the original Highnam, laid out when the house was built in 1658. The garden was, however, very famous 100 years ago for the features designed or commissioned by Thomas Gambier-Parry in the middle of the 19th century: the terraces, the broad walk, the arboretum and, above all, the winter garden where natural stone is supplemented by Pulhamite – the largest and earliest surviving example of the artificial stone from which the rock garden at Wisley is also made. The estate was neglected for nearly 100 years, but the present owner started in 1994 first to restore it and then to add new features. The results are very impressive, and worth a long visit. They include a new, one-acre rose garden between the ha-ha and the lake, two new lakes (one with a Giverny-inspired bridge and plantings), tree sculptures, a knot garden, one million bulbs and innumerable new island beds.
Pulhamite rock garden; fine conifers; tallest *Quercus acutissima* and *Fraxinus excelsior* 'Jaspidea' in the British Isles; historic garden in restoration; tea and cakes

Owned by Roger Head
Number of gardeners 2
Size 12ha (30 acres)
English Heritage Grade II*

HODGES BARN

Shipton Moyne, Tetbury GL8 8PR

Tel 01666 880202 **Fax** 01666 880373
Location 3 miles south of Tetbury on Malmesbury road from Shipton Moyne
Opening hours For NGS: 2pm to 6pm, 11, 13 and 14 May, 8, 10 and 11 June
Admission fee Adults £5; children free

This is a large garden – six acres surrounding a converted 15th-century columbarium – all intensively planted. The terraces, courtyards and gardens are divided into rooms (surrounded either by walls or by tapestry, laurel or yew hedges) to give year-round colour. Old-fashioned rose beds are underplanted with tulips for spring and with alliums and campanulas for summer. There is a formal herbaceous border, a water garden and a swimming pool area with large planted pots. Shrub roses and climbers are another Hornby passion and are to be found winding up walls and trees. The plantings reflect a desire to create an informal feeling within a formal framework. The woodland garden is almost an arboretum of ornamental trees (especially birches, maples, whitebeams and many different magnolias), underplanted with spring bulbs. In summer the grass is left long in the wood and wildflowers are encouraged to naturalise. Hodges Barn is a garden of great energy and diversity.
woodland garden; topiary; roses (mainly old-fashioned and climbers); plantsman's collection of plants; good herbaceous borders; daffodils; bluebells; cyclamen

HIDCOTE MANOR GARDEN

Hidcote Bartrim, Chipping Campden GL55 6LR

Tel 01386 438333 **Fax** 01386 438817
www.nationaltrust.org.uk
Location Signed from B4632, Stratford/Broadway road
Opening hours 10am to 6pm (5pm from 1 October), Saturday to Wednesday and Good Friday; 24 March to 4 November; plus Fridays in July and August; last admissions one hour before closing
Admission fee Adults £8; children £4

One of England's greatest gardens, Hidcote is an Arts & Crafts masterpiece created by the American plantsman and plant collector Major Lawrence Johnston. It was designed as a series of outdoor rooms, each with a different character and separated by walls and hedges of many different species. Hidcote therefore has a firm architectural structure – many of Lawrence Johnston's ideas came from France and Italy – combined with a great love of plants. The planting is exuberant but always considers the contrasts and harmonies which can be obtained by planting different things together. Some of the rooms are very small, like Mrs Winthrop's garden – no more than a courtyard with a sundial at the centre – and others, like the long walk and the theatre lawn, give a great sense of space – though in fact the garden is no more than 10 acres in size. Among the most famous features are: the mixed borders richly planted with old roses and companion plants; the red borders, which were among the first 'hot' borders in the country when planted in 1913; the sunken 'bathing pool' garden where a huge circular swimming pool fills a hedged compartment; and the woodland area or wilderness, sometimes known as Westonbirt, where Lawrence Johnston planted long vistas which run from end to end, but which disappear and reappear as you follow the paths back and forth. The National Trust is working on a programme of renewal and regeneration – the East Court garden has just been replanted to its original design – and it is fair to say that Hidcote is now looking better than it did 10 years ago. 2007 marks the centenary of Johnson's arrival at Hidcote, and will be marked by a special exhibition.

woodland garden; topiary; roses (ancient and modern); rock garden; plantsman's collection of plants; good herbaceous borders; tallest pink acacia *Robinia* **x** *ambigua* 'Decaisneana' (19m; 62ft) in the British Isles; National Trust shop and plant centre; licensed restaurant; teas

Owned by The National Trust
Number of gardeners 7
Size 4.2ha (10.5 acres)
English Heritage Grade I

Owned by Mrs Charles Hornby
Number of gardeners 2 part-time
Size 2.4ha (6 acres)

HUNT'S COURT
North Nibley, Dursley GL11 6DZ

Tel 01453 547440 **Fax** 01453 549944
Location Turn across front of Black Horse pub and bear left for 1/4 mile
Opening hours 9am to 12.30pm and 1.45pm to 5pm, Tuesday to Saturday (and Bank Holiday Mondays in spring), all year, except August and Christmas to New Year; for NGS: 2pm to 6pm, 10, 17 and 24 June and 2 and 9 September
Admission fee Adults £3; children and Royal National Rose Society members free

The garden at Hunts Court has been planted since 1976 by something of a horticultural rarity – a plant-loving farmer, and his wife. Keith and Margaret Marshall say they have 'the collector's touch of madness': the result is a garden which is charming, peaceful and educational. Their first love was old-fashioned roses, and they moved their garden fence out into the surrounding fields as the collection of gallicas, damasks and hybrid perpetuals began to grow: it is now the best in the west of England, and still expanding. The 450 cultivars include climbers, species and a few modern shrub roses. Many are underplanted by the Marshalls' next great passion – hardy geraniums and penstemons, each of which is represented by over 100 cultivars. The fence has been moved out several times now to accommodate a large collection of ornamental trees and shrubs, underplanted in turn by more unusual herbaceous plants. These are the stock plants for the thriving nursery they now run in their old stockyard. It is surrounded by a fine plantsman's garden with something for all seasons, including good autumn colour and winter-flowering shrubs. But when the Marshalls last moved the fence, they planted a mini-arboretum – 'very rewarding' is their verdict.
roses of every kind, especially 19th-century cultivars; many other plants of interest to the plantsman; first-rate nursery attached; refreshments on NGS days

Owned by TK and MM Marshall
Number of gardeners 1
Size 1ha (21/2 acres)

KIFTSGATE COURT
Chipping Campden GL55 6LN

Tel/fax 01386 438777
www.kiftsgate.co.uk
Location 3 miles from Chipping Campden opposite Hidcote Manor
Opening hours Noon to 6pm, Saturday to Wednesday, May to July; 2pm to 6pm, Sundays, Mondays and Wednesdays, April, August and September
Admission fee Adults £5.50; children £1.50

Famous for its roses, especially the eponymous *Rosa filipes*, Kiftsgate is all about plants and the use of colour. The best example is the yellow border, where gold and orange are set off by occasional blues and purples. After some dull years, everything about Kiftsgate has revived again: new thinking, new plantings and new enthusiasm have more than restored its excellence. The latest additions are in marked contrast to the rest of the garden: the tennis court has been transformed into a contemporary water garden, full of movement and sound, by Simon Allison. Structure and form predominate here over Kiftsgate's traditional themes of colour and texture. And the garden as a whole is remarkable for its tender plants – abutilons, echiums, azaras and wonderful tree peonies in May.
roses (mainly old-fashioned); colour plantings; good borders; many interesting plants; tea room in the house; lunches May to July

Kiftsgate Court

Kiftsgate Court

Lydney Park Gardens

Owned by Mr and Mrs J Chambers
Number of gardeners 2
Size 1.6ha (4 acres)
English Heritage Grade II*

LYDNEY PARK GARDENS
Lydney Park GL15 6BU

Tel 01594 842844/842922 **Fax** 01594 842027
Location Off A48 between Lydney and Aylburton
Opening hours 10am to 5pm, Sundays, Wednesdays and Bank Holidays, 1 April to 6 May; then daily until 3 June
Admission fee Adults £4, but £3 on Wednesdays; children 50p

There are fine formal gardens around the house, but Lydney is famous for its rhododendrons: a remarkable collection planted over the last 50 years is the backbone to the extensive woodland garden. And not just rhododendrons, but azaleas and camellias, too – all are carefully planted to create distinct effects from March to June. The numbers are still growing, and include plants grown from collected seed and hybrids from distinguished breeders, many as yet unnamed, while others have yet to flower. Lydney is now recognised as one of the best rhododendron gardens in England.
rhododendrons and azaleas; woodland garden; mature conifers; deer park; daffodils; some souvenirs for sale; light teas

Owned by Viscount Bledisloe
Number of gardeners 2, plus part-time help in season
Size 3.2ha (8 acres) of woodland garden

MILL DENE GARDEN
School Lane, Blockley,
Moreton-in-Marsh GL56 9HU

Tel 01386 700457 **Fax** 01386 700526
www.milldenegarden.co.uk
Location First road on left as you come into Blockley from Bourton-on-the-Hill; follow brown tourist signs
Opening hours 10am to 5pm, Tuesday to Friday, April to October; plus occasional weekends for charity; and by appointment
Admission fee Adults £4.50; OAPs £4; children £1; RHS members free 3 to 27 April and 2 to 31 October

This Cotswold water-mill garden has been designed and planted by the owner in an English country garden style. Steep terraces rise from the mill pond, stream and grotto. Paths wander through the rose walk, flanked by standard 'Sander's White Rambler' roses and lavender, to the cricket lawn. At the top of the garden, the *potager* and the 'fantasy fruit garden' (all greys and blues) have the church as a backdrop and views of the hills.
new walk with roses chosen for scent (2005); shop; refreshments

Owned by Mr and Mrs BS Dare
Number of gardeners 1/2
Size 1ha (21/2 acres)

MISERDEN PARK
Miserden, Stroud GL6 7JA

Tel 01285 821303 **Fax** 01285 821530
Location Signed from A417, or turn off B4070 between Stroud and Birdlip
Opening hours 10am to 5pm, Tuesday to Thursday, April to September; for NGS: 9 April and 25 June
Admission fee Adults £4; children free

The Cotswold house at Miserden (Jacobean, with a Lutyens addition) has wide views across the Golden Valley, while the spacious, peaceful gardens lie to the side. Most were laid out in the 1920s using a 17th-century structure – a charming rose garden, a long yew walk and expansive herbaceous borders, currently undergoing restoration. Recent additions include a rill and summerhouse, a parterre of lavender and hebes, a shrub border, a border of silvers and greys and a blue and yellow walkway below the house. The trees around the edges are magnificent – not particularly rare, but tall, well-grown and shapely. The old kitchen gardens have a very extensive range of glasshouses, now part of a general-purpose nursery.
topiary; good trees; good herbaceous borders; martagon lilies; roses; domed yew walk; cyclamen; excellent garden nursery (closed Mondays)

Miserden Park

Owned by Major MTNH Wills
Number of gardeners 2
Size 5ha (12½ acres)
English Heritage Grade II*

OWLPEN MANOR
Uley, Dursley GL11 5BZ

Tel 01453 860261 **Fax** 01453 860819
www.owlpen.com
Location Off B4066 near Uley
Opening hours 2pm to 5pm, Tuesdays, Thursdays and Sundays, May to September
Admission fee Adults £3.25; children £1.25

Owlpen is a dreamy Cotswold manor house whose loveliness depends upon its site. It has a small formal garden which was terraced in the 16th century, altered c.1720 and restored in the Old English style by Norman Jewson in 1926. Jewson planted the box parterres and topiary yews; the present owners have added the roses and herbs since 1980. The aim is to suggest an earlier garden 're-ordered conservatively' in about 1700. Owlpen is perhaps not worth a special journey by keen plantsmen, but the restaurant, the setting and the house all add up to a good place for an outing.
topiary; roses (mainly old-fashioned); standard gooseberries; guidebooks and postcards for sale; licensed restaurant (noon to 5pm)

Owned by Sir Nicholas and Lady Mander
Number of gardeners 1
Size 0.8ha (2 acres)
English Heritage Grade II

PAINSWICK ROCOCO GARDEN
Gloucester Road, Painswick GL6 6TH

Tel 01452 813204 **Fax** 01452 814888
www.rococogarden.co.uk
Location Outside Painswick on B4073
Opening hours 11am to 5pm, daily, 10 January to 31 October
Admission fee Adults £5; OAPs £4; children £2.50; RHS members free

Years of restoration work have saved the unique rococo garden at Painswick from back-to-nature woodland. A white Venetian Gothic exedra, a Doric seat, the plunge pool, an octagonal pigeon house, a Gothic gazebo called the Eagle House, a bowling green, the fish pond and a Gothic alcove have all been reconstructed in their original positions thanks to the efforts of Lord Dickinson and the Painswick Rococo Garden Trust.
A remarkable garden and a brilliant theatrical achievement. Recent additions include the Exedra Garden (18th-century herbaceous plantings in an informal structure, best in early summer) and the kitchen garden (best in late summer). There are cyclamen everywhere in autumn, as well as hordes of snowdrops in winter. And do not miss the amazing yew topiary around the old parish church in the centre of Painswick.
woodland garden; snowdrop wood; new plant nursery; maze; gift shop; licensed restaurant, coffee, teas and light snacks

Owned by Painswick Rococo Garden Trust
Number of gardeners 4
Size 2.4ha (6 acres)
English Heritage Grade II*

RODMARTON MANOR
Rodmarton, Cirencester GL7 6PF

Tel 01285 841253 **Fax** 01285 841298
www.rodmarton-manor.co.uk
Location Off A433 between Cirencester and Tetbury
Opening hours 2pm to 5pm, Wednesdays, Saturdays and Bank Holiday Mondays, 9 April, then 1 May to 30 September; plus 11, 15 and 18 February for snowdrops (open at 1.30pm)
Admission fee Adults £4; children £1

A splendid Arts & Crafts garden, with a strong design and exuberant planting. Simon Biddulph says there are 18 different areas within the garden, from the trough garden for alpine plants to the famous double herbaceous borders (in the middle of a redesign), which lead to a Cotswold summerhouse. Highly original – contemporary, but made without any contact with Hidcote.

interesting plants; old-fashioned roses; topiary; much renovation and replanting; snowdrops

Owned by Simon Biddulph
Size 3.2ha (8 acres)
English Heritage Grade II*

SEZINCOTE

Moreton-in-Marsh GL56 9AW

Tel 01386 700444
www.sezincote.co.uk
Location On A44 to Evesham, 1½ miles out of Moreton-in-Marsh
Opening hours 2pm to 6pm (or dusk, if earlier); Thursdays, Fridays and Bank Holiday Mondays, January to November
Admission fee Adults £4; children £1.50

The house at Sezincote was the model for the Brighton Pavilion, and seems inseparable from the cruciform Moghul garden that sets off its Indian façade so well, yet this brilliant formal garden was designed as recently as 1965. On the other side are sumptuous borders planted by Graham Stuart Thomas and a luscious water garden of candelabra primulas and astilbes around the Temple to Surya, the Snake Bridge and Brahmin bulls. Humphry Repton had a hand in the original landscape, but the modern gardens are even more satisfying than the classical, 18th-century parkland setting.
good, bold plantings in the water garden; tallest maidenhair tree *Ginkgo biloba* (26m; 5ft) in the British Isles and five other record trees. These include the blue-leaved noble fir *Abies procera* Glauca Group, the weeping hornbeam *Carpinus betulus* 'Pendula' and the yellow-leaved beech *Fagus sylvatica* 'Zlatia'

Owned by Mr and Mrs D Peake
Number of gardeners 3
Size 4ha (10 acres)
English Heritage Grade I

SNOWSHILL MANOR

Snowshill, Broadway WR12 7JU

Tel 01386 852410 **Fax** 01386 842822
www.nationaltrust.org.uk
Location Brown signs from Broadway village centre
Opening hours 11am to 5.30pm, Wednesday to Sunday and Bank Holiday Mondays, 24 March to 28 October
Admission fee Gardens only: adults £4.20; children £2.10; families £10.60

Baillie Scott designed the garden at Snowshill as 'an extension of the house, a series of garden rooms'. It has often been praised for its changes of levels and collection of curious artefacts – an armillary sphere and a gilt figure of St George and the Dragon, for instance. Snowshill is as eccentric as its owner, Charles Wade, and the spooky bric-a-brac which fills his house, but many visitors find it 'charming' or 'interesting'. Snowshill was the National Trust's first organically run garden.
unusual design; good borders; National Trust shop; restaurant

Owned by The National Trust
Number of gardeners 2
Size 0.8ha (2 acres)
English Heritage Grade II

SPECIAL PLANTS

Hill Farm Barn, Greenways Lane, Cold Ashton, Chippenham SN14 8LA

Tel 01225 891686
www.specialplants.net
Location Near Bath, just south of junction of A46 and A420; not in Cold Ashton
Opening hours Nursery: 10am to 5pm, daily, March to October; and by appointment. Garden: 11am to 5pm, Wednesdays, July to September; plus third Thursday of month from June to September (for NGS)
Admission fee Adults £2.50

The collection of hardy plants at this connoisseur's nursery is excellent, but it is for her tender perennials that Derry Watkins's nursery is best known. Salvias, pelargoniums and streptocarpus are among her top lines, together with conservatory climbers and shrubs. There are also one-day courses at the nursery in autumn. In 1996, Derry Watkins and her architect husband bought a derelict barn with three acres of steeply

sloping fields. Around the barn he designed bold shapes in gravel, water and grass, terraced with dry stone walls. Then she planted it up with drifts of colour using many unusual plants (not a rose or a clematis in sight, alas). There is a 'black and white' border, a sizzling hot red and orange bed and a cooler lemon and lime slope, as well as a gravel garden, bog garden, allium alley, ponds, vegetable garden and now an orchard and a woodland walk, all set off by wonderful views down the valley.
unusual plants; home-made teas

Owned by Derry Watkins
Number of gardeners 1
Size 0.3ha (æ acre)

STANCOMBE PARK
Dursley GL11 6AU

Tel 01453 542815
Location Off B4060 between Dursley and Wotton-under-Edge
Opening hours Groups by appointment
Admission fee Adults £3; children (under 10) £1

Stancombe has everything: a handsome house above a wooded valley, a flower garden of wondrous prettiness, and a Gothic horror of a historic folly garden at the valley bottom. Start at the top. Peter Coats, Lanning Roper and Nada Jennett all worked on the rose gardens and mixed borders by the house: there is more to learn about good modern design and planting here than any other garden in Gloucestershire. Then wander down the valley where the path narrows and the incline steepens to a ferny tunnel, and start the circuit of the follies, best described as an open-air ghost-train journey without the ghosts. Highly recommended.
fine collection of trees; excellent borders; fine spring bulbs; lots of roses; some interesting and unusual plants; refreshments by arrangement

Owned by Mrs Basil Barlow
Number of gardeners 1
Size 6ha (15 acres)
English Heritage Grade I

STANWAY HOUSE
Stanway, Cheltenham GL54 5PQ

Tel 01386 584528 **Fax** 01386 584688
www.stanwayfountain.co.uk
Location On B4077.
Opening hours 2pm to 5pm, Tuesdays and Thursdays, June to August; plus Saturdays in July and August; and groups by appointment; for NGS: 1 April and 20 May
Admission fee Adults £4; OAPs £3; children £1

The important water gardens at Stanway are undergoing restoration: the 91m (300ft) gravity-fed fountain is the tallest in Britain. A pyramidal folly dominates the hillside behind the house. Repairs have begun on the 170m (558ft) cascade which runs down to a long still tank known as the Canal. On the way up to the top are some interesting trees and shrubs. If you have not been to Stanway for a few years, you will be amazed by the changes; worth another visit.
woodland garden; mature conifers

Owned by Lord Neidpath
Number of gardeners 1 1/2
Size 8ha (20 acres)
English Heritage Grade I

Highway Fountain, Stanway

Stanway House

STOWELL PARK

Northleach GL54 3LE

Tel 01285 720308 **Fax** 01285 720360
www.stowellpark.com
Location A429 between Cirencester and Northleach
Opening hours 2pm to 5pm, 20 May (plus church plant sale), 24 June for Royal British Legion
Admission fee Adults £4; no concessions; children free

(P) 🚻

The most important feature at Stowell is its peach house, 55m (180ft) long, which has been in constant use since the early 19th century. Nowhere in England does such a glasshouse produce fruit in the manner perfected by our Victorian ancestors. Stowell is in a magnificent position, with terraced gardens in front of the house looking down over the Coln valley and landscaped woodlands dating from the 18th century. The pleached lime avenue at the house's entrance was planted in 1983 and is now fully established. In the superb traditional walled gardens are substantial herbaceous borders and some plantings of old-fashioned roses.

fine kitchen garden and glasshouses; roses; good herbaceous borders; plants for sale on 21 May only; excellent teas

Owned by Lord and Lady Vestey
Number of gardeners 4
Size 3.2ha (8 acres)
English Heritage Grade II

SUDELEY CASTLE & GARDENS

Winchcombe GL54 5JD

Tel 01242 602308 **Fax** 01242 602959
www.sudeleycastle.co.uk
Location 8 miles north-east of Cheltenham on B4632
Opening hours 10.30am to 5pm, daily 31 March to 28 October
Admission fee Adults £7.20; OAPs £6.20; children £4.20

(P) 🚻 ♿

This large commercially-run garden has features by many top garden designers: Jane Fearnley-Whittingstall did the roses and Charles Chesshire

Sudeley Castle and Gardens

WESTONBIRT THE NATIONAL ARBORETUM

Westonbirt, Tetbury GL8 8QS

Tel 01666 880220 **Fax** 01666 880559
www.forestry.gov.uk/westonbirt
Location 3 miles south-west of Tetbury on A433
Opening hours 10am to 8pm (or dusk, if earlier), daily, all year. Visitor centre: 10am to 5pm, daily, March to December
Admission fee Adults £5-£7.50 according to season; children £2; RHS Members free

Westonbirt is the finest and largest arboretum in the British Isles: it contains one of the most important collections of trees and shrubs in the world. There are 18,000 of them, representing 3,700 species and cultivars, planted from 1829 to the present day, and covering some 600 acres of beautifully landscaped grounds. The maple glade is famous, and so are the bluebells in the part known as Silk Wood. Magnificent spring displays of rhododendrons, azaleas and magnolias, wildflowers in summer and architectural winter beauty are matched by the spectacular autumn colouring for which Westonbirt is justifiably famous. Westonbirt is also one of the best gardens in England for a winter walk but, with 17 miles of paths, you must equip yourself with a guidebook and a map to find your way about.

over 1,000 species of record-breaking trees, including 24 maples (*Acer* species) and 16 *Sorbus*; other champion trees include the red horse-chestnut *Aesculus* x *carnea* at 27m (88ft); the upright birch *Betula pendula* 'Fastigiata' at 29m (95ft); the handkerchief tree *Davidia involucrata* at 24m (79ft); the home-sprung *Pinus* 'Holfordiana' at 36m (118ft); and the large-leaved deciduous oak *Quercus macranthera* at 31m (102ft); gift shop; plant centre; restaurant; café

Owned by Forestry Commission
Number of gardeners 8
Size 240ha (600 acres)
NCCPG National Collections *Acer* (Japanese cvs.); *Salix*
English Heritage Grade I

replanted the 'secret garden' (originally designed by Rosemary Verey) in the Mediterranean style. New plantings continue. The whole garden is organically managed. There are fine old trees, magnificent Victorian topiary (mounds of green and gold yew) and a raised walk around the pleasure gardens that may be Elizabethan in origin. Popular and successful.
topiary; roses (ancient and modern); herbs; mature conifers; good herbaceous borders; ruins of banqueting hall, now a pretty garden; wildflower meadow; plant centre; coffee shop

Owned by Lady Ashcombe and family
Number of gardeners 4
Size 5.6ha (14 acres)
English Heritage Grade II*

THROUGHAM COURT
Througham GL6 7HG

Tel 01285 821215 **Fax** 01285 821325
www.christinefacer.com
Location Signed to right of road from Bisley to The Camp
Opening hours By appointment for groups of 20+
Admission fee £10 (plus VAT) per person

Christine Facer is a brilliant medical scientist turned garden designer. Science informs her thinking and her designs, and she shows great originality in her choice and use of materials. Charles Jencks's Garden of Cosmic Speculation is clearly an influence: one of the gardens at Througham is called the Garden of Cosmic Evolution, while others refer to mathematics ('Fibonacci's Walk') and astronomy ('Black Hole Seat'). At the heart is a pretty Jacobean house with fine Cotswold views. Miraculously, Facer holds all these contrasting elements together with a tight overall design and imaginative plantings.
important modern designs; refreshments by arrangement

Owned by Dr Christine Facer Hoffman
Number of gardeners 21/2
Size 1.2ha (3 acres)

UNIVERSITY OF BRISTOL BOTANIC GARDEN
The Holmes, Stoke Park Road, Stoke Bishop, Bristol BS9 1JQ

Tel 0117 331 4912 **Fax** 0117 331 4909
www.bris.ac.uk/depts/BotanicGardens
Location North of city centre, off Stoke Hill; 200 yards on right
Opening hours 10am to 4.30pm, Wednesday to Friday, plus Sundays, April to November
Admission fee Entrance charge for 2007 not yet known

The new University Botanic Garden opened in 2006. The design was worked out by Land Use Consultants and sets out to be both 'meandering' and 'organic', with a blend of informal and formal plantings that is both educational and aesthetically pleasing. Most of the plants at the old garden on Bracken Hill were transported to new sites here. There are four core plant collections: plant evolution; plants from the world's Mediterranean climates; useful plants; and rare and threatened native plants. The new garden has a strong evolutionary theme including a sunken dell that charts the most important stages of plant evolution on land from green algae to the diversity of flowering plants and a 'family tree' based on the latest understanding of flowering plant relationships using DNA analysis. New Chinese and European Herb Gardens contain medicinal plants, many rare in cultivation, and a new Glasshouse complex is home to five climate-controlled zones. Each zone is filled with exciting plants from subtropical ferns and orchids to exotic bulbs, cacti and succulents. *Victoria amazonica* grows in a tropical pool and many food, spice and medicinal plants are also grown. New for 2007 is a large display illustrating the numerous ways in which plants are pollinated and a rocky Mediterranean hillside planting.

Owned by The University of Bristol
Number of gardeners 5, plus volunteers
Size 1.7ha (41/4 acres)

WESTBURY COURT

Westbury-on-Severn GL14 1PD

Tel 01452 760461 **Fax** 01452 760461
www.nationaltrust.org.uk
Location 9 miles south-west of Gloucester on A48
Opening hours 10am to 5pm, Wednesday to Sunday and Bank Holiday Mondays, 7 March to 28 October; daily in July and August
Admission fee Adults £4.25; children £2.10

Westbury was restored in the 1970s to become the best example of a medium-sized 17th-century Dutch garden in England. An elegant pavilion, tall and slender, looks down along a long tank of water. On the walls are old apple, pear and plum cultivars. Parterres (now planted in the 17th-century style), fine modern topiary and a T-shaped tank with a statue of Neptune in the middle make up the rest of the garden. All the plants were known to cultivation before 1720. The garden is going through a period of consolidation; visitors should expect changes.
topiary; herbs; biggest holm oak *Quercus ilex* in the British Isles

Owned by The National Trust
Number of gardeners 1
Size 1.6ha (4 acres)
English Heritage Grade II*

WILLOW LODGE

Gloucester Road, Longhope, Gloucester GL17 0RA

Tel/fax 01452 831211
www.willowgardens.fsnet.co.uk
Location On A40, 10 miles from Gloucester and 6 miles from Ross-on-Wye, 1/2 mile west of Dursley Cross
Opening hours 1pm to 5pm, 6, 7, 27 and 28 May, 12 and 13 August; groups and private visits by appointment between April and August
Admission fee Adults £3; children free

This garden has been entirely made by the owners, enthusiastic plantsmen, since they moved here in 1987. At first they developed just an acre around the house: it remains a good garden of mixed herbaceous and shrubby plantings, with some particularly fine shade-lovers – trilliums, erythroniums and dodecatheons. Then they started to plant the adjoining field as an arboretum, underplanted with native daffodils, snowdrops and ground orchids, *Dactylorhiza* species. Among the many interesting plants here are *Sinocalycanthus chinensis* and several *Lespedeza* species; some have been collected on their travels in China and North America. The stream that runs from end to end of the garden has been used to create a bog garden (lots of different primulas) and a pond, alongside a large alpine bed. There is much to enjoy and learn throughout the garden.
a good young arboretum; bog garden; maples; teas

Owned by Mr and Mrs JH Wood
Number of gardeners 3
Size 1.6ha (4 acres)

HAMPSHIRE

For such a prosperous county, Hampshire has comparatively few historic gardens of the highest importance: only Hackwood Park (not open to the public) and Highclere Park (right in the north) are listed as Grade I. But Hampshire compensates with a wealth of 20th-century plantsmen's gardens and nurseries. Indeed, the Sir Harold Hillier Gardens at Ampfield – the world's greatest collection of temperate trees and shrubs – was founded as recently as 1953 and grew out of the commercial activities of Hillier's Nursery. When modern gardens like Brandy Mount, Exbury, Longstock, Spinners and Meon Orchard are taken into account, and some of the small specialist nurseries like Blackthorn and Langley Boxwood, Hampshire emerges as one of the best places in Europe for plants and gardens, plantsmen and gardeners. Unfortunately, however, the well-known organic garden at Longmead House will not be opening again in 2007. The National Gardens Scheme is extremely well represented in the county, with a very large number of gardens opening for charity. There are many good gardens that do not open often enough for us to list in this guide: Pylewell Park, Rotherfield Park and Conholt Park among them. And deep in the New Forest, at Rhinefield, is the best late-Victorian pinetum in southern England. The Hampshire Group of the NCCPG is strong – always a good measure of the interest in gardening with plants – with 47 National Collections. And the Hampshire Gardens Trust, founded more than 20 years ago by the energy and foresight of Gilly Drummond, has been the model for every county-based gardens trust since then. Sparsholt College, between Winchester and Stockbridge, is a RHS Partner College.

53 LADYWOOD

Eastleigh SO50 4RW

Tel 023 8061 5389
Location M3, Jct 12; along A335, right at first roundabout (Woodside Ave); 2nd right into Bosville; Ladywood is 5th on right
Opening hours 2pm to 5pm, Tuesdays (by prior appointment), 3 April to 28 August; plus 14 May and 25 June; also 11am to 5pm on 13 May and 24 June
Admission fee Adults £3; garden not suitable for children under 16

Mrs Ward's garden is a model of how to design a very small garden to look much bigger than it really is, and then to fill it with interesting plants and attractive colour combinations. Screens and trellis work divide up the space, and the compartments are so ornamented with decorative details that you have to stop and go round it very slowly, in case you might miss something. Contrasts of textures are another feature – brick, stone, concrete, gravel and pebbles are mixed up to maximise variety – and so are flowering plants in pots. Leaves are as important as flowers; most of the shrubs are evergreen, and chosen for their foliage. The range of herbaceous and woodland plants is truly amazing, and they are all extremely well grown. A garden to admire and learn from.

plants from the garden for sale; refreshments on Sundays

Owned by Mrs Sue Ward
Number of gardeners owner only
Size 14m x 14m

ABBEY COTTAGE

Rectory Lane, Itchen Abbas, Winchester SO21 1BN

Tel 01962 779575
www.abbeycottage.net
Location On B3047, 1 mile east of the Trout Inn at Itchen Abbas

Abbey Cottage

Opening hours Noon to 5pm, 6 and 7 May, 11 June, 26 and 27 August; and by appointment
Admission fee Adults £2.50; children free

Abbey Cottage would be a fine garden by any standards – it has a firm design, beautiful flint and brick walls, good lines, interesting plants, good colour schemes and immaculate standards of tidiness – but what makes it especially interesting is that Colonel Daniell is a recent convert to organic gardening. He says that 'organic gardening was the element missing from my gardening... now the garden feels complete'. The garden is maintained as much for the pleasure of his many friends and visitors as for his own pleasure.
organic garden; good structure; excellent maintenance; teas and plants for sale at weekend openings

Owned by Col Patrick Daniell CBE
Number of gardeners 1 part-time
Size 0.6ha (1 1/2 acres)

APPLE COURT

Hordle Lane, Hordle, Lymington SO41 0HU

Tel 01590 642130 **Fax** 01590 694220
www.applecourt.com
Location South of New Forest, just north of A337 at Downton crossroads
Opening hours 10am to 5pm, Friday to Sunday and Bank Holiday Mondays, March to October
Admission fee Adults £3; children free

The display gardens attached to this specialist nursery are firmly designed and would be worth a visit even without plants. They include exotic borders, a woodland walk and a new Japanese garden. The white garden has at its heart an oval-shaped lawn, surrounded by pleached hornbeams. The white plantings lie *outside* this oval of limes. Elsewhere are about 300 cultivars of *Hosta*, many of them – like the daylilies – were bred in the USA and are offered for sale by Apple Court but by no other UK nursery. There are 400 *Hemerocallis* cultivars, including spider and other unusual forms.
tea and coffee

Owned by Charles and Angela Meads
Number of gardeners 2
Size 0.6ha (1 1/2 acres)

BLACKTHORN NURSERY

Kilmeston, Alresford SO24 0NL

Tel 01962 771796 **Fax** 01962 771071
Location 1 mile south of Cheriton, off A272
Opening hours 10am to 4pm, 12, 13, 26 and 27 January, 9, 10, 23 and 24 February, 9, 10, 23 and 24 March, 7, 8, 21 and 22 September

Blackthorn's plants tend to be spring beauties: the nursery's three specialities are hellebores, epimediums and daphnes, all of which they breed, as well as introducing new species. Their most striking hellebores are semi-doubles called 'Party Dress' hybrids. The list of epimediums is the best in England – over 40 different names: their rarities include a large number of collected species like *E. fargesii* Og. 93057 and *E. franchetii* 'Brimstone Butterfly' Og. 87001. The daphnes are no less remarkable: over 50 different names, including such little-known hybrids as *D.* x *thauma* and no fewer than seven cultivars of *D.* x *hendersonii*. Their general list of alpines and herbaceous plants is equally exciting: they have a covetable and ever-changing selection of good plants. For dedicated plantsmen, a visit to Blackthorn on an open day is one of the social highlights of early spring: every fellow-plantsman in the country seems to be there too. But the Whites intend to retire next year, in the spring of 2008, so do not leave your visit until it is too late.

Owned by R and S White
Size 0.1ha (1/4-acre) woodland walk

BRAMDEAN HOUSE

Bramdean, Alresford SO24 0JU

Tel 01962 771214 **Fax** 01962 771095
Location On A272, between Winchester and Petersfield
Opening hours 2pm to 5pm, 18 February, 15 April, 13 May, 10 June, 15 July, 12 August, 9 September and by appointment
Admission fee Adults £4.50; children free; for NGS: adults £3.50

The gardens at Bramdean are much admired, and rightly so. Against a backdrop of mature trees, two wide mirror-image borders lead away from the back of the house. They are full of unusual shrubs, plants, bulbs and climbers. At the end of the central axis, steps lead to a one-acre walled kitchen garden whose central beds are planted with a range of herbaceous plants, roses, perennials and bulbs. Here, too, is a large collection of sweet peas, a trial of hardy nerines, and flowers, fruit and vegetables grown for the house. The vista runs yet further, through an orchard underplanted with massed daffodils to an apple house some 300 yards from the house.

climbing roses; herbaceous plants; peonies; ornamental shrubs; bulbs of every sort; climbing roses; clematis; sweet peas; vegetables; fruit; tender nerines; refreshments on NGS days

Owned by Mr and Mrs H Wakefield
Number of gardeners 2
Size 2.6ha (6 1/2 acres)
English Heritage Grade II

CADLAND GARDENS

Cadland House, Fawley, Southampton SO45 1AA

Tel 023 8089 1543 **Fax** 023 8024 3308
Location 16 miles south-east of Southampton off A326/B2053
Opening hours Parties by appointment from May to July and in September and October
Admission fee £5 per head

Cadland has a miniature Capability Brown landscape, designed around a fishing cottage that burnt down in 1916. Though much larger, the present Cadland House stands on the same site. Since 1983, the gardens have been restored as closely as possible to Brown's original layout. Ponder the contrasts of openness and closure, light and shade. And note that Brown chose as his eye-catcher the steeple of Ryde church across the Solent on the Isle of Wight. In the walled gardens is much of horticultural interest: the lean-to fruit house is the longest in Hampshire, bursting with apricots, peaches, nectarines and 'Muscat of Alexandria' grapes.

BRANDY MOUNT HOUSE

East Street, Alresford SO24 9EG

Tel 01962 732189
www.brandymount.co.uk
Location Left into East Street from Broad Street, 50 yards, first right
Opening hours 11am to 4pm, 7, 10 and 11 February; 2pm to 5pm, 4 March; and by appointment
Admission fee Adults £2; children free

Brandy Mount is the garden of plantsmen – but plantsmen who are also distinguished cultivators and exhibitors of alpine plants. The first surprise is to find quite such a large and secluded garden so near the centre of a busy town. Then you discover that, although the underlying soil is chalky, a great variety of the rarer shade-loving plants thrive in the rich soil under the trees – as well as the snowdrops, for which the garden is famous among galanthophiles. The herbaceous borders in the sunnier parts support the many species of geranium, peonies, daphnes and spring-flowering bulbs which are happy in the warm, free-draining soil. The planting of all these areas is informal, with wide sweeps of lawn between the borders. The vegetable area has been reorganised as a formal *potager* with traditional box hedges and small beds to allow the owners to grow a greater variety of salad crops and more unusual vegetables, interspersed with flowering plants. Alpines have always been a speciality: they flourish around the terrace in front of the house, where there are over 30 kinds of smaller daphnes. Many alpines are also grown in troughs and sinks, which are organised as a group and replanted as small crevice gardens. These support many rare and tricky species which are also grown in frames and in the Alpine House. There is a fine collection of European primulas and saxifrages and an ever-increasing one of dwarf narcissi. A new raised bed, which can be covered with an Access frame, is used for special snowdrops, narcissi and daphnes. This garden is fascinating, immaculately maintained, and forever changing, as the collection of rare plants grows ever larger. Strongly recommended.

plantsman's garden; woodland and herbaceous plants on a chalk soil; terrace and troughs for alpines; snowdrops; daphnes; peony species; European primulas; Alpine House; extensive plant sales area full of good plants; teas

Owned by Caryl and Michael Baron
Number of gardeners part-time (very)
Size 0.5ha (1¼ acres)
NCCPG National Collections *Daphne*; *Galanthus*

Capability Brown landscape; refreshments by arrangement

Owned by Mr and Mrs Maldwin Drummond
Number of gardeners 2
Size 6ha (15 acres)
English Heritage Grade II*

EXBURY GARDENS

Exbury, Southampton SO45 1AZ

Tel 023 8089 1203 **Fax** 023 8089 9940
www.exbury.co.uk
Location 3 miles south of Beaulieu
Opening hours 10am to 5.30pm (or dusk, if earlier), daily, 17 March to 4 November; open until 8.30pm from 14 to 18 May
Admission fee Adults £6.50; OAPs £6; children £1; but in high season (17 March to 10 June): adults £7.50; OAPs £7; children £1.50; RHS members free 17 to 31 March and all September

Rhododendrons, rhododendrons, rhododendrons: over one million of them in 200 acres of natural woodland. More than 40 have won awards from the Royal Horticultural Society. But there are magnolias, camellias and rare trees too, many grown from the original seed introduced by famous plant collectors. A place of wonder in May, but beautiful at every time of the year. The collection of nerines which Lionel de Rothschild bred between the wars was dispersed after his death but reassembled and developed by Sir Peter Smithers in Switzerland. A few years ago he returned them to Exbury where they may be seen once again in October. A new garden has been created in the style of Piet Oudolf and James Van Sweden – huge swathes of herbaceous perennials and grasses within a strong woodland structure.
good herbaceous borders; candelabra primulas; rare trees; rose garden; water garden; daffodils; massive two-acre rock garden; *Nerine* hybrids; hydrangea walk; plant centre; gift shop; hot and cold lunches; new tea room

Owned by Edmund de Rothschild
Number of gardeners 9
Size 80ha (200 acres)
English Heritage Grade II*

FARLEIGH HOUSE

Farleigh Wallop, Basingstoke RG25 2HT

Tel 01256 842684 **Fax** 01256 810048
Location South-east of Basingstoke, off B3046 to Preston Candover
Opening hours For NGS and by appointment
Admission fee For NGS: adults £3.50; private visits: adults £5

The garden at Farleigh House has been stylishly remade in recent years. The park still comes up close to the house, but yew hedges frame the views out and there are new installations every year – wire sheep, lily ponds and even new lakes. It is all very spacious, unfussy and restrained. The kitchen garden has been divided into three parts. One is an old rose garden, with slabs of nepeta and alchemilla round a central pool and fountain. Another has wild roses and some good modern sculptures. Best of all is the section with a deep herbaceous border and large pots of agapanthus running down to a splendid series of new conservatories, planted with bougainvilleas, daturas, passion flowers and other tender shrubs.
refreshments

Owned by The Earl and Countess of Portsmouth
Number of gardeners 3
Size 4ha (10 acres)

FURZEY GARDENS

Minstead, Lyndhurst SO43 7GL

Tel 023 8081 2464 **Fax** 023 8081 2297
www.furzey-gardens.org
Location Off A31 or A337 to Minstead
Opening hours 10am to 5pm (dusk in winter), daily, except 25 and 26 December
Admission fee March to October: adults £4.50; OAPs £3.50; children £1.50; reductions in winter; RHS members free

Furzey demonstrates how woodland garden effects can be created in quite small areas. Parts are a maze of narrow curving paths running between hedges of Kurume azaleas, unforgettable in April

Exbury Gardens

Farleigh House

Gilbert White's House

and May, but the late-summer flowering of eucryphias runs them close and the autumn colours of nyssas, parrotias and enkianthus are worth a visit in October.
rhododendrons and azaleas; mature conifers; camellias; bluebells; naturalised dieramas; heathers; spring bulbs; small shop; refreshments

Owned by Furzey Gardens Charitable Trust
Number of gardeners 2 horticultural instructors with teams of students with learning difficulties
Size 3.2ha (8 acres)

GILBERT WHITE'S HOUSE
High Street, Selborne, Alton GU34 3JH

Tel 01420 511275 **Fax** 01420 511040
www.gilbertwhiteshouse.org.uk
Location In centre of Selborne, on B3006
Opening hours 11am to 5pm, daily, April to September; 11am to 5pm, daily, except Mondays, October to March
Admission fee Adults £6.50; OAPs £5.50; children free

The house (on the village street) was bought some years ago, and the museum founded to commemorate the life and work of Gilbert White, author of *The Natural History and Antiquities of Selborne*. The garden provides a very good example of how a person of modest means might construct a scaled-down landscaped park in the mid-18th century. The flower borders display plants and features described by White, including an arbour of laburnums, spacious lawns, a ha-ha and spacious views across the valley. *Jasminum humile*, old roses and hollyhocks are to the fore, while a tangle of perennials grows in beds cut out of the turf. The 'wild' garden, orchard and vegetable garden, with a 'wine pipe' and a herb garden, complete the idyll. The simplicity is very moving.
plants associated with Gilbert White; gift shop; tea parlour

Owned by Oates Memorial Trust
Number of gardeners 2, plus volunteers
Size 12ha (30 acres)

Hambledon House

HAMBLEDON HOUSE

Hambledon, Waterlooville PO7 4RU

Tel 023 9263 2380
Location In village centre, 8 miles south-west of Petersfield
Opening hours For NGS: 2pm to 5.30pm, 25 March, 22 April, 22 May, 15 and 16 June, 27 August and 16 September; and for groups by appointment
Admission fee Adults £3; children free

Hambledon House sits in a frost pocket on thin chalky soil, but Mrs Hart Dyke has created a garden which is thick with colour all through the year. She is a great plantswoman, but it is the placing of plants that interests her most. Brick and flint walls, and wonderful hedges of yew and box divide the garden into smaller areas; it is especially interesting for its unusual trees and shrubs. Colour, shape and form determine where plants look best: highlights include clematis, salvias, lavender, hardy geraniums, grasses and a great choice of herbaceous plants.
plants for plantsmen; good colour combinations; plants from garden for sale; home-made teas

Owned by Captain and Mrs David Hart Dyke
Number of gardeners owners only
Size 1ha (2 1/2 acres)

HARDY'S COTTAGE GARDEN PLANTS

Priory Lane, Freefolk, Whitchurch RG28 7NT

Tel 01256 896533 **Fax** 01256 896572
www.hardys-plants.co.uk
Location Off B3400 Whitchurch to Overton road: 1 1/2 mile on left, up Priory Lane, past Watership Down pub
Opening hours 10am to 5pm, daily, March to October; evening visits by appointment

This family-run nursery, started in 1987, offers over 1,200 different cottage garden perennials. Its attractive exhibits are a regular highlight of RHS shows, including Chelsea and Hampton Court. It is one of the best nurseries in southern England for a really wide choice of good plants – the sort you do not find in most garden centres.

Owned by Rosy and Rob Hardy

HEATHLANDS

47 Locks Road, Locks Heath, Southampton SO31 6NS

Tel 01489 573598 **Fax** 01489 557884
Location 2 miles from M27, Jct 9; Locks Road is main north-south road through middle of Locks Heath
Opening hours 2pm to 5.30pm, 4 March, 1 April, 6 May and 26 August
Admission fee Adults £3; children free

Since building his house in 1967, Dr Burwell has filled his acre of stony soil with a wonderful choice of immaculately grown plants of every type. It is the embodiment of careful plantsmanship, a garden to go round slowly – looking, studying and thinking. Your first sight is an 80m (262ft) line of *Paulownia tomentosa* grown from seed in about 1970, flowering (in May) all along the road and thought to be the longest line in England. Next comes *Garrya elliptica* trained as a small tree. Round the side of the house is a tall yew hedge, topped by a brooding topiary peacock. The design is a mixture of formal and informal, with a large number of different habitats. Under a canopy of light oak woodland thrives a shady fernery with orchids and *Rhododendron sinogrande*. *Ostrowskia magnifica* is planted against a wall of the house. Cyclamen and bulbs are everywhere. The climate is mild – the sea is less than two miles away – so there are hedges of griselinia, a plant of *Pittosporum* 'Garnettii' 5m (16ft) high, and *Cleyera japonica* growing in the open. The vegetable garden has a new cutting garden, and an area for standing pots. In a narrow alley between tall hedges of yew and rhododendron is the National Collection of Japanese Anemones. Dr Burwell will tell you that, though first described in 1695, they were not introduced (from mainland Asia) until the 1840s by Robert Fortune. The collection has about 40 cultivars, including a seedling which will shortly be introduced as 'Heathlands Ruby'.
many different habitats; a very wide range of plants of every kind; some good combinations of colour and form

Owned by Dr John Burwell
Number of gardeners owner, with help one day a week
Size 0.4ha (1 acre)
NCCPG National Collections *Anemone* (Japanese)

HIGHCLERE CASTLE

Highclere, Newbury RG20 9RN

Tel 01635 253210 **Fax** 01635 255315
www.highclerecastle.co.uk
Location South of Newbury off A34
Opening hours 11am to 4.30pm, Sunday to Thursday, 1 to 15 April and 1 July to 30 August; plus 6, 7, 28 and 29 May
Admission fee Gardens only: free

A major historic garden – when Capability Brown landscaped it in the 1770s he left intact the avenues and follies of the early 18th century, but the park is dominated now by hundreds of huge cedars. Jim Russell advised on the planting in the walled garden. The 'Secret Garden' is not among his best, but the espaliered medlars and quince trees are good.
rhododendrons and azaleas; herbaceous borders; good collection of cedars; long avenues; gift shop; self-service restaurant

Owned by The Earl of Carnarvon
Number of gardeners 2
Size 2400ha (6000 acres) of parkland
English Heritage Grade I

HINTON AMPNER

Bramdean, Alresford SO24 0LA

Tel 01962 771305 **Fax** 01962 793101
www.nationaltrust.org.uk
Location On A272, 1 mile west of Bramdean
Opening hours 11am to 5pm, Saturday to Wednesday, 17 March to 31 October; plus 6 April; and noon to 4pm on 1, 2, 8, 9, 15 and 16 December
Admission fee Adults £5.50; children £2.75

The gardens at Hinton Ampner were laid out by the scholarly Ralph Dutton in the middle of the 20th century with great regard to line, landscape and historical propriety. Statues, buildings, axes and views have been placed with exquisite judgement to lead you subtly along the exact route that Dutton intended. He was also careful to choose plants that would do well on chalk and then planted lots of them – using always the best forms: among them are buddlejas, lilacs, philadelphus, cotoneasters, weigelas and shrub roses. It is one of England's best mid-20th-century gardens, maintained to a high specification. The Trust has now begun to restore the old walled garden and visitors are welcome to see the work in progress.
topiary; daffodils; yew trees; good plants; teas and home-made cakes

Owned by The National Trust
Number of gardeners 3
Size 5ha (12½ acres)
English Heritage Grade II

HOUGHTON LODGE

Stockbridge SO20 6LQ

Tel 01264 810502 **Fax** 01264 810063
www.houghtonlodge.co.uk
Location Off A30 at Stockbridge; well signed
Opening hours 10am to 5pm, Wednesdays (and other days by appointment), March to October
Admission fee Garden and Hydroponicum: £5; groups at special rates; children free

Houghton is a lovely, 18th-century Gothic *cottage ornée* on a ledge above the River Test, with long spacious views down the river and across the water meadows. Part of the BBC's *David Copperfield* was shot here. In the traditional walled garden are espaliered fruit trees, herbs, a glasshouse filled with tropical orchids and a topiary known as the snorting dragon. The owner has been restoring the 18th-century shrubbery: this means clearing seedling trees to open up the view across the river and replanting with trees and shrubs which were grown there 200 years ago. Houghton also boasts the leading hydroponic greenhouse in England, where plants are grown in nutrient-rich solutions instead of soil – salad vegetables and herbs, as well as bougainvilleas and bananas. The garden makes a great effort to be educational and entertaining. Mown paths through the water meadows bring you up close to the natural flora of chalk valleys.
plants under glass; daffodils; cyclamen; topiary snorting dragon; refreshments; windfall apples (free!)

THE SIR HAROLD HILLIER GARDENS

Jermyns Lane, Ampfield, Romsey SO51 0QA

Tel 01794 368787 **Fax** 01794 368027
www.hilliergardens.org.uk
Location Signed from A3090 and A3057
Opening hours 10am to 6pm (dusk if earlier), daily, except 25 and 26 December
Admission fee Adults £7.50; concessions £6.50; children (under 16) free

Ignore the word 'gardens': this is quite the most important modern arboretum in the UK. It has the greatest collection of wild and cultivated woody plants in the world: over 12,000 taxa in 180 acres, totalling 42,000 plants. The arboretum was established in 1953 by the late Sir Harold Hillier: Hillier's Nursery aimed at the time to offer for sale every cultivar of every tree or shrub that was hardy in the British Isles. Sir Harold himself was an active importer and collector of new species from all over the world, at a time (of relative economic depression) when few British horticulturists had the impetus to look outside the United Kingdom for plants of any kind. Every part of the arboretum is an education and a pleasure, whatever the season or weather. It has so many unique features that the visitor needs all day to see more than a fraction of its riches: the collection of poplar trees called the Populetum; more than 100 pines (*Pinus* species), including the 'big cone' pine *P. coulteri* whose cones may weigh as much as 2kg; a maple valley; the largest winter garden of its kind in Europe and a Gurkha memorial garden. But it is the sheer number of trees and shrubs here that makes the most lasting impression: every time you visit, and wherever you walk, you see interesting plants that you have never seen before. The labelling is exemplary and a helpful guide is available. Hillier Plant Centre shares a car park with the arboretum. Details of seasonal special events, workshops, evening talks, guided tours and children's activities can be obtained on request.
a plantsman's collection of trees and shrubs; mature conifers; good mixed borders; 51 record trees, including 11 *Sorbus*; plant centre; gift shop; restaurant

Owned by Hampshire County Council
Number of gardeners 14, plus volunteers
Size 72ha (180 acres)
NCCPG National Collections *Carpinus*; *Cornus*; *Corylus*; *Cotoneaster*; *Hamamelis*; *Ligustrum*; *Lithocarpus*; *Photinia*; *Pinus* (excl dwarf cvs.); *Quercus*; 'Hillier' plants

Owned by Martin Busk
Number of gardeners 3 part-time
Size 7.2ha (18 acres)
English Heritage Grade II*

LANGLEY BOXWOOD NURSERY
Langley Lane, Rake, Liss GU33 7JN

Tel 01730 894467 **Fax** 01730 894703
www.boxwood.co.uk
Location 5 miles north of Petersfield; ring for map or directions (B2070)
Opening hours 8am to 4.30pm, Monday to Friday; 10am to 4pm, Saturdays
Admission fee Free

These specialist growers of box have a comprehensive range of box plants for hedging, edging and topiary. There are over 50 cultivars of *Buxus* in their delightful catalogue, and some yew *Taxus* also. Both are available in a wide variety of topiary shapes, from simple balls to complex crowns and animals, and (given sufficient notice) they will create individual designs. Rare free-form specimens are also offered.
box, yew and evergreen topiary

Owned by Russell Coates
Number of gardeners 7
Size 2ha (5 acres)
NCCPG National Collections *Buxus*

LITTLE COURT
Crawley, Winchester SO21 2PU

Tel 01962 776365 **Fax** 01962 776842
Location On main street through Crawley village, 300 yards from church or pond
Opening hours 2pm to 5.30pm, 11, 18 to 21 February, 1 and 2 April, 1 and 30 May, 21 and 24 June (for eremurus display), 9 September; plus 17, 19, 24 and 26 February 2008; and by appointment at other times
Admission fee Adults £3; children free

Little Court fits a lot into its three acres: the design allows for several distinct areas which are linked by spacious vistas and judiciously placed seats to emphasise the many views and axes. A sunken lawn, flint walls, orchards, fine trees, a copse (with a large tree house), a grass labyrinth, and a 'proper' old-fashioned kitchen garden are some of the features. The plantings are colour-themed, but some plants (like cyclamen and *Crocus tommasinianus*) have naturalised, too. The range of herbaceous plants is fairly impressive, especially hellebores, clematis and hardy geraniums. There is much to be learned and enjoyed here.
plantsman's plants; herbaceous perennials; teas

Owned by Professor and Mrs AR Elkington
Number of gardeners 1 part-time
Size 1.2ha (3 acres)

MACPENNYS NURSERIES
154 Burley Road, Bransgore, Christchurch BH23 8DB

Tel 01425 672348
www.macpennys.co.uk
Location On the Burley road, on north-west edge of Bransgore
Opening hours 9am to 5pm, Monday to Saturday; 10am to 5pm, Sundays and Bank Holidays; closed at Christmas and New Year
Admission fee Donation to NGS

This long-established nursery ('old-fashioned' in the best sense) has a reliable general range across the plant spectrum, plus a few rarities. It is particularly good for conifers, rhododendrons and shrubs. The large woodland garden next to the nursery is open for the National Gardens Scheme and full of interesting plants. Many have grown to a considerable size. The garden is perhaps at its best in late spring, when the rhododendrons and azaleas overlap with the last camellias.

Owned by Mr and Mrs TM Lowndes
Size 1.6ha (4 acres)

THE MANOR HOUSE
Upton Grey, Basingstoke RG25 2RD

Tel 01256 862827 **Fax** 01256 861035
www.gertrudejekyllgarden.co.uk

LONGSTOCK WATER GARDENS

Longstock, Stockbridge SO20 6EH

Tel 01264 810894/01264 810904 **Fax** 01264 810924
www.longstockpark.co.uk
Location 1½ miles north-east of Longstock village
Opening hours 2pm to 5pm, first and third Sundays in the month, April to September
Admission fee Adults £4; children 50p

Longstock has quite the most extraordinary and beautiful water garden in England, a little Venice where dozens of islands and all-but-islands are linked by an apparently endless number of small bridges and intensely planted with water-loving plants: drifts of astilbes, primulas, kingcups, hemerocallis, musks, water irises and lilies. The ground is so soft that the islands seem to float, and a remarkable accumulation of peat has allowed such calcifuge plants as *Meconopsis betonicifolia* to flourish in this chalky valley. But the garden as a whole has an exceptional variety of habitats: parts are very dry. A seam of acid soil supports a collection of *Rhododendron orbiculare* and *R. williamsianum* cultivars and their hybrids like 'Temple Belle'. Around the perimeter are swamp cypresses and liquidambars: further away are oaks and Scots pines. On the other side of the road lies the splendid arboretum, open at the same time and with a vast collection of well-spaced specimen trees now approaching the prime of their life. Both the water gardens and the arboretum are open only rarely, so that they can be maintained principally for the benefit of partners of John Lewis, but up at the top, along a wooded drive, is an excellent nursery which is open daily throughout the year. It specialises in rare trees and shrubs, but also has a constantly changing stock of other interesting plants. Nearby is a beautiful, long pergola of fruit and clematis, and the National Collection of *Buddleja*. Every part of the Longstock estate – water gardens, arboretum, nursery and walled garden – are models of their kind, beautifully maintained and in top condition.

plantsman's collection of plants; good herbaceous borders; arboretum

Owned by John Lewis Partnership
Number of gardeners 3 at water garden; 3 in arboretum
Size 4ha (10 acres) of water garden; 26ha (65 acres) in arboretum
NCCPG National Collections *Buddleja*; *Clematis viticella*

Meon Orchard

Location In Upton Grey village above and beside the church
Opening hours By appointment only: 9am to 4pm, Monday to Friday, April to July
Admission fee £5, to include a copy of the guidebook and complete plant list; groups of 20+ receive a personal guided tour and tea/coffee at £5 each

Ros Wallinger has restored this Jekyll garden since 1984 using the original planting plans (now at Berkeley University, California, though copies are on display at Upton Grey). She has gone to great pains to recreate it exactly in all its Edwardian loveliness. In the wild garden, grass paths meander through wildflowers, rambling roses, shrubs and walnut trees to a water lily pond. In the formal garden the rich herbaceous borders drift from cool blues, white and pinks at either end to hot reds, oranges and yellows in the middle. There is no better place to study Gertrude Jekyll's plantings, but what makes it so special is that it is a 'young' garden again. And the restoration continues. Read more about it in Ros Wallinger's *Gertrude Jekyll's Lost Garden* (Garden Art Press, 2000).
roses (mainly old-fashioned and climbers); good herbaceous borders; refreshments for groups

Owned by Mrs John Wallinger
Number of gardeners 1, plus very keen owners
Size 2ha (5 acres)
English Heritage Grade II

MEON ORCHARD

Kingsmead, Wickham, Fareham PO17 5AU

Tel/fax 01329 833253
Location A32 north from Wickham for 1½ miles; left at Roebuck; ½ mile on left; well signed on open days
Opening hours 2pm to 6pm, 3 June and 29 July; plus 2pm to 6pm on 2 September for NCCPG and specialist nursery plant sale; groups welcome by appointment
Admission fee Adults £3

This stylish garden is a plantaholic paradise. The emphasis is upon difficult and tender plants which look their best in late summer. An extraordinary number of plants survive the winter outside with a little protection: bananas, hedychiums, *Impatiens tinctoria* and *Dahlia imperialis*, for example. The Smiths bought the property in 1986 and designed the garden as a series of interlinking paths and glades which radiate out and give the whole layout the impression of being much larger than it really is. It is not a quiet or refined garden, but exuberant and experimental, full of dramatic plants and contrasts. The 40 or so *Eucalyptus* species in their National Collection have grown quickly and give the garden an air of maturity. The speed has been extraordinary; a *Eucalyptus nitens*, planted a mere 10 years ago is now a staggering 22m (70ft) tall. Cordylines, Italian cypresses and *Ligustrum japonicum* 'Rotundifolium' also recur throughout the garden and bind it together. In 2005, an overgrown bed of cypresses was cleared, allowing further planting of wild-sourced and hybrid *Podocarpus*, plus additions to their collection of *Araliaceae*, especially of *Pseudopanax*. These two collections were both awarded official National Collection status in 2005. A vast number of pots are planted out for the summer or grouped together. Some may be put in a strategic position for only a few weeks while their flowers associate well with another plant. The owners' plantsmanship is very broad and encompasses hardy plants and alpines, too: a laburnum hedge as you come down the drive, bulbs of every kind, a quincunx of Japanese anemones, a water garden, a pond and hundreds of hardy trees and shrubs. This is a most imaginative and creative garden to visit for ideas about what to grow and how to display it.
southern hemisphere plants; tea/coffee and biscuits

Owned by Dr DJ and Mrs LA Smith
Number of gardeners owners, plus 3 hours' help a week
Size 0.6ha (1½ acres)
NCCPG National Collections *Eucalyptus*; *Podocarpaceae*; *Araliaceae*

MOTTISFONT ABBEY

Mottisfont, Romsey SO51 0LP

Tel 01794 340757 **Fax** 01794 341492
www.nationaltrust.org.uk
Location 4½ miles north-west of Romsey
Opening hours 11am to 4pm, Saturdays and Sundays, 1 to 18 March; 11am to 5pm, Saturday to Wednesday and Good Friday, 19 March to 27 May and 3 September to

Mottisfont Abbey

28 October; 11am to 5pm, daily, 28 May to 1 June; 11am to 8.30pm, daily, 2 June to 1 July for roses; 11am to 6pm, Saturday to Thursday, 2 July to 2 September
Admission fee Adults £7.50 (£8 in June rose season); children £3.80
Owned by The National Trust
Number of gardeners 4
Size 11.1ha (28 acres)
NCCPG National Collections *Platanus*; *Rosa*
English Heritage Grade II

The park and gardens near the house are stately: Russell Page, Geoffrey Jellicoe and Norah Lindsay all worked here. A broad chalk spring surges out in the grounds and runs down to feed the River Test. One of the London planes *Platanus* x *hispanica* near the river has two huge trunks fused together, though nobody can work out whether the two stems are on the same roots. But it is the old rose collection in the walled garden which has made Mottisfont's name. It is Graham Stuart Thomas's best-known work, a collection of all the roses he discovered, assembled, preserved and made popular through his writings. Mottisfont is surely the loveliest rose garden in Britain.
roses (mainly old-fashioned and climbers); good herbaceous borders; guided walks and 'rose clinics' in season; tallest *Platanus* x *hispanica* (42m; 138ft) in the British Isles; good shop selling books; licensed restaurant

SIR GEORGE STAUNTON COUNTRY PARK
Middle Park Way, Havant PO9 5HB

Tel 023 9245 3405 **Fax** 023 9249 8156
www.hants.gov.uk/countryside/staunton
Location North of Havant on B2149
Opening hours Glasshouses: 10am to 5pm (4pm in winter), daily, all year; park: dawn to dusk, daily, except 25 December
Admission fee Adults £5; concessions £4.10; children £3.60; parkland free; prices to be reviewed in April 2007

The historic heart of this landscape garden is a Regency walled garden, pleasure grounds and *ferme ornée*, but the local authority has also restored and developed the Victorian

glasshouses as an educational resource. Here you can see useful plants like tea, coffee, pineapple, coconut palms, papyrus and rice plants, as well as such ornamentals as passion flowers, sarracenias, *Nepenthes* and strelitzias. Recent additions include a Golden Jubilee maze and puzzle garden.
Chinese bridge; good trees; shell house; lakes; Regency farm; Victorian glasshouses; tea room; light lunches and refreshments

Owned by Hampshire County Council
English Heritage Grade II*

SPINNERS
Boldre, Lymington SO41 5QE

Tel 01590 673347
Location Signed off A337 between Brockenhurst and Lymington
Opening hours 10am to 5pm, Tuesday to Saturday, 1 April to 14 September; nursery and part of garden open all year, but only by appointment in December and January
Admission fee £2.50 from 1 April to 14 September; free at other times; RHS members free at all times

Only two acres, but what a garden! Spinners is a plantsman's paradise, where the enthusiast can spend many happy hours browsing at any time of the year. The habitat plantings and plant associations are particularly interesting to study. Much of the garden is light woodland, so it has good collections of hydrangeas, lilies, hostas, rodgersias and ferns. Peter Chappell's nursery sells an extraordinary range of good plants: you always come away with a bootful of novelties. Trilliums are one of the nursery's specialities: they include such rarities as *T. chloropetalum*. The list of magnolias is perhaps even more impressive: over 80 cultivars, including a great range of *M. acuminata* hybrids, Gresham hybrids and the new *M. stellata* x *liliiflora* hybrids, as well as such introductions as *M.* x *loebneri* 'Pirouette' and *M.* x *loebneri* 'Donna'.
woodland garden; an important plantsman's garden; fine collection of trees; rhododendrons; magnolias; woodland plants; rarities and novelties; new peat beds and bog garden; biggest *Eucalyptus perriniana* in the British Isles

Owned by Peter Chappell
Number of gardeners several part-time helpers
Size 1ha (21/2 acres)

STRATFIELD SAYE HOUSE
Stratfield Saye, Basingstoke RG7 2BZ

Tel 01256 882882 **Fax** 01256 881466
www.stratfield-saye.co.uk
Location 1 mile west of A33 between Reading and Basingstoke
Opening hours 11.30am to 5pm (last admissions 3.30pm), daily, 5 to 10 April and 5 to 30 July; plus groups by prior arrangement
Admission fee Garden only: £3 (weekdays); £3.50 (weekends)

Not a famous garden, but there are some fine incidents: a huge kitchen garden, a large and cheerful rose garden, rhododendrons in the park, and magnificent trees, including wellingtonias, named after the Iron Duke.
tallest Hungarian oak *Quercus frainetto* (33m; 108ft) in the British Isles; gift shop; light refreshments

Owned by The Duke of Wellington
Number of gardeners 2
English Heritage Grade II

TUDOR HOUSE GARDEN
Bugle Street, Southampton SO14 2AD

Tel 023 8063 5904 **Fax** 023 8033 9601
www.southampton.gov.uk/leisure
Location Bugle Street runs parallel to the High Street in the old town
Opening hours By arrangement for groups
Admission fee Free

The house and garden are both closed for urgent repair to the house, but are due to reopen in phases from 2008. Pre-booked groups can however still be accommodated. Sylvia Landsberg's reconstruction of a Tudor garden has a knot garden, a fountain, a secret garden and contemporary plantings of herbs and flowering plants all crammed into a tiny area.
Tudor-style knot garden; herbs

Owned by Southampton City Council
Number of gardeners 1
Size 30m x 30m (100ft x 100ft)

TYLNEY HALL

Rotherwick, Hook RG27 9AZ

Tel 01256 764881 **Fax** 01256 768141
www.tylneyhall.com
Location 3 miles north-west of Hook
Opening hours For NGS and hotel guests
Admission fee NGS: adults £3; children free

Gertrude Jekyll collaborated with Seldon Wornum in the design and planting of the Italian garden and water garden at Tylney. Both have been meticulously restored and maintained by the modern owners of the house, now a luxury hotel. The rose pergola has been rebuilt, the iris border replanted. The water garden with its lakes, streams, stepping stones, kiosk and water-loving plants is of extraordinary beauty. In the woods are rhododendrons, fine trees and a magnificent avenue of wellingtonias.
Jekyll design; restaurant

Owned by Elite Hotels
Number of gardeners 7
Size 26.4ha (66 acres)
English Heritage Grade II*

THE VYNE

Sherborne St John, Basingstoke RG24 9HL

Tel 01256 883858 **Fax** 01256 881720
www.nationaltrust.org.uk
Location 4 miles north of Basingstoke
Opening hours 11am to 5pm, Saturdays and Sundays, 4 February to 18 March; 11am to 5pm, Saturday to Wednesday, and Good Friday, 24 March to 28 October
Admission fee Adults £5; children £2.50

This historic garden has many fine features, including a 17th-century summerhouse which is said to be the earliest domed garden building in England. The horticultural interest lies in its fine old trees, an avenue of red-twigged limes, walnuts, and a venerable tree known as the 'Hundred Guinea Oak' because that was the price which a passing timber merchant offered for it nearly 200 years ago. In the 1960s, Graham Stuart Thomas added herbaceous borders and old shrub roses.
herbaceous borders; annuals; good trees; wild garden; restaurant

Owned by The National Trust
Number of gardeners 21/2
Size 5ha (121/2 acres)
English Heritage Grade II

WATER MEADOW NURSERY AND HERB FARM

Cheriton, Alresford SO24 0QB

Tel 01962 771895 **Fax** 01962 771985
www.plantaholic.co.uk
Location Just off A272, on B3046 to Alresford
Opening hours 10am to 5pm, Wednesday to Saturday, March to July; Fridays and Saturdays, August to October; and by appointment
Admission fee Garden: adults £2.50; nursery: free

The display garden is beautifully laid out with many of the unusual plants in the nursery's list. As well as a long herbaceous border, there are bog gardens and damp gardens, water lily canals and a wildflower meadow. The National Collection of *Papaver orientale* has more than 100 cultivars and is augmented by many of the nursery's so-called 'Super Poppies'. These are displayed in a continuous planting that they call the 'Poppy Necklace'. The owners run several 'Poppy Days' in May and June with walks and talks about the collection. Agapanthus are another speciality, and the nursery has recently embarked on a very promising breeding programme; unnamed seedlings of agapanthus and poppies are displayed in a special trials ground. Photographers are always welcome.

Owned by Roy and Sandy Worth
Number of gardeners 2 part-time
Size 1ha (21/2 acres)
NCCPG National Collections *Papaver orientale*

WEST GREEN HOUSE

Hartley Wintney, Basingstoke RG27 8JB

Tel/fax 01252 844611
www.westgreenhouse.co.uk
Location In West Green village; follow brown tourist signs
Opening hours 11am to 4.30pm, Wednesday to Sunday, and Bank Holiday Mondays, 6 April to 30 September
Admission fee Adults £5; Children £2.50

West Green house is 1720s, brick and ashlar, with classical busts along its garden façade. It looks onto a plain lawn, whose sides are hedged in yew and hornbeam, running gently up to a woodland. This 'theatre lawn' is used for concerts and dramatic performances, with the house as a baroque backdrop. Marylyn Abbott took a 99-year tenancy of West Green from the National Trust in 1993. The previous tenant was Lord McAlpine, who employed Quinlan Terry to create a modern Elysium which was pretty enough in its way, but nothing like as good as the garden that Marylyn Abbott has now made. His garden was already going back when McAlpine left in 1990, so Abbott found the seats, and other structures buried in four or five years of undergrowth. Taming the inherited jungle was only a beginning: what the garden needed was vision, knowledge, taste, energy, expertise and imagination. Marylyn Abbott had all those qualities. She learned her gardening in New South Wales, where her garden at Mittagong is the most visited in Australia. She found the quality of the light in England so different from Australia that she made a special study of its effects upon colour in the garden. Her book *Gardening with Light and Colour* is a modern classic. It is in the mellow, 18th-century walled kitchen garden that Marylyn Abbott's sense of design and colour finds its fullest expression. Here, within neat clipped box hedges, the borders overflow with plants in stunning colour combinations that change from year to year and throughout the seasons. Elegant trellis-work fruit cages and attractive terracotta pots draw you up to the *potager* where fruit and vegetables are grown in a decorative way – always ornamental but never chi-chi. A grand water staircase (inherited from McAlpine but much improved by Abbott) provides a focal point to the nymphaeum designed by Quinlan Terry. West Green has many other features which are original and inspirational. By the house is a charming small topiary garden – anyone could copy it – where water lilies flourish in small water tanks sunk in the ground. It runs up to a handsome aviary inhabited by unusual breeds of bantams and chickens. Beyond, are a dramatic new Persian water garden in a woodland glade, a newly restored lake, more follies and fancies, new walks and massive plantings – 10,000 lilies, for example, snowdrops, daffodils and fritillaries. Lavishness is a hallmark of the Abbott style – 20,000 tulip bulbs are planted every year – but she also emphasises the importance of drama, colour, innovation and humour in the garden. The lessons for the visitor are endless: you cannot fail to be inspired, cheered, amused and delighted by this extraordinary garden.
exuberant plantings; colour combinations; woodland garden; parterre; great sense of style; new nursery; restaurant

Owned by Marylyn Abbott
Number of gardeners 4
Size 3.2ha (8 acres)

HEREFORDSHIRE

There is, of course, no such county as Herefordshire – not any more. It was dissolved in 1974, when the old county was linked to its neighbour as 'Hereford & Worcester'. This was never a popular union, and Herefordshire people were always quick to point out that they retained their own identity and Lord Lieutenant. Herefordshire is now a District Council but, so distinct does it consider itself, that we list it as a county again. It is a pity that so few of its historic gardens are open to the public. Hergest Croft has by far the most important collection of trees, with a large number of 'record-breakers' among them; Eastnor Castle also has some magnificent conifers, the largest of their kind in England. There are comparatively few top-class modern gardens – Arrow Cottage is a memorable exception (as is Sir Roy Strong's private garden at Much Birch) – and the county does not do conspicuously well for the National Gardens Scheme. Likewise, it has comparatively few National Collections and National Collection holders and no RHS Partner Colleges. But good nurseries exist – Kenchester Water Gardens is one of the best – and the extensive fruit orchards testify to the county's suitability for horticulture. The NCCPG group has worked with the Marcher Apple Network to identify old trees, propagate them and establish new orchards to preserve them.

ABBEY DORE COURT GARDEN

Abbey Dore, Hereford HR2 0AD

Tel/fax 01981 240419
www.abbeydorecourt.co.uk
Location 3 miles west of A465, midway between Hereford and Abergavenny
Opening hours 11am to 5.30pm, Tuesdays, Thursdays, Saturdays and Sundays and Bank Holidays, 1 April to 1 October
Admission fee Adults £3.50; children 50p

This is a splendid plant-lover's garden on a difficult site, with fine borders leading down to the ferny river walk and a meadow on the other side planted with interesting trees. Mrs Ward says her 'rambling garden' has 'stopped getting any bigger', but the truth is that the garden grows, changes and improves with every visit. The walled garden now has nine different herbaceous borders, as well as clematis arches and a great number of pathways. Mrs Ward recently took in another acre of field – bamboos, trees, shrubs and more perennials than ever: very exciting.

good herbaceous borders; handsome wellingtonias; ferns; hellebores; good nursery; restaurant

Owned by Mrs Charis Ward
Number of gardeners 1
Size 2.4ha (6 acres)

ARROW COTTAGE

Ledgemoor, Weobley HR4 8RN

Tel 01344 622181
www.arrowcottagegarden.co.uk
Location 1 mile from Weobley: off Wormsley road, signed Ledgemoor and second right, first house on left
Opening hours 11am (1pm on Saturdays) to 4pm, Wednesdays and Friday to Sunday, May to August
Admission fee Adults £3.50; children £1

Arrow Cottage was made in the 1990s by Lance Hattatt, a garden stylist who specialised in contemporary design, with a penchant for the surrealist. There are 24 garden rooms of immense variety, but all exhibit a large measure of plantsmanship. All are maintained to the highest standard. The keen plantsman will find *Baptisia tasmanica* flourishing outside, and pots of *Agapanthus africanus* along the rill in summer. The Martins are starting to stamp their own ideas on the garden while always retaining its unique charm

and character. They created a new gravel garden in 2006, and have carefully opened out some fine views to the distant hills.

good herbaceous borders; stream; wildflower orchard; 50m (164ft) yew-enclosed rill; good plants throughout; old roses; refreshments and light lunches

Owned by David and Janet Martin
Size 0.8ha (2 acres)

AULDEN FARM

Aulden, Leominster HR6 0JJ

Tel 01568 720129
www.auldenfarm.co.uk
Location 4miles south-west of Leominster, near Ivington
Opening hours 10am to 5pm, Tuesdays and Thursdays, April to August; plus Thursdays in March and September; for NGS: 2pm to 5.30pm, 29 April, 27 May; 1 July, 26 August
Admission fee Adults £2.50; children free

The garden at Aulden Farm is an adjunct to a promising young nursery – both were started in 1997. Irises are very well represented, with *I. ensata* cultivars along the edge of a dry stream and *I. sibirica* around a pond. But the hemerocallis collection is also very extensive and, because the owners are enthusiastic plantsmen, there is always lots to see at every season.

irises; hemerocallis; nursery; teas by arrangement for groups

Owned by Alun and Jill Whitehead
Number of gardeners owners only
Size 1.2ha (3 acres)

THE BANNUT

Bringsty, Bromyard WR6 5TA

Tel/fax 01885 482206
www.bannut.co.uk
Location On A44, 2½ miles east of Bromyard
Opening hours 12.30pm to 5pm, Wednesdays, Saturdays, Sundays and Bank Holidays, Easter to September
Admission fee Adults £3; children £1.50

Unlike many plantsman's gardens, the plants at The Bannut have been used to great decorative effect. The best example is the knot garden made

from the contrasting leaf colours of different heathers, though the Everetts are fond of all heathers and grow a large number (over 10,000) in the summer heather garden. They are, however, interested in all types of plants and how to display them in the garden. The beds and borders are planted for colour harmonies and contrasts, mainly of herbaceous plants near the house, but with more shrubs towards the little copse where cowslips flower in spring. Near the house are a formal yellow and white garden and an 'arbour garden' in silver, pink and blue. An old paddock is now planted with rhododendrons, azaleas, camellias and pieris, plus hydrangeas for late-summer interest. Recent additions include a laburnum and clematis walk and a 'secret' garden, with water features and a willow house. The standard of maintenance throughout is excellent and the owners make a point of telling visitors that the garden is wheelchair-friendly and that there are plenty of seats from which to enjoy vistas.
over 300 different heathers; colour-themed plantings; island beds of shrubs and herbaceous plants; knot garden; cowslips; light lunches; teas

Owned by Maurice and Daphne Everett
Number of gardeners owners, plus part-time help
Size 1ha (2½ acres)

BERRINGTON HALL
Leominster HR6 0DW

Tel 01568 615721 **Fax** 01568 613263
www.nationaltrust.org.uk
Location On A49, 3 miles north of Leominster
Opening hours 11am to 5pm, Saturday to Wednesday and Good Friday, 19 March to 4 November; plus weekends only from 3 March to 18 March and from 1 to 16 December
Admission fee Adults £4.20; children £2.10

This majestic park is classic Capability Brown. The National Trust has laid out a one-mile parkland walk which takes in the best vantage points and shows you how the landscape would have looked when young. The pleasure gardens around the house are Victorian – laurel walks and an avenue of golden yews. In the old walled garden, the Hereford & Marches Historic Apple Collection is supplemented by old pear varieties, quinces and medlars.
classic parkland; apples and pears; National Trust shop; licensed tea room for lunch and teas

Owned by The National Trust
Number of gardeners 2
Size 4.6ha (11½ acres)
English Heritage Grade II*

EASTNOR CASTLE
Eastnor, Ledbury HR8 1RL

Tel 01531 633160 **Fax** 01531 631776
www.eastnorcastle.com
Location 2 miles east of Ledbury on A438 Tewkesbury road
Opening hours 11am to 4.30pm, 5 to 9 April, then on Sundays and Bank Holiday Mondays to 30 September; also daily except Saturdays from 16 July to 31 August
Admission fee Adults £3.30; OAPs £2.50; children £1.50

Eastnor is all about trees. The arboretum planted by Lord Somers from 1852 to 1883 is now mature, and full of champion specimens. Many are rare, including a tall American beech (*Fagus grandifolia*) and an enormous red hickory (*Carya ovalis*). It is, however, the conifers which dominate the setting for the neo-Norman castle, largely because they were planted so thickly and in such great numbers. Miles Hadfield wrote that Eastnor was 'embowered by vast conifers – plantations which spill out into the surrounding hills and fields'. Quite apart from the many hundreds of cedars, the record-breaking specimens include the Shensi fir (*Abies chensiensis*), the purple-coned fir (*Picea purpurea*) from south-east China, and *Pinus hartwegii* from Mexico. The rest of the garden is less interesting, but tree-lovers will find Eastnor a real treat.
mature conifers; fine collection of trees; spring bulbs; tallest deodar *Cedrus deodara* (38m; 125ft) in the British Isles, plus 11 more record trees; souvenirs and gift shop; lunches and teas

Owned by James Hervey-Bathurst
Number of gardeners 2
Size 16ha (40 acres)
English Heritage Grade II*

HERGEST CROFT GARDENS
Kington HR5 3EG

Tel 01544 230160 **Fax** 01544 232031
www.hergest.co.uk
Location Signed from A44
Opening hours Noon to 5.30pm, daily, 1 April to 29 October
Admission fee Adults £5.50; children free. RHS members free except in May and June

Hergest Croft is an extremely important woodland garden and arboretum around an Edwardian house. It has over 4,000 rare trees and shrubs, but there seems no end to the garden's marvels: huge conifers, magnificent birches, scores of interesting oaks, many acres of billowing rhododendrons – Hergest Croft is one of the best rhododendron gardens in Britain. But it is also worth visiting for its double herbaceous borders, alpine collections, roses, autumn gentians and kitchen garden, all on a scale that most of us have forgotten.
fine collection of trees; rhododendrons; tallest *Cercidiphyllum japonicum* (25m; 82ft) in the British Isles, among some 50 record trees; gift shop; home-made teas

Owned by WL Banks
Number of gardeners 6
Size 22ha (56 acres)
NCCPG National Collections {*Acer*}; {*Betula*}; {*Zelkova*}
English Heritage Grade II*

HOW CAPLE COURT
How Caple, Hereford HR1 4SX

Tel 01989 740626 **Fax** 01989 740611
www.howcaplecourt.com
Location Signed on B4224 and A449 junction
Opening hours 10am to 5pm, daily, 12 March to 14 October
Admission fee Adults £3; children free

Spectacular formal gardens laid out about 100 years ago (some Italianate, others more Arts & Crafts), and now undergoing restoration. Pergolas, loggias, dramatic terraces and *giardini segreti* with stunning views across a lushly wooded valley. How Caple is a garden of national importance, but little known even locally.
mature conifers; Italian terraces surrounded by restored pergolas; old roses; topiary; woodland gardens; stable shop; tea room

Owned by Mr and Mrs Roger Lee
Number of gardeners 1
Size 4.4ha (11 acres)

IVY CROFT
Ivington Green, Leominster HR6 0JA

Tel 01568 720344
www.ivycroft.freeserve.co.uk
Location Halfway between Ivington and Coldharbour, on north side of road
Opening hours 9am to 4pm, Thursdays, April to September; and by appointment at other times; for NGS: 2pm to 5.30pm, 22 April, 27 May, 1 July, 26 August and 16 September; plus 9am to 4pm on 7, 14, 21 and 28 February 2008
Admission fee Adults £2.50; Children free

Ivy Croft is a plantsman's garden, with a strong line in willows, snowdrops and cyclamen – and therefore especially good in late winter. But there is colour and interest at every season, and the nursery is always worth a visit.
nursery

Owned by Sue and Roger Norman
Number of gardeners owners, plus 2 part-time
Size 0.8ha (2 acres)

KENCHESTER WATER GARDENS

Church Road, Lyde, Hereford HR1 3AB

Tel 01432 270981 **Fax** 01432 342243
Location On A49, 1 mile north of Hereford
Opening hours 9am to 6pm (5.30pm from October to March), daily, all year; 10.30am to 4.30pm on Sundays; closed Christmas Day
Admission fee Free

The gardens and the nursery at Kenchester are equally important for anyone interested in water plants. The range of plants grown and offered for sale is excellent, and includes nearly 210 cultivars of *Nymphaea*, of which they have a National Collection. The gardens have pools and ponds over a large area. This is a dynamic nursery which is getting bigger and better all the time.
water plants and water gardens; light lunches and teas

Owned by Mr and Mrs MR Edwards
Number of gardeners 2
Size 2.4ha (6 acres)
NCCPG National Collections *Nymphaea*

KINGSTONE COTTAGE PLANTS

Weston under Penyard, Ross-on-Wye HR9 7PH

Tel 01989 565267
Location Off A40, north of Weston under Penyard, on road to Rudhall
Opening hours 10am to 5pm, Sunday to Friday, 7 May to 6 July; and by appointment
Admission fee Adults £2 for NGS

The main feature of this garden is its National Collection of old *Dianthus*, some 140 cultivars, which flower in early summer. This is the place to see such rarities as *D.* 'Fenbow Nutmeg Clove' and *D.* 'Cranborne Seedling'. Mr and Mrs Hughes also sell plants which they have propagated from their collection – the best way to promote a wider interest in old cultivars and guarantee their future survival. But there is much more to see as well as the pinks, including a sunken terrace garden, a large pond and a grotto.
ponds; grotto; summerhouse; pinks

Owned by Michael and Sophie Hughes
Number of gardeners 2
Size 0.8ha (2 acres)
NCCPG National Collections *Dianthus*

MOORS MEADOW

Collington, Bromyard HR7 4LZ

Tel 01885 410318
www.moorsmeadow.co.uk
Location 4 miles north of Bromyard on B4214
Opening hours 11am to 5pm, Friday to Tuesday, March to September
Admission fee Adults £4; children £1

Ros Bissell recently took over the plantsman's garden that her parents began in 1955. The real horticultural interest starts just behind the house – a remarkable collection of trees, shrubs, rhododendrons, grasses and bulbs, mainly in a woodland setting, with newer, extensive plantings in the meadows. All the plants sold in the small nursery are propagated from the garden itself. The richness of its plantings means that there is much to see at every season.
plant nursery

Owned by Ros Bissell
Number of gardeners 2
Size 2.8ha (7 acres)

THE PICTON GARDEN

Old Court Nurseries, Walwyn Road, Colwall, Malvern WR13 6QE

Tel 01684 540416
www.autumnasters.co.uk
Location 3 miles west of Great Malvern; 5 miles east of Ledbury on B4218
Opening hours 11am to 5pm, Wednesday to Sunday, August; and daily from 1 September to mid-October; thereafter by prior appointment only
Admission fee Adults £3 for NGS (in 2006)

The Picton Garden at Old Court Nurseries holds the National Collection of Michaelmas daisies (*Aster*). This is also the nurseries' speciality: the extensive collection is fully described in Paul Picton's excellent book *The Gardener's Guide to Growing Asters* (1999). When the Michaelmas daisies are in flower, the banks of colour, graded for height, recall the grandest of Edwardian gardens and the Picton Garden becomes one of the great showpieces of English horticulture. There are many other interesting perennials and cottagey plants here, some arranged in 'prairie-style' plantings.
magnificent collection of asters; herbaceous plants

Owned by Paul and Meriel Picton
Number of gardeners 2
Size 0.6ha (1½ acres)
NCCPG National Collections *Aster* (autumn-flowering)

QUEEN'S WOOD ARBORETUM & COUNTRY PARK

Dinmore Hill, Leominster HR6 0PY

Tel 01568 798320 **Fax** 01568 798329
Location Midway between Leominster and Hereford on A49
Opening hours 9am to dusk, daily, all year
Admission fee Free

A vigorous young arboretum, first planted in 1953 with public amenity in mind. Wonderful for walking, whatever the season, and well run in a friendly, efficient manner so that visitors get the most from it. The rangers say that spring and autumn are the best time for colour, but there are lots of early purple orchids and spotted orchids in summer, too.
a fine collection of trees, including mature conifers; bluebells; wood anemones; gift shop; light meals from 9am to 5pm

Owned by Hereford Council
Number of gardeners 4
Size 24ha (60 acres)

STAUNTON PARK

Staunton-on-Arrow, Leominster HR6 9LE

Tel 01544 388556
Location In Staunton Green, *not* Staunton-on-Arrow
Opening hours 11am to 5pm, Thursdays, 17 May to 30 August; charity days: 11am to 5.30pm on 20 June and 2pm to 5.30pm on 24 June, 1 and 14 July
Admission fee Adults £3; Children free

Much of the structure of the grounds at Staunton dates back to Victorian times – wellingtonias, rhododendron woodlands, a rock garden and a lake – but the modern plantings are what makes it a garden worth visiting. A rose garden and fine mixed borders are the highlights.
home-made teas

Owned by Susan Fode
Number of gardeners 3
Size 4ha (10 acres)

STOCKTON BURY

Kimbolton, Leominster HR6 0HB

Tel 01568 613432
www.stocktonbury.co.uk
Location 1 mile north of Leominster on A49 and A4112, then signed
Opening hours Noon to 5pm, Wednesday to Sunday, and Bank Holiday Mondays, 1 April to 1 October
Admission fee £4 (flat rate)

Stockton Bury is an extraordinary garden, made over many years by a working farmer who is also a plantsman. The design is fairly firm, with a large number of different enclosures and walks in different styles. The buildings include a pigeon house, a cider press and a tithe barn. The planting is fairly controlled, so that rarities can be appreciated and the architectural features are enhanced. Ornamental details are everywhere, and often inspirational.
plants for sale; restaurant

Owned by Raymond Treasure
Number of gardeners 2
Size 1.6ha (4 acres)

WESTONBURY MILL WATER GARDENS

Pembridge HR6 9HZ

Tel/fax 01544 388650
www.westonburymillwatergardens.com
Location On A44, 11/2 miles west of Pembridge
Opening hours 11am to 5pm, daily, April to September
Admission fee Adults £3.50; children £1

The gardens at Westonbury are informally laid out around a muddle of streams and ponds behind an old corn mill. There are massed displays of candelabra primulas, mimulus hemerocallis, astilbes and water irises, as well as gunneras and water lilies. But the garden is transported into quite a different league by the series of dotty follies that the owner has built. They include an African hut, a castellated dovecote that spurts out water and a hemispherical dome made of old wine bottles.
light refreshments

Owned by Richard Pim
Number of gardeners owner only
Size 1.2ha (3 acres)

WHITFIELD

Wormbridge HR2 9BA

Tel 01981 570727 **Fax** 01981 570745
Location 8 miles south-west of Hereford on A465
Opening hours For NGS: 2pm to 6pm, 18 March and 13 May; and parties by appointment
Admission fee Adults £3

Whitfield has magnificent trees, most of them planted by the Clives over the last 200 years. *Zelkova serrata*, a weeping oak, and a ginkgo planted as early as 1778 are some of the highlights, but there is nothing to beat the grove of 20 or so *Sequoia sempervirens* now pushing 46m (150ft) in height.
topiary; mature conifers; fine collection of trees; huge grove of redwoods; tallest dwarf alder *Alnus nitida* and durmast oak *Quercus petraea* in the British Isles; teas

Owned by Mr and Mrs Edward Clive
Number of gardeners 1 full-time, 2 part-time
Size 5.2ha (13 acres)
English Heritage Grade II

ventnor botanic garden
*free admission
to gardens,
gift shop, cafe,
plant sales, exhibitions
*green house excepted
carpark rates apply
ISLE of WIGHT
undercliff drive ventnor PO38 1UL ph.(01983) 855397
photograph courtesy of Julian Winslow

HERTFORDSHIRE

Hertfordshire has two great historic gardens (Hatfield House and St Paul's Walden Bury) that are open to the public, and a couple of lesser ones (Ashridge and Knebworth), but few of the others admit visitors. Nor does Hertfordshire have as many good modern gardens as its proximity to London might suggest. However, the Royal National Rose Society's new display garden around its old offices near St Albans will open officially for the first time this year. The only garden with really good herbaceous plantings in Hertfordshire is Benington Lordship. There is a sprinkling of fine trees at such gardens as Bayfordbury (sometimes open for the National Gardens Scheme) and Aldenham – both relics of keen gardening owners in the past – but no old-established arboretum or pinetum of special merit. The National Gardens Scheme can muster only about two thirds of the number of gardens that open for charity in such a county as Northamptonshire and there are only eight National Collections in the county. But Hertfordshire has some good nurseries and a large number of excellent garden centres. Nevertheless, it remains difficult to explain why a county so close to London should not be endowed with horticultural wealth on anything like the scale of Surrey or Kent.

AYLETT NURSERIES LTD

North Orbital Road, London Colney, St Albans AL2 1DH

Tel 01727 822255 **Fax** 01727 823024
www.aylettnurseries.co.uk
Location On A414, on left-hand side when driving towards Hatfield
Opening hours 8.30am to 5.30pm, Monday to Saturday; 10.30am to 4.30pm, Sunday
Admission fee Free

This huge (and very successful) general garden centre has a prime trading position with a vast range of plants and every imaginable sundry. It also offers a design service and delivery. But Ayletts also has a speciality – its award-winning dahlias which have been a feature of RHS shows for many years and won 36 consecutive gold medals. The growing fields are well worth a visit in late summer or early autumn. All the different classes of dahlia hybrids are represented in both quantity and quality. There will be a special dahlia festival from 15 to 23 September 2007.
gift shop; coffee shop

Owned by The Aylett family
Size 2.8ha (7 acres)

BENINGTON LORDSHIP

Benington, Stevenage SG2 7BS

Tel 08701 261709 **Fax** 01438 869622
www.beningtonlordship.co.uk
Location Off A602 Stevenage to Hertford, in Benington village, next to church
Opening hours Noon to 4pm, daily, 3 to 25 February, for snowdrops; 2pm to 5pm, Easter, spring and summer Bank Holiday weekends, Sundays; noon to 5pm, Bank Holiday Mondays; Herbaceous Border week: 2pm to 5pm, daily, 17 to 24 June; on request, all year (please telephone)
Admission fee Adults £3.50; children free; Sundays in February £4.50; RHS members free 3 to 18 February and 17 to 22 June

Benington Lordship is a Georgian house with an Edwardian add-on, a mock Norman gateway and the ruins of a real Norman castle in the grounds. The extensive gardens have been revived and replanted in recent years without destroying the older features: a Pulhamite folly, an Edwardian rock garden (now a grass dell with bulbs and small specimen trees) and a sense of spacious parkland. The late winter, the drifts of snowdrops and, a little later, of *Scilla bithynica* are quite spectacular. But the highlight of a visit today is the stupendous double herbaceous border that Mrs Bott has planted in gentle pastel shades: the best we know.

roses (ancient and modern); rock garden; very good herbaceous borders; heather garden; cowslip bank; water features (and kingfishers); kitchen garden; refreshments

Owned by Richard Bott
Number of gardeners 1
Size 2.8ha (7 acres)
English Heritage Grade II

THE GARDENS OF THE ROSE
Chiswell Green, St Albans AL2 3NR

Tel 01727 850461 **Fax** 01727 850360
www.rnrs.org.uk
Location 1 mile from junction of M1 and M25; 2 miles south of St Albans
Opening hours Not yet decided, but probably 10am-5pm; daily; 9 June to 30 September
Admission fee Not known as we went to press; RNRS members free

The gardens of the Royal National Rose Society have risen from the ashes of its well-publicised financial troubles. The Society is remaking the gardens on the old site, with a stunning design by Michael Balston and companion plantings. The idea is to show, on a large scale, just how good roses can look in a garden setting. Although the construction of the first phase (six acres) is complete, the roses and plantings went in only last winter, so everything is very much in its infancy – and there may be gaps in the planting, too. Elsewhere on-site are the international rose trials.

roses of every kind; Adrian Fisher maze

Owned by The Royal National Rose Society
Number of gardeners 2
Size 10.7ha (27 acres)
NCCPG National Collections *Rosa* (species and cultivars)

HILL HOUSE GARDEN
Stanstead Abbots, Ware SG12 8BX

Tel 01920 870013
Location Next to Parish Church in Capell Lane
Opening hours Groups by appointment
Admission fee Adults £4; children 50p

Outstanding plantings in the old kitchen garden include colour borders, weeping pears and vegetables, all as neat as imaginable. Pretty woodland garden and lush growth around the pond.

woodland garden; 6m (20ft) high original Victorian conservatory; good herbaceous borders; rose species; home-made teas

Owned by Mr and Mrs Jonathan Pilkington
Number of gardeners 1, plus some extra help
Size 3.2ha (8 acres)

HOPLEYS PLANTS
High Street, Much Hadham SG10 6BU

Tel 01279 842509 **Fax** 01279 843784
www.hopleys.co.uk
Location 50 yards north of The Bull pub
Opening hours 9am (2pm on Sundays) to 5pm, daily, except Tuesdays; closed in January, February, November and December
Admission fee Donation; coaches £1.50 per person

Hopleys has a fine four-acre garden with some excellent plants (notable conifers and an ash tree said to be the fourth largest in the UK), but the nursery is its principal draw. It offers an extensive choice of hardy shrubs and perennials, with many half-hardy plants too – being particularly strong on

HATFIELD HOUSE

Hatfield AL9 5NQ

Tel 01707 287010 **Fax** 01707 287033
www.hatfield-house.co.uk
Location Off A1(M), Jct 4
Opening hours 11am to 5.30pm, daily, 7 April to end of September; East Garden open only on Thursdays (closed in August)
Admission fee Park and garden: Adults £5; children £4; plus £3.50 for East Garden; RHS members free except during special events

(P) 🚻 ♿ ✿

The gardens at Hatfield are mainly late 19th- and 20th-century. An 1890s parterre called the East Gardens is the outstanding feature: in 1977 The Dowager Marchioness of Salisbury enclosed it on either side with avenues of evergreen oaks – now grown as a high hedge-on-stilts – and replanted the formal beds. Two years later she started on the Knot Garden, a historical re-creation in front of the Old Palace. The designs are extracted from traditional English patterns in such herbaries as Parkinson's. Four central beds surround a small pool: the corners of the beds are marked by pyramids of box. Three are knots; the fourth is a gravel maze, to remind us that Hatfield already had a maze when Queen Elizabeth I visited it. The Elizabethan fruit garden is represented by pomegranates, which are put out in the summer: another link to the earliest gardens at Hatfield. The planting is true to the period, too: every plant is one that would have been introduced to England before 1620. They include clove carnations, ancient roses and a collection of historical tulips given by the *Hortus Bulborum* in Holland. The Dowager's intention was to make the gardens as they might have been, and bring them back into sympathy with the great unchanging house. 'It is my dream,' she wrote, 'that one day they will become again a place of fancies and conceits, where not only pleasure and peace can be found but a measure of surprise and mystery.' The gardens are now run by her daughter-in-law, the present Marchioness.
good herbaceous borders; knot gardens and good topiary; physic garden; organic kitchen garden (whole garden organically managed); souvenirs and gift shop; licensed restaurant, coffee shop, snacks and hot lunches

Owned by The Marquess of Salisbury
Number of gardeners 6
Size 16.8ha (42 acres)
English Heritage Grade I

diascias, osteospermums, penstemons and salvias. Since its foundation in 1968, the nursery has been responsible for numerous introductions: the most famous are *Lavatera* 'Barnsley' and *Potentilla fruticosa* 'Red Ace'. The tradition continues with its new *Abelia* x *grandiflora* 'Hopleys'. The website is excellent – very comprehensive and informative. There will be four RHS Special Events at Hopleys Plants in 2007; details from 020 7821 3408.
self-service refreshments

Owned by Aubrey Barker
Number of gardeners 1/2
Size 1.6ha (4 acres)

KNEBWORTH HOUSE

Knebworth, Stevenage SG3 6PY

Tel 01438 812661 **Fax** 01438 811908
www.knebworthhouse.com
Location Off A1(M), Jct 7
Opening hours 11am to 5.30pm, daily, 31 March to 15 April, 28 April to 7 May; 26 May to 3 June, 30 June to 5 September; plus weekends from 24 March to 30 September
Admission fee Adults, concessions and children all £7 (excluding house)

(P) 🚻 ♿ ✿

Most of the garden was laid out by Lutyens, who married a daughter of the house. It has been well restored in recent years, with Jekyll plantings where appropriate. These include some inventive and harmonious colour-themed gardens and a herb garden made from Jekyll's original plans. In the park are fine Victorian conifers and handsome avenues of lime and horse-chestnut.
rose garden with herbaceous borders; sunken lawn; gold garden; wilderness; maze; ponds; herb garden; licensed tea room

Owned by The Hon Henry Lytton Cobbold
Number of gardeners 4
Size 10ha (25 acres)
English Heritage Grade II*

ST PAUL'S WALDEN BURY
Whitwell, Hitchin SG4 8BP

Tel 01438 871218 **Fax** 01438 871229
Location B651, 5 miles south of Hitchin
Opening hours For NGS: 2pm to 7pm, 22 April, 13 May, 3 June; and by arrangement at other times for groups
Admission fee Adults £3.50; concessions £2; children 50p; private visits £6 per person

St Paul's Walden Bury garden is highly important as a unique example of the French 18th-century style – hedged *allées* forming a *patte d'oie* lead into the woodland towards temples, statues and pools. The present owner and his father (the Queen Mother's brother and a past President of the Royal Horticultural Society) added rhododendrons, camellias, maples and magnolias (plus much more besides) into parts of the woodland. It is therefore a garden that appeals to historians, plantsmen and artists alike. The snowdrops, daffodils, cowslips, spotted orchids, woodland peonies and wildflowers are all very fine in due season.
woodland garden; formal French landscape; rhododendrons; teas on NGS days

Owned by Sir Simon Bowes Lyon
Size 24ha (60 acres)
English Heritage Grade I

ISLE OF WIGHT

The Isle of Wight ('the Island' to its residents) may be small and deficient in wealth-creating industries, but it has two exceptional gardens: the 19th-century royal palace of Osborne, which overlooks the Solent on the northern shores of the island, and the modern botanic garden at Ventnor on the sunny southern side. The two gardens have an unusual link: the head gardener at Osborne is married to the head gardener at Ventnor. The Isle of Wight also has some fine plantsman's gardens (most notably John Harrison's at North Court), an active Historic Gardens Trust and NCCPG group, several National Collections and some good nurseries. In addition to those listed below, there is a magnificent choice of daylilies available from A la Carte Daylilies (Little Hermitage, St Catherine's Down, Ventnor PO38 2PD – by appointment only), including many of the new American hybrids: the nursery has two National Collections of *Hemerocallis*, large-flowered cultivars that have received awards since 1960, and miniature and small-flowered cultivars. Another National Collection is held by Springbank Nurseries (Winford Road, Newchurch, Sandown PO36 0JX), whose nerines have won several awards at RHS shows in recent years and extend to over 600 cultivars.

DEACON'S NURSERY

Moor View, Godshill PO38 3HW

Tel 01983 840750/522243 **Fax** 01983 523575
www.deaconsnurseryfruits.co.uk
Location Moor View is next to school, down School Crescent
Opening hours 8am to 4pm, Monday to Friday, all year; boots advisable in winter

Deacon's is one of the leading fruit tree nurseries in England, with trees and soft fruit of every size and variety, including 'family' trees. The very comprehensive list has over 600 different cultivars, including 300 apples: many are not listed elsewhere – including such regional specialities as 'Devonshire Crimson Queen' and 'Welsh Russet'. They are particularly proud of the 20 tree fruits they list, which originated in the Isle of Wight. All rootstocks are of virus-free origin. They mail anywhere in the UK and abroad.

Owned by Brian and Grahame Deacon
Number of gardeners 5, plus owners
Size 6.7ha (17 acres)

MOTTISTONE MANOR

Mottistone, Newport PO30 4ED

Tel 01983 741302
www.nationaltrust.org.uk
Location On B3399 west of Brighstone
Opening hours 11am to 5.30pm, Sunday to Thursday, 26 March to 29 October
Admission fee Adults £3.30; children £1.70; families £8.30

Mottistone has a cleverly designed modern garden on a difficult site – steep and narrow. Much has been terraced and enclosed to allow a rose garden and good herbaceous borders. Most of the rest is given to a wide variety of fruit trees, trained to make avenues and underplanted with vegetables or spring bulbs. It is a model for this type of planting, but made long before the current fashion for ornamental *potagers*.
roses (mainly modern); fruit; mature conifers; good herbaceous borders; bluebells; irises; teas

Owned by The National Trust
Number of gardeners 2
Size 2.4ha (6 acres)

NORTH COURT
Shorwell PO30 3JG

Tel 01983 740415 **Fax** 01983 821257
www.northcourt.info
Location 4 miles south-west of Newport, off B3323
Opening hours 2pm to 5.30pm, 23 June; and by appointment
Admission fee Adults £3; children free

The Harrison family which owns the substantial 17th-century North Court, inherited fine grounds with some magnificent trees and a clear stream at the bottom. John Harrison has extensively replanted it with a plantsman's enthusiasm and a special interest in tender exotica. It is now the best private garden on 'the Island'.
woodland garden; subtropical plants; roses (ancient and modern); plantsman's collection of plants; fruit; good herbaceous borders; large plane trees; B and B for garden lovers; refreshments; lunches for groups

Owned by Mr and Mrs John Harrison
Number of gardeners 2 part-time
Size 6ha (15 acres)

NUNWELL HOUSE
Brading, Ryde PO36 0JQ

Tel 01983 407240
Location Signed off A3055, 1 mile west of Brading
Opening hours 1pm to 5pm, 27 and 28 May, and 10 June; then Monday to Wednesday from 3 July to 5 September
Admission fee Gardens only: £2.50

The garden at Nunwell, with its peaceful views across the Solent, dates back to about 1600. The walled garden was built about 100 years later and still has its original paths, flanked by excellent double herbaceous borders. Vernon Russell-Smith planted a small arboretum about 30 years ago. The present owners have added some highly attractive garden ornaments and have restored the fabric and the plantings after some years of neglect. The mass of 'Frensham' roses along the front of the house (rather too hard-pruned) and the long stone steps lined with lavender are two of the more striking features. Good ornamental trees flower in spring – Japanese cherries, malus and magnolias. But it is perhaps the overall peace of the garden that is most attractive about Nunwell, worlds away from the downmarket razzmatazz of the Wightian coast.
roses (old-fashioned and modern); plantsman's collection of plants; herbs; fine collection of trees; statuary; 50m (164ft) border of 'Frensham' roses

Owned by Colonel and Mrs JA Aylmer
Number of gardeners owners, plus 1/2
Size 2.4ha (6 acres)
English Heritage Grade II

OSBORNE HOUSE
East Cowes PO32 6JY

Tel 01983 200022 **Fax** 01983 281380
www.english-heritage.org.uk
Location Follow brown tourist signs
Opening hours 10am to 5pm (4pm in October), daily, 24 March to 31 October
Admission fee Garden only: adults £5.90; concessions £4.40; children £3; families £14.80

Prince Albert laid out the stupendous Italianate terraces between the elegant Italianate palace and the parkland below. Starting in 1847, he embellished the terraces with balustrades, urns, steps, bronzes, statues and fountains, all based on designs he had seen in northern and central Italy. The seasonal displays of massed bedding are mighty impressive, especially as they reach their peak from April to May and from August to October: they employ Victorian period plants and designs. In the park are many fine trees, including

Osborne House

stately cedars, cork oaks and holm oaks; ilex, viburnum, rhododendrons and tall bay trees create a handsome evergreen landscape. The walled kitchen garden has been restored to use: English Heritage has repaired the wall and the old glasshouses, reinstated the original paths, started to train fruit trees against the walls (including 'Lane's Prince Albert' apples), and filled the beds with annual and perennial flowers for cutting. The colour effects are very effective, too. Heritage vegetables and fruit are grown organically at the royal children's gardens surrounding the Swiss cottage. Prince Albert used to pay them for their produce.

Italianate terraces; working walled garden - cut flowers and fruit; Victorian pleasure gardens; English Heritage shop; restaurant; tea room

Owned by English Heritage
Number of gardeners 9, plus seasonal extras
Size 20ha (50 acres)
English Heritage Grade II*

VENTNOR BOTANIC GARDEN

Undercliff Drive, Ventnor PO38 1UL

Tel 01983 855397 **Fax** 01983 856756
www.botanic.co.uk
Location 1½ miles west of Ventnor on A3055
Opening hours Dawn to dusk, daily, all year; show-house and plant sales open daily, 10am to 5pm (but weekend only in winter, and closing at 4pm); visitor centre open 10am to 6pm (4pm in winter and closed on Mondays and Fridays from November to March)
Admission fee Garden: free; small charge to visit show-house; car-parking charges

Originally an offshoot of Hillier's Nursery, the Ventnor Botanic Garden is devoted to exotic plants. It is not strictly a *botanic* garden, but it has a remarkable collection. Many of the plants – perhaps most – are from the southern hemisphere but flourish in the unique microclimate of the 'Undercliff': widdringtonias from Zimbabwe and Tasmanian olearias, for instance, as well as astelias, *Sophora microphylla* and *Griselinia lucida*

from New Zealand. Parts of the garden are composed entirely of foreign plants, with no European species in sight – even the background trees are exotics. *Geranium maderense* has naturalised on the sunny slopes and so has an amazing colony of 4m (13ft) *Echium pininana*. There are some fine specimens of *Puya chilensis* that flower most years in the scree garden. Elsewhere are such Mediterranean natives as acanthus, cistus and *Coronilla valentina*, and a remarkable area called the Palm Garden, where stately foliage plants like yuccas, cordylines, phormiums and beschornerias are underplanted with watsonias, cannas and kniphofias. Almost destroyed by the gales of 1987 and 1990, the collections were rapidly remade and the garden now looks wonderfully vigorous again. The Mediterranean garden has been extensively re-landscaped. A new southern hemisphere garden is planted mainly with South African and Australian species. A long glade is entirely planted with New Zealand plants and there is a new tree-fern valley. Seasonal planting is geared to the summer months, when the garden receives most visitors, and is often dramatic and inspirational. The energetic head gardener has a splendid eye for planting and works marvels despite the obviously inadequate funding. A magnificent visitor centre offers the venue for exhibitions and a programme of events, as well as a restaurant for visitors. The nursery sells some very interesting and often tender plants which are surplus to the garden's own requirements. Most are seed-raised and come from all around the world, wherever there is a Mediterranean-type climate.

subtropical plants; plantsman's collection of plants; good herbaceous borders; palms; olives; bananas; medicinal herbs from all over the world; largest collection of New Zealand plants in the UK; new nursery specialising in rare plants from the garden; licensed café with snacks, tea/coffee, lunches

Owned by Isle of Wight Council
Number of gardeners 8
Size 8.7ha (22 acres)

KENT

Kent is thick with good gardens and nurseries: the Garden of England has the oldest market gardens in the country. These were developed in the 16th century to supply fresh fruit and vegetables to the fast-growing population of London: the men of Kent filled their barges up with the capital's night soil on the return journey and applied this bounty to their orchards. Kent has long been a rich county, not only because of its soil and climate, but also because many Londoners have traditionally spent the fortunes they made in the City on the acquisition of houses and gardens there. The number of arboreta and record-sized trees in Kent testifies to its long tradition of ornamental gardening. Not only does it have an exceptional number of important historic gardens, but all six of those which are rated Grade I by English Heritage are open regularly to the public – Godinton, Hever, Knole, Penshurst, Scotney and Sissinghurst. Many of the other graded gardens are also open throughout the summer – among them are Chartwell, Emmetts, Goodnestone, Leeds Castle, Mount Ephraim, Port Lympne and Walmer Castle. Kent's historic gardens are supplemented by fine modern ones with important horticultural collections: the national pinetum at Bedgebury, for example, and the extensive fruit collections at Brogdale. The gardens at Yalding and Broadview are important examples respectively of organic gardening, and a teaching garden. The National Gardens Scheme thrives in Kent. Gardens and gardening flourish in every town and village: a great number of good garden centres and nurseries exist to satisfy the demand for plants. The nurseries include some of the leading specialists in their field: Brenda Hyatt, for example, has won many awards over the years for her auriculas, while Downderry Nursery (another regular at RHS shows in season) has National Collections of lavender and rosemary.

BEDGEBURY NATIONAL PINETUM

Park Lane, Goudhurst, Cranbrook TN17 2SL

Tel 01580 879820 **Fax** 01580 212423
www.forestry.gov.uk/bedgebury
Location 1 mile east of A21 at Flimwell on B2079
Opening hours 8am to dusk, daily, all year
Admission fee Free, but £5 for a car and £20 for a coach

Bedgebury Pinetum is the national conifer collection: the International Dendrological Research Institute considers it the best conifer collection in the world. It was founded as a joint venture between the Forestry Commission and the Royal Botanic Gardens at Kew: the first plants for the pinetum were raised at Kew in 1921 and planted out at Bedgebury four years later. The collection boasts some 330 different species and more than 2,000 cultivars growing in landscaped woodland around a series of lakes and streams – stunning when reflected by the water. But Bedgebury is not just for conifer lovers. The woodland garden is also known for its deciduous trees: it has fine collections of oaks and maples, azaleas and rhododendrons. A new Japanese glade was added in 1996. Bedgebury is also good for its autumn colour and one of the best places we know for a winter walk. Good for wildlife, too.

mature conifers; rhododendrons; fungi; new Japanese maple glade; 18 record tree species, including two broadleaves; shop and visitor centre; tea room

Owned by Forestry Commission
Number of gardeners 6
Size 130ha (320 acres)
NCCPG National Collections *Chamaecyparis lawsoniana* (cvs.); *Juniperus*; *Taxus*; *Thuja*; x *Cupressocyparis*
English Heritage Grade II*

BEECH COURT GARDENS

Canterbury Road, Challock, Ashford TN25 4DJ

Tel 01233 740735 **Fax** 01233 740842
www.beechcourtgardens.co.uk
Location On A252 1 mile west of Challock (left-hand side)
Opening hours 10.30am to 5.30pm, daily, except Fridays, April to September; plus 13 May, 5 August and (noon to dusk) 11 November for NGS; and by appointment in October and November for autumn colour
Admission fee Adults £4.50; OAPs £3.80; wheelchair-bound £2; children £1; groups of 12+ £3.50 each

Beech Court is a fine woodland garden, very enjoyable to visit and explore. It was mainly laid out in 1947, though parts have some much older trees and the property dates back to medieval times. There is lots to discover along its paths and glades at every season – hydrangeas, azaleas, maples, magnolias, shrub roses, viburnums, climbing roses and magnificent rhododendrons. Nearer the house are expansive lawns (rather bumpy – visitors must be careful), pools and well-planted, fluid island beds.
plant nursery; lunches and teas

Owned by Mr and Mrs Vyvyan Harmsworth
Number of gardeners 3 part-time
Size 4ha (10 acres)

BELMONT PARK

Belmont, Throwley, Faversham ME13 0HH

Tel 01795 890202 **Fax** 01795 840042
www.belmont-house.org
Location Signed from A251 at Badlesmere
Opening hours 10am to 6pm, daily from 31 March 2007, all year
Admission fee Garden: adults £3; children £1

Quiet parkland and the relics of a 200-year-old arboretum surround this handsome Samuel Wyatt house. The pleasure gardens include a pinetum with a Victorian grotto, an ancient rock garden and a walled garden with herbaceous borders and a 7m (23ft) tree of *Ilex aquifolium* 'Ferox Argentea'. The Coronation Avenue was planted in 1937: a dead-straight, 300 yard pathway, lined with immaculately-clipped yew hedges and leading to a Gothic flint folly. The old kitchen garden was prettily remade for the millennium by Arabella Lennox-Boyd. Pergolas hung with apples, pears, roses and vines lead to the central pool and flower garden. Further afield are metal arbours dressed with golden hop and a Victorian greenhouse. The standard of maintenance everywhere is extremely high.
rock garden; shell grotto; rhododendrons; pinetum; teas

Owned by The Harris (Belmont) Charity
Number of gardeners 3
Size 16ha (40 acres)
English Heritage Grade II

BROADVIEW GARDENS

Hadlow College, Hadlow, Tonbridge TN11 0AL

Tel 01732 853211 **Fax** 01732 853207
www.hadlow.ac.uk
Location Signed from A26, 3 miles north-east of Tonbridge
Opening hours 10am to 5pm (4pm on Sundays), daily, all year
Admission fee Adults £2; children free; RHS members free in September and October

These new gardens attached to Hadlow College include a series of model designs and plantings which are intended to help students to learn the skills of garden design and horticulture. They are, of course, extremely interesting and inspiring for ordinary visitors: they include a subtropical garden, a low-maintenance garden, long herbaceous borders, an oriental garden and a

medicinal garden.
garden centre; café

Owned by Hadlow College
Size 3.2ha (8 acres)
NCCPG National Collections *Anemone* (Japanese); *Helleborus*

BROGDALE
Brogdale Road, Faversham ME13 8XZ

Tel 01795 535286 **Fax** 01795 531710
www.brogdale.org
Location 1 mile south-west of Faversham
Opening hours 10am to 5pm, daily, 26 March to 29 October; 10am to 4.30pm, daily, winter; closed over Christmas period
Admission fee Guided walks: adults £5; OAPs £4.50; children £3; RHS members free except during special events

Brogdale describes itself as 'a living museum' and claims to have the largest collection of fruit cultivars in the world: more than 2,200 apples, 500 pears and 350 plums. There are demonstrations, exhibitions, workshops and events throughout the year. Fruit from the collections is sold and scion wood supplied.
hardy fruit of every kind - the biggest collection in Europe; excellent shop with rare fruit varieties for sale in season; light lunches and teas

Owned by Brogdale Horticultural Trust
Size 60ha (150 acres)
NCCPG National Collections *Corylus* (cobnuts and filberts); *Malus* (apples, ornamental cvs. and cider apples); *Prunus* (cherries); *Prunus* (plums); *Pyrus*; *Ribes grossularia* (gooseberries); *Ribes nigrum* (blackcurrants); *Ribes sativum* (currants other than blackcurrants); *Vitis vinifera* (grapes)

CHARTS EDGE
Hosey Hill, Westerham TN16 1PL

Tel 01732 504556 (evenings)
www.chartsedgegardens.co.uk
Location 1/2 mile south of Westerham, just off A25 and onto B2026
Opening hours 2pm to 5pm, Fridays and Sundays, mid-April to mid-September; for NGS: 20 May, 17 June and 15 July
Admission fee Adults £3.50; OAPs £3; children free

Charts Edge is a fine old plantsman's garden, which is currently undergoing restoration and improvement. It has a fine show of spring-flowering trees and shrubs, especially camellias, rhododendrons, azaleas and magnolias, but they are accompanied by eucryphias and hydrangeas which make a good show in late summer. The gardens have many different features, including a large rock garden, a bog garden and a handsome new cascade.
rhododendrons and azaleas; tea and cakes

Owned by Mrs J Bigwood
Number of gardeners 3
Size 4ha (10 acres)

CHARTWELL
Westerham TN16 1PS

Tel 01732 868381 **Fax** 01732 868193
www.nationaltrust.org.uk/chartwell
Location A25 to Westerham, then signed from B2026
Opening hours 11am to 5pm, Wednesday to Sunday and Bank Holiday Mondays (plus Tuesdays in July and August), 17 March to 28 October
Admission fee House and gardens: adults £10.80; children £5.40

Sir Winston Churchill lived here from 1924 on and laid out the spacious and extensive gardens in a slightly old-fashioned style. One of the rose gardens has the cultivar 'Winston Churchill' but every part has a deep sense of history and all is maintained to a very high standard. The Trust has started to restore the garden to a closer representation of the way it was in Churchill's time; the kitchen garden has just been reinstated.
roses (mainly modern); National Trust shop; restaurant

Owned by The National Trust
Number of gardeners 5
Size 33ha (82 acres)
English Heritage Grade II*

COBHAM HALL
Cobham DA12 3BL

Tel 01474 823371 **Fax** 01474 825902
www.cobhamhall.com
Location In Cobham, close to M2 and A2
Opening hours 2pm to 5pm, Wednesdays and Sundays, March, April, July and August; but please telephone to check; groups by arrangement
Admission fee Adults £4.50; concessions £3.50

Humphry Repton laid out the park at Cobham for the Earl of Darnley in the 1790s but the older trees date back to its previous use as a medieval deer park. James Wyatt designed a Gothic dairy and a rustic cow byre. There are further buildings in Lady Darnley's Garden, including a Tuscan temple, an aviary and an orangery. All are currently under restoration after a £5 million grant from the Heritage Lottery Fund – the largest HLF project in the South East. Cobham Hall is now a private school for girls.
souvenir shop; cream teas

Owned by The Trustees of Cobham Hall
Size 58ha (125 acres)
English Heritage Grade II*

COPTON ASH GARDENS
105 Ashford Road, Faversham ME13 8XW

Tel 01795 535919
Location On A251, opposite M2 eastbound exit
Opening hours By appointment
Admission fee Adults £2.50; children free

This is a first-rate plantsman's garden, started in 1978 and now with over 3,000 different plants growing in 1½ acres – the fruit of Tim Ingram's constant quest for new things to try out. His interests are omnivorous, with unusual plants from every corner of the globe and endless different microhabitats within the garden. Recent developments include extensive plantings of small bulbs, like snowdrops, cyclamen and crocuses (species only – no hybrids), and the best woodland perennials, especially hellebores, erythroniums and trilliums. Seldom have so many good plants been grown in such a small area. Visitors are especially welcome early in spring when the garden starts to wake up, but there is much of interest at every season. It is a garden to explore slowly – a paradise for plantsmen.
important collection of dry-land plants of every kind

Owned by Tim and Gillian Ingram
Number of gardeners 1½
Size 0.6ha (1½ acres)

DODDINGTON PLACE GARDENS
Sittingbourne ME9 0BB

Tel 01795 886101
www.doddingtonplacegardens.co.uk
Location Follow brown tourist signs from A2
Opening hours 2pm to 5pm, Sundays and Bank Holiday Mondays, 8 April to 24 June; plus other dates for NGS
Admission fee Adults £4; children £1.50

The house and garden both date back to the 1870s: Markham Nesfield had a hand in the original formal gardens. The handsome *Sequoiadendron giganteum* and billowing yew hedges are also 19th-century, but this is a garden to which every generation has added something. From the Edwardian era dates the rock garden of local stone: cyclamen have naturalised all through it. The woodland garden was developed in the 1960s on a small outcrop of greensand: rhododendrons, camellias, styrax, eucryphias and maples flourish here. More recent are a paved rose garden (*very* pretty), an avenue of *Betula utilis* var (jacquemontii) 'Grayswood Ghost' planted for its winter bark, and excellent colour borders (red and white). And the present owners are restoring the Edwardian rock garden and adding new architectural features and plantings with great verve.
woodland gardens (4 acres); magnificent lumpy yew hedges; fine old wellingtonias; rhododendrons and azaleas

Owned by Mr and Mrs R Oldfield
Number of gardeners 2, plus 1 part-time
Size 4ha (10 acres)
English Heritage Grade II

DOWNDERRY NURSERY
Pillar Box Lane, Hadlow, Tonbridge TN11 9SW

Tel 01732 810081 **Fax** 01732 811398
www.downderry-nursery.co.uk
Location Follow brown tourist signs off A26 north-east of Hadlow
Opening hours 10am to 5pm, Tuesday to Sunday and Bank Holiday Mondays, May to October
Admission fee Free; tours (including distillation demonstration) available at £5 per adult

This nursery in an old walled garden has the widest imaginable list of lavender and rosemary cultivars. Almost all the species are here, including the most unusual ones, and a wide number of hybrids and selections, some of them bred or chosen by the owner Dr Charlesworth himself. His exhibits at the major RHS summer shows have been a source of inspiration to many gardeners, and hurried them to visit his nursery, where his display garden has come together very well. Customers speak well of the quality of his plants. He has now started to distil lavender oils and sell the products. There will be a special 'Lavender Weekend' on 23 and 24 June 2007, when an admission price of £2 will include free tours and light refreshments.
lavender and rosemary; light refreshments (free with a tour)

Owned by Dr Simon J Charlesworth
Size 0.4ha (1 acre) and 1ha (2½-acre) field of lavender
NCCPG National Collections *Lavandula*; *Rosmarinus*

EAST NORTHDOWN FARM NURSERY
Margate CT9 3TS

Tel 01843 862060 **Fax** 01843 860206
www.botanyplants.co.uk
Location On east fringes of town, along George Hill Road (B2052) between Cliftonville and Kingsgate
Opening hours 10am to 5pm, daily, all year, except Christmas week
Admission fee Free

East Northdown Farm Nursery specialises in plants that will tolerate chalk soil, low rainfall and drying sea winds. There are many Mediterranean species, but the emphasis is always upon their toughness in cultivation. The farmhouse garden is worth a visit in its own right – many rare plants grown in a charming and traditional setting.
snacks and drinks

Owned by William and Louise Friend
Number of gardeners Owners only
Size 0.8ha (2 acres)

EDENBRIDGE HOUSE
Main Road, Edenbridge TN8 6SJ

Tel 01732 862122 **Fax** 01732 867385
Location On B2026, 1½ miles north of Edenbridge, near Marlpit Hill
Opening hours 2pm to 6pm, 15 April, 6 May, 17 June, 1 July and 9 September; 1pm to 5pm, 16 May and 12 September; 6pm to 9pm, 29 June; plus 2pm to 5pm, Tuesdays and Thursdays, April to September; and groups by appointment
Admission fee Adults £3; children 25p

This 1930s garden has been renewed and replanted by the present owner as a series of garden rooms to offer something of interest at every season. The spacious terraces are home to a rich mix of tender plants, many of them put out in pots for the summer months. A stream with bog plants along its edges runs down to a small pool. Rare exotics flourish in a gravel garden. In the kitchen garden is a fine greenhouse and small collection of ornamental trees, as well as apples and an appetising vegetable garden.
plantsman's garden; roses; herbaceous plants; orchard; gravel garden; teas (not on Tuesdays or Thursdays)

Owned by Mrs MT Lloyd
Size 2ha (5 acres)

EMMETTS GARDEN
Ide Hill, Sevenoaks TN14 6AY

Tel 01732 868381 **Fax** 01732 750490
www.nationaltrust.org.uk
Location Between Sundridge and Ide Hill off B2042
Opening hours 11am to 5pm (last admission 4.15pm),

Tuesday to Sunday, 17 March to 3 June; Wednesday to Sunday, 6 June to 1 July; Wednesdays, Saturdays and Sundays, 4 July to 28 October
Admission fee Adults £5.50; children £1

A short, stiff walk (or buggy ride) up from the car park brings you to this windswept hilltop garden, laid out in Edwardian times and maintained on a slim budget. The formal Italianate rose garden is pretty in July, but better still is the informal woodland garden laid out with unusual trees and shrubs in the William Robinson style. The bluebells are good; so is the autumn colour.
rock garden; bluebells; Italianate rose garden; rare trees and shrubs; autumn colour; azaleas; tea room

Owned by The National Trust
Number of gardeners 2
Size 7ha (17 1/2 acres)
English Heritage Grade II

GARDEN ORGANIC YALDING
Yalding, Maidstone ME18 6EX

Tel/fax 01622 814650
www.gardenorganic.org.uk
Location On B2162, 1/2 mile south of village
Opening hours 10am to 5pm, Wednesday to Sunday and Bank Holidays, April to October
Admission fee Adults £4; concessions £3.50; children £1; RHS members free

This is the new name for Yalding Organic Gardens, though it still has a series of 14 historically themed gardens run organically by Garden Organic (the new name for the HDRA). They include an apothecary's garden in the 13th-century style, a late 19th-century artisan's garden and a post-war allotment: all very stylish and educational. Others show the influence of William Cobbett and Gertrude Jekyll through the centuries. There is a central hop-pole pergola – a good example of how design features should come out of their surrounding landscape. The garden sets out to inspire, to educate and to give pleasure – and succeeds.
gardens through the ages - modern reconstructions; shop café

Garden Organic Yalding

Owned by Henry Doubleday Research Association
Number of gardeners 4
Size 2ha (5 acres)

GODINTON HOUSE & GARDENS
Ashford TN23 3BP

Tel 01233 620773 **Fax** 01233 647351
www.godinton-house-gardens.co.uk
Location A20 to Charing, then follow brown tourist signs
Opening hours 2pm to 5.30pm, Thursday to Monday, 25 March to 28 October; tours by arrangement; house open from 6 April to 9 October; NGS days: 25 March and 1 April (plant sale); also open on 29 July for the Red Cross
Admission fee Gardens only: adults £3; children free; honesty box

Godinton is the prettiest house in Kent, a Jacobean mansion reworked in the 1920s by Sir Reginald Blomfield, who advised on the spacious gardens for over 20 years. The charming Italian garden is his: statues, loggia, summerhouse, Persian rill, marble colonnade and Italian cypresses. The magnificent yew hedge dates from his first plantings in the 1900s: Dutch gables have been cut along its top to match the architecture of the house. Elsewhere are a sunken pool fringed with elegant weeping willows, a recently redesigned rose garden, herbaceous borders, sweeping lawns, a stupendous 18th-century park and a topiary garden with a statue of Pan at the centre. The wild garden is a carpet of daffodils and fritillaries in spring. In the kitchen garden are rows of fruit, vegetables and cut flowers, and a border with rare cultivars planted by members of the Delphinium Society. Every part has recently been restored and maintained to a very high standard.

topiary; formal Italianate garden; redesigned rose garden; teas; lunches for booked groups

Owned by The Godinton House Preservation Trust
Number of gardeners 4
Size 5ha (12½ acres)
English Heritage Grade I

GOODNESTONE PARK

Wingham, Canterbury CT3 1PL

Tel/fax 01304 840107
www.goodnestoneparkgardens.co.uk
Location Follow brown tourist signs from B2046
Opening hours 11am to 5pm, Wednesday to Friday and Bank Holidays, 29 March to 30 September; plus noon to 5pm on Sundays from 19 February
Admission fee Adults £4.50; OAPs £4; children (under 12) £1; wheelchair-bound £1; groups (20+) £4; guided groups £6; RHS members free in April, May and September, except during special events

Goodnestone is a handsome Palladian building. Jane Austen's brother married a daughter of the house: she will have known the fine chestnut avenue dating from about 1800 and the 18th-century parkland beyond. Later came the formal 19th-century terraces around the house, a 1920s woodland garden (best in spring when the rhododendrons and camellias are in flower) and the sloping cricket ground below the house. Very recent are a gravel garden on the edge of the wood, and a formal parterre on one of the terraces. The walled garden is quite exceptional. Actually there are three walled gardens, one after another, each of about one acre and enclosed by beautiful, worn old bricks. A long, broad, grass walk runs right down the middle and connects them to one another, with the flint tower of the parish church as a focal point beyond. Drifts of shrub roses, peonies, penstemons, clematis and herbaceous plants fill the borders, stuffed with interesting plants and arranged to create pretty colour plantings. Here, above all, you see the passionate plantsmanship which has imbued the present owner since she first started to garden here nearly 50 years ago.
woodland garden; topiary; snowdrops; roses (mainly old-fashioned); good herbaceous borders; teas; light lunches

Owned by Lady FitzWalter
Number of gardeners 2 full-time, 2 part-time
Size 5.6ha (14 acres)
English Heritage Grade II*

GREAT COMP

St Mary's Platt, Borough Green, Sevenoaks TN15 8QS

Tel 01732 886154
www.greatcomp.co.uk
Location 2 miles east of Borough Green: take B2016 off A20
Opening hours 11am to 5pm, daily, April to October
Admission fee Adults £4.50 children £1

Great Comp is a monument to the energy and enthusiasm of Eric Cameron, who has built up the garden since he first acquired it in 1957 – exactly 50 years ago. The design is a fine mix of the formal and the informal, and benefits greatly from a number of modern follies, built mainly as ruined cottages. The main ride down from the house is especially impressive, but it is fairly easy to get lost on some of the woodland paths at the sides. The plant content is of considerable horticultural interest and includes some 30 magnolia cultivars and a good range of rhododendrons, conifers, heathers and herbaceous plants: over 3,000 different plants in all. Late in the season come spectacular colour effects from dahlias, cannas and other exotics. A lavish use of bulbs, bedding and annuals ensures that the garden is colourful at every season. But the most interesting thing about the garden is the way in which large areas have been planted for minimum maintenance. There is much to learn and admire here. Dysons Nurseries, best known for their salvias, are also based within the grounds and the salvias too are a great feature of the garden.
woodland garden; plantsman's collection of plants; good herbaceous borders; ground cover; dwarf conifers; salvias; gifts, plants and souvenirs; refreshments

Owned by Great Comp Charitable Trust
Number of gardeners 3
Size 2.8ha (7 acres)

Great Comp

Groombridge Place Gardens

Hever Castle

GROOMBRIDGE PLACE GARDENS
Groombridge, Tunbridge Wells TN3 9QG

Tel 01892 861444 **Fax** 01892 863996
www.groombridge.co.uk
Location On B2110, 4 miles south-west of Tunbridge Wells
Opening hours 10am to 5.30pm, daily, 31 March to 3 November
Admission fee Adults £8.95; OAPs and children £7.45

Groombridge has lots to offer: a drunken garden where the yews lean at tipsy angles, an oriental garden, a white rose garden, a 'draughtsman's garden', a secret garden and a chessboard garden. Ivan Hicks has been at work in the 'Enchanted Forest', where the gardens are said to be 'interactive'. Best of all are the brilliant colour plantings, among the best we know. But the entry price is high and some may question whether the garden offers good value.
good colour plantings; gift shop; light lunches and teas

Owned by Groombridge Asset Management Ltd
Number of gardeners 2 full-time, plus several part-time
Size 0.6ha (1 1/2 acres), plus 80ha (200 acres) of park and woods

HEVER CASTLE
Edenbridge TN8 7NG

Tel 01732 865224 **Fax** 01732 866796
www.hevercastle.co.uk
Location 3 miles south-east of Edenbridge, signed from M25, Jct 5 and 6
Opening hours 11am to 5pm (3.30pm in November), daily, March to November
Admission fee Adults £7.80; OAPs £6.70; children £5

Hever is one of the most important Edwardian gardens in England, and maintained to a very high standard. The pretty moated castle sits in a park of oaks and firs (underplanted with rhododendrons) with a yew maze and formal neo-Tudor garden to one side. The best part is a spectacular five-acre Italian garden, where a long pergola (cool, dripping fountains all along) leads past a series of exquisite Italian gardens, stuffed with outstanding sculptures, urns, sarcophagi and other loot brought by William Waldorf Astor from Rome in 1903; it finally bursts onto a theatrical terrace, known as the Piazza, and a 35-acre lake, hand-dug by 800 workmen in less than two years.
woodland garden; topiary; 3,000 roses (old-fashioned and modern, with some climbers too); rhododendrons and azaleas; snowdrops; crocuses; daffodils; bluebells; tulips; dahlias; autumn colour; Christie's/HHA Garden of the Year in 1995; garden, gift and book shops; two restaurants

Owned by Broadland Properties Ltd
Number of gardeners 10
Size 16ha (40 acres)
English Heritage Grade I

HOLE PARK
Rolvenden, Cranbrook TN17 4JB

Tel 01580 241344 **Fax** 01580 241882
www.holepark.com

Location Off B2086 between Rolvenden and Cranbrook
Opening hours 2pm to 6pm, Sundays and Bank Holiday Mondays, 1 April to 1 July and 7, 14 and 21 October; plus Wednesdays and Thursdays from April to October; also days for NGS and other charities (see website); guided tours and groups by appointment at other times
Admission fee Adults £4; children 50p

This great garden is far too little known. The drive runs under an avenue of horse-chestnuts through classical parkland with wonderful views. The pleasure garden is Edwardian in origin, but has been revived and replanted by the present owner. Solid hedges and clipped specimens of yew are everywhere: backing the excellent herbaceous borders, around the water lily pond and framing a croquet lawn with standard wisterias. The flowery woodlands have palm trees in the dell, surrounded by purple rhododendrons and orange azaleas. Daffodils abound from March onwards and the millions of bluebells in the woodland walk never cease to astonish in early May. Autumn colours are especially good, too.
good design and good plants; new millennium water garden; bluebells; plant stall on Sundays; teas on Sundays and Bank Holidays

Owned by Mr and Mrs Edward Barham
Number of gardeners 2
Size 6ha (15 acres)

IDEN CROFT HERBS
Frittenden Road, Staplehurst TN12 0DH

Tel 01580 891432 **Fax** 01580 892416
www.herbs-uk.com
Location Signed from A229, south of Staplehurst
Opening hours 9am (11am on Sundays and Bank Holidays) to 5pm, daily, March to September; 9am to 4pm, Monday to Friday, October to February
Admission fee Adults £4; concessions £3; children free

This nursery display garden has been developed over the last 30 years and planted as a series of demonstration areas. These incorporate a 16th-century walled garden, originally attached to Staplehurst Manor. Other gardens include a cottage garden near the café, and a 'sensory garden', which shows how herbs may be arranged and appreciated by scent, colour, shape, form and texture. The intention is to provide design and planting ideas for all visitors, whatever the size of their garden. Part of it now appears rather run down and weedy, but all herb gardens have a tendency to look like that – just enjoy the garden's good points.
herbs

Owned by Philip Haynes
Number of gardeners 1
Size 0.6ha (1½ acres)
NCCPG National Collections *Mentha*; *Origanum*; *Nepeta*

IGHTHAM MOTE
Ivy Hatch, Sevenoaks TN15 0NT

Tel 01732 810378 **Fax** 01732 811029
www.nationaltrust.org.uk
Location Signed from A25 in Ightham village
Opening hours 10am to 5.30pm, daily, except Tuesdays and Saturdays, 14 March to 28 October
Admission fee Adults £9.50; children £4.75

Ightham Mote is a moated medieval manor in a wooded Kentish valley, with cottage-garden borders of pinks, old roses and lilies. These were remade about 100 years ago in a dreamily English style and give colour throughout the season. Fine lawns, natural springs, orchards and a kitchen or cut-flower garden are some of the other features. In the woodland parts are fine specimen trees, thick rhododendrons and a substantial collection of hydrangeas and philadelphus. Now that the house is restored, the rest of the estate is due to be upgraded and much more attention given to the gardens.
woodland garden; National Trust shop; restaurant

Owned by The National Trust
Number of gardeners 4, plus volunteers
Size 5.6ha (14 acres)
English Heritage Grade II

LADHAM HOUSE
Ladham Road, Goudhurst TN17 1DB

Tel 01580 212511
Location Left at Chequers Inn on Cranbrook Road, then

2nd right into Ladham Road
Opening hours 2pm to 5pm, 20 May
Admission fee Adults £3.50; children (under 12) 50p

Ladham was laid out by a botanist Master of the Rolls in the mid-19th century, and has been enthusiastically restored and updated in recent years. There is a good mixture of new planting and old: the latter includes the deep red form of *Magnolia campbellii* which has been named 'Betty Jessel' and is now available commercially.
woodland garden; good herbaceous borders; fine collection of trees; magnolias; teas

Owned by CG Johnson
Number of gardeners 2
Size 4ha (10 acres)

LEEDS CASTLE

Maidstone ME17 1PL

Tel 01622 765400 **Fax** 01622 735616
www.leeds-castle.com
Location M20, Jct 8
Opening hours 10am to 5pm (last admission 3pm), April to October; 10am to 3pm, November to March; closed on 7 July, 3 and 4 November and 25 December
Admission fee Castle, park and gardens: adults £13.50; OAPs and students £11; children £8

More a romantic castle than a garden, Leeds is best seen across the lake (the 'Great Water') which Russell Page created in the 1930s. Page also designed and planted the Culpeper Garden, which takes its name partly from Sir Thomas Colepeper, who bought the castle in 1632, and partly from Nicholas Culpeper, the 17th-century herbalist. It could be said that the Culpeper Garden does not show the 20th century's greatest garden designer at his best. The standard of maintenance is, however, very high: informal plantings of old garden flowers – roses, pinks, lavender, poppies and lupins. Here, too, is the National Collection of bergamot (*Monarda*) cultivars. The latest development is the 'Lady Baillie Garden', a series of sheltered terraces between the Culpeper Garden and the lake. In this part of the garden the planting is more Mediterranean in character. The nearby maze, planted in 1988, is fun to visit: it resembles a

Leeds Castle

topiary castle with towers and bastions and, when you get to its centre, you find the entrance to an underground grotto. The 'wood garden' is planted with rhododendrons and azaleas and underplanted with daffodils and anemones and there are further rhododendrons to the west of the moat. Leeds is run by a high-profile charitable trust which receives no government funding or grant aid, which may help to explain the high entry charges. Are they worth it for someone who is principally interested in gardens and plants? The answer – paradoxically – is yes, provided you also visit the castle and some of the many other attractions here. The owners say you need at least three hours to experience and enjoy them properly.
woodland garden; roses (mainly old-fashioned); herbs; good herbaceous borders; vineyard; plant centre; refreshments

Owned by Leeds Castle Foundation
Number of gardeners 13
Size 5ha (12½ acres), plus 200ha (500 acres) of parkland
NCCPG National Collections *Monarda*
English Heritage Grade II*

LULLINGSTONE CASTLE
Eynsford DA4 0JA

Tel 01322 862114 **Fax** 01322 862115
www.lullingstonecastle.co.uk
Location On A225, south of Eynsford Station
Opening hours Noon to 5pm, Fridays and Saturdays; 2pm to 6pm, Sundays and Bank Holiday Mondays, April to September; groups by arrangement at other times
Admission fee Adults £6; concessions £5.50; children £2.50; families £12.50

Lullingstone houses the 'World Garden of Plants', Tom Hart Dyke's vision of a garden whose design resembles the world's continents. Every part is planted only with plants from its country of origin. The collection is still growing, but the Wollemi pine is already in place, somewhere between Sydney and Ayers Rock in the Australian border. Eventually the garden will extend to some 10,000 different plants and have a strong educational content.

Owned by Guy Hart Dyke
Number of gardeners 1
Size 0.3ha (3/4 acre)

MADRONA NURSERY
Pluckley Road, Bethersden TN26 3DD

Tel 01233 820100 **Fax** 01233 820091
www.madrona.co.uk
Location Halfway between Bethersden village and Pluckley railway station
Opening hours 10am to 5pm, Saturday to Tuesday, mid-March to end of October

This is a first-rate general nursery, with a good choice of unusual cultivars across the range. Trees and shrubs are perhaps its main speciality – it is particularly strong on arbutus, birches, *Aesculus* and unusual conifers like *Podocarpus macrophyllus* and several forms of *Sequoiadendron giganteum* – but Madrona also offers a fine choice of herbaceous perennials. All are well grown and well displayed: a thoroughly satisfying nursery to visit.
light refreshments

MARLE PLACE GARDENS
Brenchley, Tonbridge TN12 7HS

Tel 01892 722304 **Fax** 01892 724099
www.marleplace.co.uk
Location Follow brown tourist signs from Brenchley or Forstal Farm roundabout off A21
Opening hours 10am to 5pm, Friday to Monday, 25 March to 3 October; and by appointment
Admission fee Adults £4.50; concessions £4

The gardens around the Jacobean house are mainly formal. They were imaginatively designed and planted in the 1930s and have been well preserved and improved by the present owners since the early 1960s. The sunken garden, laid out with scented plants, is particularly charming. The Edwardian kitchen garden has been redesigned with exotic planters and the Victorian greenhouse holds a collection of over 200 orchids. Recent additions include some unusual sculptures, a 'mosaic terrace',

a nut plat and a bog garden. The wilder parts are full of natural flowers, especially alliums. And all around are orchards of Kentish apples and pears.
good herbaceous borders; unusual plants; Victorian gazebo; Edwardian rock garden; tea, coffee and cakes

Owned by Mrs Lindel Williams
Number of gardeners 2
Size 6ha (15 acres)

MOUNT EPHRAIM
Hernhill, Faversham ME13 9TX

Tel 01227 751496 **Fax** 01227 750940
www.mountephraimgardens.co.uk
Location Brown tourist signs from A2 and A299
Opening hours 1pm to 5pm, Wednesdays, Thursdays, Saturdays, Sundays and Bank Holidays, Easter to 30 September; opens at 11am on Bank Holiday weekends
Admission fee Adults £4; children £1

Mount Ephraim is a handsome Edwardian garden, in a spacious position surrounded by orchards of apples and pears. The very substantial rock garden, with pools of water and Japanese influences, was laid out by Waterers in about 1910. The formal garden has a series of terraces with yew topiary in combinations of gold and green. Beyond are a lake, a stream, good conifers and rhododendron woods. The park trees include a venerable, gnarled *Robinia pseudoacacia* on the lawn in front of the house. Behind the house is a magnificent topiary garden, with geometric shapes, animals, birds and Great War regimental badges. Beyond is the millennium rose garden, pretty with old and David Austin roses. Everything has been restored and brought to life again in recent years, with some good new plantings. The newest feature (opened in 2006) is the 'mizmaze', a maze composed of exotic grasses interplanted with colourful perennials, but designed to look like the spokes of a wheel. The design came from a picture of a medieval labyrinth.
rock garden; topiary; maze of grasses and perennials; small shop; plants for sale; teas

Owned by Mrs Lesley Dawes
Number of gardeners 2½
Size 4ha (10 acres)
English Heritage Grade II

Mount Ephraim Gardens

OLD BUCKHURST
Markbeech, Edenbridge TN8 5PH

Tel 01342 850825
www.oldbuckhurst.co.uk
Location East of village on right-hand side of road to Chiddingstone Hoath
Opening hours 11am to 5.30pm, Wednesdays, plus first and last Saturdays of month, May to September; plus 21, 22, 25, 28 and 29 April, 5 May, and 1, 2, 5, 8 and 9 September
Admission fee Adults £3; children free

There was nothing but lawns and paving when the Gladstones started the garden at Old Buckhurst in 1988. It has been designed and planted as a series of compartments, each with its own character and colour scheme – colours and textures hold the garden together. Shrub roses, clematis and foliage plants are special favourites, but the garden is thickly planted, and intended to have as much interest as possible at every season of the year. A garden to enjoy and learn from.

Owned by Mr and Mrs John Gladstone
Number of gardeners owners only
Size 0.4ha (1 acre)

PENSHURST PLACE
Penshurst, Tonbridge TN11 8DG

Tel 01892 870307 **Fax** 01892 870866
www.penshurstplace.com
Location Follow brown tourist signs from A21 Hildenborough exit
Opening hours 10.30am to 6pm, daily, 26 March to

28 October; plus weekends in March
Admission fee Gardens only: adults £6; OAPs £5.50; children £4.50; RHS members free in April, September and October

This is a historic garden of great importance: it has substantial genuine Tudor remains. Nevertheless, much of what we see now was developed in the mid-19th century as a re-creation of the ideal Elizabethan garden, divided into small self-contained garden rooms, each with its own style and character. They have been well restored and developed in recent years. A vast Italianate parterre dominates the immediate pleasure garden: it is planted with *Rosa* 'Surrey' – another is planted as a Union Jack. There are borders by Lanning Roper and John Codrington, a 100m (328ft) bed of peonies and thick yew hedging – more than one mile of it.
roses (mainly modern and climbers); daffodils; good herbaceous borders; formal Italian garden; spring bulbs; gift shop; tea room

Owned by Viscount De L'Isle
Number of gardeners 6
Size 4.4ha (11 acres)
English Heritage Grade I

PORT LYMPNE
Lympne, Hythe CT21 4PD

Tel 01303 264647 **Fax** 01303 264944
www.totallywild.net
Location Exit 11 on M20 and follow brown tourist signs
Opening hours 10am to 6pm in summer, 10am to 5pm in winter, daily, except 25 December; last admissions 90 mins before closing
Admission fee Adults £13.95; OAPs £11.95; children £10.95; (2006 prices)

Ignore the zoo: Port Lympne is a stylish and luxurious house, with a seriously important 20th-century garden. It was laid out by Philip Tilden for Sir Philip Sassoon in 1911 on the steepest of slopes above Romney Marshes and worked on by Russell Page in the 1950s. The modern approach is nothing if not dramatic – an absolutely straight 100m (328ft) walk lined with hydrangeas, which brings you suddenly to the top of

Penshurst Place

the stupendously-long stone staircase known as the Trojan stairs. Around the front door is a forecourt with 16 statues acquired from the sale at Stowe, in Buckinghamshire, in 1921; castellations in the yew hedges give views to the south. The slopes are terraced into five levels and include a vineyard and 'figyard'. The chessboard garden – oblong rather than square – has squares of grass contrasted with beds for bulbs and annual displays: it is matched by a 'striped' garden on the other side of the main terrace. Down one side are the Long Borders, planted as mixtures of shrubs and perennials, and leading to the magnolia walk, the bowling green, the rose terrace, the dahlia terrace and the herbaceous border. Standards of maintenance remain high: a good garden for grandparents who want to see something more than animals.
topiary; good herbaceous borders; bedding out; dahlias; shop; restaurant

Owned by The John Aspinall Foundation
Number of gardeners 9
Size 6.2ha (15 1/2 acres)

RIVERHILL HOUSE GARDENS
Sevenoaks TN15 0RR

Tel 01732 452557/458802 **Fax** 01732 458802
www.kentattractions.co.uk/Riverhill.htm

Location 2 miles south of Sevenoaks on A225
Opening hours 11am to 5pm, Sundays and Bank Holiday weekends, April to 17 June
Admission fee Gardens only: adults £3; children 50p; house open by appointment to groups

Ⓟ 👫

Riverhill is a handsome Queen Anne house with grand views over the Weald. The garden suffered badly in the Great Storm of 1987. In the middle of the 19th century it belonged to John Rogers the botanist, who planted many of the surviving conifers and specimen trees. The vast billowing rhododendrons include original introductions by Hooker and Fortune. The azaleas and bluebells are stunning. Rogers's descendants made the rose walk.

rhododendrons and azaleas; mature conifers; bluebells; tallest *Magnolia* x *soulangeana* (13m; 43ft) in the British Isles; small gift shop; home-made teas

Owned by The Rogers family
Number of gardeners 1
Size 3.2ha (8 acres)
English Heritage Grade II

ROCK FARM

Gibbs Hill, Nettlestead, Maidstone ME18 5HT

Tel/fax 01622 812244
Location 1 mile south of Wateringbury, turn right up Gibbs Hill
Opening hours 11am to 5pm, 16 and 19 May; 13, 16, 20, 23, 27 and 30 June; 4, 7 and 11 July; 2pm to 6pm, 9 September; and private visits by appointment
Admission fee Adults £4; children free

Ⓟ 👫 ✿

Rock Farm is a plantsman's garden, made over many years by a (now retired) nurserywoman on alkaline soil. There are natural springs and ponds, a bog garden, iris beds, interesting trees and shrubs and a spectacular herbaceous border designed to be at its best in high summer. All is maintained to a very high standard.

Owned by Mrs SE Corfe
Number of gardeners Owner only
Size 1ha (21/2 acres)

ROSEWOOD DAYLILIES

70 Deansway Avenue, Sturry, Canterbury CT2 0NN

Tel 01227 711071
Location Off to right of Herne Bay Road, the main road leading north out of Sturry
Opening hours By appointment; special open day for NCCPG on 31 July (2pm to 5 pm)
Admission fee Free

Ⓟ ✿

Here is a splendid place to see more than 1,000 different daylilies, especially those bred and introduced since 1970. These include many of the hundreds of modern American hybrids: the owner trials new cultivars and then offers the best for sale. The nursery's list grows every year: a lot of cultivars with an RHS Award of Garden Merit have recently been added, as have many new spider forms and other specialities. It also offers a range of companion plants: agapanthus (80 cvs.), crocosmias (30 cvs.) and hardy geraniums.

Hemerocallis; *Agapanthus*

Owned by Chris Searle
NCCPG National Collections *Hemerocallis* (cvs. post-1970)

SCOTNEY CASTLE GARDEN

Lamberhurst, Tunbridge Wells TN3 8JN

Tel 01892 893868 **Fax** 01892 890110
www.nationaltrust.org.uk/scotneycastle
Location On A21, south of Lamberhurst
Opening hours 11am to 5.30pm, Wednesday to Sunday and Bank Holidays, 17 March to 28 October; plus 3, 4, 10 and 11 March
Admission fee Adults £5.80; children £2.90; guided tours by arrangement (extra fee)

Ⓟ 👫 ♿ ✿

The house (opening to the public for the first time in Summer 2007) was designed by Salvin in the late 1830s: the quarry where they extracted the stone for building is now a sheltered woodland dell. During the 19th century, many specimen trees were added to the parkland – cypresses, cedars and wellingtonias: those that survived the gales of 1987 still give structure to the gardens in their maturity. But the slopes between the house and the moated and ruined castle at the bottom are covered with ornamental trees and shrubs planted by Christopher Hussey in the 1950s – among them are many rhododendrons, azaleas, hydrangeas, kalmias and maples. The ruined castle is the focus of the whole picturesque composition and the way it has been richly draped in wisteria, clematis, honeysuckles and roses is both romantic and photogenic. Among the ruins are a herb garden and a cottage garden designed by Lanning Roper in about 1970, surprisingly appropriate and effective. The views of the castle as you meander round the edge of the moat are little short of miraculous.

woodland garden; plantsman's collection of plants; rhododendrons; azaleas; water lilies; wisteria; good autumn colour; plantings in ruins of 14th-century castle; shop

Owned by The National Trust
Number of gardeners 4
Size 8ha (20 acres)
English Heritage Grade I

SISSINGHURST CASTLE GARDEN
Sissinghurst, Cranbrook TN17 2AB

Tel 01580 710700 **Fax** 01580 710702
www.nationaltrust.org.uk/sissinghurst
Location 1 mile east of Sissinghurst village, 1/2 mile off A262; cross-country footpath from village
Opening hours 11am to 6.30pm, Friday to Tuesday, 17 March to 28 October; opens at 10am on Saturdays, Sundays and Bank Holidays
Admission fee Adults £8.60; children £4; families £22

P ♿ ✿

So important, influential and well known is Sissinghurst that it comes as a shock to realise that Harold Nicolson and Vita Sackville-West began to make the garden there as recently as 1930. Sackville-West's writings made it famous right from the beginning so that it is possible to trace the history of such features as the white garden in her many books still in print. Harold Nicolson was a careful designer who understood the importance of line and measure: he was very much a classicist in taste. Vita Sackville-West was a romantic, exuberant, poetic plantswoman. It was the combination of these two complementary talents that made the garden a source of wonder and inspiration. Sissinghurst is now part of every English gardener's education, and one to which it is important to return time and again. The garden is always changing and developing. It was the Nicolsons' intention that the garden should continue to develop after they gave it to the National Trust, and this principle – that the garden must be kept up to date with new plants – is inherent in the way that it has been managed. The design is unaltered and unalterable, and the plantings continue to be governed by the Gertrude Jekyll principles of which Sissinghurst is a supremely beautiful interpretation. But the plants are always changing and Sissinghurst therefore remains an influential plantsman's garden, too. All the plants sold by the little nursery are propagated from the garden; thus can visitors with a sense of history take a piece of Sissinghurst with them.

influential 20th-century garden; roses (mainly old-fashioned); plantsman's collection of plants; herbs; good herbaceous borders; National Trust gift shop; self-service restaurant; coffee shop

Sissinghurst

Owned by The National Trust
Number of gardeners 8
Size 2.2ha (5 1/2 acres)
English Heritage Grade I

SQUERRYES COURT

Westerham TN16 1SJ

Tel 01959 562345 **Fax** 01959 565949
www.squerryes.co.uk
Location 1/2 mile from A25, signed from Westerham
Opening hours 11.30am to 5pm, Wednesdays, Thursdays, Sundays and Bank Holiday Mondays, April to September
Admission fee Garden only: adults £4; OAPs £3.50; children £2

The gardens have been excellently restored with advice from Tom Wright since 1987, guided by a Badeslade plan of the original garden made in 1719, before they were landscaped later in the century. The main feature is a formal garden behind the house, where box-edged beds are filled with santolina, lavender and sage, alongside the beautifully-planted Edwardian borders. The outline of the old formal garden is still apparent in the terracing and paths, and new borders have been added for year-round interest. The modern design and planting are inevitably a compromise, but Squerryes is a place of great beauty and variety. Beyond the formal gardens is a woodland garden planted with rhododendrons and azaleas, and the whole is surrounded by an 18th-century park.
parterres; topiary; roses (mainly old-fashioned); herbaceous borders; formal design; gazebo; dovecote; woodland walks; lake; small shop in house; teas and light refreshments

Owned by J and A Warde
Number of gardeners 1, plus 2 part-time
Size 10ha (25 acres)
English Heritage Grade II

STARBOROUGH NURSERY

Starborough Road, Marsh Green, Edenbridge TN8 5RB

Tel 01732 865614 **Fax** 01732 862166
Location On B2028 Edenbridge to Lingfield road
Opening hours 9.30am to 4pm, daily, except Wednesdays and Sundays; closed in January, July and August

Starborough has for long been an important nursery for its wide range of trees and shrubs and, since it took over G Reuthe Ltd in the 1990s, for its rhododendrons and azaleas, too. Its list of liquidambars, cornus, camellias and magnolias is particularly good.

Owned by Mr and Mrs CB Tomlin

STONEACRE

Otham, Maidstone ME15 8RS

Tel 01622 862871 **Fax** 01622 862157
www.nationaltrust.org.uk
Location 1 mile south of A20; north end of Otham village
Opening hours 11am to 6pm (last admissions 5pm), Saturdays and Bank Holiday Mondays, 31 March to 6 October
Admission fee Adults £3.50; children £1.50; groups £3

Stoneacre is an important and influential garden because the tenant until 2000 was Rosemary Alexander, Principal of the English Gardening School at the Chelsea Physic Garden. It was where she worked out her ideas and showed her students how the principles of design and planting look 'on the ground'. The present tenants came to gardening from the fashion world and have made considerable alterations to the plantings around the house. They have incorporated their passion for strong textures and dark subtle colouring – for example, by contrasting dainty grasses with large-leaved shrubs. The old *potager* has been transformed into an intimate green and white garden. The back courtyard has an unusual collection of plants and flowers grouped around the doors. It is still one of the most exciting new gardens in southern England, and in perfect harmony with the Tudorised house.
spring bulbs; autumn colour; strong design

Owned by The National Trust
Number of gardeners 2

TILE BARN NURSERY
Standen Street, Iden Green, Benenden TN17 4LB

Tel/fax 01580 240221
www.tilebarn-cyclamen.co.uk
Location 2 miles south of Benenden; turn left at crossroads in Iden Green
Opening hours 9am to 5pm, Wednesday to Saturday

This is a splendid garden nursery devoted to one genus – *Cyclamen*. Cyclamen are everywhere: they have spread through the lawns and into the drive, as well as under the shelter trees, shrubs and hedges. In the glasshouses are rows and rows of every imaginable hardy species and cultivar of cyclamen of different ages, all pot-grown and all of flowering size – a wonderful sight from August to April. Visitors will also find pots of some other unusual bulbs species, particularly the smaller, daintier colchicums, crocuses, fritillarias, snowflakes and narcissi.

Owned by Peter and Liz Moore

WALMER CASTLE & GARDENS
Kingsdown Road, Walmer, Deal CT14 7LJ

Tel 01304 364288 **Fax** 01304 364826
Location Follow brown tourist signs
Opening hours 10am to 6pm (4pm in March and on Saturdays), daily, March to October; open Wednesday to Sunday only in March and October; closed when the Lord Warden is in residence: 13 to 15 July
Admission fee Adults £6.30; concessions £4.70; children £3.30; families £15.80

The gardens at Walmer Castle are well worth a visit, partly for their horticultural interest and partly for their many historical associations – William Pitt, the Duke of Wellington and Winston Churchill were all Wardens of the Cinque Ports. The castle looks onto the Broad Walk, 100m (328ft) long, on either side of a wide path backed by massive mature yew hedges (3m tall x 2m wide; 10ft x 7ft), and lined with fine herbaceous borders. Beyond are a croquet lawn, magnificent 19th-century terraces, and Penelope Hobhouse's new Queen Elizabeth The Queen Mother's Garden. To the north of the Broad Walk is the Kitchen Garden – an enclosed orchard with espaliered fruit trees, a cutting garden and glasshouses. Further away are drifts of daffodils, a lawnful of specimen trees planted by famous visitors from the 19th century onwards, a wildflower meadow, a thickly wooded quarry and a holm oak avenue planted in 1866.
magnificent old yew hedges; new garden by Penelope Hobhouse; English Heritage shop; tea room

Owned by English Heritage
Number of gardeners 4
Size 3.2ha (8 acres)
English Heritage Grade II

WAYSTRODE MANOR
Spode Lane, Cowden TN8 7HW

Tel 01342 850695
Location In village
Opening hours 2pm to 5.30pm on 20 May, 13 and 24 June
Admission fee Adults £3; children 50p

The garden at Waystrode Manor has been developed over the last 35 years. You approach it along an avenue of pink horse-chestnuts, but the garden has a good collection of plants and is laid out in the cottage style. Highlights include a bog garden, an old-fashioned rose garden, a white garden, irises, geraniums, ornamental trees and tender plants put out for the summer.
good borders; interesting plants; unusual trees; small shop; plant stall; teas and cakes

Owned by Mrs Jill Wright
Number of gardeners 2
Size 3.2ha (8 acres)

LANCASHIRE, MERSEYSIDE & GREATER MANCHESTER

There are few historic gardens in this industrial corner of the North West, but several public parks whose importance is both historical and contemporary: Sefton Park in Liverpool was designed by Edouard André, Birkenhead Park by Sir Joseph Paxton, and Heaton Park in Manchester by William Emes. The public gardens at the seaside resorts of Blackpool and Southport are famous for their summer displays. Few private gardens are open to the public, though the National Gardens Scheme has in several villages managed to persuade a cluster of gardens to open simultaneously and make up a good afternoon's visiting. Myerscough College near Preston is a RHS Partner College, with lectures and workshops all through the year. It also has a National Collection of *Eryngium* and is hoping for provisional acceptance for its collection of *Aesculus* (horse-chestnut) species and cultivars, of which it holds around 60. There is a handful of other National Collections in the three counties, but this is not a corner of England with any established interest in plants apart, perhaps, from alpines: Reginald Kaye at Carnforth and Holden Clough near Clitheroe are both long-established nurseries specialising in plants for cold climates. The new garden of the Lennox-Boyds at Gresgarth is a rising star.

COBBLE HEY FARM

Hobbs Lane, Claughton on Brock, Preston PR3 0QN

Tel 01995 602643
www.cobblehey.co.uk
Location 6 miles east of Garstang, signed from B6430
Opening hours 10.30am to 4.30pm, Thursday to Monday, February to Christmas
Admission fee Adults £3; concessions £2.50; children £1.50

Cobble Hey is a working farm, with rare breeds and a commitment to conservation. The garden is young, but has many different features, including three ponds (connected by 100 yards of stream), a fernery, heather garden, herbaceous border, parterre and much else. A garden to watch.
shop; small nursery; refreshments and light meals

Owned by Edwina Miller
Number of gardeners 3
Size 1ha (2 1/2 acres)

CROXTETH HALL & COUNTRY PARK

Croxteth Hall Lane, Liverpool L12 0HB

Tel 0151 233 6910 **Fax** 0151 228 2817
www.croxteth.co.uk
Location Muirhead Avenue East
Opening hours 10.30am to 5pm, daily, Easter to September
Admission fee Walled garden: adults £1.40; OAPs and children 80p; grounds: free

Very much a public amenity, Croxteth Hall has a fine woodland trail along the River Alt, but the main interest for gardeners is the Victorian walled garden. This aims to show visitors what they can achieve at home. There are lines of trained fruit trees, growing either against the walls or free-standing, a large vegetable garden (lots of varieties grown from the HDRA), an area for soft fruit, a herb garden, and a mushroom house – to remind people how mushrooms were once cultivated in grand gardens. These are interplanted with more ornamental features – a bedding display, a rose

garden, some herbaceous borders and the collection of fuchsias. There are also working greenhouses and some beehives, which add to the garden's interest.
herbs; plants under glass; fruit; good herbaceous borders; current holder of Sandford Award; shop; café

Owned by City of Liverpool
Number of gardeners 4
Size 1.5ha (3¾-acre) walled garden
NCCPG National Collections *Fuchsia* (hardy)
English Heritage Grade II

DUNHAM MASSEY
Altrincham WA14 4SJ

Tel 0161 941 1025 **Fax** 0161 929 7508
www.nationaltrust.org.uk
Location 3 miles south-west of Altrincham off A56; well signed (Dunham Massey Hall and Park)
Opening hours 11am to 5.30pm (4.30pm from 24 October), daily, 17 March to 28 October
Admission fee Gardens only: adults £5; children £2.50; car park £4

Dunham Massey's 250 acres include an ancient deer park, a medieval moat made into a lake in the 18th century, an Elizabethan mount, an 18th-century orangery, a pump house and some early landscape avenues. All remain as features of the grounds, but the National Trust has decided to major on its even more interesting Victorian relics – evergreen shrubberies, a bark house, ferns and colourful bedding-out schemes. Serpentine paths lead between borders thickly planted for texture and colour. The bog garden and moss garden take advantage of the unusual opportunities of the site. The woodlands are planted with Professor Pratt's azaleas, cardiocrinums, meconopsis, and more than 60 different hydrangeas. There are more unusual trees in the extensive lawns. The result is a potent cross-section of historical and modern styles with a solid core of Victorian excellence, while the standard of maintenance is one of the highest in any National Trust garden.
topiary; good herbaceous borders; hydrangeas; skimmias; Edwardian parterre; garden shop; large restaurant

Owned by The National Trust
Number of gardeners 5
Size 10ha (25 acres) of garden and 90ha (222-acre) park
English Heritage Grade II*

FLETCHER MOSS BOTANICAL GARDENS
Mill Gate Lane, Didsbury M20 8SD

Tel 0161 434 1877
Location In East Didsbury, off A5145
Opening hours 8am (9am at weekends and Bank Holidays) to dusk, daily, all year
Admission fee Free

Fletcher Moss is a model municipal botanic garden, beautifully maintained but open free to the public. In the rock garden, which is substantially constructed on three levels with a pool at the bottom, is a rich collection of alpine plants, small conifers, maples and aquatics. The woodland areas have excellent autumn colour, but are almost as good in spring.
rock garden; mature conifers; bulbs; heathers; rhododendrons; café

Owned by Manchester City Council
Size 8.5ha (21 acres)

HOGHTON TOWER
Hoghton, Preston PR5 0SH

Tel 01254 852986 **Fax** 01254 852109
www.hoghtontower.co.uk
Location A675 midway between Preston and Blackburn
Opening hours 11am to 4pm, Monday to Thursday, July to September; 1pm to 5pm, Sundays, July to September; also Bank Holiday Mondays from Easter to August
Admission fee Adults £3; children (under 5) free

A series of spacious courtyards and walled gardens surround this Tudor-Elizabethan castellated house, which is approached up a one-mile avenue. Its gardens are now undergoing restoration and upgrading. Their setting is impressive and there are fine spring walks in the rhododendron woods below.

GRESGARTH HALL

Caton, Lancaster LA2 9NB

Tel 01524 771838 **Fax** 01524 771281
www.arabellalennoxboyd.com/gresgarth
Location 1/2 mile south of Caton
Opening hours 11am to 5pm, 8 April, 13 May, 10 June, 8 July, 12 August, 9 September and 14 October
Admission fee Adults £5; children free

Mark and Arabella Lennox-Boyd bought Gresgarth Hall near Lancaster in 1978. Arabella is a distinguished garden designer, with a wonderful eye for structure, line and colour. The main formal gardens lie to the side of the house – terraces elegantly laid out with octagonal platforms, angled staircases and neat box edgings. Much of the planting here is white: *Clematis* 'Duchess of Edinburgh' and *Rosa* 'Climbing Mrs Herbert Stevens' grow against the retaining wall. Here and throughout the garden are magnificent hellebores, all the best modern cultivars from Ashwood Nurseries, Helen Ballard, Elizabeth Strangman and Will McLewin in Cheshire. The main herbaceous borders are in pastel shades (pink, blue and white) and designed to flower from April to October – ending with a splendid show of Michaelmas daisies and grasses. A new yellow border is planned for 2007: the herbaceous plantings are constantly changing as Arabella experiments and tests out new ideas and new combinations. The terraces run down to the lake, which the Lennox-Boyds re-landscaped. The damp border on its far side has glorious blue meconopsis, candelabra primulas in vast drifts, gunneras for late-summer effect and both species of *Lysichiton*. A handsome bridge crosses the river to a long woodland garden, which stretches along the valley bottom for about 400m (1,312ft). Springs are everywhere, and a great variety of soils which, together with the steep banks of the valley, make for an infinite number of microhabitats. The dominant species is English oak but there are also remnants of a Victorian planting of sequoias and wellingtonias. The principal underplanting is of winter-flowering witch hazels – *Hamamelis* 'Pallida', *H.* 'Diane' and many new cultivars: they now have more than 50 different cultivars. The hillside across the river is laid out with an extensive collection of young rhododendrons and azaleas. The Lennox-Boyds have also planted a very large number of magnolias (over 300 different cultivars), an avenue of filberts and cobs along the outside of the walled garden and a substantial group of the different cultivars of lilac. Microhabitats support some surprisingly tender plants. *Drimys lanceolata* and *Olearia scillonensis* both grow out in the open: so does the sweet-scented *Daphne bholua*, which has started to seed around – there are over 60 bushes now, some grown from Sir Peter Smithers's garden in Switzerland and others of their own raising. Among the rarest plants are a fine *Emmenopterys henryi*, micropropagated by Kew. Lilies also flourish, particularly the tall white *Cardiocrinum yunnanense*. More and more plants are being added from seed collected all over the world. But it is above all the energy and the scale of the Lennox-Boyds' endeavours which create the greatest impression. They have successfully combined good design, passionate plantsmanship and a fine eye for decoration in a uniquely romantic natural setting. There can be no doubt that Gresgarth is one of the greatest gardens of our times.

good design; colour plantings; rhododendrons; plant sales; teas and cakes

Owned by The Hon Sir Mark and Lady Lennox-Boyd
Number of gardeners 4 1/2
Size 5ha (12 acres)

good herbaceous borders; rhododendrons and azaleas; gift shop; tea room

Owned by Hoghton Tower Preservation Trust
Number of gardeners Contractors
English Heritage Grade II

HOLDEN CLOUGH NURSERY
Holden, Bolton by Bowland, Clitheroe BB7 4PF

Tel 01200 447615 **Fax** 01200 447197
www.holdencloughnursery.co.uk
Location 8 miles north-east of Clitheroe, off A59
Opening hours 9am to 5pm, Monday to Friday, March to October; plus Saturdays all year; other times by appointment
Admission fee Free

This long-established working nursery (founded in 1927) has a large range of interesting alpines, perennials, crocosmias (including some new cultivars), dwarf conifers, shrubs, ferns, grasses and foliage plants. It is well known at shows all over the country. Two of its best introductions are the hardy and vigorous hybrid *Iris* 'Holden Clough' and the dwarf-growing *Pieris japonica* 'Little Heath'. Others, now available once again, are the rare and beautiful *Astilbe* 'Holden Clough' and the double-flowered *Rhodohypoxis* 'Holden Rose'. The display garden is still expanding, with new plantings and a new alpine bed for 2007.

Owned by Peter Foley
Size 0.8ha (2 acres)

LEIGHTON HALL
Carnforth LA5 9ST

Tel 01524 734474 **Fax** 01524 720357
www.leightonhall.co.uk
Location Signed from A6 junction with M6
Opening hours 2pm to 5pm, Tuesday to Friday and Bank Holiday Sundays and Mondays, May to September; plus all Sundays in August; open at 12.30am in August
Admission fee House and gardens: adults £6; OAPs £5

The handsome semi-castellated house at Leighton is set in lush parkland with the Lakeland Fells as a backdrop: the Victorian conservatory to the side of the house has recently been restored. The main garden features are in the 19th-century walled garden, whose formal paths contrast with the exuberant informality of the planting. Here are herbaceous borders, a herb garden, fruit trees, a vegetable plot and masses of climbing roses – as well as the unusual gravel maze.
roses (mainly old-fashioned); herbs; fruit; good herbaceous borders; 'caterpillar' path maze; Victorian conservatory; gift shop; tea room

Owned by RG Reynolds
Number of gardeners 1½
Size 2ha (5 acres)

RUFFORD OLD HALL
Rufford, Ormskirk L40 1SG

Tel 01704 821254 **Fax** 01704 823813
www.nationaltrust.org.uk
Location 7 miles north of Ormskirk on A59
Opening hours Noon to 4pm, Saturdays and Sundays, 3 to 18 March; 11am to 5.30pm, Saturday to Wednesday and Good Friday, 24 March to 28 October
Admission fee Garden only: adults £3.50; children £1.70

One of the National Trust's most successful re-creations, the gardens are laid out in the Victorian style around a remarkable 15th-century timber-framed house. The garden had little character when the National Trust took over, but Graham Stuart Thomas was charged with adding exotic shrubs and plants to make it more interesting to visitors. The results include box and yew topiary, a mixed border of roses and herbaceous plants, and an explosion of crocuses, daffodils, bluebells and rhododendrons in spring.
roses (mainly old-fashioned); rhododendrons and azaleas; good herbaceous borders; National Trust shop; lunches and teas

Owned by The National Trust
Number of gardeners 1
Size 5.6ha (14 acres)

SPEKE HALL

The Walk, Liverpool L24 1XD

Tel 0151 427 7231 **Fax** 0151 427 9860
www.nationaltrust.org.uk
Location 1 mile off A561, on west side of Liverpool Airport
Opening hours 11am to 5.30pm (dusk from mid-October to March), daily, all year, except 1 January and 24 to 26 and 31 December
Admission fee Grounds and Home Farm only: adults £4; children £1.90

Speke is an oasis among the concrete deserts of Merseyside's suburbs. At its heart is a substantial half-timbered house, dating back to the 14th century and surrounded by a moat, now dry. The garden is mainly modern, a sympathetic restoration of the one which a rich Liverpool merchant made in the mid-19th century. On the south lawn, three Victorian island beds have recently been remade. The nearby rose garden was planted in 1984 with shrubs and floribundas. All around are rhododendrons, daffodils and bluebells in spring.
roses; spring bulbs; summer borders; stream garden; shop; restaurant

Owned by The National Trust
Number of gardeners 3
Size 7ha (17½ acres)
English Heritage Grade II

LEICESTERSHIRE

One of the reasons why there are so few historic gardens in Leicestershire (no Grade I gardens and only two Grade II*) is that much of the county was open and unenclosed until the latter half of the 18th century. Even today, it is not as rich in interesting gardens as its neighbours, Northamptonshire and Warwickshire. However, the National Gardens Scheme offers a respectable number of gardens to visit in its Yellow Book, and the first-rate gardens at Wartnaby and Long Close show just how much can be grown by an adventurous plantsman – so does the excellent University of Leicester Botanic Garden. Leicestershire has some good garden centres and a handful of first-rate specialist nurseries. Brooksby Melton College is a RHS Partner College with a fine teaching garden and collection of plants. It also has two National Collections: *Liriope* and *Ophiopogon*. Contrary to local belief, there is no such county as Rutland: it was dissolved in 1974 and absorbed into Leicestershire until eventually it re-emerged as a unitary authority. We include its gardens here for convenience.

BARNSDALE GARDENS

The Avenue, Exton, Oakham LE15 8AH

Tel 01572 813200 **Fax** 01572 813346
www.barnsdalegardens.co.uk
Location The Avenue is on south-west edge of Exton
Opening hours 9am to 5pm (7pm from June to August), daily, March to October; 10am to 4pm, daily, November to February; last admissions 2 hours before closure; closed on 24 and 25 December
Admission fee Adults £6; concessions £5; children £2; families £15; groups £4.50; RHS members free except in group visits

Barnsdale was famous for 20 years as Geoff Hamilton's BBC *Gardeners' World* garden. Within it are 37 smaller individual gardens and garden features, laid out and maintained with the same intention – to encourage people to make the most of their opportunities as garden owners. The gardens are of every kind. Some have descriptive names like the Tranquil Garden and the Town Paradise: others are more specific like the Japanese Garden, the Rose Garden, the Stream and Bog Garden. But for many visitors, the most interesting are those which match their own particular circumstances and inspire them to become better gardeners – the Cottage Garden, the Small Town Garden, the Ornamental Kitchen Garden and the Allotment Garden. All are maintained to the highest standard and continue to educate, delight and inspire. The attached specialist nursery sells over 2,000 different plants, many of them rare and unusual. Owned and run by Geoff Hamilton's son and daughter-in-law, its policy is to offer the widest possible choice of good plants to its customers. There will be four RHS Special Events at Barnsdale Gardens in 2007; details from 020 7821 3408.
gift shop; nursery; licensed coffee shop

Owned by Sue and Nick Hamilton
Number of gardeners 6
Size 3.2ha (8 acres)

BELVOIR CASTLE

Belvoir, Grantham NG32 1PD

Tel 01476 871002 **Fax** 01476 871018
www.belvoircastle.com
Location 6 miles west of Grantham
Opening hours 11am and 5pm, 3 to 12 April and weekends in April; daily, except Mondays and Fridays, in May and June (but open on Bank Holiday Mondays); daily, except Fridays in July and August; Saturdays and Sundays in September
Admission fee Gardens: adults £6; RHS members free from April to July

Barnsdale Gardens

Belvoir has formal gardens along the Victorian terraces beneath the castle and a Broad Walk overlooking the restored 19th-century rose garden. Some way off is a hedged enclosure with seven statues by Caius Cibber. The Spring Garden has recently been restored to its early 19th-century form. woodland garden; roses (mainly modern); tallest bird cherry *Prunus avium* (28m; 92ft) and yew tree *Taxus baccata* (29m; 95ft) in the British Isles; gift shop; lunches and teas; picnic site

Owned by The Duke of Rutland
Number of gardeners 4
English Heritage Grade II

GOSCOTE NURSERIES LTD

Syston Road, Cossington LE7 4UZ

Tel 01509 812121 **Fax** 01509 814231
www.goscote.co.uk
Location 5 miles north of Leicester, on B5328
Opening hours 9am to 5pm, Monday to Saturday; 10am to 5pm, Sundays; closes at 4.30pm in winter and between Christmas and New Year
Admission fee Free

(P) 👪 ✿

Goscote has a wide range of reasonably priced plants of all types – more than 1,500 different kinds are propagated on-site. They offer an extensive collection of trees and shrubs, including acers, azaleas, clematis, conifers and roses, many of them rare or unusual. Plants can also be seen in the show gardens, laid out as island beds and borders, with a rock garden, a water garden and a 20m (66ft) pergola. The website is very helpful. mature show gardens

Owned by Frank James Toone
Size 0.3ha (3/4 acre)

THE HERB NURSERY

Thistleton, Oakham LE15 7RE

Tel 01572 767658 **Fax** 01572 768021
www.herbnursery.co.uk
Location In middle of village
Opening hours 9am to 6pm (or dusk, if earlier), daily; closed from Christmas to New Year; open weekend: 16 and 17 June
Admission fee Donation

This family-run nursery lists nearly 500 herbs and wildflower plants, with a special emphasis upon lavender, mint and thyme. The range of scented-leaf pelargoniums is particularly good (80+ cultivars), and there is an extensive range of cottage garden plants. The demonstration beds and borders around the nursery are a bonus. Ask to see the new knot garden.

Owned by Peter and Christine Bench

KAYES GARDEN NURSERY

1700 Melton Road, Rearsby, Leicester LE7 4YR

Tel: 01664 424578
Location On A607, north-east of Leicester
Opening hours 10am to 5pm (10am to noon on Sundays), Tuesday to Sunday, March to October; by appointment from November to February
Admission fee Garden: £2; nursery: free

This popular nursery has an excellent, mature display garden, densely planted with a wide range of interesting plants. It also opens for the National Gardens Scheme. The nursery's specialities are hardy herbaceous plants, grasses, aquatics and climbers. Hazel Kaye has a plantsman's eye for quality, and the list includes many of the best forms of a wide range of plants.
eryngiums; tradescantias; teas

Owned by Hazel Kaye
Number of gardeners 2
Size 0.6ha (1½ acres)
NCCPG National Collections *Tradescantia* (Andersoniana Group)

LONG CLOSE

Main Street, Woodhouse Eaves, Loughborough LE12 8RZ

Tel 01509 890616 (daytime)
www.longclose.org.uk
Location 4 miles south of Loughborough
Opening hours 9.30am to 5.30pm, Tuesday to Saturday and Bank Holiday Mondays, March to October, but closed in August; groups also welcome at other times by appointment; for NGS: 1pm to 5pm on 5 April (plant fair), 2pm to 6pm on 27 May (plants for sale)
Admission fee Adults £3.50; children 50p; tickets from Pene Crafts Gift Shop, opposite (9.30am to 1pm and 2pm to 5.30pm); groups and on Sundays pay at garden

This is a plantsman's garden, made over many years and now magnificently mature. Some of the plants might be thought too tender for so far north: it has been called 'a Cornish garden in Leicestershire'. The entrance courtyard has *Crinum* x *powellii* 'Album', *Sophora tetraptera* and *Clematis armandii*. You go round the side of the house and suddenly a spacious series of terraced gardens opens out below you, lined by clouds of rhododendrons and venerable conifers. The terraced lawns lead to a fine woodland garden, underplanted with bulbs, magnolias, camellias and massed rhododendrons and azaleas. Elsewhere are good herbaceous plantings, a thicket of *Prunus tenella*, penstemons (quite a collection), a box-edged *potager*, a very handsome, bulging, pendulous ash *Fraxinus excelsior* 'Pendula', aged wisterias, *Azara microphylla* 6m (20ft) tall, Italian cypresses *Cupressus sempervirens* Stricta Group, a stream and pond, thickly planted with both species of *Lysichiton*, a wildflower meadow with orchids in June and *Lathraea clandestina* spreading upon the roots of an old poplar. Soaring above are huge English oaks, and arborescent hawthorns (*Crataegus monogyna*) as much as 20m (66ft) high. The whole garden is run organically.
woodland garden; rhododendrons; azaleas; spring bulbs; lots of other interesting plants; plants for sale, especially penstemons; tea and coffee; refreshments for groups by arrangement; teas on Sundays

Owned by John Oakland and Pene Johnson
Size 2.2ha (5½ acres) plus 1.2ha (3-acre) meadow

ORCHARDS

Hall Lane, Walton, Lutterworth LE17 5RP

Tel 01455 556958
www5e.biglobe.ne.jp/~orchards/
Location In the centre of Walton
Opening hours For NGS: 11am to 5pm, 3 June and 15 July; groups at other times by appointment
Admission fee Adults £2.50; children free

The most interesting thing about this modern garden is that all its plants have *green* leaves. The owners believe that coloured or variegated leaves compete with the flowers for our attention, and that the best way to enjoy them is against their natural foliage. The underlying principle – this is a very thoughtful and intensely designed garden – is to imitate the contrasting light effect of our native woodlands and meadows. There is a preference for plants with a fleeting season of flower, which makes them all the more precious; so there are no repeat-flowering roses or ever-blooming osteospermums here. The result is quite unlike any other garden, and makes you realise how important it is to take in the surrounding countryside and to reflect the sky.
teas

Owned by Mr and Mrs Graham Cousins
Number of gardeners Owners only
Size 0.5ha (1¼ acres)

UNIVERSITY OF LEICESTER BOTANIC GARDEN

Beaumont Hall, Stoughton Drive, Oadby LE2 2NA

Tel 0116 271 7725/2933
www.le.ac.uk/biology/botanicgarden
Location 3 miles south of Leicester on A6 London Road opposite racecourse; visitor entrance at The Knoll, Glebe Road
Opening hours 10am to 4pm, Monday to Friday, all year; plus Saturdays and Sundays from 17 March to 11 November; closed 1 January, 25 and 26 December; special Open Days: 11am to 4pm, 1 and 29 July and 2 September
Admission fee Free, but charge for special events

The University of Leicester Botanic Garden moved to its present site in 1947. It fills the grounds surrounding four houses, which were built early in the 20th century and are now used as student residences. The four (once separate) gardens have been merged into a single entity – the University Botanic Garden with some 16 acres. They now support a wide variety of plants, from historic trees to a 1980s ecological meadow. A pretty Edwardian pergola draped with roses, a well-planted rock garden and a splendid display of hardy fuchsias from the National Collection all add to its interest. In 1997 the garden opened an out-station at Knighton, known as the Attenborough Arboretum. Though its plantings are still few and the trees very young, it is designed to display the native tree flora of England in a historical sequence of arrival dates – ending with beech (*Fagus sylvatica*) after the last Ice Age.
rock garden; rhododendrons and azaleas; plants under glass; mature conifers; cacti; succulents; heathers; fuchsias

Owned by The University of Leicester
Number of gardeners 5
Size 6.4ha (16 acres)
NCCPG National Collections *Aubrieta*; *Chamaecyparis lawsoniana*; *Fuchsia*; *Skimmia*

WARREN HILLS COTTAGE

Warren Hills Road, Coalville LE67 4UY

Tel 01530 812350
www.warrenhills.co.uk
Location On B587 near the schools on the Copt Oak to Whitwick road
Opening hours Noon to 5pm, 20 May, 24 June and 29 July; and by appointment; groups welcome; all for NGS
Admission fee Adults £2; children 50p

This maturing garden is attached to a small nursery specialising in hardy plants, many of them unusual. The owner describes it as 'a plantaholic's garden', planted to provide year-round interest. The main feature is the collection of over 55 different astrantias, each growing in its own labelled bed. Other features include hellebores, bulbs and early perennials underscoring the rhododendrons.
astrantias; campanulas; penstemons; salvias; cream teas on open days

Owned by Graham Waters
Number of gardeners 2 part-time
Size 0.8ha (2 acres)
NCCPG National Collections *Astrantia*

WARTNABY GARDENS

Wartnaby, Melton Mowbray LE14 3HY

Tel 01664 822549 (best between 10.30am and 1pm)
www.wartnabygardenlabels.co.uk
Location 3 miles north of Melton Mowbray on A606; left at A6 Kettley then 1 mile
Opening hours 9.30am to 12.30pm, Tuesdays, April to July; for NGS (plant fairs): 11am to 3pm on 25 February and 11am to 4pm on 29 April and 17 June; and parties by appointment
Admission fee Adults £3; children free; RHS members free on Tuesdays; adults £2.50 on 25 February

Wartnaby is the garden of someone who loves roses and is prepared to make them one of the principal elements of her garden design: the result is one of the best modern examples of how to grow roses in mixed borders. Even in the so-called rose garden, the roses do not dominate: they are interplanted instead with other shrubs, like ceanothus, hebes and tree peonies, and underplanted with geraniums and bulbs. Foliage, shapes, colours and textures take over when the roses are not in flower. The long central path in the substantial kitchen garden is flanked by massed plantings of hybrid musks, including 'Cornelia', 'Prosperity' and 'Pink Prosperity', underplanted with the grey-leaved *Stachys byzantina* and *Lychnis flos-jovis*, and edged with lavender and box. Recent developments include spring plantings around the ponds and pools in the woodland and a new walk through the young arboretum. Wartnaby is a garden of enormous interest and charm.
roses (mainly old-fashioned) used in mixed borders; fruit; fine collection of trees; colour borders; many new features; refreshments

Owned by Lady King
Size 2ha (5 acres)

WHATTON HOUSE

Long Whatton, Loughborough LE12 5BG

Tel/fax 01509 842268
www.whattongardens.co.uk
Location 3 miles from Jct 24, Kegworth A6 towards Hathern
Opening hours 11am to 4pm, Sunday to Friday, March to October; groups welcome by arrangement
Admission fee Adults £2.50; children free

The garden at Whatton was started in 1880 and many of the older features date from about 1900, but there has been much replanting over the years, especially recently. A rose garden, a fine herbaceous border and some magnificent specimen trees are among the attractions. It is particularly interesting in spring when the bulbs and flowering shrubs are in full display.
roses (ancient and modern); good herbaceous borders; arboretum; climbing plants; bark temple; canyon garden; bulbs; teas on Sunday afternoons

Owned by Lord Crawshaw
Number of gardeners 1 1/2, plus owners
Size 6ha (15 acres)
English Heritage Grade II

LINCOLNSHIRE

Lincolnshire, with which we include what was for a while South Humberside, has long been known for its horticultural industry based on bulb-growing, and it still has a high number of producers, both wholesale and retail. The show garden at Springfields is one of the great attractions of Lincolnshire in spring. The county has its fair share of important historic gardens: Belton House and Grimsthorpe Castle are both open to the public, though the third Grade I garden at Brocklesby Park (Capability Brown, Humphry Repton and Reginald Blomfield all worked there) remains strictly private. The National Gardens Scheme has a fair number of gardens opening for charity and the county is blessed with several specialist nurseries of national importance. Pottertons Nursery near Caistor is a leading source of alpine plants and Kathleen Muncaster on the north-west outskirts of Gainsborough has a very impressive range of fuchsias. Unfortunately, the Japanese maple specialist Hippopottering Nursery is moving to a new site, and its new arboretum will not be open to visitors for a few years. RHS members have free access to Normanby Hall Country Park, one of the most interesting restoration projects on the east coast of England. Easton Walled Garden, a private initiative, has also achieved near-miracles since restoration began in 2002.

AUBOURN HALL

Auborn, Lincoln LN5 9DZ

Tel 01522 788224 **Fax** 01522 788199
Location Signed off A46, 8 miles south-west of Lincoln
Opening hours 1pm to 5pm, Monday to Friday, 14 May to 6 July; charity openings: 22 April (NCCPG sale), 13 May (St John Ambulance) and 16 and 17 June (sculpture weekend)
Admission fee Adults £4; children £2

Aubourn has spring bulbs, colour-themed borders, a rose garden, sweeping lawns and handsome old trees (especially cedars) around a Jacobean mansion.
refreshments

Owned by Mr and Mrs Christopher Nevile
Number of gardeners 2
Size 4ha (10 acres)

BAYTREE NURSERIES

High Road, Weston, Spalding PE12 6JU

Tel 01406 370242 **Fax** 01406 372829
www.baytree-gardencentre.com
Location 1½ miles east of Spalding, on A151
Opening hours 9am to 6pm, summer; 9am to 5pm, winter; closed for Easter Day, Christmas Day and Boxing Day

Baytree won the Garden Centre of Excellence Award some years ago: in 2000 it also won the trade's Retailer of the Year Award. Its 15 acres include a pets and aquatic department, a leisure complex devoted to selling garden furniture and an owl centre. But it also aims to carry the largest selection of bulbs available at retail level anywhere in the country and a very large stock of plants, many of them grown on-site. Roses are a speciality: Baytree lists over 300 cultivars including some which it has bred and introduced itself.
self-service licensed restaurant

Owned by Reinhard Biehler
Size 6.2ha (15½ acres)

BELTON HOUSE

Grantham NG32 2LS

Tel 01476 566116 **Fax** 01476 579071
www.nationaltrust.org.uk
Location 3 miles north-east of Grantham on A607
Opening hours 11am (10.30am in August) to 5.30pm, Wednesday to Sunday and Bank Holiday Mondays,

17 March to 28 October (closed on 14 July); plus noon to 4pm, Friday to Sunday, 2 November to 16 December
Admission fee Adults £7; children £4.50; families £18.50

Grandeur and amenity go hand in hand at Belton. There are 1,000 acres of wooded deer park, a Wyattville orangery, a Dutch garden and an Italian garden with statues and parterres. But the adventure playground and other facilities make it popular with all ages.
woodland garden; topiary; snowdrops; daffodils; bluebells; good herbaceous borders; biggest sugar maple *Acer saccharum* in the British Isles; gift shop; lunches, teas, licensed restaurant

Owned by The National Trust
Number of gardeners 4
Size 14ha (35 acres)
English Heritage Grade I

DODDINGTON HALL

Doddington, Lincoln LN6 4RU

Tel 01522 694308 **Fax** 01522 682584
www.doddingtonhall.com
Location Signed off A46 Lincoln bypass
Opening hours 1pm to 5pm, Sundays and Bank Holiday Mondays, 19 February to 30 September; plus Wednesdays from May to September; gardens open at noon from May onwards
Admission fee Garden only: adults £3.90; children £1.95; RHS members free; tours by arrangement

Doddington is a ravishing Elizabethan house around which successive generations have made a successful Tudor-style garden. The owners keep it simple and formal at the front, but in the walled garden (thickly and richly planted) are Edwardian knots and parterres, a modern herb garden and pleached hornbeams. Wonderfully harmonious and strongly recommended in early summer. There will be five RHS Special Events at Doddington Hall in 2007; details from 020 7821 3408.
good herbaceous borders; long succession of spring bulbs; irises; peonies; box-edged parterres; topiary; farm shop; café

Doddington Hall Gardens

Owned by Claire Birch
Number of gardeners 3
Size 2.4ha (6 acres)
English Heritage Grade II*

EASTON WALLED GARDENS

Easton, Grantham NG33 5AP

Tel 01476 530063 **Fax** 01476 550116
www.eastonwalledgardens.co.uk
Location Between A1 and B6403, 2 miles north of Colsterworth
Opening hours 11am to 4pm, daily, 10 to 23 February for snowdrops; 11am to 4pm, Wednesdays, Fridays, Sundays and Bank Holiday Mondays, April to September; Sundays only from October to December
Admission fee Adults £4.50; children 50p; coaches by appointment only

Easton has a spectacular display of snowdrops in late winter, and the garden is always open for a week or ten days when they are at their peak. But there is even more to see at other times of the year, because the whole garden is undergoing a substantial restoration and reinterpretation by its young, enthusiastic owners. Easton Hall, the house, was pulled down in 1951 and the garden abandoned. Now – starting in 2002 – the avenues have been cleared, stonework restored and new planting schemes devised. Do not expect an instant garden, but visit Easton now as it emerges from 50 years of neglect, and then return to measure the progress. Work continues – new in 2006 were a David Austin rose garden, a turf maze, an iris collection and some sweet pea trials. This year (2007) sees the addition of trial beds for

Grimsthorpe Castle

annuals, 5,000 tulips and extensive plantings in the raised vegetable beds. There will be two RHS Special Events at Easton Walled Gardens in 2007, one for snowdrops and the other for sweet peas; details from 020 7821 3408.
plants for sale; gift shop; sweet pea seeds; tea room

Owned by Sir Fred and Lady Cholmeley
Number of gardeners 3
Size 4.8ha (12 acres)
English Heritage Grade II

GRIMSTHORPE CASTLE
Grimsthorpe, Bourne PE10 0LY

Tel 01778 591205 **Fax** 01778 591259
www.grimsthorpe.co.uk
Location On A151, 4 miles north-west of Bourne
Opening hours 11am to 6pm, Thursdays, Sundays and Bank Holiday Mondays; April to September; plus daily from June to August except Fridays and Saturdays
Admission fee Adults £3.50; concessions £3; children £2

Much is happening at Grimsthorpe. Recent researches have unearthed traces of the Stephen Switzer garden design from about 1700 and shown that it was probably a local engineer called John Grundy who designed the lake in 1771, not Capability Brown. Yew hedges have been planted to enclose the Victorian Italian garden, which is stylishly maintained with summer bedding among the topiary, urns and sculptures. The most interesting horticultural feature is a formal vegetable garden, made in the 1960s before the craze for *potagers*, right below the Italian garden. The ornamental ponds, complete with fountains, have just (2005) been re-instated within the topiary squares, and further developments are planned for the near future.
topiary; roses (mainly modern); fine collection of trees; shop; tea room (licensed)

Owned by Grimsthorpe and Drummond Castle Trust Ltd
Number of gardeners 4
Size 10.7ha (27 acres)
English Heritage Grade I

GUNBY HALL
Gunby, Spilsby PE23 5SS

Tel 01909 486411 **Fax** 01909 486377
www.nationaltrust.org.uk
Location 2 1/2 miles north-west of Burgh-le-Marsh
Opening hours 2pm to 5pm, Tuesday to Thursday, June to August; plus Wednesdays in May; by written appointment only: Tuesday to Thursday in April and September, and Tuesdays and Thursdays in May
Admission fee Adults £3.50; children £2; families £9

Rich herbaceous borders, an arched apple walk, shrub roses, herbs and traditional English vegetables are planted in the exquisite walled garden.
roses (mainly old-fashioned); herbs; fruit; good herbaceous borders

Owned by The National Trust
Number of gardeners 2, plus volunteers
Size 2.8ha (7 acres)
English Heritage Grade II

HALL FARM & NURSERY
Harpswell, Gainsborough DN21 5UU

Tel 01427 668412 **Fax** 01427 667478
www.hall-farm.co.uk/nursery
Location On A361, 7 miles east of Gainsborough
Opening hours 10am to 5.30pm (or dusk, if earlier), weekdays, all year; for NGS: 10am to 5.30pm on 3 September
Admission fee Adults £3; children 50p on NGS day; otherwise a charity donation is requested

This garden is intensely planted and beautifully maintained as an adjunct to the nursery, and for the owners' pleasure. There are plants of every kind – trees, shrubs, bulbs and herbaceous plants – and over 100 different roses. The National Gardens Scheme day (always on the first Sunday in September) is a 'free seed collection' day.
roses (mainly old-fashioned) in a newly-made rose garden; plantsman's collection of plants; good herbaceous borders; sunken garden; good nursery next door

Owned by Pam and Mark Tatam
Size 0.6ha (1 1/2 acres)

KATHLEEN MUNCASTER FUCHSIAS
18 Field Lane, Morton, Gainsborough DN21 3BY

Tel 01427 612329
www.kathleenmuncasterfuchsias.co.uk
Location North-west of Gainsborough; Field Lane is off the minor road to Walkerith
Opening hours 10am to 5pm, Thursday to Tuesday, February to mid-June; phone first at other times
Admission fee Free

This is the nursery of a fuchsia specialist who began as an amateur and now has a National Collection of hardy cultivars and one of the largest nurseries in the country which specialises in the genus. The fuchsias can be seen in the garden, together with the stock plants: almost all the glasshouses may also be visited. The list is impressive, though not all the cultivars in the collection are propagated regularly – ask if they have a cutting available. They will introduce four new fuchsias in 2007: long-flowering 'Carole Hipkin', well-branched 'Emmakins', semi-erect 'Lincoln Castle' and all-purpose 'Marilyn Jane'.
teas for pre-arranged groups

Owned by Kathleen Muncaster
Number of gardeners owner only
Size 0.25ha (2/3 acre)
NCCPG National Collections *Fuchsia* (hardy)

NORMANBY HALL COUNTRY PARK
Normanby, Scunthorpe DN15 9HU

Tel 01724 720588 **Fax** 01724 721248
www.northlincs.gov.uk/normanby
Location 3 miles north of Scunthorpe
Opening hours Walled garden: 10.30am to 5pm (4.30pm in winter), daily, all year, except 1 January and 25 and 26 December; park: 9am to dusk, daily, all year
Admission fee Adults £4.40; children £2.20 (2006 prices); RHS members free

The Victorian Walled Garden (actually built in 1817, before Queen Victoria was even born) has been restored and planted – with help from the National Lottery – as a living museum of 19th-century horticulture. Old varieties of fruit and vegetables are grown organically. The glasshouses have recently been rebuilt to house peaches and other fruit. Ferns and exotic ornamentals fill a display house. Recent developments include a bog garden along the base of the ha-ha (125m; 410ft long), a Christmas garden of hollies, ivies, hellebores and ferns, and herbaceous borders in the Secret Garden and Sunken Garden. Now they are developing a Victorian woodland garden. Two RHS Special Events will take place during 2007; details from 020 7821 3408.
fruit and vegetables; herbaceous borders; woodland walks and parkland outside; deer park; shop; refreshments

Owned by Sir Reginald Sheffield (leased to North Lincs Council)
Number of gardeners 4
Size 0.4ha (1 acre), plus 120ha (300 acres) of parkland

POTTERTONS NURSERY
Moortown Road, Nettleton,
Market Rasen LN7 6HX

Tel 01472 851714 **Fax** 01472 852580
www.pottertons.co.uk
Location 20 miles north-east of Lincoln, on B1205; leave A46 at Nettleton
Opening hours 9am to 4pm, daily; special opening weekends 19 and 20 May and 8 and 9 September
Admission fee Free

This alpine, bulb and rock plant specialist (formerly known as Potterton and Martin) has an interesting and extensive range of plants for sale, running from the easy to the unusual. All are propagated on-site, and most can be seen in the extensive display garden. The rock garden has a stream course, waterfalls and pools: elsewhere are raised beds, troughs, woodland and peat beds. The nursery holds many Chelsea gold medals, and has won the RHS Farrer Trophy (best alpine display) on several occasions. Satisfied customers praise not only the nursery's wide choice of plants, but also its cultivation skills and reasonable pricing policy.
large rock garden

Owned by Robert and Jackie Potterton
Number of gardeners 1 part-time
Size 2ha (5 acres)

SPRINGFIELDS FESTIVAL GARDENS
Camelgate, Spalding PE12 6ET

Tel 01775 724843 **Fax** 01775 711209
www.springfieldsgardens.co.uk
Location 1 mile from Spalding, signed off A16 bypass
Opening hours 10am to 6pm (8pm on Thursdays), Monday to Saturday; 11am to 5pm on Sundays, all year, except 25 December
Admission fee Free; parking charge

Springfields Horticultural Society, a registered charity, owns and maintains the show gardens for the UK flower bulb industry. They were re-landscaped as part of a major out-of-town retail centre in 2003 to 2004. They include formal gardens, seasonal flowerbeds, celebrity gardens (Charlie Dimmock, Chris Beardshaw, Kim Wilde), a Japanese garden, woodland walks, natural wetlands and water features. But best of all are the spectacular displays of bulbs – daffodils, tulips, hyacinths and many others, all donated by the industry.
millions of bulbs; shopping mall; restaurant and café

Owned by Springfields Horticultural Society Ltd
Number of gardeners 5
Size 8ha (20 acres)

LONDON

London gardeners are much more fortunate than they would have you believe. They have a micro-climate that enables them to grow plants that are tender anywhere except in the mildest corners of the south-west, and they enjoy a good choice of suitably stylish plants from garden centres and other outlets within the city itself. Some of the world's greatest gardens are within a short journey: among them are the Chelsea Physic Garden, Chiswick House, the Royal Botanic Gardens at Kew, Richmond Park and Syon Park. The Royal Parks Agency manages the inner-city green spaces like Hyde Park and Regent's Park with immense horticultural skill: almost all the parks contain acres of well-kept grass and trees of record size. London is, of course, the seat of the Royal Horticultural Society, whose Chelsea Flower Show is traditionally regarded as the start of the London summer season. The Hampton Court Palace Flower Show in July is, if possible, even more of a Londoners' show, while the regular London shows at the RHS's own halls in Westminster are attended by thousands of London gardeners keen to see plants and buy them. Nowhere has so many lectures and other educational garden events as London does. The RHS's Partner College at Capel Manor has a long programme of lectures, demonstrations and workshops throughout the year. Many of the specialist plant societies have their shows and administrative offices in London, too: if you want to see plants as diverse as orchids, carnations, vegetables, daffodils or camellias, London is the place to do so. The National Gardens Scheme thrives there; the Museum of Garden History is based there – just across the river from the Houses of Parliament; the Association of Gardens Trusts has its office in London and so does the Institute of Horticulture. The London Historic Parks & Gardens Trust is one of the country's most successful conservation societies. The greater part of the RHS's Lindley Library – Britain's largest collection of horticultural books and primary sources about gardening – is based in London and now housed in spacious purpose-built accommodation at 80 Vincent Square. Perhaps the only thing that a Londoner cannot do is to garden on a large scale. That apart, there is no better place to be a garden-lover.

BEALE ARBORETUM

West Lodge Park Hotel, Cockfosters Road, Hadley Wood EN4 0PY

Tel 020 8216 3904 **Fax** 020 8449 9916
www.bealeshotels.co.uk
Location A111 1 mile south of M25, Jct 24
Opening hours 2pm to 5pm, Monday to Friday, April to October; for NGS: 13 May (2pm to 5pm) and 28 October (1pm to 4pm)
Admission fee £3

The Beales have been developing their arboretum since 1963 by adding to the original plantings around the house. It is now run by Andrew Beale, the third generation to be involved. Young trees are planted among much older specimens – Victorian cedars and redwoods – with a view to the overall effect. A grassy glade runs down from the hotel terrace to a classical cupola at the bottom, inviting exploration. There are fine collections of oaks, hornbeams, liquidambars and nyssas, as well as buddlejas, elaeagnus and rhododendrons. The arboretum is maintained to a high standard, primarily as a facility for hotel guests. It is an excellent example of what can be achieved by an enthusiastic individual.

20-acre arboretum; mature conifers; fine collection of young trees; 200-year-old *Arbutus unedo*; refreshments in hotel

Owned by Beales Hotels
Number of gardeners 2
Size 12ha (30 acres)
NCCPG National Collections *Carpinus betulus* (cvs.); *Elaeagnus*

CANNIZARO PARK
West Side Common, Wimbledon SW19 4UE

Tel 020 8545 3657
www.cannizaropark.org.uk
Location West side of Wimbledon Common
Opening hours 8am to sunset, Monday to Friday, 9am to sunset, Saturday, Sunday and Bank Holidays; all year
Admission fee Free

Cannizaro is well known among connoisseurs for its azaleas, planted about 40 years ago and a magnificent spectacle when in full flower. It is one of the best woodland gardens of its type in the country and especially beautiful when the underplantings of bulbs are in flower. There are some fine specimen trees, including birches, horse-chestnuts and the tall sassafras.
woodland garden; mature conifers; azaleas; magnolias; several *Sassafras albidum* 15m (49ft) or more; some refreshments at summer weekends

Owned by London Borough of Merton
Size 15.5ha (39 acres)
English Heritage Grade II*

CAPEL MANOR
Bullsmoor Lane, Enfield EN1 4RQ

Tel 08456 122 122 **Fax** 01992 717544
www.capel.ac.uk
Location A10 by M25, Jct 25
Opening hours 10am to 6pm (or dusk, if earlier), daily, March to October; weekdays only from November to February
Admission fee Adults £5; OAPs £4; children £2

Capel Manor gardens

There are three main areas at this high-profile demonstration garden attached to a horticultural college 'where the City meets the Countryside'. First, there is the National Gardening Centre, where dozens of small model gardens are designed and planted to give people state-of-the-art ideas for their own gardens. Second, there are the trial grounds run by *Gardening Which?*, where this influential monthly magazine carries out all its trials and experiments, long term and seasonal. Third, there is the series of themed gardens laid out for students to learn from: a walled garden, a herb garden, a knot garden, a disabled person's garden, a shade garden, an Italianate holly maze, a magnolia border, a pergola, a Japanese garden, alpine beds and some historical re-creations. Other themes include Mediterranean, modern, cottage, rustic, family and minimalist gardens. The latest additions are model gardens which include a 'Sunflower Street' taken from the Chelsea Flower Show, a 'Diana, Princess of Wales Garden' and a 'HM The Queen Mother Garden', featuring some of the favourite plants of the two royal ladies. Whatever your interests and whatever the time of year, Capel Manor is a garden which educates and delights. And it is brilliant for new ideas, especially for small gardens. There is a substantial programme of RHS workshops, lectures and garden walks at Capel Manor during 2007; details from 020 7821 3408.
vegetables and fruit; topiary; plantsman's collection of plants; herbs; plants under glass; daffodils; good herbaceous borders; fine collection of trees; alpine plants; roses of every kind; small shop; restaurant

Owned by Capel Manor Corporation
Number of gardeners 8
Size 12ha (30 acres)
NCCPG National Collections *Achillea*, *Sarcococca*

CHELSEA PHYSIC GARDEN
66 Royal Hospital Road SW3 4HS

Tel 020 7352 5646 **Fax** 020 7376 3910
www.chelseaphysicgarden.co.uk
Location Entrance in Swan Walk, off western end of Royal Hospital Road
Opening hours Noon to dusk, Wednesdays; noon to 5pm, Thursdays and Fridays; noon to 6pm, Sundays and Bank Holidays, April to October; plus noon to 5pm on 21 to 26 May (for Chelsea Flower Show)

Admission fee Adults £7; children £4

This oasis of peace between Royal Hospital Road and the Chelsea Embankment started life in 1673 as a pharmacological collection, and has kept its original design – hence the word 'Physic' in its name. But it also has the oldest rock garden in Europe, the largest olive tree in Britain (with three trunks), extensive botanical order beds, a vast number of rare, tender and interesting plants, including *Eucalyptus leucoxylon* var. *rosea*, *Washingtonia filifera* and the long-flowering form of *Rosa chinensis* known as 'Crimson Bengal'. A historical walk emphasises the importance of the garden through the ages by drawing attention to the number of plants first introduced to Britain by the garden and its curators.
herbs; plants under glass; good herbaceous borders; 18th-century rock garden; large olive tree growing outside; light refreshments

Owned by Chelsea Physic Garden Company
Number of gardeners 5
Size 1.6ha (4 acres)
English Heritage Grade I

CHISWICK HOUSE

Burlington Lane, Chiswick W4 2RP

Tel 020 8742 1225
Location South-west London on A4 and A316
Opening hours 8am to dusk, daily, all year
Admission fee Free

Laid out by Bridgeman and Kent for Lord Burlington, Chiswick is the best baroque garden in southern England, and the exquisite house is pure Palladian. The bachelor Duke of Devonshire added an Italian renaissance garden early in the 19th century, and a Camellia House with slate benches and huge bushes, mainly of old Japonica hybrids. But it is the layout and buildings which are so exceptional: the Ionic temple, the Inigo Jones gateway, the obelisk and the statues. Forget the dogs and the joggers – almost all free-entry gardens have a municipal heart – but explore the *pattes d'oie*, *allées* and ilex groves of the main garden on a hot July morning and you might be doing a Grand Tour of Italy 250 years ago.
plants under glass; camellias; parterres; summer bedding; luxuriant evergreens; refreshments

Owned by London Borough of Hounslow
Number of gardeners 5
Size 16ha (40 acres)
English Heritage Grade I

CLIFTON NURSERIES

5A Clifton Villas, Little Venice W9 2PH

Tel 020 7289 6851 **Fax** 020 7286 4215
www.clifton.co.uk
Location In Little Venice, 100 yards from Warwick Avenue tube station
Opening hours 8.30am to 6pm (5.30pm from October to February), Monday to Saturday; 10.30am to 4.30pm, Sundays, all year
Admission fee Free

Clifton Nurseries were founded in 1854 and are now the capital's oldest garden centre. They have become one of the smartest and most stylish sources of good plants and designer sundries for Londoners. They concentrate on supplying town gardens with containers, statuary, climbers and

shrubs in specimen sizes, indoor and conservatory plants. Topiary is one of their specialities: so are mature plants for instant gratification.
everything for London gardeners

DOWN HOUSE
Luxted Road, Downe, Orpington BR6 7JT

Tel 01689 859119 **Fax** 01689 862755
www.english-heritage.org.uk
Location In Downe, on right side of Luxted Road
Opening hours 10am to 5pm, Wednesday to Sunday, and Bank Holiday Mondays, 7 February to 16 December; closes at 4pm in February and March, November and December; open daily and closes at 6pm in July and August
Admission fee Adults £7.20; concessions £5.40; children £3.60

Ⓟ 🚻 ♿
Charles Darwin's house and garden have been restored as they were in the great scientist's lifetime. It is a thoughtful, practical, middle-class garden with none of the extravagances of 'great' gardens. The borders, orchards and kitchen gardens are just as they were in the 1860s: there are orchids and carnivorous plants in the greenhouse and grassland fungi in the lawns. Visitors can also explore the 'sandwalk' where Darwin thought through his ideas as he paced along.
Charles Darwin's garden; gift shop; tea room

Owned by English Heritage
Number of gardeners 2, plus many volunteers
Size 1.6ha (4 acres)

ELTHAM PALACE
Court Yard, Eltham SE9 5QE

Tel 020 8294 2548 **Fax** 020 8294 2621
www.elthampalace.org.uk
Location Follow English Heritage signs off Court Road (A208)
Opening hours 10am to 5pm, Sunday to Wednesday, April to October; 10am to 4pm, Sundays, February, March, November and December; closed from 21 December to 3 February
Admission fee Adults £4.60; concessions £3.50; children £2.30 (2006 prices)

Ⓟ 🚻 ♿
The ramparts and moat of the old royal palace give structure to the modern garden. There are fine rose gardens, herbaceous borders, rock gardens and shade borders dating from the 1930s, but restored recently. Also from the pre-war period are several huge specimens of *Ligustrum lucidum*. Perhaps the best modern planting is the 110m (360ft) South Moat border by Isabelle van Groeningen, which won the English Heritage Contemporary Gardens competition, though climate change has required some alterations to the original choice of plants.
historic royal palace; unusual 1930s garden; modern prairie-style garden; tea room

Owned by English Heritage
Number of gardeners 3, plus volunteers
Size 7.6ha (19 acres)
English Heritage Grade II*

FENTON HOUSE
Windmill Hill, Hampstead NW3 6RT

Tel/fax 020 7435 3471
www.nationaltrust.org.uk
Location Entrances in Hampstead Grove near Hampstead station
Opening hours 2pm to 5pm, Saturdays and Sundays, 3 to 25 March; then 2pm to 5pm, Wednesday to Sunday and Bank Holiday Mondays, 28 March to 28 October; opens at 11am on Saturdays, Sundays and Bank Holiday Mondays
Admission fee Adults £2; children £1

🚻 ♿
Fenton House is a country house in Hampstead, approached along an avenue of robinias. The garden makes excellent use of space: a broad terrace runs along two sides of the enclosing brick wall and looks down on the neat enclosed gardens below. The 300-year-old apple orchard boasts 30 cultivars of English apples (largely local ones), and there is a working organic kitchen garden, complete with compost heaps. It is not outstandingly flowerful, but the hedges are good and plants are firmly trained. The standards of maintenance are very high, and there is something to see throughout the year: definitely worth knowing, and popular both with visitors and with the many volunteers who enjoy working there.

HAMPTON COURT PALACE

Hampton KT8 9AU

Tel 0870 752 7777
www.hrp.org.uk
Location North side of Kingston Bridge over the Thames on A308 junction with A309
Opening hours 10am to 6pm (4.30pm from November to March), daily, all year
Admission fee Formal gardens: adults £4; concessions £3; children £2.50; maze: adults £3.50; children £2.50 (prices under review)

William III was responsible for the main features at Hampton Court today. His Privy Garden has been reconstructed as it was in 1702 and remains the outstanding example of a successful historic restoration from the 1990s. Even the planting is accurate – roses, fritillaries and other flowering plants chosen and cultivated exactly as they would have been 300 years ago. Note how widely spaced they are in their slightly raised beds, an exact copy of horticultural practices of the time. Next to the vast Privy Garden is the Pond Garden, a sunken formal garden with magnificent displays of bedding – tulips in spring and tender perennials in summer. Nearby is the Great Vine – actually 'Black Hamburgh' – planted in 1768 on the advice of Capability Brown: it is the world's oldest known vine and produces, on average, 300kg of grapes every year. As from July this year (2007), William III's restored Exotic Garden, opposite the Pond Garden, will also be open to visitors. To one side of the Privy Garden lies the great formal East Garden. Its central feature is the Long Water which cuts right through the deer park: the Hampton Court Palace Flower Show (organised by the Royal Horticultural Society) takes place astride its banks on 3 to 8 July 2007 (tickets from 0870 906 3791). The garden at the palace end of the Long Water was laid out as a parterre by William III with 12 marble fountains: Queen Anne added the semi-circular canals in 1710. On the other side of the palace are the Wilderness gardens, extending over a considerable area, and a mass of naturalised daffodils in spring. Here, too, is the famous Hampton Court Maze, which covers about one third of an acre and has yew hedges totalling nearly half a mile. Other areas in the Wilderness also have considerable horticultural interest, including the rose garden, a herbaceous garden, and walls covered with climbing plants. Hampton Court is large and you need several hours to appreciate all the gardens, their different styles and what they offer. The website is excellent – educational and helpful.
topiary; roses (ancient and modern); herbs; fruit trees; good herbaceous borders; the famous maze; laburnum walk; knot gardens; the Great Vine; the Wilderness; shop; café; coffee shop

Owned by Historic Royal Palaces
Number of gardeners 40
Size 24ha (60 acres) of formal gardens and 240ha (600 acres) of deer park
NCCPG National Collections *Heliotropium*
English Heritage Grade I

Fenton House

roses (mainly old-fashioned); herbs; good herbaceous borders; restored Edwardian garden

Owned by The National Trust
Number of gardeners 1, plus several volunteers
Size 0.6ha (1 1/2 acres)

HAM HOUSE
Ham, Richmond TW10 7RS

Tel 020 8940 1950 **Fax** 020 8439 8241
www.nationaltrust.org.uk
Location On River Thames, signed from A307
Opening hours 11am to 6pm (or dusk, if earlier), Saturday to Wednesday, all year except 1 January and 25 and 26 December
Admission fee Adults £3; children £2; families £7

Ham is a modern re-creation of the original 17th-century garden. It is not a literal copy, but more of a free-handed reinterpretation. The best part is a grand series of hornbeam enclosures with white summerhouses and seats, known as the Wilderness. The borders are all planted, so far as possible, in the 17th-century style. There are plans to redevelop the kitchen garden in front of the orangery to contrast its 17th-century design and plantings with the better-known 19th-century ones that are commonly seen elsewhere. The garden buildings include a dairy, ice house and still house.
formal gardens in 17th-century style; roses (mainly modern and climbers); herbs; fruit; parterres; holm oak avenue; National Trust shop; tea room

Owned by The National Trust
Number of gardeners 4
Size 8ha (20 acres)
English Heritage Grade II*

ISABELLA PLANTATION
Richmond Park, Richmond TW10 5HS

Tel 020 8948 3209 **Fax** 020 8332 2730
www.royalparks.gov.uk
Location Richmond Park
Opening hours Dawn to dusk, daily, all year
Admission fee Free

The Isabella Plantation in Richmond Park is at last getting the recognition it deserves: these 42 acres of rhododendrons and azaleas under a mature deciduous canopy are one of the finest woodland gardens in the country. They are probably best visited in late April and May, when the azaleas are accompanied by lush streamside plantings of candelabra primulas, ferns and hostas. And it all gets better still: the new bog garden is a great addition.
woodland garden; rhododendrons and azaleas; camellias and magnolias; good ornamental trees; primulas

Owned by The Royal Parks
Number of gardeners 5
Size 17.2ha (42 acres)
NCCPG National Collections *Rhododendron* (Kurume azaleas, the Wilson 50)
English Heritage Grade I

KENWOOD
Hampstead Lane NW3 7JR

Tel 020 8348 1286 **Fax** 020 7873 3891
www.english-heritage.org.uk/parksandgardens
Location North side of Hampstead Heath, off B519
Opening hours 8am to dusk (8.30pm, if earlier), daily, all year
Admission fee Free

Parts of this superb 18th-century parkland around two glittering lakes have recently been restored to Repton's original designs. There are splendid plantings of rhododendrons, fine azaleas, a

mature *Davidia involucrata* and wonderful landscaped views to London and Westminster. Work continues.
woodland garden; good herbaceous borders; fine collection of trees; restaurant; café

Owned by English Heritage (Iveagh Bequest)
Number of gardeners 5
Size 44ha (112 acres)
English Heritage Grade II*

MUSEUM OF GARDEN HISTORY
Lambeth Palace Road SE1 7LB

Tel 020 7401 8865 **Fax** 020 7401 8869
www.museumgardenhistory.org
Location Between Lambeth Bridge and Lambeth Palace
Opening hours 10.30am to 5pm, daily, all year, except Christmas and New Year period
Admission fee £3 voluntary admission charge (£2.50 concessions)

The garden is small, and complements the museum's fascinating collections and excellent exhibitions. It was designed as a knot garden by the Marchioness of Salisbury in the early 1980s in homage to John Tradescant the Elder, who laid out the gardens at Hatfield in the early 17th century and is buried in the museum grounds. The plants are those imported by Tradescant and his son from their travels to Virginia, Muscovy and the Barbary coast, or known to have flourished in their garden at Lambeth. It is therefore a garden for contemplation, though the museum's events, exhibitions, lectures and courses are well worth knowing about. The museum is now being redeveloped with the aim of becoming a first-class information resource about the history of gardening in Britain.
17th-century plants; good exhibitions; historic tool collection; books, cards and gifts; light refreshments

Owned by Museum of Garden History
Number of gardeners 10 part-time volunteers

MYDDELTON HOUSE
Bulls Cross, Enfield EN2 9HG

Tel 01992 702200 **Fax** 01992 650714
Location Off A10 onto Bullsmoor Lane: right at Bulls Cross; train to Turkey Street station
Opening hours 10am to 4.30pm (3pm from October to March), weekdays, except Christmas Holidays, all year; plus noon to 4pm, Sundays and Bank Holiday Mondays, Easter Sunday to 31 October; for NGS: noon to 4pm on 29 April, 27 May, and 24 February 2008
Admission fee Adults £2.60; concessions £2 (subject to review)

Holy ground for plantsmen with a sense of history, EA Bowles's garden was abandoned for 30 years: Lee Valley Regional Park Authority has started to restore it. Thousands of naturalised bulbs have survived: snowdrops, crocus and narcissi in spring, and cyclamen, colchicums and sternbergias in autumn. The large wisteria planted in 1903 has also survived, while the rose garden has been replanted with varieties that Bowles grew. The iris borders are spectacular in May but it is true to say that, as with all plantsman's gardens, there is much to see throughout the year. A current project is to restore the Lunatic Asylum, Bowles's collection of freak plants like the double-flowered (but non-berrying) blackberry *Rubus ulmifolius* 'Bellidiflorus'. The RHS thought so highly of this part of the garden that, even in the cash-strapped 1950s, it propagated the plants and created its own Lunatic Asylum corner at Wisley. And the Lee Valley Regional Park Authority has just reacquired the kitchen garden and has plans to restore it, too. There is a Friends group called the EA Bowles of Myddelton House Society which has an active programme of events: details from Mr A Pettitt, 2(A) Plough Hill, Cuffley, Potters Bar, Hertfordshire EN6 4DR or from *rogerwkholland@btinternet.com*.
snowdrops; roses (mainly old-fashioned and climbers); plantsman's collection of plants; daffodils; good herbaceous borders; fine collection of trees

Owned by Lee Valley Regional Park Authority
Number of gardeners 3
Size 2.4ha (6 acres)
NCCPG National Collections *Iris*
English Heritage Grade II

ROYAL BOTANIC GARDENS, KEW

Kew, Richmond TW9 3AB

Tel 020 8332 5655
www.kew.org
Location Kew Green (parking), tube to Kew Gardens tube station, or train from Waterloo to Kew Bridge
Opening hours 9.30am to 6.30pm (7.30pm at weekends), but closes at 5.30pm from mid-February to last Saturday in March and 6pm from early September to end of October, and at 4.15pm in November to December, daily, all year except 24 and 25 December; last admissions 30 minutes before closing
Admission fee Adults £12.25; concessions £10.25; children free (subject to review)

Kew's gardens are enormous – the guidebook advises people to allow a whole day for their visit – and have one of the largest collections of plants in the world. Kew is also full of historical, artistic and landscape interest, as well as its botanic and horticultural glories. The emphasis is upon species rather than garden cultivars, but there is an immense amount for gardeners to see and admire and – of course – to learn from. There are seasonal features like the crocus carpet and historic areas like the Queen's garden behind Kew Palace which was designed in the 1960s as a reconstructed 17th-century garden. Nor should the famous Pagoda (now open to visitors again) and Japanese gateway garden be forgotten. There are also many horticulturally themed gardens. The azalea garden divides azaleas into 12 distinct horticultural groups, eg the Ghent hybrids and the Knap Hill hybrids, and arranges them all systematically in historic order. The bamboo garden has over 120 cultivars arranged to maximise the contrast between their forms and leaf shapes. The berberis dell is a unique feature with a comprehensive collection of berberis and mahonia – the tallest is a 5m (16ft) specimen of *Berberis lycoides*. Kew has one of the best bluebell woods in the London area, behind Queen Charlotte's cottage. The grass garden has over 550 species and is being added to continuously: although the scientific purpose is to display the diversity and importance of grasses, the garden is arranged ornamentally. The holly walk was laid out in 1874 by Sir Joseph Hooker: the original specimens are therefore over 130 years old and as high as 30m (98ft). The collection has over 600 hollies. The juniper collection is the largest in Europe. The lilac garden ('Go down to Kew in lilac time') was renovated in 1993 and has over 100 specimens in 10 separate beds. The rhododendron dell (700 plants) includes some unique Kew hybrids as well as hardy species. The rose garden was created in 1923 and is very popular in high summer: it has roses of all types and an area which illustrates the history of roses in cultivation. There is also a rose pergola running through the order beds, which were originally designed as a living library of flowering plants systematically arranged for students of botany. The Mediterranean garden has been extended and replanted for the 2007 summer festival entitled 'Mediterranean Year'. The pinetum has an important collection of conifers and there are many record-breakers among the deciduous species at Kew, too. The rock garden was rebuilt in the 1980s to include more microhabitats. It has over 2,500 different plants roughly arranged in geographical areas, eg the mountains of Europe, the Mediterranean and Patagonia. The glasshouses also contain a vast collection of plants. The Palm House was built in the 1840s to house tropical trees and shrubs – these include coconuts, bananas, breadfruit, mangoes and pawpaws. The Princess of Wales Conservatory opened in 1987 and has 10 distinct climatic zones ranging from arid to moist tropical: here are such plants as ginger, pineapple and orchids. The Temperate House is set out geographically: among its most striking plants are proteas from South Africa. In the hot and humid water lily house are tropical *Nymphaea* and *Victoria cruziana*, as well as such economic plants as rice and lemon grass. The Davies alpine house (*very* elegant) was opened in 2006 and its systems of refrigeration and ventilation enable Kew to grow plants which

would not otherwise survive the damp, mild climate of England. Other glasshouses to visit include the Evolution House, which tells the story of plant evolution over the last 3,500 million years and the unique filmy fern house. There are twice-daily hour-long guided tours which leave from the Guides' Desk, just inside the Victoria Gate Visitors Centre, at 11am and 2pm (no extra fee payable). Kew has every imaginable facility for visits by schools, groups, tourists and students of botany. In summer it also has many bedding-out schemes – generous, lush and highly successful – but the garden is somewhat bedevilled by Canada geese, which foul the grass, and by aircraft noise.

woodland garden; subtropical plants; snowdrops; roses; rock garden; plantsman's collection of plants; herbs; plants under glass; fruit; mature conifers; alpine plants; good herbaceous borders; fine collection of trees; heather gardens; 138 record trees - more than any other garden in the British Isles - including 38 different oaks (*Quercus spp.*); giftshop; book shop; two restaurants; two cafés

Owned by Trustees of the Royal Botanic Gardens
Number of gardeners 150
Size 121ha (300 acres)
NCCPG National Collections *Amorphophallus*; *Encephalartos*; *Heliconia*; *Iris* (subgenus Scorpiris); *Musa*
English Heritage Grade I

OSTERLEY PARK
Jersey Road, Isleworth TW7 4RB

Tel 020 8232 5050 **Fax** 020 8232 5080
www.nationaltrust.org.uk/osterley
Location 5 miles west of central London on A4
Opening hours Garden: 11am to 5pm, Wednesday to Sunday, 14 March to 28 October; park: 8am to 7.30pm (6pm from 30 October to 24 March), daily, all year; closed 25 and 26 December
Admission fee Garden: adults £3; children £1.50. Park: free; car park: £3.50

Osterley has much of its 18th-century design intact. Within the park are formal gardens, meadows, lakes and garden buildings: the Temple of Pan is especially fine. The Pleasure Grounds served as a garden to the neo-classical house, one of Robert Adam's best, and have recently been restored. Adam also built the semi-circular Garden House (1780) at the centre of the design. The many fine trees include cedars, oaks and an oriental plane planted in 1755, while the American garden has unusual conifers and rhododendrons.
woodland garden; herbs; fruit; fine rare oaks; autumn colour; tallest variegated chestnut *Castanea sativa* 'Albomarginata' (16m; 52ft) in the British Isles; National Trust shop; tea room

Owned by The National Trust
Size 56ha (140 acres)
English Heritage Grade II*

THE PALM CENTRE
Ham Nursery, Ham Street, Ham, Richmond TW10 7HA

Tel 020 8255 6191 **Fax** 020 8255 6192
www.thepalmcentre.co.uk
Location Near Ham House, on right-hand side of Ham Street, opposite Riverside Drive
Opening hours 9am to 5pm (or dusk, if earlier), daily, all year
Admission fee Free

The Palm Centre, close to Ham House, is a five-acre nursery with half an acre of glass. It specialises in hardy exotic plants, especially palms, bamboos, tree ferns, cycads, yuccas, cordylines, Mediterranean plants and grasses. It lists over 300 species. There are planted-out areas which display hardy palms and some impressive mature trees to admire. Customers are encouraged to browse.

Owned by Martin Gibbons
Size 2ha (5 acres)

QUEEN MARY'S GARDENS
Inner Circle, Regent's Park NW1 4NR

Tel 020 7486 7905
Location In the middle of Regent's Park
Opening hours Dawn to dusk, daily, all year
Admission fee Free

Queen Mary's Gardens are contained within Regent's Park's Inner Circle. Originally a display garden for the Royal Botanic Society (a 19th-century rival to the Royal Horticultural Society; Robert Marnock and William Robinson both worked there), the Japanese garden, the lake and the mound made from the excavations all date from the 1850s. The horticultural interest comes from the excellent herbaceous borders, tender bedding plants, displays of annuals and spring bulbs. Above all, Queen Mary's Gardens are known for their rose gardens, where large beds are planted each with just one cultivar – mainly modern hybrid teas and floribundas, though there are English roses and old-fashioned ones, too, often in mixed borders. At one end is a circular catenary of climbing and rambling roses around yet more beds of bright modern roses: a spectacular sight in early June – roses flower earlier in the London parks than anywhere else in England, and are worth a visit at any time after about the middle of May.
massed displays of roses; fine herbaceous borders

Owned by Royal Parks Agency

SYON PARK
Brentford TW8 8JF

Tel 020 8560 0881 **Fax** 020 8568 0936
www.syonpark.co.uk

Location Between Brentford and Isleworth, north bank of Thames
Opening hours 10.30am to 5pm, daily, March to October; 10.30am to 4pm, Saturdays and Sundays, November to February; closed 1 January and 25 and 26 December
Admission fee Adults £4; concessions £2.50; RHS members free

Syon is a wonderful mixture of 18th-century landscape, 19th-century horticultural seriousness, 20th-century plantsmanship and 21st-century theme park. The Great Conservatory was designed by Charles Fowler in the 1820s; the formal terraces followed in the 1830s. But one of the nicest details about Syon is the way the water meadows along the banks of the Thames are still grazed by cows: it creates a unique rural prospect so close to the heart of London. There are fine trees, too, the relic of a botanical collection dating back to the 1820s: some, including four species of oak, are record-breakers.

spectacular Great Conservatory; woodland garden; mature conifers; good herbaceous borders; fine collection of trees; cacti; ferns; tallest *Catalpa ovata* (22m; 72ft) in the British Isles (and 14 further record trees); Wyevale Garden Centre on site; shop; café

Owned by The Duke of Northumberland
Number of gardeners 7
Size 16ha (40 acres)
English Heritage Grade I

NORFOLK

Norfolk has a large number of important historic gardens. Only a few are open to the public, but they include Blickling, Felbrigg, Holkham, Sheringham and the royal gardens at Sandringham – an impressive list. The garden with the finest collection of trees is Ryston Hall, but it is not open to the public. The same is true of Talbot Manor, which was planted from about 1950 onwards by the late Maurice Mason with advice from Sir Harold Hillier. Nevertheless, the National Gardens Scheme does fairly well in Norfolk and the county also has a good number of first-rate nurseries: Peter Beales Roses, Norfolk Lavender, PW Plants, Reads Nursery at Hales Hall Gardens and the Romantic Garden Nursery are all of national importance. There are 13 National Collections in the county, including a collection of *Elaeagnus* which is spread among several members of the Norfolk Group of the NCCPG. The Royal Horticultural Society has good links with Norfolk: Easton College near Norwich is a RHS Partner College, while Sandringham and Mannington are RHS Free Access gardens. Many people consider that East Ruston Old Vicarage is the most important new garden to have been made in the UK during the last 20 years. And there is no doubt that both the Dell Garden and Foggy Bottom (now jointly known as Bressingham Gardens) at Bressingham continue to be immensely influential: the Bloom family at Bressingham was largely responsible for the enormous renewal of interest in herbaceous plants from about 1970 onwards. Unfortunately, however, Thorncroft Clematis Nursery at Reymerston has decided not to open its display garden in 2007, though the nursery flourishes and now stocks nearly 400 species and cultivars. And the walled garden at Holkham, laid by Samuel Wyatt in the 1780s, is no longer open to the public.

AFRICAN VIOLET & GARDEN CENTRE

Station Road, Terrington St Clement, King's Lynn PE34 4PL

Tel 01553 828374 **Fax** 01553 828376
www.africanvioletcentre.biz
Location 3 miles west of King's Lynn, on A17
Opening hours 9am (10am on Sundays) to 5pm, daily, all year; closed for New Year's Day, Christmas Day and Boxing Day
Admission fee Free

This nursery built its reputation on African violets, and its Chelsea exhibits have been memorable. It offers 140+ cultivars and one of the largest collections of *Saintpaulia* species in the UK. The display house always has a good showing.
African violets; house plants; gift shop; café

Owned by AKR Services Ltd

BLICKLING HALL

Blickling, Norwich NR11 6NF

Tel 01263 738030 **Fax** 01263 738035
www.nationaltrust.org.uk
Location 1½ miles north-west of Aylsham on B1354
Opening hours 10.15am to 5.15pm, Wednesday to Sunday and Bank Holiday Mondays, 17 March to 28 October; plus Mondays from 23 July to 2 September; 11am to 4pm, Thursday to Sunday, 1 November to 29 February 2008
Admission fee Adults £5.50; children £2.75

Blickling is the garden with everything: a Jacobean mansion, handsomely symmetrical; an early landscape layout (the Doric Temple was built in about 1735); a pretty orangery by Samuel Wyatt; a large mid-19th-century parterre, later simplified, with fine yew hedges and topiary; and 1930s herbaceous plantings by Norah Lindsay (her masterpiece). The spring bulbs are magnificent,

BRESSINGHAM GARDENS

Bressingham, Diss IP22 2AB

Tel 01379 686900 **Fax** 01379 688085
www.bressinghamgardens.co.uk
Location On A1066, 3 miles west of Diss
Opening hours 10.30am to 4.30pm (5.30pm from May to August), daily, 24 March to 28 October; groups by appointment at other times
Admission fee Adults £6; concessions £5; children £3; RHS members free in May and September

Bressingham Gardens consists of two major gardens made by the Bloom family which were until recently open at different times – Alan Bloom's Dell Garden, and Adrian Bloom's Foggy Bottom. There is no better place to learn about herbaceous plants – what they look like, how they grow and how to place them – than the Dell. This is a six-acre complex of about 50 island beds, which act as a trial ground and conservation resource for the herbaceous and alpine plants (over 5,000 of them) for which Alan Bloom is famous. The new Summer Garden was designed by Adrian Bloom to provide a new and more dramatic entrance to the garden. It has a stunning display of *Crocosmia* and *Miscanthus* cultivars interplanted with other perennials. The Blooms are keen to emphasise that the Dell Garden is not a museum piece but a carefully tended collection of perennials, developing and growing all the time. The same is true of Foggy Bottom, which Adrian Bloom started planting in about 1975 as a garden for year-round seasonal colour and interest. Its centrepiece was his unique collection of conifers, collected from all over the world and tested for English conditions. They were, for many years, the dominant plants in the garden, and he used them to show off the innumerable contrasts of form, colour, texture and shape between different cultivars. Then he began to use them in other plant combinations – with ornamental grasses, perennials and shrubs – chosen to give a succession of colour, texture and other interest throughout the year. Renovation and renewal are ongoing – new beds are constantly developed and new plant associations created. The All-Seasons Bed is a recent example: its 'river of blood' is a meandering 9m (30ft) planting of *Imperata cylindrica* 'Rubra'. A new winter garden was planted in 2006. Another new feature is Adrian's Wood, two acres connecting the two gardens which is being planted with North American natives. The net result is that all parts of Bressingham Gardens continue to be an inspirational source of ideas for the smaller garden.

superb herbaceous borders; some alpine plants; beautiful plantings; island beds; plantsman's collection of plants; mature dwarf conifers; plant centre; tea room; restaurant

Owned by Adrian Bloom
Number of gardeners 4
Size 4.8ha (15 acres)
NCCPG National Collections *Miscanthus*

and there are sheets of bluebells in the woods, but Blickling is a garden to visit at all seasons.
woodland garden; rhododendrons and azaleas; bluebells; herbaceous borders at peak July/August; shops; plant sales in season; restaurant

Owned by The National Trust
Number of gardeners 5, plus volunteers
Size 20ha (50 acres)
English Heritage Grade II*

BRADENHAM HALL
Bradenham, Thetford IP25 7QR

Tel: 01362 687279/687243 **Fax:** 01362 687669
www.bradenhamhall.co.uk
Location West of East Dereham, north of Bradenham
Opening hours 2pm to 5.30pm, second and fourth Sundays of month, April to September; groups at other times by appointment; and for NGS
Admission fee Adults £4; children free

This is an exceptional plant-lover's garden for all seasons, made over the last 40 years in a windy, open position at the top of what passes in Norfolk for a hill. The first thing you notice is that the house (early Georgian) and garden walls are covered with unusual shrubs, climbers and fruit. The flower gardens are formally designed and richly planted within beautiful yew hedges: formal rose gardens, a paved garden, and herbaceous and shrub borders. The arboretum has a remarkable collection of trees – more than 800 different species and forms, many of them rare or very rare. All are labelled. The walled kitchen gardens are traditionally managed, with vegetables, cut flowers, mixed borders and two glasshouses. In spring, the parkland and arboretum are filled with daffodils – massed plantings of more than 90 carefully chosen and graded cultivars. A delight and an education.
roses (mainly old-fashioned); plantsman's collection of plants; daffodils; good herbaceous borders; fine collection of trees; tea room

Owned by Chris and Panda Allhusen
Number of gardeners 3
Size 8.3ha (21 acres)

CHANTICLEER
Dereham Road, Ovington, Thetford IP25 6SA

Tel 01953 881194
Location On A1075, 2 miles from Watton on the Dereham road
Opening hours 10am to 4pm, 9 and 10 June, 7 and 8 July, 4 and 5 August
Admission fee Adults £2; OAPs £1.50; children free

Chanticleer is a former 1830s public house, converted to a private dwelling in the 1950s and since extended. The present owners have lived and gardened here for 25 years, originally in just under two acres, but then with three further acres for a small flock of Jacob sheep, Vietnamese pot-bellied pigs, goats, geese, chickens and ducks. The main garden includes a kitchen garden, greenhouses, orchard, herb garden and a large wildlife garden with a pond: all are managed organically. Great emphasis is placed on working with nature: the wildlife garden is frequented by birds, insects and small mammals, including breeding water voles. Most native shrubs and trees are represented, as are many wildflowers – including two species of orchid, which have colonised parts of the wildlife area. A small willow plantation supplies materials for hurdle-making. There are demonstrations of how to make compost (including the use of wormeries and liquid compost) during open weekends.
organic garden of great interest; refreshments

Owned by Mr and Mrs T Rands
Number of gardeners owners only
Size 2ha (5 acres)

CORPUSTY MILL GARDEN
The Mill House, Corpusty, Norwich NR11 6QB

Tel 01263 587223
www.corpustymillgarden.co.uk
Location In middle of village on B1149
Opening hours Groups by appointment
Admission fee Adults £6

Corpusty Mill has been made and developed by Roger Last and his late brother John since 1965.

Water is used extensively and there are strong architectural elements, garden buildings or follies, including a vast flint wall with the heads of Roman emperors, a Gothic arch and window, a grotto (with four chambers), a ruined tower, a classical pavilion and stainless steel spire. The planting is knowledgeable, varied and controlled. Most visitors come away quite amazed by the beauty and ingenuity of what they have seen.
stylish design

Owned by Roger Last
Number of gardeners owner only
Size 1.6ha (4 acres)

COURTYARD FARM
Ringstead, Hunstanton PE36 5LQ

Tel 01485 525251 **Fax** 01485 525211
Location 1 1/2 miles east of Ringstead on Docking road
Opening hours dawn to dusk; daily; all year
Admission fee Free

Courtyard Farm is not so much a garden as a model farm, owned by an organic activist. New public footpaths have been made to enable visitors to see the benefits of cultivating land without artificial fertilisers or pesticides. Acres of colourful wildflowers (over 100 different species) are the reward of this return to traditional husbandry and should be compulsory viewing for any garden owner who doubts the beauty and diversity that results from a conversion to the organic. Some sculptures and installations are a recent addition.

Owned by Lord Melchett
Size 320ha (800 acres)

EAST LODE
Nursery Lane, Hockwold, Thetford IP26 4ND

Tel 01842 827096
Location Down Church Lane in Hockwold, left at iron seat, then first house on right
Opening hours By arrangement. Special Hellebore and Spring Bulbs Open Day: 10am to 4pm on Saturday 24 March
Admission fee Adults £2

This half-acre cottage garden is absolutely full of interest – shrubs, roses, clematis and many unusual plants – all put together in the cottage style. Mrs Mansey is a skilful plantswoman and fills it with colour throughout the year: many hellebores in spring, roses and clematis in summer, evergreens and silvers for autumn and winter, and tremendous underplantings of bulbs. There is a small pond, a greenhouse, some scree beds and a conservatory. It is also intended to be a haven for bees, birds and butterflies.
plantsman's garden with many unusual plants; cottagey mix

Owned by Mrs P Mansey
Number of gardeners 1
Size 0.2ha (1/2 acre)

FAIRHAVEN WOODLAND & WATER GARDEN
School Road, South Walsham, Norwich NR13 6DZ

Tel/fax 01603 270449
www.fairhavengarden.co.uk
Location Follow brown signs off A47 on to B1140
Opening hours 10am to 5pm, daily, all year, except 25 December; closes 9pm on Wednesdays and Thursdays from May to August
Admission fee Adults £4.50; OAPs £4; children £2; RHS members free from February to April and in October

This is a vast woodland garden of naturalised rhododendrons under a canopy of ancient oaks – one pollarded specimen known as the King Oak is estimated to be 950 years old. In 1946, Lord Fairhaven laid two fairly narrow paths straight across a section of boggy land where sheets of candelabra primulas flourish in alder woodland. On the drier ground he planted masses of rhododendrons and azaleas among the naturalised *R. ponticum*. The garden is at its loveliest throughout May and June, when the rhododendrons and candelabras are reflected in the still waters of the dykes and private Broad. It is a bit short on follow-up later in the year, though there are effective plantings of hydrangeas, hostas, *Osmunda regalis*, ligularias and gunneras. The snowdrops, too, are good in February, and the

EAST RUSTON OLD VICARAGE

East Ruston, Norwich NR12 9HN

Tel 01692 650432 **Fax** 01692 651246
www.eastrustonoldvicarage.co.uk
Location Turn off A149 near Stalham or to B1159 signed Walcott, Bacton, Happisburgh; left at T-junction; on right after 2 miles, next to East Ruston Church
Opening hours 2pm to 5.30pm, Wednesdays, Fridays, Saturdays, Sundays and Bank Holidays, 25 March to 27 October
Admission fee Adults £5; children £1; RHS members free in September and October

This fine modern garden has been conceived on the grand scale. The owners, Graham Robeson and Alan Gray, combine the rare qualities of superb architectural design and exceptional plantsmanship. The house was built by a Surrey architect in 1913 in the Arts & Crafts style, which is uncommon in Norfolk. When the owners started to make their garden in 1988, it sat in an empty field. It was then that they planted the shelter belts, almost all tough evergreens. One of the most exciting things about the garden is to see so many tender exotics growing happily outside – literally thousands of them – which would not have been possible without the shelter belts. This is helped by the garden's location close to the North Sea with its maritime influence. The garden has been designed as a series of 'rooms', getting larger the further you move from the house. There are fine views borrowed from the landscape of two local churches and a whimsical porthole view of Happisburgh lighthouse. The gardens and grounds include superb long borders abundantly and richly planted, a box parterre annually bedded out with unusual and original plant combinations, a gravelled forecourt with large groups of *Aeonium* 'Zwartkop' and various echeverias, a sunken garden containing many varieties including a large group of *Lobelia tupa*, and the newly relocated and much extended exotic garden with fabulously bold plantings of palms, bananas, shrubby salvias and many tender exotics which are propagated on the premises. Much thought has gone into the design and preparation of beds for plants. The Mediterranean garden, for example, faces south and has a lot of brickwork and paving to preserve the warmth which plants need to survive through the winter. The beds are heavily mulched with gravel, and the result is that many plants survive which are typical of the Mediterranean *maquis*, the Californian chaparral and Australasia – clouds of yellow Australian mimosa, a very dark blue rosemary from the Mediterranean and *Beschorneria yuccoides* from Mexico. Even more impressive is the newly planted desert wash, made from over 350 tons of flints of varying sizes and covering an acre. It is intended to imitate the Arizona desert where the only rainfall is one of tumultuous thunderstorms every year. The plantings include some great specimens of palm trees, *Trithrinax campestris* from Argentina and *Brahea armata*, the Mexican blue palm, plus dasylirions, agaves, aloes and other succulents, some of which were grown from seed imported by the owners. East Ruston also has a pretty no-nonsense vegetable garden, a cutting garden, woodland walks, wildflower meadows, a walled garden and a spectacular corn field, brimming with field poppies, cornflowers and corn marigold. There will be two RHS Special Events at East Ruston Old Vicarage in 2007; details directly from the property on 01692 650432.

a young garden on a large scale; architectural plants; tea room

Owned by Graham Robeson and Alan Gray
Size 12.5ha (32 acres)

lysichitons in March and April. 2007 sees the addition of a new 'sensory' garden. The garden is managed organically. Many people are more interested in the wildlife and the Broad than the garden, so that even in high season the horticultural visitor may be almost alone in the woodland garden. There will be two RHS Special Events at Fairhaven in 2007; details from 020 7821 3408.
woodland garden; bluebells; snowdrops; rhododendrons; lilies; candelabra primulas; shop; excellent plant sales area; tea room

Owned by Fairhaven Garden Trust
Number of gardeners 2 full-time; 2 part-time
Size 52ha (130 acres)

FELBRIGG HALL

Felbrigg, Norwich NR11 8PR

Tel 01263 837444 **Fax** 01263 837032
www.nationaltrust.org.uk
Location Entrance off B1436, signed from A148 and A140
Opening hours 11am to 5pm, Saturday to Wednesday, 17 March to 21 October; daily from 28 May to 3 June, 23 July to 31 August and 22 to 28 October; plus 11am to 4pm, 27 to 31 December
Admission fee Adults £3.50; children £1.50

There are fine trees in the park, but the best bit of Felbrigg is the walled kitchen garden, oriented on a large brick dovecote flanked by Victorian vineries. Fruit trees are trained against the walls (figs, pears, plums) and the garden laid to neatly grown vegetables with herbaceous borders, ribbon borders and a hot border enclosed by box-edged gravel paths.
fruit; good herbaceous borders; National Trust shop; restaurant and tea room

Owned by The National Trust
Number of gardeners 3, plus 1 trainee
Size 2.4ha (6 acres)
NCCPG National Collections *Colchicum*
English Heritage Grade II*

HALES HALL GARDENS & READS NURSERY

Hales Hall, Loddon NR14 6QW

Tel 01508 548395 **Fax** 01508 548040
www.readsnursey.co.uk
Location Off A146, 1 mile south of Loddon
Opening hours 10am to 5pm (4pm in winter), Monday to Saturday, all year; plus 11am to 4pm on Sundays from April to October
Admission fee Garden: £2; nursery: free

This important and long-established family nursery specialises in citrus fruit trees and conservatory plants. Its extensive list of *Citrus* cultivars is based upon the centuries-old collection made by Rivers of Sawbridgeworth. Rivers were famous fruit-breeders in the 19th century, and their citrus trees supplied the scions needed to start the California fruit industry. Reads acquired their stock when Rivers closed in 1983. They also grow and sell over 70 different grape cultivars, including many more English-raised vines than any other nursery: this is the place to find such Victorian delicacies as 'Lady Downe's Seedling' and 'Mrs Pince's Black Muscat'. Their list of figs is equally extensive, and unparalleled among UK nurserymen: 'Goutte d'Or', 'Malcolm's Giant' and 'White Ischia' are among their specialities. In the adjoining two-acre garden are the moated remains of a mediaeval hall, planted with topiary, a 'potted' fruit orchard, a *potager*, a vegetable garden and a plantsman's collection of shrubs, herbaceous plants and bulbs.
conservatory plants; fruit; teas by arrangement for groups

Owned by The Read Family
Number of gardeners 1
Size 0.8ha (2 acres)
NCCPG National Collections *Citrus*; *Ficus*; *Vitis vinifera* (grapes)

HOECROFT PLANTS

Severals Grange, Holt Road, Wood Norton, Dereham NR20 5BL

Tel/fax 01362 684206
www.hoecroft.co.uk
Location 2 miles north of Guist on B1110 (not in Wood Norton village)

Opening hours 10am to 4pm, Thursday to Sunday, April to October; for NGS: 13 August
Admission fee Donation to NGS

Hoecroft is a small but well-known specialist nursery which began by concentrating upon variegated and coloured foliage plants. These range from the smallest alpines to large shrubs. Perhaps more prominent now is its list of ornamental grasses, rushes, sedges and bamboos: it offers over 250 different cultivars, which may be seen in the attached display gardens. These were started in 1991 with the specific purpose of showing how to achieve year-round colour with foliage rather than flowers. They also incorporate grasses to give movement and a sense of lightness between the more solid shapes of the shrubs. New this year (2007) is a gravel garden.
grasses; mixed borders

Owned by Jane Lister
Size 0.4ha (1 acre)

HOLKHAM HALL

Holkham, Wells-next-the-Sea NR23 1AB

Tel 01328 710227 **Fax** 01328 711707
www.holkham.co.uk
Location Off A149, 2 miles west of Wells
Opening hours Park: 9am, daily, except Christmas Day
Admission fee Park: free

Holkham is a big landscape park, worked on by Kent, Brown and Repton, with a 35-acre lake. WA Nesfield added the formal terraces in the 1850s. The horticultural content is minimal, but the estate goes out of its way to make visitors welcome. The website is excellent.
gift shop; café

Owned by The Earl of Leicester
Number of gardeners 6
English Heritage Grade I

HOUGHTON HALL

King's Lynn PE31 6UE

Tel 01485 528569 **Fax** 01485 528167
www.houghtonhall.com
Location Signed from A148 between King's Lynn and Cromer
Opening hours 11am to 5.30pm, Wednesdays, Thursdays, Sundays and Bank Holidays, Easter Sunday to 30 September; for NGS: 1 July
Admission fee Adults £5; children £2; families £12; RHS members free in June

Sir Robert Walpole made the park, now stocked with white fallow deer and contemporary sculptures, but it is the new plantings which draw visitors to Houghton today. The huge old kitchen garden at Houghton has been transformed by the present Marquess in memory of his grandmother Sybil Sassoon, an enthusiastic gardener. The new layout is modern but formal, drawing on the best Italianate tradition of design and a family fondness for lavish planting. The herbaceous borders (130m – 427ft – long) are stupendous – so are the roses; both depend for their effect upon big designs and large-scale planting. The results are inspirational, and very impressive.
shop; tea room

Owned by The Marquess of Cholmondeley
Size 2ha (5 acres) plus 160ha (400 acres) parkland

HOVETON HALL

Wroxham, Norwich NR12 8RJ

Tel 01603 782798 **Fax** 01603 784564
www.hovetonhallgardens.co.uk
Location 9 miles north of Norwich: follow brown tourist signs from A1151
Opening hours 10.30am to 5pm, Wednesday to Friday, Sundays and Bank Holiday Mondays, May to September; also Sundays and Bank Holiday Mondays from 8 to 19 April and from 2 to 16 September
Admission fee Adults £4.50; wheelchair-bound and carers £2.50; children £2

The gardens are laid out around a series of streams, with beautiful waterside plantings,

gunneras and candelabra primulas. Rhododendrons and azaleas fill the woodland gardens – at their peak in May. Daffodils are a spring feature, and the many-coloured hydrangeas are impressive later in the year. A moon-gate in the shape of a spider's web was added in 1936 to enclose the walled herbaceous garden. The walled kitchen garden is divided into three: a knot garden, a circular herb garden (designed by Tessa Hobbs) and a vegetable garden. Old fruit trees line the walks, and the peonies are a sight in June.
rhododendrons and azaleas; daffodils; good herbaceous borders; water garden; light lunches and teas

Owned by Mr and Mrs Andrew Buxton
Number of gardeners 3
Size 6ha (15 acres)

LYNFORD ARBORETUM
Munford, Thetford IP26 5HW

Tel 01842 810271
Location Turn right off A1065 just north of Munford
Opening hours Dawn to dusk, daily, all year
Admission fee Free

P

The Lynford Arboretum was started in 1947 by students at the Forester Training School who at that time occupied nearby Lynford Hall. They planted about 100 species of conifers and broadleaves, some in forestry plots, but mostly as individual specimens within the parkland and policies surrounding the house. The soil is thin and sandy, but some of those original plantings are already handsome specimens, including a *Nothofagus obliqua* and a *Pinus banksiana* each 20m (66ft) tall. Rather simply maintained by the Forestry Commission, the arboretum has considerable potential for development. Lynford Hall is now a hotel: the extensive formal garden (rather gone back) was laid out by William Burn in the 1860s and was famous for its bedding until 1914. Beyond is a curving lake. Rather surprisingly, the Forestry Commission does not permit dogs in the arboretum.
trees, deciduous and evergreen

Owned by Forestry Commission

MANNINGTON GARDENS
Mannington Hall, Norwich NR11 7BB

Tel 01263 584175 **Fax** 01263 761214
www.manningtongardens.co.uk
Location Signed from B1149 at Saxthorpe
Opening hours Noon to 5pm, Sundays,May to September; and 11am to 5pm, Wednesday to Friday, June to August
Admission fee Adults £4; concessions £3; children free; RHS members free except during special events

P

The gardens at Mannington embrace a moated house, the ruins of Mannington Church, two lakes, a scented garden, an arboretum of native trees, a new 'sensory garden', genuine wildflower meadows and handsome herbaceous borders. But the best part is the Heritage Rose Garden, made in association with Peter Beales, where thousands of old-fashioned roses are planted to illustrate the history of roses in cultivation. The developments are represented by beds which display roses according to their periods, from the 15th century up to today. There will be one RHS Special Event at Mannington in 2007; details from 020 7821 3408.
roses (mainly old-fashioned and climbers); natural surroundings; colour borders; lakes; wildflowers; roses for sale; light refreshments, teas

Owned by Lord Walpole
Number of gardeners 2 full-time, 3 part-time
Size 8ha (20 acres)
English Heritage Grade II

OXBURGH HALL
Oxborough, King's Lynn PE33 9PS

Tel 01366 328258 **Fax** 01366 328066
www.nationaltrust.org.uk
Location 7 miles south-west of Swaffham on Stoke Ferry road
Opening hours 11am to 4pm, Saturdays and Sundays, 6 January to 11 March and 3 November to 23 December; 11am to 5.30pm (4.30pm after 30 September), Saturday to Wednesday, 17 March to 28 October; daily in August
Admission fee Adults £3.50; children £2

P

The baroque 19th-century parterre has been replanted by the National Trust with such herbs as rue and cineraria making permanent companions for annuals and bedding plants. Good fruit trees in the walled garden, especially medlars and quinces.
roses (mainly modern); good herbaceous borders; French-style parterre; trained fruit trees; woodland walks; vegetable garden; gift shop; licensed restaurant

Owned by The National Trust
Number of gardeners 2, plus volunteers
Size 6.2ha (151/2 acres)
English Heritage Grade II

PW PLANTS

Sunnyside, Heath Road, Kenninghall NR16 2DS

Tel/fax 01953 888212
www.hardybamboo.com
Location South-west of Norwich, between Kenninghall and North Lopham
Opening hours 9am to 5pm, Fridays, all year; plus the last Saturday of the month from October to March and every Saturday from April to September
Admission fee Free

This enterprising nursery offers a wide range of plants chosen for their general garden-worthiness, interesting foliage and shape. It is perhaps best known for its bamboos, which have won the nursery many medals at RHS shows, but PW Plants also stock grasses, shrubs, perennials and climbers. Most are growing in the display gardens.
bamboos

Owned by Paul Whittaker
Number of gardeners 1
Size 0.6ha (11/2 acres)

PENSTHORPE MILLENNIUM GARDEN

Pensthorpe, Fakenham NR21 0LN

Tel 01328 851465 **Fax** 01328 855905
www.pensthorpe.com
Location 1 mile from Fakenham on A1067
Opening hours 10am to 5pm (4pm from January to March), daily, all year; closed 25 and 26 December
Admission fee Adults £7; OAPs £5.50; children £3.50

Piet Oudolf designed the Millennium garden (said to be the largest showcase of Oudolf's work in England) at Pensthorpe, and Judy Toll laid out the Wave garden; both are best in July and August.
gift shop; café

Owned by Bill and Deb Jordan
Number of gardeners 2
Size 0.4ha (1 acre)

PETER BEALES ROSES

London Road, Attleborough NR17 1AY

Tel 01953 454707 **Fax** 01953 456845
www.classicroses.co.uk
Location 2 miles south of Attleborough: leave A11 at Breckland Lodge; follow brown tourist signs
Opening hours 9am to 5pm (4.30pm from October to March, and 4pm in January), Monday to Saturday; 10am to 4pm, Sundays and Bank Holidays
Admission fee Free

There is a small display garden attached to this well-known rose nursery and latest reports say that it is well maintained. A good range of older and classic roses is offered for sale, both at the nursery and from its mail-order catalogue and website, which list over 1,300 species and cultivars.
roses (mainly old-fashioned); garden sundries and gift shop; licensed bistro

Owned by Peter Beales
Number of gardeners 2
Size 1ha (21/2 acres)
NCCPG National Collections *Rosa* (species)

PLANTATION GARDEN

4 Earlham Road, Norwich NR2 3DB

Tel 01508 482552/01603 621868 **Fax** 01603 631166
www.plantationgarden.co.uk
Location Between The Beeches Hotel and the Roman Catholic Cathedral
Opening hours 9am to 6pm (or dusk, if earlier), daily, all year
Admission fee Adults £2; children free; honesty box when unattended

The Plantation Garden was made in an abandoned chalk quarry by Henry Trevor, a successful Norwich businessman, between 1856 until his death in 1897. In the ensuing years the garden passed through various hands until, in 1980, it was totally overgrown, abandoned and forgotten. In that year it was rediscovered and the Plantation Garden Preservation Trust formed to save and restore the garden. Its many features include woodland walkways, flowerbeds, lawns, a Gothic fountain, an Italianate terrace, a 'medieval' terrace wall, a rustic bridge and a reconstruction of the original thatched summerhouse. Sir Roy Strong is patron of the Trust and points out that the garden is 'something of a rarity, for in most cases it is usually only the grandest of gardens which survive from earlier periods'. The original house, designed by Edward Boardman for Henry Trevor, is now part of The Beeches Hotel. Modern interest comes from summer and winter bedding schemes, period perennial plantings and tender exotics.

historic Victorian suburban garden undergoing restoration; crocosmias; tea and cakes (on Sunday afternoons, May to September)

Owned by The Plantation Garden Preservation Trust
Number of gardeners 1 part-time, plus volunteers
Size 1.2ha (3 acres) approx.
English Heritage Grade II

RAVENINGHAM HALL GARDENS

Raveningham, Norwich NR14 6NS

Tel 01508 548152 **Fax** 01508 548958
www.raveningham.com
Location Signed off A146 at Hales
Opening hours 11am to 4pm, Monday to Friday, Bank Holiday Sundays and Mondays, Easter to August
Admission fee Adults £4; OAPs £3; children free

The house at Raveningham is partly Georgian and partly 20th-century: the 14th-century church of St Andrew near the house is an integral part of the landscape. Both are set in a splendid 18th-century park and enhanced by 19th-century tree plantings. Despite all this history, the main attraction now is the modern plantings. These were largely the work of Priscilla, Lady Bacon, who collected rare plants and arranged them beautifully in areas like the long herbaceous border. She was also a keen dendrologist and planted the young arboretum. In the working walled garden (very pretty) is a recently restored Victorian glasshouse. Outside the walled garden are an orchard, a herb garden and a new 'time' garden. A new lake has also been made in the park, and there are contemporary sculptures by the present owner's wife throughout.

roses (mainly modern); good herbaceous borders; fine collection of trees; splendid 18th-century walled garden and Victorian glasshouses; home-made teas on Bank Holiday Sundays and Mondays

Owned by Sir Nicholas Bacon Bt
Number of gardeners 3
Size 2ha (5 acres)
English Heritage Grade II

SANDRINGHAM HOUSE

Sandringham, King's Lynn PE35 6EN

Tel 01553 612908 **Fax** 01485 541571
www.sandringhamestate.co.uk
Location Signed from A148
Opening hours 10.30am to 5pm (4pm in October), daily, 15 April to 20 July and 31 July to 28 October
Admission fee Adults £6; OAPs £5; children £3.50; RHS members free

This is the best of the royal gardens, with much of interest at all seasons. The woodland and lakes are rich with ornamental plantings. The splendid herbaceous borders were designed by Eric Savill and the North Garden by Geoffrey Jellicoe, but it is the scale of it all that most impresses, and the grandeur, too. There will be two RHS Special Events at Sandringham in 2007; details from 020 7821 3408.

good herbaceous borders; rhododendrons; azaleas; maples; hydrangeas; gift shop; plant centre; restaurant and tea rooms

Owned by HM The Queen
Number of gardeners 8
Size 24ha (60 acres)
English Heritage Grade II*

SHERINGHAM PARK
Sheringham NR26 8TB

Tel: 01263 820550 **Fax:** 01263 820556
www.nationaltrust.org.uk
Location Junction of A148 and B1157
Opening hours Dawn to dusk, daily, all year
Admission fee Cars £3.60 (National Trust members free)

This is one of the best Repton landscapes to have survived the last 200 years, but it was also fleshed out with a great 19th- and 20th-century collection of rhododendrons. The owners also subscribed to EH Wilson's expeditions and bought a splendid variety of choice trees and shrubs from the Surrey nurseries between the wars. The elegant classical temple was built in 1975 to a design by Repton. Recent clearing and replanting have opened up the rhododendron woods very successfully.
woodland garden; mature conifers; rhododendrons; refreshments

Owned by The National Trust
Number of gardeners 3
Size 20ha (50 acres)
English Heritage Grade II*

STODY LODGE
Melton Constable NR24 2EW

Tel 01263 860572 **Fax** 01263 861179
www.stodyestate.co.uk
Location 3 miles south-west of Holt
Opening hours 2pm to 5pm, 6, 13, 30, 27 and 18 May, and 3 June; and by appointment on Wednesday afternoons (min. 2 people)
Admission fee Adults £4.50; children free

Stody has the largest collection of rhododendrons and azaleas in East Anglia. They were first planted by Lord Rothermere in the 1920s and fill the walks and woodlands around the handsome house. In the 1980s, the present owners started to plant Mollis hybrids and they have multiplied through the area called the Water Garden until they alone amount to some 2,000 plants. Throughout the garden are fine ornamental trees, from a vast and ancient cedar of Lebanon to a mass of liquidambars, sorbus, magnolias, eucryphias and davidias dating for the most part from the mid-20th century. Stody deserves to be much better known; its scents and colours during the flowering season are almost overpowering.
rhododendrons and azaleas; home-made teas

Owned by Mrs AJ MacNicol
Number of gardeners 1½
Size 4ha (10 acres)

STOW HALL
Stow Bardolph, King's Lynn PE34 3HU

Tel 01366 383194
Location 2 miles north of Downham Market, off A10
Opening hours 5pm to 9pm, 22 June (plus flower or cookery demonstration); and by appointment
Admission fee Adults £3.50; children free

Although the Hares have lived here for 450 years, the gardens at Stow Hall are largely modern. Little remains of earlier gardens except for their outline and the magnificent, mature trees. These include London plane trees, cedars of Lebanon and vast beeches, many supplied by Lee & Kennedy of Hammersmith, the leading nursery of the day. The outbuildings, stables and walled gardens are covered in climbing roses and tender plants like *Azara microphylla*. There is a working kitchen garden, and a young collection of old apple cultivars. Old-fashioned roses are everywhere.
roses; kitchen garden; plant stall; home-made teas and light suppers

Owned by Lady Rose Hare
Number of gardeners 1½
Size 8ha (20 acres)

NORTHAMPTONSHIRE

Despite its industrial importance and its proximity to London, Northamptonshire is still a county of large estates. Three of the four Grade I historic gardens are open to the public (Althorp, Boughton House and Castle Ashby), while the fourth (Drayton) is occasionally open to groups from organisations like the Garden History Society. Althorp and Boughton House also have good arboreta, each with a few champion trees. The National Gardens Scheme does well in Northamptonshire: it is particularly successful in persuading groups of gardens, as many as eight or nine in a village, to open together on the same day. It is therefore something of a paradox that there appear to be comparatively few nurseries in the county and only two National Collections. On the other hand, its RHS Free Access garden – Cottesbrooke – is a modern classic, a historic landscape with a really good horticultural garden inserted into it.

ALTHORP
Northampton NN7 4HQ

Tel 01604 770107 **Fax** 01604 770042
www.althorp.com
Location Signed from M1, Jct 16
Opening hours 11am to 5pm, daily, 30 June to 2 September; closed 31 August
Admission fee Adults £3.50; OAPs £2.50; children £1.50

Althorp is interesting more for its ex-royal associations than as a great garden. However, the 19th-century formal gardens are impressive and the traditional parkland deeply pastoral. In the arboretum are some fine mature trees, including a record-breaking Santa Lucia fir (*Abies bracteata*) over 30m high.
mature conifers; formal gardens; biggest *Abies bracteata* (38m; 125ft) in the British Isles; gift shop; café

Owned by Earl Spencer
English Heritage Grade I

BOUGHTON HOUSE
Kettering NN14 1BJ

Tel 01536 515731 **Fax** 01536 417255
www.boughtonhouse.org.uk
Location A43, 3 miles north of Kettering, signed through Geddington
Opening hours Noon to 5pm, Sunday to Friday, 1 May to 1 September; daily in August
Admission fee Adults £1.50; OAPs and children £1

Boughton has an important landscaped park dating from the early 18th century. The layout is intact, as are some of the plantings – one of the lime avenues was planted in 1715. The original landscaping features have been purposefully restored over the last 20 years or so: rides, avenues, *allées*, lakes, canals and prospects – the restoration plan is ongoing. There is little of horticultural interest, but the sense of history is strongly felt.
roses (mainly modern); good herbaceous borders; good website; current holder of Sandford Award; shop; tea rooms (Sunday; daily in August)

Owned by The Duke and Duchess of Buccleuch and The Living Landscape Trust
Number of gardeners 5
Size 8ha (20 acres) garden; 140ha (350 acres) park
English Heritage Grade I

CANONS ASHBY HOUSE
Daventry NN11 3SD

Tel 01327 861900 **Fax** 01327 861909
www.nationaltrust.org.uk
Location Signed from A5 and A422
Opening hours 11am to 5.30pm (4.30pm in October and November), Saturday to Wednesday, 17 March

to 4 November; 11am to 4pm, Saturdays and Sundays, 10 November to 16 December
Admission fee Garden only: adults £2.50

(P) (♿)

Canons Ashby is a rare survivor among gardens. The Drydens, who owned it, never really took to the landscape movement. The early 18th-century layout is intact and has been carefully restored by the National Trust. The terraces below the house (*very* pretty) are planted with clipped Portugal laurel (*Prunus lusitanica*) and period fruit trees. A place to contemplate old Tory values.
topiary; fruit; good herbaceous borders; light lunches and teas

Owned by The National Trust
Number of gardeners 2
Size 1.4ha (3 1/2 acres)
English Heritage Grade II*

CASTLE ASHBY GARDENS

Castle Ashby, Northampton NN7 1LQ

Tel 01604 696696 **Fax** 01604 696516
www.castleashby.co.uk
Location Off A428 between Northampton and Bedford
Opening hours 10am to 5.30pm, daily, all year; closes at 4.30pm from October to March
Admission fee Adults £2.80; OAPs and children £1.90

(P) (♦) (♿) (✺)

Much thought and money has recently been spent on restoring the gardens at Castle Ashby. The Italian formal gardens were among the first to be renewed, and the arboretum has been restocked. There are stylish terraces, an orangery and greenhouses built by Sir Matthew Digby Wyatt in the 1860s, but perhaps the best thing about Castle Ashby is the park – 200 acres of it, designed by Capability Brown.
topiary; fine collection of trees; gift shops; plant centre; new tea rooms (2007)

Owned by The Marquess of Northampton
Number of gardeners 5
Size 8ha (20 acres)
English Heritage Grade I

COTON MANOR

Guilsborough NN6 8RQ

Tel 01604 740219 **Fax** 01604 740838
www.cotonmanor.co.uk
Location Signed from A5199 (formerly A50) and A428
Opening hours Noon to 5.30pm, Tuesday to Saturday and Bank Holiday weekends, April to September; plus Sundays in April and May
Admission fee Adults £5; OAPs £4.50; children £2

(P) (🚻) (♿) (✺)

The Pasley-Tylers have lived at Coton since the 1920s, and every generation has left its mark upon the garden. Among the best features are a rose garden, a herb garden, a woodland garden, colour plantings (including a wonderful crimson and pink border), a Mediterranean bank, a five-acre bluebell wood, an apple orchard with 80 English cultivars, and a wildflower meadow. Water is everywhere: pools, streams and ponds support hostas, primulas and the black and yellow flowers of *Kirengeshoma palmata*. There are surprises too: one might suppose that the sweet-scented *Trachelospermum asiaticum* and long-flowering *Fremontodendron californicum* were too tender for Northamptonshire, but they both grow against the walls of the house. Recent plantings include a bog garden and an extension to the woodland garden. The whole garden comes together nicely because the plants are chosen for their overall contribution as well as their intrinsic merits. The standard of maintenance is excellent, while the presence of a few ornamental birds adds quite another dimension to a visit.
roses (mainly old cultivars); good herbaceous borders; bluebells; waterfowl; lots of pots; home produce and gifts; excellent small nursery; light lunches and teas

Owned by Ian Pasley-Tyler
Number of gardeners 3
Size 4ha (10 acres)

COTTESBROOKE HALL

Cottesbrooke, Northampton NN6 8PF

Tel 01604 505808 **Fax** 01604 505619
www.cottesbrookehall.co.uk
Location 10 miles north of Northampton
Opening hours 2pm to 5.30pm, Thursdays, May to

September; plus Wednesdays in May and June; for NGS: 2pm to 5pm, 5 August
Admission fee Gardens only: adults £5; concessions £4; children £2.50; RHS members free, except on special event days

Ⓟ 👪 ♿ ❁

Cottesbrooke is the garden with everything: a two-mile drive, majestic parkland, a classical bridge, a fabulously pretty house, an 18th-century park, lakes, waterfalls, bluebell woods, rhododendrons, drifts of daffodils and primulas, 27 cultivars of naturalised snowdrops, half a dozen garden rooms, Scheemakers's statues from Stowe, an armillary garden, pergolas, *allées*, 300-year-old cedars, new developments every year, immaculate maintenance, plants aplenty, and the signatures of Geoffrey Jellicoe, Sylvia Crowe and James Alexander Sinclair among the designers who have helped to develop it.
roses (mainly old-fashioned); good herbaceous borders; exceptionally harmonious design; thoughtful plantings; water gardens; wild gardens; HHA/Christie's Garden of the Year in 2000; tea room

Owned by Mr and Mrs AR Macdonald-Buchanan
Number of gardeners 6
Size 5ha (12 1/2 acres)
English Heritage Grade II

DEENE PARK
Corby NN17 3EW

Tel 01780 450278 **Fax** 01780 450282
www.deenepark.com
Location Off A43 between Corby and Stamford
Opening hours 11am to 4pm, 18 and 25 February; 2pm to 5pm, Sundays, June to August; plus Bank Holiday Sundays and Mondays from Easter to August; groups by arrangement
Admission fee Adults £4; children £1; groups by arrangement

Ⓟ 👪 ♿ ❁

Deene Park has beautiful 18th-century parkland around the rambling, castellated house. The gardens are modern, made since the 1970s, with help from David Hicks. The mixed borders of shrub roses and herbaceous plants are especially beautiful in late June. Much old trees and a lush river walk are added attractions.
parkland; roses; formal garden; tea room

Cottesbrooke Hall and gardens

Owned by Edmund Brudnell
Number of gardeners 2
Size 8ha (20 acres)
English Heritage Grade II

HOLDENBY HOUSE GARDENS

Holdenby, Northampton NN6 8DJ

Tel 01604 770074 **Fax** 01604 770962
www.holdenby.com
Location 6 miles north-west of Northampton, off A5199 or A428
Opening hours 1pm to 5pm, Sundays and Bank Holiday Mondays, April to September
Admission fee Adults £3; OAPs £2.50; children £2; but adults £5; OAPs £4.50; children £3.50 from May to August when the falconry centre is open

The outlines of the garden at Holdenby are Elizabethan: a bowling alley, some parterres and terraces were built in 1580 to impress Queen Elizabeth on one of her progresses through England. They explain why Holdenby is highly regarded as a historical garden. The Elizabethan-style garden was planted by Rosemary Verey, using only those plants which were available in 1580. Rupert Golby planted the 'fragrant border' and there is a charming 'silver border' made to display the owners' ever-growing collection of silver- and grey-leaved plants.

roses (mainly old-fashioned); herbs; good herbaceous borders; Elizabethan-style garden; fragrant and silver borders; kitchen garden; current holder of Sandford Award; souvenirs and crafts for sale; tea room in original Victorian kitchen

Owned by Mr and Mrs James Lowther
Number of gardeners 2
Size 6ha (15 acres)
English Heritage Grade II*

KELMARSH HALL

Northampton NN6 9LU

Tel 01604 686543 **Fax** 01604 686437
www.kelmarsh.com
Location On A508 at crossroads in Kelmarsh
Opening hours 2pm to 5pm, Tuesday to Thursday and Bank Holiday Sundays and Mondays, 8 April to 30 September; snowdrop opening: 10am to 3pm, 11 February; for NGS: 22 April and 1 July

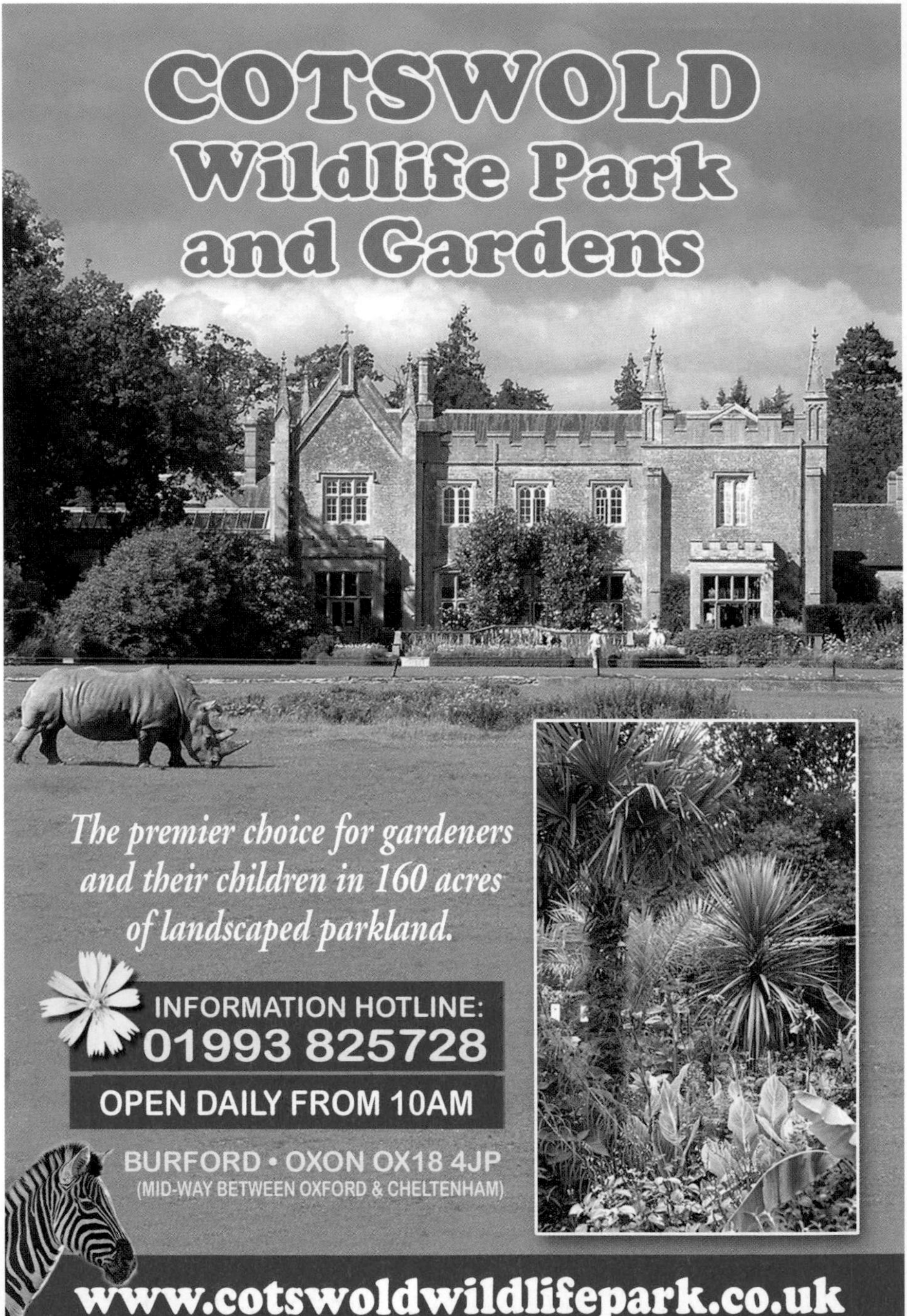

Admission fee Adults £4; concessions £3.50; children £2.50; RHS members free

Kelmarsh is a handsome Palladian house: it looks out over a formal terrace, designed by Geoffrey Jellicoe in 1936, to formalised parkland. The view extends across a meadow lined with horse-chestnuts to a lake before wilder, open semi-parkland carries the eye to the horizon. Most of the horticultural interest is off to the side, around the outside of a triangular walled garden. First come lumpy box hedges, pleached limes and a pretty sunken garden, designed as a quincunx and planted with white and scented flowers. Further on, *Tropaeolum speciosum* clambers through the hedges which flank a sequence of narrow, intimate beds, designed by Nancy Lancaster with help from Norah Lindsay and currently (2007) undergoing restoration. Some of the yew hedges have been breached by cutting the yew trees back to the trunks and letting them grow into curious hump-backed shapes – a very effective and unique feature of the garden. At the furthest extremity, the narrow path bursts out into a fan-shaped old-fashioned rose garden, recently remade, with a splendid view of the parish church across parkland. On the way back (outside the walled garden again) is the long border, another Lancaster-Lindsay collaboration, which has just been replanted. This is a fine garden, which will be interesting to watch as it develops in years to come. A Heritage Lottery grant has funded the restoration of the vinery and back sheds, which means that the walled garden with its cut-flower borders is now fully accessible.

spring bulbs; old hedges; lots of recent restoration; teas

Owned by The Kelmarsh Trust
Number of gardeners 3 1/2
Size 5.6ha (14 acres)

OLD RECTORY

Sudborough NN14 3BX

Tel 01832 733247 **Fax** 01832 733832
www.oldrectorygardens.co.uk
Location A14, Exit 12; in village centre, by church, off A6116
Opening hours 2pm to 6pm, Tuesdays, April to September; and by appointment
Admission fee Adults £4; children free

This immaculately maintained modern garden has been made around a handsome Georgian rectory with a bit of advice from Rosemary Verey and Rupert Golby. In front of the house, on the edge of the lawn, is a handsome and ancient *Robinia pseudoacacia*: everything else is fairly recent and extremely well grown. The garden is thickly and thoughtfully planted so that every season is rich in interest. Few of the plants are rare, but all are well chosen – some for their flowers, some for their foliage and others because they look good in mixed groups. Roses are much in evidence throughout the garden and in a dedicated rose garden. The best feature is an extensive and very pretty *potager*, designed by Rosemary Verey, which has an infinite number of beds edged and fairly narrow brick paths between them. Clematis and roses cover the framework of a tunnel: they are joined, in season, by ornamental gourds which are encouraged to grow up the same structure. The fruit trees are trained in many different ways and good use is made of flowers in pots to ensure that the *potager* has colour at all seasons.

roses (ancient and modern); herbs; fruit; good herbaceous borders; handsome new *potager*; tea, coffee and biscuits

Owned by Mr and Mrs AP Huntington
Number of gardeners 2
Size 1.2ha (3 acres)

ROCKINGHAM CASTLE

Market Harborough LE16 8TH

Tel 01536 770240 **Fax** 01536 771692
www.rockinghamcastle.com
Location 2 miles north of Corby on A6003
Opening hours Noon to 5pm, Sundays and Bank Holiday Mondays, 8 April to September; plus Tuesdays from June to September
Admission fee £4.50

Rockingham has centuries of garden history in its layout: the park was landscaped in the 18th century but goes back to the 13th century as a deer park. The formal circular rose garden on the site of the old keep was added in the 19th century: it is surrounded by a billowing, castellated yew hedge

400 years old, known as the 'Elephant Hedge'. The wild garden in a ravine was replanted 20 years ago as a mini-arboretum. The most recent improvements are a series garden 'rooms', enclosed by young yew hedges, each most stylishly designed and planted.
roses (mainly old-fashioned); good herbaceous borders; fine collection of trees; gift shop; tea room

Owned by James Saunders Watson
Number of gardeners 3
Size 5ha (12 1/2 acres)
English Heritage Grade II*

STOKE ALBANY HOUSE
Market Harborough LE16 8PT

Tel 01858 535227 **Fax** 01858 535580
Location 1/2 mile south of Stoke Albany village
Opening hours 2pm to 4.30pm, Sundays, 1 April and 6 June to 18 July; groups by prior arrangement
Admission fee Adults £3; children free

Stoke Albany has an opulent traditional garden serenely set around a handsome house. Its elements incorporate lots of roses, herbaceous plants, a grey garden for silver plants, an avenue of catmint, a box-edged *potager* and a wildflower meadow. A more contemporary note is struck by the Mediterranean garden, planted largely with grasses.
daffodils; roses

Owned by Mr and Mrs AM Vinton
Number of gardeners 2
Size 1.6ha (4 acres)

SULGRAVE MANOR
Sulgrave, Banbury OX17 2SD

Tel 01295 760205 **Fax** 01295 76805
www.sulgravemanor.org.uk
Location 7 miles from Banbury
Opening hours Noon to 5.30pm, Saturdays and Sundays, April; 2pm to 5.30pm, Tuesday to Thursday, Saturdays and Sundays, May to October; closed Mondays and Fridays except Bank Holidays; groups at other times by appointment; last entry 4 pm
Admission fee Adults £6.50; concessions £5.75; children £3; families £17.50; special prices for special events

There are two reasons for visiting Sulgrave. The first is that it belonged to George Washington's family or, at least, to his ancestors. This places the Great American firmly among the English minor gentry. The second is that, after the estate was underwritten by the Colonial Dames in 1924, Sir Reginald Blomfield was called in to design a period garden. In his day, Blomfield was one of England's foremost architect-designers, and the garden he made for Sulgrave is formally laid out in a simple, 17th-century style, to complement the old house. The plantings are suitably olde worlde. The Herb Society moved its headquarters to Sulgrave in 2001 and has planted a herb garden which is full of interest but rather spoils the spirit of the place.
herbs; tea room

Owned by Sulgrave Manor Board
Number of gardeners 1
Size 2ha (5 acres)
English Heritage Grade II

NORTHUMBERLAND AND TYNE & WEAR

Northumberland and Tyne & Wear are two sides of the same historical phenomenon: men made their fortunes in Newcastle or Sunderland, both now in Tyne & Wear, and then moved out to build houses and plant gardens in Northumberland. Belsay, Cragside and Lindisfarne all owe their gardens to this social pattern. Belsay is a Grade I garden: the only other one in Northumberland is Alnwick, where the Duchess of Northumberland's spectacular new garden is now complete. The greatest 19th-century garden in Northumberland is Cragside, which now has a collection of champion conifers. There are record-breakers, too, at Alnwick, and a very good arboretum at Howick, where many new plantings have also been made in recent years. The National Gardens Scheme does not have a large portfolio of gardens in Northumberland and Tyne & Wear, but there are several first-rate nurseries in the two counties, including Halls of Heddon, Herterton House and Hexham Herbs. The real interests of ordinary gardeners in Northumberland and Tyne & Wear are quite different: alpines and leeks. Both the Alpine Garden Society and the Scottish Rock Garden Club are well supported here, while the National Pot Leek Society could be described as a uniquely Geordie success story.

THE ALNWICK GARDEN

Denwick Lane, Alnwick NE66 1YU

Tel 01665 511350 **Fax** 01665 511351
www.alnwickgarden.com
Location Signed in Alnwick and from A1
Opening hours 10am to 7pm (4pm in winter), daily, all year, closed Christmas Day
Admission fee Adults £8; concessions £7.50; children free

The Alnwick Garden has become a major tourist attraction in a very short time – and deservedly so, because it is wonderful to visit. First open to the public in 2001, it is a continuing project, with new features appearing all the time. The Duchess of Northumberland is the driving force behind it, and the gifted Jacques Wirtz is its designer. The main feature is already impressive – a grand neo-baroque water cascade flanked by hornbeam arcades in the Belgian style and ending in fountains. At the top, you enter the Ornamental Garden, a place of box-lined paths, pleached apples, tender climbers (tea roses and ceanothus against the walls) and the best continental-style of planting outside Belgium. Here, too, are rare roses from Lens in Belgium, like 'Frisson Frais' and 'Lieve Louise', seldom seen in England. Whole beds are dedicated to a single genus, like hellebores, irises, Japanese anemones and delphiniums, so that there is always something to see, whatever the season. Down the hill again (the cascade flows down a north-facing slope and is difficult to photograph well – photographers, please note) is an excellent, thickly planted David Austin rose garden, with pergolas, climbers, shrub roses and a few mixed plantings – very beautiful. In fact the whole garden is probably best when all the roses are out in high summer. But there are fun features, too: the poison garden, the serpent garden, the bamboo labyrinth and the largest wooden tree house in the world. The standard of maintenance is exemplary. The lack of a decent horticultural guidebook is regrettable, but this should not detract from the enormous pleasure of a visit to this enormous, sumptuous, inspirational and fascinating garden.

grand cascade; roses; shops; café; restaurant

Owned by The Alnwick Garden Trust
Number of gardeners 8
Size 16ha (40 acres) including 4.8ha (12 acres) of walled garden

BEDE'S WORLD HERB GARDEN

Bede's World, Church Bank, Jarrow NE32 3DY

Tel 0191 489 2106 **Fax** 0191 428 2361
www.bedesworld.co.uk
Location Signed from A185 and A19
Opening hours 10am to 5.30pm, daily, all year; opens noon on Sundays; closes 4.30pm from November to March; Christmas opening hours not yet known
Admission fee Herb garden only: free

Bede's World is an educational experience: one of its main parts is an 'Anglo-Saxon farm' with a vegetable garden where early cultivars of vegetables are grown. But there is also a herb garden, based on a plan of the 9th-century original at St Gall in Switzerland, where culinary, aromatic and medicinal herbs are grown. It is a small part of an ambitious enterprise which seeks to impart a feeling for the Anglo-Saxon world.
herbs; shop for herbal products; lunches and light refreshments

Owned by Bede's World

BELSAY HALL

Belsay, Newcastle-upon-Tyne NE20 0DX

Tel 01661 881636 **Fax** 01661 881043
www.english-heritage.org.uk
Location At Belsay on A696 Ponteland to Jedburgh road
Opening hours 10am to 5pm (4pm in October), daily, April to October; 10am to 4pm, Thursday to Monday, November to March; closed 1 January and 24 to 26 December
Admission fee Adults £5.50; concessions £4.10; children £2.80

The wildly picturesque gardens at Belsay were created by Sir Charles Monck in the 19th century around his new Greek Revival house. The outstanding feature is 11 acres of disused quarry with a sequence of gloomy chasms, corridors and pinnacles, which house all manner of exotic and rare plants. Rhododendron species flower here from November to August, climbers scramble 10m (33ft) up the quarry faces, spring bulbs carpet the meadow and modern underplantings like lilies flower from May to September. The ravines create a microclimate which allows such plants as *Trachycarpus* palms and eucryphias to flourish in a cold upland site: Belsay is of great interest to plantsmen. The house is very austere – inspired by ancient Athens – but underpinned by fine formal terraces where the gardeners arrange magnificent displays of bedding. Down the valley are splendid woods planted with two acres of hardy hybrid rhododendrons – not open to the public, but a magnificent sight from the terraces. Elsewhere are fine weed-free lawns (one is for croquet), intensive modern herbaceous plantings, a magnolia terrace, a recently restored rose border, tall heathers, brooding conifers (some of the earliest Douglas firs in England) and the stately ruins of Belsay Castle. The standard of maintenance is superb.
snowdrops; rhododendrons and azaleas (species and hardy hybrids); formal terraces; winter garden; unique quarry garden; gift shop; refreshments in summer

Owned by Managed by English Heritage on behalf of the Belsay Trust
Number of gardeners 4, plus 1 trainee
Size 16ha (40 acres)
NCCPG National Collections *Iris spuria*
English Heritage Grade I

BIRKHEADS SECRET GARDENS & NURSERY

Marley Hill, Newcastle-upon-Tyne NE16 5EL

Tel 01207 232262/07778 447920 **Fax** 01207 232262
www.birkheadsnursery.co.uk
Location Follow brown tourist signs on A6076 between Sunniside and Stanley
Opening hours 10am to 5pm, daily, except Mondays, March to October; and by appointment at other times and seasons; groups by appointment
Admission fee Garden: £2.50; nursery: free

This nursery offers a varied and informed selection of alpines, perennials and shrubs, all of which can be seen growing in the adjoining gardens; the owner is a garden designer with a passion for plants. The gardens include an avenue of soft blue, pink and silver perennials, the Bowes railway heritage garden, over half a

BIDE-A-WEE COTTAGE

Stanton, Netherwitton, Morpeth NE65 8PR

Tel/fax 01670 772238
www.bideawee.co.uk
Location 7 miles north-west of Morpeth
Opening hours 1.30pm to 5pm, Wednesdays and Saturdays, 21 April to 29 August; parties by arrangement at other times
Admission fee £2.50; RHS members free

The situation of the garden at Bide-a-Wee Cottage is extraordinary: most of the garden is hidden in a disused quarry on the edge of a 160m (500ft) ridge. The unusual site means that there are enormous variations within its two acres – variations of aspect, topography, soil type and moisture. Over the last 20 years, Mark Robson has seized on this natural diversity to plant a remarkably wide spectrum of plants. In the wet, shaded quarry bottom, by the ponds, are swathes of primulas, rodgersias, ostrich ferns, sensitive ferns and gunneras. Away from the water, on the north-facing slopes of the quarry and in the shade of trees, are meconopsis, rhododendrons and gentians. Quite a different type of plant grows on the south-facing slopes: abutilons, agapanthus and eryngiums, for example. Throughout the garden, the natural rock walls are contrasted with hedges and complemented by evergreens – conifers, rhododendrons and grasses. Then more ephemeral perennials and wildflowers are woven into the design, as are the more unusual plants that are the hallmark of a plantsman. Robson describes his garden as 'bold perennial plantings linked with a network of winding paths and steps, all associated with dramatic changes of level'. These are designed to create views across the garden or down onto lower levels, as well as into the countryside beyond. To the east, above the quarry, drifts of late-flowering perennials (including lythrum, eupatorium and helianthus) melt into the half-acre wildflower meadow that is also home to the beehives. Then the garden opens out and blends into the rough landscape of Northumberland – tough grassland grazed by sheep.
rock garden; plantsman's collection of plants; excellent nursery selling plants from garden

Owned by Mark Robson
Size 0.8ha (2 acres)
NCCPG National Collections *Centaurea*

mile of colour-themed borders, a mini-arboretum underplanted with spring bulbs, the slate garden with old roses and scented shrubs, a wildflower meadow, an oriental-style meditation garden with pond, the spring garden planted with a woodland theme for all-year interest, a wildlife pond, the beachcombers' garden, a gravel and rock garden.
a plantsman's garden attached to a plantsman's nursery; small coffee shop

Owned by Christine Liddle
Number of gardeners 3
Size 1.2ha (3 acres)

CHESTERS WALLED GARDEN

Chollerford, Hexham NE46 4BQ

Tel 01434 681483
www.chesterswalledgarden.co.uk
Location 6 miles north of Hexham, off B6318 near Chollerford
Opening hours 10am to 5pm, daily, mid-March to October; telephone for winter opening times
Admission fee Adults £3; children (under 10) free

This energetic and successful garden nursery is strategically placed near the fort at Chesters. The original name of the nursery was 'Hexham Herbs'. Now the garden is a tourist attraction in its own

right, and the nursery is better than ever. The herb collection is remarkable (over 900 cultivars) and the design within a two-acre brick-walled garden is charming. Dye plants, a Mediterranean garden, two ponds, an astilbe bed and a knot garden are just some of the features. Much of the structure comes from box hedges, but wildflowers have been allowed to seed alongside the more exotic plants, which gives an air of naturalness. In addition to their National Collections of *Origanum*, *Thymus* and *Sanguisorba*, the nursery has a very good collection of mint cultivars. The garden has over 3,000 different plant cultivars growing in it, and the owner aims to propagate and sell them all in rotation, which means that if they do not have something just at the moment, you should be able to buy it from them in the future.
thyme bank; roses (mainly old-fashioned); herbs; 'Roman' garden; grass garden; wildlife ponds; nursery attached; gift and produce shop

Owned by Mrs S White
Size 0.8ha (2 acres)
NCCPG National Collections *Origanum*; *Thymus*; *Sanguisorba*

CRAGSIDE

Rothbury, Morpeth NE65 7PX

Tel 01669 620333 **Fax** 01669 620066
www.nationaltrust.org.uk
Location 13 miles south of Alnwick
Opening hours Gardens: 10.30am to 7pm (last admissions 5pm), Tuesday to Sunday and Bank Holiday Mondays, 17 March to 4 November; 11am to 4pm, Wednesday to Sunday, 7 November to 16 December
Admission fee Adults £7.70; children £3.30; families £18.70

There are three gardens at Cragside: all were made by the armaments millionaire Lord Armstrong when he started to build the house in 1863. First comes the Italianate formal garden with splendid carpet bedding, ferneries and an orchard house with rotating pots. Then there is the large, semi-natural rock garden by the house. But most impressive of all are the rhododendron woods – hundreds of acres of 19th-century hybrids, plus trusty *R. ponticum* and *R. luteum*. The estate drives take you for six miles all the way round, past granite boulders, moorland, heather and conifers – but the rhododendrons dominate the journey, breathtaking in early June.
fruit; mature conifers; massive rock garden; tallest *Abies nordmanniana* (50m; 164ft), *Cupressus nootkatensis* (33m; 108ft) and *Picea glauca* (28m; 92ft) in the British Isles; National Trust shop; refreshments

Owned by The National Trust
Number of gardeners 5
Size 250ha (1,000 acres)
English Heritage Grade II*

THE GARDEN STATION

Langley, Hexham NE47 5LA

Tel 01434 684391
www.thegardenstation.co.uk
Location A686 Alston road off A69, then follow yellow signs to left
Opening hours 10am to 5pm, Tuesday to Sunday, plus Bank Holiday Mondays, May to August
Admission fee Free; donations welcome

This is a small centre for gardening, art courses and exhibitions, with some interesting sculptures and water features. The Garden Station is a very attractive restored Victorian railway station in a sheltered and tranquil woodland garden. Following along the old track under stone arched bridges, the garden is planted with bold foliage plants, including *Meconopsis* and primulas.
plants for sale; light refreshments

Owned by Jane Torday
Number of gardeners 2 part-time
Size 1ha (2 1/2 acres)

HALLS OF HEDDON

West Heddon Nurseries, Heddon on the Wall, Newcastle-upon-Tyne NE15 0JS

Tel 01661 852445 **Fax** 01661 852398
www.hallsofheddon.co.uk
Location 1 mile north-west of Heddon, off B6318
Opening hours 9am to 5pm, Monday to Saturday; 10am to 5pm, Sundays
Admission fee Free

Ⓟ 👫 ❁

Halls produced their first dahlia and chrysanthemum catalogue in 1931. Now they offer over 400 cultivars for many purposes, including showing, cutting, garden display, greenhouse cultivation and growing in pots and containers. Their extensive list includes many cultivars which are unique to them. Their magnificent show fields are open from the end of August to mid-October (unless the plants are cut down earlier by frost). They have over 15,000 plants on display, including plants of up to 50 new cultivars being trialled for possible introduction.

Owned by David Hall
Number of gardeners 4
Size 0.4ha (1 acre)

HERTERTON HOUSE GARDENS & NURSERY

Hartington, Cambo NE61 4BN

Tel 01670 774278
Location 2 miles north of Cambo (B6342)
Opening hours 1.30pm to 5.30pm, daily except Tuesdays and Thursdays, April to September; for NGS: 14 June, 12 July and 2 August
Admission fee Adults £3; Children £1

Ⓟ 👫 ❁

This excellent plantsman's garden is firmly designed and meticulously planted. The formal garden (very simple, very full) relies on contrasts of colour, texture and shape of clipped evergreens – a model of how to impart a sense of size and space to a very small space. There is topiary throughout the garden; it also provides shelter for tender plants like 'Gloire de Dijon' roses. The knot garden is famous, and much photographed, full of herbs and pharmacological plants. The main garden is best seen from the staircase at the back of the house; it has a very firm structure, furnished with evergreen shrubs clipped into endless inventive forms to give interest all through the year. More impressive still are the cottagey herbaceous plantings, all weaving through each other in beautifully coordinated colours. In the gazebo at the top are photographs showing how the garden has developed, expanded, grown up and intensified over the years: a most inspirational display. A modern masterpiece.

plantsman's collection of plants; small formal garden; physic garden; nursery garden; first-class nursery attached

Owned by Mr and Mrs Frank Lawley
Number of gardeners 2
Size 0.4ha (1 acre)

HOWICK HALL GARDENS

Alnwick NE66 3LB

Tel 01665 577285
www.howickhallgardens.org.uk
Location Off B1399 between Longhoughton and Craster
Opening hours Noon to 4pm, Saturdays and Sundays, mid-February to March; noon to 6pm, daily, April to October
Admission fee February and March: adults £3.50; OAPs £2.50; children free; April to October: adults £4.50; OAPs £3.50; children free

Ⓟ 👫 ♿

Howick is a very good garden, full of interesting plants. It is also rather un-Northumbrian, because its closeness to the sea makes possible the cultivation of such tender plants as tree fuchsias, carpenterias, olearias and ceanothus. The handsome Palladian house has well-planted formal terraces below – you cannot miss the 70m (230ft) ribbon of agapanthus in high summer – and there is a rock garden to one side. The woodland garden has acid soil, and was planted in the 1930s with a fine collection of rhododendrons and camellias together with shrubs like linderas and underplantings of lilies, hellebores and candelabra primulas. Elsewhere are fine parkland, a large bog garden, lots of new plantings (groves of cercidiphyllums) from collected seed, daffodils, colchicums and curiosities like an oak tree and a beech tree all intermingled because they were planted in the 19th century in the same hole. The present Lord Howick is an avid plant collector: the new arboretum is planted with some 11,000 trees and shrubs (1,700 taxa) all grown from wild-collected seed.

roses (mainly old-fashioned); rhododendrons and azaleas; plantsman's collection of plants; mature conifers; spring bulbs; eucryphias; much new planting; champion *Magnolia wilsonii*; tea room

Owned by Howick Trustees Ltd
Number of gardeners 5
English Heritage Grade II

KIRKLEY HALL GARDENS

Ponteland NE20 0AQ

Tel 01670 841200 **Fax** 01661 860047
Location Signed in Ponteland
Opening hours 10am to 5pm, weekdays, all year; and by appointment at weekends; closes at 3pm from October to March
Admission fee Free

The Victorian, walled garden at Kirkley Hall is one of the best in the North of England in which to learn how to garden. The emphasis is on plants – their selection, cultivation and enjoyment – though cutbacks mean that standards of maintenance are somewhat relaxed. Further demonstration gardens have been laid out between the walled garden and the house, with some interesting trees and shrubs along the way.
woodland garden; plantsman's collection of plants; plants under glass; fruit; mature conifers; good herbaceous borders; plant centre

Owned by Northumberland College at Kirkley Hall
Number of gardeners 3
Size 4ha (10 acres)
NCCPG National Collections *Fagus*

LONGFRAMLINGTON GARDENS

Swarland Road, Longframlington, Morpeth NE65 8BE

Tel/fax 01665 570382
www.longframlingtongardens.co.uk
Location 3/4 mile east of Longframlington along B6345
Opening hours 8.30am to 5pm (or dusk, if earlier), daily, all year; closed Christmas to New Year; evenings by appointment
Admission fee Adults £3.95; nursery free

This young garden was started in 1998 in a cold, open, windy, greenfield position and has a chirpy, modern design where low maintenance is important. The design reflects the modern need for low maintenance and year-round interest, and the designer's preference for informality. It is worth visiting to see how many plants have survived recent winters in this unpromising site – including cistus, hebes and *Olearia macrodonta*. The main problem at this stage is to acquire sufficient shelter to allow ornamentals to grow and establish well. The nursery is said to offer over 2,500 different plants, all of them suitable for the Northumbrian climate.
young nursery; new garden; coffee shop

Owned by Hazel Huddleston
Size 5ha (12 1/2 acres)

SEATON DELAVAL HALL

Seaton Sluice, Whitley Bay NE26 4QR

Tel 0191 237 1493
Location 1/2 mile from coast between Whitley Bay and Blyth
Opening hours 2pm to 6pm, Wednesdays and Sundays, June to September; plus Bank Holidays in May and August
Admission fee Adults £4; OAPs £3.50; children £1

The garden is modern: one of Jim Russell's earliest works, it dates from 1948 and is stylish, expansive and easy to maintain. Parterres and topiary of yew and box are used to enclose old-fashioned roses, handsome ornaments and a fountain: a fair match for the sumptuous house – Vanbrugh's masterpiece. The horticultural interest comes from a fine weeping ash (it dates back to before 1750), good plantings of rhododendrons and azaleas, and a laburnum walk.
rhododendrons and azaleas; laburnum tunnel; ice house; roses

Owned by Lord Hastings
Number of gardeners 2
Size 0.8ha (2 acres)
English Heritage Grade II*

ST LUKE'S COTTAGE
North Road, Wooley, Hexham NE46 1TN

Tel 01434 673445
Location 3 miles south of Hexham (A69); 3 miles east of A68
Opening hours By appointment
Admission fee Donation to Multiple Sclerosis Society

Alan Furness is a long-standing stalwart of the Alpine Garden Society, that most august of specialist horticultural societies. His garden in a cool valley in southern Northumberland illustrates the enormous opportunities for growing alpine plants which such a situation offers. Within his garden is a wide range of specially constructed habitats to suit an equally wide range of plants: a large limestone scree, and one for acid-loving plants; several high humus beds and meadow beds; a tufa rock bed; a crevice bed, a raised bed and several damp areas; and four alpine houses. Celmisias (species and garden hybrids), primulas, saxifrages, gentians and pulsatillas are especially well represented, but the whole garden is both a revelation and an inspiration.
alpine plants; screes; many different microhabitats

Owned by Alan Furness
Size 0.3ha (3/4 acre)
NCCPG National Collections *Celmisia*

WALLINGTON
Cambo, Morpeth NE61 4AR

Tel 01670 773600 **Fax** 01670 774420
www.nationaltrust.org.uk
Location 6 miles north-west of Belsay (A696)
Opening hours 10am to 7pm, daily, all year; closes at 6pm in October and 4pm between November and March; grounds open daily in daylight hours
Admission fee Adults £6.05; children £3.05

There are three reasons to visit Wallington. First, because Capability Brown was born in nearby Kirkharle. Second, to gawp at the ancient tree-like specimen of *Fuchsia* 'Rose of Castile' in the conservatory. Third, to admire the modern mixed borders (*very* Graham Stuart Thomas) in the long, irregular, walled garden, in a sheltered valley far from the house. Worth the journey for any of them, but prepare for a longish walk to the walled garden.
woodland garden; roses (mainly old-fashioned and climbers); rhododendrons and azaleas; plants under glass; daffodils; good herbaceous borders; tallest *Sorbus discolor* (7m; 23ft) in the British Isles; shop; restaurant

Owned by The National Trust
Number of gardeners 6, plus 2 students
Size 26ha (65 acres)
NCCPG National Collections {Sambucus}
English Heritage Grade II*

NOTTINGHAMSHIRE

For a county of such historic importance, Nottinghamshire has comparatively few historic gardens. Clumber Park has lost the house that was once at its centre, and Newstead Abbey has long lost its most famous owner, Lord Byron. Nevertheless, there are some interesting 19th-century gardens in Nottinghamshire, including the curious little arboretum at Papplewick Pumping Station. One of the best civic parks in England is the Nottingham Arboretum, 8ha (20 acres) in extent, which opened in 1852: the architect Sir Joseph Paxton and the nurseryman Samuel Curtis both advised the founders. Nowadays there are few nurseries of national importance in the county. Nevertheless, the *RHS Plant Finder* had its origins in the list of nurseries prepared by the Nottingham Group of the Hardy Plant Society in the 1970s and early 1980s. The county also has some eight National Collections. The National Gardens Scheme lists a fair number of gardens of all sizes that open in Nottinghamshire for charity: the RHS Free Access garden at Felley Priory is one of exceptional interest and beauty, and a good example of what can be achieved on an unpromising site in only a few years. One further sight should not be missed – the incredible hulk of the Major Oak, also known as Robin Hood's Oak, in Sherwood Forest.

CLUMBER PARK

Worksop S80 3AZ

Tel 01909 476592/544917 **Fax** 01909 500721
www.nationaltrust.org.uk
Location Off A614 Nottingham road, 4 miles south of Worksop
Opening hours Park: dawn to dusk, daily, all year, but closed on 18 August and 25 December; walled garden: 10am to 5pm, Monday to Friday; 10am to 6pm, Saturdays, Sundays and Bank Holidays, 31 March to 30 September
Admission fee Walled garden: adults £2; cars £4.50; pedestrians, cyclists and coaches free

Clumber has over 3,800 acres of thickly wooded parkland with a Gothic chapel, classical bridge, temples, an avenue of cedars, a heroic double avenue of limes and masses of rhododendrons. There are good conservatories and a garden tools exhibition in the old walled garden. The main glasshouse range, at 150m (492ft), is the longest owned by the National Trust. But the scale of everything at Clumber is enormous: very impressive.

woodland garden; autumn colour; vineries; old rhubarb cultivars; superb trees; tallest *Ilex aquifolium* 'Laurifolia' (20m; 66ft) in the British Isles; National Trust shop; restaurant

Owned by The National Trust
Number of gardeners 4, plus seasonal help
Size 13ha (32 acres) of gardens in 1,500ha (3,800 acres) of park
English Heritage Grade I

HODSOCK PRIORY

Blyth, Worksop S81 0TY

Tel 01909 591204 **Fax** 01909 591578
www.snowdrops.co.uk
Location Signed off B6045 between Blyth and Worksop
Opening hours 10am to 4pm, daily, 1 February to 4 March
Admission fee Adults £4; children £1

The gardens at Hodsock are unique in February when visitors can see a remarkable winter feature – thousands of snowdrops. They have also been planting ferns, hollies, white-stemmed rubus and lots of winter-flowering plants: aconites, *Cyclamen coum*, sarcococcas, prunus and loniceras.

aconites; hellebores; hepaticas; winter-flowering plants of all kinds; large *Catalpa* (Indian bean tree); tea room

Owned by Sir Andrew and Lady Buchanan
Number of gardeners 1 full-time, 3 part-time
Size 2ha (5 acres) plus woodland

FELLEY PRIORY

Underwood NG16 5FJ

Tel 01773 810230 **Fax** 01773 580440
Location 1/2 mile west of M1, Jct 27, on A608
Opening hours 9am to 12.30pm, Tuesdays, Wednesdays and Fridays, all year; plus 9am to 4pm, second and fourth Wednesday of every month, March to October; and 11am to 4pm, 11 February (for snowdrops) then every third Sunday of month, March to October; for NGS: 11am to 4pm, 9 April; NCCPG plants fairs: noon to 4pm, 3 June and 7 October; parties welcome, by appointment
Admission fee Adults £3; OAPs £2.50; children and RHS members free

Parts of the house at Felley Priory – a wonderful brick and dark red sandstone building – date back to 1150. One link with the 16th century is a venerable pear tree which grows against the house: the Royal Horticultural Society has identified it as 'Jargonelle', an ancient cultivar well known before 1600. Major and Mrs Chaworth-Musters started work on the garden in 1976 and were, from the start, adventurous gardeners, willing to try plants which might be considered doubtfully hardy at 180m (590ft) so far inland. The results are astonishing. Against the garden walls are *Buddleja colvilei*, nandinas, eucryphias, several hebes and *Drimys winteri*: elsewhere in the garden are *Podocarpus salignus* and *Correa backhouseana*. Felley Priory is an excellent garden for plants, with a very large number of interesting ones in flower at every season – enough to start a nursery where everything is propagated from the garden. Shrubs are a major interest, and Felley has good collections of magnolias, cornus, hydrangeas, *Paeonia suffruticosa* and viburnums. Bulbs are planted in great numbers: as well as snowdrops and cyclamen there are massive displays of daffodils in spring. The handsome yew hedges are little more than 20 years old, yet they fill the garden with their bulk: some have been turned into objects of topiary, with curvy tops and bobbles and birds. In the rose garden is a good display of well-grown old-fashioned roses: there are about 90 different cultivars, some imported directly from French nurseries. The rarities include a pink and white form of *Rosa multiflora* which was collected in Korea by Jamie Compton. The medieval garden harks back to the original priory which was lost at the time of the Reformation: it is planted with plants that were known in the 15th century – among them are lilies, roses, violas, columbines, irises, tulips and *Phillyrea latifolia*. Everything at Felley is charming, stylish well trained and well grown. New plants arrive constantly from all the best nurseries: the garden gets better all the time.

old-fashioned rose gardens; good herbaceous borders; knot gardens, two pergolas and thousands of daffodils; new pleached hedge of *Crataegus tanacetifolia*; unusual trees and shrubs; nursery attached; refreshments

Owned by The Hon Mrs Chaworth-Musters
Size 1ha (2 1/2 acres)

HOLME PIERREPONT HALL

Holme Pierrepont, Nottingham NG12 2LD

Tel/fax 0115 933 2371
www.holmepierrepontthall.com
Location 3 miles east of Trent Bridge
Opening hours 2pm to 5pm, Monday to Wednesday, 5 February to 28 March; plus 18 February for snowdrops, 18 March for hellebores, 1 April for daffodils, 15 April for tulips and 30 September for NGS; groups welcome by appointment at other times
Admission fee Adults £3

The house at Holme Pierrepont is both beautiful and historic. The main attraction of the garden is a large courtyard garden, designed in 1875, whose box parterre is filled with modern plantings. But there are fine recent additions, too, including splendid herbaceous borders and interesting fruit trees. The rare English tulip *Tulipa sylvestris* grows wild in a remote part of the fields. The main openings, in late winter and early spring, are planned for when the snowdrops and winter-flowering plants are at their peak. The April opening is when the rare wild English tulip *Tulipa sylvestris* is at its peak in the meadows; Holme Pierrepont is thought to have the largest colony in the country.
roses (mainly old-fashioned); formal gardens; good topiary; teas in the long gallery

Owned by Mr and Mrs Robin Brackenbury
Number of gardeners 2½ part-time
Size 1ha (2½ acres)
English Heritage Grade II

MILL HILL PLANTS

Mill Hill House, Elston Lane, East Stoke, Newark NG23 5QJ

Tel 01636 525460
www.come.to/mill.hill.plants&garden
Location 5 miles south-west of Newark; leave A46 at East Stoke, for Elston; ½ mile down, on right
Opening hours 11am to 5pm, 28 May and by appointment; April to September
Admission fee Garden: £2

The garden is generously planted for year-round interest with hardy and half-hardy perennials, annuals and shrubs. Wildlife is encouraged. The nursery has now closed down, but the garden gets better and better.

Owned by Mr and Mrs RJ Gregory
Size 0.2ha (½ acre)
NCCPG National Collections *Berberis*

NATURESCAPE

Lapwing Meadows, Coach Gap Lane, Langar NG13 9HP

Tel 01949 860592 **Fax** 01949 869047
www.naturescape.co.uk
Location Signed off A46 and A52
Opening hours 11am to 5.30pm, daily, April to September
Admission fee Free

Naturescape is a significant nursery, specialising in British wild plants. These include wildflowers, bulbs, native shrubs and trees, pond and marsh species and cottage garden favourites: many are available both as plants and as seeds. The principle behind the nursery is the realisation that many garden owners want to attract wildlife to their gardens, and that growing native plant species is the best way to do so. The visitor centre opened in 1990 and is set in a wildlife garden showing different habitats. Meadows, hedges, ponds, woodland edges and wetlands are supplemented by cottage gardens and such features as a bee garden.
wildflowers; native plants; tea room

Owned by Brian, Liz and Mark Scarborough
Number of gardeners 2½
Size 18ha (45 acres)

NEWSTEAD ABBEY

Newstead Abbey Park, Ravenshead NG15 8NA

Tel 01623 455900 **Fax** 01623 455904
www.newsteadabbey.org.uk
Location 4 miles south of Mansfield on A60; 12 miles north of Nottingham

Opening hours 9am to 6pm (or dusk if earlier), daily, except the last Friday in November and Christmas Day
Admission fee Adults £3; concessions £2.50; children £1.50; families £8.50

Chiefly of interest for being the debt-ridden estate which Lord Byron the poet inherited and had to sell, Newstead has a good modern garden. Features include a Spanish garden, a tropical garden, an iris garden, a rose garden, a heather garden, a fern garden, ponds and lakes. Best are the Japanese garden and the substantial rockery. The council has restored and extensively replanted it as a public amenity: lots of cheerful roses and summer bedding.
rock garden; herbs; Japanese garden; water features; shop; café

Owned by Nottingham City Council
Number of gardeners 5
Size 120ha (300 acres) of parkland
English Heritage Grade I

SALLEY GARDENS
Simkins Farm, Adbolton Lane, West Bridgford NG2 5AS

Tel 0115 923 3878
Location Just off A52 from Nottingham to Grantham
Opening hours 9am to 5pm, Sundays, April to September; and by appointment
Admission fee Free

Salley Gardens is a nursery which concentrates upon plants that are especially beneficial to mankind: all are organically grown. They include dye and beverage plants, and culinary and aromatic herbs and spices. The main emphasis, however, is on plants with medicinal properties. Three major herbal traditions are represented: North American, European and Traditional Chinese Medicine. Plants used in homeopathy, ayurveda and conventional medicine are also listed. 2003 saw an expanded section of culinary herbs, including some 30 different types of basil.
herbal and medicinal plants

Owned by Richard Lewin
Size 0.2ha (1/2 acre)

TEVERSAL MANOR
Buttery Lane, Teversal Old Village, Sutton-in-Ashfield NG17 3JN

Tel 01623 554569 **Fax** 01623 555373
www.teversalmanor.co.uk
Location In middle of village; tree-lined drive near church
Opening hours 10am to 5.30pm (or dusk, if earlier), Thursday to Saturday, 8 March to 24 December; plus 11am to 5pm (or dusk) on Sundays and Bank Holiday Mondays
Admission fee Adults £4.50; concessions £3.50; children £2.50

The present owners have given the gardens at Teversal an extensive makeover. Four broad terraces, each 57m (187ft) wide, have been imaginatively planted in various styles, including a parterre, a rose garden, a tropical garden and a mini-arboretum. Other features include a Thai house, a stumpery, a dry river bed garden and some exciting modern sculptures. The bulbs are good in spring.
gift shop; light lunches; cream teas

Owned by John and Janet Marples

OXFORDSHIRE

Oxfordshire is one of the best counties for keen gardeners. The natives may grumble about the cold, wet, heavy, clay soils of the Thames Valley, but they have some of the finest English gardens, ancient and modern, to show what those soils can do for them. There are no fewer than nine Grade I historic gardens in the county, and all are open to the public. Both the Oxford Botanic Garden and its country offshoot the Harcourt Arboretum at Nuneham Courtenay have seriously important plant collections, laid out to attract the ordinary garden owner. It is in these two collections, too, that many of the county's record-breaking trees grow. Several 20th-century gardens were also laid out on a grand scale, including Sutton Courtenay, Buscot, Garsington, Waterperry and Pusey – the latter, alas, is no longer open to the public. The county also has a host of good small gardens: it has long been a matter of pride that Oxfordshire should have more gardens open for the National Gardens Scheme and raise more money for its charities than any other English county. Nevertheless, it has only a handful of National Collections and comparatively few first-rate nurseries – Mattocks Roses, now part of the Notcutt chain, is perhaps the best known. It is as if Oxford were relying for its horticultural reputation more upon its past achievements than its present – rather like its university, some would say. Nevertheless it was at Oxford University that the Garden History Society was born, thanks to the energy and acumen of Mavis Batey. And the many college gardens that open to the public are another of the city's gifts to garden lovers: Robin Lane-Fox looks after the Fellows' garden at New College.

BLENHEIM PALACE

Woodstock, Oxford OX20 1PX

Tel 01993 811091 **Fax** 01993 810570
www.blenheimpalace.com
Location 8 miles north of Oxford
Opening hours 10am to 6pm (or dusk, if earlier; last admissions 4.45 pm), daily, 10 February to 28 October; and daily, except Mondays and Tuesdays, from 31 October to 9 December; park open daily all year, except Christmas Day
Admission fee Park, gardens and pleasure gardens: adults £9.30; OAPs £7.30; children £4.70; RHS members free 10 February to 25 May (excluding Easter) and 10 September to 9 December

Blenheim is the grandest of grand gardens. Vanbrugh, Bridgeman, Blenheim Palace is huge – the incarnation of classical triumphalism. Hawksmoor and Wise worked on the grand layout of the gardens: the monumental bridge, the triumphal arch and the column of victory (axially aligned on the main entrance to the palace) all date from the 1720s. The huge park (800ha/2,000 acres) was landscaped by 'Capability' Brown. Achille Duchêne designed the formal gardens in the 1920s: the Water Terraces centre on a Bernini fountain and took five years to build. The Italian garden focuses on the neo-classical mermaid fountain. There is a pretty Victorian rose garden and, in the 'Pleasure Gardens', a maze and a lavender garden. The 'Secret' Garden has been restored as a garden for all seasons with original trees, plants and water features. The arboretum has some interesting trees, including four fine upright incense cedars (*Calocedrus decurrens*). In 1908, Winston Churchill proposed to his wife Clementine in the Temple of Diana. There will be a number RHS Special Events at Blenheim in 2007; details from 020 7821 3408.

formal gardens; new maze; current holder of Sandford Award; good shops; restaurant and two self-service cafés

Owned by The Duke of Marlborough
Number of gardeners 12
Size 40ha (100 acres)
English Heritage Grade I

BROOK COTTAGE

Well Lane, Alkerton, Banbury OX15 6NL

Tel 01295 670303/670590 **Fax** 01295 730362
www.brookcottagegarden.co.uk
Location 6 miles north-west of Banbury, 1/2 mile off A422
Opening hours 9am to 6pm, Monday to Friday, Easter Monday to 31 October; group, evening and weekend visits by appointment
Admission fee Adults £4; OAPs £3; children free

Brook Cottage is *not* a dinky little cottage garden: it is a first-rate plantsman's garden, made by the present owner and her husband since 1964, on four acres of sloping pasture. The good plants are moreover displayed with a fine sense of colour and form. Parts of the garden are winding and cottagey, parts more spacious and open. Beautiful flowering trees in spring are followed by opulent old roses in summer and rich autumn colour. A recent addition is a border of blue and white agapanthus interspersed with kniphofias in shades of lemon and lime. The yellow border is backed by a hedge of copper beech, while the white border is brought to life by a dark hedge of yew. The diversity of planting is supplemented by tender perennials displayed in numerous ornamental containers. All the wooden furniture has been designed and hand-made to complement the character of the different areas. There is much to study and enjoy here.
plantsman's collection of plants; roses (over 200, mainly species and shrubs); good herbaceous borders (colour coordinated); 50 different clematis; gravel and water gardens; plants for sale; DIY tea and coffee; refreshments for groups by arrangement

Owned by Mrs DM Hodges
Number of gardeners 1, plus some part-time help
Size 1.6ha (4 acres)

BROUGHTON CASTLE

Banbury OX15 5EB

Tel/fax 01295 276070
www.broughtoncastle.demon.co.uk
Location 21/2 miles west of Banbury on B4035

BUSCOT PARK

Faringdon SN7 8BU

Tel 01367 240786 **Fax** 01367 241794
www.buscotpark.com
Location On A417 west of Faringdon
Opening hours Garden only: 2pm to 6pm, Monday to Friday, 3 April to 29 September; plus Saturdays and Sundays on second and fourth weekends of the month from May to September; also 7, 8, 14 and 15 April, and 5 and 6 May
Admission fee Adults £5; children £2.50

There are three fairly distinct gardens at Buscot. You enter through the newest – a series of colour plantings and horticultural features created by Lord Faringdon over the last 20 years. Here is the 'Parents' Walk', a lush double herbaceous border designed by Peter Coats in 1986: lots of yellow foliage is contrasted with purple, to create a sense of lightness and brightness even on the dullest of days. Next to it is the old kitchen garden which was turned into a 'Four Seasons' garden in the early 1980s: the four quadrants planted by Tim Rees in the early 1990s have recently been further developed and revised to represent each of the four seasons. It also has prettily trained fruit trees, vegetables used as climbing plants and gooseberries grown as standards. You climb out of the walled garden, up a steep staircase lined with yews, and walk past the front of the house on your way to the second of the gardens: a perfect *patte d'oie*, focused on the Theatre Arch. The temptation is to explore all three avenues of the *patte d'oie* at once, but they are linked by cross-paths which run between further gardens cut out of the woodland: these include a circular sunken garden furnished in summer with orange and lemon trees in pots, and a pretty white and green garden which is known as the 'Swinging Garden' because of the swinging seats which surround it. But the third and best-known garden at Buscot is Harold Peto's water garden, which dates from the 1900s and stretches down over hundreds of yards in a series of steps and then through a long, narrow, straight canal punctuated towards the end by a chunky Italianate bridge until it bursts out into the view of the lake at the bottom. The canal – little more than a rill, really – is framed first by Irish yews and then by clipped box hedges. It has an amazing dynamism and strength of design which makes it an entirely self-contained garden. The only downside to a visit is that the lake is actually the furthest point of the garden, and there is then no other way out except to retrace your steps across the park and through the modern gardens. But Peter Coats's borders look even better as you approach them again from outside the walled gardens. And a word of warning: Buscot is a big garden, so allow lots of time for your visit.

topiary; roses (mainly old-fashioned); fruit; good herbaceous borders; tallest *Pinus nigra* var. *cebennensis* (32m; 105ft) in the British Isles; light refreshments

Owned by The National Trust (administered by Lord Faringdon)
English Heritage Grade II*v

Opening hours 2pm to 5pm, Wednesdays and Sundays, 1 May to 14 September; plus Thursdays in July and August, Bank Holiday Sundays and Mondays (including Easter); for NGS: 30 July
Admission fee Castle and gardens: adults £6.50; OAPs and students £5.50; children £2.50

The garden at Broughton Castle dates back to the 19th century: the neat formal garden with roses and lavender (best seen from the house) was designed by Lady Algernon Gordon-Lennox in the 1890s. The modern garden was established in 1970 with advice from Lanning Roper. It has two pretty colour-themed mixed borders – blue-yellow and white and pink and silver – both at their best towards the end of June when the roses are in full flower. The plants play second fiddle to the stupendous setting – the castle, the moat and the spacious parkland beyond.
roses (mainly old-fashioned and climbers); good herbaceous borders; shop; tea room

Owned by Lord Saye and Sele
Number of gardeners 1
Size 0.8ha (2 acres)
English Heritage Grade II*

BROUGHTON GRANGE
Wykeham Lane, Broughton, Banbury OX15 5DS

Tel 0770 1098161
Location East end of village, on road to Bodicote
Opening hours For NGS: 10.30am to 4.30pm, 6 May and 1 July; and groups by appointment
Admission fee Adults £5

The gardens at Broughton Grange are new and very impressive. Tom Stuart Smith has made a walled garden that is actually open to the landscape but uses clipped trees to give a sense of enclosure. Fruit and vegetable are here in plenty, but it is the thick plantings of perennials and grasses that one notices most, and the illusion of space that comes from reflecting pools on three different levels. All the fashionable features of modern gardens are also here at Broughton, including a knot garden, a laburnum tunnel, wildflower meadows, a rose parterre, a stumpery and a young arboretum, but they are made and maintained to an outstanding level of excellence. A triumph.
perennial plantings; teas on NGS days

Owned by Stephen Hester
Number of gardeners 10
Size 10ha (25 acres), plus 60ha (150 acres) park and arboretum

COTSWOLD WILDLIFE PARK
Burford OX18 4JP

Tel 01993 823006 **Fax** 01993 823807
www.cotswoldwildlifepark.co.uk
Location 2 1/2 miles south of Burford on A40
Opening hours 10am to 4.30pm (last admissions), daily, all year; last admission 3.30pm from October to February
Admission fee Adults £9.50; OAPs £7; children £7

Although mainly the reserve of animals and birds, Cotswold Wildlife Park has some splendidly exotic plantings to match. There is a lot of floral colour throughout the estate, especially annuals, bright bedding and large-leaved plants to simulate the jungle, but it is very well integrated into the whole. The floral displays in the walled garden are exceptionally good.
shop; restaurant; café

Owned by John Heyworth
Number of gardeners 6, plus 2 part-time
Size 56ha (120 acres) wildlife park

GARSINGTON MANOR
Garsington, Oxford OX44 9DH

Tel 01865 361234 **Fax** 01865 361566
Location East of B480 Oxford to Watlington road
Opening hours For NGS: 2pm to 5pm, 29 April and 23 September
Admission fee Adults £3; children free

The gardens at Garsington Manor were laid out in the 1920s in the Italian style by Lady Ottoline Morrell and her architect husband Philip. The parterre has 24 square beds with Irish yews at the corners; the Italian garden has a large ornamental pool enclosed by yew hedges and set about with statues; beyond, is a wild garden, with lime tree avenues, shrubs, a stream and pond. They make an incomparable setting for the summer opera season.
Italianate gardens; modern plantings; teas

Owned by Mrs RA Ingrams
Number of gardeners 3
Size 1.6ha (4 acres)
English Heritage Grade II*

GREENWAYS
40 Osler Road, Headington, Oxford OX3 9BJ

Tel 01865 767680 (after dark) **Fax** 01865 767922
Location Osler Road is in Headington, off A420 London Road, within the ring road
Opening hours By appointment for individuals and groups
Admission fee Adults £2.50; children free

This garden is totally different and – incredibly – now 30 years old. The Cootes have emphasised the Provençal look of the house by planting a rich Mediterranean garden – glittering evergreens, terracotta pots, old oil jars, gravel, parterres, mosaic water garden – with an exuberance of tender plants including olives, brugmansias, yuccas, oleanders, palms, bougainvillea, agaves, lantana and echiums. It is quite the most stylish small garden in England, and intensively maintained to the highest standard.
beautiful modern Italianate garden; subtropical plants; plantsman's collection of plants; good herbaceous borders; painted obelisks; long view to monumental classical vase

Owned by Mr and Mrs NHN Coote
Number of gardeners owners only
Size 0.3ha (3/4 acre)

HARCOURT ARBORETUM
Nuneham Courtenay OX44 9PQ

Tel 01865 343501 **Fax** 01865 341828
www.botanic-garden.ox.ac.uk
Location On A4074, just south of village of Nuneham Courtenay
Opening hours 10am to 5pm, daily, April to November; 10am to 4.30pm, Monday to Friday, December to March; closed over the Christmas period
Admission fee Free; car park £3

Although it belongs to the University of Oxford Botanic Garden, Harcourt Arboretum is best regarded as a standalone woodland garden with a distinct history and character. It has been developed since 1950 around a nucleus of magnificent American conifers planted about 1840 in a corner of the Nuneham Courtenay estate. The new plantings include 'plants from high places' (geographically arranged), conservation areas, an extensive glade of ornamental maples, and fine modern features like collections of *Nothofagus*, magnolias and camellias. The labelling is fairly good and there are useful information boards. It is perhaps best visited in May, when the mature oak woodland which surrounds the conifers is filled with vast oceans of bluebells.
woodland garden; rhododendrons and azaleas; mature conifers; camellias; fine collection of trees; bluebells

Owned by The University of Oxford
Number of gardeners 4 1/2
Size 32ha (80 acres)

KELMSCOTT MANOR
Kelmscott, Lechlade GL7 3HJ

Tel 01367 252486 **Fax** 01367 253754
www.kelmscottmanor.co.uk
Location Signed from B4449 and A4095
Opening hours House and garden: 11am to 5pm (gates open 10.30am), Wednesdays, April to September; garden only: 2pm to 5pm (gates open 1.15pm) on Thursdays from June to September; plus the third Saturday of the month from April to September and the first Saturday of the month in July and August
Admission fee Adults £8.50; students £4.25; gardens only: adults £2; children free

Kelmscott Manor was the summer home of William Morris, an unspoilt Tudor farmhouse on the banks of the Thames. The surrounding countryside, river and garden were inspirational to Morris's designs and writings. Work on restoring the garden started in 1996 and the result is something that Morris would recognise – all typical of the 1890s, with rustic fencing, herbaceous borders edged by box, and an orchard and pergola. The planting reflects the rich botanical content of his designs – wild tulips (*T. sylvestris*) and fritillaries (*F. meleagris*) grow thickly under the original mulberry tree. Elsewhere are crocuses, aconites and snowdrops, followed by roses, hollyhocks, cottage annuals, poppies, pinks and China asters. Morris's original topiary dragon 'Fafnir' is currently being restored and the standard rose bushes flanking the garden path featured in his most famous book *News from Nowhere*.
gift shop; licensed restaurant for coffee, lunches and teas

Owned by The Society of Antiquaries of London
Number of gardeners 1 part-time
Size 1.3ha (3 1/4 acres)
English Heritage Grade II

KINGSTON BAGPUIZE HOUSE
Kingston Bagpuize, Abingdon OX13 5AX

Tel 01865 820259 **Fax** 01865 821659
www.kingstonbagpuizehouse.org.uk
Location On A415, 1/2 mile south of junction with A420
Opening hours 2pm to 5.30pm, the first Sunday and Monday and the third Thursday of the month from February to September; plus Bank Holiday Mondays; plus 1, 8, 18-19 and 22 February, 8 to 9 April, 27 and 28 May, 15 and 16 July, 26 and 27 August, 16 and 17 September; rare plant fair on 26 May
Admission fee Adults £3; children free; groups by arrangement

Most of the garden at Kingston Bagpuize dates from the 1950s, when Nancy Lindsay and Sir Harold Hillier advised on plantings. Some surprisingly rare and tender trees and shrubs have survived from that period, including *Albizia julibrissin*, *Itea ilicifolia* and *Xanthoceras sorbifolium*. Many are now handsome specimens, spectacular in flower. There are traces of older plantings in the park, notably 19th-century redwoods, while some of the yews date back even further. There has been much new planting in recent years and there is a lot to enjoy at every season. The garden opens early for its snowdrops, which include a green-tipped variant of *Galanthus elwesii* named 'Marlie Raphael' after a former owner.
good trees and shrubs; tea room

Owned by Mrs Virginia Grant
Number of gardeners 2 part-time
Size 3.2ha (8 acres)

LIME CLOSE
35 Henley's Lane, Drayton, Abingdon OX14 4HU

Tel 07831 861463
Location 2 miles south of Abingdon, off main road through Drayton
Opening hours 2pm to 5.30pm, 15 April and 3 June; and groups by prior appointment
Admission fee Adults £3; children free

This modern garden has been much praised, and deservedly, for its wide range of plants and the way in which they are grouped. As well as rare trees, shrubs, alpines, perennials and bulbs, it can boast a recently planted shade border, a pond, a pergola, some unusual topiary, a herb garden designed by Rosemary Verey and a wonderful selection of raised beds and troughs planted by the owner's

aunt Miss C Christie-Miller. A new cottage garden has just been made with beds planted in different tones of single colours and a collection of 100+ cultivars of irises from France has been planted in the ornamental kitchen garden.
good mixed borders; unusual plants; cream teas

Owned by M-C de Laubarède
Size 1.2ha (3 acres)

MAGDALEN COLLEGE
High Street, Oxford OX1 4AU

Tel 01865 276000 **Fax** 01895 276030
www.magd.ox.ac.uk
Location In centre of Oxford
Opening hours Noon (1pm from October to 21 June) to 6pm (or dusk, if earlier), daily, all year; closed 22 to 31 December
Admission fee Adults £3; concessions £2; Oxford residents free

The fame of Magdalen's gardens rests mainly on its ancient deer park and the meadows across the Cherwell that house an enormous colony of naturalised *Fritillaria meleagris*. There are fine trees and borders in the Fellows' Garden, too.
light lunches and teas from July to September

Owned by The President and Fellows
Number of gardeners 6
Size 40ha (100 acres)
English Heritage Grade I

LE MANOIR AUX QUAT'SAISONS
Church Road, Great Milton, Oxford OX44 7PD

Tel 01844 278881 **Fax** 01844 278847
www.manoir.com
Location Signed in village
Opening hours All year; patrons only
Admission fee Free to patrons

Raymond Blanc insists that the gardens at Le Manoir aux Quat'Saisons are 'very much a part of the Le Manoir experience and are as important as the cuisine'. Features include a Japanese water garden and a 17th-century pond, but the soul of the garden is a two-acre kitchen garden. It is organically run, and registered with the Soil Association. The herb garden grows about 120 different herbs, alongside some 90 different vegetables. There will be several RHS Special Events at Le Manoir aux Quat'Saisons in 2007; details from the restaurant directly on 01844 278881.
2-star Michelin restaurant

Owned by Raymond Blanc
Number of gardeners 6
Size 11ha (27 acres)

MATTOCKS ROSES
Nuneham Courtenay, Oxford OX44 9PY

Tel 01865 343454 **Fax** 01865 343267
www.mattocks.co.uk
Location On B4015, Golden Balls Roundabout (A4074)
Opening hours 9am to 6pm, Monday to Saturday; 10.30am to 4.30pm, Sundays
Admission fee Free

This is one of the oldest nurseries in England, founded in 1875 and now part of the Notcutts Group. Mattocks have been particularly successful in promoting their 'County' series of groundcover roses, though most of them were actually raised in Germany and Denmark. They offer a large choice of all kinds of roses, and online ordering, too, as well as a fine display garden. One of their specialities, bred by John Mattock and introduced in 1973, is the yellow repeat-flowering climber 'Dreaming Spires'.

Owned by Notcutts Garden Centre

NUFFIELD PLACE
Huntercombe, Henley-on-Thames RG9 5RY

Tel 01491 641224
www.nuffield-place.com
Location Signed from A4130
Opening hours 2pm to 5pm, 29 April (bluebell opening); then the second and fourth Sundays of the month, May to September
Admission fee Adults £1; children free

Nuffield Place belonged to William Morris, Lord Nuffield, the founder of Morris Motors. Most of the garden (including the rose pergola, rock garden, yew hedges and many of the trees) was laid out in 1914 before Lord Nuffield bought the house. It is currently being restored as it was in its heyday, the 1930s and 1950s. Expect some slippage for the next year or so, or visit it now and return as it improves.
home-made teas

Owned by Nuffield College, Oxford
Number of gardeners $1\frac{1}{2}$
Size 1.6ha (4 acres)

OXFORD BOTANIC GARDEN
Rose Lane, Oxford OX1 4AZ

Tel 01865 286690 **Fax** 01865 286693
www.botanic-garden.ox.ac.uk
Location East end of High Street next to river, opposite Magdalen College tower
Opening hours 9am to 5pm (4.30pm from November to February; 6pm from May to August), daily, all year, except Good Friday and Christmas Day; glasshouses: 10am to 4pm
Admission fee Adults £3; OAPs £2.50; children free

This is the oldest botanic garden in England, first laid out in 1621: the handsome gateways were added a few years later. It has kept its original rectangular design and many of the statues and garden ornaments. It also has a calm that is far from the bustle outside and has proved a refuge for generations of undergraduates. There are good and representative collections of almost every type of plant, including a grass garden, carnivorous plants, a water garden, fernery, orangery and several conservatories. Everything is well labelled, of course, and designed not only as an aesthetically pleasing living collection of plants for the university botanists but, much more generally, as an educational resource. In recent years the area outside the walled garden has been developed as a garden to inspire gardeners: here are a water garden, rock garden, herbaceous border and autumn border. The glasshouses have recently been redesigned so that visiting schoolchildren can enjoy 'the ultimate rainforest and desert experience'. The garden is very good on education, and its website is brilliant.
roses (mainly old-fashioned); rock garden; herbs; plants under glass; systematic beds; huge *Sorbus domestica* service tree; *Victoria amazonica*

Owned by The University of Oxford
Number of gardeners 9
Size 1.8ha ($4\frac{1}{2}$ acres)
NCCPG National Collections *Euphorbia*
English Heritage Grade I

PETTIFERS
Lower Wardington, Banbury OX17 1RU

Tel 01295 750232
Location Just off A361 in centre of village
Opening hours By appointment
Admission fee Adults £6; groups £5 per head

This is the garden of a plantswoman with a good eye for form and colour. Gina Price has been making it since 1989 and manages to combine foreground interest with fine views of the landscape outside. The firm architectural structure of hedges, clipped evergreens and terraces enables her to plant late-summer grasses with confidence. The colour contrasts within her perennial plantings are fairly cutting-edge, too.
grasses; herbaceous plants; tea and biscuits for groups

Owned by Mr James and The Hon Mrs Price
Number of gardeners 1
Size 0.6ha ($1\frac{1}{2}$ acres)

ROUSHAM HOUSE
Steeple Aston, Bicester OX25 4QX

Tel/fax 01869 347110
www.rousham.org
Location A4260 then off B4030
Opening hours 10am to 4.30pm, daily, all year
Admission fee Adults £4; no children under 15

Waterperry Gardens

Rousham is the most perfect surviving example of William Kent's landscaping: *Kentissimo*, according to Horace Walpole. The main axis brings you to Scheemakers' statue of a lion devouring a horse, high above the infant River Cherwell. Follow the correct circuit: the serpentine landscape lies away to the side. Here are Venus's Vale, the Cold Bath and Townsend's Building, from which a lime walk will lead you to the Praeneste. Rousham is an Arcadian experience. The pretty herbaceous border in the walled garden and the modern rose garden by the dovecote seem almost an irrelevance.
early 18th-century landscape; important sculptures and garden buildings

Owned by C Cottrell-Dormer
Number of gardeners 4
Size 10ha (25 acres)
English Heritage Grade I

ST JOHN'S COLLEGE
St Giles, Oxford OX1 3JP

Tel 01865 277300
Location Enter by Porter's Lodge
Opening hours 1pm to 5pm (dusk, in winter), daily, all year
Admission fee Free

The gardens at St John's were last overhauled in the 1770s. Good trees, expansive lawns and a famous rock garden are the highlights of a visit today.

Owned by The President and Fellows
Number of gardeners 5
Size 2ha (5 acres)
English Heritage Grade II*

STANSFIELD
49 High Street, Stanford-in-the-Vale SN7 8NQ

Tel 01367 710340
Location Off A417 opposite Vale garage
Opening hours 10am to 4pm, first Tuesday of the month, April to September; and by appointment, including evenings; garden clubs especially welcome
Admission fee Adults £2; children free

Stansfield is a modern plantsman's garden, and a fascinating model of what an enthusiastic collector and cultivator of plants can achieve in a few years. Over 2,000 different plants grow in just over one acre. The special features include troughs, screes, open borders and endless microhabitats.
plantsman's collection of plants; good herbaceous borders; Mediterranean garden; teas

Owned by Mr and Mrs D Keeble
Number of gardeners owners only

STONOR
Henley-on-Thames RG9 6HF

Tel 01491 638587 **Fax** 01491 639348
www.stonor.com
Location On B480, 5 miles north of Henley-on-Thames
Opening hours 1pm to 5.30pm, Sundays and Bank Holiday Mondays, 1 April to 16 September; plus Wednesdays in July and August
Admission fee Adults £3.50; first child £1.50; other children free

Stonor fills a hillside: classical parkland (with a deer park, too), the Elizabethan house, lawns, terraces, a 17th-century walled garden and finally the wood with wonderful views at the top. Nothing appears to have changed for 200 years: the effect is miraculous.
roses (mainly old-fashioned); rock garden; daffodils; souvenir shop; tea room

Owned by Lord Camoys
Number of gardeners 1
English Heritage Grade I

WATERPERRY GARDENS
Waterperry, Wheatley, Oxford OX33 1JZ

Tel 01844 339226 **Fax** 01844 339883
www.waterperrygardens.co.uk
Location M40, Jct 8 or 8a; well signed locally with brown tourist rosettes
Opening hours 9am (10am in winter) to 5pm, daily, all year, except 19 to 22 July and Christmas/New Year period

Admission fee April to October: adults £4.50; OAPs £3.75; children £3; November to March: all £3; RHS members free in September

The gardens at Waterperry are extensive, well-maintained and full of interesting plants. Much has been redesigned and replanted in recent years, with some fine formal features and pleasing plant combinations. The Virgin's Walk is a good place to study shade-loving plants, but the main feature of this area is a long classical herbaceous border brilliantly colourful from late May until October. The Mary Rose Garden, enclosed by yew hedges, illustrates both modern and older roses, and the formal garden is particularly neatly designed and colourful, with a small knot garden, herb border and wisteria tunnel. Nearby are some interesting ways of training apples and roses, but the main part of the garden is the extensive shrub borders, alpine beds and flower borders. Waterperry offers much to enjoy and learn from at every season.
roses; rock garden; herbs; good herbaceous borders; apple orchards; irises; home produce, stoneware, books; excellent plant centre; tea shop; wine licence

Owned by School of Economic Science
Number of gardeners 3½
Size 2.8ha (7 acres)
NCCPG National Collections *Saxifraga* (Kabschia)

WESTWELL MANOR
Burford OX18 4JT

Location 2 miles from A40, west of Burford roundabout
Opening hours 2pm to 6.30pm, 1 July; and by prior appointment for serious horticultural groups of 20+
Admission fee Adults £3; children 50p

Westwell is a large and peaceful Cotswold garden with several distinct 'rooms'. The features include rills, a water garden, herbaceous borders, an orchard, a lavender meadow, lots of hazel and willow fencing, a vegetable garden, a moonlight garden, a clematis wall and a small rice paddy.
topiary; roses (mainly old-fashioned); good herbaceous borders; water garden

Owned by Mr and Mrs TH Gibson
Number of gardeners 2
Size 2.8ha (7 acres)

SHROPSHIRE

Shropshire has the reputation of being a remote and quasi-feudal county. It is certainly true that very few of its historic gardens are ever open to the public. Hawkstone is the most notable exception, but this – the county's only Grade I garden – is now in multiple occupation: nevertheless, its principal parts are still highly visitable and also have the best collection of trees, mainly conifers, in Shropshire. Among 20th-century gardens, Hodnet Hall is of national importance, and a sizeable achievement by modern standards; we are pleased to note that it will be open much more often in 2007 than in 2006. Three further recent gardens are also outstanding, each in its own way – Burford House, David Austin Roses and Wollerton Old Hall. There are 26 National Collections in Shropshire and the National Gardens Scheme is well supported, mainly by gardens that are large or medium-sized.

ANGEL GARDENS

Springfield, Angel Lane, Bitterley, Ludlow SY8 3HZ

Tel/fax 01584 890381
www.stmem.com/angelgardens
Location 5 miles east of Ludlow, signed from A4117
Opening hours Noon (2pm on Saturdays) to 5pm, Saturday to Monday, April to October; see website for possible further openings; groups at other times by arrangement
Admission fee Adults £4; children £1

Angel Gardens are perched high up on the edge of the Clee hill, with views across to the mountains of Wales, yet its lake and pools are so convincing that they seem completely natural. The Chinese bridge across the lake is a *tour de force*, matched by the rustic tea house on the water's edge. The damper parts are lushly planted with hostas, crocosmias, hemerocallis and water irises. But there are also rock gardens for alpine plants, a fine collection of rhododendrons, good mixed borders, a fern garden and an area around the house where – most improbably – tender cordylines, phormiums and trachycarpus flourish. Seldom are good design and good plants so well combined with a spirit of adventure and true sense of style.
souvenir shop; tea room

Owned by Dr KC and Mrs JAV Elliott
Number of gardeners Owners only
Size 1.2ha (3 acres)

ATTINGHAM PARK

Shrewsbury SY4 4TP

Tel 01743 708162 **Fax** 01743 708155
www.nationaltrust.org.uk
Location 4 miles south-east of Shrewsbury on B4380
Opening hours 10am to 5.30pm (4pm from November to February), Friday to Tuesday, all year
Admission fee Adults £3.30; children £1.65

No garden to speak of, but the classical late 18th-century parkland round the vast Georgian house is a joy to walk around at any time of the year.
rhododendrons and azaleas; daffodils; newly restored orangery; National Trust shop; light lunches and teas

Owned by The National Trust
Number of gardeners 1
Size 20ha (50 acres)
English Heritage Grade II*

BENTHALL HALL

Broseley TF12 5RX

Tel/fax 01952 882159
www.nationaltrust.org.uk
Location 1 mile north-west of Broseley (B4375)
Opening hours 1.30pm to 5.30pm, Tuesdays and Wednesdays, 3 April to 30 September; plus Sundays and Bank Holiday Mondays from July to September
Admission fee Adults £3; children £1.50

Benthall Hall

Ⓟ 🚻 ♿ ❁

Benthall was the home of the 19th-century botanist George Maw. His Mediterranean collection is still the backbone of the garden – crocuses naturalised everywhere and a surprising number of 'Mediterranean' plants, including acanthus, cistus and *Clematis cirrhosa*. There is good topiary – clipped yews and holly – and some high-summer surprises like *Primula florindae*. Skilful plantings have more or less screened out the enormous electricity pylons that should never have been placed so close to the house.
Arts and Crafts design; spring bulbs

Owned by The National Trust
Number of gardeners 1
Size 1.2ha (3 acres)

BURFORD HOUSE GARDENS
Tenbury Wells WR15 8HQ

Tel 01584 810777 **Fax** 01584 810673
www.burford.co.uk
Location A456 between Tenbury Wells and Ludlow
Opening hours 9am to 6pm (gardens close at dusk, if earlier), daily, all year; closed 25 and 26 December
Admission fee Adults £3.95; children £1; groups (20+) £3; RHS members free

Ⓟ 🚻 ♿ ❁ ✉

This glamorous seven-acre garden, made to complement a stylish Georgian house, is now beautiful and mature. The fluid design is enhanced by interesting plants, imaginatively used and comprehensively labelled. There are good roses and herbaceous borders, the original *Wisteria*

'Burford' on the back of the house, and a magnificent series of water gardens, but Burford is famous above all for its *Clematis* – over 500 cultivars – cleverly trained, grown and displayed among shrubs and in the new Clematis Maze near the coach house. Charles Chesshire has renewed and reordered much of the planting, and the results are excellent. There are new developments on the other side of the river, too: bulbs and wildflower plantings in particular.
clematis; roses (mainly old-fashioned and climbers); plantsman's collection of plants; mature conifers; good herbaceous borders; *Rosa* 'Treasure Trove'; new wildflower garden; new collection of bamboos; café; morning coffee, lunches and teas

Owned by Burford Garden Company
Number of gardeners 4
Size 2.8ha (7 acres)
NCCPG National Collections *Clematis*

DAVID AUSTIN ROSES

Bowling Green Lane, Albrighton, Wolverhampton WV7 3HB

Tel 01902 376376 **Fax** 01902 372142
www.davidaustinroses.com
Location M54, Jct 3; follow brown tourist signs
Opening hours 9am to 5pm, daily, all year, except Christmas to New Year; for NGS: last Sunday in June
Admission fee Free

David Austin has developed an entirely new strain of 'English' roses which combine the shape and scent of old-fashioned roses with the colours, health and floriferousness of modern types. The display gardens adjoining his nursery are impressive: five different sections, each extensive and thickly planted with old-fashioned roses and his own hybrids – over 700 different cultivars of English Roses, old roses, shrub roses, climbers, ramblers and species, as well as some modern hybrid teas and floribundas. From mid-June to mid-July, and later in the summer, it is a place of great beauty. The garden is maintained to an extremely high standard: all the roses look happy and healthy, and flower profusely. Sculptures by David Austin's wife add a further dimension to a visit. Groups are sometimes allowed to see the breeding houses and trial grounds. There will be two RHS Special Events at David Austin Roses during 2007; details from 020 7821 3408.
roses of every kind, especially 'English' roses; important rose nursery and plant centre; tea room and light refreshments

Owned by David Austin
Number of gardeners 1
Size 0.8ha (2 acres)
NCCPG National Collections *Rosa* (David Austin 'English Rose' cultivars)

THE DOWER HOUSE

Morville Hall, Morville, Bridgnorth WV16 5NB

Tel 01746 714407
www.stmem.com/dower-house-garden
Location At junction of A458 and B4368, 3 miles from Bridgnorth
Opening hours 2pm to 6pm, Wednesdays, Sundays and Bank Holiday Mondays, 1 April to 30 September; groups by appointment at other times
Admission fee Adults £4; children £1

Dr Swift is a distinguished garden writer with a special gift for putting our gardening practices in a historical context. Her own garden is intricately designed, immensely stylish and full of allusions. The aim is to tell the story of English gardening in a series of gardens which represent the styles and aspirations of different historical periods. The oldest feature, in spirit, is a turf maze, followed by a medieval cloister garden of clipped yew. Then come the Elizabethan-style knot garden, a 17th-century 'plat', a William and Mary canal garden and so on, up to a stupendous Victorian rose border. The planting shows the discerning eye of a knowledgeable plantsman. Dr Swift is also a dedicated conservationist, not just of historical style, but also of old garden cultivars of everything from roses to apples and vegetables. The Dower House is therefore a first-rate garden which is extremely satisfying on many different levels.
home-made teas

Owned by Dr Katherine Swift, as tenant of the National Trust
Number of gardeners Owner, plus part-time help
Size 0.6ha (1/2 acres)

The Dower House gardens

DUDMASTON
Quatt, Bridgnorth WV15 6QN

Tel 01746 780866 **Fax** 01746 780744
www.nationaltrust.org.uk
Location 4 miles south-east of Bridgnorth on A442
Opening hours Noon to 6pm, Sunday to Wednesday, April to September
Admission fee Adults £4.50; children £3.60

Dudmaston has a fine collection of trees and shrubs, put together by several generations of keen plantsmen in the 19th and 20th centuries. Rhododendrons form the background: there are many magnolias, cherries, kalmias, maples and roses, underplanted with daffodils and primroses, which makes this a particularly fine garden in spring. But there is also a natural rock garden made of the local red sandstone. Elsewhere are a bog garden and a good herbaceous border, recently replanted.
rhododendrons and azaleas; fine trees; sculptures; shop; plant sales; tea room

Owned by The National Trust
Number of gardeners 2
Size 3.2ha (8 acres)
English Heritage Grade II

HALL FARM NURSERY
Vicarage Lane, Kinnerley, Oswestry SY10 8DH

Tel/fax 01691 682135
www.hallfarmnursery.co.uk
Location 2 miles from A5, between Shrewsbury and Oswestry
Opening hours 10am to 5pm, Tuesday to Saturday, 1 March to 31 October
Admission fee Free

Hall Farm Nursery carries a good range of fashionable herbaceous perennials, including a great number of ornamental grasses, echinaceas, bog plants, asters and heleniums. All its plants are grown and propagated on-site: requests for cultural advice are therefore welcome. The display borders around the nursery are attractive and well

maintained. Two RHS Special Events will take place at Hall Farm Nursery during 2007; details from 020 7821 3408.
herbaceous plants; ornamental grasses

Owned by Christine and Nick Ffoulkes Jones

HAWKSTONE HISTORIC PARK & FOLLIES

Weston under Redcastle, Shrewsbury SY4 5UY

Tel 01939 200611 **Fax** 01939 200311
www.hawkstone.co.uk
Location Off A49 between Shrewsbury and Whitchurch
Opening hours 10am to 4.30pm, daily, 6 January to 25 March; 10am to 5.30pm, Wednesday to Sunday, 31 March to 27 May and 12 to 28 October; 10am to 6pm, daily, 28 May to 9 September
Admission fee Adults £5.75; OAPs £4.75; children £3.75

Sir Rowland Hill began landscaping Hawkstone in the 1750s, but most of what remains was initiated by his elder son Sir Richard and completed by his grandson, another Sir Rowland Hill, best known for inventing the postage stamp. It is a fine example of the 'sublime' movement, which sought to create contrasts of emotion in the natural landscape. Hawkstone has deep ravines and gloomy chasms, accompanied by dizzying pinnacles, soaring sandstone rocks, and ornamental follies which fill the whole estate, once more than 700 acres in extent. It is the contrasts which make this landscape unique: the mosses, ferns and dampness of its dark gullies turn suddenly into dramatic cliffs, tunnels, crags and bridges, while the peaks of the precipitous outcrops offer views across 13 counties. But allow lots of time for your visit – the owner recommends at least three hours.
remarkable series of landscaped follies; some good trees; gift shop; tea room

Owned by MC Boler
Number of gardeners 3
Size 40ha (100 acres)
English Heritage Grade I

HILLVIEW HARDY PLANTS

Worfield, Bridgnorth WV15 5NT

Tel/fax 01746 716454
www.hillviewhardyplants.com
Location Between Worfield and Albrighton, off B4176
Opening hours 9am to 5pm, Monday to Saturday, March to mid-October; and by appointment
Admission fee Free

This is a good nursery for hardy herbaceous perennials. Its range of primulas and auriculas, aquilegias and South African plants is especially noteworthy. Guided tours of the nursery and well-planted display garden can be arranged for groups. Several RHS Special Events will take place at Hillview Hardy Plants during 2007; details from 020 7821 3408.
refreshments by arrangement

Owned by John and Ingrid Millington
Number of gardeners 31/2
Size 0.4ha (1 acre)
NCCPG National Collections *Acanthus*

HODNET HALL GARDENS

Hodnet, Market Drayton TF9 3NN

Tel 01630 685786 **Fax** 01630 685853
www.hodnethallgardens.org
Location Near junction of A53 and A442
Opening hours Noon to 5pm, 8 and 9 April, 7, 20, 27 and 28 May, 3, 10 and 24 June, 22, 26 and 27 July and 16 September; for NGS: 13 May; and by appointment for groups of 20+

In the 1950s, *The RHS Journal* (forerunner of *The Garden*) described Hodnet as a 'small modern garden'. Now it has more than 60 acres of woodland garden around a chain of ornamental pools. The woodlands are planted with exotic trees, like magnolias, maples and davidias, against a background of native oaks, sycamores, limes and beech trees. Underneath are rhododendrons, azaleas, camellias, prunus and berberis, themselves underplanted when they flower in spring with a wide variety of herbaceous plants, especially hostas, primulas, daffodils and

bluebells. The spacious mixed borders near the house are particularly interesting in July, when they are complemented by the beds of old-fashioned roses and modern floribundas. But Hodnet is a garden for everyone and every season – good in late summer, too, when the hydrangeas and astilbes flower. Allow lots of time for a thorough visit to one of the greatest 20th-century gardens.
woodland garden; roses (mainly old-fashioned); good herbaceous borders; camellias; primulas; rhododendrons; HHA/Christie's Garden of the Year in 1985; tea room

Owned by AEH Heber-Percy
Number of gardeners 4
Size 24+ha (60+ acres)
English Heritage Grade II

LOWER HALL
Worfield, Bridgnorth WV15 5LH

Tel 01746 716607 **Fax** 01746 716325
Location In centre of village of Worfield
Opening hours By appointment; groups welcome
Admission fee Adults £4; children free

Lanning Roper helped to get this splendid garden going in the 1960s. It bestrides the River Worfe and every part has a distinct character. There are lush streamside plantings (some replanted in 2002 to 2003), infinite colour schemes, and a woodland area at the bottom. These contrast with formal designs, straight brick paths, a pergola and more colour themes in the old walled garden. It is one of the best gardens to be made since World War II, still evolving and neatly kept.
roses (all sorts); plantsman's collection of plants; good herbaceous borders

Owned by CF Dumbell
Number of gardeners 2
Size 1.7ha (4 1/4 acres)

PREEN MANOR
Church Preen, Church Stretton SY6 7LQ

Tel/fax 01694 771207
Location Signed from B4371 Much Wenlock/ Church Stretton
Opening hours 2pm to 6pm, 8 April, 31 May, 28 June, 19 July and 7 October (4.30pm Harvest Thanksgiving); and parties by appointment in June and July
Admission fee Adults £3.50; Children 50p

P

Preen has a stylish new garden with some original ideas to complement the historic old site. These include a chess garden, a collection of plants in handsome old pots, a pebble garden, a fern garden and that symbol of the 1990s – a gravel garden. In the woodland garden are rhododendrons and candelabra primulas. And it gets better every year.
woodland garden; fruit; fern garden; home-made teas

Owned by Mrs Philip Trevor-Jones
Number of gardeners 2 1/2
Size 2.4ha (6 acres), plus woodland

SWALLOW HAYES
Rectory Road, Albrighton, Wolverhampton WV7 3EP

Tel 01902 372624 **Fax** 01902 373151
Location M54, Jct 3, then A41 towards Wolverhampton and first right after garden centre
Opening hours 2pm to 5pm, 6 and 20 May, 3 June; and by appointment
Admission fee Adults £3; children 10p; £3.50 per head for groups, to include tea and biscuits

P

Swallow Hayes is a plantswoman's garden (3,000 plants) entirely made since 1968 and a model of its kind, where groundcover helps to minimise labour and maximise enjoyment. The garden started life as a stock-ground and trial-ground for the owner's wholesale nursery. Mrs Edwards has more than 100 different cultivars of *Geranium* in a garden which is packed with different microhabitats, each of them themed and exploited as fully as possible. There is much to see and enjoy at every season. The garden is open every January for about a week to view the National Collection of winter-flowering witch hazels *Hamamelis* of which there are over 50 cultivars. Please telephone for January 2008 dates.

rock garden; herbs; fruit; mature conifers; good herbaceous borders; ferns; geraniums; trees and shrubs; teas on open days

Owned by Mrs P Edwards
Number of gardeners Owner, plus some very part-time help
Size 0.8ha (2 acres)
NCCPG National Collections *Hamamelis*; *Lupinus* (Russell strains)

WOLLERTON OLD HALL

Wollerton, Market Drayton TF9 3NA

Tel 01630 685760 **Fax** 01630 685583
www.wollertonoldhallgarden.com
Location Follow brown tourist signs from A53/A442 or A53/A41 junctions
Opening hours Noon to 5pm, Fridays, Sundays and Bank Holidays; Good Friday to end of September
Admission fee Adults £4.50; children £1; RHS members free in April, May and September

Started in 1984, this RHS Partner Garden seeks to combine horticultural excellence with unrestrained planting of perennials, careful colour design with strong contrasts, and intimacy with bold design structure. As well as good design features to ponder and copy, there are extensive collections of salvias, clematis and the more unusual perennials.

plantsman's collection of plants; good herbaceous borders; deciduous euonymus; salvias; clematis; shrub roses; crocosmias; lunches and teas

Owned by Lesley Jenkins
Number of gardeners 2½
Size 1.6ha (4 acres)

SOMERSET

Like its neighbour Devon, Somerset is rich in both gardens and nurseries: it is a county where gardeners are well served. Four of its five Grade I historic gardens – Dunster, East Lambrook, Hestercombe and Montacute – are regularly open to the public. Somerset also has an exceptional number of good small and medium-sized gardens, often made by the present owners – as witness the large number (in quite a small county) that open in aid of the National Gardens Scheme. Somerset is famous for its mild climate – warm and wet – and the rich soils that are put to cider and dairying: they also induce good growth in gardens. It has long been recognised that along the coast – at Porlock and Cannington, for example – plants flourish that would not survive in any but the mildest parts of Devon and Cornwall. The Popes have decided not to renew their lease and so the garden at Hadspen House remains closed, though Niall Hobhouse (son of Penelope) has exciting plans for its future. Nevertheless, the county has no arboreta of note and few trees that are thought to be among the tallest or largest of their kind. Somerset has many nurseries and among them are several of national or international importance: Avon Bulbs and Broadleigh Gardens for bulbs, Kelways for peonies, Mallet Court for rare trees and P.M.A. Plants for Japanese maples. Somerset also has a large number (over 20) of National Collections, which is always a good indicator of the general level of interest in gardening. And it has long been well served by the county horticultural college at Cannington, which is one of the leading centres in all England for the teaching of amenity horticulture.

THE AMERICAN MUSEUM

Claverton Manor, Bath BA2 7BD

Tel 01225 460503 **Fax** 01225 469160
www.americanmuseum.org
Location Off A36 south of Bath
Opening hours Noon to 6pm, daily, except Mondays, 17 March to 28 October
Admission fee Adults £5; concessions £4; children £3; private tours by prior arrangement

The 15 enchanting acres of garden at Claverton Manor were created by two artistic Americans, Dallas Pratt and John Judkyn, from about 1960 onwards. They bought the handsome classical house, built in 1820, to hold their collection of early American domestic art and artefacts: the American Museum is now the largest of its kind outside the USA and well worth a visit. The house has a stunning situation with wide views across to the west-facing slopes of the Avon valley, yet is sheltered and screened from all but the prettiest eye-catchers on the other side. Tea is served on the terrace in front of the house, next to the little colonial herb garden ('colonial' = pre-1778). Sloping lawns lead to the Mount Vernon garden, a box-edged re-creation of George Washington's own original. The first enclosure has beds of old roses: the main section is a herbaceous garden. Despite a little historical latitude with the choice of 18th-century plants, it is all very neat and instructive, and prettily enclosed by white picket fencing. Also of horticultural interest is a young arboretum, which opened in 1985 on the slopes below and recently expanded. This celebration of hardy American trees and shrubs adds up to a fine, well-labelled collection and includes (among many other rarities) *Alnus rhombifolia*, *Salix mackenziana* and *Philadelphus insignis*. The new part is planted with trees discovered on the first expedition across America – the Lewis and Clark Trail. Also worth discovering are the new (2006) woodland and parkland walks, a ferny dell at the bottom of the arboretum and a collection of American apple cultivars, with such names as 'Smokehouse' and 'Sheep's Nose'. The American Museum is a well-endowed foundation and its

gardens are very well maintained, which adds enormously to the pleasure of a visit, though rabbits and deer are a problem.
topiary; roses (mainly old-fashioned); herbs; fruit; good herbaceous borders; fine collection of trees; bookshop, herb shop and country store; light lunches; tea, coffee and American cookies

Owned by Trustees of the American Museum in Britain
Number of gardeners 4
Size 6ha (15 acres)
English Heritage Grade II

AMMERDOWN PARK
Kilmersdon, Radstock, Bath BA3 5SH

Tel 01761 432227 **Fax** 01761 433094
Location West of Terry Hill crossroads: A362/A366
Opening hours 11am to 5pm, 9 April, 7 and 28 May, 27 August
Admission fee Adults £4; OAPs £3; children free

Ammerdown's layout is Lutyens at his most ingenious. The lie of the land precludes right angles, but long, straight views cover up the irregularities. It has some nice plants, particularly trees, but the design is everything and there are good spring bulbs. A restoration plan has recently got underway.
major Lutyens garden; good design; refreshments in May and August

Owned by The Hon Andrew Jolliffe
Number of gardeners 2 1/2
Size 6ha (15 acres)
English Heritage Grade II*

AVON BULBS
Burnt House Farm, Mid-Lambrook, South Petherton TA13 5HE

Tel/fax 01460 242177
www.avonbulbs.co.uk
Location Turn south, down 'no through road', halfway between West Lambrook and East Lambrook
Opening hours 9am to 4.30pm, Thursday to Saturday, mid-February to end of March and mid-September to end of October
Admission fee Free

Avon Bulbs offers an impressive variety of bulbs (and close relatives) of all sizes, types and seasons – mainly by mail order. The nursery is well run and the plants are beautifully grown. It is well worth a visit early in the year to see the wide range of its stock, including much which is not listed in the catalogue. The opening hours are limited because of the seasonal nature of the business and the nursery's show commitments. It is a good idea to check with them before visiting. There will be two RHS Special Events at Avon Bulbs in 2007; details from 020 7821 3408.
hardy bulbs of every kind

Owned by Chris Ireland-Jones
Number of gardeners 4
Size 1.2ha (3 acres)

BARRINGTON COURT
Barrington, Ilminster TA19 0NQ

Tel 01460 241938 **Fax** 01460 243133
www.nationaltrust.org.uk
Location In Barrington village, 5 miles north-east of Ilchester, on B3168
Opening hours 11am to 4.30pm (5pm from April to September), Thursday to Tuesday, 1 March to 30 October; 11am to 4pm, 1, 2, 8, 9, 15 and 16 December
Admission fee Adults £7.70; children £3.30

There is still an Edwardian opulence about Barrington. Massive plantings of irises, lilies and rich dark dahlias. And good design detail, too: the patterns of the brick paving are a study in themselves.

roses (mainly old-fashioned); fruit; fine collection of trees; shop; tea room; licensed restaurant

Owned by The National Trust
Number of gardeners 3, plus 2 trainees and 1 seasonal gardener
Size 4ha (10 acres)
English Heritage Grade II*

BATH BOTANIC GARDENS
Royal Victoria Park, Bath BA1 2NQ

Tel 01225 396386 **Fax** 01225 480072
Location West of city centre by Upper Bristol Road
Opening hours 8.30am to dusk, daily, all year, except Christmas Day
Admission fee Free

Bath Botanic Gardens was founded in 1887, extended in 1926 and again in 1987. It has nine acres of trees, shrubs, borders, limestone-loving plants and scented walks. It has never been attached to a university or institute, so it is more of a horticultural collection than a botanic garden, and public amenity is its main function. The central feature is a rocky pool designed in the Japanese style, surrounded by venerable not-so-dwarf maples. Standards are high, maintenance is good, and the seasonal highlights of bulbs, bedding and herbaceous plants are among the best. The excellent guidebook is a model of visitor-friendliness.
rock garden; autumn colour; fine bedding displays; good *Scilla* collection; tallest tree of heaven *Ailanthus altissima* (31m; 102ft) and tallest hornbeam *Carpinus betulus* (27m; 89ft) in England (and 11 other record trees)

Owned by Bath and North East Somerset Council
Number of gardeners 3
Size 3.8ha (9 1/2 acres)
English Heritage Grade II

BLACKMORE & LANGDON
Stanton Nurseries, Pensford, Bristol BS39 4JL

Tel 01275 332300 **Fax** 01275 331207
www.blackmore-langdon.com
Location 8 miles south of Bristol on B3130, between A37 Wells road and A38
Opening hours 9am to 5pm, Monday to Friday, all year; 10am to 4pm, Saturdays and Sundays, April to September; special Plant Sale from 11 to 13 May

This family business was started in 1901 and is now run by the founder's grandsons. It has a long tradition of breeding and growing showy border plants – huge begonias and tall delphiniums, in particular. The nursery's immaculately grown flowers have been a feature of RHS Flower Shows – and especially the Chelsea Flower Show – for many years. What is not so well known is that the nursery also produces phlox, aquilegias and polyanthus. All its plants are grown on-site.
The begonias and delphiniums fill a one-acre glasshouse; there are also delphiniums in flower in the field from the end of May until September. There will be an annual plant sale (combined with a Chelsea preview) from 12 to 14 May.
delphiniums; begonias

Owned by The Langdon family

BROADLEIGH GARDENS
Bishops Hull, Taunton TA4 1AE

Tel 01823 286231 **Fax** 01823 232464
www.broadleighbulbs.co.uk
Location At Barr, 3/4 mile north-west of Bishops Hull
Opening hours 9am to 4pm, Monday to Friday; viewing and collection of pre-booked orders
Admission fee £1 charity donation

This nursery, with strong RHS connections, is best known for its small bulbs, though it now grows almost as many foliage and woodland perennials. Look out for the agapanthus, crocosmias, snowdrops, the many miniature narcissus and species tulips, and Broadleigh's own Pacific Coast hybrid irises. The three-acre display garden is planted for year-round effect, and includes formal and informal areas.
spring bulbs (especially miniature narcissus); agapanthus

Owned by Christine Skelmersdale
Number of gardeners 4
Size 2ha (5 acres)
NCCPG National Collections *Narcissus* (miniature)

Cothay Manor gardens

CLEEVE NURSERY
Cleeve, Bristol BS49 4PW

Tel 01934 832134 **Fax** 01934 876498
www.cleevenursery.co.uk
Location On A370 between Bristol and Weston-super-Mare
Opening hours 9am to 6pm (5pm in winter), Monday to Saturday, all year; plus 10am to 5pm on Sundays and Bank Holidays; closed 25 December to 1 January
Admission fee Free

P 🚻 ♿
This is a well-regarded garden centre with a wide range of home-grown plants for sale. There will be an RHS Special Event here during 2007; details from 020 7821 3408.
garden centre; coffee shop

Owned by Alan and Felicity Down

COTHAY MANOR
Greenham, Wellington TA21 0JR

Tel 01823 672283 **Fax** 01823 672345
www.cothaymanor.co.uk
Location Off A38, 1½ miles from Greenham
Opening hours 2pm to 6pm, Wednesdays, Thursdays, Sundays and Bank Holiday Mondays, Easter to September; groups (21+) by appointment throughout the season
Admission fee Adults £4.50; children £2.50; special rates for pre-booked groups

P 🚻 ♿ ●
Cothay is an exciting old/new garden on either side of the River Tone. The seven acres of formal gardens designed in the 1920s by Reggie Cooper (a friend of Lawrence Johnston, Harold Nicolson and Vita Sackville-West) have now been completely replanted, room by room, colour by colour, since the Robbs came here in 1993. Cothay makes a model study of how a garden can be rejuvenated. It is now in the prime of life, brimming with vigour. The avenue of mop-headed acacias (*Robinia pseudoacacia* 'Umbraculifera'), nearly 100m (328ft) long, looks stunning underplanted with nepeta and a thousand white tulips. New for 2004 were a mount, planted with wildflowers and bulbs, and a lake – work continues.
stylish 1920s design; good plants; cream teas

Owned by Mr and Mrs Alastair Robb
Number of gardeners 1½
Size 2.8ha (7 acres); plus 2ha (5 acres) of new trees
English Heritage Grade II*

CROWE HALL
Widcombe Hill, Bath BA2 6AR

Tel 01225 310322
Location Off A36 up Widcombe Hill
Opening hours 2pm to 6pm, 15 April, 13 May, 3 June and by appointment
Admission fee Adults £3; children £1

P ♠ 🚻 ♿
Crowe Hall is a most extraordinary and exciting garden. It looks straight out at the Capability Brown landscape at Prior Park, and 'borrows' it. Mown grass paths have been cut through the meadows above the house to create an ever-changing view of the park and Palladian bridge. Below the house is an Italianate terrace, which

leads to a ferny rock garden (real rocky outcrops here) and down into a semi-woodland garden. Recent developments include a 'Sauce' garden, in memory of Lady Barratt (a former owner), a 'Hercules' garden and the 'Teazle' garden with a cascade, pool and pergola in memory of a much-loved dog.
roses (mainly old-fashioned); fine greenhouse and grotto; teas

Owned by John Barratt
Number of gardeners 2
Size 4.4ha (11 acres)
English Heritage Grade II

DUNSTER CASTLE
Dunster, Minehead TA24 6SL

Tel 01643 821314 **Fax** 01643 823000
www.nationaltrust.org.uk
Location 3 miles south-east of Minehead on A39
Opening hours 11am to 4pm, daily, 1 to 22 March and 1 November to 31 December; closed 25 and 26 December; 10am to 5pm, daily, 23 March to 31 October
Admission fee Adults £4.30; children £2.20

Ⓟ 🚻 ♿

Dunster is a Victorian woodland (with older features) on a steep slope, terraced in places and planted with tender exotica – mimosa, *Beschorneria* and a collection of citrus plants in an unheated conservatory.
Arbutus grove; woodland garden; subtropical plants; National Trust shop; tea room at Dunster Mill

Owned by The National Trust
Number of gardeners 4
Size 6.7ha (17 acres)
NCCPG National Collections *Arbutus*
English Heritage Grade I

EAST LAMBROOK MANOR
East Lambrook, South Petherton TA13 5HL

Tel 01460 240328 **Fax** 01460 242344
www.eastlambrook.com
Location Signed from A303 at South Petherton
Opening hours 10am to 5pm, daily, all year; for NGS: 20 May and 10 June

East Lambrook Manor

Admission fee Adults £3.95; OAPs £3.50; children free; RHS members free from November to February

Ⓟ 🚻

East Lambrook is the archetypal cottage garden, made by Margery Fish, the popular gardening writer, and charmingly restored in recent years. Margery Fish was an important influence in British gardening in the 1950s and 1960s. She learnt about gardening not from books but from her own observations, so that she developed her own unselfconscious style of gardening. As a journalist, she knew how to communicate, and her books about the garden she made at East Lambrook have been very influential. The present owners are continuing the work of restoration begun in the 1980s, and have updated the plantings while respecting the original spirit. They have returned Margery Fish's nursery to its original site, made a special bed for hardy geraniums and restored the malthouse. They also run RHS courses for gardeners all through the year.
Margery Fish's garden; plantsman's collection of plants; good herbaceous borders; 150 different snowdrops; hellebores; euphorbias; geraniums; cottage garden plants; lunches and teas

Owned by Marianne and Robert Williams
Number of gardeners 1
Size 0.8ha (2 acres)
English Heritage Grade I

ELWORTHY COTTAGE PLANTS

Elworthy Cottage, Elworthy, Lydeard St Lawrence, Taunton TA4 3PX

Tel 01984 656427
www.elworthy-cottage.co.uk
Location 10 miles north-west of Taunton, on B3188 in Elworthy village centre
Opening hours 10am to 4pm, Thursdays, late-March to end of July; and by appointment at any time from February to October; groups welcome
Admission fee £2

Elworthy offers a pleasant selection of perennials and cottage garden plants, including quite a number which are uncommon or hard to find, as well as old favourites. The nursery is strong on geraniums, clematis and pulmonarias, as well as geums, violas, crocosmias and grasses. Some of the nursery's plants are not available from any other source. It has also introduced new plants, including *Geranium* x *oxonianum* 'Elworthy Misty', G. 'Elworthy Tiger' and G. 'Elworthy Eyecatcher'. Most of the plants can be seen in the garden, which is neatly laid out with island beds and themed colours for year-round interest but also to blend in with the surrounding countryside (Exmoor National Park) and to encourage wildlife. Other features include a gravel area for shade-tolerant plants, a decorative vegetable garden, an autumn bed of hot colours, hedges of native species, wildflower areas and a living willow screen.
raised beds; troughs; wildflowers

Owned by Mike and Jenny Spiller
Number of gardeners Owners only
Size 0.4ha (1 acre)

GAULDEN MANOR

Tolland, Lydeard St Lawrence TA4 3PN

Tel 01984 667213
Location 1 mile east of Tolland Church, off B3224
Opening hours 2pm to 5pm, Thursdays, Sundays and Bank Holidays, June to August; and groups by appointment at other times
Admission fee £3.25

Gaulden is a modern garden, well designed and well planted. It has a series of small garden rooms, each devoted to a different theme (roses, herbs etc.) which makes it seem much larger than it really is and a pleasure to explore. The stream garden – very pretty – is below the monks' pond, its sides planted with candelabra primulas, ferns and gunneras. Fun for children, too.
woodland garden; roses (ancient and modern); herbs; good herbaceous borders; scent gardens; secret garden

Owned by James Starkie
Number of gardeners 2
Size 0.8ha (2 acres)

GREENCOMBE GARDENS

Porlock TA24 8NU

Tel 01643 862363
www.greencombe.org.uk
Location 1/2 mile west of Porlock on left of road to Porlock Weir.
Opening hours 2pm to 6pm, Saturday to Wednesday, April to July and again in autumn.
Admission fee Adults £5; Children (under 16) £1.

Greencombe is an organic showpiece of international renown. The garden stretches across a sheltered hillside, which looks up to the tree-covered slopes of Exmoor, behind and down across ancient fields to Porlock Bay and an uninterrupted view of the sea. It is a woodland garden, long and narrow, with a rich underplanting of ornamental plants beneath an outstanding canopy of oaks, hollies, conifers and sweet chestnuts. Camellias, rhododendrons, azaleas, maples, lilies, roses, clematis, and hydrangeas all flower in turn among many ferns, and the garden's four National Collections: *Erythronium*, which are small mountain lilies; *Vaccinium*, which the curator Joan Loraine calls 'whortleberries worldwide'; *Gaultheria*, which she refers to as 'whortleberries for bears'; and

Hestercombe Gardens

Polystichum, the 'thumbs-up' fern. The garden is completely organic, with compost heaps and leaf mould pits on show, and a riot of birds, butterflies and lesser insects. But, above all, like all good plantsmen's gardens, Greencombe is full of rare plants and has lots to interest the visitor at every time of the year.
woodland garden; plantsman's collection of plants; good herbaceous borders; organically run

Owned by Greencombe Garden Trust
Number of gardeners 1 part-time
Size 1.4ha (3 1/2 acres)
NCCPG National Collections *Erythronium*; *Gaultheria*; *Polystichum*; *Vaccinium*

HESTERCOMBE GARDENS
Cheddon Fitzpaine, Taunton TA2 8LG

Tel 01823 413923 **Fax** 01823 413747
www.hestercombegardens.com
Location 4 miles north of Taunton
Opening hours 10am to 5pm, daily, all year; closed 25 December
Admission fee Adults £6.95; OAPs £6.25; children £2.50; RHS members free from October to February

Ignore the house – a Victorian mansion now used as council offices – and look at the famously restored garden. Lutyens's hallmarks are everywhere: iris-choked rills, pergolas, seats, relieved staircases and pools where reflections twinkle on recessed apses. Gertrude Jekyll's planting is bold and simple, which adds to the vigour. The combination of Lutyens design and Jekyll plants is extremely photogenic: Hestercombe is a highly rewarding garden to learn about symmetry, balance and proportion. The secret landscape garden, which Coplestone Warre Bampfylde laid out in the late 18th century, reopened in 1997: 40 acres of lakes, temples, combes and woodlands which have not been seen for over 100 years. The Heritage Lottery Fund has made a grant of £3.7m to be paid between 2003 and 2008, which will confirm Hestercombe as Somerset's most visited garden.
good herbaceous borders; classical landscaping; Lutyens design and Jekyll planting; gift shop; plant sales (March to October); café

Owned by Hestercombe Gardens Trust
Number of gardeners 8
Size 20ha (50 acres)
English Heritage Grade I

KELWAYS LTD
Barrymore Farm, Langport TA10 9EZ

Tel 01458 250521 **Fax** 01458 253351
www.kelways.co.uk
Location On B3153, just east of Langport
Opening hours 9am to 5pm, Monday to Saturday; 10am to 4pm, Sundays

Long famous for its peonies (500+ herbaceous and 35 tree peonies), Kelways also has a large range of irises (700+) and an expanding range of perennials, shrubs and bedding plants. An orchid house displays and sells English-grown orchids. The peony fields will be open at their peak – usually the first two weeks of June, but please telephone before travelling to check the dates.
peonies; irises; orchids

Owned by C Johnson
NCCPG National Collections *Paeonia lactiflora*

LOWER SEVERALLS GARDENS & NURSERY
Crewkerne TA18 7NX

Tel 01460 73234 **Fax** 01460 76105
www.lowerseveralls.co.uk
Location 1 1/2 miles north-east of Crewkerne; signed from A30 and A352
Opening hours 10am to 5pm, Tuesdays, Wednesdays, Fridays, Saturdays and all Bank Holiday Mondays, 1 March to 30 September; for NGS: 30 April, 7 and 14 May, 11 and 18 June and 10 September
Admission fee Adults £3; children free

Both the garden and nursery started in 1985. At first, the nursery specialised in herbs, of which it still has a wide range. However, there are also good selections of hardy geraniums, salvias and lots more besides. The garden is set in front of an 18th-century Hamstone farmhouse: it has fine

herbaceous borders, island beds, a living 'dogwood basket' and an area for bog plants known as 'the Wadi'.
herbaceous borders; island beds; herbs; self-service teas; lunches and teas for groups by arrangement

Owned by Mary Pring
Number of gardeners 2
Size 1.2ha (3 acres)

LYTES CARY MANOR
Charlton Mackrell, Somerton TA11 7HU

Tel/fax 01458 224471
www.nationaltrust.org.uk
Location Near A303 junction with A372 and A37
Opening hours 11am to 5pm, Wednesdays, Friday to Sunday and Bank Holiday Mondays, 24 March to 28 October
Admission fee Adults £4; children £2; families £15

Lytes Cary has a neo-Elizabethan garden to go with the prettiest of manor houses: yew hedges, hornbeam walks, alleys and lawns, medlars, quinces and a simple Elizabethan flower border.
topiary; good herbaceous borders

Owned by The National Trust
Number of gardeners 1, plus seasonal help and volunteers
Size 2.4ha (6 acres)
English Heritage Grade II

MALLET COURT NURSERY
Curry Mallet, Taunton TA3 6SY

Tel/fax 01823 481493
www.malletcourt.co.uk
Location In centre of Curry Mallet
Opening hours 10am to 4pm, Mondays to Fridays; plus special open days in April and October; weekends by appointment
Admission fee Free

This is a wonderful specialist tree nursery with an excellent list of unusual trees. Its displays at RHS Flower Shows, including Chelsea and Hampton Court, have been a delight and a revelation over many years now. Many of the species it sells are offered by no other nursery anywhere in the world. It is particularly good for *Quercus* and *Acer*, and strong on species from China and Korea, but the nursery's list is full of species of every imaginable genus of rare tree. Every dendrophile in Britain knows of it and buys from it: the array of plants to be seen at the nursery is itself an education. Two RHS Special Events will take place at Mallet Court during 2007; details from 020 7821 3408.

Owned by JGS Harris and Mrs PME Mallet-Harris

MEADOWS NURSERY
5 Rectory Cottages, Selwood Street, Mells, Frome BA11 3PN

Tel 01373 812268
Location In centre of village
Opening hours 10am to 6pm, Wednesday to Sunday and Bank Holiday Mondays, February to October
Admission fee Free

Meadows Nursery has a pretty, cottage-style garden, well maintained and boosted by putting out some spectacular succulents and other glasshouse plants in summer. The nursery specialises in perennials, all grown in peat-free, loam-based compost, and has a particularly good line in kniphofias. Both the nursery and the garden make very good use of a confined space.
good nursery

Owned by Sue Lees and Eddie Wheatley
Number of gardeners Owners only
Size 0.2ha (1/2 acre)

MILL COTTAGE PLANTS
Henley Mill, Wookey BA5 1AW

Tel/fax 01749 676966
www.millcottageplants.co.uk
Location 2 miles from Wells, off A371; left into Henley Lane, then 50 yards on left
Opening hours Nursery: 10am to 5.30pm, Wednesdays, March to September; garden also open by appointment
Admission fee Garden: £3; nursery: free

The nursery grows a selection of unusual perennials, including a wide range of arisaemas, hellebores, oriental poppies, epimediums, ferns and grasses. It also has a good line in rare hydrangea cultivars. The garden is well worth seeing, though it is best to ask if you can see it in advance of your visit. It includes a sunny formal garden, a shaded 'folly' garden, a kitchen garden, 'hot red' borders, and a late-summer bed (mainly grasses and perennials). Groups are especially welcome.
beautiful waterside setting; hardy perennials

Owned by Peter and Sally Gregson
Number of gardeners 2½
Size 1ha (2½ acres)

MILTON LODGE
Old Bristol Road, Wells BA5 3AQ

Tel 01749 672168
www.miltonlodgegardens.co.uk
Location Old Bristol Road off A39
Opening hours 2pm to 5pm, Tuesdays, Wednesdays, Sundays and Bank Holidays, Easter to 31 October
Admission fee Adults £4; children (under 14) free; groups by arrangement

This impressive Edwardian garden is terraced down a hillside against a backdrop of Wells Cathedral. Most of the plantings are modern and look good against the walls and bulky yew hedges. In a combe, across the main road, is an eight-acre 19th-century arboretum. Both parts are full of interesting plants, excellently maintained and constantly improving, with considerable new planting in recent years.
roses (mainly modern); good herbaceous borders; fine collection of trees; tallest *Populus alba* (20m; 66ft) in the British Isles; teas on Sundays (May to August)

Owned by The Trustees of the late DC Tudway Quilter
Size 1.6ha (4 acres)
English Heritage Grade II

MONTACUTE HOUSE
Montacute, Yeovil TA15 6XP

Tel 01935 823289 **Fax** 01935 826921
www.nationaltrust.org.uk
Location In Montacute village, 4 miles west of Yeovil
Opening hours 11am to 6pm (or dusk, if earlier), daily, except Tuesday, 17 March to 28 October; 11am to 4pm, Wednesday to Sunday, 29 October to 30 December
Admission fee Adults £5; children £2. 20

The sunken gardens at Montacute are a perfect foil for the amazing Elizabethan mansion, and are beautifully maintained. They cannot be beaten for the sense of English renaissance grandeur they impart. The National Trust has recently had the courage to replant the borders not as they were originally planned by Vita Sackville-West, nor as subsequently laid out by Graham Stuart Thomas in pretty pastel shades, but using the brilliant colours devised by Phyllis Reiss of nearby Tintinhull in the 1950s. The vivid colours of 'Frensham' roses, purple berberis and late-summer dahlias are the ideal complement to the Hamstone house.
good herbaceous borders; exquisite gazebos; shop; light lunches and teas; licensed restaurant

Owned by The National Trust
Number of gardeners 4
Size 5ha (12½ acres), plus 10.2ha (26 acres) of parkland
English Heritage Grade I

P.M.A. PLANT SPECIALITIES
Junker's Nursery Ltd, Lower Mead, West Hatch, Taunton TA3 5RN

Tel 01823 480774 **Fax** 01823 481046
www.junker.co.uk
Location West Hatch is 4 miles south of Taunton
Opening hours By appointment only
Admission fee Free

P.M.A. has some interesting container-grown trees and shrubs. It is particularly strong on Japanese and snakebark acers, daphnes, magnolias and the ornamental tree *Cornus* (flowering dogwoods). Some plants are available in larger sizes for instant impact. The display borders are particularly instructive – new areas are planted and developed every year – and visitors also have free access to the stock plants. The new *Betula* glades are shaping up well. Look out for the many epimediums and hellebores in the woodland plantings.

Owned by Nick and Karan Junker
Number of gardeners Owners only
Size 1.2ha (3 acres)

PRIOR PARK LANDSCAPE GARDEN

Ralph Allen Drive, Bath BA2 5AH

Tel 01225 833422
www.nationaltrust.org.uk
Location 1½ miles south of Bath city centre; no on-site or nearby parking
Opening hours 11am to 5.30pm (or dusk, if earlier), Wednesday to Monday, 3 March to 28 October; 11am to dusk, Saturdays and Sundays, 3 to 25 February and 3 November to 24 February 2008
Admission fee Adults £4.50; children £2.50

The classical landscape at Prior Park was laid out between 1734 and 1764 by a property developer called Ralph Allen, who was a friend of Pope and Burlington. Pope advised extensively on the original layout and buildings before Capability Brown gave them a makeover in the early 1760s. The park is no more than 28 acres, stretching from the extremely handsome Palladian house (not National Trust) at the top of the steep valley, to the exquisite Palladian bridge right at the bottom, which is the focus of the entire landscape and reflected in three lakes. It is reached by a rugged and sometimes slippery path through the woods on either side, quite unfitted for wheelchairs and buggies and only suitable for the sure-footed and confident. Now the National Trust has started on its final programme of restoration, by reviving the Wilderness, its Gothic temple, serpentine lake and cascade. There is nothing of horticultural interest, but some fine trees – mainly beech, with some yew, sycamore and seedling ashes, underplanted with ferns and laurels. Nevertheless, it is hard to imagine a more elegant landscape than this one, which uses the busy and fashionable city of Bath as its background. Photographers may wish to visit it early in the afternoon, when the sun shines on the Palladian bridge. There is one snag, however: the Trust can offer no on-site parking, except for disabled visitors; Bus No 2 runs from Dorchester Street every 30 minutes daily, and the City Sightseeing Tour bus runs from the railway station every 30 minutes in summer and every hour in winter; further details on the National Trust's website.
Palladian bridge; handsome parkland; refreshments at weekends in summer

Owned by The National Trust
Number of gardeners 3, plus volunteers
Size 11.1ha (28 acres)
English Heritage Grade I

SHERBORNE GARDEN

Pear Tree House, Litton BA3 4PP

Tel 01761 241220
Location On B3114, ½ mile west of Litton village, 7 miles north of Wells
Opening hours 11am to 5pm, Sundays and Mondays, June to October; for NGS: 10 to 14 February for snowdrops, and 3 June
Admission fee Adults £3; children free; groups welcome by appointment

This plantsman's garden started in a modest enough way in 1964 but now extends to more than six acres. It is very thickly planted, yet it also seems to sit very well in the countryside. The owners are particularly interested in trees and plant them in groups for comparison: hence the 'prickly wood' (of hollies), the pinetum and an acer glade, as well as some 40 different oaks. Recent additions include a 'dell walk' underplanted with heucheras, ferns and snowdrops, and some 20 phormiums in the gravel garden. But there are also good herbaceous plantings and bulbs, and a fine collection of *Rosa* species, hemerocallis (250) and ferns (200), which make it an excellent garden to dawdle in and learn from.
woodland garden; roses (ancient and modern, plus many species); plantsman's collection of plants; small

pinetum; collection of hollies (180 varieties) and hardy ferns (250 varieties); 29 different water lilies; tea/coffee

Owned by Mr and Mrs John Southwell
Number of gardeners Owners, with part-time help
Size 2.4ha (6 acres)

STON EASTON PARK
Ston Easton, Bath BA3 4DF

Tel 01761 241631 **Fax** 01761 241377
www.stoneaston.co.uk
Location On A37, 11 miles from Bath
Opening hours Dawn to dusk, daily, all year; residents and guests of the hotel only
Admission fee Free to residents and guests

Humphry Repton laid out the splendid park at Ston Easton; a sham castle dates from his time. Penelope Hobhouse worked on the modern gardens. The extensive kitchen garden and cutting gardens supply the hotel's vegetables and flowers.
luxury hotel; Humphry Repton landscape; restaurant

Owned by Andrew Davis
Number of gardeners 5
Size 14.4ha (36 acres)
English Heritage Grade II

TINTINHULL HOUSE
Tintinhull, Yeovil BA22 8PZ

Tel 01935 823289 **Fax** 01935 826357
www.nationaltrust.org.uk
Location In Tintinhull village, 5 miles north-west of Yeovil
Opening hours 11am to 5pm, Wednesday to Sunday and Bank Holiday Mondays, 17 March to 28 October
Admission fee Adults £5.30; children £2.70; families £13.30

This garden is the most famous example of a Jekyll-style garden on a small scale. It combines great design with a wide range of plants and the most skilful use of colour combinations in planting them. The garden looks larger than it really is because it has been divided into a sequence of small rooms of different size, all of them hedged or walled. Perhaps the most famous part is the largest, around a formal rectangular pool in front of a pillared summerhouse. The borders on either side are in complete contrast to each other: one is made in the bright, bold colours of scarlet, yellow, orange and white, while the other is dominated by pastel pinks, mauves, blues and pale yellows. Yet they are also mirror images of each other, because each uses grey-leaved plants and striking leaf shapes as well as colour. No garden employs such a wide palette of plants so rigorously as elements of design. There has been much cutting back, clearing, renewal and replanting recently.
topiary; roses (mainly old-fashioned); good herbaceous borders; colour borders; kitchen garden; light refreshments

Owned by The National Trust
Number of gardeners 1
Size 0.8ha (2 acres)
English Heritage Grade II

TYNTESFIELD
Wraxall BS48 1NT

Tel 01275 461900 **Fax** 01275 461907
Location On B3128 at Wraxall
Opening hours 10am to 5.30pm, Saturday to Wednesday, 17 March to 4 November
Admission fee Adults £5; children £2.50; families £12.50

The National Trust has made a good start to restoring the gardens and parkland at Tyntesfield. It was laid out in the 1860s and 1870s in a mixture of Gothic and Italianate styles. The formal garden is Italianate, with eight cruciform beds set into a grass terrace and enclosed by gravel paths. Beyond is a choice of three paths leading to the arboretum known as Paradise. One has hollies cut as mushrooms, another Irish yews and the third an avenue of Portugal laurel. Paradise itself is a Victorian collection of oaks, cedars, hollies and conifers. The walled garden, remodelled in 1889 in the Classical style, has a cut-flower garden, a vegetable garden, an orangery (built for Queen Victoria's Diamond Jubilee), and a series of glasshouses, bothies and sheds.
light refreshments

Owned by The National Trust
Number of gardeners 4
Size 8ha (20 acres)

WAYFORD MANOR
Crewkerne TA18 8QG

Tel 01460 73253 **Fax** 01460 76365
Location 3 miles south-west of Crewkerne off A30 or B3165
Opening hours For NGS: 2pm to 5pm, 1 and 22 April, 6, 7 and 27 May, 11 and 24 June; and parties by appointment
Admission fee Adults £3; children £1

Ⓟ

Wayford is one of the best gardens designed by Harold Peto: terraces and courtyards, pools and arbours, balustrades and staircases, Tuscan and Byzantine. Down in the wild garden is an extensive collection of mature acers and magnolias, as well as many rhododendrons, dogwoods, candelabra primulas, bog plants and daffodils. The whole garden is being restored by the enthusiastic and knowledgeable owners: they recently reinstated the pergola with stone Tuscan columns as Peto originally designed it.
good herbaceous borders; rhododendrons; spring bulbs; maples; tallest *Photinia davidiana* (13m; 43ft) in the British Isles; plants for sale; teas

Owned by Mr and Mrs RL Goffe
Number of gardeners 1
Size 1.6ha (4 acres)
English Heritage Grade II

STAFFORDSHIRE

Staffordshire has three historic gardens to which English Heritage has accorded Grade I status: Alton Towers, Biddulph Grange and Shugborough. All are open to the public. The county is not, however, a magnet for garden visitors with horticultural interests. The Dorothy Clive Garden is the only really first-rate garden in Staffordshire to have come out of the 20th century. There are only three National Collections and the National Garden Scheme has comparatively little success within the county. Why this should be remains a puzzle: the county is fairly wealthy, its soils are fertile, and its climate is not too subject to extremes. The Staffordshire Gardens and Parks Trust is, however, very active and its historic gardens are well visited – Shugborough, Weston and Trentham have all enjoyed long traditions of popular participation in their public events. There are few arboreta of note and practically no record-sized trees anywhere in the county. Even the Royal Horticultural Society seems unable to stir up enthusiasm for gardening: Staffordshire is one of the few counties where it has no partners, except for the Dorothy Clive Garden. But Ashwood Nurseries, on the borders of West Midlands, is a place of international standing.

ALTON TOWERS

Alton, Stoke-on-Trent ST10 4DB

Tel 0870 5204060 **Fax** 01538 704092
www.altontowers.com
Location Signed for miles around
Opening hours 9.30am to 5pm, 6pm or 7pm, depending on season, daily, 17 March to 4 November
Admission fee Tickets vary in cost according to season but are always fairly expensive; the owners say that Alton Towers offers much more than gardens to visit and that the best ticket deals are available online

Alton has 300 acres of dotty and exuberant display, best seen from the Sky-ride. The gardens are by and large detached from the razzmatazz of the theme park. There are splendid Victorian conifers and gaudy bedding, magnificently done. The highlights include a Swiss Cottage, a Roman bridge, a Chinese pagoda, a flag tower and a corkscrew fountain. It is seriously important to garden historians and excellent entertainment still – but not for contemplative souls. Best in term time.

woodland garden; roses (mainly modern); rock garden; mature conifers; good herbaceous borders; many restaurants

Owned by Tussauds Group
Number of gardeners 10
Size 120ha (300 acres)
English Heritage Grade I

ASHWOOD NURSERIES LTD

Ashwood Lower Lane, Kingswinford DY6 0AE

Tel 01384 401996 **Fax** 01308 401108
www.ashwood-nurseries.co.uk
Location 2 miles west of Kingswinford, near A449
Opening hours Nursery: 9am to 5.30pm, Monday to Saturday, 9.30am to 5.30pm, Sundays, all year, except 25 and 26 December; John Massey's private garden: 11am to 4pm on 31 March, 5 May and 29 September; 10am to 4.30pm on 28 July
Admission fee Free to nursery and show garden; £3.50 (for charity) for private garden days

Ashwood is a rising star among nurseries. The owner and his associates have the happy knack of anticipating trends in horticultural fashion: then they put a lot of thought into developing new plants and, thus, new markets. They began in the 1970s with lewisias, crossing and selecting them until they could offer a remarkable range of colours. In 1996 they were awarded a gold medal for their lewisias at the Chelsea Flower Show, their

first ever exhibit at the Royal Horticultural Society's most prestigious event. Next they began to breed hellebores – strains of *H. orientalis* in particular. The Ashwood hybrids are remarkable for their purity of colour, vigour and form – but, above all, for the new developments that they have brought to the genus: doubles, anemone-centred and upright forms. Now they are turning their attention to hybrids of *H. niger*. 'Hellebore Weekends' have been planned for 3 and 4 February and 17 and 18 February 2007, with guided tours of the collection in return for a donation of £1.50 to charity. More recent, but no less promising, has been their involvement with hardy cyclamen, auriculas, hepaticas and salvias. Hepaticas are extremely fashionable in Japan, where rare cultivars may cost the equivalent of several hundred pounds, and there is clearly money to be made from developing this genus yet further. Above all, Ashwood means quality: the exhibits the nursery brings to RHS Flower Shows are beautifully grown. The hydrangeas they brought to the Chelsea Flower Show in 2005 were a real eye-opener. A visit to their nursery is strongly recommended. There will be four RHS Special Events at Ashwood Nurseries in 2007; details from 020 7821 3408. And John Massey's private garden is worth a long journey to see on one of its four open days.
hellebores; cyclamen; lewisias; hepaticas; auriculas; gift shop; tea room

Owned by John Massey
Size 2ha (5 acres)
NCCPG National Collections *Lewisia*

BIDDULPH GRANGE GARDENS

Grange Road, Biddulph,
Stoke-on-Trent ST8 7SD

Tel 01782 517999 **Fax** 01782 510624
www.nationaltrust.org.uk
Location 1/2 mile north of Biddulph, 3 1/2 miles south-east of Congleton
Opening hours 11.30am to 6pm, Wednesday to Sunday and Bank Holiday Mondays, 17 March to 28 October; 11am to 3pm, Saturdays and Sundays, 3 November to 16 December
Admission fee Adults £6; children £3; (adults £2.30; children £1.10; 3 November to 16 December)

The garden at Biddulph was made in the middle of the 19th century by James Bateman – an important amateur garden designer, plantsman and writer. His wife Maria and their friend Edward Cooke also had a hand in it. Their garden has several microclimates, compartments, follies and whimsies: it is, in fact, the earliest example of a garden being divided into a series of smaller rooms, each designed and planted to a different theme. Some are so original and inventive that they still strike us as frankly rather wacky – the Dragon Parterre, for example, which is dominated by a golden buffalo, or the stumpery, where a pile of carefully excavated and inverted tree stumps form a framework for trailing ivies and other plants. One of the more eccentric novelties is the 'upside-down tree' replanted with its roots in the air between the Rhododendron ground and the lime avenue. Others are the Egyptian courtyard with its own pyramid, a bowling green and quoits ground, the Chinese garden (surprisingly large and beautiful, with a joss house, temple and section of the Great Wall) and the Scottish glen. Elsewhere are areas devoted to collections of plants – a wellingtonia avenue, a pinetum and the dahlia walk. The estate suffered 50 years of neglect when the house was used as a hospital but a core of devoted gardeners kept the garden so well that, when the National Trust began to restore it, much of the original garden and many of its quirkier features were still in place. They are now as good as ever.
Victorian garden with many different styles and rooms; excellent plants and plantings; mature conifers; mosaic parterre; gift shop; tea room

Owned by The National Trust
Number of gardeners 4, plus 1 student
Size 6ha (15 acres)
English Heritage Grade I

CONSALL HALL LANDSCAPE GARDENS

Consall, Wetley Rocks, Stoke-on-Trent ST9 0AG

Tel 01782 551947/01782 749994
www.consallgardens.co.uk
Location 3/4 mile east of Consall village

Opening hours 10am to 5pm, Wednesday, Sunday and Bank Holiday Mondays, Easter to 30 September; for NGS: 29 May
Admission fee Adults £4; children £1; families £10

William Podmore has made the extensive gardens at Consall Hall over the last 50 years. They are landscaped on the grand scale around a sequence of lakes and wooded valleys. Beech and exotic trees form the framework, with colourful shrubs, especially azaleas, as the underplanting. There are four miles of walks, each designed as a sequence of views, but with lots of foreground too.
plant shop; tea room

Owned by William Podmore
Number of gardeners 2
Size 28ha (70 acres)

DOROTHY CLIVE GARDEN
Willoughbridge, Market Drayton TF9 4EU

Tel 01630 647237 **Fax** 01630 647902
www.dorothyclivegarden.co.uk
Location A51, midway between Nantwich and Stone
Opening hours 10am to 5.30pm, daily, mid-March to October
Admission fee Adults £4.50; OAPs and groups (20+) £3.80; children £1 (under 11s free); RHS members free in July and August

This well maintained garden was begun in 1940 with advice on plants and planting from Frank Knight, then director of Wisley. The layout is informal, yet full of incidents, each with a distinct character. They include a superb woodland garden, an alpine scree, a gravel garden, a fine collection of trees and spectacular flower borders. The Dorothy Clive Garden first reaches a peak in May, when the woodland quarry is brilliant with rhododendrons, but new mixed borders ensure that midsummer and August are also high points. The great range and variety of plants mean that there is always much to see whatever the season.
woodland garden; mature conifers; camellias; good herbaceous borders; heather; cyclamen; tea room with beverages and home-baked food

Owned by Willoughbridge Garden Trust
Number of gardeners 3
Size 5ha (12 acres)

MOSELEY OLD HALL
Moseley Old Hall Lane, Fordhouses WV10 7HY

Tel 01902 782808
www.nationaltrust.org.uk
Location South of M54 between A449 and A460
Opening hours Noon to 5pm (11am to 5pm on Bank Holiday Mondays), Wednesdays, Saturdays, Sundays, Bank Holiday Mondays and the following Tuesdays, 3 March to 31 October; noon to 4pm, Sundays, 4 November to 16 December
Admission fee Adults £5.80

This is a modern reconstruction of a 17th-century, walled, town garden: neat box parterres, a nut walk and an arched pergola hung with clematis and vines. The plantings are all of the period, including the fruit trees: quietly inspirational.
topiary; snowdrops; herbs; current holder of Sandford Award; gift shop; tea room

Owned by The National Trust
Number of gardeners 1 part-time
Size 0.4ha (1 acre)

OULTON HOUSE
Oulton, Stone ST15 8UR

Tel 01785 813556 **Fax** 01785 816141
Location From Stone take Oulton Road and turn left after Oulton sign; 3rd driveway on right; steep, winding drive; house at top of hill
Opening hours By appointment, February to end of July
Admission fee Adults £3; children 75p

This three-acre garden has been made by Mrs Fairbairn over many years, essentially for private enjoyment, not for public display. It is full of good plants – roses, rhododendrons, geraniums and clematis – arranged in colour groupings. The snowdrops and hellebores are especially good early in the year, followed by more spring bulbs and a field of daffodils, but the high point comes

with the herbaceous borders and roses in June and July.
snowdrops; roses (mainly old-fashioned); rock garden; plants under glass; good herbaceous borders; hellebores; spring bulbs; plants for sale sometimes; teas

Owned by Mr and Mrs WA Fairbairn
Number of gardeners Owners, plus part-time help
Size 1.4ha (3 1/2 acres)

SHUGBOROUGH
Milford, Stafford ST17 0XB

Tel 01889 881388 **Fax** 01889 881323
www.shugborough.org.uk
Location On A513 from Stafford to Lichfield; signed from M6, Jct 13
Opening hours 11am to 5pm (last admissions 4.30pm), daily, 16 March to 26 October
Admission fee House and garden: adults £10; concessions £8; children £6; families £25

Shugborough has a classical landscape park with Longhorn cattle and some fine follies, notably the Chinese house and a classical summerhouse. The finest feature is a handsome William Andrews Nesfield terrace where clipped dumplings of golden yew are set off by lavish plantings of lavender and yellow floribunda roses – simple but very effective. Steps descend slowly to a sluggish tributary of the river Trent, where yellow water lilies bloom. Horticultural features include vast ancient wisterias on the stable block, a yew that claims to be the widest tree in Europe and masses of rhododendrons – the garden is probably at its best in late May. The walled garden was re-opened in 2006 and its bothy is worth exploring, but more needs to be done to bring them up to the same high standards of the rest of the estate.
majestic parkland; good herbaceous borders; topiary; current holder of Sandford Award; National Trust shop; licensed restaurant; tea rooms

Owned by The National Trust (managed by Staffordshire County Council)
Number of gardeners 4
Size 8.7ha (22 acres)
English Heritage Grade I

TRENTHAM GARDENS
Stone Road, Stoke-on-Trent ST4 8AX

Tel 01782 646646 **Fax** 01782 644536
www.trenthamleisure.co.uk
Location Signed from M6
Opening hours 10am to 6pm (closes at 4pm in winter; last admissions one hour before closing), daily, all year; closed 25 December
Admission fee Adults £6.50; OAPs £6; children £5.50

Visitors who remember the old Trentham gardens are in for a shock. The scale of the new garden centre and Trentham village shopping complex befits a new Jerusalem. The entrance is no longer where it should be, by the site of the Duke of Sutherland's now demolished mansion, though the latest news is that the mansion itself will shortly be rebuilt to Sir Charles Barry's original designs. Instead, you have to negotiate your way through the shopping complex and enter the gardens from the side, by the lake. Tom Stuart-Smith and Piet Oudolf have replanted the entire Italian garden with grasses and perennials on a massive scale. At the moment, the effects are stunning – a model of how to employ the 'new planting' in a historic setting – but it is too early to know whether the garden will live up to its early promise. Perennials and grasses all grow at different rates and this sort of gardening requires very careful management and maintenance if it is not to degenerate into a complete mess in a few years' time. But the fountains are still there, and working well now, and Portuguese laurels in Versailles cases flank the avenue down to the statue of Perseus. Meanwhile, a new seven-acre

Trentham Gardens

garden designed by Piet Oudolf is due to open this year (2007).
important formal gardens; modern herbaceous plantings; shops; garden centre; tea room

Owned by Trentham Leisure Ltd
Number of gardeners 16
English Heritage Grade II*

WESTON PARK
Weston-under-Lizard, Shifnal TF11 8LE

Tel 01952 852100 **Fax** 01952 850430
www.weston-park.com
Location On A5
Opening hours 11am to 6.30pm (last admissions 5pm), Saturdays and Sundays from 21 April to 2 September; but daily 1 to 15 April, 26 May to 1 June and throughout July and August; closed 28 July and 16 to 23 August; open 7 May
Admission fee Adults £4.50; OAPs £3.50; children £2.50

Weston has a fine 18th-century landscape (Capability Brown worked there) and a 19th-century Italianate parterre, a temple of Diana, a grotto called Pendrill's Cave, and a handsome orangery by James Paine. It is not of major horticultural interest, but the rose walk and rhododendrons are worth seeing. It is perhaps best for its fine collection of trees, some of them record-breakers, and the collection of *Nothofagus* planted by the late Lord Bradford.
fine collection of trees; landscaped park; rhododendrons; gift shop; restaurant

Owned by The Weston Park Foundation
Number of gardeners 3
English Heritage Grade II*

SUFFOLK

Suffolk has comparatively few historic gardens of national importance but, such as they are, they are of great interest to the garden lover. Both Helmingham and Shrubland are rated as Grade I gardens, while Euston, Ickworth and Somerleyton are all Grade II*. Shrubland was sold last year (2006), but is expected to reopen as a hotel later this year or in 2008. There is a particularly fine collection of trees at East Bergholt Place, which has a good nursery attached. Suffolk is a rich county but was, until recently, rather cut off from London and its markets, which may help in part to explain why it has so many good nurseries. Notcutts is one of the largest quality nurseries in the country, with a long and distinguished history of plant introductions and exhibits at RHS Flower Shows. The leading seedsmen Thompson & Morgan have been at Ipswich for over 100 years: their trial-grounds may also be visited in season. But it is the sheer number of good small, modern nurseries which is so surprising: we list Park Green and Rougham Hall among others – but Gardiner's Hall Plants at Braiseworth (over 3,000 different plants) and North Green Snowdrops (sent 'in the green') are also worth knowing. Suffolk has many good modern gardens like Wyken Hall and others that we do not list. The National Garden Scheme does well in the county and the Suffolk Gardens Trust is an active organisation. The NCCPG is represented by about a dozen National Collections, including some horticulturally important genera like lilacs (*Syringa*), delphiniums and fuchsias. Otley College near Ipswich is a RHS Partner College, with lectures, workshops and garden walks throughout the year: further details from 020 7821 3408.

BLAKENHAM WOODLAND GARDEN

Little Blakenham, Ipswich IP8 4LZ

Tel 07760 342131 **Fax** 0207 730 1902
Location 4 miles north-west of Ipswich
Opening hours 10am to 5pm, daily, March to July
Admission fee Adults £3; children £1.50

Ⓟ ♿

In the 1960s, the late Lord Blakenham, Treasurer of the RHS, planted up this woodland of ancient oak and hazel coppice with rhododendrons, azaleas, magnolias and flowering trees and shrubs. When his son took over the development of the garden in 1982, the present Lady Blakenham intensified the plantings and added her own features and installations. Best of all is the spiralling grassy arena, circling down to a chalky bottom, a wonderfully fluid and exciting addition. Visit it in bluebell time, when the combination of natural beauty and artistic genius is most alluring.
rhododendrons; bluebells

Owned by Blakenham Woodland Garden Ltd
Number of gardeners 2
Size 2.4ha (6 acres)

EAST BERGHOLT PLACE

East Bergholt CO7 6UP

Tel/fax 01206 299224
Location 2 miles east of A12, on B1070, east-north-east of East Bergholt
Opening hours 10am to 5pm, daily, March to October; closed Easter Sunday
Admission fee Adults £3; children free; RHS members free except on Sundays

Ⓟ 👪 ♿ ✿

East Bergholt has a wonderful woodland garden (best in spring) planted by Charles Eley, the present owner's great-grandfather, at the start of the 20th century. It is the home of *Malus* x *purpurea* 'Eleyi' and has been called a 'Cornish Garden in Suffolk'. Of greatest interest is a collection of trees known as the 'Swale', around a gentle valley with a small brook running down the middle. Many of the older trees and shrubs were grown from original collections by George Forrest: others represent modern plantings and replantings. The collection is well labelled and well maintained – a fine place to see a wide range of trees and shrubs. Good specimens include a very handsome variegated cherry laurel *Prunus laurocerasus* 'Castlewellan' 5m (16ft) high, a magnificent *Quercus castaneifolia* and a fine three-stemmed *Davidia involucrata* var. *vilmoriniana*. Some are record-breakers, including a *Lithocarpus densiflorus* 12m (39ft) tall. The valley is sheltered by hedges of holly and yew and a mature collection of hardy rhododendrons. And it is good for insects and wildlife, too. Restoration and replanting continue. There will be two RHS Special Events at East Bergholt Place in 2007; details from 020 7821 3408.

topiary; rhododendrons and azaleas; camellias; fine collection of trees; specialist plant centre in walled garden

Owned by Mr and Mrs Rupert Eley
Number of gardeners 2
Size 6ha (15 acres)
NCCPG National Collections *Euonymus* (deciduous)

EUSTON HALL

Euston, Thetford IP24 2QP

Tel 01842 766366 **Fax** 01842 766764
www.eustonhall.co.uk
Location On A1088 3 miles south of Thetford and 12 miles north of Bury St Edmunds
Opening hours 2.30pm to 5pm, Thursdays, 14 June to 13 September; plus 24 June, 15 July and 2 September
Admission fee £3

P 🚻 ♿

The classical 18th-century landscaping at Euston is very beautiful. William Kent made the serpentine lake, though it was later modified by Capability Brown. Kent also built the elegant banqueting house. There are avenues of beech and lime, and clumps, spinneys and belts of mature trees. The formal terraces by the house lead to herbaceous borders and rose gardens. It all adds up to a most satisfying composition,

Euston Hall gardens

where horticulture plays second fiddle to landscaping.

roses (mainly old-fashioned); William Kent temple and summerhouse; new 'Monet' bridge on lake; river walk and watermill; craft shop; home-made teas

Owned by The Duke of Grafton
Number of gardeners 2
Size 28ha (70 acres)
English Heritage Grade II*

GLEMHAM HALL

Little Glemham, Woodbridge IP13 0BT

Tel 01728 748289
www.glemhamhall.co.uk
Location Signed from A12 between Woodbridge and Saxmundham
Opening hours For NGS, and by appointment
Admission fee Adults £3.50

P 🚻 ♿

Humphry Repton had a hand in the park at Glemham, but the horticultural interest is all fairly recent. The owners have remade the garden completely since they took over in 1994. Perhaps the best features are a David Austin rose garden with some 450 plants and the herbaceous borders which have been planted to create colour effects. The orchard and bulky old yew hedges also contribute much to the pleasure of a visit.

teas on NGS days

Owned by Mr and Mrs Philip Hope-Cobbold
Number of gardeners 2
Size 1.2ha (3 acres), plus parkland

HARVEYS GARDEN PLANTS

Great Green, Thurston,
Bury St Edmunds IP31 3SJ

Tel/fax 01359 233363
www.harveysgardenplants.co.uk
Location In middle of Great Green, on road between Thurston and Norton
Opening hours 9.30am to 4.30pm, Tuesday to Saturday, 11 January to 31 December
Admission fee Free

(P)

Harveys Garden Plants is a family-run nursery and grows an extensive range of hardy herbaceous plants. It specialises in unusual perennials, particularly those not commonly found in garden centres. The specialities include hellebores, snowdrops, heleniums and shade-loving and woodland plants. New display borders and a woodland area are promised for this year (2007). There will be six RHS Special Events at Harveys Garden Plants in 2007; details from 020 7821 3408.

Korean chrysanthemums; excellent specialist nursery; refreshments (Thursday to Saturday); new visitor centre

Owned by Roger and Teresa Harvey
Size 4ha (10 acres)

HAUGHLEY PARK

Stowmarket IP14 3JY

Tel 01359 240701 **Fax** 01359 243001
www.haughleyparkbarn.co.uk
Location Signed Haughley Park (*not* Haughley) from A14
Opening hours 2pm to 5.30pm, Tuesdays, May to September, plus 29 April and 6 May ('bluebell Sundays')
Admission fee Adults £3; children free

Haughley has a Grade I Jacobean mansion with well-kept modern flower gardens and fine trees set in a natural landscape. On the main lawn is a magnolia, probably *Magnolia denudata*, 8m (26ft) high and 11m (36ft) across and, beside it, the largest oak in Suffolk with a trunk girth of over 9m (30ft). In the walled garden are vegetables, trained fruit trees, a rose arbour and other ornamental

features. In 2006, a new lawn was laid out near the restored 17th-century barn, on which are displayed four astounding stacked-glass sculptures by the American artist Danny Lane. In the woodland garden, the lily-of-the-valley and acres of bluebells (special Sunday openings) are worth the journey, no matter how far. There is a choice of three woodland walks, from 1½ to 2½ miles long: the camellias are good in May and the rhododendrons in June. On the long walk, through West Woods, it is interesting to see the progress of different ways of regenerating those parts damaged by the great gale of 1987. Some areas were clear felled and replanted, some cut as coppice wood and some left to regenerate naturally.

woodland garden; rhododendrons and azaleas; good herbaceous borders; bluebells; lily-of-the-valley; 1,000-year-old oak with 9.15m (30ft) girth; teas on Sunday openings

Owned by Robert Williams
Number of gardeners 3
Size 3.2ha (8 acres), plus 105ha (265 acres) of park and woods

ICKWORTH

Horringer, Bury St Edmunds IP29 5QE

Tel 01284 735270 **Fax** 01284 735175
www.nationaltrust.org.uk/ickworth
Location 3 miles south-west of Bury St Edmunds
Opening hours 10am to 5pm, Friday to Tuesday, 20 March to 1 October; 11am to 4pm, Friday to Tuesday, 2 October to 18 March 2007; open daily during half-term holidays, Easter holidays and summer holidays (24 July to 3 September); closed 25 December
Admission fee Adults £3.40; children 90p

HELMINGHAM HALL

Stowmarket IP14 6EF

Tel 01473 890799 **Fax** 01473 890776
www.helmingham.com
Location 9 miles north of Ipswich on B1077
Opening hours 2pm to 6pm, Wednesdays and Sundays, 6 May to 16 September; 10am to 4pm on 27 May
Admission fee Adults £4.50; concessions £4; children £2.50

A visit to Helmingham is a step back into history, to a time of ancient certainties, order and peace. The Tollemaches have lived here since 1487. The house is a moated manor, half-timbered when built in 1480, but given a cladding of bricks and tiles in the 18th century. It is set in the most spacious 400-acre deer park, loosely studded with vast centennial oaks grown to their full spread. Helmingham's formal garden lies beyond the moat to the south of the house. It is surrounded by 60 hybrid musks, lightly pruned and allowed to billow out, to fill the beds. The entire garden, about 100m (328ft) long, is edged with 'Hidcote' lavender, underplanted with variegated London pride, and complemented by *Campanula lactiflora*, alstroemerias, foxgloves and peonies. This is gardening on a large scale, and makes its impact through simplicity and repetition: it is immensely grand. Beyond the formal garden is the walled garden proper, built of brick in 1745. On either side of the central grassy path runs a broad and stately double herbaceous border, perhaps 120m (394ft) long. Climbing roses are tied to straining wires all along its back: they include 'Guinée', 'Long John Silver', and *Rosa multiflora* var. *cathayensis*. The roses are underplanted with herbaceous plantings chosen to blend with the soft colours of the roses: pinks, blues, mauves, whites and the palest of creamy-yellows. Not until the main rose-flowering has finished in mid-August do yellows, bronzes, oranges and reds come to the fore. A spring border runs the whole way along one of the outer walls of the walled garden and is planted mainly with irises, tulips and peonies, backed by more climbing roses, vines, clematis, chaenomeles, ceanothus and myrtle from Queen Victoria's wedding posy. Nearer the house is a new series of knot gardens planted in 1982, which look as if they have been here for hundreds of years. The knots include the Tollemaches' heraldic device, a fret or interlacing pattern of bands, which has been made to interweave by pruning the strips of box at different levels. It leads to another rose garden: albas and species roses, centifolias and mosses, a large choice of gallicas and so on, underplanted with spring bulbs, white foxgloves, *Campanula persicifolia*, *Alchemilla mollis*, purple violas and geraniums. One reason why the garden is so successful is that the roses and their companion plantings all fall within a narrow colour range: it is a discipline from which every garden owner can learn. But everything here is carefully thought through and controlled: you see this firmness again in the immaculately edged lawns and weedless borders. Everywhere at Helmingham order prevails over anarchy.

roses (mainly old-fashioned); good herbaceous borders; deer park; moat; fine walled garden; good parterres and knots; shop; tea room

Owned by Lord Tollemache
Number of gardeners 3 full-time, 1 part-time
Size 4ha (10 acres)
English Heritage Grade I

Ickworth is an extraordinary garden for an extraordinary house: both were influenced by Italy. The main borders follow the curves of the house. There is also an Italian garden with Mediterranean plants and long vistas in the park. Capability Brown had a hand in it. Please note that parts may be closed off from time to time for essential work.
autumn colour; Italian garden; Victorian 'stumpery'; display of lemon trees in orangery; tallest *Quercus pubescens* (29m; 95ft) in the British Isles; National Trust shop; large, self-service restaurant

Owned by The National Trust
Number of gardeners 5, plus a trainee
Size 28ha (70 acres)
NCCPG National Collections *Buxus*
English Heritage Grade II*

MAGNOLIA HOUSE

Yoxford, Saxmundham IP17 3EP

Tel 01728 668321
Location In centre of village on B1120
Opening hours For NGS: 2pm to 5.30pm, 17 June; and by appointment
Admission fee Adults £3

Mark Rumary has been one of England's leading designers and landscapers for many years. His garden is a masterly example of how to plan and plant a small garden to make it seem much larger than it really is. He also has the knack of knowing when and how to renew it so that it always looks fresh and controlled. The design is tight, with small, enclosed features, like a Moorish pool, and a profusion of pots to supply interest throughout the year. Scent and form are important to him, and a sense of maturity comes from an ancient mulberry tree and a *Magnolia* x *loebneri* that he planted himself nearly 40 years ago.
tea and biscuits

Owned by Mark Rumary
Number of gardeners Owner only

PARK GREEN NURSERIES

Wetheringsett, Stowmarket IP14 5QH

Tel 01728 860139 **Fax** 01728 861277
www.parkgreen.co.uk
Location 6 miles north-east of Stowmarket
Opening hours 10am to 4pm, Monday to Saturday, 1 March to 30 September; groups welcome by appointment
Admission fee Free

This excellent nursery specialises in hostas. It stocks over 200 different cultivars and introduces new ones every year. Recent home-raised releases include *Hosta* 'Delia', *H.* 'Fran Godfrey', *H.* 'Sarah Kennedy', *H.* 'Gay Search' and *H.* 'Royal Golden Jubilee'. A very large number can be seen in the demonstration beds. It also stocks a wide range of ornamental grasses and hardy perennials. Park Green Nurseries will host two RHS Special Events in 2007, on 24 May and 21 June; details from 020 7821 3408.
light refreshments

Owned by Richard and Mary Ford

ROUGHAM HALL NURSERIES

A14 Rougham, Bury St Edmunds IP30 9LZ

Tel 0800 970 7516 **Fax** 01359 271149
www.roughamhallnurseries.co.uk
Location Off the west-bound carriageway of the A14; signed from new junction
Opening hours 10am to 4pm, daily, all year, except Christmas to New Year

Rougham Hall Nurseries – always very popular when they come to RHS Flower Shows – are breeders, introducers and growers of an extensive and interesting range of perennials. Their selection of asters is particularly good, as is their list of delphiniums, of which they have a National Collection. Their other National Collection is of gooseberries: they have by far the most extensive list anywhere in the world. The whole history of this most highly prized of dessert fruits is contained within the hundreds of cultivars which they list. The range is always increasing, too: it is worthwhile enquiring if they do not appear to have one that you are looking for. Rougham Hall Nurseries will be hosting two RHS Special Events during 2007; details from 020 7821 3408.

Owned by K Harbutt
Size 2ha (5 acres)
NCCPG National Collections *Delphinium*; *Ribes grossularia* (gooseberries)

SOMERLEYTON HALL

Somerleyton, Lowestoft NR32 5QQ

Tel 01502 730224 **Fax** 01502 732143
www.somerleyton.co.uk
Location 4 miles north-west of Lowestoft on B1074
Opening hours 10am to 5pm, Thursdays, Sundays and Bank Holidays, plus Tuesdays and Wednesdays in July and August, 1 April to 28 October
Admission fee Adults £4.75; OAPs £3.75; children £2.75

Somerleyton is a splendid place to visit: there is much for the garden and plant lover to see and enjoy. In front of the house (palatial, Victorian) is an extremely grand formal garden. William Andrews Nesfield laid out the terraces and the yew maze, which was planted in 1846: it is not too difficult to get to the centre, which is less than 400m (1,312ft) from the entrance. The gardens are full of topiary and good statuary, including a great equatorial sundial, encircled by signs of the zodiac. Near the house are quantities of roses, herbaceous borders and seasonal bedding. Further afield are large plantings of rhododendrons and azaleas. Though none is actually a record-breaker, Somerleyton has some very fine specimen trees, including a giant redwood (*Sequoiadendron giganteum*), *Eucalyptus gunnii*, Monterey pine (*Pinus radiata*), Atlas cedar (*Cedrus atlantica*) and a particularly good maidenhair tree (*Ginkgo biloba*). There has been much replanting since the hurricane of 1987 and the new plantings are already making quite an impact. The walled garden was once the kitchen garden but is now planted with flowers: on the walls are many different climbers including roses, clematis, figs, climbing hydrangeas and such wall shrubs as *Hoheria sexstylosa*. The glasshouses and peach cases were designed by Sir Joseph Paxton, architect of the Crystal Palace, with his characteristic ridge-and-furrow roofs. They are now planted with tender ornamentals like Meyer's lemon, abutilons, *Cassia* (*Senna*) *corymbosa* and the sweetly-scented *Dregea sinensis*. An old boiler house has a collection of old garden equipment in it. Other good features include an elegant, long, metal pergola with lots of different wisterias and a young avenue of lime trees along the driveway, planted in 1981. The whole estate is well kept and well run for visitors' enjoyment.
roses (mainly modern); plants under glass; maze; new bamboo bed; fine statues; magnificent trees; pergola; formal garden; walled garden; souvenir gift shop; tea room for light lunches and teas

Owned by The Hon Hugh Crossley
Number of gardeners 3
Size 5ha (12½ acres)
English Heritage Grade II*

WHITE HALL PLANTS

Southolt Road, Worlingworth IP13 7HW

Tel 01728 628490 **Fax** 01728 628160
Location Follow brown tourist signs on A1120 from Earl Soham
Opening hours 10am to 5pm, Thursday to Sunday, Easter to October
Admission fee Free

There are stock beds and sale displays for over 2,000 different plants in this excellent nursery. There are good numbers of heucheras, ligularias, dicentras, grasses, salvias, penstemons, lilies, hellebores, foxgloves, cardamines and epimediums – and much else besides.
excellent plantsman's nursery

Owned by Charles Walker
Number of gardeners 3
Size 1.2ha (3 acres)

WYKEN HALL

Stanton, Bury St Edmunds IP31 2DW

Tel 01359 250287 **Fax** 01359 253420
Location 9 miles north-east from Bury St Edmunds; follow brown tourist signs from A143 at Ixworth to Wyken Vineyards
Opening hours 2pm to 6pm, Sunday to Friday, 1 April to 1 October; for NGS: 12 and 13 May
Admission fee Adults £3; OAPs £2.50; children free; RHS members free

The garden at Wyken is ingeniously designed: a series of old-style gardens to complement the Elizabethan house. These include a knot garden, a herb garden, a traditional English kitchen garden, wildflower meadows, a nuttery and a copper beech maze. All are in scale with the house and the farmland around. Stylish and well maintained, this is one of the best modern private gardens in the country. The restaurant features in the *Good Food Guide*. The 'Giant Stride' (a sort of revolving maypole) was added to commemorate the millennium.

woodland garden; roses (ancient and modern); plantsman's collection of plants; herbs; fruit; good shrubs; good herbaceous borders; award-winning seven-acre vineyard; country store shop; lunches and teas at excellent Vineyard Restaurant

Owned by Sir Kenneth and Lady Carlisle
Number of gardeners 2
Size 1.6ha (4 acres)

SURREY

A Martian could be excused for thinking that Surrey was the centre of the horticultural universe. It is the county with everything that gardeners could ever want. Its six Grade I gardens include two very important landscapes – Claremont and Painshill – and two highly influential 20th-century gardens – Munstead Wood and the Savill Garden. Because of its closeness to London, it has become a very rich county during the last 100 years, which means that people have the time and money to garden on a large scale. The National Gardens Scheme does extremely well in Surrey, with a large number of medium-sized gardens opening for charity, as well as a handful of intensely-cultivated smaller gardens. It is the county where the National Gardens Scheme has its headquarters. Surrey has many of the country's best known nurseries – the light soils being poor for agriculture but excellent for growing plants: the floral mile along the A30 is a famous landmark, where some of the trees and shrubs in the old Waterer nurseries have grown to exceptional size. There are good trees – and many record-breakers – at Winkworth Arboretum, the Savill Garden and the RHS Garden Wisley. Surrey still has a large number of first-class nurseries. Those that we do not have space to list but which are well worth visiting include Secretts near Godalming and Lincluden at Bisley. The Surrey Gardens Trust and the Surrey Group of the NCCPG are both very active in the county: the NCCPG has its base at Wisley. There are some 35 National Collections in Surrey, including seven at Wisley and nine at the Savill Garden. And of course, the Royal Horticultural Society's own flagship garden at Wisley dominates every aspect of gardens and gardening in the county: as many as 20 per cent of the Society's members live in Surrey.

CADENZA

Butterfly Walk, Warlingham CR6 9JA

Tel 01883 623565
Location M25, Jct 6; A22 northbound for 4 miles; fourth exit at large roundabout; uphill and turn right
Opening hours By appointment only, at most times
Admission fee Free

This is the private garden of keen plantsmen. Their special interest is small bulbs, and they have one of England's most interesting collections of hardy cyclamen and *Fritillaria* species. Frames and greenhouses extend the range of what is grown. An education and an inspiration.
cyclamen; fritillaries; bulbs

Owned by Mr and Mrs Ronald Frank
Number of gardeners Part-time help
Size 0.3ha (3/4 acre)

CLANDON PARK

West Clandon, Guildford GU4 7RQ

Tel 01483 222482 **Fax** 01483 223479
www.nationaltrust.org.uk/clandonpark
Location Off A247 at West Clandon
Opening hours 11am to 5pm, Tuesdays to Thursdays and Sundays, 18 March to 28 October
Admission fee House and garden: adults £7.20; children £3.60; no garden only prices

Capability Brown's magnificent mature beeches are now underplanted with sombre Victorian shrubberies and slabs of comfrey, bergenias and *Geranium macrorrhizum* – the apotheosis of National Trust groundcover. There is a modern pastiche of a Dutch garden at the east end of the grounds but the daffodils in spring are breathtaking. A recent addition are several dicksonias, fresh from the New Zealand garden at Chelsea in 2004. Unfortunately, the National

Trust no longer sells garden only tickets, and £6.50 is expensive for what the garden offers.
parterres; grotto; Dutch garden; Maori meeting house; Clandon Park Garden Centre is nearby; restaurant; shop

Owned by The National Trust
Number of gardeners 1
Size 3.8ha (9 1/2 acres)
English Heritage Grade II

CLAREMONT LANDSCAPE GARDEN
Portsmouth Road, Esher KT10 9JG

Tel 01372 467806 **Fax** 01372 476420
www.nationaltrust.org.uk/claremont
Location On southern edge of town (A307)
Opening hours 10am to 6pm (but dusk from November to March and 6pm or sunset if earlier on Saturdays, Sundays and Bank Holiday Mondays, from April to October), daily, all year, but closed on Mondays from November to March; closed on 25 December and at 4pm on Thursday 19 July
Admission fee Adults £5.60; children £2.80

P 🚻 ♿
This vast historic landscape – now much reduced – was worked over by Vanbrugh, Bridgeman, Kent and Capability Brown and has been energetically restored in recent years. The elegant green theatre is best seen flanked by spreading cedars from across the dark lake. Very popular locally, it is apt to get crowded at summer weekends.
laurel lawns; tallest service tree *Sorbus domestica* (23m; 75ft) in the British Isles, and two further record trees; shop; tea room

Owned by The National Trust
Number of gardeners 3, plus volunteers
Size 19.6ha (49 acres)
English Heritage Grade I

GREAT FOSTERS
Stroude Road, Egham TW20 9UR

Tel 01784 433822 **Fax** 01784 472455
www.greatfosters.co.uk
Location 2 miles south of Egham
Opening hours For hotel guests: dawn to dusk, daily, all year; and by appointment
Admission fee By arrangement

P 🚻 ♿
The Tudor royal hunting lodge is now a luxury hotel, and its gardens are among England's most immaculately maintained. No other formal garden can claim to be surrounded on three sides by a Saxon moat populated by black swans. It was designed by Romaine-Walker in 1918 and its mature yew hedges and topiary are regularly filled with seasonal bedding plants. Elsewhere are a large lake, a rose garden, a Japanese-style bridge (complete with wisteria) and an awesome modern amphitheatre designed by Kim Wilkie.
topiary; restaurant

Owned by The Sutcliffe family
Number of gardeners 5
Size 20ha (50 acres)
English Heritage Grade II*

HANNAH PESCHAR SCULPTURE GARDEN
Black and White Cottage, Standon Lane, Ockley RH5 5QR

Tel 01306 627269 **Fax** 01306 627662
www.hannahpescharsculpture.com
Location Turn off A29 down Cathill Lane, left at T-junction, over bridge and entrance is 400 yards on right
Opening hours 11am to 6pm, Fridays and Saturdays, 2pm to 5pm, Sundays and Bank Holidays, May to October; and by appointment
Admission fee Adults £9; concessions £7; children £6

P 🚻 ♿
The lush water garden and woodlands surrounding a black and white cottage are the setting for this remarkable and ever-changing collection, mainly of contemporary British sculpture. The water garden has been revamped by Anthony Paul with lots of architectural plants. There are pools and a stream, and surprisingly few flowers, but lots of contrasts of light and shade. The background is more important for sculpture than any transient colour. An earlier owner was the distinguished horticulturist Dick Trotter,

Mr Bowles's 'nephew Dick' and sometime Treasurer of the RHS.
sculptures; water; glass

Owned by Hannah Peschar
Number of gardeners 2 part-time
Size 4ha (10 acres)

HATCHLANDS PARK
East Clandon, Guildford GU4 7RT

Tel 01483 222482 **Fax** 01483 223176
www.nationaltrust.org.uk/hatchlands
Location Off A246 Guildford to Leatherhead
Opening hours House: 2pm to 5.30pm, Tuesday to Thursday, Sundays and Bank Holiday Mondays, April to October; also Fridays in August; park walks: 11am to 6pm, daily, April to October
Admission fee Park walks: adults £3.30; children £1.70

Apart from the Jekyll garden (roses, lupins, box and columbines) Hatchlands is an 18th-century landscape with parkland. Four marked ways include a magnificent bluebell wood. The garden buildings are charming and the National Trust has made some progress with restoration and replanting.
woodland garden; National Trust
shop; restaurant

Owned by The National Trust
Number of gardeners 2
Size 180ha (450 acres) of parkland

HERONS BONSAI LTD
Wire Mill Lane, Newchapel, Lingfield RH7 6HJ

Tel 01342 832657
www.herons.co.uk
Location Turn left off the A22, 1/4 mile south of junction with B2028
Opening hours 9.30am to 5.30pm, Monday to Saturday; 10.30am to 4.30pm on Sundays; closes at dusk in winter months
Admission fee £1 donation to charity; nursery free

This bonsai nursery has a string of gold medals behind it from Chelsea Flower Shows. As well as trees for indoors and outdoors, there are ornaments, pots, tools and accessories (retail and wholesale). The Chans are recognised experts and donated the bonsai collection and Japanese garden at RHS Garden Wisley. They run bonsai classes and offer Japanese garden design. The whole nursery is landscaped in the Japanese style, with several examples of different types of Japanese gardens.

Owned by Peter and Dawn Chan
Number of gardeners 3
Size 3ha (7 1/2 acres)

HYDON NURSERIES
Clock Barn Lane, Hydon Heath, Godalming GU8 4AZ

Tel 01483 860252 **Fax** 01483 419937
Location 2 miles east of A3, Milford exit; near Cheshire Home
Opening hours 8.30am to 5pm (4pm in winter), Monday to Friday; plus Saturdays 9.30am to 12.45pm (5pm from 1 March to 15 June and from late September to October); Sundays by appointment; closed for lunch 12.45pm to 2pm; conducted tours for small groups by prior appointment
Admission fee Free; parties by arrangement

These rhododendron and azalea specialists have an extensive range of all classes, including some tender species and their own hybrids of *Rhododendron yakushimanum* and others. They have a comprehensive stock of evergreen azaleas, including 36 of the Wilson Kurume azaleas. They also sell trees and shrubs that combine well with rhododendrons and azaleas, especially camellias (another speciality – 100+ cultivars). The nursery extends over 25 acres: among the many fine trees are five large specimens of the dark pink form of *Magnolia campbellii* and fine mature *Nothofagus dombeyi* and *N. antarctica*, as well as the two record-breakers. Visitors are particularly welcome to see the magnolias in early spring; the gardens (not suitable for wheelchairs) are at their best between mid-March and June and there is an annual sale of plants during March.

rhododendrons and azaleas; tallest *Eucalyptus pauciflora* subsp. *niphophila* and *Sorbus* 'Joseph Rock' in the British Isles

Number of gardeners 5
Size 10ha (25 acres)

LOSELEY PARK
Guildford GU3 1HS

Tel 01483 304440 **Fax** 01483 302036
www.loseley-park.com
Location Off B3000 at Compton, south of Guildford
Opening hours 11am to 5pm, Tuesday to Sunday, 1 May to 30 September; plus Bank Holiday Mondays in May and August
Admission fee Adults £4; OAPs £3.50; children £2; RHS members free in May and September, except on NGS days and during special events

The walled garden attached to this fine Elizabethan house has recently been re-made and replanted in the Jekyll style, with 1,000 old-fashioned roses framed by long, low, box hedges. Other good features include a herb garden, a fruit and flower garden, a fountain garden (planted in cream, white and silver), a cut-flower garden, an organic vegetable garden and a new wildflower meadow. There will be several RHS Special Events at Loseley Park in 2007; details from 020 7821 3408.
roses (mainly old-fashioned); herbs; fruit; lakeside walk; gift shop; courtyard tea room; restaurant

Owned by Michael More-Molyneux
Number of gardeners 3
Size 1ha (2 1/2 acres)

MILLAIS NURSERIES
Crosswater Farm, Crosswater Lane, Churt, Farnham GU10 2JN

Tel 01252 792698 **Fax** 01252 792526
www.rhododendrons.co.uk
Location Off Jumps Road, 1/2 mile north of Churt village
Opening hours Nursery: 10am to 1pm and 2pm to 5pm, Monday to Friday; also Saturdays in spring and autumn; and daily in May; garden: mid-April to early June
Admission fee Garden: £3; nursery: free

This important and dynamic rhododendron and azalea nursery has an extensive range of species and hybrids, including some new Himalayan species, late-flowering cultivars chosen to avoid the frost, large-leaved species for sheltered gardens, scented deciduous azaleas, *R. yakushimanum* hybrids for the smaller garden, dwarf cultivars for the rock garden and Maddenia series rhododendrons for the conservatory. The six-acre garden (ponds, stream and companion plantings) has an extensive collection of new magnolias and acers. There is also a trials garden where hundreds of new cultivars from around the world are labelled and tested.
rhododendrons; sorbus; tea and coffee

Owned by The Millais family
Size 2.4ha (6 acres)

MUNSTEAD WOOD
Heath Lane, Busbridge, Godalming GU7 1UN

Tel 01483 417867 **Fax** 01483 425041
Location 1 mile south of Godalming on B2130: turn along Heath Lane; parking in field 300 yards along on left
Opening hours 2pm to 6pm, 22 April, 27 May and 1 July
Admission fee Adults £3; OAPs £1.50; children free

Munstead Wood is important for being Gertrude Jekyll's own garden. Here she worked out the principles she expounded in her best-known books *Wood and Garden* (1899) and *Colour in the Flower Garden* (1908). Her garden has now been split into several smaller holdings, each in separate ownership, but the main parts are still attached to the house which Lutyens designed in 1896. The

Painshill Park

wood garden is fairly intact: the views up and down its main path to and from the lawn in front of the house seem just as they were a hundred years ago: birches underplanted mainly with rhododendrons and azaleas. Closer to the house is a block of borders full of good plantings – herbaceous plants, in particular. The nut walk and its nearby borders have recently been replanted: the Clarks have spent many years restoring the garden – and the results are admirable.

woodland garden; roses (mainly old-fashioned); sunken rock garden; good herbaceous borders; rhododendrons and azaleas; spring garden; cream teas

Owned by Sir Robert and Lady Clark
Number of gardeners 2
Size 4ha (10 acres)
English Heritage Grade I

PAINSHILL PARK

Portsmouth Road, Cobham KT11 1JE

Tel 01932 868113 **Fax** 01932 868001
www.painshill.co.uk
Location Signed from M25, Jct 10 and A3
Opening hours 10.30am to 6pm (last admissions 4.30pm), daily, March to October; 11am to 4pm (last admissions 3pm), daily, November to February; closed 25 and 26 December
Admission fee Adults £6.60; concessions £5.80; children (under 16) £3.85

Charles Hamilton was the plantsman, painter and designer who created Painshill between 1738 and 1773, when he finally went bankrupt. His lasting achievement was to transform a barren heathland into ornamental pleasure grounds and parkland of dramatic beauty. A 14-acre lake is at the centre of the design: it offers a focus for the garden's most famous features, the white Gothic temple and the grotto, which is approached across a 'Chinese' bridge. Hamilton sought to provoke the greatest variety of moods: other features included a ruined abbey, a Turkish tent, a hermitage and a vineyard on a south-facing slope above the lake. Hamilton was a pioneer of the naturalistic landscape style, and very influential, but never a rich man: he leased Painshill from the Crown and had little to spend, which makes his achievement all the more remarkable. He was also a great plantsman,

RHS GARDEN WISLEY

Woking GU23 6QB

Tel 01483 224234 **Fax** 01483 211750
www.rhs.org.uk/gardens/wisley
Location M25, Jct 10; follow brown tourist signs
Opening hours 10am (but 9am at weekends and bank holidays) to 6pm, daily, all year, except Christmas Day; closes at 4.30pm from November to February; last admissions one hour before closing
Admission fee Adults £7.50; children £2; discounts for groups – telephone 01483 212307 or 212308; RHS members (plus one guest) free

Wisley is the most important horticultural demonstration garden in Europe – perhaps in the world. It has many incidents of great intrinsic value – the vast Pulhamite rock garden which fills an entire hillside, for example – but its true worth lies in its comprehensiveness: everything that a gardener could possibly want to see and learn from is here within its 240 acres. The only problem is its very size: Wisley is not a garden you could ever hope to get round properly in just a day, let alone a few hours. It is somewhere to explore over many visits at different times of the year, until the layout and the principal features become familiar and you learn where you should go to see what is good and instructive at the time of your visit. Sir Thomas Hanbury bought the Wisley estate and gave it to the Society in 1903 for 'the encouragement and improvement of the science and practice of horticulture in all its branches'. When the Society moved its experimental garden from Chiswick, Wisley was in a remote part of Surrey with no public transport to serve it. The move would not have been possible without the invention of the motor car: 6,000 Fellows (as members were then called) visited it during its first 12 months. Now more than 700,000 visitors come to the garden every year. Wisley was unashamedly a trials garden, where the Society practised the perfect cultivation of every type of plant that could be grown in the British Isles, from alpines to hothouse orchids, whether in the open ground or in artificial conditions. This was backed up – then, as now – by an important system of trials which grew, tested, examined and made awards to flowers, fruit and vegetables. Those trials remain one of the garden's most important activities. Wisley was, above all, conceived as a scientific garden: to this day, the main building which dominates the formal garden near the entrance is known as the Laboratory and contains scientific and administrative offices. Sir Simon Hornby, past-President of the RHS, describes Wisley as 'a garden to delight, instruct and inspire'. His assertion is true at every time of the year. For many visitors, the pulling power of Wisley is greatest in the short, dark days of winter. That is the time when such plants as cyclamen and narcissi fill the alpine pan house: there is always colour and interest here because suitable pots are brought from the growing-frames and plunged into its sandy benches specifically to maintain the display through every week of the year. In the landscaped alpine house, too, there is much of interest even in deep midwinter. Wisley really begins to come into its own in spring. The alpine meadow is the best of its kind anywhere in Britain: from about the middle of March onwards, for at least four weeks, it is completely carpeted with hoop-petticoat narcissi (forms of *N. bulbocodium*). In September, the same meadows are thick with autumn-flowering crocuses. Beyond them is the Pulhamite rock garden, constructed in 1911 to 1912, which is probably the finest in Britain. It does not provide the variety of habitats that more modern rock gardens offer, but it is a majestic and beautiful construction. It covers the whole hillside from the 'monocot border' (full of such plants as agapanthus, daylilies, amaryllis, nerines and kniphofias – best in late summer) at the top to the stream at the bottom of the valley, whose margins are thick with such plants as *Lobelia cardinalis* and lysichitons. Beyond is an area of light woodland where magnolias and tall rhododendrons give shelter to such woodlanders as meconopsis, hellebores and snowdrops and huge patches of candelabra primulas. By late spring, one of the best areas is Battleston Hill, the highest point in the

CLAY PERRY

gardens, where winding paths take you through a beautifully laid out woodland garden underplanted with rhododendrons, azaleas, magnolias and camellias. Crocuses in late winter, lilies in high summer and colchicums in autumn extend the season so that this is always an area of colour and interest. Here, and throughout the garden, are many unusual rare and interesting plants which add so much to the horticultural quality of Wisley. Also on Battleston Hill is a 'Mediterranean' garden, where an extensive collection of plants with a reputation for tenderness shows what can be grown successfully on light, well-drained soil when trees provide shelter and frost rolls away downhill. Wisley has a fine collection of roses, from rare species to the massed ranks of modern roses which fill the beds around the Bowes-Lyon Pavilion and in behind the mixed borders. Wisley is, in short, one of the best places in Britain to see roses of every sort, including some which are rare elsewhere in English gardens open to the public. The mixed borders also come into their own from midsummer onwards: there are two of them, and they face each other on either side of the broad, grass ride which leads up to Battleston Hill. These borders are 130m (427ft) long, backed by beech hedges and have a light framework of shrubs as a background for deep plantings of all the traditional perennials of the English herbaceous border. In contrast to the mixed borders are the new borders, designed by the Dutch plantsman Piet Oudolf, who has used the modern style of perennial planting. The borders, 147m (482ft) long and 11m (36ft) wide, are planted with over 16,000 perennials and grasses. The plants are chosen for their movement and colour and planted in diagonal 'rivers' across the borders, which gives a feeling of walking in a meadow. Wisley has many other areas dedicated to the cultivation and display of particular plants. The pinetum is one example – an under-visited area of stately conifers, some of them record-breakers and all of them interesting at every season. The heather garden in Howard's Field is another dedicated garden, a National Collection with probably the best collection of heathers in England. The fruit fields are a part of the garden that far too few venture into: over 1,400 cultivars of top, bush and soft fruit are grown here, including more than 670 apple cultivars. The Society has been associated with the cultivation of fruit ever since its foundation in 1804, and displays of Wisley fruit have long been a feature of RHS London shows. Wisley also has its formal gardens. These centre upon the long rectangular canal

continued on page 318

continued from page 317

newly relined in the winter of 2006-7 in front of the Laboratory and the walled gardens beyond. Designed by Geoffrey Jellicoe and Lanning Roper, the canal is a formal setting for water lilies while the walled enclosures have spectacular summer and winter bedding displays. Rare and tender climbers cover their walls. Formal in a different sense are the model gardens which seem to grow and develop every year. The first were model fruit gardens, which showed people how to grow a great variety of fruit (and grow it well) in a small area. Nearby are model vegetable gardens, now supplemented by many ornamental model gardens, which serve the same function – to show visitors what may be achieved in their own gardens. Each is full of design ideas on a realisable scale, reflecting changing styles and new techniques. Up by the Orchard Café, eight small gardens are under construction, aimed at young professionals who may be moving into new starter homes but whose interest in gardening is tempered by limited spare time at weekends. These gardens – six are already open – offer a dramatic choice of design, materials, features and planting styles.For many people, one of the most fascinating areas is the main Trials Field – over the brow of Battleston Hill and down towards the furthest boundary with the A3. This is where the RHS runs most of its trials (more than 50 every year, some short- and some long-term) on a very wide selection of annuals, perennials, shrubs, bulbs, fruit and vegetables. The permanent trials are conducted (among others) with border carnations, chrysanthemums, daffodils, dahlias, daylilies, delphiniums, garden pinks, irises and sweet peas. These trials continue from year to year with periodic replanting, at which time additions and removals are made. They are of exceptional interest to visitors and often of remarkable beauty. There can be few horticultural experiences more exciting than to walk through the

CLAY PERRY

massed ranks of thickly planted delphiniums or sweet peas that tower over you in July or August. Wisley is always changing. The biggest project at the moment is the Bicentenary Glasshouse, open for the first time in mid-June. It incorporates a learning-centre where a classroom, 'Growing Lab' and teaching garden will give hands-on experience of growing plants to visitors from primary school-age upwards. At 3,000 sq. metres, the Bicentenary Glasshouse is near the Piet Oudolf borders and is more than twice the size of the current display glasshouses. The 12m (39ft) high glasshouse will display plants from all five continents and visitors will be able to see them from a viewing platform. It incorporates several water features (waterfalls, rock cliffs, scree and still ponds) and is divided into three main planting zones – desert, tropical and temperate climates. Here, and throughout the garden, the RHS sets out to delight, instruct and inspire.

woodland garden; snowdrops; roses (ancient and modern); rock garden; plantsman's collection of plants; plants under glass; fruit; mature conifers; good herbaceous borders; fine collection of trees; heather garden; herb garden; horticultural trials; vegetable gardens; tallest *Ostrya virginiana* (15.5m; 51ft) in the British Isles and 25 further record trees; impressive book and gift shop; major plant centre; restaurant and café

Owned by The Royal Horticultural Society
Number of gardeners c.80
Size 96ha (240 acres)
NCCPG National Collections *Calluna vulgaris*; *Crocus*; *Daboecia*; *Epimedium*; *Erica*; *Galanthus*; *Rheum* (culinary)
English Heritage Grade II*

importing many new species from North America for his shrubberies. After 1948 the garden fell into dereliction, but it has now been meticulously restored – a historic landscape with a unique sequence of exquisite garden follies – simple, classical and very harmonious. And a splendid place for a winter walk.
'American' garden; grotto; Turkish tent; vineyard; tallest *Juniperus virginiana* (26m; 85ft) in the British Isles; gift shop; visitor centre; licensed tea room

Owned by Painshill Park Trust
Number of gardeners 4
Size 63ha (158 acres)
NCCPG National Collections Plants collected by John Bartram
English Heritage Grade I

PANTILES NURSERIES
Almners Road, Lyne, Chertsey KT16 0BJ

Tel 01932 872195 **Fax** 01923 874030
www.pantiles-nurseries.co.uk
Location 5 mins from M25 Jct 11
Opening hours 9am to 6pm (5pm in winter), Monday to Saturday, all year; plus 10.30am to 4.30pm on Sundays
Admission fee Free

The nursery specialises in semi-mature container-grown specimens up to 7m (23ft) high. It is popular with professionals and impatient amateurs alike – anyone, in fact, in search of that instant air of maturity which a large and well-grown tree can bring. The range of specimen trees and shrubs is very impressive and includes acers, liquidambars and magnolias, as well as large specimens of yew and box, cloud-pruned in the Japanese style.
large plants; tree ferns; aquatics

Size 4.4ha (11 acres)

POLESDEN LACEY
Great Bookham, Dorking RH5 6BD

Tel 01372 452048 **Fax** 01372 452023
www.nationaltrust.org.uk/polesdenlacey
Location Off A246 between Leatherhead and Guildford
Opening hours 11am to 5pm (4pm from November to February), daily, all year; closed 24 December to 2 January 2007
Admission fee Adults £6.50; children £3.20; families £16.20

Polesden Lacey is best for the long terraced walk, laid out by Sheridan, and the return through an Edwardian-style rose garden whose pergolas drip with rambling roses. But there is good walking around the whole estate and the Regency house has splendid views across its wooded valley.
snowdrops; roses of every kind; good herbaceous borders; lavender garden; large National Trust shop; self-service tea room

Owned by The National Trust
Number of gardeners 4, plus seasonal help
Size 12ha (30 acres)
English Heritage Grade II*

RAMSTER
Chiddingfold GU8 4SN

Tel 01428 654167 **Fax** 01428 658345
Location 1½ miles south of Chiddingfold on A283
Opening hours 10am to 5pm, daily, 6 April to 24 June; 11am to 4pm, 20, 21, 27 and 28 October for autumn colour; parties by appointment at other times
Admission fee Adults £4; children free

Ramster was first laid out in 1890, with help from a local nursery, Gauntletts of Chiddingfold, who were known for their interest in flowering shrubs and especially for Japanese plants and planting. From this original influence date the ornamental stone lanterns, the large plantings of bamboos, and the avenue of *Acer palmatum* var. *dissectum* seedlings, now over 100 years old. In 1922 the property was bought by Miranda Gunn's grandparents, Sir Henry and Lady Norman. Lady Norman was a keen gardener, the sister of the 2nd Lord Aberconway, who was President of the RHS. She had been brought up at Bodnant, where she imbibed the family's great love of rhododendrons: many of the plants at Ramster came from Bodnant, and some of the rhododendrons and azaleas are her own hybrids. Ramster is an

SAVILL GARDEN

Wick Lane, Englefield Green, Windsor TW20 0UU

Tel 01753 435544 **Fax** 01753 847536
www.theroyallandscape.co.uk
Location Off Wick Lane at Englefield Green, 3 miles west of Egham off A30 and 5 miles from Windsor
Opening hours 10am to 6pm (4.30pm from November to February), daily, except 25 and 26 December
Admission fee Adults £6.50; OAPs £6; groups (10+) £5.25 each; children (6 to 16) £3.25; families (2 adults and 2 children) £17 from March to October; children under 6 free

This is the finest woodland garden in England, developed since 1932 on an undulating site framed by deciduous trees. There are several gardens here, some formal, some informal, but all are seamlessly linked together. The woodlands contain unrivalled spring plantings with masses of camellias, rhododendrons, azaleas, maples and flowering dogwoods underplanted with subtle drifts of bulbs, ferns and herbaceous plants. Refurbishment of the bog garden has allowed the development of stunning associations of meconopsis, primulas, astilbes, hostas and wild narcissi. The primulas come in monospecific masses, from the earliest *P. rosea* and *P. denticulata* through to *P. florindae* in July and August. In high summer, the rose garden and set-piece double herbaceous borders are worth a long trip to see. The gravel garden is one of England's oldest and largest: parts have been replanted with a fine display of drought-tolerant plants and plants which benefit from the mulching effect of the gravel. Extensive and intelligent use is made of a wide range of summer perennials in the borders and in containers. The Golden Jubilee Garden has a formal structure, informal planting, and exquisite pastel shades. The New Zealand Garden was recently completely re-designed and replanted with many additional plants. By late summer the woods are filled with hydrangeas. Then the deciduous broad-leaved trees begin their autumn spectacle. From November to March the newly created winter beds display flowers, stems and berries in effective colour groupings. But there are many reasons to visit the garden at other times, such as the drifts of *Narcissus bulbocodium* in March and the floods of lysichitons in April. The raised beds, greenhouse and monocot border are each full of interest in due season.

roses (mainly modern); camellias; fine collection of trees; mahonias; magnificent late-summer borders; tallest silver birch *Betula pendula* (30m; 98ft) in the British Isles (and 13 other record trees); gift and plant shop; splendid new visitor centre; licensed restaurant

Owned by Crown Estate
Number of gardeners 12
Size 14ha (35 acres)
NCCPG National Collections *Ilex*; *Magnolia*; *Mahonia*; *Pernettya*; *Rhododendron* (species and Glenn Dale azaleas); ferns; dwarf and slow-growing conifers
English Heritage Grade I

important garden for rhododendrons and, in the part known as Ant Wood, the Gunns have been building up a comprehensive collection of the old Hardy Hybrids – over 200 plants. But the garden is full of other projects and developments: the bog garden has come together very quickly since it was planted in 1998, and there is a new Millennium Garden. The garden is maintained in such a way as to allow meadow grasses, wildflowers and orchids to flourish and flower later in the year, but Ramster is essentially a garden for spring and early summer.

mature woodland garden with rhododendrons, magnolias, camellias, azaleas; bluebells; largest *Euonymus europaeus* (6m; 20ft) in the British Isles; home-made teas in May and at weekends

Owned by Mr and Mrs Paul Gunn
Number of gardeners 1
Size 10ha (25 acres)

TITSEY PLACE
Oxted RH8 0SD

Tel 01273 407056 **Fax** 01273 478995
www.titsey.com
Location Off the B269 north of Limpsfield
Opening hours 1pm to 5pm, Wednesdays, Sundays and Bank Holiday Mondays, 9 May to 30 September; plus 9 April and 7 May; NGS days: 23 June, 21 July and 11 August
Admission fee Adults £2.50; children £1

The historic garden at Titsey has been well restored with advice from Elizabeth Banks since it first opened to the public in 1993. The layout is gardenesque and most of the plantings date from the middle of the 19th century. The large triple-trunked horse-chestnut (*Aesculus hippocastanum*) on the upper terrace dates from that time. The formal gardens are planted with roses (replanted in 2002) and herbaceous plants, while the old walled kitchen garden has been planted as an example of how fruit, vegetables and flowers were grown in Victorian times.

fine parkland

Owned by The Trustees of the Titsey Foundation
Number of gardeners 5
Size 5ha (12 1/2 acres)

VALE END
Albury, Guildford GU5 9BE

Tel/fax 01483 202296
www.ngs.org.uk
Location 500 yards west of Albury on A248
Opening hours 2pm to 5pm, 17 June and 11 July; 6pm to 8.30pm, 16 June (music); groups by arrangement
Admission fee Adults £3; children free; 17 June and 11 July; adults £4; children free; 16 June

Vale End is a traditional plantsman's garden, one of the best on Bagshot sand, where a love of plants has not been allowed to obscure either the design or the landscape beyond. It is walled around, and made on many levels, on a site that faces south-west: the owners have taken the opportunity to grow sun-loving and Mediterranean plants. Daphne Foulsham is a Vice President (and a very successful ex-Chairman) of the National Gardens Scheme.

plantsman's collection of plants; good herbaceous borders; roses (mainly old-fashioned); vegetables; fruit; herbs; refreshments

Owned by Mr and Mrs John Foulsham
Size 0.4ha (1 acre)

VALLEY GARDENS
Wick Road, Englefield Green,
Windsor TW20 0UU

Tel 01784 485400 **Fax** 01753 847536
www.theroyallandscape.co.uk
Location At Englefield Green, 5 miles from Windsor, off A30: follow signs for Savill Garden
Opening hours 8am to 7pm (3.30pm in winter), daily, all year
Admission fee Cars £5 (£6 in April and May); occupants free

This is a woodland garden on a royal scale. The Valley Gardens have over 200 acres of plantings across a site of great natural beauty which falls in vast sweeps to the open expanse of Virginia Water. As in the Savill Garden, huge trees of oak, beech, sweet chestnut and Scots pine provide a magnificent framework and have been used with

great sensitivity. The whole composition conveys the feeling of a flowering forest from some far-off corner of Asia. From March and April until the end of June, a succession of camellias, rhododendrons and azaleas provide an unbelievable kaleidoscope of colour, most notably in the Punch Bowl where a natural combe is filled with terrace upon terrace of brightly-coloured Japanese Kurume azaleas. Giant magnolias garland themselves overhead with thousands of chalice-shaped blooms. A huge array of supporting trees, shrubs and perennials jostles for attention. Enormous groups of hydrangeas provide late-summer colour, from the white foaming flowers of *H. paniculata* to the blues and pale pinks of the lacecaps and mopheads. In autumn, the hillsides light up in a spectacle unrivalled this side of the Appalachian Mountains. In the nearby heather garden an old gravel pit has been transformed into a horticultural wonder to rival the Punch Bowl: ostensibly dominated by heathers and dwarf conifers (there is a National Collection here), the garden contains unrivalled collections of exotic and native birches, whitebeams and rowans, wild roses, cotoneasters and cistus. Recent plantings have made extensive use of ornamental grasses to provide relief among the stolid conifers. On the next hillside is to be found the National Collection of *Rhododendron* species, brought here in the 1950s from the famous garden of Tower Court near Ascot. A sweeping valley also contains a pinetum of some note, carpeted by countless thousands of dwarf narcissi in March and April.
outstanding collection of trees; hydrangeas; heathers; primulas; magnolias; rhododendrons and azaleas; all visitor facilities at the Savill Garden

Owned by Crown Estate
Number of gardeners 16
Size 87ha (220 acres)
NCCPG National Collections *Ilex*; *Magnolia*; *Mahonia*; *Pernettya*; *Rhododendron* (species and Glenn Dale azaleas); ferns; dwarf and slow-growing conifers

VANN
Hambledon, Godalming GU8 4EF

Tel/fax 01428 683413
www.vanngarden.co.uk
Location 2 miles from Chiddingfold; signs from A283 at Hambledon on NGS days
Opening hours 2pm to 6pm, daily, 7 to 13 May and 3 to 10 June; and by appointment; opens at 2pm on 7 May
Admission fee Adults £4; children free; pre-booked groups welcome

This high-profile Jekyll garden has been well restored and meticulously maintained by the present Caroes, the third generation to live here. Start with the old cottage garden at the front of the house and move round the house to the Arts and Crafts pergola straight to the lake. This is the heart of the garden, from which several distinct gardens lead from one to the next and melt into the Surrey woods: among them, a yew walk (1909), island beds, mixed borders, the Jekyll water garden (1911) and a woodland garden under vast oaks leading to a hazel coppice. The plantings are dense and thoughtful.
woodland garden; good herbaceous borders; bluebells; fritillaries; wood anemones; teas on 7 May

Owned by Mrs Martin Caroe
Number of gardeners 1/2
Size 2ha (5 acres)
English Heritage Grade II

THE VERNON GERANIUM NURSERY
Cuddington Way, Cheam, Sutton SM2 7JB

Tel 020 8393 7616 **Fax** 020 8786 7437
www.geraniumsuk.com
Location South-west of Cheam
Opening hours 9.30am to 5.30pm, Monday to Saturday; 10am to 4pm, Sundays, March to June

As it names indicates, this is a specialist pelargonium nursery. The number of pelargonium cultivars here speaks for itself – over 1,100 doubles and semi-doubles, Deacons, stellars, rosebuds, finger-flowered, fancy-leaved, speckled, uniques, dwarfs, miniatures, angels and regals – the list seems endless. Guided tours are given daily at 11am and 2.30pm on 23 and 24 June 2007.
pelargoniums

WINKWORTH ARBORETUM
Hascombe Road, Godalming GU8 4AD

Tel 01483 208477 **Fax** 01483 208252
www.nationaltrust.org.uk/winkwortharboretum
Location 2 miles south-east of Godalming, off B2130
Opening hours Dawn to dusk, daily, all year; groups *must* pre-book in writing
Admission fee Adults £5; children £2.50; families £12.50

Winkworth is a true arboretum in the sense that it has a large collection of full-sized trees – over 600 taxa – planted liberally over a large area. Many of the plantings are now in their prime. The red oaks (*Quercus coccinea*), tupelos *Nyssa sylvatica* and sweet gums *Liquidambar styraciflua* are quite spectacular in autumn.

woodland garden; fine collection of trees; bluebells; wood anemones; autumn colour; tallest *Acer davidii* (19m; 62ft) in the British Isles, and five further record trees; shop; tea room

Owned by The National Trust
Number of gardeners 3
Size 49ha (123 acres)
NCCPG National Collections *Sorbus* (Aria and Micromeles groups)

SUSSEX, EAST

The two historic gardens in East Sussex that English Heritage has rated Grade I could not be more different – Great Dixter and Sheffield Park. Yet they have one thing in common which is typical of East Sussex gardens generally – they are gardens whose historic features have been overlaid with plants. Few of the other historic gardens in the county are open to the public, but plant lovers are almost spoiled for choice. Every corner of East Sussex seems to brim with good modern gardens – those like Pashley Manor and Merriments have been widely recognised for their beauty and invention – and good collections of trees, including those at Sheffield Park and Stanmer Park, near Brighton. The National Gardens Scheme does well in East Sussex, especially in the area around Crowborough where there are many medium-sized gardens to see. Nurseries, too, are good and fairly plentiful: some of the best are attached to gardens, like Great Dixter, or have a fine display garden attached to them, like Merriments. There are comparatively few National Collections: one of the most interesting is the collection of lilacs (*Syringa* cvs.) kept by the City of Brighton & Hove Parks Department.

BATEMAN'S

Burwash, Etchingham TN19 7DS

Tel 01435 882302 **Fax** 01435 882811
www.nationaltrust.org.uk/batemans
Location Signed at west end of village
Opening hours 11am to 5pm, Saturday to Wednesday, 17 March to 28 October
Admission fee Adults £6.85; children £3.45

These ten acres on the banks of the River Dudwell were Rudyard Kipling's home from 1902 until his death in 1936. The garden is fun for children, because there is a working flour mill, but not spectacular for the knowledgeable gardener, except for the *Campsis grandiflora* on the house and the herbaceous borders designed by Graham Stuart Thomas.

roses (mainly old-fashioned); herbs; good herbaceous borders; Kipling pear arch; National Trust shop; tea room

Owned by The National Trust
Number of gardeners 2
Size 4ha (10 acres)
English Heritage Grade II

BATES GREEN FARM

Tye Hill Road, Arlington, Polegate BN26 6SH

Tel 01323 485152 **Fax** 01323 485151
Location 3 miles south-west of Hailsham
Opening hours For NGS: 11am to 5pm, 8 April, 10 June and 16 September; and by appointment
Admission fee Adults £4; children free

Made by the present owners since the mid-1970s, the garden at Bates Green Farm has several different areas. These include: a shady garden with narcissus, geraniums and cyclamen; a vegetable garden with raised beds; a monocot border; and mixed borders planted for year-round colour associations.

woodland garden; good herbaceous borders; colour borders; bluebells; rockery; pond; light lunches and teas on NGS days

Owned by Mr and Mrs JR McCutchan
Number of gardeners 1 part-time
Size 0.8ha (2 acres)

BRICKWALL HOUSE & GARDENS

Frewen College, Northiam TN31 6NL

Tel 01797 253388 **Fax** 01797 252567
Location Off B2088
Opening hours By appointment for groups; for NGS: 2pm to 5pm on 27 May
Admission fee Gardens: £3

This is an important historic garden, with 17th-century features that were reworked in the 19th century, a chess garden where green and yellow yew shapes are grown in squares of black or white chips, and attractive mixed plantings of perennials and annuals. The bluebells in the arboretum are magnificent.
topiary; herbs; good herbaceous borders; fine collection of trees; bluebells; extensively redesigned since 1980; teas by arrangement

Owned by Frewen Educational Trust
English Heritage Grade II*

CLINTON LODGE

Fletching, Uckfield TN22 3ST

Tel 01825 722952 **Fax** 01825 723967
Location In main village street
Opening hours 2pm to 5.30pm, 6 May, 10, 11, 18 and 25 June, 2, 9 and 30 July and 6 August for NGS
Admission fee Adults £4; children free

Clinton Lodge is a rising star among new gardens, designed round a handsome 17th-century house. There are formal gardens of different periods, starting with a 'medieval' *potager* and an Elizabethan-style herb garden with camomile paths and turf seats. The most successful parts are the pre-Raphaelite walk of lilies and pale roses, the Victorian-style herbaceous borders in soft pastel shades and a very cheerful garden of old roses. A canal garden and an *allée* of fastigiate hornbeams were added in 2001, and a knot garden and 'shade glade' in 2003.
roses (mainly old-fashioned); herbs; good herbaceous borders; yew hedges; lime walks; *potager*; knot gardens; teas

Owned by Sir Hugh and Lady Collum
Number of gardeners 2
Size 2.4ha (6 acres)

HAILSHAM GRANGE

Hailsham BN27 1BL

Tel 01323 844248
Location In village centre, next to church
Opening hours 2pm to 5.30pm, 3 June and 2 July; and by appointment
Admission fee Adults £3.50

Hailsham Grange – actually the former vicarage – has a series of formal gardens that are richly planted in the modern manner. Box, yew and hornbeam (on stilts) divide the space to make the whole seem much larger than the sum of its parts. Look out for the Gothic summerhouse, topiary and colour-themed plantings, all constructed with exquisite taste.
home-made teas

Owned by Noel Thompson
Number of gardeners 1
Size 0.4ha (1 acre)

MARCHANTS HARDY PLANTS

2 Marchants Cottages, Ripe Road, Laughton BN8 6AJ

Tel/fax 01323 811737
Location 1/2 mile east of Laughton; take right turn signed to Ripe
Opening hours Mid-March to end of October
Admission fee Adults £2.25

This acclaimed young garden is especially good from June onwards, and peaks early in autumn. It is attached to a nursery with an excellent selection of herbaceous plants and grasses. Their many introductions include *Sedum* 'Purple Emperor'.
herbaceous plants; grasses; good nursery

Owned by Graham Gough and Lucy Goffin
Number of gardeners 1
Size 0.4ha (1 acre)

GREAT DIXTER

Dixter Road, Northiam TN31 6PH

Tel 01797 252878 **Fax** 01797 252879
www.greatdixter.co.uk
Location Off A28 at Northiam Post Office
Opening hours 2pm (11am from May to September) to 5pm, Tuesday to Sunday and Bank Holiday Mondays, 1 April to 29 October
Admission fee Adults £6; children £2

Nathaniel Lloyd bought Great Dixter in 1910: Lutyens did a conversion job on the house and laid out part of the gardens. Most of the brickwork, yew hedges, steps, walls, doorways and Arts and Crafts details date back to the original design – contemporary with Hidcote and earlier than Sissinghurst. The topiary was Nathaniel Lloyd's contribution – he wrote a book about it. But the main reason for the garden's pre-eminent reputation is the decades of horticultural skill which Nathaniel's son, the late Christopher Lloyd, put into its planting. He was a knowledgeable plantsman who once taught horticulture at Wye College and had a remarkable eye for combining plants in harmonious groupings throughout the year. His books – especially the compilation of articles from *Country Life* published as *The Well-Tempered Garden* – are immensely popular and influential, so the Lloyd style of planting and maintaining a garden is probably more widely copied now than any other. The heart of the garden is the Long Border, about 65m (213ft) long and 4½m (15ft) deep, which became a showcase and trial ground for his experiments. It is a series of compositions loosely strung together with a wide variety of weaving colours, heights and textures, but unified as much by good foliage as by flowers. Every section of it teaches you something new that could be made to work in your own garden. One of Lloyd's strengths was his fondness for change – his desire to refine and improve his garden all the time. He was one of the first garden owners to use lots of annuals and tender perennials to extend the summer season right through into autumn. He shocked the country's rosarians by replacing his parents' collection of old-fashioned roses with a late-summer explosion of dahlias, cannas and exotic foliage. And nobody practised the gentle, patient art of long-term meadow gardening so successfully as Christopher Lloyd: indeed, he wrote so eloquently and prolifically about the principles and practices of meadow gardening that, even if he had never penned a word on any other aspect of ornamental horticulture, he would be established as a great apostle of this charming and relaxed art form which he sometimes referred to as 'tapestry gardening'. Visiting Great Dixter should be a compulsory part of every gardener's ongoing education.

topiary; subtropical plants; plantsman's collection of plants; good herbaceous borders; meadow garden; colour schemes; gift shop

Owned by Great Dixter Charitable Trust and Olivia Eller
Number of gardeners 5
Size 2ha (5 acres)
English Heritage Grade I

Merriments Gardens

MERRIMENTS GARDENS

Hawkhurst Road, Hurst Green TN19 7RA

Tel 01580 860666 **Fax** 01580 860324
www.merriments.co.uk
Location On A229
Opening hours 10am (10.30am on Sundays) to 5 .30pm, daily, 31 March to early October
Admission fee Adults £4.50; children £2

The gardens at this nursery are young – started in 1991 on a bare clay field – but the tail is already wagging the dog. Four remarkable acres of imaginative design and striking planting are kept meticulously tidy. The planting has been chosen so that each area blends seamlessly into the next and creates a satisfying and harmonious whole. The deep sweeping borders are designed and planted to combine colour, form and texture in endlessly imaginative planting schemes. The blue garden is the best we know. The features include foliage borders, two ponds, a border for spring, several borders designed to peak in summer and autumn – and dozens more. Everything is mulched, and the plantings are never allowed to get too thick. Recent developments include a dry area which has been transformed into a Mediterranean-inspired scree garden and a waterlogged area which has been turned into a bog garden and planted with moisture-loving plants. The nursery is excellent, a good complement to one of the best show gardens in England.

plantsman's collection of plants; good herbaceous borders; brilliant modern design; tropical border; first-rate nursery attached; garden café

Owned by David and Peggy Weeks
Number of gardeners 3
Size 1.6ha (4 acres)

MICHELHAM PRIORY

Upper Dicker, Hailsham BN27 3QS

Tel 01323 844224 **Fax** 01323 844030
www.sussexpast.co.uk/michelham
Location Signed from A22 and A27

Opening hours 10.30am to 4.30pm, Tuesday to Sunday, March and October; 10.30am to 5pm, Tuesday to Sunday, April to July and September; 10.30am to 5.30pm, daily, August (2006 details)
Admission fee Adults £6; OAPs £5; children £3

The old Augustinian priory has an Elizabethan barn, a blacksmith's shop, a rope museum, a working watermill and England's largest medieval water-filled moat. Within the garden are several distinct areas, including a physic garden and cloister garden, with medieval plantings (faithful, if a little dull), some very good borders, a bog garden, a kitchen garden and several wildflower areas. It all makes for an enjoyable visit, highly educational for children and interesting for parents.
herbs; mature conifers; good herbaceous borders; sculpture trail; dovecote gift shop; licensed restaurant and tea room

Owned by The Sussex Archaeological Society (Sussex Past)
Number of gardeners 2, plus volunteers
Size 2.8ha (7 acres)

MOORLANDS
Friars Gate, Crowborough TN6 1XF

Tel 01892 652474
Location 2 miles north of Crowborough, at Friar's Gate
Opening hours 11am to 5pm, Wednesdays, 1 April to 1 October; for NGS: 2pm to 6pm, 24 June
Admission fee Adults £4; children free

The garden at Moorlands was begun by Dr Smith's parents in 1929: Dr Smith took over in 1974, made a lake and ponds, and planted a lot of woodland and bog-loving plants. The garden now combines mature trees with modern herbaceous plantings. By the house, on a sloping site, is a long herbaceous border. This leads to the main stream, red with iron ore but clean enough for trout and protected enough for kingfishers. It is spring-fed, full of waterfalls, and planted with grasses and bamboos. Moorlands is a plantsman's garden of fine trees, rhododendrons and collectors' shrubs, underplanted with bog plants as well as wildflowers, such as native daffodils (*Narcissus pseudonarcissus*) and orchids.
good plants for plantsmen; Japanese anemones; teas on NGS open day

Owned by Dr and Mrs Steven Smith
Number of gardeners 3 part-time
Size 1.6ha (4 acres)

PARADISE PARK
Avis Road, Newhaven BN9 0DH

Tel 01273 512123 **Fax** 01273 616000
www.paradisepark.co.uk
Location Signed from A26 and A259
Opening hours 9am to 6pm, daily, all year, except 25 and 26 December
Admission fee Adults £7.99; children £5.99

Part of a leisure complex attached to a garden centre, the most interesting features are a tropical house and a cactus house, each landscaped with handsome plant collections chosen for display. There are some imaginative garden designs – Caribbean, seaside, desert and oriental, for example. It is a haven in winter, and the outside gardens are a pleasure to explore in summer, full of contrasting designs and splendid water features. They contain a Sussex History trail – beautiful models of important historic buildings in the county, each in a different setting. Other attractions include a hemerocallis collection, a fuchsia border and an alpine rock garden.
plants under glass; hydroponic demonstration area; *Streptocarpus* collection; plant centre; large coffee shop

Owned by Jonathan Tate
Number of gardeners 3
Size 1ha (2½ acres) of garden and 0.1ha (¼ acre) under glass

PASHLEY MANOR GARDENS
Ticehurst TN5 7HE

Tel 01580 200888 **Fax** 01580 200102
www.pashleymanorgardens.com
Location On B2099 between A21 and Ticehurst village

Opening hours 11am to 5pm, Tuesday to Thursday, Saturdays and Bank Holiday Mondays, 3 April to 29 September
Admission fee Adults £6.50; children £5

Pashley Manor is a new/old garden, made or remade in the Victorian style over the last ten years or so with advice from the brilliant Anthony du Gard Pasley. The original structure came from fine old trees, fountains, springs and large ponds or small lakes. The modern plantings have added gentle shapes, spacious expanses, harmonious colours and solid plantings. There is a sumptuous series of new enclosed gardens where colour gardening is practised to brilliant effect. And it gets better every year.
roses (mainly old-fashioned and climbers); mature conifers; Victorian shrubberies; hydrangeas; irises; HHA/Christie's Garden of the Year in 1999; lunches and teas

Owned by James and Angela Sellick
Number of gardeners 5
Size 5ha (121/2 acres)

SARAH RAVEN'S CUTTING GARDEN
Perch Hill Farm, Willingford Lane, Brightling, Robertsbridge TN32 5HP

Tel 08450 504849 **Fax** 01424 838020
www.thecuttinggarden.com
Location 2 miles south-east of Burwash Weald
Opening hours 9.30am to 5pm, 28 April, 16 June and 25 August; 11am to 5pm 23 September; private groups of 18+ by arrangement at other times
Admission fee Adults £4; groups by arrangement

Sarah Raven's Cutting Garden is a very intensive and productive garden which she uses as the basis for the courses she teaches and her column in *The Daily Telegraph*. It is laid out as a series of garden rooms, some planted with annuals and biennials, and others for the production of vegetables and fruit. The colour combinations are brilliant and there are extraordinary features, like a hazel tunnel covered in sweet peas. But it is the profusion of flowers and colours that stays in the memory – and the realisation that they are all grown for cutting. Inspirational.
refreshments by arrangement

Owned by Sarah Raven and Adam Nicolson
Number of gardeners 2
Size 0.8ha (2 acres)

SHEFFIELD PARK GARDEN
Uckfield TN22 3QX

Tel 01825 790231 **Fax** 01825 791264
www.nationaltrust.org.uk/sheffieldpark
Location Between East Grinstead and Lewes on A275
Opening hours 10.30am to 5.30pm, Tuesday to Sunday and Bank Holidays, 27 February to 23 December; open daily from 1 May to 3 June and from 1 October to 4 November; closes at 4pm from 6 November to 28 February 2008
Admission fee Adults £7; children £3.50; RHS members free except during special events

Sheffield Park is a beautiful 120-acre garden around five lakes. These were laid out in the 18th century by Capability Brown and Humphry Repton. The result is landscaping on the grandest of scales, though the lakes now reflect the 20th-century plantings of exotics. Carpeted with daffodils and bluebells in spring, its rhododendrons and azaleas are spectacular in early summer. In autumn, the garden is ablaze with wonderful leaf colours, but the collection of rare trees and shrubs makes it a fascinating visit at any time of year. The National Trust is in the middle of a major restoration project which will involve planting 9,000 trees and shrubs between 2003 and 2008. There will be two RHS Special Events at Sheffield Park in 2007; details from 020 7821 3408.
mature conifers; fine collection of trees; bluebells; daffodils; kalmias; autumn crocuses; rhododendrons; tallest *Nyssa sylvatica* (21m; 69ft) in the British Isles, plus two other record trees; National Trust shop

Owned by The National Trust
Number of gardeners 5
Size 48ha (120 acres)
NCCPG National Collections *Rhododendron* (Ghent azaleas)
English Heritage Grade I

STANDEN

West Hoathly, East Grinstead RH19 4NE

Tel 01342 323029 **Fax** 01342 316424
www.nationaltrust.org.uk/standen
Location 2 miles south of East Grinstead, signed from B2110
Opening hours 11am to 5.30pm, Wednesday to Sunday and Bank Holidays, 17 March to 28 October; plus Mondays from 16 July to 2 September; 11am to 3pm, Saturdays and Sundays, 3 to 11 March and 3 November to 16 December
Admission fee Adults £4.40; children £2.20; families £10; less in winter

This early Edwardian garden has a compartmentalised structure (very Arts and Crafts) but also enjoys magnificent views across the Medway valley. It is currently undergoing restoration, and the croquet lawn is being remade in 2007. A series of enclosed gardens around the house gives way to woodland slopes and an old quarry furnished with ferns and azaleas.
roses (mainly rugosas and old-fashioned); rock garden; mature conifers; good herbaceous borders; rhododendrons; azaleas; woodland shrubs; National Trust shop; restaurant

Owned by The National Trust
Number of gardeners 2½
Size 5ha (12½ acres)

SUSSEX, WEST

West Sussex is even better endowed with fine gardens and interesting nurseries than East Sussex. All five Grade I gardens are open to the public – Goodwood, Leonardslee, Parham, Petworth House and Stansted Park – though only Leonardslee and Parham are of great horticultural interest. However, there is also a glut of Grade II* gardens open to the public, and all of them chiefly of importance for their plant collections – Borde Hill, Cowdray, Gravetye, Highdown, Nymans, High Beeches, Wakehurst and West Dean. These are matched by a great number of good medium-sized gardens that open for the National Gardens Scheme and a large number of good nurseries and garden centres. Architectural Plants, Rotherview Nursery and Ingwersens are all nurseries of national or international status and often seen at RHS flower shows. The NCCPG has a good number of National Collections in the county. The horticultural college at Brinsbury, now part of Chichester College, is a RHS Partner College with a series of public lectures, demonstrations and workshops throughout the year: details from 020 7821 3408.

ARCHITECTURAL PLANTS

Cooks Farm, Nuthurst, Horsham RH13 6LH

Tel 01403 891772 **Fax** 01403 891056
www.architecturalplants.com
Location 3 miles south of Horsham, behind the Black Horse pub in Nuthurst
Opening hours 9am to 5pm, Monday to Saturday
Admission fee Free

Somewhat out of the ordinary, Architectural Plants specialises in exotic-looking, evergreen foliage plants, often with architectural or sculptural shapes. 'Architectural' means that the plants themselves have strong, sometimes spectacular, shapes which bring a distinctive year-round presence to a garden. Examples include eucalyptus, bamboos, hardy palms, hardy bananas and evergreen magnolias. Larger specimens are available for immediate impact. The display area around the nursery is stylishly laid out and a pleasure to visit in its own right. The nursery also has a branch at Lidsey Road, Woodgate, Chichester PO20 3SU (open 10am to 4pm, Sunday to Friday. Tel 01243 545008); it has phillyreas, arbutus and many rare trees, plus seaside exotics, but no display garden.
architectural plants; large specimens

Owned by Angus White
Size 1.2ha (3 acres)

ARUNDEL CASTLE

Arundel BN18 9AB

Tel 01903 882173 **Fax** 01903 884581
www.arundelcastle.org
Location In centre of town; use town car park
Opening hours 10am to 5pm, Tuesday to Sunday and Bank Holiday Mondays, 31 March to 28 October
Admission fee £6.50 for all

The grounds at Arundel date back to the 18th century, and were first opened to the public in 1854. Most of the gardens are modern, made by the Duchess of Norfolk since she and the Duke moved here in 1987. She has taken advantage of the mild climate to grow a wide choice of exotic plants – cannas and Mexican salvias are perennials here. The borders are planted for their contrasts and harmonies of colour and form. The traditional kitchen garden produces fruit, vegetables and cut flowers for the castle, and two Victorian glasshouses have recently been restored for grapes and peaches.
gift shop; restaurant

Owned by Arundel Castle Trustees Ltd
Number of gardeners 5
Size 1.2ha (3 acres), plus 16ha (40 acres) parkland
English Heritage Grade II*

BORDE HILL GARDEN
Balcombe Road, Haywards Heath RH16 1XP

Tel 01444 450326 **Fax** 01444 440427
www.bordehill.co.uk
Location 1½ miles north of Haywards Heath
Opening hours 10am to 6pm (or dusk, if earlier), daily, April to October
Admission fee Adults £6.50; OAPs £5; Children £3.50

This important woodland garden has been significantly developed and improved in recent years. It was originally planted in the early 1900s with exotic trees and shrubs, notably a large collection of rhododendron species grown from seed introduced by such collectors as Forrest and Kingdon Ward. Some of those trees are record-breakers, including *Sorbus hupehensis*, a splendid *Magnolia hypoleuca* and the rare Chinese tulip tree (*Liriodendron chinense*) now 19m (62ft). The garden has recently been substantially redeveloped for the recreation market and is all the better for the new capital. The gardens surrounding the house are divided into 'rooms'. These include the Garden of Allah with a new wildlife pool; a ring of Knap Hill azaleas backed by rhododendrons from Farrer and Cox's expedition to Burma and China in 1919; the newly restored Victorian greenhouses, one of which is a peach house and another devoted to South African plants (including nerines); a small Mediterranean garden; a rose garden designed by Robin Williams and planted with 500 David Austin roses; the Italian garden and two dells with *Trachycarpus* palms.
woodland garden; plantsman's collection of plants; fine collection of trees; rhododendrons; azaleas; magnolias; plants from original seed; 80 champion trees, one of the largest collections in the British Isles; gift shop; tea room and restaurant

Owned by Borde Hill Garden Ltd
Number of gardeners 5
Size 6.7ha (17 acres) of formal gardens, plus 8ha (20 acres) of woodland and 150 acres of parkland
English Heritage Grade II*

CHAMPS HILL
Coldwaltham, Pulborough RH20 1LY

Tel 01798 831868 **Fax** 01798 831536
Location West of Coldwaltham, on road to Fittleworth (Waltham Park Road)
Opening hours 2pm to 5pm, 18 March, 13 May and 12 August
Admission fee Adults £4; children free

This garden has been developed around three disused sand quarries since 1960. The woodlands are full of beautiful rhododendrons and azaleas, but the most striking feature is the collection of heathers – over 300 cultivars – interplanted with dwarf conifers. The garden also has some interesting sculptures, and stupendous views.
heathers; rhododendrons and azaleas; teas

Owned by Mr and Mrs David Bowerman
Number of gardeners 2
Size 10.7ha (27 acres), including woodland

COWDRAY PARK
Midhurst GU29 0AY

Tel 01730 812461 **Fax** 01730 812122
www.cowdraypark.co.uk
Location South of A272, 1 mile east of Midhurst
Opening hours For NGS: 2pm to 5pm, 20 May; and possibly in the autumn, too
Admission fee Adults £3; children free

Cowdray is seldom open, but worth a long journey to see the ornate house and its contemporary (100-year-old) collection of trees, particularly conifers – don't miss the avenue of wellingtonias up at the top. Some are now record-breakers, and the sweeps of rhododendrons and azaleas, especially the hardy hybrids down 'the dell', are on the grand scale. There are also two lakes, waterfalls, wildflower areas and a lot of new planting, including a valley garden.
300-year-old Lebanon cedar; wellingtonia avenue; rhododendrons; grapes and fruit in the glasshouses; valley garden; tallest *Abies concolor* f. *violacea* (28m; 92ft) and *Chamaecyparis pisifera* (29m; 95ft) in the UK; refreshments

Denmans Garden

Owned by Viscount and Viscountess Cowdray
Size 10ha (25 acres)
English Heritage Grade II*

DENMANS GARDEN
Fontwell, Arundel BN18 0SU

Tel 01243 542808 **Fax** 01243 544064
www.denmans-garden.co.uk
Location Off A29 or A27, near Fontwell racecourse
Opening hours 9am to 5pm (dusk in winter), daily, all year; closed 1 January, 24 and 25 December
Admission fee Adults £4.25; OAPs £3.80; children (4-16) £2.50; RHS members free from November to February

This modern garden is a showpiece for John Brookes's ideas and commitment to easy care. He uses foliage, gravel mulches, contrasts of form, coloured stems, winter bark and plants as elements of design. The garden's design is so fluid that you feel carried along by its momentum and, of course, it is a brilliant source of ideas for your own garden.
excellent modern design; gravel and grass; roses (mainly old-fashioned); herbs; good herbaceous borders; spring bulbs; shop; plant centre; lunches and teas

Owned by John Brookes and Michael Neve
Size 1.6ha (4 acres)

GRAVETYE MANOR HOTEL
East Grinstead RH19 4LJ

Tel 01342 810567 **Fax** 01342 810080
www.gravetyemanor.co.uk
Location 4 miles south-west of East Grinstead
Opening hours Hotel and restaurant guests only, all year; the perimeter path is open to the public free of charge from 10am to 5pm on Tuesdays and Fridays

Gravetye was William Robinson's own garden, very influential about 100 years ago, and scrupulously maintained as it was in its prime. It was here that Robinson put into practice the natural style of gardening which he promoted so vigorously in his magazines and books. Robinson's own original woodland garden has many of the trees he planted – fine davidias and nyssas, for example. And the meadows below the house are planted with naturalised bulbs in the style that Robinson made popular through his writings. Gravetye is still a garden to learn from: there is much to admire and copy.
William Robinson's woodland garden; topiary; roses (mainly old-fashioned); plantsman's collection of plants; good herbaceous borders; fine collection of trees; alpine meadow; gazebo

Owned by Mark Raffan and Andrew Russell
Number of gardeners 4
Size 12ha (30 acres)
English Heritage Grade II*

HIGH BEECHES
Handcross RH17 6HQ

Tel 01444 400589 **Fax** 01444 401543
www.highbeeches.com
Location South of B2110, 1 mile east of M23 at Handcross
Opening hours 1pm to 5pm, daily, except Wednesdays, 17 March to 31 October
Admission fee Adults £5.50; reductions for groups of 30+; coaches by appointment

One of the best (and most magical) of the famous Sussex woodland gardens, High Beeches was originally laid out by Colonel Giles Loder, a cousin of the Loders of Wakehurst. In 1966 it was acquired by Anne and Edward Boscawen, who devoted many years to its maintenance and improvement. Now it is managed by a non-profit-making charitable trust. The original woodland has been thinned and underplanted with exotics, many of them rare. Some are trees like nyssas,

High Beeches gardens

High Beeches gardens

magnolias, *Tetracentron sinense* and davidias; others are shrubs – there is a 'Loderi Walk' planted with *Rhododendron* x *loderi* cultivars. A valley of ponds and woodland glades is beautifully planted with splendid rhododendrons, azaleas and camellias for spring, and swathes of native bluebells. The garden has wonderful autumn colours, too, and a policy of letting good plants naturalise – cowslips, wild orchids, willow gentians and *Primula helodoxa*. The clock in the Clock Tower (now the restaurant) was installed to commemorate Colonel Loder's Derby winner, Spion Cop.
woodland garden; plantsman's collection of plants; mature conifers; fine collection of trees; rhododendrons; five-acre natural wildflower meadow; tallest *Stewartia monodelpha* (11m; 36ft) in the British Isles; restaurant open from noon; pretty tea garden

Owned by High Beeches Gardens Conservation Trust
Number of gardeners 2
Size 10ha (25 acres)
NCCPG National Collections *Stewartia*
English Heritage Grade II*

HIGHDOWN
Littlehampton Road, Goring-by-Sea BN12 6PE

Tel 01903 221112 **Fax** 01903 821384
Location Signed from A259
Opening hours 10am to 6pm (4.30pm in February, March, October and November, and 4pm in January and December), daily (but not weekends from October to March), all year
Admission fee Free; donations welcome

(P) 🚻

This is the most famous garden to be made on chalk, and one of the best. It was actually laid out in a disused chalk quarry and on the surrounding, south-facing downland. Its maker, Sir Frederick Stern, was determined to try anything that might grow in these unusual conditions. Eighty years on, the results are some handsome trees, vigorous roses, and long-forgotten peony hybrids. The gardens are designed on a large grid and planted mainly as mixed borders. Mediterranean plants do especially well: hellebores, tulips, daffodils and anemones have naturalised over large areas. Stern was a fine plantsman and scholar, and wrote the classic book A *Chalk Garden* as a memoir of his gardening experiences. He was also a distinguished plant breeder: Highdown has given us two very fine roses in *Rosa* 'Highdownensis' and 'Wedding Day'. The garden is now well maintained by Worthing Borough Council and a pleasure to visit at any season, but perhaps especially in spring.
woodland garden; roses (mainly old-fashioned); rock garden; plantsman's collection of plants; mature conifers; good herbaceous borders; fine collection of trees; tallest specimen of *Carpinus turczaninowii* in the UK, a handsome tree; refreshments (March to September)

Owned by Worthing Borough Council
Number of gardeners 4
Size 4ha (10 acres)
NCCPG National Collections plants introduced by Sir Frederick Stern
English Heritage Grade II*

HOLLY GATE CACTUS NURSERY
Billingshurst Road, Ashington RH20 3BB

Tel 01903 892930
www.hollygatecactus.co.uk
Location 1/2 mile from Ashington, on B2133 to Billingshurst
Opening hours 9am to 5pm (4pm from November to January), daily; closed 25 to 27 December
Admission fee Adults £2.50; OAPs and children £2 (2006 prices)

(P) 🚻 ✿

Holly Gate specialises in cacti and succulents. It carries over 50,000 plants of all types in stock and sells them both retail and wholesale. Many are also planted in the cactus garden, which has some fine specimens and a wide range of taxa – fascinating for the *cognoscenti* and an eye-opener for the uninitiated, whatever the weather.
cacti; succulents

LEONARDSLEE LAKES & GARDENS

Lower Beeding, Horsham RH13 6PP

Tel 01403 891212 **Fax** 01403 891305
www.leonardslee.com
Location 4 miles south-west of Handcross at junction of B2110 and A281
Opening hours 9.30am to 6pm, daily April to October; last admissions 4.30pm
Admission fee Adults £6 (but, in May, £8 on weekdays and £9 at weekends and Bank Holidays); children £4 at all times

Ⓟ 👫 ✿

Leonardslee is a plantsman's garden on an enormous scale. It was begun in 1801 and enlarged from 1889 by Sir Edmund Loder – and still belongs to his descendants. It is important historically as one of the earliest examples of a collection of rare plants in a designed setting – a series of woodland valleys with panoramic views on the edge of the Wealden Forest. The gardens are beautiful when they first open in April with magnificent magnolias and camellias. Autumn colour is another feature: from the middle of September onwards maples, azaleas, liquidambars, caryas and nyssas produce one of the finest arrays of autumn colour in England. But Leonardslee is famous above all for its rhododendrons and azaleas which line the many miles of paths up and down the hillsides and around the seven lakes. Sheets of bluebells accompany their main flowering in May, while the banks of the lakes and streams are densely planted with candelabra primulas, lysichitons and gunneras. There are many other fascinating features: magnificent conifers; large plantings of modern *Rhododendron yakushimanum* hybrids; several original plants of *Rhododendron* x *loderi* hybrids; a large area naturalised by *Scilla liliohyacinthus*; rare shrubs like *Ilex dipyrena*; a European cork oak (*Quercus suber*) and the Amur cork oak (*Phellodendron amurense*); a magnificent Pulhamite rock garden about 100 years old, which has a very striking clump of the hardy Chusan palm (*Trachycarpus fortunei* and a fine form of *T. fortunei* var. *surculosa*) and a bright mixture of evergreen azaleas; and a truly beautiful valley on the other side of the main lake which is filled from top to bottom with a flood of sweet-scented yellow azaleas (*Rhododendron luteum*). The garden is very large – allow lots of time – and the labelling sparse.

rock garden; plantsman's collection of plants; mature conifers; new millennium plantings (100 oak species; 100 maple species; many flowering *Cornus*); bonsai; tallest fossil tree *Metasequoia glyptostroboides* (28m; 92ft) and *Magnolia campbellii* (27m 98ft) in the British Isles, and five further champion trees; gift shop; licensed restaurant/café

Owned by The Loder family
Number of gardeners 7
Size 100ha (250 acres)
English Heritage Grade I

Owned by JM Hewitt
Number of gardeners 2
Size 930 sq m (10,000 sq ft)

W.E.TH. INGWERSEN LTD

Birch Farm Nursery, Gravetye,
East Grinstead RH19 4LE

Tel 01342 810236
www.ingwersen.co.uk
Location 4 miles south-west of East Grinstead off B2110
Opening hours 9am to 1pm and 1.30pm to 4pm, daily, except Sundays and Bank Holidays, March to September; weekdays only from October to February; closed for two weeks at Christmas
Admission fee Free

This is probably the oldest, and certainly the most distinguished, alpine nursery in the south of England: when it started – exactly 80 years ago – in 1927, Walter Ingwersen was a tenant of William Robinson at nearby Gravetye Manor. The company's exhibits at RHS flower shows have been a source of much praise. It still has one of the best collections in the country of traditional alpines, especially European primulas, sempervivums and autumn-flowering gentians, but it is also a good place to find less common rock plants, the smaller perennials, dwarf shrubs and conifers. There are many raised beds and troughs to see at the nursery (which is in a most beautiful setting): one can spend a long and very happy time here looking at alpines and browsing through possible purchases. And the Bluebell Line runs right past the nursery.
rock plants; troughs; lots of small plants for interested plantsmen

Owned by Paul Ingwersen
Number of gardeners 4
Size 0.4ha (1 acre)

NYMANS

Handcross, Haywards Heath RH17 6EB

Tel 01444 400321 **Fax** 01444 400253
www.nationaltrust.org.uk/nymans
Location On B2114
Opening hours 11am to 6pm, Wednesday to Sunday and Bank Holiday Mondays, 15 February to 23 December; closes at 4pm in November and December
Admission fee Adults £7.70; children £3.80; reductions in winter; RHS members free

The garden at Nymans was made in the early years of the 20th century by Leonard Messel, and his head gardener James Comber. Although it is now owned by the National Trust, there is still a substantial input from latter-day members of the Messel family. Nymans is a stupendous plantsman's garden with a wonderful collection of plants of every type which have been marshalled with a fair degree of artistry and made to fit within a strong overall design. It is one of the best gardens of the Sussex Weald, and one which retains much of the distinctive style dictated by its historic collection of shrubs and trees. There are opulent yellow and blue herbaceous borders in the walled garden, vivid displays of annuals, a pioneering collection of old roses, a magnificent wisteria pergola and vast collections of magnolias and camellias. Further afield, the woodland and wild garden have a great collection of rare trees and shrubs. Nymans suffered very severely from the great storm of 1987, but has since made a brilliant recovery and many would say now that the garden looks better than ever.
woodland garden; topiary; roses (mainly old-fashioned); plantsman's collection of plants; good herbaceous borders; fine collection of trees; eight different record-breaking trees; shop; plant centre; licensed restaurant

Owned by The National Trust
Number of gardeners 8
Size 12ha (30 acres)
English Heritage Grade II*

PARHAM

Storrington, Pulborough RH20 4HS

Tel 01903 742021/744888 **Fax** 01903 746557
www.parhaminsussex.co.uk
Location On A283 midway between Pulborough and Storrington
Opening hours Noon to 5pm, Wednesdays, Thursdays, Sundays and Bank Holiday Mondays, Easter to September; plus Saturday 7 July (Garden Weekend), and Tuesdays and Fridays in August

Parham gardens

Admission fee Gardens only: Adults £5; OAPs and disabled £4.50; children £1.50; prices under review

Ⓟ ✦ 👪 ♿ ✿

Parham is an ethereal English garden for the loveliest of Elizabethan manor houses. In the deer park are ancient oaks, a landscaped lake and a cricket ground, but no suggestion of a garden as you approach the house. The fun for garden-lovers is hidden in the old walled garden: four acres of lush borders, colour plantings in yellow, blue and mauve, old and new fruit trees, and all maintained to a high standard. The aim is to achieve: 'Edwardian opulence... without being too purist.' There are striking colour combinations within the vegetable garden, while extensive cutting borders supply material for the arrangements of cut flowers for which the house is famous. The long, lean-to conservatory has charming displays of fuchsias and old-fashioned pelargonium cultivars.
roses (mainly old-fashioned); trained fruit; good herbaceous borders; organic kitchen garden; HHA/ Christie's Garden of the Year in 1990; shop; light lunches and teas

Owned by Parham Park Trust
Number of gardeners 41/2, plus volunteers
Size 4.4ha (11 acres)
English Heritage Grade I

PETWORTH HOUSE
Petworth GU28 0AE

Tel 01798 342207 **Fax** 01798 342963
www.nationaltrust.org.uk/petworth
Location At Petworth, well signed
Opening hours Garden: 11am to 6pm, Saturday to Wednesday and Good Friday, 18 March to 29 October; park: 8am to dusk, daily, all year (but may close at noon on concert days)
Admission fee Garden ('Pleasure Grounds'): adults £3.50; children £1.80; park: free

Ⓟ 👪 ♿

One of the best Capability Brown landscapes in England sweeps right up to the windows of Petworth House. The National Trust has added acres of bright azaleas to the woodland garden. Both park and garden have enjoyed a renaissance since the damage caused by the great storm of 1987. The Pleasure Ground is one of the most historically interesting parts of Petworth: the layout dates back to Elizabethan times. Winding pathways lead through shrubberies, punctuated by unexpected vistas and areas for quiet contemplation.
Capability Brown landscape; woodland garden; good herbaceous borders; deer park; one million daffodils; shop; restaurant

Owned by The National Trust
Number of gardeners 4
Size 12ha (30 acres) of pleasure grounds; 280ha (700-acre) park
English Heritage Grade I

RYMANS
Apuldram, Chichester PO20 7EG

Tel 01243 783147
Location 11/2 miles south-west of Chichester
Opening hours For NGS and by appointment
Admission fee £3.50, for charity

Ⓟ ✦ ✿

The house at Rymans is *very* old (c.1410), but the garden is almost completely modern, apart from a huge ancient plane tree near the house. The main excitements are in the walled garden, dominated by double borders of old Hybrid Musk roses that are backed by clipped lime trees on stilts. Around the edges are mixed borders where unusual plants are elegantly combined for colour effect. A modern pergola is profusely planted with white wisterias. Outside the gate, an avenue of black poplars, underplanted with daffodils, leads to the parish church.
refreshments on NGS days

Owned by Mrs Michael Gayford
Number of gardeners 3
Size 2ha (5 acres) garden and 6ha (15 acres) grounds

ST MARY'S HOUSE
Bramber BN44 3WE

Tel/fax 01903 816205
www.stmarysbramber.co.uk
Location In village centre, opposite castle

Opening hours 2pm to 6pm, Thursdays, Sundays and Bank Holiday Mondays, May to September
Admission fee Adults £3

The gardens at St Mary's House have all been restored and remade by the owners since 1997. They are the perfect complement for the magnificent Grade I half-timbered house. Box-edges beds and yew topiary set off the house itself, while the cottagey plants include roses and hollyhocks. There are more roses in the walled garden, planted in the shape of a union jack to celebrate Queen Elizabeth II's jubilee in 2002. The old orchards and woodland gardens are now undergoing restoration, too.
topiary; gift shop; refreshments

Owned by Peter Thorogood and Roger Linton
Number of gardeners 6 part-time volunteers
Size 2ha (5 acres)

TOWN PLACE

Freshfield, Scaynes Hill RH17 7NR

Tel 01825 790221
www.townplacegarden.org.uk
Location Turn west off A275 at Sheffield Green; 13/4 miles on left
Opening hours 2pm to 6pm, 14, 16 and 24 June, 1, 8 and 12 July; and by appointment
Admission fee Adults £4; children free; £6 by appointment

Most of the garden at Town Place has been carved out of extensive lawns since the McGraths moved here in 1990. Now it is full of neat, self-contained features, including a *potager*, a hornbeam walk, a herb garden and a spring garden. Two of the best are the English rose garden, planted with David Austin's roses, and the sunken rose garden by the house. The long border is an essay in how to handle colour, with mainly blue- and purple-flowered herbaceous plants in front of a green-and-yellow 'tapestry' conifer hedge. The garden is still expanding and developing, but the results are already very impressive.
good design; roses; colour plantings; cream teas on open days

Owned by Mr and Mrs Anthony McGrath
Number of gardeners 3
Size 1.2ha (3 acres)

WAKEHURST PLACE

Ardingly, Haywards Heath RH17 6TN

Tel 01444 894066 **Fax** 01444 894069
www.kew.org
Location On B2028 between Turners Hill and Ardingly
Opening hours 10am to 6pm (4.30pm in winter), daily, except 24 and 25 December, all year; last admissions 30 minutes before closing
Admission fee Adults £9; children free; free to National Trust members

Wakehurst Place, now managed by the Royal Botanic Gardens at Kew as a country outlier, has a long horticultural history. Most of the planting, however, began after Gerald Loder bought the estate in 1903 and began to introduce exotic trees and shrubs – a development which continued throughout the mid-20th century under the next owner, Sir Henry Price. The planting suffered badly in the great storm of 1987, but the survivors include many rare trees including the King William pine (*Athrotaxis selaginoides*). Among the record-breaking trees which survived the gales are *Cornus nuttallii* and *Torreya nucifera*, both 17m (56ft) high, *Carya tomentosa* at 27m (89ft), and two cultivars of *Chamaecyparis lawsoniana* – 'President Roosevelt' at 15m (49ft) and 'Winston Churchill', slightly shorter, at 13m (43ft). A recent addition has been the 'iris dell', planted with authentic Japanese cultivars of water iris (*Iris ensata*), against a brilliant background of Kurume azaleas – Wakehurst has significant connections with Japan. The water garden is surrounded by sheets of blue meconopsis and the giant Himalayan *Cardiocrinum giganteum*. Wakehurst also has its botanic collections, including a lily border, wonderful ginger plants (*Hedychium*) in autumn and specimen beds with especially comprehensive collections of hypericums, hydrangeas and agapanthus. Many parts of the woodland garden are underplanted with rhododendrons, which are at their best in April and May. Wakehurst has also benefited from major funding by the Millennium Commission, which has enabled it to develop the world's largest seed bank: it

aims to collect and conserve some 10 per cent of the world's flora – 24,000 species – by the year 2010.
ornamental woodland garden; roses (mainly old-fashioned and climbers); rhododendrons and azaleas; plantsman's collection of plants; daffodils; camellias; fine collection of trees; alpine plants; bluebells; Asian heath garden; pinetum; cardiocrinums; good autumn colour; *Iris ensata* dell; water garden; tallest *Ostrya japonica* (15m; 49ft) in the British Isles, plus 25 further tree records; gift shop; plant sales (March to October); light refreshments and restaurant

Owned by RBG Kew, on lease from the National Trust
Number of gardeners 30
Size 127ha (316 acres)
NCCPG National Collections *Betula*; *Hypericum*; *Nothofagus*; *Skimmia*
English Heritage Grade II*

WEST DEAN GARDENS
West Dean, Chichester PO18 0QZ

Tel 01243 818210 **Fax** 01243 811342
www.westdean.org.uk
Location 6 miles north of Chichester on A286
Opening hours 10.30am to 5pm, daily, March to October; 10.30am to 4pm, Wednesday to Sunday, November to February; closed over Christmas and New Year period
Admission fee Adults £6; OAPs £5.50; children £3; half price from November to February; RHS members free from November to March except during special events

Laid out in the 1890s and 1900s, West Dean has now been extensively restored. Harold Peto's 100m

West Dean Gardens

West Dean Gardens

(328ft) pergola has been replanted with roses. Much of the damage to the 20ha (50-acre) St Roche's arboretum caused by the 1987 storm has been made good. The great range of glasshouses in the walled garden has been repaired and the garden itself planted as a working kitchen garden which is now the crowning glory of West Dean. A huge variety of plants – from peaches to peppers, cucumbers to coleus, aubergines to orchids – grows in the 16 glasshouses and frames. Out of doors are orderly rows of cabbage, carrots, lettuce and beetroot, alongside herbaceous borders. No space is wasted: the kitchen garden has over one mile of walls covered in trained fruit trees – over 200 different apples, pears and plums. No private garden has so many beautifully grown fruit and vegetables. Beyond the walled garden (21/4 acres in size) are 35 acres of ornamental gardens, the St Roche's arboretum (now really coming into its own, with broad paths and splendid trees) and 240 acres of landscaped park – all linked by a 21/2-mile walk. Herbaceous borders and annual bedding schemes have been reinstated and over 400,000 bulbs planted. The redevelopment of the spring garden, including the 1820s rustic thatched summerhouse with its moss- and heather-lined interior and its floor of knapped flints and horses' molars is now complete. In the wild garden are new woodland and herbaceous plantings (lots of grasses), a pond and wetland area.
roses (mainly old-fashioned and climbers); plants under glass; museum of old lawn mowers; long pergola with roses and clematis; tallest *Cupressus goveniana* (22m; 72ft) and *Ailanthus vilmoriniana* (26m; 85ft) in the UK; amazing kitchen garden; good shop; licensed restaurant

Owned by The Edward James Foundation
Number of gardeners 10
Size 36ha (90 acres) in all
NCCPG National Collections *Aesculus*; *Liriodendron*
English Heritage Grade II*

WARWICKSHIRE

Warwickshire has for centuries been a prosperous county: it has the rich clay soils, the country estates and the gardens to prove it. Many of its historic gardens are open to the public throughout the season, including such top attractions as Arbury Hall, Charlecote Park, Farnborough Hall, Packwood House, Upton House and Warwick Castle. The National Gardens Scheme is very successful in persuading the owners of modern gardens to open them to the public, especially by grouping several together within a village. Warwickshire has many first-rate garden centres and a few top-class specialist nurseries – notably Fibrex Nurseries, who specialise in pelargoniums, ivies, hardy ferns and hellebores. Fibrex also have two of the county's National Collections. The Henry Doubleday Research Association, now known as Garden Organic, has its headquarters at Ryton near Coventry. Its garden offers free access to RHS members throughout the year.

ARBURY HALL

Nuneaton CV10 7PT

Tel 024 7638 2804 **Fax** 024 7664 1147
Location 3 miles south-west of Nuneaton off the B4102
Opening hours 2pm to 6pm, Bank Holiday Sundays and Mondays (8 days in total), Easter Sunday to August
Admission fee Adults £5; children £3.50

Arbury is more important historically than horticulturally: Sanderson Miller was involved in some 18th-century improvements and there is a wonderfully landscaped sequence of canals and lakes. During the 19th century, many good trees were planted, now in the full-grown beauty of their maturity: purple beeches and a golden sycamore, for example. Then there are bluebell woods, pollarded limes, a large rose garden, a walled garden and a huge wisteria. Nothing is outstanding in itself, but the ensemble is an oasis of peace on the edge of industrial Daventry and worth the journey from far away.
woodland garden; roses (mainly modern); rhododendrons and azaleas; daffodils; bluebells; gift and crafts shop; tea room

Owned by Viscount Daventry
Number of gardeners 4
English Heritage Grade II*

BADDESLEY CLINTON

Baddesley Clinton Village, Knowle, Solihull B93 0DQ

Tel 01564 783294 **Fax** 01564 782706
www.nationaltrust.org.uk
Location 1 mile west of A4141
Opening hours Noon to 5.30pm, Wednesday to Sunday, 28 February to 16 December; also open on Bank Holiday Mondays; closes at 5pm in February, March, April, October and 1 to 4 November; closes at 4pm from 7 November to 16 December
Admission fee Adults £4; children £2

The walled garden at Baddesley Clinton has fine mixed plantings, including a good collection of shrub roses, herbaceous plants, herbs and annuals. One of the Victorian lean-to glasshouses has recently been restored. In front of the house (an ancient manor house) is a formal courtyard garden. Further away are woodland walks, a lake, stew ponds and wildflower meadows.
formal courtyard garden; walled garden; shop; plant sales; restaurant

Owned by The National Trust
Number of gardeners 2
Size 4.4ha (11 acres)
English Heritage Grade II

BARTON HOUSE

Barton-on-the-Heath, Moreton-in-Marsh GL56 0PJ

Tel 01608 674303 **Fax** 01608 674365
Location 5 miles east of Moreton-in-Marsh
Opening hours For NGS: 2pm to 6pm, 27 May; and groups (25+) by appointment

Barton is a real gem – worth travelling a long distance for its all too rare open days. The woodlands are thick with rhododendrons, azaleas, maples, camellias, magnolias and rare plants that are more often associated with Surrey than the Cotswolds. But Barton has a good collection of rare trees and shrubs, as well as its National Collection of *Arbutus*. It is a garden of enthusiasms: Mouton paeonies are one passion, and a recent addition has been an exotic Mediterranean-inspired courtyard planted with palms, cypresses and olives. Add in a Japanese garden, a colour-graded rose garden and masses of architectural bric-à-brac, each piece with its own story (the conservatory roof that came from the Royal Exchange in the City of London) and it is clear why no one can fail to respond to the bravura of it all.
teas on NGS days

Owned by Mr and Mrs IHB Cathie
Number of gardeners 3
Size 2.6ha (61/2 acres)
NCCPG National Collections *Arbutus*

CHARLECOTE PARK

Wellesbourne, Warwick CV35 9ER

Tel 01789 470277 **Fax** 01789 470544
www.nationaltrust.org.uk
Location Signed from A429
Opening hours 10.30am to 6pm, Friday to Tuesday, 3 March to 28 October; 11am to 4pm, Saturdays and Sundays, 3 November to 22 December
Admission fee Adults £4; children £2

Fine cedars and a Capability Brown park are Charlecote's main claims to fame, but the young William Shakespeare is reputed to have poached deer from the park, so the National Trust has planted a border with plants mentioned in his works. Recent additions include a parterre, a large herbaceous border, a sensory garden and 'green court' garden designed by the tenant, Sir Edmund Fairfax-Lucy.
topiary; parterre; mature conifers; deer park; orangery; National Trust shop; restaurant

Owned by The National Trust
Number of gardeners 2
Size 1.6ha (4 acres)
English Heritage Grade II*

COUGHTON COURT

Alcester B49 5JA

Tel 01789 762542 **Fax** 01789 764369
www.coughtoncourt.co.uk
Location 2 miles north of Alcester on A435
Opening hours 11am to 5.30pm, Wednesday to Sunday, plus Bank Holiday Mondays and Tuesdays, April to September; plus Tuesdays in July and August and Saturdays and Sundays in October; walled garden closes at 4.30pm
Admission fee Adults £6.20; children £3.10; RHS members free, except on Tuesdays

The garden at Coughton has all been made since 1992, designed by Christina Williams, Mrs Throckmorton's daughter. The Throckmortons have lived at Coughton for 300 years. An Elizabethan-style knot garden fills the courtyard, and extensive new plantings beyond lead the eye out to the distant landscape. The walled garden has a rose labyrinth, a new vegetable garden, fine herbaceous borders and a bog garden, as well as an orchard planted with local varieties of fruit. The family is building up a collection of daffodil cultivars bred by their American namesake Dr Tom Throckmorton.
interesting historic gardens (new) around the house (old); pretty plants and plantings; gift shop and plant centre; restaurant/café

Owned by Mrs Clare Throckmorton and the National Trust
Number of gardeners 6
Size 10ha (25 acres)

FARNBOROUGH HALL
Banbury OX17 1DU

Tel 01295 690002
www.nationaltrust.org.uk
Location Off A423, 6 miles north of Banbury
Opening hours 2pm to 5.30pm, Wednesdays and Saturdays, 7 April to 29 September, and 6 and 7 May
Admission fee Adults £4.50; children £2.25

Farnborough Hall is Sanderson Miller's masterpiece – a broad grass walk leads gently uphill for 3/4 mile to an obelisk erected in 1751. On the way are an Ionic temple and the Oval Pavilion that have gradually been freed from their surrounding vegetation. Below the house lies a pretty series of landscaped lakes – the views and walks below the terraces invite you to explore. There is no garden, as such, but a sense of space and peace: only the distant roar of the M40 takes the edge off the sense of awe. The National Trust suggests taking the woodland walk back – pretty with wildflowers in spring.
historic landscape

Owned by The National Trust
Number of gardeners 1 full-time, 1 part-time
Size 4.8ha (12 acres)
English Heritage Grade I

FIBREX NURSERIES LTD
Honeybourne Road, Pebworth, Stratford-upon-Avon CV37 8XP

Tel 01789 720788 **Fax** 01789 721162
www.fibrex.co.uk
Location South-east edge of village, on road to Honeybourne
Opening hours 9am to 4pm, Monday to Friday, all year; plus weekends (10.30am to 4pm) from March to July; closed for last two weeks of December and first week of January; also closed on Easter Sunday and August Bank Holiday Monday
Admission fee Free

Fibrex is a family nursery, built up over more than 40 years and a regular prize winner at RHS flower shows. It has four specialities – pelargoniums, ivies, hardy ferns and hellebores – and holds National Collections of two of them. The National Collection of pelargoniums has over 2,000 different species and cultivars and claims to be the largest in the world. The National Collection of ivies (*Hedera*) has over 300 different species and cultivars. The ferns are planted out in the show garden in a natural manner using mature plants: the ivies can be seen growing both outside and in a covered exhibition area.
pelargoniums; ivies; hardy ferns; hellebores; tea and coffee

NCCPG National Collections *Hedera*; *Pelargonium*

GARDEN ORGANIC RYTON
Ryton, Coventry CV8 3LG

Tel 024 7630 3517 **Fax** 024 7663 9229
www.gardenorganic.org.uk
Location 5 miles south-east of Coventry off A45
Opening hours 9am to 5pm, daily, all year, except Christmas week
Admission fee Adults £5; concessions £4.50; children £2.50; RHS members free (except for some special events, when £1.50)

This is the new name for Ryton Organic gardens, though it remains the UK's centre of excellence for organic gardening. It is very well laid out and landscaped, with 30 different small gardens, all highly instructive. The gardens include herb gardens, rose gardens, fruit and vegetable displays plus wildlife and conservation areas. A new development is the area called the Vegetable Kingdom, which tells the history of British vegetables. The website is good.
organic gardens; considerable educational interest; shop with gardening products, books, food, wine and gifts; organic whole-food restaurant

Owned by Henry Doubleday Research Association
Number of gardeners 7
Size 4ha (10 acres)

THE HILLER GARDEN

Dunnington Heath Farm, Dunnington, Alcester B49 5PD

Tel 01789 491342 **Fax** 01789 490439
Location On B4088 near Ragley Hall, 2 miles south of Alcester
Opening hours 10am to 5pm (4pm in winter), daily, all year; nursery open from March to November
Admission fee Free

This is an unusually fine display garden, with colour and interest all the year round. There are roses from medieval times through to the latest David Austin English roses. The nursery specialises in a wide range of old roses and perennial plants.
gift shop; garden centre; farm shop; restaurant

Owned by Richard Beach
Number of gardeners 1 1/2
Size 0.8ha (2 acres)

THE MILL GARDEN

55 Mill Street, Warwick CV34 4HB

Tel 01926 492877
Location Off A425, beside the old castle gate, at the bottom of Mill Street; use St Nicholas car park
Opening hours 9am to 6pm, daily, April to October
Admission fee Adults £1.50; children free

No garden has such an idyllic setting, on the banks of the Avon at the foot of Warwick Castle: the views in all directions are superb. The garden is planted in the cottage style and seems much larger than its half acre: it burgeons with plants, and the use of annuals to supplement the varied permanent planting enables it to have colour and form, contrasts and harmonies, at every season. The garden was made by Arthur Measures in the 1950s: it remains open in his memory.
plantsman's collection of plants; water plants; magnificent riverside position

Owned by J Measures and DGF Russell
Number of gardeners owners and part-time help
Size 0.2ha (1/2 acre)

PACKWOOD HOUSE

Packwood Lane, Lapworth, Solihull B94 6AT

Tel 01564 783294 **Fax** 01564 782706
www.nationaltrust.org.uk
Location 2 miles east of Hockley Heath: signed from A3400

The Mill Garden

Opening hours 11am to 5.30pm, Wednesday to Sunday and Bank Holiday Mondays, 28 February to 4 November; closes at 4.30pm in February, March, April, October and November
Admission fee Garden only: adults £4; children £2

Long famous for its topiary, Packwood also has magnificent herbaceous borders which make a visit in July or August particularly rewarding.
shop; plants for sale

Owned by The National Trust
Number of gardeners 3 1/2
Size 2.8ha (7 acres)
English Heritage Grade I

RAGLEY HALL
Alcester B49 5NJ

Tel 01789 762090 **Fax** 01789 764791
www.ragleyhall.com
Location 2 miles south-west of Alcester, signed from A46 and A435
Opening hours 10am to 6pm, daily, 22 March to 30 September; closed Monday to Wednesday in term time
Admission fee Adults £8; OAPs £6.50; children £4.50; families £25; RHS members free on Thursdays and Fridays from May to September and at weekends in July and August

Ragley Hall has a Capability Brown park, overlaid by a horticultural landscape started by Robert Marnock in the 1860s. Mature trees, including vast wellingtonias, are the background for modern gardens – roses, thousands of bulbs, azaleas, bog plants and mixed borders.
café; restaurant

Owned by The Marquess of Hertford
Number of gardeners 4
Size 10ha (25 acres)
English Heritage Grade II*

UPTON HOUSE & GARDENS
Banbury OX15 6HT

Tel 01295 670266 **Fax** 01295 671144
www.nationaltrust.org.uk
Location A422, 7 miles north-west of Banbury and 12 miles south-east of Stratford-upon-Avon
Opening hours 11am to 5pm, Saturday to Wednesday (daily in August), 3 March to 31 October; noon to 4pm, Saturdays and Sundays, 3 November to 16 December
Admission fee Adults £4.80; children £2.40; RHS members free (but not all the time)

Upton House is set off by a flat and spacious expanse of grass; only when you reach the far side of this immense lawn do the real gardens appear, tumbling down the terraced hillside to the pool at the bottom. The structure is early 1700s: the gardens are 1930s – Kitty Lloyd-Jones's masterpiece. It is dominated by a sloping kitchen garden, reached by flights of Italianate stairs. There are also small formal gardens, one with standard *Hibiscus syriacus* 'Bluebird' underplanted with eryngiums, and another planted with roses. One way back runs through good herbaceous borders – simply planted, but effective. The best area for interesting plants is the bog garden, once a medieval fish pond, with fine cercidiphyllums, gunneras, magnolias and an *Acer carpinifolium* leaning low over another pool. Be prepared for quite a long walk from the car park – and be careful on the slopes in wet weather.
good herbaceous borders; bog garden; National Trust shop; licensed restaurant

Owned by The National Trust
Number of gardeners 5, plus 1 student
Size 14ha (35 acres)
NCCPG National Collections *Aster*
English Heritage Grade II*

Conservatory at Warwick Castle

Warwick Castle

WARWICK CASTLE
Warwick CV34 4QU

Tel 0870 442 2000 **Fax** 0870 442 2394
www.warwick-castle.com
Location In town centre
Opening hours 10am to 6pm (5pm from October to March), daily, all year, except 25 December
Admission fee Peak season (22 July to 3 September): adults £17.95; OAPs £12.95; children £10.95; slightly less out of season; ticket price includes entry to castle (no 'garden only' price)

This classic 18th-century landscape looks good after some recent restoration, as do the late 19th-century formal garden (the 'Peacock' garden) and the recreated Victorian rose garden, both by Robert Marnock. But the price is expensive unless you take in the castle, too.
topiary; roses (mainly old-fashioned); rhododendrons and azaleas; mature conifers; Capability Brown landscape; handsome conservatory; shop; refreshments

Owned by The Tussauds Group
Number of gardeners 9
Size 23ha (58 acres)
English Heritage Grade I

WOODPECKERS
The Bank, Marlcliff, Bidford-on-Avon B50 4NT

Tel 01789 773416
Location Off B4086 between Bidford-on-Avon and Cleeve Prior
Opening hours By appointment at any time
Admission fee Adults £4

Woodpeckers is an outstanding plantsman's garden, with some very interesting design ideas – it is unusual for a garden to combine plants and structure so well. The owners have been making it since 1965 and, over the years, daffodils, fritillaries and snowdrops have naturalised throughout the garden above the river Avon. There are good collections of clematis, roses and, above all, alpine plants, as well as areas of woodland, orchard and wildflower meadows. The knot garden in three different cultivars of box is a model of how to create striking formal effects within a small, confined space.
refreshments by arrangement

Owned by Drs Andrew and Lallie Cox
Number of gardeners owners only
Size 1ha (2½ acres)

WEST MIDLANDS

As an administrative entity, West Midlands was a short-lived county: created in 1974 from parts of Warwickshire and Staffordshire, it is now entirely split up into unitary authorities. Its historic gardens are few, but they include what is left of the poet Shenstone's The Leasowes, together with the Birmingham Botanical Gardens and Castle Bromwich Hall. The latter are both highly visitable and highly visited – excellent gardens, deservedly popular still. Being such an urban county, West Midlands is short on old estates, landscaped parks and arboreta, but full of large villa gardens like the one in Edgbaston that became the University of Birmingham Botanic Garden. This is also the area where the National Gardens Scheme does best. The biggest RHS event in the Midlands takes place at the NEC from 13 to 17 June 2007: *BBC Gardeners' World Live* is very different from such shows as Chelsea and Hampton Court, though the great draw is the enormously long floral marquee that the Royal Horticultural Society runs with great aplomb. The county, though small, also has a surprisingly large number of National Collections, including two, *Ceanothus* and *Rudbeckia*, held by Dudley Metropolitan Borough Council.

BIRMINGHAM BOTANICAL GARDENS & GLASSHOUSES

Westbourne Road, Edgbaston, Birmingham B15 3TR

Tel 0121 454 1860 **Fax** 0121 454 7835
www.birminghambotanicalgardens.org.uk
Location Follow brown tourist signs in Edgbaston
Opening hours 9am (10am on Sundays) to 7pm (5pm or dusk from October to March), daily, all year, except Christmas Day
Admission fee Adults £6.50; concessions £3.90

Part botanic garden, part public park, wholly delightful, the Birmingham Botanical Gardens & Glasshouses can boast a historic layout (John Claudius Loudon), rare trees and shrubs, gardens for rhododendrons, roses, herbs and alpines, and four glasshouses (tropical, subtropical, Mediterranean and arid) as well as a good tea room, brilliant standards of maintenance and a brass band playing on Sunday afternoons in summer. The plant highlights are innumerable, but include water hyacinths (the weed that is choking the Nile), rice plants, papyrus plants, coffee and sugar, bananas and pineapples, many cycads, insectivorous plants, 'living stones', *Paulownia tomentosa*, good herbaceous plants (phlox, euphorbias, geraniums, delphiniums) and the National Collection of bonsai housed in a secure courtyard.

roses (ancient and modern); rock garden; plantsman's collection of plants; plants under glass; fruit; mature conifers; good herbaceous borders; alpine yard; bonsai; three 'historic' gardens: Roman, medieval and Tudor; gift shop; tea room and light refreshments

Owned by Birmingham Botanical & Horticultural Society
Number of gardeners 10, plus students
Size 6ha (15 acres)
NCCPG National Collections Bonsai
English Heritage Grade II*

CASTLE BROMWICH HALL GARDENS

Chester Road, Castle Bromwich B36 9BT

Tel/fax 0121 749 4100
www.cbhgt.org.uk
Location 5 miles from city centre, just off B4114
Opening hours 11am to 4.30pm, Tuesday to Thursday; 1.30pm to 5.30pm, Saturdays, Sundays and Bank Holiday Mondays; 11am to 3.30pm, Thursdays, April to September
Admission fee Adults £3.50; concessions £3; children 50p

The gardens at Castle Bromwich Hall are garden archaeology at work – educational, instructive and

Castle Bromwich Hall Gardens

highly enjoyable. They are being restored as they were in about 1700 by a privately funded trust. For many years they were neglected, lost beneath a tangled mass of vegetation. Work began in 1985 and has been very successful: the result is both beautiful, inspiring and educational. The gardens contain a large collection of unusual period plants, and a 19th-century holly maze. There is also a holly walk – a broad path lined with variegated hollies. At its end, the elegant Summer House looks across to an early orangery known as the Green House. Nearby is the formal vegetable garden, laid out to the design of Batty Langley's *New Principles of Gardening* (1728). Many historic vegetables and herbs are grown, along with unusual varieties like the black 'Congo' potato and white carrot. Fruit trees are formally trained – apples, pears, apricots, figs and cherries. The Upper and Lower Wildernesses have grown to maturity, with period underplanting. The North Garden has recently been restored to the design shown in Henry Beighton's Prospect of 1726, its parterre outlined with yew, mown grass and gravel.
walled gardens; historic vegetables, fruit and herbs; holly maze; gift shop; coffee shop

Owned by Castle Bromwich Hall Gardens Trust
Number of gardeners 3, plus volunteers
Size 4ha (10 acres)
English Heritage Grade II*

WIGHTWICK MANOR
Wightwick, Wolverhampton WV6 8EE

Tel 01902 761400 **Fax** 01902 764663
www.nationaltrust.org.uk
Location 3 miles west of Wolverhampton on A454
Opening hours 11am to 6pm, Wednesday to Saturday and Bank Holidays, 1 March to 22 December
Admission fee Adults £3.70; children free

Wightwick is a substantial Victorian garden, designed by Alfred Parsons and Thomas Mawson. The upper garden is held together by yew hedges, which separate it into a series of smaller gardens. The Victorian peach house, topiary, rose arbour and avenues of Irish yews are also worth seeing.
topiary; roses (mainly old-fashioned and climbers); rock garden; good herbaceous borders; current holder of Sandford Award; shop; tea room

Owned by The National Trust
Number of gardeners 3, plus 6 volunteers
Size 6.7ha (17 acres)

WINTERBOURNE BOTANIC GARDEN, UNIVERSITY OF BIRMINGHAM
58 Edgbaston Park Road, Edgbaston B15 2RT

Tel 0121 414 5590/3882 **Fax** 0121 414 8128
www.botanic.bham.ac.uk
Location Off A38 Bristol Road, 1/2 mile
Opening hours 11am to 4pm, Monday to Friday, April to September; plus 1pm to 5pm on Sundays; noon to 3.30pm, Monday to Friday only, January to March and October to December
Admission fee Adults £3; children £1.50

This was originally a private garden, belonging to one of Birmingham's great and good families: it was given to the university in 1944, but still has the 'feel' of a private garden – one with a fine collection of plants. The rhododendrons and naturalised bulbs are very pretty: even the roses, chosen to illustrate their history in cultivation, fit

Winterbourne Botanic Gardens

well into an ornamental garden. There are some geographic beds which put together plants that combine naturally in the wild, and an interesting sandstone rock garden. The garden went back a little during the 1980s and early 1990s, but has now been fully restored and redeveloped most effectively. It is a charming place to spend a couple of hours at almost any time of the year.

roses of every kind; a good collection of plants of every kind; shop; tea and coffee

Owned by The University of Birmingham
Number of gardeners 5, plus 1 student
Size 2.4ha (6 acres)
NCCPG National Collections *Anthemis*; *Rosa* (History of European roses); *Iris unguicularis* (provisional)

WILTSHIRE

Wiltshire is the county that people travel through on their way to somewhere else. For gardeners, this is a mistake. Unlike so many counties whose great Grade I historic gardens are often rather dull, Wiltshire's are all supremely beautiful – Bowood, Iford, Longleat, Stourhead and Wilton. All are open to the public, as are many of the other graded gardens. Wiltshire also has a number of very good plantsman's gardens – notably Broadleas and Home Covert near Devizes, and the Old Vicarage at nearby Edington. It has some fine arboreta: tree enthusiasts should also try to see the record-breaking multi-stemmed specimen of *Zelkova carpinifolia* at Wardour Castle – 35m (115ft) high when last officially measured in 1977. The National Gardens Scheme does well in the county, particularly among the owners of medium-sized and large gardens. The Wiltshire Gardens Trust is active in conservation and also represents the NCCPG in the county: there is a sprinkling of National Collections among its members. Wiltshire does not, however, do so well for nurseries: perhaps only the Botanic Nursery at Atworth can be said to have a national profile. It is worth noting that, contrary to widespread belief, both Shute House and Larmer Tree Gardens are actually in Wiltshire, not in Dorset.

THE ABBEY HOUSE

Market Cross, Malmesbury SN16 9AS

Tel 01666 822212 (information) **Fax** 01666 822782
www.abbeyhousegardens.co.uk
Location In town centre, behind abbey; public car parks nearby
Opening hours 11am to 5.30pm, daily, 21 March to 21 October
Admission fee Adults £5.50; concessions £5; children £2

This remarkable five-acre garden has all been made by the Pollards since 1995. They planted 2,000 different roses to celebrate the millennium, and 2,000 different herb cultivars. The roses are now underplanted with 100,000 tulips. Other features include an arcaded fruit walk, a knot garden, huge herbaceous borders, a striking laburnum tunnel, an auricula theatre, a fuchsia gallery and a formal garden. But it is the design and planting which are so distinctive: bold, varied and inspirational. The woodland garden running down to the river is home to more than 40,000 spring bulbs, 60 different hellebore cultivars and a collection of rare trees. At the bottom are fish ponds, a 6m (20ft) waterfall, heather banks, 10,000 narcissi and a fernery. Alan Titchmarsh came here for *BBC Gardeners' World* in June 2002. His verdict: 'The Wow factor is here in abundance!' But that was five years ago, and the development since then is amazing: the Wow factor is now here in *super* abundance!

plantsman's collection of plants; herbaceous borders; roses of every kind; good design; colour contrasts; light refreshments

Owned by Ian Pollard
Number of gardeners 1 full-time, 2 part-time, plus enthusiastic owners
Size 2ha (5 acres)

AVEBURY MANOR GARDEN

Avebury, Marlborough SN8 1RF

Tel 01672 539250 **Fax** 01672 538038
www.nationaltrust.org.uk
Location In village, well signed
Opening hours 11am to 5pm, daily, except Wednesdays and Thursdays, 1 April to 31 October; open Bank Holiday Mondays
Admission fee Adults £3; children £1.50

P

The National Trust is continuing restoration work at this great Edwardian garden. The 'garden rooms' are being replanted and the stupendous topiary revived: the results are well worth another visit.

The Abbey House

topiary; roses (mainly old-fashioned); good herbaceous borders; double lavender walk; shop; National Trust restaurant in village

Owned by The National Trust
Number of gardeners 2 1/2
Size 2.4ha (6 acres)

BOLEHYDE MANOR
Allington, Chippenham SN14 6LW

Tel 01249 652105 **Fax** 01249 659296
Location 2 miles west of Chippenham
Opening hours 2.30pm to 6pm, 17 June; and by appointment
Admission fee Adults £3.50; children free

This charming house is surrounded by outbuildings and walls of old Cotswold stone, which form the background to a series of enclosed gardens. Each is very prettily designed and planted in the modern style – using plants for their contrasts and combinations of flower, shape, colour and form. The gardens seem to brim over with flowers and an abundance of beauty. If only it were open more often.
roses (mainly old-fashioned); pretty *potager*; good herbaceous borders; climbing roses; teas on 17 June

Owned by Earl and Countess Cairns
Number of gardeners 1
Size 1.2ha (3 acres)

THE BOTANIC NURSERY
Cottles Lane, Atworth, Melksham SN12 8NU

Tel 07850 328756 **Fax** 01225 700953
www.thebotanicnursery.com
Location Next to grounds of Stonar School, just outside Atworth on road to South Wraxall
Opening hours 10am to 5pm, Tuesday to Saturday, March to October; and by appointment
Admission fee Free

The Botanic Nursery built its reputation on growing lime-tolerant plants, but has become better known as a plantsman's nursery, where a long browse will winkle out all sorts of rarities. It is best known at RHS flower shows for its spectacular displays of foxgloves (*Digitalis*) from its National Collection, though it also has very good collections of unusual shrubs, eryngiums and dieramas. The one-acre display garden (mainly trees and shrubs) is well worth a visit, too.
2,000 different plants, many rare, all lime-tolerant

Owned by Terence and Mary Baker
Number of gardeners 1
Size 0.8ha (2 acres)
NCCPG National Collections *Digitalis*

BOWOOD HOUSE & GARDENS
Calne SN11 0LZ

Tel 01249 812102 **Fax** 01249 821757
www.bowood.org
Location Off A4 in Derry Hill village between Calne and Chippenham
Opening hours 11am to 6pm, daily, 31 March to 31 October; rhododendron walks: mid April to early June (telephone for exact dates, which depend upon the flowering season)
Admission fee Main gardens: adults £7.70; OAPs £6.70; children (under 15) £5.20; children (2-4 yrs) £4; rhododendron walks: adults £4.95; OAPs £4.45; children free

Beautifully maintained and welcoming, Bowood has something from every period of English garden history. Capability Brown made the lake and planted many of the trees and lawns which give such a beautiful setting to the house. Charles Hamilton added the famous cascade below the lake in the picturesque style. There is an important 19th-century pinetum, laid out on pre-Linnaean principles – geographically – with oceans of grass to separate the continents. It is not just a collection of magnificent conifers, but also contains many rare and beautiful deciduous trees, including the tallest specimen of the cut-leaved horse-chestnut (*Aesculus hippocastanum* 'Laciniata') in the British Isles. By the house are handsome Italianate formal gardens designed by Smirke and Kennedy in the 19th century and recently replanted by Lady Mary Keen. Up in the woods in a separate part of the estate, and entered directly from the A342, is a magnificent display of modern

Bowood House and Gardens

rhododendrons around the beautiful Robert Adam mausoleum. The ocean of bluebells which surround these rhododendron drives is one of the finest in the South of England. Be sure to miss the reclining nude above the formal gardens.
lake; 100-acre Capability Brown landscaped parkland; famous old arboretum; topiary; mature conifers; modern borders; rhododendrons, azaleas and bluebells (separate garden); tallest *Thuya occidentalis* 'Wareana' in the UK; gift shop; coffee shop; buffet lunches and afternoon teas in licensed restaurant

Owned by The Marquis of Lansdowne
Number of gardeners 4
Size 80ha (200 acres) of grounds
English Heritage Grade I

BROADLEAS
Devizes SN10 5JQ

Tel 01380 722035 **Fax** 01380 722970
Location 1 mile south of Devizes
Opening hours 2pm to 6pm, Wednesdays, Thursdays and Sundays, April to October
Admission fee Adults £5; children £1.50; groups (10+) £4.50; RHS members free

Lady Anne Cowdray started to make this garden – now owned by a charitable trust – in 1947. Since then it has grown into a very fine plantsman's garden, with lots of different kinds of plants but an especially good collection of ornamental trees and shrubs. Broadleas has a rose garden, a grey border, a rock garden and a perennial garden, all near the Regency house. But the main attraction is the Dell, a greensand combe that stretches down to the valley below, its sides just stuffed with good things. At the top are two tall magnolias, M. *sargentiana* var. *robusta* and the very rare cultivar now known as 'Broadleas'. Pass between them, and past a very tall paulownia, and you come into a world of rare trees, a large yellow magnolia, sheets of unusual bulbs, trilliums, erythroniums and many others. And Broadleas has two characteristics common to all good plantsman's gardens: it is worth visiting at any time of the year and it gets better all the time. The nursery sells surplus plants propagated from the garden.
a plantsman's collection of plants; woodland garden; roses (ancient and modern); good herbaceous borders; fine ornamental trees; excellent small nursery for rare plants; teas for groups by arrangement

Owned by Lady Anne Cowdray and Broadleas Gardens Charitable Trust
Number of gardeners 2 1/2
Size 3.6ha (9 acres)
English Heritage Grade II

CONOCK MANOR
Devizes SN10 3QQ

Tel 01380 840227
Location 5 miles south-east of Devizes off A342
Opening hours For NGS: 2pm to 6pm, 20 May; and by appointment
Admission fee Adults £3; children free

Beautiful flat parkland surrounds this covetable Georgian house. Behind the copper-domed stables, an elegant shrub walk meanders past *Sorbus*, maples and magnolias. Some of the trees which have been planted in recent years are already making a good show. A recent addition is a Persian garden – brickwork in stylised script with water runnels and small fountains.
cottages orneés; fine trees and mixed borders; good *Sorbus* and *Eucalyptus*; woodland walk; cream teas

Owned by Mrs Bonar Sykes
Number of gardeners 1 part-time
Size 0.8ha (2 acres), plus parkland
English Heritage Grade II

CORSHAM COURT
Corsham SN13 0BZ

Tel/fax 01249 701610
www.corsham-court.co.uk
Location Signed from A4 Bath to Chippenham
Opening hours 2pm to 5.30pm, Tuesday to Thursday, plus Saturdays, Sundays and Bank Holiday Mondays, 20 March to 30 September; 2pm to 4.30pm, Saturdays and Sundays, 1 October to 19 March; closed in December

Admission fee Adults £2.50; OAPs £2; children £1.50; RHS members and wheelchair-bound (plus one helper) free

Corsham is a major 18th-century landscape garden, one of the few where both Capability Brown and Humphry Repton worked. Then the flower garden was developed in the middle of the 19th century: box-edged borders and a pretty fountain, all kept up with some good modern planting. A large arboretum was planted in the 1980s: there are plans to landscape it and enlarge its collections.
fine trees; designed by Capability Brown and Humphry Repton; young arboretum; magnolias; amazing oriental plane *Platanus orientalis* whose sweeping limbs have rooted over a huge area

Owned by James Methuen-Campbell
Number of gardeners 4
English Heritage Grade II*

THE COURTS GARDEN
Holt, Bradford-on-Avon BA14 6RR

Tel 01225 782875 **Fax** 01225 782340
www.nationaltrust.org.uk
Location In middle of Holt village, 2 1/2 miles east of Bradford-on-Avon
Opening hours 11am to 5.30pm, Thursday to Tuesday, 17 March to 28 October
Admission fee Adults £5.50; children £2.70

Holt Court (as it used to be called) is a 1920s masterpiece in the Hidcote style. It has rich colour plantings in a series of garden rooms and excellent plants, beautifully used. The design is asymmetrical, with both formal and informal lines.
plantsman's collection of plants; good herbaceous borders; fine collection of trees; tea room

Owned by The National Trust
Number of gardeners 2
Size 2.8ha (7 acres)
English Heritage Grade II

HAZELBURY MANOR
Box SN13 8HX

Tel 01225 812952 **Fax** 01225 810875
Location Due east of Box, off the B3709
Opening hours For NGS. And by appointment
Admission fee Adults £4

The grand Edwardian-style gardens at Hazelbury were laid out by a previous owner in the 1970s and 1980s. Fine topiary, deep and colourful herbaceous borders, a circle of menhirs and a laburnum walk are the principal relics, but the garden is now improving again and visitors can expect to see more in the years to come.
topiary; refreshments on NGS days

Owned by Hazelbury Partners
Size 4.8ha (12 acres)
English Heritage Grade II

HEALE HOUSE GARDEN
Middle Woodford, Salisbury SP4 6NT

Tel/fax 01722 782504
www.healegarden.co.uk
Location Signed off the western Woodford valley road, and from A345 and A360
Opening hours 10am to 5pm, Wednesday to Sunday, plus Bank Holidays, February to October
Admission fee Adults £4; OAPs £3.75; children £1.50

Many would agree that Heale is the prettiest garden in southern England. It sits at the bottom of a broad, chalk valley, with the River Avon and its leats flowing through. The house is Carolean, with substantial additions so sympathetically designed by Detmar Blow that it is difficult to know which parts belong to the original house. Harold Peto laid out the garden: you see his handiwork in the formal pools, terraces, balustrades and Italianate garden architecture. Alongside the river are more balustrading, old rambling roses and a lawn which is richly planted with hybrid musk roses and herbaceous plants. On an island in the river is a Japanese garden, laid out in 1901 and much altered by the sheer growth of the original Japanese maples: however, the scarlet lacquered bridge and the neat tea house seem almost new. Perhaps the best part of the garden is the old kitchen garden, surrounded by cob walls and designed around 100-year-old box balls and tunnels of trained apples and pears. Here, over 30 years from the mid-1960s onwards, Lady Anne Rasch developed a wonderful series of mixed borders, exuberantly planted with roses, clematis and herbaceous plants, though her plantings here have recently been updated and intensified. Heale is one of those gardens that can genuinely be called a garden for all seasons; there are swarms of cyclamen in autumn, and woodlands full of snowdrops and aconites in winter.

roses (mainly old-fashioned); good herbaceous borders; Japanese garden; good plant associations; first HHA/ Christie's Garden of the Year in 1984; plant centre; garden and gift shop; coffee shop, with teas and light lunches

Owned by Mr and Mrs Guy Rasch
Number of gardeners 2, plus owners
Size 3.2ha (8 acres)
English Heritage Grade II*

HOME COVERT GARDEN & ARBORETUM

Roundway, Devizes SN10 2JA

Tel 01380 723407
Location 1 mile north of Devizes in Roundway village
Opening hours For NGS; and groups welcome at any time by appointment
Admission fee Adults £3; children free

Home Covert is one of the most influential and largest plantsman's gardens in England. The knowledge and taste of the owners – together with their generosity towards visitors – have made it a cult garden among *cognoscenti* and learner gardeners alike. The Phillips describe it as 'a botanical mad house'; it would be truer to call it a horticultural treasure house. Every type of plant is grown but, above all, rare trees: *Cercis racemosa*, for example, and hundreds of plants – perhaps thousands – grown from seeds collected by such friends as Roy Lancaster, Martyn Rix and Maurice Foster. An older generation of plantsmen is also commemorated here – Maurice Mason, Norman Haddon and Margery Fish, for example. Home Covert is a large garden, informally laid out within natural oak woodland, and it needs a long time to see round. Down in the bog garden are collections of willows and alders, naturalised *Lathraea clandestina* and swathes of candelabra primulas. Near the house is an enormous lawn, completely free of weeds, with a view for miles down the Avon valley. Raised beds, a rock garden, shade borders, protected beds for tender plants, swarms of erythroniums, fat clumps of lilies, old-fashioned roses and wild species – there seems no end to the number and variety of what is grown here.

woodland garden; plantsman's plants of every kind

Owned by Mr and Mrs John Phillips
Number of gardeners owners only, plus part-time help
Size 13ha (33 acres)

IFORD MANOR

Bradford-on-Avon BA15 2BA

Tel 01225 863146 **Fax** 01225 852364
www.ifordmanor.co.uk
Location 7 miles south-east of Bath, signed from A36 and Bradford-on-Avon on B3109
Opening hours 2pm to 5pm, Sundays and Easter Monday, April and October; plus Tuesday to Thursday, Saturdays, Sundays and Bank Holiday Mondays from May to September
Admission fee Adults £4.50; OAPs and children (over 10) £4; children under 10 free, but weekdays preferred for safety reasons

Harold Peto's own Italianate garden on a steep wooded hillside is meticulously maintained and a delight to visit. Peto was a fashionable architect with a passion for classical Italian architecture and landscaping. When he returned from working in France and Italy, he bought Iford to house his collections of statues and architectural marbles. He planted phillyreas, Italian cypresses and other Mediterranean species and laid out the garden as a series of formal terraces on the steep hillside behind the house. The architectural highlights include a Romanesque cloister, an octagonal gazebo and a gloriously colonnaded terrace. Every detail is wonderfully photogenic, especially when contrasted with wisterias, roses or well-chosen acanthus. The woodland garden is worth exploring

Iford Manor

(it hides a recently restored Japanese garden) and there is much of horticultural interest at Iford, notably a meadow of naturalised martagon lilies.
Harold Peto's own garden; opulent Edwardian design; Italian cypresses and handsome *Phillyrea*; martagon lilies; cyclamen; roses; teas on Bank Holidays and weekends from May to August

Owned by Mrs E Cartwright-Hignett
Number of gardeners 2
Size 0.6ha (1½ acres), plus 5ha (12 acres) of woodland
English Heritage Grade I

LACKHAM COUNTRY PARK
Lacock, Chippenham SN15 2NY

Tel 01249 466800 **Fax** 01249 444474
www.lackhamcountrypark.co.uk
Location 3 miles south of Chippenham on A350
Opening hours 10am to 5pm, 17 and 18 March, 8 and 9 April, 7 and 13 May, 3, 10, 17 and 24 June, 8 and 22 July, 12, 26 and 27 August, 9 and 16 September, 7 October
Admission fee Adults £2; concessions £1.50; children free; more for some events

Lackham is among the best of the old county college gardens. Its response to the usual shortfall in funding has been to establish a Museum of Agriculture, which now also shelters the historic teaching garden. Its open days cater for every interest, from the 'lambing weekend' on 17 and 18 March to the NGS day on 22 July which is entitled 'woodcraft in action'. The gardens are open during all these events and featured in the 13-part TV gardening programme *Gardeners to Be*. The heart of Lackham is its walled garden of flowers, ornamentals, herbs, fruit and vegetables, beautifully laid out to educate and delight. In one of the glasshouses is the champion plant of *Citrus medica* which grew the largest citron (over 10lb) ever seen in Britain (according to the *Guinness Book of Records*). The grounds are good for an exploration, especially in bluebell time: there has been a lot of attractive companion planting for the National Collection of poplars.
plantsman's collection of plants; herbs; fruit and vegetables; plants under glass; daffodils; good herbaceous borders; fine collection of trees; alpine plants; bluebells; roses of every kind; sensory garden; laurel maze; woodland walk; souvenirs for sale; refreshments

Owned by Wiltshire College Lackham
Number of gardeners 4, plus students
Size 8ha (20 acres)
NCCPG National Collections *Populus*

LACOCK ABBEY
Lacock, Chippenham SN15 2LG

Tel 01249 730459 **Fax** 01249 730501
www.nationaltrust.org.uk
Location 3 miles south of Chippenham, just east of A350
Opening hours 11am to 5.30pm, daily, 24 February to 28 October; closed on Good Friday
Admission fee Adults £5.10; children £2.50

The National Trust has recently laid out a 'botanic garden' in the style of an earlier one planted by Lacock's most famous past owner, William Fox Talbot, the 'inventor' of photography. It was he who planted many of the mature trees in the park, including the London plane (*Platanus* x *hispanica*), swamp cypress (*Taxodium distichum*) and walnut (*Juglans nigra*). Part of the *Harry Potter* series was filmed at Lacock.
snowdrops; crocuses; parkland; tea room

Owned by The National Trust
Number of gardeners 1, plus 1 part-time
Size 3.4ha (8 1/2 acres)

LANDFORD TREES
Landford Lodge, Landford, Salisbury SP5 2EH

Tel 01794 390808 **Fax** 01794 390037
www.landfordtrees.co.uk
Location By junction of A36 and B3079
Opening hours By appointment for groups at weekends; visitors to nursery and tree collection at all times
Admission fee Free

This is an excellent tree nursery, with over 700 lines on sale. These include 40 different acers, 20 birches, 15 crataegus, 10 beech, 90 *Malus*, 40 *Prunus*, 50 *Sorbus* and 30 different pines. There will be a RHS Special Event at Landford Trees on 24 May 2007: details from 020 7821 3408.
well-known tree nursery

Owned by Christopher Pilkington
Size 12ha (30 acres)

LARMER TREE GARDENS
Tollard Royal, Salisbury SP5 5PT

Tel 01725 516971 **Fax** 01725 516321
www.larmertree.co.uk
Location Follow brown tourist signs from A354 or B3081
Opening hours 11am to 4.30pm, Sunday to Thursday, April to September
Admission fee Adults £3.75; OAPs £3; children £2.50

The Larmer Tree Gardens were laid out by General Augustus Pitt-Rivers as a public amenity. He put up a series of eccentric garden buildings around a spacious lawn of perhaps two acres: they include the Singing Theatre, the Indian Room, the Roman Temple and the Lower Indian Building in the Nepalese style, brought here in 1880 after the Colonial Exhibition in London. In the 1880s and 1890s, trainloads of East Enders were brought there by the philanthropic owner for a jolly cultural day in the country. His descendants have entirely restored the gardens since about 1990 and added some modern horticultural features. The best of these is a series of artificial pools in an artificial dell, surrounded by multicoloured hydrangeas. All is set in light oak woodland with splendid thickets of cherry laurel. It is not a garden of the highest horticultural interest, though there are some venerable eucryphias, crinodendrons and stewartias. It is, however, spaciously laid out and very enjoyable to visit.
hydrangeas; woodland gardens; remarkable series of follies; tea room on Sundays in season

Owned by W Gronow-Davies and Trustees
Number of gardeners 2
Size 4.4ha (11 acres)
English Heritage Grade II

LONGLEAT HOUSE
Warminster BA12 7NW

Tel 01985 844400 **Fax** 01985 844885
www.longleat.co.uk
Location Off A362 Warminster to Frome road
Opening hours 10am to 5.30pm, daily, all year, except 25 December
Admission fee Grounds and gardens: adults £3; OAPs and children £2

Ⓟ ♠ 👪

Longleat has a classic 18th-century landscape by Capability Brown, a home park of 900 acres best seen from Heaven's Gate and a grand Victorian garden reworked by Russell Page in the 1930s. Capability Brown's landscape has been carefully managed and replanted over many years, so that it keeps its intended form. The Victorian garden between the house and the elegant conservatory built by Wyatville in the 1820s is now a very beautiful rose garden. The plantings of ornamental trees and rhododendron woodlands have been thickened and updated with many new introductions. In short, Lord Bath (like his father before him) has conserved the best of Longleat and reinvigorated the rest. Worth another visit.

woodland garden; topiary; rhododendrons and azaleas; fine collection of trees; orangery; rose garden planted as a 'love labyrinth'; sun maze and lunar labyrinth; shops; cafés and restaurants

Owned by 7th Marquess of Bath
Number of gardeners 8
Size 8ha (20 acres)
English Heritage Grade I

THE MEAD NURSERY

Brokerswood, Westbury BA13 4EG

Tel 01373 859990
www.themeadnursery.co.uk
Location Off A36 or A361, between Rudge and Brokerswood Country Park
Opening hours 9am to 5pm, Wednesday to Saturday and Bank Holiday Mondays, noon to 5pm, Sundays, 1 February to 10 October; for NGS: noon to 5pm, 19 August
Admission fee £2.50 (tea and cake included) on 19 August, otherwise free

Ⓟ 👪 ♿ ✿

The Mead Nursery specialises in alpine plants (including varieties suitable for trough plantings), pot-grown bulbs and herbaceous perennials. All plants are grown in peat-free compost. The display garden is excellent: raised alpine beds, a sink garden, a bog bed, a small wildlife pond, a Mediterranean raised bed and herbaceous borders planted with colour combinations in mind.

perennials; alpines; bulbs; all plants grown on-site; pretty demonstration garden

Owned by Stephen and Emma Lewis-Dale
Size 0.3ha (3/4 acre)

OLD VICARAGE

Edington, Westbury BA13 4QF

Tel 01380 830512
Location On B3098 in Edington village
Opening hours 2pm to 6pm; 17 June, for NGS; and by appointment
Admission fee Adults £5; children free

Ⓟ ✿

John d'Arcy bought the Old Vicarage in 1982: it is now one of the best examples of a plantsman's garden in southern England. The site offers a surprising range of mini-habitats, and d'Arcy took advantage of their potential to grow the widest possible number of plants. The features now include a sunken garden, a shady pergola, an avenue of fastigiate hornbeams *Carpinus betulus* 'Fastigiata', a gravel garden where *Morina afghanica* and *Ptilostemon afer* seed around, hot walls, raised beds, peat beds and shady beds – all blended with the rest of the garden so that no feature dominates any part of it. John d'Arcy's great skill is as a cultivator: the fact that there is so much colour and interest at every time of the year proves that good plantsmanship can produce effects to challenge the most carefully designed and planted of gardens. Trees are underplanted with shrubs, which are underscored in turn by herbaceous plants and bulbs, several different plants being placed together to give a succession of interest throughout the year. John d'Arcy's special interests include mahonias, cyclamen, nerines and hollies. He is also well known as a plant collector. *Corydalis flexuosa* came from Sichuan in 1989; several new species of *Dierama* came from South Africa, together with such new species of *Geranium* as *G. harveyi* and *G. pulchrum*. All are still here, together with the living holotype of *Salvia darcyi*.

plantsman's plants – a collector's collection; herbaceous borders; alpine plants; shade plants; gravel garden; small arboretum

Owned by John d'Arcy
Number of gardeners 1
Size 1ha (2½ acres)
NCCPG National Collections *Oenothera*

SHARCOTT MANOR

Pewsey SN9 5PA

Tel 01672 563485
Location Off A345, one mile south-west of Pewsey
Opening hours 11am to 5pm, first Wednesday of every month, April to September; for NGS: 2pm to 6pm, 1 April and 9 September; and by appointment
Admission fee Adults £3; children free; all for NGS

This extensive modern garden has been quite transformed over the last 30 years into a densely planted plantsman's paradise. There is much to see as you move gently between the garden rooms near the house and out into the spacious lawns and woodland garden. There are harmonies and contrasts to please the most colour-conscious, while the dark shady lake at the bottom is a haven of romantic broodiness. A recent addition is an avenue of *Pyrus calleryana* 'Chanticleer'. Sharcott is an excellent garden which deserves to be better known.

plantsman's collection of plants; good herbaceous borders; woodland and stream gardens; good plant sales area, all propagated from garden; home-made teas

Owned by Captain and Mrs David Armytage
Number of gardeners 2 part-time
Size 2.4ha (6 acres)

SHUTE HOUSE

Donhead St Mary, Shaftesbury SP7 9DG

Tel 01935 814389 **Fax** 01935 815535
Location In village, near church
Opening hours By appointment, for groups of 20+; must be 10am to noon or 2pm to 4pm
Admission fee Adults £3.50

Geoffrey Jellicoe's favourite garden – and his masterpiece – is open to groups by special arrangement. The most famous feature is the rill garden, where water runs straight down the hillside, over copper waterfalls to the hexagonal bubble fountain. But it is all a place of rare enchantment.

meals by arrangement

Owned by Mr and Mrs John Lewis
Number of gardeners 1, plus 2 part-time
Size 2.8ha (7 acres)

STOURHEAD

Stourton BA12 6QD

Tel 01747 841152 **Fax** 01747 842006
www.nationaltrust.org.uk
Location 3 miles north-west of Mere, signed off A303/B3092
Opening hours 9am to 7pm (or dusk, if earlier), daily, all year
Admission fee Adults £6.60; children £3.60

Whatever the weather or season, Stourhead conveys a sense of majesty and harmony. Try it early on a May morning, when the air is sweet with azaleas. Or scuff the fallen leaves in late November. Admire the champion trees, and the thick evergreen plantings. Think of it 200 years ago, without the rhododendrons or exotic trees, when all the beech trees were interplanted with spruces and the colours came all from shades of green. Ponder the 18th-century aesthetic, which esteemed tones and shades more highly than colours, and follow the iconographic tour inspired (they say) by Virgil. Spot the change from Classical to Gothic, from Pope to Walpole, and wonder at the National Trust's ability to maintain it so well with only six gardeners.

Stourhead

Stourhead

snowdrops; rhododendrons and azaleas; mature conifers; fine collection of trees; good autumn colour; tallest tulip tree *Liriodendron tulipifera* (37m; 121ft) in the British Isles, and seven other record tree species; shop and plant centre; restaurant

Owned by The National Trust
Number of gardeners 6, plus 2 students
Size 40ha (100 acres)
English Heritage Grade I

WILTON HOUSE
Wilton, Salisbury SP2 0BJ

Tel 01722 746720 **Fax** 01722 744447
www.wiltonhouse.com
Location In village, 3 miles west of Salisbury by A36
Opening hours 10.30am to 5.30pm, daily, April to September
Admission fee Adults £5; children £3.50; RHS members free

Wilton has a sublime 18th-century park around its classical Inigo Jones house, which is famous for its paintings. It is this stupendous parkland setting above the River Nadder which is the chief delight of visiting the gardens at Wilton. There are comparatively few horticultural excitements, though the house has pleasant mixed borders along one of its sides and an elegant knot garden in the entrance court designed by Xa Tollemache. On the edge of the park are a pretty new garden of old-fashioned roses and an oriental water garden: opinions are divided as to the merits of the new millennium water feature.
roses; handsome cedars; famous Palladian bridge; magnificent golden-leaved oak; self-service restaurant

Owned by The Earl of Pembroke and Wilton House Trust
Number of gardeners 3
Size 8.3ha (21 acres)
English Heritage Grade I

WORCESTERSHIRE

Worcestershire has been reconstituted not as a county (which it was until 1974) but as a District Council. But such is its feeling of distinct identity that we have treated it in this book as a legal county again: the same applies to Herefordshire, to which it was yoked for 25 years. Worcestershire has a lot going for it: a flourishing National Gardens Scheme, the site of the only dedicated horticultural college in England at Pershore (a RHS Partner College), the headquarters of the Alpine Garden Society, 11 National Collection holders, and two of the most popular gardening shows in the country – the Spring Gardening Show (10-13 May 2007) and the Autumn Garden & Country Show (29-30 September 2007), both at the Three Counties Showground at Malvern. Worcestershire also has some excellent specialist nurseries, including Cotswold Garden Flowers, Old Court Nurseries and Stone House Cottage Garden. Though few of its historic parks and gardens are open to the public, they include that great plantsman's garden Spetchley Park (substantially remade by a great-nephew of Miss Ellen Willmott) and Witley Court (now undergoing extensive renovation by English Heritage).

ARLEY ARBORETUM

Arley, Bewdley DY12 1XG

Tel 01299 861368 **Fax** 01299 861330
www.arley-arboretum.org.uk
Location Follow brown tourist signs from A442
Opening hours 11am to 5pm, Wednesday to Sunday and Bank Holiday Mondays, 14 March to 11 November
Admission fee Adults £4; children £1; RHS members free on Thursdays

This beautiful arboretum opened to the public in 2002. It was first planted in the 1820s (very early for arboreta) and has been continuously expanded and replanted since. There are very fine Crimean pines *Pinus nigra* var. *caramanica*, one of which is the tallest in the United Kingdom. In all there are over 300 different taxa. Within the arboretum is a walled garden with a formal Italian garden and fine herbaceous borders – quite a contrast to the awesome trees outside.
tea room and light refreshments

Owned by RD Turner Charitable Trust
Number of gardeners 4
Size 14ha (35 acres)

BODENHAM ARBORETUM

Wolverley, Kidderminster DY11 5SY

Tel 01562 852444 **Fax** 01562 852777
www.bodenham-arboretum.co.uk
Location B4189 or B4190 to Wolverley village and follow brown tourist signs
Opening hours 11am to 5pm or dusk, Wednesday to Sunday and Bank Holiday Mondays, all year to Christmas; daily in October; weekends only in January and February
Admission fee Adults £5; children £2

Bodenham Arboretum has more than 2,700 different trees and shrubs in a total of 156 acres, containing 11 pools and five miles of footpaths. In May and early June, the rhododendrons, azaleas and laburnum tunnel are spectacular but, like all arboreta, there is much to enjoy in all seasons.
light refreshments and lunches

Owned by David Binnian
Size 62ha (156 acres)

COTSWOLD GARDEN FLOWERS

Sands Lane, Badsey, Evesham WR11 5EZ

Tel 01386 422829 **Fax** 01386 49844
www.cgf.net
Location On south-east edge of village (signed off Willersley Road)
Opening hours 9am to 5.30pm, Monday to Friday; 10am to 5.30pm, Saturday to Sunday; closed at weekends from October to March; other times by appointment
Admission fee Free

Don't be put off by the bumpy driveway – the nursery is right at the end of Sands Lane. Cotswold Garden Flowers is a treasure house of rare plants: over 8,000 different cultivars are grown in the display garden. Actually the garden is no more than the nursery's stock beds, but quite spectacular, because the owner has a knack for seeking out and introducing plants which are highly 'garden worthy'. The catalogue is both amusing and informative, but it is nothing compared to the joy of visiting the nursery and having the opportunity to see so many well-grown, new and interesting plants.

Owned by Bob Brown
Number of gardeners 3
Size 0.4ha (1 acre)
NCCPG National Collections *Lysimachia*

EASTGROVE COTTAGE GARDEN

Sankyns Green, Shrawley, Little Witley, Worcester WR6 6LQ

Tel 01299 896389
www.eastgrove.co.uk
Location On road between Great Witley (on A443) and Shrawley (on B4196)
Opening hours 2pm to 5pm, Thursday to Saturday and Bank Holiday Sundays and Mondays in May, 26 April to 14 July and 6 September to 6 October
Admission fee Adults £4; children free; RHS members free

Eastgrove is a very attractive, 17th-century, half-timbered, black and white cottage in a beautiful country setting. It has an equally pretty cottage garden that has been entirely made by the Skinners since they bought the near-derelict property in 1970. The scale is small, but the quality and variety of the plantings are stunning. There is a developing collection of trees, a raised bed (known as the 'Great Wall of China') and, above all, thickly planted herbaceous plants. The design and planting of the borders is carefully thought through, with curving borders and several enclosed rooms. The 'secret garden' concentrates on mauves, pinks, silvers and crimsons. Although perhaps best in high summer, the garden is worth visiting at any season, and beautifully maintained. Beyond the garden is a two-acre field planted with trees in 2004, complete with a ride and a grass labyrinth. The nursery propagates only plants from the garden. Specialities include aquilegias, hardy chrysanthemums, dianthus, heleniums, irises, peonies, rosemary, salvias and violas.
cottage garden; rose arches; plantsman's plants; herbaceous borders; wall plantings; pots and containers; good small nursery; home-made ice-cream

Owned by Malcolm and Carol Skinner
Number of gardeners owners only
Size 0.6ha (1½ acres), plus 0.8ha (2 acres) arboretum

HANBURY HALL

School Road, Hanbury, Droitwich Spa WR9 7EA

Tel 01527 821214 **Fax** 01527 821251
www.nationaltrust.org.uk
Location 1 mile west of A4141
Opening hours 11am to 5.30pm, Saturday to Wednesday, 17 March to 31 October; daily in July in August; plus 3, 4, 10 and 11 March
Admission fee Adults £4.50; children £2.25

Hanbury's 400-acre park explains why it is a registered Grade II garden, but it has recently had its formal garden restored, too. This was originally made by George London, and incorporates a parterre, a fruit garden and a formal wilderness. Elsewhere are a working mushroom house, an orangery, and a restored 18th-century bowling green.
gift shop; refreshments

Owned by The National Trust
Number of gardeners 4, plus volunteers
Size 8ha (20 acres)
English Heritage Grade II

OVERBURY COURT
Tewkesbury GL20 7NP

Tel 01386 725111 **Fax** 01386 725678
Location 5 miles north-east of Tewkesbury
Opening hours By appointment
Admission fee Adults £2.50; minimum charge for groups £15

A peaceful and expansive garden laid out around the large, handsome, Georgian house, with a view of the Parish church worked in. Aubrey Waterfield, Geoffrey Jellicoe, Russell Page, Peter Coates and James Alexander Sinclair all worked on the design and planting. Their work is not always distinguishable, because the result is a garden of exceptional harmony.
topiary; landscaped park; daffodils

Owned by Mr and Mrs Bruce Bossom
Number of gardeners 2

PERSHORE COLLEGE
Pershore WR10 3JP

Tel 01386 552443 **Fax** 01386 556528
www.pershore.ac.uk
Location On B4084 (formerly A44)
Opening hours 10am to 4.30pm, daily, all year; AGS garden closed at weekends
Admission fee Free

Pershore College specialises in horticultural education. Within its grounds are a 15ha (38-acre) fruit and vegetable production unit, an 8ha (20-acre) nursery stock and specialist plant unit, and a plant centre. The garden centre sells a selection of college-grown trees and shrubs including plants from the National Collection of penstemons, alpines, herbaceous plants, climbers, roses, house plants and fruit trees and bushes in season. It is open daily from 9am to 5pm (10.30pm to 4.30pm on Sundays; 4pm in winter). The college also has show gardens designed and maintained by the Hardy Plant Society and the Alpine Garden Society. Both are full of interesting plants and ideas for design and cultivation. The RHS Centre at Pershore was established in 1989 to offer a variety of courses, lectures and workshops on all aspects of horticulture for both members and non-members in the Central Region. There is a long list of RHS Special Events at Pershore in 2007.

Size 54ha (135 acres)
NCCPG National Collections *Penstemon*; *Philadelphus*

SPETCHLEY PARK
Worcester WR5 1RS

Tel 01453 810303 **Fax** 01453 511915
www.spetchleygardens.co.uk
Location 3 miles east of Worcester on A44
Opening hours 11am to 6pm, Wednesday to Sunday and Bank Holiday Mondays, 21 March to 30 September; plus 11am to 4pm at weekends in October; last admissions one hour before closing
Admission fee Adults £6; concessions £5.50; children free

In a classic English landscaped park, three generations of Berkeleys have created one of the best plantsman's gardens in the Midlands. Ellen Willmott was the owner's great-aunt and many of the most exciting trees and shrubs date from her time – a gnarled specimen of the laciniate walnut (*Juglans nigra* 'Laciniata'), for example. In the Fountain Gardens, *Tulipa sprengeri* has seeded and naturalised over a large area. Other spring flowers include peonies, columbines and masses of bulbs. In summer, there are hundreds of different roses – old-fashioned roses, tea roses, David Austin roses, floribunda roses – every type of rose is here. Martagon lilies have naturalised in large quantities. The conservatory is crammed with unusual plants. The planting continues: everywhere in the garden are new designs, new plants and new combinations. A whole new garden has been planted to commemorate the millennium, with tunnels of *Cercis canadensis* 'Forest Pansy' and *Robinia hispida* 'Macrophylla'. Because of its scale and variety, this garden offers something to everyone, but most especially to the plantsman.

Spetchley Park

many good plants of every kind for plantsmen; roses (ancient and modern); rhododendrons and azaleas; daffodils; good herbaceous borders; fine trees; deer park; good new plantings in the kitchen garden; naturalised lilies; teas and refreshments

Owned by RJ Berkeley
Number of gardeners 4
Size 12ha (30 acres)
English Heritage Grade II*

STONE HOUSE COTTAGE GARDEN
Stone, Kidderminster DY10 4BG

Tel 01562 69902
www.shcn.co.uk
Location In village, 2 miles from Kidderminster on A448
Opening hours 10am to 5pm, Wednesday to Saturday, mid-March to mid-September; and by appointment between mid-September and March
Admission fee Adults £3; children free; RHS members free

This is the garden of a famous nursery, which it matches for the range of beautiful and unusual plants it offers. The owners are compulsive plantsmen and, as the garden is small, they have to move plants around or replace them altogether to make room for new arrivals. This means that the garden is constantly developing and improving – especially since much thought is given to the way each plant will associate with its neighbours. Around the walls is an eccentric collection of follies built as towers, which makes this garden quite unique.
plantsman's plants; herbs; good herbaceous borders; alpine plants; unusual climbing plants; roses (mainly old-fashioned and climbers); excellent nursery attached

Owned by James and Louisa Arbuthnott
Number of gardeners 1
Size 0.3ha (3/4 acre)

THE WALLED GARDEN
6 Rose Terrace, Worcester WR5 1BU

Tel/fax 01905 354629
Location Off Fort Royal Hill (which is off A44); 1/2 mile from Cathedral
Opening hours 1pm to 5pm, 28 April, 12 and 26 May, 9 and 23 June and 14 July
Admission fee Adults £2; children free

This all-organic private garden has an integrated mixture of flowers, fruits and herbs. The owners have reclaimed the walled garden, dating from Victorian times, and planted a series of areas for studying and demonstrating organic gardening techniques and the uses of herbs.
herb gardens

Owned by William and Julia Scott
Number of gardeners owners only
Size 0.3ha (1/4 acre)

WEBBS
Wychbold, Droitwich Spa WR9 0DG

Tel 01527 860000 **Fax** 01527 861284
www.webbsofwychbold.co.uk
Location 1 mile from M5, Jct 5: follow brown tourist signs
Opening hours 9am (8pm from spring to Christmas) to 6pm, Monday to Friday; 9am to 6pm; Saturdays and Bank Holidays; 10.30am to 4.30pm, Sundays; closed Easter Sunday, 25 and 26 December
Admission fee Free

Webbs is a major garden centre, a regional heavyweight with several trade awards for excellence. There is an extremely large stock of plants of every kind, as well as a range of in-house retail opportunities of interest to gardeners and non-gardeners alike. They also have a reputation as plant introducers: *Diascia fetcaniensis* 'Daydream' and *Dianthus* 'Tickled Pink' are two of their plant introductions. Their Riverside display gardens (over 2 acres of them) include a National Collection of *Potentilla fruticosa* cultivars, colour spectrum and white gardens, plantings for dry, sunny and damp, shady conditions, and displays of grasses and bamboos. The adjacent New Wave Gardens, designed in conjunction with Noel Kingsbury, mix perennials, shrubs and grasses in a series of different naturalistic styles. They also contain trial beds of mixed annuals from Suttons and a bog garden.
model gardens; award-winning garden centre;

gift shop; restaurant

Size 10ha (25 acres)
NCCPG National Collections *Potentilla fruticosa* (cvs.)

WHITLENGE GARDENS
Hartlebury DY10 4HD

Tel 01299 250720 **Fax** 01299 251259
www.whit-lenge.co.uk
Location 5 miles south of Kidderminster, on A442
Opening hours 9am (10am on Sundays) to 5pm, daily, all year; closed Christmas and New Year; six days for NGS
Admission fee £1.50; children free; £2 on NGS days

The gardens are a showcase not only for the adjoining nursery but also for Keith Southall's design services. They have been developed over some 25 years and are full of interesting ideas for structural landscaping and planting. The barley sugar pergola, planted with fan-trained apples and pears, is especially attractive, but there are also many rock gardens and a large bog garden with *Gunnera manicata*. All the plants are chosen to ensure that there is colour and interest at every season.
nursery; tea room

Owned by Keith Southall
Number of gardeners 2
Size 1.2ha (3 acres)

WITLEY COURT
Great Witley WR6 6JT

Tel/fax 01299 896636
www.english-heritage.org.uk
Location 10 miles north-west of Worcester on A443
Opening hours 10am to 5pm (6pm from June to August), daily, March to October; 10am to 4pm, Wednesday to Sunday, November to February; closed 1 January, 24 to 26 December
Admission fee Adults £5.40; concessions £4.10; children £2.70; discounts for pre-booked groups of 11+

The gardens at Witley Court have undergone extensive restoration and are increasingly in good condition. You enter through rhododendron woods, planted mainly with hardy hybrids under a canopy of American conifers. More interesting, though, is the spectacular ruined mansion and the immense formal gardens behind. They are one of William Andrews Nesfield's masterpieces, built on a monumental scale by the first Earl of Dudley: English Heritage has restored the gardens and the famous Perseus and Andromeda fountain. The fountains start running from about Easter onwards – usually at noon, 2pm and 4pm on weekdays, but hourly (on the hour) from 11am to 4pm at weekends. The focus of restoration now is the east fountain and its surrounding parterres, which have been replanted with box plants taken from the original hedges and filled with gravel. A system of bedding plants will follow shortly. The house remains as it was: the sheer size of the roofless conservatory is remarkable – a place to fantasise about life among the plutocrats 100 years ago.
Victorian formal garden; rhododendron woodlands; sculpture

Owned by English Heritage
Number of gardeners 4
Size 16ha (40 acres)
English Heritage Grade II*

YORKSHIRE, EAST RIDING OF

Since the demise of much-disliked Humberside, the East Riding has been reconstituted as an administrative area. Many of Yorkshire's gardening institutions are organised on an all-Yorkshire basis: thus, for example, the Yorkshire Gardens Trust and the Yorkshire Group of the NCCPG are county-wide societies. Sledmere House is the outstanding historic garden in East Yorkshire, though Burton Constable is also well known for its Capability Brown landscape garden. There are comparatively few good modern gardens in East Yorkshire, apart from the charming water gardens at Burnby, where a National Collection of water lilies (*Nymphaea*) is displayed in a beautifully landscaped site. There are four further National Collections in East Yorkshire, including a collection of *Crataegus laevigata* and *C. monogyna* cultivars at the University of Hull's garden at Cottingham – a botanic garden that has lost the botany department that was once the reason for its existence. There is a sprinkling of gardens that open for the National Gardens Scheme in East Yorkshire, which has its own county organiser. There are few nurseries of national repute: one that is not listed below is Swanland Nurseries, which has a good collection of *Pelargonium* cultivars – over 800 of them. Burnby Hall and Burton Agnes offer free entry to RHS members (Burton Agnes won the HHA/Christie's Garden of the Year 2005 award) and the garden at Bishop Burton College is a stunner.

BISHOP BURTON BOTANIC GARDEN

Bishop Burton College, Beverley HU17 8QG

Tel 01964 553000 **Fax** 01964 553101
Location In Bishop Burton: entrance to west of village green
Opening hours 9am to 5pm, Monday to Friday, all year
Admission fee Free

Bishop Burton is a college where horticulture is taught, so this is not so much a botanic garden as a demonstration garden to teach students about plants – and a very good one, too. There are areas for fruit, vegetables and herbs, fine herbaceous borders supplemented by annuals and bedding, hot-colour borders, a heather collection, dwarf conifers, trees, shrubs, ponds and show gardens, some of them designed by students. The glasshouses include a cactus house and tropical house. Outside, in the park, is a 19th-century landscape with good wellingtonias, cedars and a cucumber tree (*Magnolia acuminata*). good collection of plants; fine trees in park; *Gardening Which?* Garden Trials; café open in term time

Owned by Bishop Burton College
Number of gardeners 4, plus students
Size 0.8ha (2 acres), plus park

BURNBY HALL GARDENS

Pocklington YO42 2QF

Tel 01759 307125 **Fax** 01377 288359
www.burnbyhallgardens.com
Location Off A1079, 13 miles east of York
Opening hours 10am to 6pm, daily, 31 March to 7 October
Admission fee Adults £3.75; OAPs £3; children £1.80; RHS members free from April to June

Burnby Hall is famed for its water lilies, planted by Amos Perry in the 1930s and now totalling over 100 different cultivars. They are grown in two long, landscaped lakes. But there is much

more to Burnby: a large, walled Victorian garden, a rock garden, a woodland walk, heather beds, a 'secret garden', seasonal bedding and a good collection of conifers all contribute to its visitor-friendly air. Follow the tarmac path around the lakes: Burnby is a grand place for a promenade, especially when a brass band is playing on Sunday afternoons in summer.
water lilies; rock garden; mature conifers; plants for sale; café; gift shop

Owned by Stewarts Trust
Number of gardeners 3
Size 3.2ha (8 acres)
NCCPG National Collections *Nymphaea*

BURTON AGNES HALL GARDENS
Burton Agnes, Driffield YO25 0ND

Tel 01262 490324 **Fax** 01262 490513
www.burton-agnes.com
Location On A614 Driffield to Bridlington road
Opening hours 11am to 5pm, daily, April to October
Admission fee Adults £3; OAPs £2.75; children £1.50; RHS members free; house extra

The old walled garden has been redesigned in a neo-Elizabethan style (to complement the nearby house) and cut up into numerous, thickly planted gardens with narrow paths and changes of level. As well as a *potager* and herb garden it has such unconventional features as life-size games boards for chess, draughts and snakes and ladders, a jungle garden and a maze with a riddle. Rather more conventional are the colour-schemed gardens and sumptuous plantings of shrub roses, clematis and herbaceous plants. There are also some enjoyable horticultural surprises, including cordylines and *Echium pininana* growing outside, and lots of furcraeas put out in pots for the summer.
good modern plantings; inventive design; HHA/Christie's Garden of the Year 2005; flower and produce shop; gift shop; café and ice-cream parlour

Owned by Burton Agnes Hall Preservation Trust Ltd
Number of gardeners 3 1/2
NCCPG National Collections *Campanula*

Burton Agnes

BURTON CONSTABLE

Skirlaugh, Hull HU11 4LN

Tel 01964 562400 **Fax** 01964 563229
www.burtonconstable.com
Location Via Hull, A165 Bridlington road, then B1238 to Sproatley to follow brown tourist signs
Opening hours 12.30pm to 5pm (last admissions 4pm), Saturday to Thursday, Easter Saturday to 31 October
Admission fee Grounds only: adults £1.50; children 75p

The main feature around the massive house is a Capability Brown landscape: his original plans are still shown. However, the foundation has recently received support from the Heritage Lottery Fund for a major restoration of the gardens, including the four acres of 19th-century pleasure grounds, so this is a garden to watch in future.
woodland garden; fine 18th-century orangery; Victorian parterre; shop; light snacks

Owned by Burton Constable Foundation
Number of gardeners 3
English Heritage Grade II

SLEDMERE HOUSE

Sledmere, Driffield YO25 3XG

Tel 01377 236637 **Fax** 01377 236500
www.sledmerehouse.com
Location Off A166 between York and Bridlington
Opening hours 10am to 5pm, Tuesday to Thursday, Sundays and Bank Holiday Mondays, Easter weekend, then from 29 April to 30 September; plus Fridays from June to August
Admission fee Adults £4; children £1

Sledmere has a classical Capability Brown landscape: his original plans can be seen in the museum. An Italianate formal garden was added in 1911, with Greek and Roman busts swathed in climbing roses. In recent years, Sledmere has enjoyed extensive replanting in the 18th-century walled garden: a new rose and clematis arcade; young roses and fruit trees on the walls; a dedicated rose garden; and a Mediterranean border. And it gets better every year as the head gardener restores, improves, takes more borders in hand and adds more plants. There are fine purple beeches in the park.
roses; Capability Brown landscape; craft and gift shop; tea terrace and licensed café

Owned by Sir Tatton Sykes Bt
Number of gardeners 3
Size 40ha (100 acres)
English Heritage Grade I

YORKSHIRE, NORTH

North Yorkshire corresponds with the old North Riding of Yorkshire: it is a county of large estates and small market towns. Among its historic gardens are some of the grandest landscapes in England: Castle Howard, Duncombe Park and Studley Royal are all Grade I gardens. North Yorkshire also has three very important modern gardens – Harlow Carr, Newby Hall and Thorp Perrow – each quite different in character but all horticultural heavyweights. Harlow Carr, for years the flagship of the Northern Horticultural Society, joined the RHS's growing fleet of top gardens in 2001 and has been substantially redeveloped and improved at the RHS's hands. The National Gardens Scheme does well in North Yorkshire and so does the NCCPG, which has over 20 National Collections in the county. The best nurseries are also in North Yorkshire, including R.V. Roger Ltd, which has a good line in exotic 'architectural' plants, and the *Pulmonaria* and rare plant specialist Stillingfleet Lodge Nurseries: Stillingfleet also has a good garden that RHS members can visit free. There are many others that offer free access to RHS members for all or part of their open season: Duncombe Park, Harewood House, Millgate House, Newby Hall, Parceval Hall, Ripley Castle and Thorp Perrow.

ALDBY PARK

Buttercrambe, York YO41 1XU

Tel 01759 371398
Location Off A166, 11 miles north-east of York
Opening hours By appointment; for Red Cross: 3 and 17 June
Admission fee Adults £3

Mark Winn has restored and improved the garden at Aldby entirely, after 20 years of neglect – the tennis lawn he remembered from the 1930s had 6m (20ft) sycamores on it. Jim Russell advised on some of the plantings. Rhododendrons, azaleas, lilies and paeonies are among the highlights.

Owned by Mark Winn
Number of gardeners 1
Size 6.4ha (16 acres)

BENINGBROUGH HALL & GARDENS

Beningbrough, York YO30 1DD

Tel 01904 472027 **Fax** 01904 472020
www.nationaltrust.org.uk
Location 8 miles north-west of York off the A19
Opening hours 11am to 5.30pm, Saturday to Wednesday, 17 March to 31 October; plus Good Friday, and Fridays from 3 July to 1 September; plus 11am to 3.30pm, Saturdays and Sundays, 3 November to 16 December
Admission fee Adults £7.70; children £3.90; families £17.60; reduced rates in winter

The National Trust calls Beningbrough 'York's Country House and Garden'. It is approached by an avenue of limes through stately parkland. Apart from a Victorian shrubbery, the gardens are modern and pretty. Two small formal gardens, one with reds and oranges and the other with pastel shades, lie on either side of the early Georgian house. A sumptuous mixed border, graded from hot colours to cool, runs right to the gate of the walled kitchen garden.
fruit; good herbaceous borders; American garden; good conservatory on house; traditional Victorian kitchen garden undergoing restoration; 'Lady Downe's Seedling' grape, raised at Beningbrough in 1835; vast Portuguese laurel *Prunus lusitanica*; National Trust gift shop; morning coffee, hot and cold lunches, afternoon teas

Owned by The National Trust
Number of gardeners 4½, plus volunteers
Size 2.8ha (7 acres)
English Heritage Grade II

CASTLE HOWARD

York YO6 7DA

Tel 01653 648333 **Fax** 01653 648529
www.castlehoward.co.uk
Location 15 miles north-east of York, off A64
Opening hours 10am to 6pm (or dusk, if earlier), daily, all year
Admission fee Adults £7.50; concessions £7; children £5

Be prepared to spend all day at Castle Howard: it is essential visiting both for plantsmen and for anyone with a sense of history. At every time of the year, there are really good walks through woodlands and formal gardens, along the terraces and beside the water, and views of the buildings and sculptures in the landscape. The heroic megapark was first laid out by the 3rd Earl of Carlisle in 1700. Vanbrugh filled the five axes with landscapings and important buildings: the south lake, the terraces, the statues and the waterfalls down to the new river are all his. Vanbrugh's masterpiece, built in 1724-26, is the Temple of the Four Winds. The Mausoleum was designed by Hawksmoor in 1728. In front of the house are the remains of a vast 19th-century parterre, whose central point is the Atlas fountain built by William Andrews Nesfield in the 1850s. Within a walled garden are a 1980s rose garden (slightly Surrey) designed by Jim Russell, with every type of rose from ancient to modern, and an ornamental vegetable garden. Of more interest to gardeners and plantsmen is Ray Wood, where a fine and historic collection of rhododendrons and other ericaceous plants (all meticulously labelled) is destined to develop as one of the greatest woodland gardens in Europe. The rhododendrons and other plants of 20th-century plant hunters are here in abundance – collections by Forrest, Rock, Kingdon Ward, Ludlow and Sheriff are all represented, as are more recent collections from Nepal, Bhutan, Japan and China. Since 1999 the wood has been managed jointly by Castle Howard and the Royal Botanic Gardens at Kew: there is a small additional charge to visit it.

important buildings; impressive landscape; sculptures; woodland garden; roses (ancient and modern); good herbaceous borders; tallest elm *Ulmus glabra* (37m; 121ft) in the British Isles; gift shop; plant centre; café

Owned by Castle Howard Estates Ltd
Size 400ha (1,000 acres)
English Heritage Grade I

DUNCOMBE PARK
Helmsley YO62 5EB

Tel 01439 772625 **Fax** 01439 771114
www.duncombepark.com
Location Off A170; signed from Helmsley
Opening hours 11am to 5.30pm (or dusk, if earlier), Sunday to Thursday, 6 May to 28 October; closed 6, 7 and 11 June
Admission fee Adults £3.50; OAPs £3; children £1.75; RHS members free, except on event days

Christopher Hussey wrote that 'the grass terraces of Duncombe are unique, and perhaps the most spectacularly beautiful among English landscape conceptions of the 18th century'. They were probably completed between 1713 and 1730 to the designs of either Charles Bridgeman or Stephen Switzer, or both. A long, broad, grass terrace curves along the edge of a steep escarpment from an Ionic rotunda to the north. Woodland clothes the hillside: you see nothing until you reach the Doric temple at the southern end and look down to the ruins of Rievaulx Abbey. Hidden in more woodland is a small, classical conservatory fronting the ruins of a Victorian rose garden. Duncombe has little or nothing of horticultural interest, but it can scarcely be bettered for Palladian grandeur.
stately 18th-century landscape; gift shop; licensed tea room

Owned by Lord Feversham
Number of gardeners 1
Size 14ha (35 acres), within 160ha (400 acres) of parkland
English Heritage Grade I

FIR TREES PELARGONIUM NURSERY
Fir Trees Cottage, Stokesley TS9 5LD

Tel/fax 01642 713066
www.firtreespelargoniums.co.uk
Location South of Stokesley, by junction of A172 and B1365
Opening hours 10am to 4pm, daily, all year; closed at weekends between October and February
Admission fee Free

This family-run nursery specialises in pelargoniums, and stocks more than 370 cultivars. A recent development is a strong line in *Dierama* species and cultivars – some 17 offered for sale. Visitors are free to wander around the nursery, including its stock and show plant areas and propagation unit. Two RHS Special Events will take place at Fir Trees Pelargonium Nursery during 2007; details from 020 7821 3408.

Owned by Helen Bainbridge
Number of gardeners 3
Size 0.4ha (1 acre) of glass

HELMSLEY WALLED GARDEN
Cleveland Way, Helmsley YO62 5AH

Tel/fax 01439 771427
www.helmsleywalledgarden.org.uk
Location Behind castle; park in Cleveland Way long-stay car park
Opening hours 10.30am to 5pm, daily, April to October
Admission fee Adults £4; concessions £3; children free

This was originally the walled kitchen garden of Duncombe Park; it is now run by a charitable trust devoted to horticultural therapy which received a £fim grant from the Heritage Lottery Fund, principally for the restoration of the glasshouses. Apart from its sheer size and splendour, the main features of horticultural interest in the walled garden are some 300 clematis cultivars, 52 different Yorkshire apples, 34 Victorian vines and a splendid Orchid House. The nursery has some interesting and unusual plants.
rare plant nursery; restaurant

Owned by Helmsley Walled Garden Ltd
Number of gardeners 3, plus volunteers
Size 2ha (5 acres)
English Heritage Grade I

MIDDLETHORPE HALL & SPA
Bishopthorpe Road, York YO23 2GB

Tel 01904 641241 **Fax** 01904 620176
www.middlethorpe.com
Location 11/2 miles south of city centre, by York racecourse
Opening hours Residents and restaurant guests: free

Ⓟ 🚻
Middlethorpe Hall is a William III country house close to the city, set in its own gardens and parkland. After a period of neglect, the gardens have been carefully restored to their 18th-century splendour and include ha-has, a white garden, a walled garden, a small lake and some beautiful specimen trees. Four RHS Special Events will take place during 2007; details from 020 7821 3408.
renowned hotel and restaurant

Owned by Historic House Hotels Ltd
Number of gardeners 2
Size 8ha (20 acres)

MILLGATE HOUSE
Richmond DL10 4JN

Tel 01748 823571 **Fax** 01748 823571
www.millgatehouse.com
Location Bottom of Market Place; first house in Millgate on left
Opening hours 10am to 4pm, daily, April to October; and by appointment on Sundays in February and March for snowdrops
Admission fee Adults £2; children free; RHS members free except on charity days

This is a walled garden in the middle of the town, and thus very sheltered. Since starting work in the garden in 1980, the owners' aim has been to create structure, bulk, year-round interest and a sense of profusion. They have achieved this by redesigning the garden to suggest that it is much larger than it really is, and by planting only the best plants of every type. The most prominent are roses, clematis, hostas, snowdrops, hellebores, ferns and foliage shrubs. By 1995 the owners had won the National Garden Competition, against 3,200 other entries. The garden continues to improve: Professor David Stevens calls it 'a sophisticated study in both the manipulation of spatial concepts and [in] planting design'. It is stylish and closely planted, a model for all town gardens. Only one caveat – it is so dense that your trousers will get soaked by brushing against plants in wet weather!

Owned by Tim Culkin and Austin Lynch
Number of gardeners owners and students
Size 0.15ha (1/3 of an acre)

MOUNT GRACE PRIORY
Osmotherley, Northallerton DL6 3JG

Tel 01609 883494 **Fax** 01609 883361
www.nationaltrust.org.uk
Location 12 miles north of Thirsk on A19
Opening hours 10am to 6pm, daily, April to September; 10am to 4pm, Thursday to Monday, October to March 2008; closed 1 January and 24 to 26 December
Admission fee Adults £4; children £2; families £10

Ⓟ 🚻 ♿
The herb garden, designed by Stephen Anderton in 1994, is of most interest to gardeners. It is a re-creation of a 15th-century monastic garden. Around the house, the 1920s flower borders are being restored: there are terraces, acers, rhododendrons and azaleas. It is not a garden in which to dally, but an interesting add-on to the whole experience of a visit to the property.
herbs; shop; hot and cold drinks

Owned by The National Trust (managed by English Heritage)
Number of gardeners 2
Size 5ha (121/2 acres)

NEWBY HALL
Ripon HG4 5AE

Tel 01423 322583 **Fax** 01423 324452
www.newbyhall.co.uk
Location Off B6265, 2 miles from A1 between Boroughbridge and Ripon
Opening hours 11am to 5.30pm, Tuesday to Sunday and Bank Holiday Mondays, April to September; plus Mondays in July and August
Admission fee Adults £7; OAPs £6; children £5.50; RHS members free in April, May and September, except during special events

Newby is the garden with everything: firm design, an endless variety of features, great plantsmanship and immaculate maintenance. Its axis is a bold, wide, double border stretching gently down to the River Ure. The National Collection of *Cornus* now extends to 32 species and 53 cultivars, planted to give colour, beauty and interest. Newby also has a large number of other rare trees and shrubs and a comprehensive collection of shrubby salvias, many of them collected in Central and southern America by the owner's brother Dr James Compton. Newby is second only to Hidcote as an example of 20th-century gardening, but very much grander: visit at any season and expect to spend all day there.
woodland garden; roses (mainly old-fashioned and climbers); rock garden; plantsman's collection of plants; daffodils; good herbaceous borders; HHA/Christie's Garden of the Year in 1986; tallest *Acer griseum* (15m; 49ft) in the UK; adventure garden for children; shop and plant centre; licensed restaurant

Owned by Richard Compton
Number of gardeners 7
Size 10ha (25 acres)
NCCPG National Collections *Cornus* (excluding *C. florida* cvs.)
English Heritage Grade II*

NORTON CONYERS
Wath, Ripon HG4 5EQ

Tel/fax 01765 640333
Location 4 miles north of Ripon
Opening hours 2pm to 5pm, Bank Holiday Sundays and Mondays, April to August; plus Sundays and Monday in June and July and daily from 4 to 7 July
Admission fee Donation to charity

Norton Conyers thrives on being one of the houses that inspired Emily Bronte's *Jane Eyre*, but it also has a stylish 18th-century park and a good walled garden. The main feature is a long, straight double herbaceous border, backed by hedges and topiarised lumps of yew, that leads to the orangery. To one side is a good collection of irises and a long, deep border of old paeonies.
teas on charity days

Owned by Sir James and Lady Graham
Number of gardeners part-time help only
Size 1.4ha (3½ acres)
English Heritage Grade II

PARCEVALL HALL GARDENS
Skyreholme, Skipton BD23 6DE

Tel/fax 01756 720311
www.parcevallhallgardens.co.uk
Location Off B6160 from Burnsall
Opening hours 10am to 6pm, daily, April to October; for NGS: 6 June; winter visits by appointment
Admission fee Adults £5; children 75p; RHS members free (but not all the time)

The gardens at Parcevall Hall have a breathtaking architectural layout and views of the Yorkshire dales. They were largely designed and planted by Sir William Milner in 1927 and benefit from a great variety of soils (limestone and gritstone) which means that rhododendrons and camellias grow alongside limestone outcrops. It is also something of a plantsman's garden: the naturalised daffodils in the orchard include 'WP Milner' while the *Primula florindae* given by Kingdon Ward has now naturalised around the lily pond. Within the grounds are 14 Stations of the Cross.
woodland garden; climbing roses; rock garden; rhododendrons and azaleas; water features; candelabra primulas; tea room

Owned by Walsingham College (Yorkshire Properties) Ltd
Number of gardeners 3
Size 6.4ha (16 acres), plus woodland

RIPLEY CASTLE GARDENS
Ripley, Harrogate HG3 3AY

Tel 01423 770152 **Fax** 01423 771745
www.ripleycastle.co.uk
Location 3½ miles north of Harrogate, off A61
Opening hours 9am to 5pm (or dusk, if earlier), daily, all year
Admission fee Adults £4.50; OAPs £4; children £3; RHS members free except during special events

RHS GARDEN HARLOW CARR

Crag Lane, Beckwithshaw, Harrogate HG3 1QB

Tel 01423 565418 **Fax** 01423 530663
www.rhs.org.uk/harlowcarr
Location Crag Lane is off Otley Road (B6162), 1½ miles from Harrogate centre
Opening hours 9.30am to 6pm (4pm from November to February), daily, all year; closed 25 December; last admissions one hour before closing
Admission fee Adults £6; students £2.20; children (6-16) £2; children (under 6) free; pre-booked groups (10) £5; RHS members (plus one guest) free

For more than 50 years, Harlow Carr has set itself the challenge of educating, inspiring and delighting northern gardeners. The garden was opened in 1950, by the Northern Horticultural Society, as a trial ground for assessing the suitability of various plants for growing in northern climates. The gardens are comprehensive and spectacular. One of the highlights is the famous Streamside Garden – possibly one of the longest in the country – a breathtaking sight from spring onwards. It peaks in June and July with the vivid colours of the famous Harlow Carr hybrid candelabra primulas, along with blue Himalayan poppies, astilbes and hostas. The woodland, arboretum and wildflower meadow are home to insects, birds, squirrels, stoats and roe deer, and, as such, form a pivotal role in encouraging biodiversity. The ornamental gardens include scented, foliage, herb, grasses and winter gardens, alpine display houses and herbaceous beds. The newly redesigned scented garden mixes contemporary planting with rustic willow elements. New features appear every year: look out for the new kitchen garden, the redesigned main borders, and the new mixed border which combines herbaceous plants with grasses and roses in a contemporary design. Another significant addition are the Gardens Through Time – seven historical gardens created to commemorate the RHS bicentenary in 2004; they were the centrepiece of a BBC television series. Each garden represents a different phase in gardening history: c.1804, the 1850s, the end of the 19th century, a garden in the style of Gertrude Jekyll, a modern garden from the Festival of Britain (1951), a scene from the 1970s and finally a contemporary garden by Diarmuid Gavin. The Royal Horticultural Society also ensures that Harlow Carr is an important centre for horticultural learning, with a full programme of workshops and longer courses on all aspects of gardening and horticulture, plus year-round events for all the family.
fruit; vegetables; herbs; daffodils; fine collection of trees; alpines; good autumn colour; gift shop; large book shop; plant centre; Betty's Café Tea Rooms

Owned by The Royal Horticultural Society
Number of gardeners 17
Size 23ha (58 acres)
NCCPG National Collections *Dryopteris*; *Fuchsia* section Quelusia; *Polypodium*; *Rheum* (viewable on request)

Ripley has a garden with something for everyone: a 15th-century castle (restored); a 120-acre deer park; 1,000-year-old oaks; temples; a landscaped park (115 acres) designed by Capability Brown; 25 acres of lakes; a fine Regency conservatory; a Victorian formal garden; evergreen shrubberies (handsome yews); rare vegetables from Henry Doubleday Research Association; colour at every season; over 2,000 hyacinths in 40 varieties; woodland walks; herbaceous borders; and hundreds of thousands of bulbs – daffodils in hosts.
hyacinths; subtropical plants; parkland; bluebells; gift shop with plants, fruit and vegetables; castle tea room

Owned by Sir Thomas Ingilby Bt
Number of gardeners 4
Size 2ha (5 acres) walled garden, plus 4ha (10 acres) woodland
NCCPG National Collections *Hyacinthus orientalis*
English Heritage Grade II

WALLED GARDEN AT SCAMPSTON
Malton YO17 8NG

Tel 01944 759111 **Fax** 01944 758700
www.scampston.co.uk
Location 4 miles east of Malton on north side of A64
Opening hours 10am to 5pm, daily, except Mondays, 7 April to 28 October; plus Bank Holiday Mondays
Admission fee Adults £5; concessions £4.50; children £3; RHS members free in April, May and October

Scampston is a Georgian house with a Capability Brown landscape, but the reason for visiting is the new Piet Oudolf garden, open for the first time in 2004. It occupies the old kitchen garden and has been divided into sections, each with a distinct but complementary character. Most spectacular is the perennial flower meadow, planted with rich reds, yellows, oranges and purples, in a modern mix of salvias, echinaceas, achilleas, monardas and grasses. There are also good herbaceous borders, avenues and hedges, and a grassy pyramid from which to survey the splendour.
modern plantings; shop; restaurant

Owned by Sir Charles and Lady Legard
Number of gardeners 4
Size 1.8ha (4½ acres), plus parkland
English Heritage Grade II*

SLEIGHTHOLMEDALE LODGE
Fadmoor, Kirkbymoorside YO62 7JG

Tel 01751 431942 **Fax** 01751 430106
www.shdcottages.co.uk
Location Signed from Fadmoor
Opening hours For NGS: 26 May, 4 June, 14 and 15 July; and by written appointment at any time
Admission fee Adults £3; children 50p

This family garden – Mrs James is the third generation to garden here – is a plantsman's paradise. The walled garden was built on a south-facing slope, which makes it possible to grow a wide range of plants that might not otherwise survive. As well as magnificent meconopsis and hardy herbaceous plants, it has Mexican and Mediterranean rarities (a cistus walk, for example) which are a triumph for good cultivation and manipulation of the microclimate. The herbaceous borders are held together by repeating certain plants throughout: foxgloves and martagon lilies, for example. Outside the walled garden is an orchard underplanted with snowdrops and narcissi. And there are roses of every sort – hundreds of them.
roses (ancient and modern); plantsman's collection of plants; good herbaceous borders; teas in July

Owned by Mrs R James
Number of gardeners 1, plus 2 very part-time
Size 1.2ha (3 acres)

STILLINGFLEET LODGE NURSERIES
Stillingfleet, York YO19 6HP

Tel/fax 01904 728506
www.stillingfleetlodgenurseries.co.uk
Location 6 miles south of York: turn opposite the church
Opening hours 1pm to 4pm, Wednesdays and Fridays, May to September; plus Saturdays from May to July, and in September; for NGS: 1.30pm to 5pm, 13 May, 24 June and 16 September
Admission fee Adults £3; children 50p; RHS members free except on Saturdays

Stillingfleet is a series of small gardens surrounding a late 18th-century farmhouse. The emphasis is on a cottage garden style of planting, and every part is maintained organically. Foliage is used to add interest and texture: the result is a sequence of sumptuous herbaceous borders – a living lesson in how to plant a garden. The collection of pulmonarias is fascinating: 13 species and over 150 cultivars flower over a long period. A walk through the wildflower meadow leads to a pond planted for natural effect. The nursery has an excellent herbaceous list with a high proportion of unusual plants: the catalogue changes each year, but is always good for geraniums and pulmonarias. There will be three RHS Special Events at Stillingfleet in 2007; details from 020 7821 3408.
herbaceous plants; wildflower walk

Owned by Vanessa Cook
Number of gardeners owner, plus a little part-time help
Size 0.6ha (1 1/2 acres)
NCCPG National Collections *Pulmonaria*

STUDLEY ROYAL WATER GARDENS

Fountains, Ripon HG4 3DY

Tel 01765 608888 **Fax** 01765 601002
www.nationaltrust.org.uk
Location 3 miles west of Ripon off B6265, via the Visitor Centre
Opening hours 10am to 4pm (5pm in summer), daily, all year, except Fridays from November to February; closed 24 and 25 December
Admission fee Adults £7.50; children £4; families £20

Studley Royal is inextricably linked to Fountains Abbey: nothing can beat the surprise view of the ruined Cistercian Abbey from Anne Boleyn's Seat. The most spectacular water garden in England was laid out between 1716 and 1781 in the sheltered flat bottom of the River Skell. The abbey is at one end, the deer park at the other. The combination of the formal canal, moon pools, grotto springs, rustic bridge, sculptures and the Temple of Piety against a dark background of trees is a supreme example of 18th-century landscaping at its most individual.
topiary; snowdrops; World Heritage site; 400-acre deer park; water garden; biggest *Prunus avium* (bird cherry) in the British Isles; National Trust visitor centre shop; tea room; restaurant

Owned by The National Trust
Number of gardeners 9, plus volunteers
Size 60ha (150 acres)
English Heritage Grade I

SUTTON PARK

Sutton-on-the-Forest, York YO6 1DP

Tel 01347 810249 **Fax** 01347 811251
www.statelyhome.co.uk
Location 8 miles north of York on B1363
Opening hours 11am to 5pm, daily, April to September
Admission fee Adults £3.50; OAPs £2.50; children £1

Capability Brown was here in the 18th century, but the joy of Sutton is the formal garden laid out on three broad terraces below the house. It was designed by Percy Cane in the 1960s and planted by the late Nancie Sheffield with exquisite taste. It was one of the first to throw off the austerity of the post-war years and insist upon floral profusion and segregated colour schemes, though it looks a little dated nowadays – rather a period piece. In the grounds are a Georgian ice house, a woodland walk, some fine Victorian conifers, and a tulip tree *Liriodendron tulipifera* planted by Prince George, later Duke of Kent, on 7 October 1933.
influential formal gardens; plantsman's plants; good herbaceous borders; plants for sale occasionally; refreshments Wednesday to Sunday in summer

Owned by Sir Reginald and Lady Sheffield
Number of gardeners 2 1/2
Size 3.2ha (8 acres), plus parkland

THORP PERROW ARBORETUM & WOODLAND GARDEN

Bedale DL8 2PR

Tel/fax 01677 425323
www.thorpperrow.com
Location On the Bedale to Ripon road, 2 miles south of Bedale
Opening hours Dawn to dusk, daily, all year
Admission fee Adults £5.95; OAPs and students £4.60;

children £3.10; RHS members free except at weekends, on bank holidays and during special events

Thorp Perrow is the most important arboretum in the North of England, with more than 20 record-breaking trees among the thousands planted since Sir Leonard Ropner started work in 1931. There was already a pinetum on the estate, planted by Lady Augusta Milbank in the 1840s and 1850s. Ropner surrounded it with his new plantings – over 1,000 different taxa still survive, to which his son Sir John has added at least another 600. There are handsome avenues to walk along, often lined with a single genus or species – red oaks, rowans, cherries or cypresses, for example. Many are thickly lined with daffodils in spring, as are the glades and bays where you can study a particular collection like acers or hollies. The only downside is that all the trees are identified only with a number, which you then have to look up in the catalogue of plantings. This minor irritation apart, Thorp Perrow is an inspiring and enjoyable place to visit.
the best collection of trees in northern England; daffodils; bluebells; new Millennium Glade; information centre; plant centre; licensed tea room

Owned by Sir John Ropner Bt
Size 34ha (85 acres)
NCCPG National Collections *Fraxinus*; *Juglans*; *Laburnum*; *Tilia*; *Cotinus*
English Heritage Grade II

VALLEY GARDENS

Valley Drive, Harrogate HG2 0QB

Tel 01423 500600 **Fax** 01423 556720
www.harrogate.gov.uk
Location Signed from town centre
Opening hours Dawn to dusk, daily, all year
Admission fee Free

The Valley Gardens at Harrogate are a good example of plantsmanship in a public garden, first laid out between 1880 and 1900. The gardens have alpine rarities in spring, a romantic rhododendron dell, good roses, a fine dahlia display in late summer and good colour bedding.
rock garden; herbaceous borders; bedding; small café

Owned by Harrogate Borough Council
Size 6.7ha (17 acres)
English Heritage Grade II

WYTHERSTONE GARDENS

Pockley, Helmsley YO62 7TE

Tel 01439 770012 **Fax** 01439 770468
www.wytherstonegardens.co.uk
Location In middle of village, on left side, coming from A170
Opening hours 1pm to 5pm, Wednesdays, 6 June to 12 September; plus 20 May, 3 and 17 June, 22 July, 19 August and 9 September for charity; and by appointment at other times
Admission fee Adults £3.50; children £1

There is a lot to see – and tender plants especially – in this remote garden, which has been boosted in recent years by the arrival of a plant-wise head gardener. In a sheltered area near the entrance are bananas, *Pinus montezumae*, trachycarpus, cordylines and phormiums. Rhododendrons thrive nearby in a specially made-up bed. Fremontodendrons and *Cytisus battandieri* have been trained against the south-facing side of the house. Around the house is a series of small, linked gardens with mixed borders, often backed by climbing roses, and good colour-schemed plantings. A garden made of old railway sleepers is terraced up with raised beds full of interesting plants – including succulents put out for the summer. Elsewhere are carpenterias, phlomis, crinums, *Melianthus major* and *Salvia greggii* and its hybrids, all apparently quite hardy in the free-draining, limestone soil. *Buddleja colvilei* is grown as a free-standing shrub. Borders of Chinese paeonies contrast with a lush garden of ferns. Further away from the house, a newly planted border of bamboos and foliage plants is reflected by a pond and surrounded by a collection of trees (including *Wollemia nobilis*) that promises to develop into a pretty domestic arboretum. The on-site nursery is excellent.
tender plants; good colour combinations; interesting nursery; teas on Sundays only

Owned by Lady Clarissa Collin
Number of gardeners 2
Size 3.2ha (8 acres)

YORKSHIRE, SOUTH

The county of South Yorkshire was invented in 1974 and is, in effect, Greater Sheffield. Nevertheless, it has a couple of good historic gardens that are open to the public – Wentworth Castle and Brodsworth Hall. The Sheffield Botanical Gardens are also of great horticultural interest, having been planted and maintained over many years as a garden of ornamental plants of every kind. Both the Sheffield Botanical Gardens and the gardens at Wentworth Castle have benefited from lottery funding in recent years and are very visitor-friendly as a result. The National Gardens Scheme has very few gardens opening for it in the county and, though it is well provided with garden centres, South Yorkshire has no specialist nurseries of national importance. There are several NCCPG National Collections – including two at Sheffield Botanical Gardens and three at Wentworth Castle.

BRODSWORTH HALL AND GARDENS

English Heritage, Brodsworth, Doncaster DN5 7XJ

Tel 01302 722598 **Fax** 01302 337165
www.english-heritage.org.uk
Location 6 miles north-west of Doncaster
Opening hours 10am to 6pm, Tuesday to Sunday and Bank Holiday Mondays, April to October; then 11am to 4pm, weekends only
Admission fee Garden only: adults £4.80; OAPs £3.75; children £2.40; cheap rates in winter

Brodsworth has proved a triumph for English Heritage – a splendid Victorian garden, unkempt for 50 years, but now spectacularly restored as first laid out in the 1860s. It offers Italianate terraces, statues and classical follies; a rose garden where the vigorous ramblers are trained on bizarre ironwork arcades and box-edged beds are filled with period roses; magnificent trees (especially cedars, pines and monkey puzzles); bright Victorian bedding in a huge formal garden; and lots of clipped evergreens – laurels, yews, aucubas and many more, even free-standing griselinias. Best of all, perhaps, are the hollies – hundreds and hundreds of them, planted to display their vast colour palette. The spring bulbs, too, are exceptional. Every part of the garden is well maintained and a joy to visit at any time of the year.

good specimen conifers; Victorian spring and summer bedding; large fern collection; significant clipped evergreen shrubberies; statuary; shop; licensed restaurant

Owned by English Heritage
Number of gardeners 6
Size 5.2ha (13 acres)
English Heritage Grade II*

SHEFFIELD BOTANICAL GARDENS

Clarkehouse Road, Sheffield S10 2LN

Tel 0114 268 6001 **Fax** 0114 255 2375
www.sbg.org.uk
Location M1, Jct 33, follow A57 signs to Glossop, left at Royal Hallamshire Hospital, 500 yards on left
Opening hours 7.30am (10am at weekends) to 7.45pm (4pm in winter), daily, all year; closed 25 December
Admission fee Free

The Sheffield Botanical Gardens were founded in 1833 by public subscription and designed by Robert Marnock in the gardenesque style. A £6.69m Heritage Lottery grant has repaired the gardens and their buildings. The glass pavilions are among the earliest curvilinear glasshouses ever built and now contain a temperate plant collection from around the world. There is much to interest the plantsman, too. The features include good camellias and magnolias; heathers; a rock garden; and good trees. The garden has splendid summer bedding and lots of seats: an exemplary combination of botany and amenity.

rock garden; mature conifers; good herbaceous borders; historic conservatories; peat garden; heath garden; roses (mainly modern); shop; restaurant; tea room

Brodsworth Hall and Gardens

Owned by Sheffield Town Trust (managed by Sheffield City Council)
Number of gardeners 6, plus 2 part-time
Size 7.6ha (19 acres)
NCCPG National Collections *Diervilla*; *Weigela*
English Heritage Grade II

WENTWORTH CASTLE GARDENS
Lowe Lane, Stainborough, Barnsley S75 3ET

Tel 01226 776040 **Fax** 01226 776042
www.wentworthcastle.org
Location 2 miles from M1, Jcts 36 and 37
Opening hours 10am to 5pm (4pm in October), daily, April to October; guided tours at 2pm; guided tours available; details from 01226 776040 or website
Admission fee Adults £3.95; concessions £3.25; children £2; families £9.95; discounts for groups; RHS members free except during special events

Wentworth Castle has a major landscape garden, one of the earliest in England, which accounts for the amazing series of buildings in the grounds – among them are an Ionic rotunda, the Gothic folly of Stainborough Castle, an obelisk to Queen Anne and another to Lady Mary Wortley-Montagu to commemorate her introduction of smallpox inoculation to England. The garden was then

Wentworth Castle Gardens

Stainborough Castle

overlaid with a seriously important collection of hardy hybrid rhododendrons at the end of the 19th century. It was in the same era that the handsome cast-iron conservatory was built: it was recently featured on BBC Two's *Restoration* series. The need to preserve the original landscape features has been the basis of an ambitious £15m restoration project. Go now to see this important landscape (South Yorkshire's only Grade I listed landscape) as it emerges from disrepair, and return to watch restoration progress. Stout footwear essential.
historic landscape; woodland garden; newly excavated 19th-century rock garden; educational collection of rhododendrons; gift shop; plants for sale; café

Owned by Wentworth Castle Trust
Number of gardeners 8
Size 20ha (50 acres) pleasure garden
NCCPG National Collections *Rhododendron* species; *Magnolia* (species); *Camellia* x *williamsii*
English Heritage Grade I

YORKSHIRE, WEST

West Yorkshire corresponds to the old West Riding. It is a county of great contrasts, from the industrial and commercial cities of Bradford and Leeds to the wool towns of Huddersfield and Halifax, with a chunk of the Peak District in the south-west and some large agricultural estates in the north. The most important historic gardens are Bramham Park – a remarkable pre-landscape garden on a big scale – and the opulent Harewood House. But they are matched for sheer horticultural value by four gardens which all have a historic past but are now owned and managed by Leeds City Council as gardens for public recreation – Lotherton Hall, Temple Newsam, The Hollies, and the Canal Gardens & Tropical World in Roundhay Park. The NCCPG has no fewer than 11 National Collections in the care of the Leeds City Parks Department. There are rather few specialist nurseries of national standing in the county, though it is well served by garden centres.

BRAMHAM PARK

Wetherby LS23 6ND

Tel 01937 846000 **Fax** 01937 846007
www.bramhampark.co.uk
Location 5 miles south of Wetherby on A1
Opening hours 11.30am to 4.30pm, daily, April to September; closed for horse trials from 4 to 10 June, Leeds Festival from 13 August to 31 August and occasionally for other events; ring before visiting
Admission fee Gardens only: adults £4; OAPs £2; children £2

Bramham is a very important pre-landscape formal garden, laid out in the grand manner in the early 18th century. A long driveway winds through the woods, turns a corner, and suddenly reveals the magnificent Palladian house, framed by the most spacious of avenues. Behind the house are long, straight rides carved through dense woodland and edged with tall beech hedges, neatly cut. Focal points include loggias, statues, temples, an obelisk and a sequence of formal cascades running down to a square, lake-sized pond. The parkland turf is speckled with cowslips and orchids, while wild onions run amok in the woods, but the scale and complexity of the design have nothing to match them anywhere in the British Isles: Bramham is the finest French garden in England – awesome, uplifting and built to impress.
very important pre-landscape park; daffodils

Owned by George Lane Fox
Number of gardeners 2
Size 27ha (68 acres)
English Heritage Grade I

GOLDEN ACRE PARK

Otley Road, Bramhope, Leeds LS16 5NZ

Tel 0113 267 3729
www.leeds.gov.uk
Location 6 miles north-west of Leeds city centre on A660 Otley Road
Opening hours Dawn to dusk, daily, all year
Admission fee Free

Golden Acre is part historic park, part botanic collection, part demonstration garden and part test ground for Fleuroselect and *Gardening Which?* It began life in the 1930s as an amusement park, but the City Council decided after the war to develop it as a public garden with a strong botanical interest. Perhaps the best of the five impressive public gardens in Leeds, it is certainly the most popular.
rock garden; large heather garden; new 'harmony' garden; herb garden; limestone rock garden; sandstone rock garden; arboretum; pinetum; display houses; rhododendrons and azaleas; cherry orchard; gifts/souvenirs; restaurant

Owned by Leeds City Council
Size 54ha (135 acres)
NCCPG National Collections *Primula auricula*; *Syringa*

HAREWOOD HOUSE

Harewood, Leeds LS17 9LQ

Tel 0113 218 1010 **Fax** 0113 218 1002
www.harewood.org
Location Between Leeds and Harrogate on A61
Opening hours 10am to 6pm, daily, 15 March to 28 October
Admission fee Grounds (weekdays): adults £8.80; OAPs £7.95; children £5.90; grounds (weekends): adults £10.90; OAPs £10; children £7.25; RHS members free (but not all the time)

Capability Brown was the first famous landscaper to work at Harewood for the super-rich Lascelles family: he was followed by Humphry Repton, John Claudius Loudon and Sir Charles Barry. The latter came in the 1840s, to build the stupendous Italianate terrace whose grand parterre and ornate fountains are the perfect link between the house and the landscaped park. Bedding out is practised here on a large scale - very impressive - and ensures colour throughout the year. The border below the parterre is planted with bold foliage plants - yuccas, phormiums, irises, artichokes, peonies, eriobotryas, bananas, callistemons and acanthus. Around the lake at the bottom are hundreds of rhododendrons, and unusual shrubs and bulbs, particularly daffodils. The waterfall at the lake head feeds a picturesque rock garden where primulas, astilbes, hostas and gunneras grow rampantly in the damp. The rose garden at the end of the lakeside walk is an extra delight in early summer. The large, traditional walled garden displays a wide selection of vegetables and economic crops from around the world: Harewood is a registered Seed Library garden.
formal terraces; good bedding; woodland garden; rhododendrons; current holder of Sandford Award; two shops; licensed café selling light lunches

Owned by Harewood House Trust Ltd
Number of gardeners 7
Size 56ha (140 acres)
English Heritage Grade I

THE HOLLIES PARK

Weetwood Lane, Leeds LS16 5NZ

Tel 0113 278 2030 **Fax** 0113 247 8277
www.leeds.gov.uk
Location 3 miles north of city off A660
Opening hours Dawn to dusk, daily, all year
Admission fee Free

Harewood House

This public park is made in a plantsman's garden, and is well run by a hard-pressed and enthusiastic team. Visitors wishing to see the National Collections are advised to make a prior appointment.
woodland garden; rhododendrons; eucryphias

Owned by Leeds City Council
Size 37ha (93 acres)
NCCPG National Collections *Deutzia*; *Hemerocallis* (Coe hybrids); *Hosta* (large-leaved); *Philadelphus*; *Syringa*

LAND FARM GARDENS
Colden, Hebden Bridge, Halifax HX7 7PJ

Tel 01422 842260
Location On right, 2 miles from Hebden Bridge on road to Colden
Opening hours 10am to 5pm, Saturdays, Sundays and Bank Holiday Mondays, May to August
Admission fee Adults £4; guided parties £5 per head, including refreshments

This is a pioneering plantsman's garden, high in the Pennines and facing north. The range of plants that can successfully be grown in such an unpromising situation is an eye-opener – lots of hardy rhododendrons, shrubs, trees and alpines, and mass plantings of cardiocrinums and meconopsis. There is also a good collection of sculpture, with more pieces arriving all the time.
garden created by owners on greenfield site; good conifers and herbaceous borders; new woodland garden (2 acres); *Meconopsis*; *Tropaeolum*; art gallery

Owned by John Williams
Number of gardeners 3 part-time
Size 2ha (5 acres)

LOTHERTON HALL
Aberford, Leeds LS25 3EB

Tel 0113 264 5535 **Fax** 0113 281 3068
www.leeds.gov.uk/lothertonhall
Location Off A1, 3/4 mile east on B1217
Opening hours 8am to 8pm (or dusk, if earlier), daily, all year
Admission fee Garden free, but charges for parking (£3.50)

This showpiece garden was laid out between 1885 and 1915 by a friend of Ellen Willmott. It was given to the council in 1968 and has been well restored in recent years. It offers gazebos, walks, yew hedging, rose gardens, and a lily pond recently replanted with period varieties. The rock garden known as the Dell is especially good. The formal garden is laid out with

gravel paths and lots of bedding. Lotherton is a garden that is on the move again, with a woodland trail recently added for disabled users and a new (2005) orchard planted in partnership with the Northern Fruit Group. Lotherton is extremely popular – over 750,000 visitors a year.
Edwardian plantswoman's garden; roses (mainly modern); good trees; fine hedges; mature layout; shop; café

Owned by Leeds City Council
Number of gardeners 2
Size 4ha (10 acres)
English Heritage Grade II

ROUNDHAY PARK & TROPICAL WORLD

Roundhay Park, Princes Avenue, Leeds LS8 2ER

Tel 0113 266 1850 **Fax** 0113 237 0077
www.leeds.gov.uk
Location 3 miles north-west of city centre, off A6120 ring road
Opening hours Open at 10am all year; close at 4pm in January and December, 5pm in February and November, 6pm in March and October, 7pm in April and September, 8pm from May to August
Admission fee Tropical World: adults £3; children £2; gardens: free

Tropical World's glasshouses contain South American rainforest plants, bromeliads, hoyas, cacti and a butterfly house. It is said to have the largest collection of tropical plants outside Kew. It is in any event a wonderful retreat from a Yorkshire winter and a triumph of municipal horticultural excellence. Roundhay Park has a £6.1m project to preserve and enhance the gardens which has received support from the Heritage Lottery Fund. Tropical World is visited by over a million people every year. The gardens outside have fine herbaceous and mixed borders, and splendid formal bedding schemes, including a clock surrounded by carpet bedding and two further raised carpet beds. Nearby is a reinterpretation of Monet's garden at Giverny and another of the Alhambra Gardens in Granada, complete with fountains. Add in two lakes and extensive woodland walks in the park and you have a most enjoyable place to visit at any time of the year.
subtropical plants; roses (mainly modern); plants under glass; good carpet bedding; orchids; desert house; souvenirs; café by lakeside

Owned by Leeds City Council
Number of gardeners 40
Size 240ha (600 acres)
English Heritage Grade II

TEMPLE NEWSAM PARK

Leeds LS15 0AD

Tel 0113 264 5535
www.leeds.gov.uk/templenewsam
Location 3 miles south-east of city, off A63 Selby road
Opening hours Dawn to dusk, daily, all year
Admission fee Free; admission charge to house

This prodigious house on a windy bluff, surrounded by 1,500 acres of parkland, has been a 'green lung' for Leeds since 1923. Somewhat dilapidated in the past, the garden is now improved by some recent plantings. These include a spring garden full of bulbs; the Italian garden with formal flowerbeds; box, yew and beech hedges; pleached laburnum walks; and a clipped hornbeam stilt hedge. A fine rhododendron and azalea walk runs down to the lakes. Nearby is a specimen tree area and a bog garden. Further on still, the old walled kitchen garden is planted with roses and wide herbaceous borders. The long conservatory has a fine display of flowering plants, ivies and cacti: its back wall (1788) still has the flues which were used to keep it warm with hot air.
spacious parkland; roses (ancient and modern); good herbaceous borders; rhododendrons; visitor centre and gift shop; tea room open daily from 10.30am

Owned by Leeds City Council
NCCPG National Collections *Aster, Chrysanthemum* (Charms and Cascade); *Delphinium, Phlox paniculata, Solenostemon*
English Heritage Grade II

YORK GATE

Back Church Lane, Adel, Leeds LS16 8DW

Tel 0113 267 8240/0845 230 1839
www.perennial.org.uk/yorkgate.html
Location 2 1/4 miles south-east of Bramhope and 1/2 mile east of A660, behind Adel Church
Opening hours 2pm to 5pm, Thursdays, Sundays and Bank Holiday Mondays, 8 April to 30 September; plus 6.30pm to 9pm on 21 and 27 June and 5 July; and by appointment
Admission fee Adults £3.50 (more for private visits); children free; RHS members free in April, May and September

This one-acre masterpiece – a modern icon – was made by the Spencer family between 1951 and 1994. It is of equal interest to the designer and the plantsman. Its marvels include a pavement maze, an arbour, a miniature pinetum, a dell with a stream, a folly, a nut walk, a peony bed, water features, a fern border, the famous herb garden, a pretty summerhouse, an alley, a white and silver garden and a kitchen garden. This combination of tight design, invention, colour sense and sheer creative opportunism is now in the care of Perennial, formerly the Gardeners' Royal Benevolent Society. Perennial has just added a new, more contemporary garden with grasses and summer-flowering perennials; visitors may wonder whether the Spencers would have approved or not.
brilliant design; plantsman's collection of plants; famous herb garden; endless inventive details; plants for sale (usually); tea and biscuits

Owned by Perennial
Number of gardeners 1, plus 1 part-time and volunteers
Size 0.4ha (1 acre)

SCOTLAND

Scottish gardens are very variable – this is a result of their soil and climate. All along the west coast, from Dumfries & Galloway up to Ullapool and beyond, are fine, subtropical woodland gardens, where one can enjoy acres of large-leaved rhododendrons and eucalyptus trees and all manner of curiosities like *Myosotidium hortensia*, which would not be hardy in any but the most favoured parts of England. There is no better place to go visiting gardens in May or June – provided the weather is kind. There are comparatively few good gardens in inland Scotland. Historically, the big estates were (and still are) in remote places where the land is unsuitable for agriculture and, in consequence, their gardens tend to be few and disappointing. In the Borders, for example, there are several estates along the valleys of Tweed and the Teviot whose gardens are open to the public: all have collections of 19th-century conifers underplanted with hardy hybrid rhododendrons or common *R. ponticum*, but little else in the way of horticultural interest. On the east coast, however, there are once again many worthy gardens, above all the superb botanic garden at Edinburgh, which (like all botanic gardens nowadays) is laid out to please visitors, and other good botanic gardens at Dundee, St Andrews and Aberdeen. There are interesting gardens, too, near Edinburgh (especially Malleny at Balerno) and on Deeside (Crathes, Kildrummy and Drum).

Trees flourish in much of Scotland – especially those North American conifers for which the cool, damp west coast provides perfect growing conditions: many of the tallest pines, firs and spruces in Britain are in Scotland. The largest collection of record-breaking trees is at the Royal Botanic Gardens in Edinburgh, which has 45.

We have listed the gardens to visit in Scotland under the old 1974 regions, rather than the historic counties or the plethora of more recent local councils. The regions divide the country into areas of acceptable size for the purpose of this book, though there is a preponderance of gardens in the old region of Strathclyde – as indeed there still is in Argyll & Bute. If readers can suggest a better way than the old regions to list gardens, we would be pleased to hear from them. Scotland's Gardens Scheme divides the country into areas that are even more confusing – 'Etterick & Lauderdale', for example, and 'Lochaber, Badenoch & Strathspey'. The 1974 regions do at least have the advantage of having been administrative areas until recently.

Scotland has many great historic gardens. The basis of the protection they enjoy is the *Inventory of Gardens & Designed Landscapes in Scotland* which was published in 1987. The Inventory listed 275 sites, which are graded in a more specific way than the gardens on the English register, for example, according to the value of their horticultural content or historic importance. Historic Scotland has recently begun to extend the Inventory.

Nobody has done more to acquire, save, restore and redevelop Scotland's great gardens than the National Trust for Scotland. Its portfolio of properties includes many of the best historic and horticultural gardens in the country: Branklyn, Brodick, Crathes, Culzean and Inverewe are gardens of international renown. It has now taken the splendid garden at Crarae into its care. The Royal Botanic Garden in Edinburgh has also developed four of the finest gardens anywhere in the world – Dawyck, Logan, Benmore (Younger Botanic Garden) and its own incomparable garden in north Edinburgh.

Members of the Royal Horticultural Society have free access for at least some months of the year to a fine list of Scottish gardens from Dunrobin Castle in the north to Harmony Garden in the Borders. More may be added during the course of the year: see the Society's website (www.rhs.org.uk) for the latest news. Scotland also has its own Yellow Book called *The Gardens of Scotland*, available from Scotland's Gardens Scheme, 31 Castle Terrace, Edinburgh EH1 2EL. It lists some 350 gardens throughout Scotland and, like its English equivalent, is the essential starting point for choosing more gardens to visit than this book recommends.

Scotland is well served by garden centres, especially by such chains as Dobbies in the Lowlands, which also has branches in northern England. Scotland has some excellent specialist nurseries: Jack Drake is Britain's premier alpine nursery; nobody has bred more or better new rhododendrons than Peter Cox at Glendoick; and Cally in Dumfries & Galloway has a great reputation for rare plants. However, it is fair to say that there are fewer nurseries per capita in Scotland as a whole than in England.

Scotland also has its own rather basic horticultural structure: this includes, for example, such societies as the Scottish Rock Garden Club, the Scottish Rhododendron Society, the Royal Caledonian Horticultural Society and the Scottish Orchid Society. All are excellent organisations and some, like the Scottish Rock Garden Club and the Scottish Rhododendron Society, are substantial societies with good programmes of events and publications of record. Scotland also has a number of horticultural training colleges, notably Threave and the Scottish Agricultural College at Auchincruive, both of them RHS Partner Colleges.

BORDERS

ABBOTSFORD
Melrose TD6 9BQ

Tel 01896 752043 **Fax** 01896 752916
www.scottsabbotsford.co.uk
Location On B6360, 2 miles west of Melrose
Opening hours 9.30am to 5pm (but 2pm to 5pm on Sundays in March, April, May and October), daily, 19 March to 31 October
Admission fee Garden only: adults £2; children free

Sir Walter Scott laid out the gardens at Abbotsford in the 1820s: he designed the formal Court garden by the house and planted the surrounding woodlands. The walled garden centres on a handsome orangery, with roses, fruit trees and herbaceous borders planted for late-summer effect.
fine walled garden; orangery; topiary; herbaceous borders; gift shop; self-service tea room

Owned by The Abbotsford Trust
Number of gardeners 2
Size 0.4ha (1 acre)

DAWYCK BOTANIC GARDEN
Stobo EH45 9JU

Tel 01721 760254 **Fax** 01721 760214
www.rbge.org.uk
Location 8 miles south-west of Peebles on B712
Opening hours 10am to 6pm (4pm in February and November, and 5pm in March and October), daily, February to November
Admission fee Adults £3.50; concessions £3; children £1

Dawyck is a woodland garden, run as a regional garden of the Royal Botanic Garden Edinburgh. It is very different from Edinburgh's other outliers: its 60 acres are high in the hills and north-facing, and the climate is more continental than temperate. The trees for which the garden is famous were first planted in the 1830s: the owners subscribed to the great plant-hunting expeditions of the day, including those of David Douglas. This explains the many fine North American conifers in the garden. In the early 20th century, the owners received plants from the early Chinese collections of EH Wilson. The gardens are also famous for their rhododendrons, berberis and cotoneasters and – of course – the Dawyck beech, an upright, fastigiate form of the common beech, first found in the policies (woodland) in the mid-19th century. Good for lichens and fungi, too – over 1,750 different fungi grow in Heron Wood.
Chinese conifers; Dawyck beech; Douglas fir from original seed; *Torreya californica*; tallest *Abies mariesii* (21m; 69ft) in the British Isles, and 12 further record trees; gift shop; light refreshments

Owned by Royal Botanic Garden Edinburgh
Size 24ha (60 acres)

Dawyck Botanic Garden

EDROM NURSERIES
Coldingham, Eyemouth TD14 5TZ

Tel 01890 771386 **Fax** 01890 771387
www.edromnurseries.co.uk
Location A1107, 5 mins from A1
Opening hours 9am to 5.30pm, daily, mid-March to mid-October
Admission fee Free

This nursery specialises in primulas, arisaemas, fritillarias, trilliums, gentians and meconopsis. The list of these genera is particularly comprehensive and includes many forms that are not available elsewhere. *Rhodohypoxis* is another speciality, and the list of Japanese *Hepatica nobilis* cultivars is stunning. As with the other plants it lists, many are new to commerce or grown under collectors' numbers. The display gardens are varied and interesting, including woodland areas, raised beds and gravel-topped troughs.

Owned by Terry Hunt and Cath Davis
Number of gardeners 2
Size 0.2ha (1/2 acre)

FLOORS CASTLE
Kelso TD5 7SF

Tel 01573 223333 **Fax** 01573 226056
www.floorscastle.com
Location Signed in Kelso
Opening hours Walled garden: 9.30am to 5pm, daily, all year; castle and grounds: 11am to 5pm, daily, Easter, then 1 May to 28 October
Admission fee Walled garden free; gardens and grounds: Adults £3; OAPs £1.50; RHS members free

Floors Castle is impressively sited in its parkland. There are some good trees in the park, including a holm oak (*Quercus ilex*) and a Dawyck beech (*Fagus sylvatica* 'Fastigiata'), and a venerable holly on the spot where King James II of Scotland was blown up while besieging Roxburgh Castle in 1460. The horticultural interest is all in the old walled garden, which has been restored as a visitor attraction. Here are old vineries and fruit houses, a rose catenary, a very long border of pink crinums and massive herbaceous borders, each designed with a different colour scheme and supplemented by dahlias and annuals so that it is full of colour even in late summer.
good borders; garden centre in walled garden; licensed restaurant; gift shop

Owned by The Duke of Roxburghe
Number of gardeners 5

HARMONY GARDEN
St Mary's Road, Melrose TD6 9LJ

Tel 01896 822493
www.nts.org.uk
Location In Melrose, opposite abbey
Opening hours 10am to 5pm, Monday to Saturday, (1pm to 5pm, Sundays), 31 March to 31 October
Admission fee Adults £3; concessions £2; RHS members free

'Harmony' takes its name from the Jamaican pimento plantation where its original builder, James Waugh, made his fortune. It is a modest, quiet, walled garden, but very much more interesting to visit than some of the private gardens in the area. There are lawns, herbaceous and mixed borders, vegetable and fruit areas, lots of spring bulbs, a turning circle edged with Scotch roses and hedges of yew with the Scottish flame flower *Tropaeolum speciosum* growing through. The views of Melrose Abbey and the Eildon Hills are a bonus.

Owned by The National Trust for Scotland
Number of gardeners 1
Size 0.8ha (2 acres)

KAILZIE GARDENS
Kailzie, Peebles EH45 9HT

Tel/fax 01721 720007
www.kailziegardens.com
Location On B7062, 2 miles east of Peebles
Opening hours 11am to 5.30pm, daily, all year
Admission fee Adults £4.50; concessions £3.50; children £1; (but £3.50, £3 and 75p respectively from November to May)

Kailzie has been revived over the last 20 years. The large walled garden has a mixture of flowers and produce: a laburnum alley, a rose garden and double herbaceous borders are some of the attractions. There are gunneras, meconopsis and primulas in the rhododendron woodland outside, and massed snowdrops along the woodland walks.
good conifers; snowdrops; daffodils; shop; restaurant and teas

Owned by Angela, Lady Buchan-Hepburn
Number of gardeners 3
Size 8ha (20 acres)

LILLIESLEAF NURSERY
Garden Cottage, Linthill, Lilliesleaf TD6 9HU

Tel/fax 01835 870415
Location On B6359 between Midlem and Lilliesleaf
Opening hours 10am to 5pm, Monday to Saturday, 10am to 4pm, Sundays, November to March; phone first
Admission fee Free

This nursery, in a pretty position on the bank of the River Ale, has a general plant range, with an emphasis on perennials and hard-to-find plants of every kind. It is particularly good for epimediums and offers a number of hybrids listed by no other nursery. The demonstration garden is also worth seeing: attractive mixed borders in a walled garden.

Owned by Teyl de Bordes
Number of gardeners 2
Size 0.4ha (1 acre)
NCCPG National Collections *Epimedium*

MANDERSTON
Duns TD11 3PP

Tel 01361 883450 **Fax** 01361 882010
www.manderston.co.uk
Location On A6105, 2 miles east of Duns
Opening hours 11.30am to dusk, Sundays and Thursdays, mid-May to September; parties at any time by appointment
Admission fee Gardens only: free; parties £4.50 per person

The house is Edwardian, built in classical neo-Georgian style, and was the location for Channel 4's *The Edwardian Country House*. Below it are four expansive terraces with rich planting around clipped yews and hollies and fountains on the upper terrace. Below is a small lake with an ornamental boathouse and an 18th-century Chinese-style bridge. On the other side of the lake are the woodland gardens with a large collection of unusual species of trees and shrubs: the extensive collection of rhododendrons and azaleas dates back 100 years. This woodland garden is criss-crossed with numerous paths so that visitors can see all parts of it. On the north side of the house, after crossing wide lawns set about with mature trees, visitors reach the formal garden and herbaceous borders, both at their best in summer.
woodland garden with rhododendrons and azaleas; mature conifers; good herbaceous borders; good bedding out on the formal terraces; tea room

Owned by Lord Palmer
Number of gardeners 2
Size 22ha (56 acres)

MELLERSTAIN
Gordon TD3 6LG

Tel 01573 410225 **Fax** 01573 410636
www.mellerstain.com
Location 1 mile west of A6089 Kelso to Edinburgh road
Opening hours For snowdrops: 11.30am to 4pm, 18 and 25 February and 4 and 11 March (guided walk at 2pm); 11.30pm to 5.30pm, 6 to 9 April; then Sundays, Wednesdays and Bank Holiday Mondays from May to September; plus Mondays and Thursdays in July and August; plus Sundays in October
Admission fee £3.50

The house has extensive views south to the Cheviots: it was built by the Adams (father and son) between 1725 and 1778. It is set off by Sir Reginald Blomfield's formal garden,

balustraded and terraced, but now rather covered by lichen. The garden is planted with floribunda roses and catmint. Beneath it runs the landscaped park, also laid out by William and Robert Adam, sauntering down to a lake. The whole picture is uncompromisingly grand.
topiary; roses (mainly modern); Italian terraced garden by Sir Reginald Blomfield; licensed restaurant

Owned by Mellerstain Trust
Number of gardeners 1, plus 1 seasonal assistant
Size 1.8ha (4 1/2 acres)

MERTOUN GARDENS
St Boswells, Melrose TD6 0EA

Tel 01835 823236 **Fax** 01835 822474
Location B6404, 2 miles north-east of St Boswells
Opening hours 2pm to 6pm, Friday to Monday, April to September
Admission fee Adults £2.50; OAPs £1.50; children 50p

Mertoun is the home of the Duke and Duchess of Sutherland, on the banks of the Tweed, with rolling lawns, herbaceous borders and azaleas. Its gardens are best known for their immaculately maintained, traditional, three-acre kitchen garden in which is situated Old Mertoun House. Here is a great variety of fruit trees, vegetables, flowers and a range of heated greenhouses and cold frames. Nearby is a circular dovecot dated 1567 and thought to be the oldest in the region. Mertoun also has a young arboretum, established since 1975, with a good selection of conifers and hardwoods, most of which have grown away very well. For many years now, the Dukes have grown a strain of pea which is said to have come from one found by Lord Carnarvon in the tomb of Tutankhamen.
vegetables; herbs; plants under glass; daffodils; good herbaceous borders

Owned by Mertoun Gardens Trust
Number of gardeners 2 1/2
Size 10.3ha (26 acres)

MONTEVIOT HOUSE GARDENS
Jedburgh TD8 6UQ

Tel 01835 830380 **Fax** 01835 830288
Location Off A68 north of Jedburgh and B6400 to Nisbet
Opening hours Noon to 4pm, daily, April to October
Admission fee Adults £3.50; children free

The gardens at Monteviot lie along a dramatic slope of the Teviot valley. The box-hedged herb garden and terrace along the front of the house have a breathtaking view of the river below. The sheltered terraced rose garden is Victorian: the river garden at the bottom was originally designed in the 1930s by Percy Cane. Italianate in inspiration, this sheltered garden slopes down between curved borders of herbaceous plants, shrubs, bulbs and roses, to a broad stone landing stage above the waters of the Teviot itself. In the nearby water garden, fed by a natural spring, three islands are linked by elegant, curved wooden bridges. Here are bog plants and bamboos. The dramatic impact of the garden as a whole is heightened by the contrast between the formal and the informal and by the way that the planting leads seamlessly through the different parts. The trees in the arboretum are exceptional – *Fagus sylvatica* 'Riversii' is 30m (98ft) high – and recent clearing has displayed them in their glory. A new water cascade sets them off beautifully.
fine collection of trees; water garden; Victorian rose garden; refreshments

Number of gardeners 3

PRIORWOOD GARDEN
Melrose TD6 9PX

Tel 01896 822493 **Fax** 01896 823181
www.nts.org.uk
Location Next to Melrose Abbey
Opening hours 10am (1pm on Sundays) to 5pm, daily, 1 April to 24 December
Admission fee Adults £3; concessions £2; honesty box

Priorwood is best known for its shop, which was recently extended and improved. Everything in the garden is geared towards dried flowers. The

plants are chosen because they are suitable for drying, but they are also very colourful. Courses on drying flowers are held here. In the orchard is a collection of historic apple cultivars, all organically grown.
dried flower shop and gift shop; plant sales

Owned by The National Trust for Scotland
Number of gardeners 1

STOBO JAPANESE WATER GARDEN
Stobo House, Peebles EH45 8NY

Tel 01721 760245 **Fax** 01721 760319
Location 7 miles west of Peebles on B712
Opening hours By appointment for groups: for SGS: usually 2nd week in June and in autumn
Admission fee Adults £3; children free

Stobo Castle is an upmarket hotel and health spa. Within its historic grounds – lots of rhododendrons and azaleas – is a Japanese garden laid out in the early 1900s. Structure comes from the tea house, arching bridge, stepping stones and the complex outlines of the lake; cherry trees and maples add seasonal interest when it is open.
teas

Owned by Hugh and Charles Seymour
Number of gardeners 1
Size 1.6ha (4 acres)

TRAQUAIR HOUSE
Innerleithen EH44 6PW

Tel 01896 830323 **Fax** 01896 830639
www.traquair.co.uk
Location Signed from Innerleithen
Opening hours Noon (10.30am from June to August) to 5pm (11am to 4pm in October), daily, 25 March to 30 October; noon to 4pm, weekends only, November
Admission fee Grounds only: adults £3.50; children £2

The main attraction is a large maze, planted in 1980, of beech and Leyland cypress. The house is a Catholic time warp, said to be the oldest inhabited and most romantic house in Scotland. The Bear Gates in the park, once the main entrance to the estate, have been closed ever since Bonnie Prince Charlie passed through them for the last time in 1746.
gift shop; restaurant serving lunch and tea; Traquair ale

Owned by Catherine Maxwell Stuart
Number of gardeners 2
Size 12ha (30 acres)

CENTRAL

DUN ARD
105b Main Street, Fintry, Stirling G63 0XE

Tel 01360 860369
Location In village, on left, 100 yds from centre towards Killearn
Opening hours By appointment
Admission fee Donation to charity

The owners have made this garden out of a sloping meadow since 1988. It has a profusion of such stylish elements as a *potager*, an old rose garden, a bog garden and 'natural' plantings of hot-coloured perennials, but these are contrasted with areas of stark and minimalist design, including a reflecting pool and a wildflower meadow. History, conservation, respect for the environment and a commitment to organic principles are the guiding forces, but the garden also exhibits great creativity and a desire to celebrate and enjoy the many arts and crafts that go into making a good garden.

Owned by Alastair Morton and Niall Manning
Number of gardeners Owners only
Size 1.2ha (3 acres)

DUMFRIES & GALLOWAY

BROUGHTON HOUSE GARDENS

12 High Street, Kirkcudbright DG6 4JX

Tel/fax 01557 330437
www.nts.org.uk
Location Signed in centre of Kirkcudbright
Opening hours 11am to 4pm, Monday to Friday, 1 February to 30 March; noon to 5pm, Thursday to Monday, 31 March to 31 October; daily in July and August
Admission fee Donations

EA Hornel, the artist, laid out the Japanese-style garden in the 1900s: it is the best-known part of the garden here and featured in many of his portraits. Most of the rest is a 'Scottish' garden with a fine position above the River Dee. The house contains many of Hornel's works and an extensive collection of Scottish books.

Owned by The National Trust for Scotland
Number of gardeners 1
Size 0.8ha (2 acres)

CALLY GARDENS

Gatehouse of Fleet, Castle Douglas DG7 2DJ

Tel 01557 815029 (info line)
www.callygardens.co.uk
Location 12 miles west of Castle Douglas, on Gatehouse road off A75
Opening hours 10am to 5.30pm, Saturdays and Sundays; 2pm to 5.30pm, Tuesday to Friday, Easter Saturday to last Sunday in September
Admission fee Adults £2.50; children free

Cally is a nursery for the horticultural *avant-garde*. It specialises in new and rare perennials, including some from wild-collected and botanic garden seed. Many are culled from a collection of over 3,000 plants, which makes it one of the most interesting in Scotland – the owner, Michael Wickenden, has an excellent eye for quality. The walled garden has 30 large borders where all these novelties and rarities can be seen growing. Unusually among Scottish gardens, it is particularly good between June and September. The list of what is for sale changes by as much as half each year.

Owned by Michael Wickenden
Number of gardeners 3, plus students
Size 1.2ha (3 acres)

CRAIGIEBURN CLASSIC PLANTS

By Moffat DG10 9LF

Tel 01683 221250
Location 21/2 miles east of Moffat, on A708; on left, beyond Craiglochan signs
Opening hours 11am to 6pm, Wednesday to Sunday, Easter to mid-October; other times by prior arrangement
Admission fee Adults £2.50; children (under 12) free

Craigieburn continues to develop and improve every year. The Wheatcrofts have close links with Nepal, and Himalayan plants – including many found by Janet – flourish in the mild, damp climate. The long (75m; 246ft) herbaceous borders are now fully planted but, as in all good gardens, the Wheatcrofts are always in the process of changing, moving and adding to the contents. Craigieburn is particularly good for *Meconopsis*, of which they used to have a National Collection, and *Primula*. The mild climate means that *Lobelia tupa* grows to 2.5m (8ft) and *Impatiens tinctoria* flourishes voluptuously. 'Meconopsis Month' from 20 May to 20 June is perhaps the peak time to visit, but there is always lots of interest to the plantsman. The nursery sells seeds and plants grown from the garden.
meconopsis; woodland plants; Himalayan plants

Owned by Janet and Andrew Wheatcroft
Number of gardeners 2
Size 3.2ha (8 acres)

CASTLE KENNEDY & GARDENS

Stair Estates, Rephad, Stranraer DG9 8BX

Tel 01776 702024 **Fax** 01776 706248
www.castlekennedygardens.co.uk
Location 5 miles east of Stranraer on A75
Opening hours 10am to 5pm, daily, April to September
Admission fee Adults £4; OAPs £3; children £1

Castle Kennedy is a ruined keep, destroyed in the first half of the 18th century when the bedding which was being aired for the return of the master, the 2nd Earl of Stair, caught fire. Its imposing bulk overlooks the walled garden, which is a riot of herbaceous colour in the summer, with gnarled old apple trees heavy with lichen in its midst, and some interesting tender shrubs, including bottle-brushes (*Callistemon* species) against its walls. The main horticultural interest lies outside, although the romantic planting continues. The 2nd Earl was a military man, and bequeathed to the garden its highly original structure of dashing rides, ridges and earthworks, which represent battle encampments. They were made by the Royal Scots Greys and the Inniskilling Fusiliers when they should have been occupied suppressing religious dissent in the area. The extensive gardens now occupy an isthmus bounded by two lochs, with the ruined castle at one end, and its 19th-century replacement, Lochinch Castle, at the other – the place where *Buddleja* 'Lochinch' originated. There is a two-acre round pond, from which an ancient, slightly decrepit avenue of monkey puzzle trees leads off. These trees, *Araucaria araucana*, were grown from original seed sent from Chile: elsewhere are plants garnered by Stair forbears who subscribed to the collecting expeditions of Sir Joseph Hooker (*Rhododendron arboreum*, for example). The gardens generally are well stocked with rhododendrons, at their best in April and May. Later in the season, in an area known as the Dancing Green, a semi-circle of crimson *Embothrium coccineum* (June) is interplanted with flower-decked *Eucryphia* x *nymansensis* (August). There are more conventional flower borders in the area beside Lochinch Castle. In gardens as old as these, time has started to take its toll, but restoration and replanting is underway. The owners recommend visitors to follow one of four graded walks to get the most out of their visit. For the energetic, this is a marvellous place just to wander at will.

woodland garden; good herbaceous borders; rhododendrons; embothriums; eucryphias; monkey puzzle avenue; tallest *Pittosporum tenuifolium* (17m; 56ft) in the British Isles, tallest *Rhododendron arboreum* (16m; 52ft) and three other record-breaking trees; plant centre; tea room

Owned by Lochinch Heritage Estate
Size 30ha (75 acres)

DRUMLANRIG CASTLE GARDENS
Drumlanrig, Thornhill DG3 4AG

Tel 01848 331555 **Fax** 01848 331682
www.drumlanrig.com
Location On A76, 4 miles north of Thornhill
Opening hours 11am to 5pm, daily, 31 March to 30 September
Admission fee Adults £4; concessions £3.75; children £3

The gardens at Drumlanrig are currently undergoing substantial restoration. The Victorian rock garden, the heather house and the grand cascade that dates back to the early 1700s are all being repaired and remade. The castle is approached along a magnificent, long, straight avenue of lime trees. The sycamore in front of the castle is one of Scotland's oldest, over 300 years old. The parterres on either side are modern reconstructions: the East parterre was remade in 1978 with the same elaborate scrolls of box and yew originally planted by the 2nd Duke of Queensberry in the late 17th century. The West parterre follows a 19th-century pattern and has been planted with topiary yews and roses, including the Gallica rose 'Duchesse de Buccleuch'. There are some fine conifers in the arboretum, notably *Calocedrus decurrens*, *Cunninghamia lanceolata* and, tallest of all, a Sitka spruce *Picea sitchensis*.
good trees; plant centre; gift shop; tea room; snack bar

Owned by The Duke of Buccleuch
Number of gardeners 4
Size 16ha (40 acres)

ELIZABETH MACGREGOR
Ellenbank, Tongland Road, Kirkcudbright DG6 4UU

Tel/fax 01557 330620
Location On A711, 1 mile north of Kirkcudbright
Opening hours 10am to 5pm, Mondays, Fridays and Saturdays, May to September
Admission fee Free

Violas – over 100 of them – are the speciality at this excellent nursery: some are not available from any other source. They are complemented by a lively selection of 500 other perennials for cottage gardens and mixed-border planting. These include a number of the nursery's own introductions, most notably eryngiums and anemones. But increasingly it is the walled garden that draws visitors to Ellenbank. Mrs MacGregor has planted it informally, with an emphasis on colour combinations and progressions – worth a visit in its own right.
violas; perennials

Owned by Elizabeth and Alasdair MacGregor
Size 0.2ha (1/2 acre), plus 0.6ha (1 1/2 acres) of stock beds and trials

GALLOWAY HOUSE GARDENS
Garlieston, Newton Stewart DG8 8HF

Tel/fax 01988 600680
www.gallowayhousegardens.co.uk
Location Off B7004 at Garlieston
Opening hours 9am to 5pm, daily, March to October
Admission fee £1 per car, plus £1 per person

Galloway House is where Neil McEacharn learnt to garden, before moving to Lake Maggiore to create the great gardens of Villa Taranto. A *Davidia involucrata* dates from his ownership, as do many of the tender trees and shrubs which he planted to take advantage of the mild maritime climate – eucryphias, for example. The fine conifers date back to the Earls of Galloway in the 19th century, while most of the *Rhododendron* species were planted after the war. The garden is still undergoing restoration, but is already a great pleasure to visit, especially in late spring.
snowdrops; rhododendrons and azaleas; daffodils; camellias; bluebells; camellia house; extensive new plantings

Owned by Galloway House Gardens Trust
Number of gardeners 1
Size 26ha (65 acres)

GLENWHAN GARDEN

Dunragit, by Stranraer DG9 8PH

Tel/fax 01581 400222
www.glenwhangardens.co.uk
Location 1 mile off A75 at Dunragit village; follow brown tourist signs
Opening hours 10am to 5.30pm, daily, March to September; and by appointment, all year
Admission fee Adults £4; OAPs £3; children £1.50; families £8.50; RHS members free in August and September

Glenwhan is a plantsman's garden which has been created since 1979 by its present owners, starting from moorland, bog and scrub. Ambitious in scale, the heart of the garden is a pair of lochans or bog lakes. Above them rises a series of roped terraces, planted with heathers, azaleas, small conifers, golden elders, hardy fuchsias and massed Rugosa roses. A small folly stands at the peak. In prospect, the whole design is beautifully composed and tranquil. From the folly there are extensive views across the garden to Luce Bay and the Mull of Galloway beyond. Tessa Knott's first plantings (in 1980) were a sturdy shelter belt of small trees, including native Scots pines, English oaks and mountain ashes. Now maturing very well, there are occasional glimpses through these lichen-stained ancients to the gorse scrub and bog which surround the garden. The shelter belt is a transitional feature: it is a refinement of the more primitive vegetation beyond the perimeter fence, and it introduces planting themes which are then developed within the garden, in the form, for example, of collections of choicer *Sorbus* and *Quercus* species (including *Q.* x *bushii* and *Q. dentata*). Pools have been cut out of the blackest peat to make an attractive sequence of grassy water gardens, planted with primula and meconopsis cultivars. Glenwhan is very much a plantsman's garden, but Tessa Knott also uses plants to create effects, and she has capitalised upon the lie of the land to produce different habitats. The new plantings include large-leaved rhododendron species (*R. fictolacteum*, for example), and some interesting southern hemisphere plants, including eucalyptus and olearias around the summerhouse, embothriums, eucryphias, callistemons and dicksonias. Another highlight is the dappled woodland walk with yet more new planting. Indeed, many parts of this garden are 'work in progress' which will be worth returning to see again as they mature. Last year (2006) they opened a 17-acre wildflower meadow outside the garden perimeter, with walks through 120 species of native plants, which makes a striking contrast with the excitements of the main garden.

woodland garden; roses (mainly old-fashioned); plantsman's collection of plants; bluebells; cistus; camellias; primulas; bog plants; trees and shrubs; many new *Rhododendron* species from collected seed; shop; nursery with interesting plants; licensed garden restaurant

Owned by Tessa and William Knott
Number of gardeners 2
Size 5ha (12½ acres)

LOGAN BOTANIC GARDEN

Port Logan, Stranraer DG9 9ND

Tel 01776 860231 **Fax** 01776 860333
www.rbge.org.uk
Location 14 miles south of Stranraer on B7065
Opening hours 10am to 6pm (5pm in March and October), daily, March to October
Admission fee Adults £3.50; concessions £3; children £1; families £8

This extraordinarily exotic garden, started by the McDouall family in the 19th century, is now part of the Royal Botanic Garden Edinburgh. Logan's sheltered aspect and proximity to the warming waters of the Atlantic enable a wide range of tender and southern hemisphere plants to be grown out of doors. The bedding out of thousands of half-hardy perennials, makes the garden a blaze of colour on bright, sunny days. In the walled garden, overlooked by the slender remains of Castle Balzieland, there is a fine collection of established tree ferns (*Dicksonia antarctica*). They are underplanted with the smaller fern, *Blechnum chilense*, which creates an impression of lush fertility, as if the dicksonias have seeded themselves everywhere. The formal lily pond is partly framed by a diagonal avenue of cabbage palms (*Cordyline australis*) 10m (33ft) high. Around the pond are waving wands of *Dierama pulcherrimum* and *Kniphofia*, and the air glints with dragonflies in summer. Among the trees which flower in the sheltered walls are a tall *Metrosideros umbellatus* and the flame tree *Embothrium coccineum*. Also flowering freely here, as it does in other gardens in south-west Scotland, is *Eucryphia* x *nymansensis* 'Nymansay'. Beyond the brilliance of the walled garden, and past an avenue of Chusan palms (*Trachycarpus fortunei*), lies Logan's woodland garden. Some of its pleasures are more hidden than others, but a spectacular specimen of *Magnolia campbellii* 'Charles Raffill' stands on the edge, in flower in April, and decked with swollen red pods by August. Look out in particular for plants from the southern hemisphere, including *Leptospermum lanigerum*, *Crinodendron hookerianum*, and the Chatham Island daisy bush *Olearia semidentata* (syn. O. 'Henry Travers'). Do not miss the gunnera bog either, where this giant rhubarb-like plant grows so tall and thick that you can lose yourself under its prickly, slightly sinister canopy. In the Discovery Centre there are reference books, computers and microscopes which the visitor can use, perhaps to learn more about the Maddenia section of the genus *Rhododendron*, in which the garden specialises. Visitors can borrow innovative free audio guides, which are keyed to numbers marked on labels throughout the gardens. It is slightly surreal to see your fellow visitors wandering around clasping these futuristic wands, but the guide is informative and chatty.

subtropical plants; good herbaceous borders; tree ferns; cardiocrinums; gunneras; cordylines; trachycarpus palms; tender perennials (diascias, fuchsias, salvias); eucalyptus; shop; café

Owned by Royal Botanic Garden Edinburgh
Size 12ha (30 acres)

LOGAN HOUSE

Port Logan, Stranraer DG9 9ND

Tel 01483 225436
Location 14 miles south of Stranraer, next to Logan Botanic Garden
Opening hours 10am to 4pm, daily, February to 1 April; 8.30am to 6pm, 2 April to 30 September; and by appointment
Admission fee Adults £3; children free

Logan Botanic Garden occupies the walled garden of Logan House. The rest of the Logan estate is still privately owned, and richly endowed with the rare plant collection built up by the McDouall family between 1870 and 1945. The real highlight is the collection of rhododendrons, including scores of self-seeded *R. augustinii*, *R. grande*, *R. maccabeanum* and *R. sinogrande*, and the original *R.* 'Logan Damaris'. But the exotic trees are stunning in all seasons: embothriums, nothofagus, araucarias, metrosideros, clethras and several UK record-holders, including *Leptospermum lanigerum* and *Eucryphia cordifolia* (20m; 66ft tall).

Owned by Mr and Mrs Andrew Roberts
Number of gardeners 1
Size 8ha (20 acres)

THREAVE GARDEN

Castle Douglas DG7 1RX

Tel 01556 502575 **Fax** 01556 502683
www.nts.org.uk
Location Off A75, 1 mile west of Castle Douglas
Opening hours 9.30am to sunset, daily, all year; walled garden and glasshouses close at 5pm (4.30pm on Fridays)
Admission fee Adults £6; concessions £4.50; RHS members free in April, May, September and October

Threave is a teaching garden with a very wide range of attractions – something to interest every gardener, in fact. It has been developed since 1960 with the needs of students at the School of Horticulture, garden owners and tourists all in mind. There are over 200 daffodil cultivars to admire in spring; roses and colourful herbaceous borders in summer; and good autumn colour. A new Victorian-style conservatory has recently been built in the walled garden.
tallest *Alnus rubra* (23m; 75ft) in the British Isles, and two other record trees; shop; plant centre; restaurant and snacks

Owned by The National Trust for Scotland
Number of gardeners 2, plus 3 instructors
Size 26ha (65 acres)

WOODFALL GARDENS

Glasserton, Whithorn, Newton Stewart DG8 8LY

Tel 01988 500692 **Fax** 01988 500080
www.woodfall-gardens.co.uk
Location By Glasserton Church, 2 miles south of Whithorn
Opening hours 2pm to 5.30pm, 10 June and 22 July for SGS and 12 August for Marie Curie; 2pm to 4.30pm on 27 August for St Ninian Festival; and by prior arrangement mid-May to August
Admission fee For SGS: adults £2.50; concessions £2; children free

After the big house at Glasserton was demolished in 1952, the large 18th-century walled garden gradually declined into disrepair. Successive owners have brought it to life again as a private garden. The garden of great interest at all seasons, with a parterre, a woodland area, a grasses garden and a fern garden, as well as colourful mixed borders and a productive *potager*.
topiary plants; *Parthenocissus*; plant sales area

Owned by Lesley and David Roberts
Number of gardeners owners only
Size 1.2ha (3 acres)

FIFE

CAMBO GARDENS
Kingsbarns, St Andrews KY16 8QD

Tel 01333 450054 **Fax** 01333 450987
www.camboestate.com
Location On A917 between Kingsbarns and Crail
Opening hours 10am to 5pm, daily, all year; guided tours by arrangement
Admission fee Adults £3.50; children free; RHS members free except in February, July and August

Cambo's large, romantic, Victorian walled garden is built around the Cambo Burn, a most unusual feature which, with its summerhouse, willows, elegant wrought iron bridges and waterfall, gives the garden its unique character. The atmosphere is informal, with naturalistic plantings of herbaceous perennials, many of them unusual. There are also masses of spring bulbs, a lilac walk, rambler roses, and fine herbaceous borders for summer and autumn. An ornamental *potager* and cutting garden add to the variety and a traditional vegetable garden supplies fruit and vegetables to the handsome Victorian house. A woodland garden with masses of colchicums in autumn is traversed by walks that lead down to the sea, spectacular in early spring when carpeted with aconites, snowflakes and snowdrops. There will be three RHS Special Events at Cambo Gardens in 2007; details from 020 7821 3408.
roses (mainly old-fashioned); daffodils; snowflakes; aconites; colchicum meadows; autumn colour; plants for sale

Owned by Mr and Mrs TPN Erskine
Number of gardeners 3
Size 1ha (2½ acres), plus 28ha (70-acre) woodland
NCCPG National Collections *Galanthus*

FALKLAND PALACE
Falkland, Cupar KY15 7BU

Tel 01337 857397 **Fax** 01337 857980
www.nts.org.uk
Location On A912, 11 miles north of Kirkcaldy; 10 miles from M90, Jct 8
Opening hours 10am to 6pm (1pm to 5.30pm on Sundays), daily, March to October
Admission fee Adults £5; concessions £4

P

The palace at Falkland is old: it dates from the first half of the 16th century. Today's flower garden was built in 1952 by Percy Cane. The pastiche of a Scottish renaissance garden has a herb garden in the Jacobean style, an astrolabe walk and formal parterres prettily planted in pastel colours.
gift shop; plant centre

Owned by The National Trust for Scotland
Number of gardeners 2
Size 4.4ha (11 acres)

HILL OF TARVIT
Cupar KY15 5PB

Tel/fax 01334 653127
www.nts.org.uk
Location Off A916, 2½ miles south of Cupar
Opening hours 9.30am to sunset, daily, all year
Admission fee Adults £2; concessions £1; honesty box; RHS members free

P

Both house and garden at Hill of Tarvit were designed by Lorimer. The formal garden is not so well planted and maintained as it used to be, but the Trust has begun to restore and replant the borders on the top terrace in an Edwardian style.
plants for sale; tea room in house (open in summer)

Owned by The National Trust for Scotland
Number of gardeners 2
Size 8ha (20 acres)

KELLIE CASTLE
Pittenween KY10 2RF

Tel 01333 720271 **Fax** 01333 720736
www.nts.org.uk
Location On B9171, 3 miles north-west of Pittenween

Opening hours 9.30am to 5.30pm, daily, all year
Admission fee Adults £4; RHS members free

Kellie Castle was Sir Robert Lorimer's own family house: it was he who initiated the reconstruction of the garden in its present form. The walled garden is no more than one acre in extent, but strong lines and thick planting create a sense of both space and enclosure. Much of the planting is a modern reinterpretation of Lorimer's original design: later family members have made alterations and additions. The organic walled garden contains a fine collection of old-fashioned roses, fruit trees and herbaceous plants: there are displays in the summerhouse about the history of the walled garden. The yew hedges are threaded with scarlet *Tropaeolum speciosum*.
extended collection of historic vegetables; gift shop; tea room

Owned by The National Trust for Scotland
Number of gardeners 2
Size 6.4ha (16 acres)

ST ANDREWS BOTANIC GARDEN

The Canongate, St Andrews KY16 8RT

Tel/fax 01334 476452
www.st-andrews-botanic.org
Location A915, Largo Road, then entrance in The Canongate
Opening hours 10am to 7pm (4pm from October to April), daily, all year
Admission fee Adults £2; OAPs and children £1; RHS members free

The botanic garden at St Andrews is currently undergoing much improvement. The garden's main asset, the peat, rock and water complex (crag, scree, moraine, alpine meadow and bog) is being repaired and replanted. The succulent house, alpine house and tropical house are now well established and there is also a house for Maddenia rhododendrons. A new Mediterranean Climate house is under development. The garden caters particularly well for children and is interesting to visit at every season.
woodland garden; rock garden; rhododendrons and azaleas; plants under glass; fine collection of trees; peat beds; ferns; heath garden; order beds; herbaceous borders; self-service tea/coffee

Owned by St Andrews University, but managed by Fife Council
Number of gardeners 4
Size 7.2ha (18 acres)

GRAMPIAN

BLACKHILLS
by Elgin, Moray IV30 3QU

Tel/fax 01343 842223
www.blackhills.co.uk
Location 1 mile south of Lhanbryde, near Elgin on B9103
Opening hours 11am to 6pm, 20 and 27 May; and by appointment
Admission fee Adults £2; children free

Blackhills is a magnificent collection of rhododendrons in two steep-sided glacial valleys: these possess a microclimate which allows many plants to grow that are normally considered too tender for the north-east coast of Scotland. The rhododendrons were planted throughout the 20th century by successive generations of the Christie family, along with many other Himalayan and Chinese plants, in a woodland garden which is now fully mature. There are about 360 different rhododendron species growing at Blackhills, all of wild origin: most were collected in the Himalayas, some came from North America, Central Asia and Northern Europe. The garden now contains one of the finest and most extensive private collections of species rhododendrons in the world.
rhododendrons

Owned by TS Christie
Number of gardeners 1
Size 20ha (50 acres)

BRODIE CASTLE
Brodie, Forres, Moray IV36 2TE

Tel 01309 641371 **Fax** 01309 641600
www.nts.org.uk
Location Signed from A96; 4½ miles west of Forres
Opening hours Grounds: 9.30am to sunset, daily, all year
Admission fee Adults £2; honesty box

Brodie Castle sits in a flat landscaped park with an ornamental woodland garden behind: here a young lime avenue leads to a polyhedral sundial and opens out attractive plantings of ornamental maples, liquidambars, sorbus, birches and rhododendrons. Brodie is however famous for its daffodils. Many were bred here at the turn of the 19th century and the Trust has tried assiduously to identify, propagate and distribute them more widely. They are a glorious sight when they bloom in the lawns around the baronial battlements.
daffodils; colchicums; NTS shop; tea room in castle (closes at 4.30pm)

Owned by The National Trust for Scotland
Number of gardeners 6, plus 2 part-time
Size 32ha (80 acres)
NCCPG National Collections *Narcissus*

CRATHES CASTLE
Banchory AB31 5QJ

Tel 01330 844525 **Fax** 01330 844797
www.nts.org.uk
Location On A93, 15 miles west of Aberdeen
Opening hours 9am to sunset, daily, all year
Admission fee Adults £8; concessions £6

Crathes is famous for its walled garden, which started as a kitchen garden and was later developed as a flower garden, both before World War I and in the 1920s and 1930s. It is divided into eight distinct gardens, each with its own character. These include a white border, a yellow enclosure known as the Golden Garden, a misty-blue garden and a dreamy high-summer border with pastel shades for long Highland evenings. The garden is intensively planted to give colour all year round. Some of the topiary yew hedges date back to 1702.
current holder of Sandford Award; tallest *Zelkova* x *verschaffeltii* in the British Isles, and four further tree records; NTS shop; plant centre; restaurant/café open most of the year

Owned by The National Trust for Scotland
Number of gardeners 5
Size 1.5ha (3¾ acres)
NCCPG National Collections *Dianthus* (Malmaison carnations)

CRUICKSHANK BOTANIC GARDEN

St Machar Drive, Aberdeen AB24 3UU

Tel 01224 272000 **Fax** 01224 272703
www.abdn.ac.uk/biologicalsci/pss/gardens
Location Follow signs for University of Aberdeen and/or Old Aberdeen; entrance in The Chanonry
Opening hours 9am to 4.30pm, Monday to Friday, all year; plus 2pm to 5pm, Saturdays and Sundays, May to September
Admission fee Free

Cruickshank Botanic Garden was founded in 1898 for the teaching and study of botany at the University of Aberdeen. Its 12 acres still have an educational element but also serve as an amenity for the wider public. Its leading features include: a rock garden for alpine plants and bulbs, where wild orchids seed around; an arboretum, planted with natives, exotics and garden cultivars, many of them now semi-mature; collections of native plants, including most of the endemic *Sorbus* species of the British Isles; and a rose garden which has been laid out to illustrate the history of the rose in cultivation. The garden is well maintained and – like all botanic gardens – worth visiting at any time of the year. It is also supported by an enthusiastic Friends organisation.
lots of plants; roses (mainly old-fashioned); rock garden; good herbaceous borders; fine collection of trees; stone troughs; peat beds; Scottish upland plants; *Meconopsis* x *sheldonii*

Owned by University of Aberdeen and Cruickshank Botanic Garden
Number of gardeners 3
Size 4.4ha (11 acres)

DRUM CASTLE

Drumoak, Banchory AB31 3EY

Tel 01330 811204 **Fax** 01330 811962
www.drum-castle.org.uk
Location Off A93, 10 miles west of Aberdeen
Opening hours Grounds: 9.30am to sunset, daily, all year; garden: 10am to 6pm, daily, 31 March to 31 October
Admission fee Adults £3; concessions £2.50

The gardens at Drum are modern – begun in 1991 with the intention of providing an appropriate historic setting for the castle and a place where old Scottish roses could be grown. There is a knot garden planted with herbs in the style of the early 17th century and a formal garden with *allées* and topiary to represent the early 18th century. The Victorian-style garden has a decorative, rose-covered catenary and the sunken garden a collection of modern roses, shrubs and perennials.
shop; small tea room

Owned by The National Trust for Scotland
Number of gardeners 2
Size 8ha (20 acres)

DUTHIE PARK

Polmuir Road, Aberdeen AB11 7SL

Tel 01224 523201
Location By river, in Ferryhill area of Aberdeen
Opening hours 9.30am to dusk, daily, all year; closed 1 January and 25 December
Admission fee Free

Duthie Park is one of Scotland's top tourist attractions: 350,000 people visit it every year – and it is free. The park was laid out in 1883, but substantially improved when David Welch was director in the 1970s and 1980s. Its main attraction in summer is the Rose Mountain, a massed display of bright modern roses, themselves quite a feature of Aberdeen's roadside landscaping. But the jewel in the crown is the Winter Gardens, a series of linked glasshouses with beautiful and instructive plant displays. They include the Bromeliad House, Cacti and Succulents Hall, Victorian Corridor, Floral Hall, Corridor of Perfumes and Fern House.

Owned by Aberdeen City Council
Number of gardeners 9

KILDRUMMY CASTLE
Kildrummy, Alford AB33 8RA

Tel: 01975 571203
www.kildrummy-castle-gardens.co.uk
Location On A97, off A944
Opening hours 10am to 5pm, daily, April to October
Admission fee Adults £2.50; children free

Kildrummy has a glen garden, laid out about 100 years ago. The richly-planted pools and ponds are complemented by a plantsman's collection on the hillside, and a large mature rock garden made from the natural sandstone. It is one of the most romantic gardens in Scotland.
roses (mainly old-fashioned); plantsman's collection of plants; fine collection of trees; autumn colour; heathers; tea and coffee

Owned by Kildrummy Castle Garden Trust
Number of gardeners 21/2
Size 8ha (20 acres)

LEITH HALL
Kennethmont, Huntly AB54 4NQ

Tel 01464 831216 **Fax** 01464 831594
www.nts.org.uk
Location On B9002, 1 mile west of Kennethmont
Opening hours 9am to sunset, daily, all year
Admission fee Adults £3; concessions £2; RHS members free

From this garden's historic past come two ponds and an ice house, but richly-planted borders are the pride of Leith Hall today: they are full of colour all through the summer. Also impressive is the rock garden, restored and replanted by that most successful of societies, the Scottish Rock Garden Club. Leith gets better and better.
sculptures in woodland walk; refreshments (noon to 5pm, May to September)

Owned by The National Trust for Scotland
Number of gardeners 2
Size 2.4ha (6 acres)

PITMEDDEN
Ellon, Aberdeen AB41 7PD

Tel 01651 842352 **Fax** 01651 843188
www.nts.org.uk
Location 1 mile west of Pitmedden on A920
Opening hours 10am to 5.30pm, daily, May to September
Admission fee Adults £5; concessions £4; children £2

The spectacular formal garden at Pitmedden was meticulously created in the 1950s by the National Trust for Scotland, using 17th-century Scottish designs. Three of the four parterres came from patterns associated with Holyroodhouse: the fourth is a heraldic design based on the coat of arms of Sir Alexander Seton, who first laid out a garden here in 1675. The result has three miles of box hedging and uses 40,000 bedding plants every summer. It may not be completely authentic, but it certainly looks genuine enough, as well as being both impressive, satisfying and peaceful.
plants for sale; tea room

Owned by The National Trust for Scotland
Number of gardeners 5
Size 6ha (15 acres)

HIGHLAND

ABRIACHAN GARDENS
Loch Ness Side, by Inverness IV3 8LA

Tel/fax 01463 861232
www.lochnessgarden.com
Location Just off A82
Opening hours 9am to 7pm (5pm in British Winter Time), daily, February to November
Admission fee Adults £2; OAPs £1; children 20p; RHS members free

Abriachan is a fine plantsman's garden, cut from native scrub – hazel, birch and rowan – on a steep, south-east-facing slope above Loch Ness. The views across to the other side and down the Great Glen are spectacular. The garden is absolutely full of interesting plants of every kind and the owners have created endless different habitats to accommodate the widest possible variety. There are lots of new projects underway. The nursery is a treasure house of good plants.
good modern garden; herbaceous plants; geraniums, helianthemums and Barnhaven primulas; hot drinks machine

Owned by Mr and Mrs D Davidson
Number of gardeners 2
Size 1.6ha (4 acres)

ARDFEARN NURSERY
Bunchrew, Inverness IV3 8RH

Tel 01463 243250 **Fax** 01463 711713
www.ardfearn-nursery.co.uk
Location On A862, 5 miles west of Inverness
Opening hours 9am to 5pm, daily

Alpines, ericaceous plants, shrubs and trees are produced at this intensive nursery in a lovely Highland farmstead. It is particularly good for plants from New Zealand and the Himalayas and, above all, for primulas. But the stock is always changing and expanding – especially of rare and unusual plants – which is what draws back both novices and the nursery's discriminating clientele year after year.
gift shop; coffee facilities

Owned by Alasdair Sutherland

ARDTORNISH GARDENS
Lochaline, Morvern PA34 5VZ

Tel 01967 421288 **Fax** 01967 421211
www.ardtornishgardens.co.uk
Location 2 miles north-east of Lochaline
Opening hours 8am to dusk, daily, March to November
Admission fee £3

This is Faith Raven's other garden – see Docwra's Manor in Cambridgeshire – and a complete contrast: 28 acres of rocky hillside full of rhododendrons and acid-loving trees and shrubs. The oldest plantings date back to the 19th century but the real horticultural interest began in the 1930s when Mrs Raven's parents began to plant a great range of species, including rhododendrons, many of which were gifts from Sir John Stirling Maxwell of Pollock House, Glasgow, and which now fill the rhododendron glen with colour. Flowering continues into August with *R.* 'Polar Bear', when the flowers also start to open on *Eucryphia* x *nymansensis* 'Nymansay' and *Hoheria lyallii*. Mrs Raven has actively improved the garden with further plantings of eucryphias, embothriums and acers and much else. The spring bulbs and early rhododendrons are fine from March onwards. Peak time for rhododendrons is May to June, but the autumn colours are also spectacular – the leaves of acers, cercidiphyllums, enkianthus, prunus, and berries of sorbus, berberis and cotoneaster.
plantsman's collection of plants; mature conifers; bluebells; kitchen garden; gunneras; rhododendrons; autumn colour

Owned by Mrs John Raven
Number of gardeners 1
Size 11.1ha (28 acres)

ATTADALE GARDENS

Strathcarron, Wester Ross IV54 8YX

Tel 01520 722217/722603 **Fax** 01520 722546
www.attadale.com
Location On A890 between Strathcarron and South Strome
Opening hours 10am to 5.30pm, Monday to Saturday, April to October; coaches by prior arrangement only; for SGS: 2pm to 5.30pm, 2 June
Admission fee Adults £4.50; OAPs £3; children £1; disabled free

The gardens at Attadale were started in the 1890s: many rhododendrons, azaleas and specimen trees date from that time. The recent expansion of planting began in the 1980s, with over 2,000 trees and shrubs, which are now underplanted with irises, candelabra primulas, gunneras and bamboos. The ponds and waterfalls are spanned by bridges and richly planted with marginals and water lilies. The whole garden is imbued with a lushness and a sense of profusion that are intensified by the quality of the light, whatever the weather. Handsome sculptures add quite a different dimension. In an old quarry, a geodesic dome houses an exotic fern collection. There is also a Japanese garden and a kitchen garden. The nursery specialises in bog plants – among them, primula, gunnera, darmera – as well as more than 80 different ferns.
rhododendrons; meconopsis; primulas; bog plants; ferns; nursery; DIY tea room

Owned by Mr and Mrs Ewen Macpherson
Number of gardeners 4 1/2
Size 8ha (20 acres)

AUCHGOURISH GARDENS & ARBORETUM

Street of Kincardine, by Boat of Garten PH24 3BY

Tel 01479 831464/07737 914292/07746 122775
Fax 01479 831672
www.thebotanicalnursery.com
Location Follow brown tourist signs from Aviemore and Inverness
Opening hours 10am to 5pm, daily, March to October; 11am to 3pm in winter
Admission fee Adults £3.50; children free

Auchgourish is a new garden, opened in 2001 as a tourist attraction with botanic and horticultural interest. It is particularly interesting to learn what will survive in extreme conditions – short summers, frost in every month of the year and a soil so poor and sandy (with a pH of 4.5) that it has neither slugs nor worms. Many East Asian plants do well, especially loniceras, malus and pyrus, and there is a slight Japanese overlay to the design. But the plants are the real interest. Most are grown from seed that is wild-collected or collected from parents of known wild origin: over 120 *Primula* species, over 80 *Sorbus*, 73 *Betula*, 67 *Iris*, 59 *Fritillaria* and even 24 *Lonicera*. And there are always surplus plants for sale which are unavailable elsewhere.
Scottish native plants; oriental gardens; surplus plants for sale

Owned by Iain Brodie of Falsyde
Number of gardeners 1
Size 4ha (10 acres)

THE CASTLE OF MEY

Thurso, Caithness KW14 8XH

Tel 01847 851473 **Fax** 01847 851475
www.castleofmey.org.uk
Location On A836 between Thurso and John O'Groats
Opening hours 10.30am to 4pm, daily, 1 May to 26 July and 8 August to 30 September
Admission fee Adults £3; concessions £2.50; children free

The Castle of Mey was Queen Elizabeth The Queen Mother's summer home and is planted largely for late-summer enjoyment, but full of interest at all seasons. The main attraction is the walled garden, enclosed by 4m (12ft) walls and protected by lots of internal hedges of thorn and flowering currant. Here are areas for soft fruit, vegetables, sweet peas and roses. On the walls are trained apples and pears – and currants, too. A long herb border has recently been planted

and there are borders devoted to *Primula florindae* and astilbes. Best of all are the spectacular glasshouses, crammed with colour. But do not overlook the primulas in the East Garden.
flowers borders; kitchen garden; plants and produce for sale

Owned by The Queen Elizabeth Castle of Mey Trust
Number of gardeners 3
Size 1.6ha (4 acres)

CAWDOR CASTLE

Cawdor, Nairn IV12 5RD

Tel 01667 404401 **Fax** 01667 404674
www.cawdorcastle.com
Location Between Inverness and Nairn on B9090
Opening hours 10am to 5.30pm, daily, 1 May to 14 October
Admission fee Gardens only: £4; RHS members free in May, June, September and October

Cawdor Castle could claim to be the most romantic castle in the Highlands – the 14th-century home of the Thanes of Cawdor. It has several gardens: the earliest dates from the 16th century. Best of all is an 18th-century flower garden with large herbaceous borders, a lavender-edged garden with shrub roses, whole borders of lilies and galtonias, spring-flowering trees and shrubs, and an arch of rambling roses. The 19th-century wild garden has a good collection of rhododendrons and spring bulbs, as well as huge lime trees and fine Victorian conifers. Recent additions to the walled garden include a holly maze, a laburnum walk, several modern designs and coloured planting schemes. The Auchindoune garden, originally planted in the 1920s with plants brought back by Lord Cawdor from his expedition to the Himalayas with Frank Kingdon Ward, is being restored with many of the species they collected in the Tsangpo Gorges: it is open from 10am to 4pm on Tuesdays and Thursdays from May to July, and by appointment at other times.
woodland garden; roses (mainly old-fashioned), fruit; good herbaceous borders; good late-summer plantings; gift shop; licensed restaurant in castle

Owned by The Dowager Countess Cawdor
Number of gardeners 4
Size 1.4ha (3½ acres)

Cawdor Castle

COILTIE GARDEN
Divach, Drumnadrochit IV63 6XW

Tel 01456 450219
Location Take the small uphill road off the A82 at Drumnadrochit to Divach for about 2 miles; garden 150m beyond Divach Lodge
Opening hours Noon to 7pm, daily, 16 June to 22 July; and by appointment
Admission fee Adults £2; children free

There was little except a few old trees and a 30m (98ft) waterfall when the Nelsons came to Coiltie in 1980 and took on the neglected and overgrown Victorian garden. They decided not to reconstruct it, but to lay a new informal one on the sloping site, and planted it with trees (100+), hedges, shrubs, climbers, herbaceous plants and lots of roses. Below is a steep ravine with ancient woodlands. Gillian Nelson tells the story of the garden and its recovery in her book *To Make a Garden*, which is available at the garden.
roses; trees; mixed borders

Owned by Mr and Mrs David Nelson
Number of gardeners 1
Size 1.6ha (4 acres)

DUNBEATH CASTLE
Dunbeath, Caithness KW6 6EY

Tel 01593 731308 **Fax** 01593 731241
www.dunbeath.co.uk
Location Off A9, at Dunbeath
Opening hours By appointment
Admission fee Adults £4; concessions £3

The descent to Dunbeath Castle is magnificent, from your first glimpse until you arrive at the castle itself, perched above the waters of the Moray Firth. The horticultural interest is all in the walled garden, redesigned by Xa Tollemache in 1998 as a haven from the rude sea winds. There are garden rooms and a profusion of fruit, vegetables and flowers for the house, but best of all are the long herbaceous borders stretching down towards the sea, and mirror-planted all along its length.
refreshments by arrangement

Owned by Mr and Mrs SW Murray Threipland
Size 0.8ha (2 acres)

DUNROBIN CASTLE GARDENS
Golspie, Sutherland KW10 6SF

Tel 01408 633177 **Fax** 01408 634081
www.great-houses-scotland.co.uk
Location 1 mile north of Golspie on A9
Opening hours Castle and gardens: 10.30am to 5.30pm (4.30pm in April, May and October), 1 April to 15 October; last admissions 30 minutes before closing
Admission fee Castle and garden: adults £7; OAPs £6; children £5; reductions for groups and families; RHS members free; gardens free in winter

The grand terraced gardens at Dunrobin were laid out in 1850 by Sir Charles Barry, architect of the Houses of Parliament. Their formal style, striding down to the Dornoch Forth, is appropriate to the enormous French-style *château*. Three immensely grand parterres surround the fountains, two traditionally bedded out (but brilliantly and colourfully done) and one planted with hardy geraniums and *Ceratostigma willmottianum*, underplanted with tulips and lilies. One of the parterres was substantially made in recent years,

Dunrobin Castle Gardens

and thereby much improved: some 20 wooden pyramids have been planted with clematis and climbing roses in a modern reinterpretation of 19th-century grandeur. Elsewhere are lots of interesting plants: *Akebia quinata*; expansive clumps of gunneras; tall fuchsias (including *F.* 'Dunrobin Bedder'); *Ceanothus thyrsiflorus* with eccremocarpus threading through it; huge maples, limes and horse-chestnuts (much taller than one might expect so far north); a long herbaceous border where plants grow unusually tall; and extensive rhododendron woodlands. New for 2007 is a long raised bed featuring more old *Fuchsia* cultivars grown in tiers alongside ferns and pale petunias.
woodland garden; topiary; roses (mainly modern); good herbaceous borders; formal gardens; gift shop; tea room in castle

Owned by The Sutherland Trust
Number of gardeners 3
Size 2ha (5 acres)

INVEREWE
Poolewe, Ross and Cromarty IV22 2LG

Tel 01445 781200 **Fax** 01445 781497
www.nts.org.uk
Location On A832, 6 miles north-east of Gairloch
Opening hours 9.30am to 9pm (4pm from 1 November to 30 March), daily, all year
Admission fee Adults £8; concessions £5.25; children £1

Inverewe is one of the wonders of the horticultural world, a subtropical garden in the north-west Highlands. Its position on a sheltered peninsular, warmed by the Gulf Stream, explains the luxuriance of its plantings. It is also the reason why, even so far north, it has much to interest the plantsman at every time of the year. The garden owes its origins to Osgood Mackenzie, who from 1862 to 1922 planted windbreaks to protect more delicate exotics within. Spectacular large-leaved Himalayan rhododendrons, magnolias, eucalyptus, tree ferns, palms and tender rarities are underplanted with drifts of blue poppies and candelabra primulas. Among Inverewe's record trees are specimens of *Eucalyptus cordata* and *Salix magnifica*, neither of

Inverewe

which would be fully hardy in the home counties of England. Inverewe is exceptionally well maintained, though perhaps best on a sunny, dry day in May, before the midges breed.
tallest *Eucalyptus cordata* (30m; 90ft) in the British Isles, and three further record trees; large shop; plant centre; excellent new restaurant

Owned by The National Trust for Scotland
Number of gardeners 8
Size 20ha (50 acres)
NCCPG National Collections *Olearia*; *Brachyglottis*; *Rhododendron* (Barbatum, Glischra and Maculifera sections)

JACK DRAKE
Inshriach Alpine Nursery, Aviemore, Inverness-shire PH22 1QS

Tel 01540 651287 **Fax** 01540 651656
www.drakesalpines.com
Location 4 miles south of Aviemore; take B970 to Inverdruie; turn right, 3/4 mile after the Spey Bridge
Opening hours 10am to 5pm, daily, March to October
Admission fee Free; donations welcome

For more than 60 years, this famous Highland nursery has been a Mecca for devotees of alpine and rock garden plants. It offers a large number of selected or collected forms. True alpines rub shoulders with herbaceous plants for wild and bog gardens. The nursery is laid out with demonstration gardens – screes, peat walls, wild

gardens and bog gardens. A new woodland walk is under development.
Scotland's premier alpine nursery; primulas; meconopsis; gentians; heathers; tea room

Owned by John and Gunnbjørg Borrowman
Size 0.8ha (2 acres)

LECKMELM ARBORETUM
by Ullapool IV23 2RH

Location 3 miles south of Ullapool on A835
Opening hours 10am to 6pm, daily, April to October
Admission fee Adults £2.50; children free

Ⓟ ♠

Leckmelm Arboretum was laid out in the 1880s, and it is from those days that many of the finest rhododendron species and trees date – wellingtonias, cedars, monkey puzzles and a huge weeping beech (*Fagus sylvatica* 'Pendula'). Some of the trees are record-breakers, including an *Abies amabilis* 40m (131ft) high, a good *Chamaecyparis lawsoniana* 'Wisselii', a *Thujopsis dolabrata* and a *Kalopanax pictus*, whose presence at such a northerly point may be explained by the mild climate. The Troughtons have taken advantage of the arboretum's position on the shores of Loch Broom to make new plantings in recent years: they have put in such large-leaved rhododendrons as *R. sinogrande* and *R. maccabeanum*, and even a selection of dicksonias and palms.
ancient trees; good rhododendrons

Owned by Mr and Mrs Peter Troughton
Number of gardeners 1
Size 5ha (12½ acres)

LOCHALSH WOODLAND GARDEN
Balmacara, By Kyle of Lochalsh, Ross IV40 8DN

Tel 01599 566325 **Fax** 01599 566359
www.nts.org.uk
Location On A87, 3 miles east of Kyle
Opening hours 9am to sunset, daily, all year
Admission fee Adults £2; honesty box

Ⓟ ♠ 🚻 ♿ ✿

This woodland garden is becoming much better known, and deservedly. The structure is about 100 years old – tall pines, oaks and larches with ornamental underplantings started in the late 1960s. Rhododendrons from Euan Cox at Glendoick came first: newer plantings include collections of hardy ferns, bamboos, fuchsias, hydrangeas and Maddenia rhododendrons, as well as plants from Tasmania and New Zealand. The season of interest extends from early spring well into autumn.
plants for sale; shop

Owned by The National Trust for Scotland
Number of gardeners 1
Size 5.2ha (13 acres)

LOTHIAN

BINNY PLANTS
Ecclesmachan Road, Broxburn EH52 6NL

Tel 01506 858931/07753 626116 **Fax** 01506 858155
www.binnyplants.co.uk
Location 2 miles north of Uphall on B8046
Opening hours 10am to 5pm, daily, all year; phone first in winter months
Admission fee Free

This excellent nursery has an expanding range. It claims to have Scotland's largest selection of ornamental grasses and a massive range of hardy ferns and other plants for the shady garden, as well as hundreds of perennials and shrubs. Its irises (100+ cultivars), peonies (200+ cultivars), astilbes (50+ cultivars), euphorbias, geraniums, hostas and small shrubs are especially noteworthy. The catalogue has good, helpful plant descriptions, with some shrewd observations that give the reader confidence. The new show gardens are coming along nicely.

Owned by Billy Carruthers
Number of gardeners 4

DALMENY HOUSE
Rosebery Estates, South Queensferry EH30 9TQ

Tel 0131 331 1888 **Fax** 0131 331 1788
www.dalmeny.co.uk
Location B924 off A90
Opening hours 2pm to 5.30pm, Sunday to Tuesday, July and August; and for SGS in snowdrop time
Admission fee Grounds only: free

The grounds at Dalmeny are extensive and visitors are encouraged to see the valley walk with rhododendrons, wellingtonias and other conifers. But the estate concentrates upon the house and its remarkable collections rather than promoting the gardens and grounds.
woodland garden; snowdrops; mature conifers; rhododendrons and azaleas; wellingtonias; refreshments

Owned by The Earl of Rosebery

INVERESK LODGE
24 Inveresk Village, Musselburgh EH21 7TE

Tel 0131 665 1855
www.nts.org.uk
Location A6124 south of Musselburgh, 6 miles east of Edinburgh
Opening hours 10am to 6pm, daily, all year
Admission fee Adults £3; concessions £2; honesty box

The modern plantings in this terraced, Victorian garden have much of horticultural interest. In the fine Edwardian conservatory are an aviary and some tree ferns. Elsewhere are good herbaceous borders and interesting climbing plants. Graham Stuart Thomas designed the rose borders.
good collection of plants

Owned by The National Trust for Scotland
Number of gardeners 1
Size 5.2ha (13 acres)
NCCPG National Collections *Tropaeolum* (species)

INWOOD GARDEN
Carberry, Musselburgh EH21 8PZ

Tel 0131 665 4550
www.inwoodgarden.com
Location Signed from A6124
Opening hours 2pm to 5pm, Tuesdays, Thursdays and Saturdays, April to September; for SGS: 1 July
Admission fee Adults £2; children free; RHS members free

This is an immaculately maintained plantsman's garden and full of interest throughout the season. It has a large number of island beds and many different plant communities: trilliums, orchids,

tricyrtis and primulas in the woodland parts; ferns, giant lilies and candelabra primulas in the bog garden; stunning bananas (*Ensete ventricosum* 'Maurelii' and *Musa basjoo*, which is left in the ground in winter), cannas and hedychiums in the small exotic garden. All has been made since 1984.
tea room

Owned by Mr and Mrs Irvine Morrison
Number of gardeners Owners only
Size 0.5ha (11/4 acres)

LAURISTON CASTLE

2A Cramond Road South, Davidsons Mains, Edinburgh EH4 5QD

Tel 0131 336 2060 **Fax** 0131 312 7165
Location 3 miles from city centre; take Queensferry Road (A90) to Davidsons Mains
Opening hours 8am to dusk, daily, all year
Admission fee Free

Lauriston Castle has a historic 30-acre garden, but the main attraction is the new Japanese garden, the largest in Britain, made to celebrate the twinning of Kyoto Prefecture with Edinburgh. Highlights include a magnificent view across the Firth of Forth, cherry trees in spring and spring-flowering bulbs.
Japanese garden

Owned by Lauriston Castle Trust
Number of gardeners 2
Size 12ha (30 acres)

MALLENY HOUSE GARDEN

Balerno EH14 7AF

Tel 0131 449 2283
www.nts.org.uk
Location In Balerno, off A70
Opening hours 10am to 6pm (or dusk, if earlier), daily, all year
Admission fee Adults £3; concessions £2; honesty box

Tel 0131 552 7171 **Fax** 0131 248 2901
www.rbge.org.uk
Location 1 mile north of Princes Street; entrances off Inverleith Row and Arboretum Place
Opening hours 10am to 7pm, daily, all year; closes at 6pm in March and October, 4pm from November to February; closed 1 January and 25 December; glasshouses close at 5pm (3.30pm from November to February)
Admission fee Gardens: free; guided tours available (£4) at 11am and 2pm, daily, from April to September; glasshouses: adults £3.50; concessions £3; children £1; families £8

The Royal Botanic Garden Edinburgh has an important amenity function for both tourists and local people, but is principally a collection of plants of scientific and educational importance. It is internationally renowned for its collection of plants from temperate and tropical regions around the world, including: plants from the Himalayas and west China; the rhododendron collection – the best in the world; the collection of orchids from South-East Asia; alpines; and the flora of Arabia. So far as possible, these have been displayed within the gardens in a naturalistic setting which hints at their native habitats. The landscaping in the glasshouses is particularly good and recreates a whole series of different environments, from arid deserts to humid tropics. The newly restored Temperate Palm House, built in 1852, is still the tallest in Britain (23m;75ft high). It goes without saying that everything is extremely well labelled and the standard of maintenance is among the highest in any garden anywhere in the world. The members of staff are also invariably courteous and helpful. The rock garden is over two acres in extent and composed of many different microhabitats, most of them helped by the naturally light sandy soil and low rainfall. More than 5,000 species (from areas as different as high mountains, the Arctic regions and the Mediterranean) flourish in the mounds and gullies of sandstone and conglomerate alongside the stream and in the screes. The heath garden has recently been restored as a Scottish moorland complete with Landrover tracks. The arboretum has nearly 2,000 different trees, many

ROYAL BOTANIC GARDEN EDINBURGH

20A Inverleith Row, Edinburgh EH3 5LR

of them seldom seen in cultivation – the sort that visitors consider attractive but are then disappointed to find unavailable commercially. There are also extensive areas dedicated to azaleas and to systematic demonstration gardens. A must for any visitor to Scotland.

woodland garden; subtropical plants; roses (ancient and modern); rock garden; rhododendrons and azaleas; herbs; plants under glass; mature conifers; good herbaceous borders; fine collection of trees; alpine plants; peat beds; 45 UK record-breaking trees, more than any other Scottish garden; shop; plant centre; licensed café

Owned by Board of Trustees
Size 29ha (72 acres)

Malleny is one of the National Trust for Scotland's best gardens, much praised for its 'personal' quality. The 19th-century shrub roses are richly underplanted with herbaceous plants which carry the display through into the autumn: there is a sense of opulence about the garden throughout the summer and autumn. The magnificent conservatory creates quite another dimension, as do the huge cones of yew topiary, relics of a 17th-century formal garden. It is, above all, a very peaceful garden – and far too little visited.

Owned by The National Trust for Scotland
Number of gardeners 1
Size 1.2ha (3 acres)
NCCPG National Collections *Rosa* (19th-century shrubs)

SHEPHERD HOUSE

Inveresk, by Musselburgh EH21 7TH

Tel 0131 665 2570
www.shepherdhousegarden.co.uk
Location Opposite Inveresk Lodge garden
Opening hours 2pm to 4pm, Tuesdays and Thursdays, 17 April to 28 June; for SGS: 2pm to 5pm, 13 May; groups by appointment
Admission fee Adults £3; children free

The Frasers bought Shepherd House in 1957 and have crammed a multitude of spacious gardens into the one-acre triangle behind the house. The outstanding feature is a slender, formal rill, that runs almost the entire length of the garden and passes under a pergola of clematis and rambling roses. Roses are a connecting theme throughout, and there is a profusion of flowers in every season, especially when the hellebores, tulips, irises and oriental poppies flower in spring and early summer. The rill runs from a formal pond to a raised pond at the back of the garden, with four fountains that circulate the water. Two symmetrical *potagers* fill one side of the garden. Elsewhere are a knot garden, a rose arbour and a Millennium garden. Wherever you look or wander lie beauty and harmony.
teas on SGS day

Owned by Sir Charles and Lady Fraser
Number of gardeners 1 part-time
Size 0.4ha (1 acre)

SUNTRAP GARDEN

43 Gogarbank, Edinburgh EH12 9BY

Tel 0131 339 7283
www.suntrap-garden.org.uk
Location 1 mile west of Edinburgh bypass, between A8 and A71
Opening hours 10am to 6pm (4pm in winter), daily, all year, but with limited facilities at weekends
Admission fee Adults £1; children and NTS members free

Suntrap is one of the best places in Lothian to learn how to be a better gardener. It has been developed as a life-long learning centre, with courses and events throughout the year. The demonstration gardens include island beds, a rock garden, a peat garden, sculptures, vegetable plots, a sensory garden, annual borders – and much more.
woodland garden; vegetables; roses (mainly modern); plants under glass; daffodils; good herbaceous borders; alpine plants; 'Italian' garden; peat walls

Owned by Oatridge College
Number of gardeners 2
Size 1.2ha (3 acres)
NCCPG National Collections Bonsai

STRATHCLYDE

ACHAMORE GARDENS
Isle of Gigha PA41 7AD

Tel 01583 505390/07766 860701 **Fax** 01583 505394
www.gigha.org.uk
Location Take Gigha ferry from Tainloan (20 mins) then easy walking for 1 1/2 miles
Opening hours Dawn to dusk, daily, all year
Admission fee Adults £3.50; children £1

Achamore is one of the best rhododendron gardens in the British Isles and started as recently as 1944. Despite such a short existence (many rhododendron gardens date well back into the 19th century), Achamore has also had its fair share of ups and downs. It was largely planted by Sir James Horlick, with advice from Jim Russell. It has about 20 distinct areas cut out of the woodland (overgrown with *R. ponticum*) but they all have rhododendrons in common: their names include the Loderi Garden, Thomson Garden and Maccabeanum Wood. Camellias, eucalyptus and nothofagus also grow well here, as do many of the Surrey-type trees recommended by Russell – flowering cherries, sorbus and birches. And there are good herbaceous plantings, from daffodils through to pulmonarias and primulas.
woodland garden; subtropical plants; rhododendrons; azaleas; biggest *Larix gmelinii* in the British Isles

Owned by Isle of Gigha Heritage Trust
Number of gardeners 3
Size 16ha (40 acres)

ACHNACLOICH
Connel, Oban PA37 1PR

Tel/fax 01631 710796 (from 9am to 5pm, Monday to Friday)
Location On A85, 3 miles east of Connel
Opening hours 10am to 6pm, daily, 25 March to 31 October
Admission fee Adults £2; OAPs £1; children free

Achnacloich is a substantial woodland garden, made in three stages. First there were the Scots pine and European larch, which have grown to great heights. Then came the large-scale plantings of rhododendrons, particularly the *triflora* species, which have begun to naturalise. The latest stage has been the creation of a plantsman's garden, using the tender shrubs and trees which flourish on the west coast of Argyll. Some of the embothriums are taller than the native oaks.
woodland garden; rhododendrons and azaleas; good shrubs; plants for sale

Owned by Mrs J Nelson
Number of gardeners 1
Size 14ha (35 acres)

AN CALA
Isle of Seil PA34 4RF

Tel/fax 01852 300237
www.gardens-of-argyll.co.uk
Location In village of Easdale, 16 miles south of Oban on A816
Opening hours 10am to 6pm, daily, April to October
Admission fee Adults £2.50; children free

This sheltered garden on the wild west coast was designed by Thomas Mawson and planted by the actress Faith Celli: it still has a 1930s feel to it. There is a natural rock garden and several streams which have been dammed and planted with moisture-loving species. Mrs Downie has recently completed a rustic temple, decorated with a mosaic of cones from all over the world. A flock of Rupert Till wire-sculpted sheep complements the straying real ones outside the garden. But the overall effect is of a garden of great lushness, with splendid views across the islets of the Inner Hebrides.
rock garden; wild garden; bog garden; waterfalls and streams

Owned by Mrs T Downie
Number of gardeners 1
Size 2ha (5 acres)

ANGUS GARDEN
Barguillean, Taynuilt PA35 1HY

Tel 01866 822335 **Fax** 01866 822539
www.barguillean.co.uk
Location Turn south off A85 at Taynuilt (signed Glen Lonan); 3 miles on right
Opening hours Dawn to dusk, daily, all year
Admission fee Adults £2; children free

This garden in a beautiful setting on the shores of Loch Angus has a particularly fine collection of modern rhododendrons in light oak woodland. It doubles up as a test ground for new hybrids introduced by Barguillean Nurseries from the USA. It has recently be acquired by the Josephine Marshall Trust, whose trustees have plans for a substantial expansion of the gardens to create more summer and autumn interest.
woodland garden; rhododendrons and azaleas; newly installed Peace Bell

Owned by Josephine Marshall Trust
Number of gardeners 1
Size 4.4ha (11 acres) plus 6ha (15-acre) lake

ARDANAISEIG HOTEL GARDEN
Ardanaiseig, Kilchrenan, by Taynuilt PA35 1HE

Tel 01866 833333 **Fax** 01866 833222
www.ardanaiseig.com
Location On Loch Awe, 4 miles up from Kilchrenan
Opening hours 9am to 5pm, daily, all year
Admission fee Adults £2; children free

Ardanaiseig has a fine woodland garden with an important collection of rhododendrons and azaleas. Most were planted about 100 years ago. The hotel is in a stunning position on a promontory. The 19th-century walled garden has just been restored and its Victorian greenhouse is being rebuilt.
woodland garden; rhododendrons and azaleas; daffodils; good herbaceous borders; bluebells; maples; magnolias; hotel open to garden visitors

Owned by Bennie Gray
Number of gardeners 1
Size 2ha (5 acres)

ARDCHATTAN PRIORY
Connel, Oban PA37 1RQ

Tel 01796 481355 **Fax** 01796 481211
www.gardens-of-argyll.co.uk
Location 5 miles east of Connel Bridge, on the north shore of Loch Etive
Opening hours 9am to 6pm, daily, April to October
Admission fee Adults £2.50; children free

Daffodils, rock plants and azaleas are the main attraction in spring, but Ardchattan is also planted for high summer, with an emphasis on roses and herbaceous borders. The garden is good in late summer and autumn, too: late-flowering *Eucryphia glutinosa* and hydrangeas are complemented by fine leaf colour from the *Sorbus* species and *Cornus kousa*.
roses (mainly old-fashioned); daffodils; good herbaceous borders; good collection of *Sorbus* species; huge *Hebe* bushes

Owned by Mrs Sarah Troughton
Number of gardeners 1½
Size 3.4ha (8 acres)

ARDKINGLAS WOODLAND GARDEN
Cairndow PA26 8BH

Tel 01499 600261 **Fax** 01499 600241
www.ardkinglas.com
Location Just off A83 at Cairndow, 8 miles north of Inverary
Opening hours Daylight hours, daily, all year
Admission fee Adults £3.50; children free

Formerly known as Strone Gardens, Ardkinglas is famous for its magnificent conifers and its fine Lorimer house. As well as one of the tallest trees in Britain, it has the 'mightiest conifer in Europe', a specimen of *Abies alba* with a huge girth. The garden has been substantially improved by recent restoration and new plantings: these include a gazebo, a lochan, an extension to the woodland garden itself and a new bridge across the River Kinglas to a 17th-century mill. The bluebells are spectacular. Among the rhododendrons are many hybrids bred by Michael Noble, Lord Glenkinglas,

Arduaine Garden

when he was Secretary of State for Scotland. The nearby Tree Shop, run by the Ardkinglas estate, is a nursery specialising in trees and shrubs – especially rhododendrons. It is open seven days a week and has a handsome list of unusual plants.

woodland garden; rhododendrons and azaleas; mature conifers; one of the tallest trees *Abies grandis* (63m; 207ft) in the British Isles; the mightiest conifer *Abies alba* in Europe; and many other champion trees; excellent nursery

Owned by Ardkinglas Estate
Number of gardeners 1
Size 10ha (25 acres)

ARDUAINE GARDEN

Arduaine, by Oban, Argyll PA34 4XQ

Tel/fax 01852 200366
www.nts.org.uk
Location On A816 between Oban and Lochgilphead
Opening hours 9.30am to sunset, daily, all year
Admission fee Adults £4; concessions £3

Ⓟ 🚻 ♿

Arduaine is a luxuriant woodland garden in a sheltered, south-facing situation at the edge of the sea. Stout conifers and 12m (39ft) thickets of *Griselinia* protect the spectacular rhododendrons which two nurserymen planted in the 1970s. *Primula denticulata* and *Narcissus cyclamineus* have naturalised in grassy glades. *Cardiocrinum giganteum* and *Myosotidium hortensia* grow

vigorously. There are several outsize and champion trees, including *Eucryphia glutinosa*, *Gevuina avellana*, *Trochodendron aralioides* and the upright form of the tulip tree known as *Liriodendron tulipifera* 'Fastigiatum'. Some of the giant rhododendrons (*R. arboreum* subsp. *zeylanicum*) are 100 years old: the plant of *R. griffithianum* must be one of the largest in existence. But the sheer variety of the plantings is an education, while the whole garden is handsomely maintained.
tallest *Nothofagus antarctica* (26m; 85ft) in the British Isles and six further records; reception centre (April to September); no refreshments in the garden, but Loch Melfort Hotel is next door

Owned by The National Trust for Scotland
Number of gardeners 3
Size 8ha (20 acres)

BARWINNOCK HERBS
Barrhill, Girvan KA26 0RB

Tel/fax 01465 821338
www.barwinnock.com
Location Off B7207, 12 miles north-west of Newton Stewart
Opening hours 10am to 5pm, daily, except Wednesdays, Easter to end of September
Admission fee Free

Although not far from such tourist destinations as Galloway Forest Park, Barwinnock Herbs is set among wonderfully wild scenery, which forms a spectacular backdrop to this beautifully laid out nursery. Primarily a nursery which specialises in organically grown culinary, medicinal and aromatic herbs, there is also a small garden in which these plants are prettily displayed. The plant yard itself is most attractive, with the pots arranged on rustic tables amidst a collection of agricultural bygones. There is a small rural museum attached, with some local produce and seed on sale and, for those who want to venture further afield, there are some enticing walks mapped out from the nursery. If you do not want to take your purchases with you, they are happy to post them for you.

Owned by Dave and Mon Holtom
Number of gardeners 1

BENMORE BOTANIC GARDEN
Dunoon PA23 8QU

Tel 01369 706261 **Fax** 01369 706369
www.rbge.org.uk
Location 7 miles north of Dunoon on A815
Opening hours 10am to 6pm, daily, March to October; closes at 5pm in March and October

Benmore Botanic Garden

Admission fee Adults £3.50; concessions £3; children £1; families £8

Benmore Botanic Garden has been a regional annexe of the Royal Botanic Garden Edinburgh since 1929, having been given to the nation a few years earlier by the brewer Harry Younger. The stupendous redwood avenue which greets the visitor at the entrance dates from 1863 and was the start of a systematic programme of planting conifers on the estate, into which the Youngers introduced ornamental trees and shrubs. The mild, wet climate makes possible the cultivation of tender plants from the lower altitudes of the Sino-Himalaya, Bhutan, China and the New World. Benmore is a living textbook of the genus *Rhododendron*: over 400 species and sub-species grow at Benmore, and hundreds of hybrids and cultivars. Their background is of conifers planted early in the 19th century, perhaps the best collection in Scotland. The conifers are at the heart of the conservation programme of the Royal Botanic Garden Edinburgh and have been supplemented by recent ecological plantings, including a Bhutanese glade and a Chilean glade. But the whole garden is spacious, educational and beautifully maintained.

woodland garden; mature conifers; fine collection of trees; giant redwood avenue planted in 1863; rhododendrons; ferns; new Chilean plant collection; ten record-breaking trees, including *Nothofagus betuloides* at over 20m (66ft); gift shop; café

Owned by Board of Trustees/Royal Botanic Garden Edinburgh
Size 60ha (150 acres)

BIGGAR PARK
Biggar ML12 6JS

Tel 01899 220185
Location 1/4 mile south-west of Biggar on A702; black iron gates and a lodge on the north side
Opening hours For SGS: 5.30pm to 8.30pm, 3 June; and by appointment for groups, May to August
Admission fee Adults £4; children £1

Biggar Park garden is a mixture of woodland (formal and informal), spacious lawns, and unusual trees, shrubs and rhododendrons. It is 225m (738ft) above sea level, so somewhat susceptible to late-spring frosts. In the traditional working walled garden are fine herbaceous borders, vegetables, fruit trees and a greenhouse. Shrub roses are a special interest: there are good collections of both old and modern cultivars. The gardens also have a good collection of meconopsis. A recent addition is a small Japanese garden. Several ornamental ponds are landscaped into the garden.

herbaceous borders; spring bulbs, especially fritillaries; rhododendrons and azaleas; meconopsis; old roses; good collection of shrubs and trees

Owned by Captain and Mrs David Barnes
Number of gardeners 1, plus owners
Size 4ha (10 acres)

Brodick Castle

BRODICK CASTLE
Isle of Arran KA27 8HY

Tel 01770 302202 **Fax** 01770 302312
www.nts.org.uk
Location Ferry from Ardrossan to Brodick; follow signs
Opening hours Park: 9.30am to sunset, daily, all year; walled garden: 10am to 4.30pm, daily, 30 March to 31 October; 10am to 3.30pm, Friday to Sunday, 1 November to 21 December
Admission fee Adults £4; concessions £3

Brodick Castle

This lush rhododendron garden was begun by Molly, Duchess of Montrose, in 1923. The climate at Brodick is mild and wet: the sloping hillside is almost frost-free. Some of the Duchess's plantings are now record-breakers, including *Embothrium coccineum* at more than 20m (66ft), the seldom-seen *Euonymus tingens*, the wild form of *Leptospermum scoparium* more than 10m (33ft) high, and the rare *Nothofagus nervosa* which is over 30m (98ft) high. In the woodland are fine magnolias, camellias, crinodendrons and olearias, but none of these plantings is a match for the rhododendrons, many of which were grown from collectors' seed. The work of collectors Forrest, Ludlow and Kingdon Ward are all represented here. The walled garden has a late-Victorian layout, but the plantings take advantage of the mild climate. For those with longer to dally, Brodick also has a fine park with further features including a restored ice house.
tallest *Drimys winteri* (21m; 69ft) and *Embothrium coccineum* (20m; 66ft) in the British Isles (and three further records); NTS shop; plant centre; restaurant and tea rooms

Owned by The National Trust for Scotland
Number of gardeners 6, plus 2 part-time
Size 32ha (80 acres)
NCCPG National Collections *Rhododendron* (subsections Falconera, Grandia and Maddenia)

COLZIUM WALLED GARDEN
off Stirling Road, Kilsyth, Glasgow G65 0PY

Tel 01236 828155 **Fax** 01236 826322
www.northlan.gov.uk
Location Signed from Kilsyth on B803
Opening hours Noon to 7pm, daily, Easter to mid-September; noon to 4pm, Saturdays and Sundays, rest of year
Admission fee Free

Colzium Walled Garden is an up-and-coming young garden, which the council has developed on an ancient site since 1976. A wide range of plants is grown within the protection of high walls, particularly conifers, rhododendrons and ornamental trees and shrubs of dwarf habit. They are intended to offer colour and interest throughout the year. The standards of maintenance and labelling are excellent.
snowdrops; over 100 different *Galanthus* cultivars

Owned by North Lanarkshire Council
Size 0.2ha (1/2 acre)

CRARAE GARDENS
Crarae, by Inveraray PA32 8YA

Tel/fax 01546 886614
www.nts.org.uk
Location South of Inverary on A83
Opening hours 9.30am to sunset, daily, all year
Admission fee Adults £4; concessions £3; children £2

Crarae was finally saved for the nation by the National Trust for Scotland, which took possession in April 2002. There are plans for extensive restoration to these 50 acres of romantic woodland, centred on a steep glen spanned by

wooden bridges. The long, narrow climb up the glen is a pilgrim's progress for plantsmen, past all manner of exotic plants displayed for effect, but especially large-leaved rhododendrons. Best in the morning and in late May.
woodland garden; camellias; rhododendrons; autumn colour; tallest *Acer pensylvanicum* in the British Isles (and 12 further tree records); visitor centre open April to September; light refreshments

Owned by The National Trust for Scotland
Number of gardeners 2½
Size 20ha (50 acres)
NCCPG National Collections *Nothofagus*

CULZEAN CASTLE & COUNTRY PARK
Maybole, Ayrshire KA19 8LE

Tel: 01655 884400 **Fax:** 01655 884503
www.culzeanexperience.org
Location Off A719, west of Maybole and south of Ayr
Opening hours Walled garden: 10.30am to 5pm (last admissions 4pm), daily, 30 March to 31 October; park: 9.30am to sunset, daily, all year
Admission fee Adults £5; concessions £3.75; children £1

Culzean is the flagship of the National Trust for Scotland, thoroughly restored and with more than 400,000 visitors a year. The gardens are important and include a deer park, a ruined arch, a viaduct, an ice house, a beautiful Gothic camellia house, gazebos, a pagoda and a vinery. The three areas of horticultural interest are the walled garden, the fountain court and 'Happy Valley', which is a woodland garden with fine specimen trees. Record-breakers include an upright Irish yew (*Taxus baccata* 'Fastigiata') at 20m (66ft), and the rare southern Japanese hemlock *Tsuga sieboldii* at 25m (82ft).
tallest Irish yew *Taxus baccata* 'Fastigiata' (20m; 66ft) in the British Isles (plus two further tree records); current holder of the Sandford Award; good shops; plant centre; restaurant; coffee shop

Owned by The National Trust for Scotland
Number of gardeners 7, plus 4 groundsmen
Size 50ha (125 acres)

FINLAYSTONE COUNTRY ESTATE
Langbank PA14 6TJ

Tel 01475 540505
www.finlaystone.co.uk
Location On A8, 10 mins west of Glasgow Airport
Opening hours 10am to 5pm, daily, all year
Admission fee Adults £3.50; OAPs and children £2.50

Much of the garden at Finlaystone was laid out in 1900. The formal gardens date from this period: the walled garden, the knot garden and the sunken garden. All were set within a natural landscape of ornamental trees and shrubs. The sunken garden is enclosed within a yew hedge which was castellated in about 1918. But much of today's imaginative and beautiful garden is more recent, including the long, winding herbaceous border. The wooded areas are thick with azaleas, as well as rhododendrons, bluebells and snowdrops. Celtic themes have inspired the MacMillans to construct two new features. The Celtic paving has an intricate pattern set into grass, using a design in the Book of Kells. In the walled garden is a 'garden

Culzean Castle and Country Park

Culzean Castle and Country Park

oasis' in the form of a Celtic cross with a pool at its centre, but all enclosed by a circular brick pergola. There is also a garden of scented plants for blind visitors, sometimes known as the 'Fragrant Garden' and on other occasions as the 'Smelly Garden'. The 'New Garden' dates from 1959: the banks of a burn are lined with *Darmera peltata*, spectacular in autumn. The rhododendrons and azaleas merge into the wilder woods on the far bank and daffodils are everywhere in spring.
rhododendrons and azaleas; daffodils; bluebells; gift shop; good play areas; light meals (11am to 5pm, April to October)

Owned by Arthur MacMillan
Number of gardeners 1, plus owner
Size 4ha (10 acres)

GEILSTON GARDEN
Cardross, Dumbarton G82 5HD

Tel: 01389 849187 **Fax:** 01389 849189
www.nts.org.uk
Location On A814, at western end of Cardross
Opening hours 9.30am to 5pm, daily, 30 March to 31 October
Admission fee Adults £4; concessions £3; RHS members free

Geilston is a nice example of the many small country houses, villas and estates which were put together by successful Glasgow industrialists along the banks of the Clyde. The garden retains a sense of being a private space in which the visitor is an invited guest. The many attractive features include a fruit and vegetable garden with a central 'dipping pond', a walled garden with traditional glasshouses and a burn which winds through the wooded glen.

Owned by The National Trust for Scotland
Number of gardeners 1
Size 2.8ha (7 acres)

GLASGOW BOTANIC GARDEN
730 Great Western Road, Glasgow G12 0UE

Tel 0141 334 2422/3354 **Fax** 0141 339 6964
Location On A82, 2 miles from city centre
Opening hours Grounds: 7am to dusk, daily, all year; glasshouses: 10am to 4.45pm (4.15pm in winter), daily, all year
Admission fee Free

Most of the elements of the traditional botanic garden are here, including chronological beds, but the glory of Glasgow is its two glasshouses – the Kibble Palace and the Main Range – which have both been restored in recent years to their former splendour. There are interesting new gardens outside, too: a fine rose garden, a herb garden, vegetable beds and the long, scented border.
roses (ancient and modern); herbs; plants under glass; mature conifers; good herbaceous borders; fine collection of trees; beautiful glasshouse (the 'Kibble Palace')

Owned by Glasgow City Council
Number of gardeners 14, plus apprentices
Size 10.7ha (27 acres)
NCCPG National Collections *Begonia*; *Dendrobium*; *Dicksoniaceae*

GLENARN
Rhu, Helensburgh G84 8LL

Tel 01436 820493 **Fax** 0141 221 8450
www.gardens-of-argyll.co.uk
Location Turn up Pier Road at Rhu Marina, first right is Glenarn Road
Opening hours Dawn to dusk, daily, 21 March to 21 September
Admission fee Adults £3; OAPs and children £1.50; guided tours for groups

Glenarn's 10 acres of woodland garden have at least one venerable old rhododendron dating from Joseph Hooker's Himalayan expedition (1849 to 1851) and many species from the 1930s trips of Kingdon Ward and Ludlow and Sherriff. The garden owes its present outline to the Gibson family who owned it from 1927 to 1982, and many of their own rhododendron hybrids still flourish here, though there are plenty of magnolias, camellias, pieris and other good plants. *Magnolia campbellii* var. *mollicomata* is 12m (39ft) tall, and *Magnolia sprengeri* var. *diva* has made 10m (33ft) so far. Other plants which date back to the Gibsons are the rare climbing gesneriad *Asterantha ovata* and the swarms of *Primula pulverulenta* which are such a splendid feature in early summer. The Thornleys took over in 1983 – both of them professional architects whose gardening was moulded by the formal gardens of Italy – but their commitment to the woodland nature of the garden is remarkable. They have relaid the steps, recut the paths, restored the vegetable garden and added a pond with a water chute. Work is still progressing in the rock garden, where the owners have completed excavating and restoring the quarry face. Meanwhile they have also propagated the unique plants, renewed the plantings, created spaces and maintained the balance between individual specimens. It is a remarkable achievement and worth a visit at any season, though especially in spring.
rock garden; plantsman's collection of plants; mature conifers; rhododendrons; embothriums; refreshments by arrangement for groups

Owned by Mr and Mrs Michael Thornley
Number of gardeners Owners only
Size 4ha (10 acres)

GREENBANK GARDEN
Flenders Road, Clarkston, Glasgow G76 8RB

Tel 0141 616 5126
www.nts.org.uk
Location 1 mile along Mearns Road from Clarkston Toll, take first left
Opening hours Garden: 9.30am to sunset, daily, all year
Admission fee Adults £4; concessions £3; children £2

Greenbank is a demonstration garden: it was left to the National Trust for Scotland in 1976 on condition that it was developed as a teaching resource for people with small gardens. The walled garden has therefore been divided into a great number of sections which represent different interests and skills: a rock garden, fruit garden, dried flower plot, raised beds, winter garden, and so on.
woodland garden; rock garden; fruit in the walled garden; good herbaceous borders; a garden for the disabled; roses of every kind; NTS gift shop; plant sales; tea room

Owned by The National Trust for Scotland
Number of gardeners 3
Size 1ha (21/2 acres) of walled garden; 6ha (15 acres) of policies
NCCPG National Collections *Bergenia*

KINLOCHLAICH HOUSE
Appin PA38 4BD

Tel 01631 730342 **Fax** 01631 730482
www.kinlochlaich-house.co.uk
Location On A828, midway between Oban and Fort William
Opening hours 9.30am (10.30am on Sundays) to 5.30pm, daily, April to mid-October; 9.30am to 5pm, daily, except Sundays, mid-October to March
Admission fee £2 donation to SGS

Kinlochlaich is one of Scotland's leading garden centres, with a very wide range of plants of every sort. But the historic walled garden, hexagonal in shape and dating back to the 1790s, is also a test ground and display garden, with an especially fine collection of camellias, rhododendrons,

unusual shrubs and Scottish totems like *Meconopsis betonicifolia*.
plant centre

Owned by Donald Hutchison
Number of gardeners 4
Size 2ha (5 acres)

LADYBURN
by Maybole KA19 7SG

Tel 01655 740585 **Fax** 01655 740580
Location 8 miles south of Maybole, by B7023
Opening hours 2pm to 5pm, Wednesdays, mid-May to September
Admission fee Adults £3.50

The old gardens at Ladyburn have been extensively revived and replanted in recent years. The walks along the burn and the new herbaceous plantings are all good, but the real horticultural interest lies with the roses – not just the national collections of Scots roses and *R. rugosa* hybrids, but also a growing collection of climbers, ramblers and Portland roses.
historic roses; teas

Owned by Jane Hepburn
Number of gardeners 2
Size 2ha (5 acres)
NCCPG National Collections *Rosa rugosa; Rosa spinosissima*

MOUNT STUART
Isle of Bute PA20 9LR

Tel 01700 503877 **Fax** 01700 505313
www.mountstuart.com
Location 5 miles south of Rothesay
Opening hours 10am to 6pm, daily, May to September; plus 6 to 9 April
Admission fee Adults £3.50; OAPs £3; children £2

Mount Stuart has a vast and fascinating garden to accompany the sumptuous house. Its 300 acres include: a mature Victorian pinetum; a two-acre rock garden designed by Thomas Mawson and thickly planted with rare collected plants; a 'wee' garden of five acres, planted with tender exotics from Australia and New Zealand; and a kitchen garden redesigned by the late Lord Bute with help from Rosemary Verey. Add in the relics of an 18th-century landscape, a tropical greenhouse, acres of bluebells and established rhododendrons, and you have the measure of a long and fascinating visit.
woodland garden; rhododendrons and azaleas; plants under glass; mature conifers; bluebells; important rock garden; tender plants; fine new visitor centre; restaurant and café

Owned by The Mount Stuart Trust
Number of gardeners 9
Size 120ha (300 acres)

TOROSAY CASTLE & GARDENS
Craignure, Isle of Mull PA65 6AY

Tel 01680 812421 **Fax** 01680 812470
www.torosay.com
Location 1 1/2 miles from Craignure on A849 to Iona
Opening hours Gardens: 9am to dusk, daily, all year
Admission fee Adults £4.75; concessions £4; children £2.50; RHS members free (gardens only); castle extra

The best feature of the gardens at Torosay is the Italian Statue Walk, lined with 19 figures by Antonio Bonazza. The formal terraces are covered with rambling roses, other climbers and perennials. The oriental garden, bog garden, greenhouses and rock garden add to the sheer variety. The woodland garden is stuffed with interesting specimens: *Eucryphia*, *Embothrium* and *Crinodendron* among many Chilean plants, underplanted with old daffodil cultivars, meconopsis and primulas.
rock garden; water garden; *Eucalyptus* walk; new conservation plantings with conifers from Royal Botanic Garden Edinburgh; eucalyptus walk; shop; tea room (April to October) with light lunches

Owned by Mr C James
Number of gardeners 1 1/2, plus seasonal extras and volunteers
Size 5ha (12 1/2 acres)

TAYSIDE

BELL'S CHERRYBANK CENTRE
Cherrybank, Perth PH2 0PF

Tel 01738 472800 **Fax** 01738 472805
Location Just off A93 Glasgow Road, Perth, between Broxden roundabout and city centre
Opening hours 10am (noon on Sundays) to 5pm (4pm in November and December), daily, April to December
Admission fee Adults £3.75; children £2.50; RHS members free

These immaculately maintained show gardens make good use of water and incorporate some striking modern sculptures. They are best known for their collection of heaths and heathers, the most comprehensive in the British Isles with plants representing over 900 cultivars. The National Heather Collection is part of a proposal by Scotland's Garden Trust to create a 45-acre garden of national importance on adjacent land.
heathers; gift shop; light refreshments and drinks

Owned by Scotland's Garden Trust
Number of gardeners 2
Size 2.6ha (61/2 acres)
NCCPG National Collections *Erica*

BLAIR CASTLE
Blair Atholl, Pitlochry PH18 5TH

Tel 01796 481207 **Fax** 01796 481487
www.blair-castle.co.uk
Location Signed from A9, north of Pitlochry
Opening hours 9.30am to 5.30pm, daily, 1 April to 27 October
Admission fee Adults £2.50; children £1.30

The landscaping around Blair Castle is some of Scotland's finest. The Hercules Garden was first laid out by the 2nd Duke of Atholl in 1744 and includes a formal water tank, 2.5 acres in extent, extensive herbaceous borders and an impressive collection of fruit trees. Nearby is Diana's Grove where axial paths and avenues radiate out from a statue of Diana. The fine conifers date from the 19th century and include the tallest Japanese larch in the United Kingdom (44m; 144ft).
shop; restaurant

Owned by The Blair Charitable Trust
Number of gardeners 3
Size 3.8ha (91/2 acres)

BOLFRACKS GARDEN
Aberfeldy PH15 2EX

Tel 01887 820344 **Fax** 01887 829522
www.bolfracks.com
Location 2 miles west of Aberfeldy on A827
Opening hours 10am to 6pm, daily, April to October
Admission fee Adults £3; children free

Bolfracks is a plantsman's garden, unusual among Scottish gardens for having a good display of flowers throughout the year. There are rhododendrons and azaleas, of course, but they are principally dwarf species and hybrids, and joined by a large number of daphnes, phyllodoces, pieris, quinces and berberis. Midsummer sees the shrub roses, of which there is a good collection, with everything from gallicas through to modern shrub roses. But Bolfracks is particularly good for its herbaceous borders: the perennials make an effective display by June and continue through until autumn, when gentians, cyclamen and colchicums take over.
herbaceous plants; roses; lots of plants at every season

Owned by RA Price
Number of gardeners 1
Size 1.2ha (3 acres)

BRANKLYN GARDEN
116 Dundee Road, Perth PH2 7BB

Tel 01738 625535
www.branklyngarden.org.uk

Location Off Dundee Road, on eastern edge of Perth, 1/2 mile from Queen's Bridge
Opening hours 10am to 5pm, daily, 31 March to 31 October
Admission fee Adults £5; concessions £4; children £2; RHS members free

The apotheosis of Scottish rock gardening, Branklyn is a suburban garden absolutely crammed with rare plants growing in a series of artificial microhabitats. This is a garden to go round slowly, looking at all the plants – small rhododendrons, alpines, herbaceous plants and peat lovers. It was built up between 1922 and 1967 by John and Dorothy Renton, who bequeathed it to the National Trust for Scotland. This sort of garden depends for its success upon the understanding and plantsmanship of the gardeners who work in it, and the Trust has been fortunate with their employees at Branklyn since they took it on.
small NTS gift shop; plant sales

Owned by The National Trust for Scotland
Number of gardeners 2
Size 0.8ha (2 acres)
NCCPG National Collections *Cassiope*; *Lilium*

CHRISTIE'S NURSERY
Downfield, Westmuir, Kirriemuir DD5 8LP

Tel/fax 01575 572977
www.christiealpines.co.uk
Location On A926 1 mile west of Kirriemuir
Opening hours By appointment from March to October; groups welcome
Admission fee Free

This alpine nursery has an impressive list, particularly strong on gentians, hardy orchids, meconopsis, corydalis and lewisias. The owners expect to have about 1,000 different items in stock at any time, and about 2,000 growing in their pretty display garden.
meconopsis; trilliums; lilies; limestone scree garden; refreshments by arrangement

Owned by Ian and Ann Christie
Size 0.6ha (11/2 acres)
NCCPG National Collections *Gentiana*

CLUNY HOUSE
by Aberfeldy, Perthshire PH15 2JT

Tel 01887 820795
Location 31/2 miles from Aberfeldy, on Weem to Strathtay road
Opening hours 10am to 6pm, daily, March to mid-November
Admission fee Adults £3.50; children (under 16) free; season ticket £6

Cluny is a plantsman's garden, largely made in the 1950s by Mrs Mattingley's father, who subscribed to the Ludlow and Sherriff expeditions. Some older trees date from the 19th century – notably two vast wellingtonias – and the Mattingleys have continued to develop the garden since they took over in 1987. It is very much a woodland garden, with a natural appearance, except that the canopy is now of rhododendrons, acers, sorbus, euonymus and birches. It has superb rhododendrons and many other ornamental trees and shrubs from the Himalayas and North America, as well as an underplanting of meconopsis, trilliums, gentians, nomocharis, cardiocrinums, erythroniums, lilies, arisaema and hellebores. But it is memorable, above all, for primulas, of which the Mattingleys used to have a National Collection. The annual display starts with the early-flowering petiolarid species – *P. whitei*, *P. tanneri*, *P. sonchifolia* and *P. nana*, for example. Then come sheets of candelabra species: the first is yellow *P. chungensis*, followed by purple *P. pulverulenta*, the dark pink and white forms of *P. japonica*, purple *P. beesiana*, orange *P. bulleyana*, yellow *P. sikkimensis* and yellow *P. florindae* – as well as naturally occurring hybrids between them. Many exotic species – and not just primulas – seed and regenerate freely in the acid, humus-rich soil. Cluny has lots to excite the visitor throughout the season: bulbs in April, followed by primulas from May to June, lilies in July, excellent autumn interest and every likelihood of seeing red squirrels. The whole garden is hand weeded and chemical free: promising seedlings are thereby spotted and protected.
plantsman's collection of plants; fine collection of trees; meconopsis; primulas; cardiocrinums; wellingtonia (*Sequoiadendron giganteum*) with the widest girth in the British Isles

Owned by Mr J and Mrs W Mattingley
Number of gardeners 1 full-time, 3 part-time
Size 2.4ha (6 acres)

DRUMMOND GARDENS
Muthill, Crieff PH7 4HZ

Tel 01764 681433/681321 **Fax** 01764 681642
www.drummondcastlegardens.co.uk
Location South of Crieff on A822
Opening hours 1pm to 6pm, daily, Easter weekend, then daily from May to October
Admission fee Adults £4; OAPs £3; children £1.50; RHS members free in May, September and October

Drummond Castle has probably the most important formal garden in Scotland, laid out in about 1830 as a St Andrew's cross, with complex parterres filled since the 1950s with roses, statues, clipped cones, herbaceous plants, gravel and lots more besides. The ongoing programme of renovation has already restored much of the garden to a very high standard. The result is order, shape, structure, mass, profusion and colour. There is also a copper beech planted by Queen Victoria to commemorate her visit in 1842. Parts of the film *Rob Roy* were shot in the gardens.
fruit; important formal garden

Owned by Grimsthorpe and Drummond Castle Trust Ltd
Number of gardeners 5
Size 6ha (15 acres)

DUNDEE BOTANIC GARDEN
Riverside Drive, Dundee DD2 1QH

Tel 01382 381190 **Fax** 01382 640574
www.dundeebotanicgarden.co.uk
Location Signed from Riverside Drive (A85), near its junction with Perth Road
Opening hours 10am to 4.30pm (3.30pm from November to February), daily, all year; closed 1 and 2 January, 25 and 26 December
Admission fee Adults £3; OAPs £2; children £1; families £7; RHS members free except during special events

Dundee has a fine modern Botanic Garden which caters well for visitors: its gentle south-facing slopes are just above the banks of the River Tay. Founded in 1971, it can boast fine collections of conifers and broad-leaved trees, good shrubs, tropical and temperate glasshouses, a water garden and a herb garden. There is a whole series of native plant communities from montane to coastal habitats. These include a collection of *Sorbus* species native to Britain. These are also plant groupings which demonstrate adaptations for survival, such as drought resistance (the Mediterranean garden) and specialised pollination. Among the more surprising collections are *Nothofagus* species from South America and a large number of *Eucalyptus* trees from Australia. There will be two RHS Special Events at Dundee Botanic Garden in 2007; details from 020 7821 3408.
subtropical plants; herbs; plants under glass; mature conifers; drought-resistant plants; carnivorous plants; shop; plant centre; café

Owned by The University of Dundee
Number of gardeners 3
Size 9.2ha (23 acres)

EDZELL CASTLE
Edzell, Angus DD9 7VE

Tel/fax 01356 648631
www.historic-scotland.gov.uk
Location On B966 to Edzell village, then signed for 1 mile
Opening hours 9.30am to 5.30pm, daily, April to September; 9am to 4pm, Saturday to Wednesday, October to March
Admission fee Adults £4.50; OAPs £3.50; children £2.25

Edzell has a 1930s formal garden in the 17th-century style, designed to be seen from the ruined keep. It is shaped like a quincunx of sorts, with yew bobbles, box edging and roses in the beds. The four main segments have the mottos of the Lindsay family *DUM SPIRO SPERO* ('While I breathe, I hope') and *ENDURE FORT* ('Endure with Strength') cut round their edges in box. In summer, niches in the garden walls are planted with lobelia and alyssum to form a *fess chequy* representing the Lindsay arms. It is a garden of considerable historic importance as the only

complete 'pleasaunce' in Scotland but, once you have seen the parterre, Edzell is not a garden to linger in.
topiary; bedding; formal garden; shop

Owned by Historic Scotland
Number of gardeners 1
Size 0.4ha (1 acre)

EXPLORERS' GARDEN

Pitlochry Festival Theatre, Pitlochry, Perth PH16 5DR

Tel 01796 484600 **Fax** 01796 484616
www.pitlochry.org.uk
Location Well-signed in Pitlochry
Opening hours 10am (11am on Sundays) to 5pm, daily, 1 April to 4 November
Admission fee Adults £3; OAPs £2.50; children £1; families £7

This is a remarkable garden – a celebration of the Scottish plant collectors who have introduced so many new plants to our gardens over the last 250 years. It has been made in a woodland setting around and above the theatre, with a striking modern layout that incorporates some excellent modern sculptures. All the plants in the garden were first found by Scots: the work of the Coxes (father and son), Don, Douglas, Drummond, Forrest, Fortune, Jeffery, Ludlow and Sherriff, Masson, Menzies and Thomson – names that attach themselves so often to plants that they discovered – are especially well represented. The garden has a strong educational and conservation purpose, but it is beautiful, too. Highlights, in late spring, are drifts of *Primula japonica* and banks of *Meconopsis betonicifolia*.
café

GLENDOICK GARDENS

Glendoick, Perth PH2 7NS

Tel 01738 860205 **Fax** 01738 860630
www.glendoick.com
Location A90 between Perth and Dundee
Opening hours 10am to 4pm, Monday to Frida,; mid-April to mid-June; buy tickets at garden centre; for SGS: 2pm to 5pm, 6 and 20 May; and pre-booked parties of 20+ between mid-April and mid-June
Admission fee Adults £3; children free

Everyone knows of the Glendoick nursery, but the garden is even more important. Started by Farrer's friend Euan Cox in the 1920s, it has one of the best collections of plants, especially rhododendron species, forms and hybrids, in the British Isles. The nursery propagates all its stock on-site. Peter Cox has specialised in breeding low-growing rhododendrons for small gardens: his successes include such well known cultivars as 'Curlew', 'Razorbill' and 'Egret', as well as evergreen azaleas like 'Panda'. He has also continued to hunt for plants in China, as his father did before him. His own son Kenneth has made ten expeditions to Tibet and Arunachal Pradesh. There is a good demonstration garden in the garden centre which is open all year. The website is very good indeed.
woodland garden; fine trees; plantsman's collection of plants; primulas; meconopsis; lilies; famous garden centre attached; restaurant

Owned by Mr and Mrs Peter A Cox and Kenneth Cox
Number of gardeners Owners, with (very) part time help
Size 4ha (10 acres), including nursery
NCCPG National Collections *Rhododendron* (section Pogonanthum, subsections Campylogyna, Glauca and Uniflora, and Cox hybrids)

HOUSE OF DUN

Montrose, Angus DD10 9LQ

Tel 01674 810264 **Fax** 01674 810722
www.nts.org.uk
Location On A395, halfway between Montrose and Brechin
Opening hours 9am to sunset, daily, all year
Admission fee Adults £2; honesty box

The first thing you notice at House of Dun, particularly in winter, is the magnificent line of mature wellingtonias, but there are also sheets of spring bulbs, a Victorian rose garden for summer, a border of *Nerine bowdenii* over 100m (328ft) long, and a collection of old fruit trees of interest in

autumn. The walled garden (next to the house) has been restored as it might have been in the late 19th century and planted with cultivars that date back to the 1880s.
NTS shop; restaurant, open with house

Owned by The National Trust for Scotland
Number of gardeners 1
Size 18ha (45 acres)

KINROSS HOUSE
Kinross KY13 8ET

Tel 01577 862900 **Fax** 01577 863372
www.kinrosshouse.com
Location M90, Jct 6, into Kinross, right at mini-roundabout, first left
Opening hours 10am to 7pm, daily, April to September
Admission fee Adults £3; OAPs £1.50; children free, if accompanied

Many consider Kinross the most beautiful house in Scotland, and its views across Loch Leven are extensive. It is approached along a magnificent avenue of lime trees. The elegant walled garden has herbaceous borders and roses and, above all, a 17th-century sense of proportion. It is one of the few Scottish gardens which are genuinely at their best in July and August. The website is excellent.
walled garden; mixed borders; lime avenue

Owned by James Montgomery
Number of gardeners 4
Size 4ha (10 acres) of walled garden

PITMUIES GARDENS
Guthrie, by Forfar, Angus DD8 2SN

Tel/fax 01241 828245
www.pitmuies.com
Location Signed off A932 Forfar to Arbroath road
Opening hours 10am to 5pm, daily, March to October; and by appointment; the garden will also be open in February 2007 as part of the new Scottish Snowdrop Festival
Admission fee Adults £2.50; children free

Pitmuies is one of the most beautiful modern gardens in Scotland. Laid out and planted in the Hidcote style, Pitmuies has wonderful shrub roses in mixed plantings, clever colour schemes, and innumerable different gardens within the garden: a delphinium border, a cherry walk, rhododendron glades, vast hollies, a superb *Acer griseum* and splendid trees inherited from Victorian times – and earlier, for there are 400-year-old Spanish chestnuts on the lawn. The spring bulbs, hellebores and the alpine meadow are a great joy when the garden opens in spring.
roses (ancient and modern); plants under glass; fruit; good herbaceous borders; alpine meadow; ferns; colour schemes; tallest *Ilex aquifolium* 'Argenteomarginata' in the British Isles; home-raised plants and produce in season

Owned by Mrs Farquhar Ogilvie
Number of gardeners 1, plus 1 groundsman
Size 10.3ha (26 acres)

SCONE PALACE
Perth PH2 6BD

Tel: 01738 552300 **Fax:** 01738 552588
www.scone-palace.co.uk
Location Signed from A93, 1½ miles north of Perth
Opening hours 9.30am to 5.30pm, daily, April to October
Admission fee Gardens only: adults £4; OAPs £3.65; children £2.75; RHS members free

Scone is best known for its large pinetum and for the Douglas firs (*Pseudotsuga menziesii*) grown from original seed sent back by their discoverer David Douglas, who was born on the estate. Lord Mansfield has the largest private collection of orchids in the country. A selection is always on view in the state rooms and there will be an orchid festival at Scone on 4 and 5 August.
established pinetum; woodland walks; rhododendrons and azaleas; daffodils; new 'Murray' maze; tallest *Tilia platyphyllos* (37m; 121ft) in the British Isles and three other record trees; handsome Douglas fir; largest private collection of orchid hybrids in Britain; gift shop; restaurant in old servants' hall

Owned by The Earl of Mansfield
Number of gardeners 5
Size 40ha (100 acres)

WALES

Most of the best-known gardens of Wales are close to the sea – as, indeed, are most of its larger centres of population. This gives the principality a reputation for being able to grow tender plants that would not be hardy, say, in Surrey. There is some truth in this, though no Welsh garden is truly subtropical in the way that Tresco and Inverewe are. The National Gardens Scheme offers gardens to visit in every part of Wales. The Royal Horticultural Society has negotiated free access for its members, for some or all of the year, to some of the principality's finest gardens, including Bodnant, the National Botanic Garden of Wales and Picton Castle.

This book lists gardens in Wales under the old 1974 counties, rather than the historic counties or the present administrative units. The 1974 counties are a useful size for the purpose of this book, and their names are readily recognised.

Wales has many historic gardens, made mainly in the 18th and 19th centuries and usually in the styles that were fashionable in England at the time. The National Trust has played an important part in preserving and restoring some of the finest. Bodnant, Plas Newydd and Powis Castle are gardens of the utmost international importance. By and large, however, they share with other Welsh gardens the characteristic of having acquired their horticultural importance during the 20th century: the same is true of other classic Welsh gardens like Portmeirion and Dyffryn. Much of that horticultural input came from England and there was, until quite recently, a sense among some that gardening was a hobby either for very rich anglicised Welshmen or for the English who came to live in Wales. Despite its troubles, and although it cannot rival such major botanic gardens as Kew and Edinburgh, the new National Botanic Garden of Wales does give a new focus to Welsh horticulture.

Wales's historic gardens are well supported by the Welsh Historic Gardens Trust which has taken action to identify, evaluate and conserve the principality's heritage. Its declared aims are to initiate and assist in the conservation of gardens, parks and designed landscapes that are of historic, cultural and aesthetic importance in the Welsh heritage, and to alert public awareness to the decline in particular places. Comparatively few historic gardens in Wales are open to the public.

CADW, the Welsh Historic Monuments Commission in Cardiff, publishes a Register of Parks and Gardens of Special Historic Interest in Wales. This is the work of Elisabeth Whittle who wrote the standard modern work on the subject *The Historic Gardens of Wales* (HMSO, 1992). The Register is modelled on English Heritage's list for England and the criteria for selection and grading gardens are comparable.

The best collection of trees in Wales is at Bodnant, which has a large number of rarities and some 20 champions among them. There are good tree collections also at Dyffryn and Margam in Glamorgan. Wales has comparatively few top-class nurseries, and practically none in South Wales near Cardiff or Swansea. However, the outstanding examples elsewhere are among Britain's best. Celyn Vale has a unique list of Australasian trees; Dibleys Nurseries is the leading nursery for *Streptocarpus* and other house plants; and Crûg Farm Plants introduces more new collected plants into cultivation than any other in Britain.

The two principal horticultural colleges are at opposite ends of Wales. Both the Welsh College of Horticulture at Mold (Tel 01352 841000) and Pencoed College at Bridgend (Tel 01656 302600) are RHS Partner Colleges with a good number of public lectures and workshops throughout the year.

Carmarthenshire
...the Garden of Wales
National Botanic Garden of Wales
Llanarthne.
The first botanic garden of the new millennium with the world's largest single-span glasshouse has been crowned the No 1 Wonder of Wales
01558 668768
www.gardenofwales.org.uk
Aberglasney Gardens
Llangathen.
Aberglasney is one of the UK's most exciting garden restoration projects. The garden has been transformed into a Plantsmans' paradise.
01558 668998
www.aberglasney.org
Dinefwr Park & Castle
Llandeilo.
Newton House - set in Dinefwr Park, steeped in history with fantastic scenery, walks & views - is now fully refurbished with extended tearooms.
01558 823902
www.thenationaltrust.org
Norwood Gardens
Llanllwni.
An opportunity to see a garden in its fourth year of development. Set in the picturesque Teifi valley. Find us on the A485 between Carmarthen and Lampeter.
01559 395386
www.norwoodgardens.co.uk
01269 590223 | www.carmarthenshire.gov.uk/tourism

CLWYD

ABERCONWY NURSERY
Graig, Glan Conwy, Colwyn Bay LL28 5TL

Tel 01492 580875
Location South of Glan Conwy, 2nd right off A470: right at top of hill, nursery is on right
Opening hours 10am to 5pm, Tuesday to Sunday, mid-February to mid-October

This is best known as one of our leading nurseries for alpine plants and a steady introducer of new cultivars, especially autumn-flowering gentians and dwarf *Saxifraga fortunei* hybrids. But it also offers unusual shrubs and herbaceous and woodland plants, including many dwarf rhododendrons and small ericaceous plants. Other specialities are cistus, primulas, small ferns, hybrids of *Helleborus niger* and an extensive choice of dionysias, androsaces and the porophylla saxifrages.

Owned by Keith Lever

BODRHYDDAN
Rhuddlan LL18 5SB

Tel 01745 590414 **Fax** 01745 590155
www.bodrhyddan.co.uk
Location On A5151, midway between Dyserth and Rhuddlan
Opening hours 2pm to 5.30pm, Tuesdays and Thursdays, June to September; also by appointment; plus special openings for groups
Admission fee Adults £2; children £1

The house and garden at Bodrhyddan date back to medieval times – the ancient oaks alongside the parterre are possibly over 500 years old – but most of what we see today was opulently laid out in the 1870s and restored in the 1980s. There is also an avenue of Monterey pines (*Pinus radiata*) dating from 1928, which leads to another avenue of limes (*Tilia platyphyllos*) planted in 1957. William Andrews Nesfield designed the long parterre, which was planted with vegetables when the present Lord Langford returned from World War II, but is now absolutely stunning with seasonal bedding. The Pleasance – abandoned since 1939 – was recreated in 1982 as a woodland garden; it has extensive shrub plantings around four ponds. In the woodlands are three short, signed walks. It is good to see such a distinguished garden on the up again.
teas

Owned by Lord Langford OBE, DL
Number of gardeners 2
Size 2.4ha (6 acres)

CELYN VALE NURSERIES
Allt-y-Celyn, Carrog, Corwen LL21 9LD

Tel/fax 01490 430671
www.eucalyptus.co.uk
Location 3 miles east of Corwen and 1 mile from Carrog, near A5
Opening hours 9am to 4pm, Monday to Friday, January to November
Admission fee Free

Specialist growers of eucalyptus and acacias: they use seed from high-altitude specimens to maximise hardiness and will advise also on suitable species for coppicing, poor drainage, alkaline soils, hedging, salt tolerance and so on. They say that the hardiest gum trees are *E. archeri*, *E. coccifera*, *E. pauciflora* subsp. *debeuzevillei*, *E. pauciflora* subsp. *niphophila*, *E. parvifolia*, *E. perriniana* and *E. subcrenulata*.
eucalyptus

Owned by Andrew McConnell

CHIRK CASTLE
Chirk LL14 5AF

Tel 01691 777701 **Fax** 01691 774706
www.nationaltrust.org.uk

BODNANT GARDEN

Tal-y-Cafn, Colwyn Bay LL28 5RE

Tel 01492 650460 **Fax** 01492 650448
www.bodnantgarden.co.uk
Location 8 miles south of Llandudno and Colwyn Bay on A470; entrance 1/2 mile along Eglwysbach Road
Opening hours 10am to 5pm, daily, 10 March to 4 November
Admission fee Adults £7; children £3.50; RHS members free

Bodnant combines dramatic formal terraces with extensive woodland plantings on the grandest of scales. It is compulsory viewing for all keen gardeners. A deep herbaceous border backing onto a high wall is instantly striking, with mature, often tender climbers rampant above bold, warm plantings. Although this is North Wales, and the views from the lawns are across the valley to the Carneddau mountains, parts of the garden feel distinctly Italianate. Beside the house, two enormous cedars overshadow a formal lily pond, on the third of five terraces, where hydrangeas abound. A crisply-shaved yew hedge curves above a mezzanine rose pergola, and there are specimens of *Magnolia grandiflora* everywhere. Below is the Pin Mill, a stately gazebo from the early 18th century, which looks across a flat pool to a grassy stage at the opposite end of its terrace, edged with cut cubes of yew topiary. Plantings of pencil-thin cypresses, and *Cistus* and *Potentilla* cultivars, help to create an intensely Mediterranean feel on clear summer days. Behind the Pin Mill, the mood changes, as the valley fills with tall specimen trees, marching beside a fast-flowing mill stream and a stern old mill. Along the stream there are hostas, bergenias and meconopsis. Some of the massive *Sequoiadendron* specimens bear planting plaques which show them to be in their second century. Winding back in an extended arc towards the house, there are gentler woodland plantings with shrubby borders, and smaller trees growing in grass. There is a magnificent collection of magnolias, rhododendrons and camellias. Other good plantings include *Viburnum* x *bodnantense*, hybrid camellias, huge rhododendrons, white wisterias, a vast *Arbutus* x *andrachnoides*, flaming embothriums and the famous laburnum tunnel. The garden is admirably maintained, and popular with visitors, too. The walled plant centre (not National Trust) is strong on many of the tender climbers from the garden, and reasonably priced.

tallest Californian redwood *Sequoia sempervirens* (47m; 154ft) in the British Isles and 18 further record-breaking tree species - more than any other garden in Wales; plant centre; light lunches, teas, refreshments (11am to 5pm)

Owned by The National Trust
Number of gardeners 18
Size 32ha (80 acres)
NCCPG National Collections *Embothrium*; *Eucryphia*; *Magnolia* (spp.); *Rhododendron forrestii*

Location 1½ miles west of Chirk off A5
Opening hours 10am to 6pm (5pm in October), Wednesday to Sunday, 24 March to 4 November; plus Tuesdays in July and August
Admission fee Adults £4.50; children £2.20; families £11.20

Chirk has a fine 18th-century landscape by William Emes and handsome 19th-century formal gardens, with yew hedges and billowing topiary. Part is planted with roses. There is also a good 1930s collection of trees and shrubs, the relics of a garden by Norah Lindsay. Elsewhere are a rock garden, a 1950s mixed border, a lime avenue and drifts of daffodils in spring.
shop; restaurant and tea room

Owned by The National Trust
Number of gardeners 3
Size 2.2ha (5 ½ acres)

DIBLEYS NURSERIES
Llanelidan, Ruthin LL15 2LG

Tel 01978 790677 **Fax** 01978 790668
www.dibleys.com
Location 6 miles south of Ruthin; follow brown tourist signs from A525
Opening hours 10am to 5pm, daily, April to September; plus weekdays in March and October
Admission fee Garden: £2.50; glasshouses: free

Dibleys is the leading British nursery for gesneriads – especially streptocarpus, of which they have a comprehensive collection of cultivars, from 'Constant Nymph' to the latest modern hybrids like 'Crystal Ice'. They will be introducing new cultivars again in 2007. Dibleys has made a great impact on RHS Flower Shows in recent years, and won 17 consecutive gold medals at Chelsea. It also has a long list of other gesneriads like *Kohleria* and *Columnea*, and a good line in foliage begonias. The garden has extensive views over the Vale of Clwyd. There will be a RHS Special Event at the nursery in 2007; details from 020 7821 3408.
café

Owned by The Dibley family
Size 0.4ha (1 acre) of glasshouses; 4ha (10-acre) garden
NCCPG National Collections *Streptocarpus*

ERDDIG
Wrexham LL13 0YT

Tel 01978 355314 **Fax** 01978 313333
www.nationaltrust.org.uk
Location Signed from A483 and A525
Opening hours 11am to 6pm, Saturday to Wednesday (plus Thursdays in July and August), 24 March to 28 October; opens at 10am in July and August; closes at 5pm in October; plus Saturdays and Sundays from 4 November to 16 December
Admission fee Gardens only: adults £5; children £2.50

More of a re-creation than a restoration, Erddig today majors on domestic life in the early 18th century. There are old-fashioned fruit trees (an excellent collection of apples, plums, pears and cherries, beautifully trained), an avenue of pleached limes and a long canal to frame the house, but all are slightly awed by the Victorian overlay – avenues of monkey puzzles and wellingtonias.
restaurant; tea room

Owned by The National Trust
Number of gardeners 4
Size 5.2ha (13 acres)
NCCPG National Collections *Hedera*

THE GARDEN HOUSE
Erbistock, Wrexham LL13 0DL

Tel 01978 781149 **Fax** 01978 781144
Location Signed in village
Opening hours 10am to 4pm, Wednesday to Friday; 2pm to 5pm, Sundays; April to September
Admission fee Adults £4; children free; RHS members free on Wednesdays

The Garden House features shrub and herbaceous borders in various colour schemes, rose pergolas, a lily pond in the Monet style (complete with bridge) and a Jekyll-style colour-circle.

Owned by The Wingett family
Size 2ha (5 acres)
NCCPG National Collections *Hydrangea*

DYFED

Aberglasney Gardens

ABERGLASNEY GARDENS

Llangathen SA32 8QH

Tel/fax 01558 668998
www.aberglasney.org
Location 4 miles west of Landeilo, signed from A40
Opening hours 10am to 6pm, daily, April to September; 10.30am to 4pm, daily, October to March; coaches by appointment only
Admission fee Adults £6.50; OAPs £6; children £3; RHS members free from January to March

Aberglasney has a garden that lay dormant for about 400 years, until plans were made to restore it in 1998. The structure remains fairly intact from that time, including a cloister right at the heart of the layout and a (very rare) parapet walk. Reproduction gardens have been inserted within that framework. There are six in all, including three walled gardens. Hal Moggridge and Penelope Hobhouse have both been involved with the project: work continues and has cost £6m to date. The modern plantings are for year-round interest and include meconopsis, trilliums, lilies and rare trees and shrubs. There will be two RHS Special Events here in 2007; details from 020 7821 3408.
important historic garden; yew tunnel; pool garden; new winter garden (2005); shop; café

Owned by Aberglasney Restoration Trust
Number of gardeners 3
Size 4ha (10 acres)

BRO-MEIGAN GARDENS

Boncath SA37 0JE

Tel 01239 841232
www.bromeigan.co.uk
Location On B4332 between Boncath and Eglwyswrw
Opening hours 11am to 5pm, daily, except Mondays and Tuesdays, Easter to 29 October; open Bank Holiday Mondays
Admission fee Adults £3.50; OAPs £3.25; children £2

There are many gardens within the garden at Bro-Meigan: a turf maze, a lime tree avenue, a cottage garden, a primrose patch, a herb garden

Aberglasney Gardens

and an oriental garden. All have been made since 1986 and are held together by the owners' plantsmanship, which ensures that there is always interest at every season. Bro-Meigan is organically maintained.
tea room

Owned by Yvonne and David Gillett
Number of gardeners 2
Size 2.6ha (6½ acres)

CAE HIR
Cribyn, Lampeter SA48 7NG

Tel/fax 01570 470839
www.caehirgardens.ws
Location In village
Opening hours 1pm to 6pm, daily, April to October
Admission fee Adults £4.50; OAPs £4; children 50p; RHS members free

This vigorous and expanding garden was begun in 1985 and has been featured many times on television. It is also an RHS partner garden. Mr Akkermans's energy and achievement are an inspiration. He has taken six acres of meadowland and made them into a series of beautiful colour-coordinated gardens. The golden garden is quite outstanding. All different types of plants are here: trees, shrubs and herbaceous plants, often used in original ways. Mr Akkermans is now experimenting with agaves, half-hardy trees and shrubs, allowing wildflowers to mix with cultivated ones in some parts of his orderly garden. Elsewhere are collections of bonsai and cacti, and a water garden fed by natural ponds and a stream.
colour gardens; bonsai; mature ornamental trees; bog garden; light refreshments

Owned by Wil Akkermans
Number of gardeners owner only, with family help
Size 2.6ha (6½ acres)

COLBY WOODLAND GARDEN
Amroth, Narberth SA67 8PP

Tel 01834 811885
www.nationaltrust.org.uk
Location Signed from A477
Opening hours 10am to 5pm, daily, 24 March to 28 October; walled garden opens at 11am
Admission fee Adults £4; children £2

Colby is an attractive woodland garden, best in late spring and early summer, when the rhododendrons and azaleas are in full flower. Among the 19th-century plantings are vast cryptomerias, clumps of *Embothrium coccineum* and a huge specimen of *Rhododendron falconeri* subsp. *eximium*, planted in 1883. In the walled garden, a rill runs down from the *trompe l'oeil* gazebo to a pool. There have been many new plantings recently throughout the garden.
shop; tea room

Owned by The National Trust
Number of gardeners 2
Size 11.1ha (28 acres)

MOORLAND COTTAGE PLANTS
Rhyd-y-Groes, Brynberian, Crymych SA41 3TT

Tel 01239 891363
www.moorlandcottageplants.co.uk
Location On B4329, 12 miles south-west of Cardigan and 16 miles north-east of Haverfordwest
Opening hours 10.30am to 5.30pm, daily, except Wednesdays, mid-May to mid-September; nursery open March to September
Admission fee Adults £1.80; children 50p; for NGS

This is a promising young nursery, attached to a charming display garden. It is high up in the Pembrokeshire Coast National Park and surrounded by hills. Perennials are the main speciality, especially geraniums, campanulas, crocosmias, geums and potentillas. Grasses and groundcover plants are also offered in a wide variety. The garden is open and windy, though now more sheltered as the early plantings grow up; its areas include a grasses garden, a cottage garden and fine mixed borders.

Owned by Jennifer Matthews
Number of gardeners 1 part-time

The National Botanic Garden of Wales

THE NATIONAL BOTANIC GARDEN OF WALES

Middleton Hall, Llanarthne, Carmarthen SA32 8HG

Tel 01558 668768 **Fax** 01558 668933
www.gardenofwales.org.uk
Location 7 miles east of Carmarthen, off A48
Opening hours 10am to 6pm (4.30pm during British Winter Time), daily, except Christmas Day
Admission fee Adults £8; concessions £6; children £3; RHS members free from October to February

The landscaped park and gardens of the original 18th-century Middleton Hall estate are the setting for this new national botanic garden which opened to the public in 2000 amid great acclamation. Near the entrance to the garden is a 'Welsh landscape' with native meadows and woodlands. Then comes the Broadwalk, 220m (722ft) long, with a rill which runs down through a geological display of Welsh rocks. The garden's collection of herbaceous plants is planted along its edges, with narrow paths leading into the plantings to facilitate access. There is also a Japanese garden and a herb garden, named after the Physicians of Myddfai, with an ethnobotanical collection of native pharmacological Welsh plants. However, it is the Great Glasshouse which has received most of the adulation, and rightly so, because it is a stunning piece of architecture – the largest single-span glasshouse in the world. It concentrates upon the Mediterranean floras of the world – cheaper to maintain than tropical floras – including Chile, California, south-west Australia, South Africa, the Mediterranean basin and the Canary Isles.
good glasshouses; herbaceous plants; herbs; shop; plant sales; café; restaurant

Owned by The National Botanic Garden of Wales
Number of gardeners 13, plus 20 students and 20 volunteers
Size 40ha (100 acres)

PICTON CASTLE

Picton, Haverfordwest, Pembrokeshire SA62 4AS

Tel/fax 01437 751326
www.pictoncastle.co.uk
Location 4 miles east of Haverfordwest off A40
Opening hours 10.30am to 5pm, Tuesday to Sunday and Bank Holiday Mondays, April to September; for NGS: 6 May and 15 July
Admission fee Adults £4.95; OAPs £4.75; children £2.50; RHS members free from April to September

This 13th-century castle has been the home of the Philipps family for some 400 years, and the 40 acres of grounds include fine collections of rhododendrons, azaleas, magnolias, camellias, myrtles, embothriums and eucryphias, some of which have been bred by the castle gardeners. Older specimens, like a vast multi-trunked *Abies alba,* have been joined by new plantings of recent introductions – *Taiwania cryptomerioides* and *Calocedrus formosana* among them. The climate is mild, and supports normally tender plants like *Pittosporum tobira* 'Variegatum' and *Vestia foetida.* The display is at its best in May to June: summer and autumn bring woodland walks among the massive oaks and giant redwoods. Recent additions include a fern walk and a collection of bamboos. The walled garden has a fish pond, an indoor fernery, rose beds, herbaceous borders and a fountain in the centre. Four RHS special events will take place at Picton during 2007; details from 020 7821 3408.

woodland garden; rhododendrons and azaleas; camellias; garden shop selling surplus garden produce; restaurant

Owned by Picton Castle Trust
Number of gardeners 4, plus 2 part-time
Size 16ha (40 acres)

TRADEWINDS

Ffynnonwen, Pen-y-Bont, Carmarthen SA33 6PX

Tel 01994 484744 **Fax** 01994 484586
www.tradewindsnursery.co.uk
Location 3 miles south-east off Trelech; signed from B4299
Opening hours 10am to 5pm, daily, all year; please telephone to confirm garden is open
Admission fee Adults £2.50

This is a young plantsman's garden, allied to a small nursery. It is planted for year-round interest, using foliage as well as flowers to create colour effects. Parts are devoted to herbaceous and mixed plantings, but there is also a Mediterranean courtyard garden and a woodland area.

home-made teas

Owned by Stuart Kemp-Gee and Eve Etheridge
Number of gardeners owners
Size 0.6ha (1½ acres)

Dyffryn Botanic Garden, Cardiff

GLAMORGAN

CLYNE GARDENS
Mill Lane, Blackpill, Swansea SA3 5BD

Tel 01792 298637/401737 **Fax** 01792 297394
www.swansea.gov.uk/clyne
Location 3 miles west of Swansea on A4067 coast road
Opening hours Dawn to dusk, daily, all year
Admission fee Free; tours available by prior arrangement

Clyne is a stupendous woodland garden, the best in South Wales, well cared for by enthusiastic and knowledgeable staff. It is supreme as a magic rhododendron valley in May, but the range of rare and tender plants provides interest all year. Bluebells, lysichitons and gunneras are among its other features. It was planted between 1921 and 1952 by a local landowner called Algernon Walker-Heneage-Vivian, who subscribed to many of the Himalayan and Chinese plant-hunting expeditions of the day. The forms and hybrids of *Rhododendron niveum* which the head gardener brought to the RHS Flower Shows in the 1990s are still remembered by the London rhododendron fraternity. The mild climate means that *R. fragrantissimum* grows happily outside, and there is a group of *R.* 'Loderi King George' 16m (52ft) high. The car park is small and tends to fill up early in the day. During May, the gardens celebrate the Clyne in Bloom Festival, with guided walks, band concerts, children's entertainments and plant sales.
woodland garden; rhododendrons and azaleas; good herbaceous borders; occasional light refreshments

Owned by City and County of Swansea
Number of gardeners 5
Size 19.6ha (49 acres)
NCCPG National Collections *Pieris*; *Enkianthus*; *Rhododendron* (subsections Triflora and Falconera)

DYFFRYN BOTANIC GARDEN
St Nicholas, Cardiff CF5 6SU

Tel 029 2059 3328 **Fax** 029 2059 1966
www.dyffryngardens.org.uk
Location M4, Jct 33 on A48 then follow signs
Opening hours 10am to 6pm (5pm in October and 4pm in winter), daily, all year; no facilities from November to March
Admission fee Adults £3.50; OAPs and children £2.50; RHS members free from April to October except during special events

Dyffryn's sumptuous gardens were designed by Thomas Mawson for Reginald Cory around an Edwardian prodigy house. They are now being restored with a chunky £3.23m millennium grant. Originally intended partly for display – there is even a Roman garden with a temple and fountain – and partly for the Corys' own pleasure, Dyffryn has a huge collection of good plants built up in the early years of the 20th century. Watch it revive over the next year: the garden as a status symbol.
woodland garden; roses (mainly modern); rhododendrons and azaleas; good herbaceous borders; spring bulbs; summer bedding; tallest purple birch *Betula pendula* 'Purpurea' in the British Isles (and 10 other record trees); plants sales area; tea rooms; visitor centre

Owned by Vale of Glamorgan Council
Size 22ha (55 acres)

MARGAM COUNTRY PARK
Port Talbot SA13 2TJ

Tel 01639 881635 **Fax** 01639 895897
www.npt.gov.uk/margampark
Location Follow directions from M4, Jct 38
Opening hours 10am to 5pm, daily, March to September; closes at 4.30pm from October to February; opens at 1pm on Monday and Tuesday in winter
Admission fee Free; charge for car park

Margam is a popular country park with lots to interest the garden historian and plantsman. The setting is a 1,000-acre park with lakes, woodlands and herds of red, fallow and Père David deer – the best collection of deer in Wales. The 18th-century

orangery, for which Margam is famous, is said to be the longest in Europe, but there is also a fine Japanese garden, a collection of rare trees and rhododendrons (some grown from Kingdon Ward's seed) and cheerful bedding out. The mature trees here are especially impressive and include several large tulip trees, a cork oak and an enormous cut-leaved beech.
roses (mainly modern); fine collection of trees; bedding out; daffodils; rhododendrons; orangery; tallest bay tree *Laurus nobilis* (21m; 69ft) in the British Isles; gift shop; restaurant and light refreshments

Owned by Neath Port Talbot County Borough Council
Number of gardeners 4
Size 24ha (60 acres)

PLANTASIA
Parc Tawe, Swansea SA1 2AL

Tel 01792 474555 **Fax** 01792 652588
www.plantasia.org
Location Off main eastern approach to Swansea
Opening hours 10am to 5pm, daily, all year; closed on Mondays in December and January
Admission fee Adults £3.30; concessions £2.30

Plantasia is a large glasshouse with three climatic zones – arid, tropical and rainforest. Each is full with colourful exotic plants – palms, strelitzias, tree ferns, nepenthes, cacti and such economic plants as giant bamboos, bananas, coconuts and pineapples. The authorities say that some of the 5,000 plants represent species which are actually extinct in the wild. It is the perfect goal for a winter expedition, provided you like the insects, birds, monkeys and reptiles, as well as the flowers.
tropical and arid glasshouses; good collection of exotic plants; educational facilities; gift shop; coffee shop

Owned by City and County of Swansea
Number of gardeners 2
Size 0.4ha (1 acre)

SINGLETON PARK & SWANSEA BOTANICAL GARDENS
Oystermouth Road, Swansea SA2 8QD

Tel 01792 298637 **Fax** 01792 297394
www.swansea.gov.uk/botanics
Location Signed from main A4067 coast road, west of Swansea
Opening hours Daily, all year; closes at 6pm from Easter to July, 8pm in August and 4.30pm at other times
Admission fee Free

Singleton Park was once part of Lord Swansea's estate, but has been a public park since 1919. The Swansea Botanical Gardens are in the top end of the park, best entered from Sketty Road and through the green gates in the high wall. The spectacular herbaceous border inside the entrance, first planted in 1921, makes good use of seasonal bedding. Elsewhere are a rose terrace, a bog garden, a sunny herb garden (lots of Mediterranean plants), and display beds with collections of irises, dahlias, chrysanthemums, sweet peas, carnations, asters, delphiniums and penstemons. In the part known as the Ornamental Gardens are a rock garden, archery lawn and excellent rhododendron collection. The glasshouses are good, too: the Cactus House, the Temperate House, the Tropical House (orchids, bromeliads, epiphytes and tillandsias), and the Economics House (economic plants like sugar cane, olives, rice, coffee and coconut palms).
good herbaceous borders; interesting greenhouse plants

Owned by City and County of Swansea
Number of gardeners 7, plus 2 trainees
Size 4ha (10 acres)
NCCPG National Collections *Rhododendron* (part)

GWENT

PENPERGWM LODGE
Abergavenny NP7 9AS

Tel/fax 01873 840208
www.penplants.com
Location 3 miles from Abergavenny on B4598, opposite King of Prussia pub
Opening hours 2pm to 6pm, Thursday to Sunday, end of March to end of September
Admission fee Adults £3; children free; RHS members free

Catriona Boyle has developed the garden at Penpergwm over the last 20 years, based on the structure created when the house was built in Edwardian times – mature trees, open lawns, some formal areas and old hedges. She has added two exuberant terraces, each planted to a colour theme and linked by an Italianate parterre and a pillared vine-walk. There is also a new *Malus* avenue centred on the house. Recent developments include an octagonal brick Golden Jubilee folly and a new summerhouse at the top of the garden: both have excellent views. The pre-war kitchen garden has been completely overhauled with new terracing and a broad, central canal. The nursery has lots of home-propagated plants, mostly unusual herbaceous plants, bulbs, climbers and shrubs, but also half-hardy perennials which flower late into autumn. Specialities include *Aconitum*, euphorbias, cistus, clematis, loniceras, camassias, erythroniums, *Melianthus major* and salvias.
colour borders; good plants; nursery for unusual plants

Owned by Mrs C Boyle
Number of gardeners 1
Size 1.6ha (4 acres)

TREDEGAR HOUSE COUNTRY PARK
Newport NP10 8YW

Tel 01633 815880 **Fax** 01633 815895
Location M4, Jct 28
Opening hours Park: 9am to dusk, daily, all year
Admission fee Park and garden: free

Tredegar is one of the great historic houses of South Wales, with a park and gardens to match. Much was lost to neglect in the mid-20th century, but the new owners have restored the walled formal gardens, the sunken garden and the orangery with parterres and espaliered fruit trees.
modern parterres; amenity parkland; refreshments in season

Owned by Newport City Council
Number of gardeners 2
Size 8.7ha (22 acres)

GWYNEDD

BODYSGALLEN HALL
Llandudno LL30 1RS

Tel 01492 584466 **Fax** 01492 582519
www.bodysgallen.com
Location On right, off A470 to Llandudno
Opening hours Dawn to dusk, daily, all year
Admission fee Open only to hotel guests; children over 6 welcome

Bodysgallen Hall is a top hotel and the gardens live up to its high standards. They include a parterre divided into eight segments, an extremely busy kitchen garden, woodland walks, a cascade garden with a lily pond and white floribundas in the old walled garden. And it is handy for Bodnant, too.
woodland garden; roses (mainly old-fashioned); rock garden; herbs; fruit; knot garden; parterres; refreshments at hotel

Owned by Historic House Hotels Ltd
Number of gardeners 4
Size 87ha (220 acres), including parkland

CRÛG FARM PLANTS
Griffith's Crossing, Caernarfon LL55 1TU

Tel/Fax: 01248 670232
www.crug-farm.co.uk
Location 2 miles north-east of Caernarfon, off A487; follow signs to Bethel
Opening hours 10am to 5pm, Thursday to Sunday and Bank Holidays, 24 February to 29 September; garden open for NGS: 27 May; for Samaritans: 30 June; closed on Sundays and Bank Holidays from July to September
Admission fee Nursery free; garden £1.50 for NGS

Crûg Farm is unusual in specialising in plants for shade: perennials, shrubs and climbers. The range is extensive and interesting. The selection of hardy geraniums equals many specialists in the genera. The owners' collecting expeditions to Korea, Sikkim, Japan, China, Vietnam, Laos, the Philippines and Taiwan are making an impact on the gardens of many discerning plantsmen: new-to-science names a-plenty. The display garden and private garden are worth seeing when they are open for the National Gardens Scheme. There will be two RHS Special Events at Crûg Farm in 2007 (details from 020 7821 3408) and a plant fair in aid of the Welsh Historic Gardens Trust on 5 May.

Owned by Bleddyn and Sue Wynn-Jones
Number of gardeners 1
Size 1.2ha (3 acres)
NCCPG National Collections *Coriaria*; *Paris*; *Polygonatum*

PENRHYN CASTLE
Bangor LL57 4HN

Tel 01248 353084 **Fax** 01248 371281
www.nationaltrust.org.uk
Location 2 miles east of Bangor on A5122, signed from A55 to A5 junction
Opening hours Noon to 5pm, daily, except Tuesdays, 31 March to 4 November; open at 11am in July and August; last admissions 4.30pm
Admission fee Adults £5.40; children £2.70 (2006 prices)

Penrhyn is a neo-Norman castle with a distant walled garden of parterres and terraces merging into slopes of rhododendrons and camellias. There is much of dendrological interest (ancient conifers, holm oaks, champion eucryphias and naturalised arbutus trees) and a 'dinosaur landscape' of tree ferns, gunneras and aralias. The snowdrops are spectacular in February.
light lunches in licensed tea room

Owned by The National Trust
Number of gardeners 3
Size 19ha (47 acres)

PLAS BRONDANW GARDENS
Llanfrothen, Panrhyndeudraeth LL48 6SW

Tel 07880 766741
www.brondanw.org
Location On Croesor Road, off A4085
Opening hours 9am to 5pm, daily, all year
Admission fee Adults £3.50; children £1;
RHS members free

Plas Brondanw is the highly original and architectural Edwardian garden laid out by Sir Clough Williams-Ellis 17 years before he began Portmeirion, and now assiduously restored by his granddaughter Menna. It is one of the best-kept secrets in North Wales, full of slate stonework and such original design ideas as the arbour of four red-twigged limes. The garden rooms are inward-looking and almost cottagey in their planting, but the mountain peaks are ever present.
arts and crafts garden; topiary; follies

Owned by Trustees of the Second Portmeirion Foundation
Number of gardeners 2

PLAS NEWYDD
Llanfairpwll, Anglesey LL61 6DQ

Tel 01248 714795 **Fax** 01248 713673
www.nationaltrust.org.uk
Location 2 miles south-west of Llanfairpwll on A4080
Opening hours 11am to 5.30pm, Saturday to Wednesday, 31 March to 31 October
Admission fee Adults £4; children £2 (2006 prices)

Plas Newydd has a grand collection of rhododendrons (plus azaleas, magnolias and acers) within a Repton landscape on a spectacular site above the Menai Straits. Its many other horticultural attractions include an avenue of *Chamaecyparis pisifera* 'Squarrosa' running down to the sea, large plantings of hydrangeas for late colour and an arboretum of Australasian plants (lots of eucalyptus and nothofagus). Some of the rhododendrons came as a wedding present to Lord and Lady Anglesey from Lord Aberconway at Bodnant: many others followed. Many tender species are of considerable size, including a *R. montroseanum*, which is probably the largest in Britain. Late-flowering hybrids like 'Polar Bear' extend the season well into July. The fine Italianate garden below the house, with its 'hot and cold' borders, is 1920s – most surprising.
National Trust shop; tea room

Owned by The National Trust
Number of gardeners 4
Size 12.3ha (31 acres)

PLAS-YN-RHIW
Rhiw, Pwllheli LL53 8AB

Tel/Fax 01758 780219
www.nationaltrust.org.uk
Location 16 miles from Pwllheli; turn off B4413 at Botwnnog and follow signs along lanes and through village
Opening hours Noon to 5pm, Thursday to Monday, 5 April to 30 September; plus Wednesdays from 1 July to 31 August; also noon to 4pm, 1 to 28 October
Admission fee Adults £2.40; children £1.10; £1.70 for snowdrops in February (telephone for exact times and dates)

This pretty garden is small and fairly formal: it is divided into a series of rooms which are hedged with cherry laurel and bay to protect them from the sea gales. Box-edged parterres are filled with rambling roses and billowing cottage garden flowers. Tender trees and shrubs flourish in the mild coastal climate.
gift shop

Owned by The National Trust
Number of gardeners 1, plus 1 trainee
Size 0.4ha (1 acre)

PORTMEIRION
Penrhyndeudraeth LL48 6ET

Tel 01766 770000 **Fax** 01766 771331
www.portmeirion-village.com
Location Signed from A487 at Minffordd, between Penrhyndeudraeth and Porthmadog
Opening hours 9.30am to 5.30pm, daily, all year

Admission fee Adults £6.50; OAPs £5.20; children £3.50; RHS members free

(P) (toilets) (plants for sale)

Portmeirion is where the architect Sir Clough Williams-Ellis worked out his Italianate fantasies. The television series *The Prisoner* was filmed here. The gardens are carved out of a rhododendron woodland but are formal, with a mixture of Mediterranean plants and exotic palms, and full of architectural bric-a-brac of every period. Other attractions include tree ferns, gunneras, phormiums, ginkgos and holm oaks. Williams-Ellis began to lay out the garden at Portmeirion as soon as he made his first purchase of land along the coastline of north-west Wales in 1926. He bought up further estates in later years, by which he acquired one of the chief attractions of the gardens at Portmeirion today – the collection of rhododendrons and azaleas which is known as the Gwyllt Gardens. *Rhododendron arboreum* has grown to enormous size and in parts of the garden is still impenetrable. The peak display comes in May: the mainstay of late summer and autumn is thousands of hydrangeas throughout the Portmeirion estate. The gardens have been further developed in the last 20 years, taking advantage of the mild climate. One garden – almost at the furthest end of the estate and planted with a background of eucalyptus trees – is known as the 'ghost garden' because of the way the wind whistles in the leaves.

woodland garden; subtropical plants; rhododendrons and azaleas; giant yuccas; exuberant summer bedding; tallest *Maytenus boaria* (18m; 59ft) in the British Isles; several shops; refreshments; hotel

Owned by Portmeirion Ltd
Number of gardeners 11
Size 28ha (70 acres)

POWYS

ASHFORD HOUSE

Talybont-on-Usk, Brecon LD3 7YR

Tel 01874 676271
Location 1 mile east of Talybont along B4588
Opening hours 2pm to 6pm, Tuesdays, April to September; and by appointment (please telephone)
Admission fee Adults £2.50; children free

(P) (dogs) (toilets) (wheelchair) (plants for sale)

There are two parts to the garden at Ashford: both have been made by the Andersons. First there is the walled garden, about an acre in extent, with raised beds (lots of alpines), and a plantsman's collection of plants of every kind in fine mixed borders. Then there is the woodland garden, which has been underplanted with suitable shrubs, especially rhododendrons, camellias and bulbs.

alpines; woodland with rhododendrons; tea, coffee and biscuits

Owned by Mr and Mrs DA Anderson
Number of gardeners 1 part-time
Size 1.4ha (3½ acres)

THE DINGLE

Frochas, Welshpool SY21 9JD

Tel 01938 555145 **Fax** 01938 555778
www.dinglenurseries.co.uk
Location Turn left to Nurseries off A490 to Llanfyllin
Opening hours 9am (2pm on Tuesdays) to 5pm, daily, all year except Christmas week
Admission fee Adults £3; children free; RHS members free except during special events

(P) (dogs) (toilets) (wheelchair) (plants for sale)

This steep garden around a tranquil lake is attached to a successful nursery and is essentially a plantsman's private garden. It is mainly made up of unusual trees and shrubs, but it has some herbaceous plantings, too. The beds are put together with a carefully coordinated colour mixtures and designed to look good all through the year.

south-facing bank; pool; north-facing woodland garden; unusual trees and shrubs; first-rate nursery attached; light refreshments

Owned by Mr and Mrs D Hamer
Number of gardeners 1, plus owner
Size 1.6ha (4 acres)

GLANSEVERN GARDENS
Glansevern, Berriew, Welshpool SY21 8AH

Tel 01686 640644 **Fax** 01686 640829
www.glansevern.co.uk
Location On A483, 4 miles south-west of Welshpool
Opening hours Noon to 6pm, Thursday to Saturday and Bank Holiday Mondays, 3 May to 29 September; parties by appointment on any day of the week
Admission fee Adults £4; OAPs £3; children free

The handsome Greek-revival house at Glansevern sits in a landscaped park (1802), complete with its lake and water garden fed by innumerable streams. There is a vast 1840s rock garden which incorporates a spooky grotto. The 'Smoker's Walk' runs down through woodland to the banks of the River Severn with a circular folly perched on a promontory. Splendid Victorian conifers are everywhere, but it is the modern planting which really distinguishes Glansevern: island beds around the house, herbaceous borders on either side of the orangery and an acre of garden rooms in the walled gardens.
rock garden and grotto; roses (mainly modern); water garden; lake; good herbaceous borders; good trees; plants for sale; licensed café

Owned by Gerran and Meriel Thomas
Number of gardeners 3
Size 8ha (20 acres)

POWIS CASTLE & GARDEN
Welshpool SY21 8RF

Tel 01938 551920 **Fax** 01938 554336
www.nationaltrust.org.uk
Location 1 mile south of Welshpool off A483
Opening hours 11am to 6pm, Thursday to Monday, 1 April to 28 October; closes at 4.30pm after 17 September
Admission fee Adults £6.60; children £3.30 (2006 prices)

The hanging terraces draped with bulky overgrown yews and exuberant summer bedding are famous. If you visit Powis in summer or early autumn, you will be completely distracted by the rare and tender plants on the walls – they include Banksia roses, hoherias and a hefty *Acca sellowiana* – and by the containers brilliantly planted with annuals and tender plants. At other times it is the structure which impresses: the 17th-century terraces, lead statues, planters and clipped yews. The views are always a big draw, but especially when the rhododendrons and azaleas are in flower on the ridge opposite the castle. There is much wonderfully rich colour planting and in early autumn the maples colour the lower slopes, as does an Edwardian garden of roses and hollyhocks in summer. The aspect is south-east, so Powis is best seen in the morning light: photographers please note.
plant shop and gift shop; restaurant for light lunches and teas

Owned by The National Trust
Number of gardeners 8
Size 9.6ha (24 acres)
NCCPG National Collections *Aralia*; *Laburnum*

CHANNEL ISLANDS

GUERNSEY

SAUSMAREZ MANOR
St Martin GY4 6SG

Tel 01481 235571 **Fax** 01481 235572
www.sausmarezmanor.co.uk
Location Well signed, off main road between St Peter Port and St Martin
Opening hours Daily, 1 March to 23 December
Admission fee Adults £4.50; OAPs, students and children £3.50; RHS members free during first week of every month

The main attraction at Sausmarez is the extensive collection of sculptures of every sort displayed for sale in the grounds. Although there may be as many as 200 around at a time, they are never intrusive. There is a lot more to see in the garden, especially in the thick, woodland jungle around the lake – 50 different bamboos, eight species of palm, tree ferns, 320 camellias, giant echiums, tree fuchsias, hydrangeas, hedychiums, gunneras and *Geranium maderense*.

sculptures; tender plants; jungly woodland; café from Easter to October

Owned by Peter de Sausmarez
Number of gardeners 1
Size 0.5ha (1.2 acres)

JERSEY

ERIC YOUNG ORCHID FOUNDATION

Victoria Village, Trinity JE3 5HH

Tel 01534 861963 **Fax** 01534 865293
www.ericyoungorchidfoundation.co.uk
Location On the western edge of Victoria Village.
Opening hours 10am to 4pm, Wednesday to Saturday, all year
Admission fee Adults £3.50; OAPs £3; children £1

Eric Young was an amateur orchid-grower who left his fortune to endow this foundation, one of the best collections in the world. The purpose-built display house shows the richness and variety of orchids in all their beauty. The foundation is also an active breeder of new orchids, for which it regularly wins international awards. No visitor can fail to be captivated by the sheer variety of colours, shapes and forms of the orchids here, and excellence of the displays.
gift shop; hot and cold drinks

Owned by The Eric Young Orchid Foundation

JUDITH QUÉRÉE'S GARDEN

Creux Baillot Cottage, Le Chemin des Garennes, St Ouen JE3 2FE

Tel/fax 01534 482191
www.judithqueree.com
Location Directions given when bookings made
Opening hours Pre-booked guided tours only: 11am or 2pm, Tuesdays, Wednesdays and Thursdays, May to September
Admission fee £5, to include guided tour

Judith Quérée started her garden in 1977: seldom have such good design and so many plants been used together so effectively. It has a true plantsman's collection of rarities – collections of tender salvias, clematis and bog plants, for example – but cultivated with great skill and assembled with artistic sensibility. The design is full of decorative details, and structural innovation like the raised wooden walkway from which you view the bog garden. Every corner has something of interest at every season. Wildlife is respected, too. It is Jersey's most original modern garden: other gardeners on the island talk of it with nothing but reverence.
some unusual plants for sale

Owned by Judith and Nigel Quérée
Number of gardeners owners only
Size 0.4ha (1 acre)

NORTHERN IRELAND

The two best gardens in Northern Ireland are the 20th-century masterpieces – Mount Stewart and Rowallane. Both are primarily of horticultural interest and well maintained as major tourist attractions by the National Trust. It is a pity that so few people from Britain know them at first hand. Given good weather, they are among the most enchanting and extensive gardens anywhere in the British Isles – and especially lovely in late spring. Northern Ireland also has some fine historic landscapes dating back to the 18th century: Florence Court in Co. Fermanagh and Castle Ward in Co. Down are two that we list.

Many trees and shrubs flourish in the mild, damp climate of Co. Down and Co. Antrim. The National Arboretum at Castlewellan has a very fine collection of mature trees: 34 of them are record-breakers. Nevertheless, it is fair to say that gardening and garden visiting are not such popular activities in Northern Ireland as on the mainland of the United Kingdom. Prices reflect this: the cost of admission to National Trust properties in Northern Ireland is substantially less than one would pay to visit a garden of equivalent quality in England.

The most comprehensive list of historic parks, gardens and demesnes in Northern Ireland was written by Belinda Jupp and published in 1992 as *The Heritage Gardens Survey*. The Northern Ireland Gardens Committee is keen to complete a more formal register.

The Ulster Gardens Scheme raises funds every year for work in National Trust gardens which would not otherwise be possible. The scheme is run by the Northern Ireland region of the National Trust at Rowallane. The gardens tend to be small and private ones made by the present owners: the Ulster Gardens Scheme also issues a second list of gardens that are open only for group visits by appointment.

Northern Ireland has a few gardening clubs and societies of its own: there is, for example, the Northern Ireland Daffodil Group and the Rose Society of Northern Ireland. Daffodils have for long been a Northern Irish speciality: Brian Duncan and Carncairn Daffodils are two of the world's leading breeders, and their owners follow in the footsteps of other great Ulster daffodil men like Sir Frank Harrison and Guy Wilson. Roses are very popular: the roses in the Sir Thomas & Lady Dixon Park in south Belfast are a great draw in summer and the Dickson rose nursery – now mainly wholesale – has been at Newtownards for over 100 years. Since the closure of the Slieve Donard nursery, there has been no outstanding plantsman's nursery in Northern Ireland, though Gary Dunlop at Ballyrogan comes close to it, and Patrick Ford at Seaforde is a particularly good source of rare trees and shrubs. There are seven National Collections in Northern Ireland, most of them held by corporate owners like the National Trust.

Northern Ireland's only horticultural college is Greenmount College of Agriculture & Horticulture in Co. Antrim, which is a RHS Partner College. RHS members also have free access to a number of gardens in Northern Ireland during the summer, most notably Benvarden Garden and Carnfunnock Country Park in Co. Antrim. And Garden Show Ireland is fast becoming the leading horticultural event in the whole island; it takes place at Hillsborough Castle in Belfast from 8 to 10 June.

ANTRIM

BENVARDEN GARDEN & GROUNDS

Benvarden, Dervock, Ballymoney BT53 6NN

Tel 028 2074 1331 **Fax** 028 2074 1955
www.benvarden.com
Location Follow brown tourist signs on B67 Coleraine to Ballycastle road; 8 miles from Giants Causeway
Opening hours Noon to 5.30pm, Tuesday to Sunday and Bank Holiday Mondays, June to September; and by appointment
Admission fee Adults £3.50; children free; RHS members free from June to August

The main feature of the two-acre walled garden is a spectacular curved red brick wall, nearly 4m (13ft) high, dating from approximately 1780. Around the walls are espalier-trained apple and pear trees. Other features include a splendid rose garden, several herbaceous borders, a new box parterre, and a fully working kitchen garden. There are also walks around a small lake, planted with rhododendrons, azaleas, magnolias and fine trees. A splendid cast-iron bridge, 35m (120ft) long and built in 1870, spans the River Bush.
roses; herbaceous plants; kitchen garden; rhododendrons and azaleas; tea room

Owned by Mr and Mrs Hugh Montgomery
Number of gardeners 2
Size 2ha (5 acres)

CARNFUNNOCK COUNTRY PARK

Drains Bay, Coast Road, Larne BT40 2QG

Tel 028 2827 0541 **Fax** 028 2827 0852
www.larne.gov.uk/carnfunnock.html
Location On Antrim coast road (A2), 31/2 miles north of Larne
Opening hours 9am to dusk (9pm in summer), daily, all year; closed 1 January and 25 December
Admission fee Parking fees apply; free for RHS members in July and August

The walled garden is set within Carnfunnock Country Park on the Antrim coast, an Area of Outstanding Natural Beauty. It was originally the cottage garden of Cairncastle Lodge, until purchased by Sir Thomas and Lady Dixon, who owned the neighbouring Cairndhu Estate. The gardens contain a wide collection of plants from all over the world and enjoy a microclimate which allows plants such as eucalyptus to flourish. The gardens are themed to include a flower garden, butterfly garden, scented walkway, herbaceous border, heather garden, rock garden and water garden. They also boast an amphitheatre, while one of the central features to the walled garden is a unique collection of sundials tracing the history of time. The park has a hornbeam maze in the shape of Northern Ireland. The new (2006) biodiversity trail features a bog garden, giant bird tables and woodland and wildflower areas.
rhododendrons and azaleas; tender plants; coffee shop (Easter to September)

Owned by Larne Borough Council
Number of gardeners 3
Size 0.6ha (11/2 acres) garden, 190ha (473 acres) park

DERRY

GUY WILSON DAFFODIL GARDEN

University of Ulster, Coleraine BT52 1SA

Tel 028 7034 4141
Location Signed from sports centre, or entry via Portstewart Road
Opening hours Dawn to dusk, daily, all year; peak flowering time mid-March to mid-April
Admission fee Free

The name says it all – this is both a celebration of Guy Wilson as a daffodil breeder and a museum of his hybrids. Drifts of his cultivars, and others of Irish raising, sweep through the university gardens – more than 1,800 cultivars. Best in April.
exceptional collection of daffodils, best in second half of April

Owned by The University of Ulster at Coleraine
NCCPG National Collections *Narcissus*

DOWN

ANNESLEY GARDENS & CASTLEWELLAN NATIONAL ARBORETUM

Castlewellan BT31 9BU

Tel 028 4377 8664 **Fax** 028 4377 1762
www.forestserviceni.gov.uk/arboretum.htm
Location 30 miles south of Belfast, 4 miles west of Newcastle
Opening hours 9am to dusk, daily, all year
Admission fee £4 per car

Castlewellan means trees: 18 oldest existing specimens in the British Isles, 49 champion trees of the British Isles and 86 champion trees of Ireland. The heart of the collection is in a 12-acre walled garden, interplanted with rhododendrons and other shrubs. The central path has mixed borders at the top: dwarf rhododendrons are prominent even here. Much has been restored in recent years: the two fountains have been repaired and lost views of the Mountains of Mourne re-opened. Labelling is good, both here and in the adjoining six-acre woodland garden, and the standard of maintenance high. In the Forest Park is the newly-planted 'Peace Maze' which represents the journey to peace in Northern Ireland. It is certified by *The Guinness Book of Records* as the longest and largest hedge maze in the world.

woodland garden; mature conifers; fine collection of trees; autumn colours; embothriums; eucryphias; tallest *Chamaecyparis nootkatensis* 'Lutea' (22m; 72ft) in the British Isles, plus 33 other tree records; new 'fragrant garden' around a Lutyensesque tea house; light refreshments at peak times

Owned by Dept of Agriculture and Rural Development, Forest Service
Number of gardeners 3
Size 40ha (100 acres)

CASTLE WARD

Strangford, Downpatrick BT30 7LS

Tel 028 4488 1204 **Fax** 028 4488 1729
www.ntni.org.uk
Location On A25, 7 miles from Downpatrick and 1/2 miles from Strangford
Opening hours 10am to 4pm (8pm from April to September), daily, all year
Admission fee Adults £4.50; children £2; families £10.50

It is the position of the house at Castle Ward which makes it so special – set among rolling parkland with stupendous views across Strangford Lough – while the house itself intrigues the visitor by having one façade in the Georgian style and the other in the Gothic. There are fine trees in the

Castlewellan National Arboretum

MOUNT STEWART

Grey Abbey, Newtownards BT22 2AD

Tel 028 4278 8387 **Fax** 028 4278 8569
www.nationaltrust.org.uk
Location East of Belfast on A20
Opening hours Lakeside gardens and walks: 10am to sunset, daily, all year; formal gardens: 10am to 8pm, daily, 10, 11, 17, 18, 24, 25 March, then from 31 March to 31 October; gardens close at 4pm in March and 6pm in April and October
Admission fee Adults £5; children £2.50; families £12.50

Mount Stewart is the greatest garden in Northern Ireland – arguably in all Ireland. There are two factors which have made this possible: the exceptional climate, which allows plants to thrive that would not survive in all but the mildest parts of the British Isles; and the willingness of the garden's principal maker, Edith, Marchioness of Londonderry, to spend money on a large scale on design, plants and staff. The formal garden in front of the house is grandly laid out with all manner of inventive details: best known are the stone carvings of animals, known as the 'dodo terrace'. Beyond the formal garden is a sunken Spanish garden and off to one side is the shamrock garden, where a bed designed by Lady Londonderry to represent the Red Hand of Ulster has been surrounded in these more politically correct times by a green shamrock. The rare plants begin on the walls of the house itself: *Rosa gigantea* covers a large area and there are huge plants of *Magnolia grandiflora*. Nearby are the wonderfully-flowing beds of the lily wood where exotic myrtles, pittosporums and phormiums are underplanted with primulas, cyclamen, narcissi and lilies, but here – as in every part of the garden – one is never far from amazing large-leaved rhododendrons, cordylines and tree ferns. Better still is the walk around the lake, where rhododendrons flood the woodlands: for many visitors in spring it is the highlight of a tour of Mount Stewart. The views across the lake are dominated by the mausoleum and the exceptional collection of rhododendrons is interplanted with rare shrubs like mimosas, clianthus, prostantheras, pittosporums and grevilleas. They are underplanted in places with meconopsis and candelabra primulas and, at one point, you catch a glimpse of a white stag in a glade. The outstanding area is the Jubilee Glade where plants in shades of red, white and blue provide colour all through the year. For design, variety, plants and plantings, Mount Stewart is a place of miracles. Allow lots of time for your visit.

Owned by The National Trust
Number of gardeners 8, plus volunteers
Size 31ha (77 acres)
NCCPG National Collections *Phormium*; *Dianella*; *Libertia*

ROWALLANE GARDEN

Saintfield, Ballynahinch BT24 7LH

Tel 028 9751 0131 **Fax** 028 9751 1242
www.nationaltrust.org.uk
Location 1 mile south of Saintfield on A7
Opening hours 10am to 8pm (4pm from 17 September to 11 April 2008), daily, all year; closed 1 January, 25 and 26 December
Admission fee Adults £4.50; children £2

The extensive gardens at Rowallane can be dated back to 1903, when Hugh Armytage Moore inherited the estate from his uncle, John Moore. Uncle John had planted some of the larger trees – wellingtonias, beeches and rhododendrons – but everything else you see today dates from the 20th century. Hugh Armytage Moore was a great plantsman – not just a collector of horticultural curiosities, but a selector of good forms. As his appetite for plants grew, so the garden expanded into the little fields which pattern the estate. The seedlings grew and needed to be planted. The hedges and walls which surround these enclosures remain as the boundary features of each compartment, so that you still have the impression of walking from field to field although each is thickly planted with ornamental trees and shrubs. Moore subscribed to the plant-collecting expeditions of EH Wilson and Frank Kingdon Ward. It is to those expeditions that the vast collection of rhododendrons owes its origins. No garden can match it on a sunny day in April or May, as you amble from a glade of *R. augustinii* forms to a line of *R. maccabeanum* or back through *R. yakushimanum* hybrids: the large-leaved species are particularly prominent. Because of the mild climate, many other good plants flourish here which are rare elsewhere – *Lomatia ferruginea*, *Grevillea rosmarinifolia* and *Nothofagus cunninghamii*, for example. Rowallane has also given us some good garden hybrids (eg *Hypericum* 'Rowallane') and selected forms (eg *Viburnum plicatum* 'Rowallane'). Another notable feature is the rock garden – an outcrop of natural whinstone rock which actually has few plants growing in it, but many around the base of the boulders, including the striking candelabra primula 'Rowallane Rose'. And the walled garden, too, is a treasure-house of rare plants, including the National Collection of *Penstemon* species, which gives colour long after the rhododendrons have faded. But it is still the rhododendrons and azaleas for which the garden is best remembered.

tallest *Cupressus duclouxiana* (14m; 46ft) in the British Isles and three other record trees; light refreshments

Owned by The National Trust
Number of gardeners 5, plus volunteers
Size 21ha (52 acres)
NCCPG National Collections *Penstemon*

park, including embothriums and an avenue of ancient limes. In the walled garden are stately cordylines, dwarf palms, pittosporums and the rare *Mitraria coccinea*. Elsewhere are yew terraces, a Victorian rock garden, a pinetum, and Temple Water, which is claimed to be Ireland's largest ornamental garden feature, dating from 300 years ago.
shop; tea room

Owned by The National Trust
Number of gardeners 1, plus volunteers
Size 16ha (40 acres), plus 334ha (840 acres) of parkland

SEAFORDE GARDENS
Seaforde, Downpatrick BT30 8PG

Tel 028 4481 1225 **Fax** 028 4481 1370
www.seafordegardens.com
Location Between Belfast and Newcastle
Opening hours 10am to 5pm, Monday to Saturday; 1pm to 6pm, Sundays, mid-March to late October; plus weekdays in winter
Admission fee Adults £3; children £2

Seaforde is a leading nursery for trees and shrubs, including Irish specialities (*Eucryphia* x *intermedia* 'Rostrevor') and tender taxa. The list now includes a growing number of rhododendrons grown from Patrick Forde's own collecting expeditions to Bhutan, Yunnan, Tibet and Vietnam. The gardens – open all year – are extensive and important: they have drifts of primulas, camassias and bluebells, as well as both pink forms of *Eucryphia lucida* and a hornbeam maze. In the tropical butterfly house is a fascinating collection of tree ferns.
rare trees; eucryphias; lots of interesting plants; tea rooms

Owned by Patrick Forde
Number of gardeners 2
Size 2ha (5 acres)
NCCPG National Collections *Eucryphia*

FERMANAGH

FLORENCE COURT
Enniskillen BT92 1DB

Tel 028 6634 8249 **Fax** 028 6634 8873
www.nationaltrust.org.uk
Location 8 miles south-west of Enniskillen
Opening hours Grounds: 10am to 8pm (4pm from October to March), daily, all year
Admission fee £3.50 per car; £16.50 per minibus; £22 per coach

Florence Court has an 18th-century parkland, with superb views of the surrounding mountains (Benaughlin and Cuilcagh) and some magnificent trees. These include the original 'Irish Yew' (*Taxus baccata* 'Fastigiata') in the adjoining Forest Park and many specimens of a beautiful form of weeping beech with a broad curving crown. The rhododendrons are, for the most part, huge ancient hybrids of *R. arboreum*, but there has been much new planting in recent years and the horticultural interest is now considerable. The roses in the walled garden are especially attractive.
National Trust shop; light lunches and teas; picnickers welcome

Owned by The National Trust
Number of gardeners 1, plus volunteers
Size 6.4ha (16 acres)

REPUBLIC OF IRELAND

Until quite recently, gardens were widely thought of in Ireland as part of the culture of the Anglo-Irish: real Irishmen possessed neither the resources nor the cultural points of reference to occupy themselves with horticulture. There was a grain of truth in this: one of the consequences of the Troubles and the land reforms has been the disappearance of many of the historic gardens, parks and demesnes that accompanied the houses of the landed gentry. It is a problem of which the Irish are acutely aware and where such groups as the Irish Georgian Society have done much to change people's perceptions. The remarkable new wealth and confidence that Ireland has found within the European Union have helped to dispel the notion that gardens are yet another manifestation of British superiority: now they are seen as something that the Irish can seize upon and adapt to their own cultural styles, traditions, needs and conditions.

The old order is still there, of course. Most of the big gardens attached to big houses and open to the public date back to the 19th century – examples are Lismore, Derreen, Tullynally and Powerscourt. But a number were also made in the middle of the 20th century, often with English pounds (Birr and Malahide) or American dollars (Glenveagh and Mount Congreve). And the best modern gardens in Ireland have most certainly been made by Irishmen.

Ireland is well supplied with garden centres, but has few specialist nurseries. Good garden plants are more difficult to come by. Irish gardeners sometimes say that their best herbaceous plants tend to come from Britain and are then more widely distributed through an informal system of gifting. The NCCPG is represented by the Irish Garden Plant Society: there are only three National Collections in the country – Garrya and *Potentilla fruticosa* (cvs.) at National Botanic Gardens, Glasnevin, and Olearia in the care of Fingal County Council at Malahide Castle. It is also to be hoped that the new Irish interest in gardening will benefit the Royal Horticultural Society of Ireland, whose 'Royal' title hints at its ties to the United Kingdom, but which has fewer than 2,000 members.

Garden restoration is a growth industry in Ireland today. During the last 10 years the Heritage Service has helped to rescue the Lutyens gardens at Heywood in Co. Laois and taken over the administration of Fota. Private enterprise has come to the rescue of other gardens: Nicholas and Susan Mosse have made a grand job of restoring the romantic landscape garden at Kilfane in Co. Kilkenny while Benedictine nuns have started to restore the high Victorian gardens at Kylemore Abbey in Connemara. But perhaps the greatest measure of the popularity of gardening in Ireland today is the success of Helen Dillon as a garden owner, horticultural guru and media star – a success that is very well deserved, for her Dublin garden is an inspiration and her ability to communicate by the written and spoken word is legendary.

CARLOW

ALTAMONT GARDEN
Altamont, Tullow

Tel 00 353 059 91 59444 **Fax** 00 353 059 91 59510
www.heritageireland.ie
Location Signed from N80 and N81
Opening hours All year; phone for opening times
Admission fee Adults €2.90; OAPs €2.10; children €1.30

Altamont is a charming and romantic woodland garden, full of rare plants, together with lakes, islands, a bog garden and a shady glen. A new double herbaceous border, 75m (246ft) long within the walled garden, was opened in 2000 with a plant sales area next to it. The woodland garden is a place of contemplation and wonder, and very olde worlde Irish.
woodland garden; rhododendrons and azaleas; cyclamen; plant centre

Owned by Office of Public Works
Number of gardeners 4, plus students
Size 16ha (40 acres)

CORK

ANNES GROVE GARDENS
Castletownroche, Mallow

Tel/fax 00 353 22 26145
www.annesgrovegardens.com
Location 1½km north of Castletownroche on N72
Opening hours 10am to 5pm, Monday to Saturday; 1pm to 6pm, Sundays, mid-March to 30 September
Admission fee Adults €6; OAPs and students €4; children €2

Annes Grove has long been famous for its 30-acre garden, begun in 1907: 'Robinsonian' is the word most often used to describe it. The walled garden is a flower garden, with a 17th-century mount and a Victorian Gothic summerhouse on top. The river garden is lushly wild with lysichiton, gunnera and candelabra primulas around the pools. In the glen garden lies a wonderfully dense collection of rhododendrons and azaleas, many from Kingdon Ward's seed.
woodland garden; plantsman's collection of plants; good herbaceous borders; rhododendrons from wild seeds; rare trees; tallest *Azara microphylla* (11m; 36ft) in the British Isles

Owned by Patrick Annesley
Number of gardeners 4
Size 12ha (30 acres)

BALLYMALOE COOKERY SCHOOL GARDEN
Ballymaloe, Shanagarry

Tel 00 353 21 4646785 **Fax** 00 353 21 4646909
www.cookingisfun.ie
Location Signed from Castlemartyr and Shanagarry
Opening hours 10am to 6pm, daily, 1 April to 1 October
Admission fee Adults €5; OAPs €2.50; children €2.50

The garden attached to the famous Ballymaloe Cookery School is full of unusual fruit, vegetables and herbs. Seldom is a functional garden so stylishly designed and planted, or so extensive. And it is organic.
vegetables; roses (mainly old-fashioned); fruit; good herbaceous borders; magnificent formal parterres for herbs; Celtic maze; shell house; garden shop

Owned by Tim and Darina Allen
Number of gardeners 6
Size 1.2ha (3 acres)

BANTRY HOUSE & GARDENS
Bantry

Tel 00 353 27 50047 **Fax** 00 353 27 50795
www.bantryhouse.com

Location Well-signed on main road into Bantry town
Opening hours 10am to 6pm; daily; March to October
Admission fee Adults €5; children free

Bantry house is a most elegant Georgian mansion in a glorious position at the water's edge. The gardens were laid out by the 2nd Earl of Bantry in the 1840s in the Italian style, creating no fewer than seven terraces up the hillside and filling them with urns, statues and classical pieces. Among the best features are a circular pergola hung with wisteria and the staircase known as the Hundred Steps, surrounded by rhododendrons and azaleas. The present owners have been restoring and remaking the gardens since 1997 and the results are astonishing.
wisteria circle; fine *Gingko biloba*; trachycarpus palms; tea room

Owned by Egerton and Brigitte Shelswell-White
Number of gardeners 2 full-time, plus 3 seasonal
Size 8ha (20 acres)

FOTA ARBORETUM & GARDEN
Fota Estate, Carrigtwohill

Tel/fax 00 353 21 4812728
www.fotahouse.com
Location 22km from Cork city; take N25 eastbound and turn off for Cobh (R624)
Opening hours Arboretum: 9am to 6pm (5pm from November to March), daily, all year; walled gardens: 9am to 6pm, Monday to Friday, April to October; plus some Sundays (ring for times and dates); closed for Christmas holidays; tours by prior appointment; ring 00 353 87 7907299.
Admission fee Free; cars €2

Fota is famous above all for its trees, most of them planted by the Smith-Barry family towards the end of the 19th century. As well as a fine collection of Victorian conifers (huge redwoods and wellingtonias), the garden and arboretum are notable for the collection of flowering mimosas (*Acacia*), a beautiful *Styrax japonica*, a magnificent collection of mature magnolias, and a spectacular specimen of *Phoenix canariensis* which was planted out over 100 years ago. Some of the record-breaking trees have been lost in recent years, but many of Fota's very rare trees still survive, including *Dacrycarpus dacrydioides* and *Phyllocladus trichomanoides*. The garden and arboretum were transferred to the State in 1996 and have since undergone much restoration, regeneration and improvement. New plants have been added, often as part of international conservation programmes. The old walled kitchen garden has been converted to a formal rose garden, with themed borders of monocots, shade-loving and South American plants, a large selection of climbers on the walls, and a collection of Irish-bred daffodils. The Victorian orangery was restored in 2000 and displays a fine collection of contemporary plants. The original formal gardens, known as the 'pleasure gardens', have also been made good – especially the Italian garden.
woodland garden; mature conifers; 160 Irish-bred daffodil cultivars

Owned by Office of Public Works
Number of gardeners 5
Size 11ha (27 acres)

HILLSIDE
Annmount, Glounthane

Tel/fax 00 353 21 4353119
www.hillsidegardens.org
Location From Cork, turn left at Glounthane Church, up hill, under bridge, 100m on right
Opening hours By appointment between May and September
Admission fee €5

This is an intensely cultivated plantsman's garden in a setting of mature trees (beech and pines) and rhododendrons, azaleas, pieris and woodland plants. It burgeons with alpine plants in every part – stone troughs, a scree bed and gravel areas. It also won the 'Top Garden in Ireland' award in 1996 and 2000 for its all-season attractions. And it is forever changing and improving – 2007 sees a new gravel garden in the old orchard.
rhododendrons and azaleas; plantsman's collection of plants; alpine plants; woodland plants

Owned by Mrs Mary Byrne
Number of gardeners owner only
Size 1.6ha (4 acres)

ILNACULLIN

Garinish Island, Glengariff, Bantry

Tel 00 353 276 3040 **Fax** 00 353 276 3149
Location 1½ km by boat from Glengariff
Opening hours 10am to 6.30pm, Monday to Saturday, March to October; opens at 9.30am in July and August, closes at 4.30pm in March and October; plus 11am to 6.30pm on Sundays (1pm to 5pm in March and October; 1pm to 6.30pm in April)
Admission fee Adults €3.70; plus boat fare (€10-12 return)

Ilnacullin is famous for its *casita*, a pavilion built by Harold Peto in 1910. It looks over an Italianate pool lined with Japanese bonsai in elegant pots. Elsewhere are a Grecian temple, a genuine Martello tower and a woodland of exotic trees and shrubs known as Happy Valley. Tree ferns, dacrydiums, and *Schima wallichii* subsp. *wallichii* var. *khasiana* are some of the best-known plants. The scent of *Rhododendron fragrantissimum* pervades the whole island in spring.
coffee shop

Owned by Heritage Ireland
Size 15ha (37 acres)

LAKEMOUNT

Barnavara Hill, Glanmire

Tel/fax 00 353 21 4821052
www.lakemountgarden.com
Location R639 from Cork through Glanmire village and left up the hill
Opening hours By appointment
Admission fee By arrangement

This modern garden has been made by the Cross family over the last 50 years, protected from southerly gales by hedges and windbreaks. The mild climate permits the cultivation of many tender plants. The rhododendrons, camellias, azaleas and hydrangeas are especially good, but they are underplanted by a great number of different plants, including hellebores, ferns and bulbs. Much thought is given to growing the best forms and associating them together for contrasts and harmony of colour and shape. There is much here to admire, enjoy and learn from.
refreshments by arrangement

Owned by Brian and Rose Cross
Number of gardeners owners only
Size 1ha (2½ acres)

DONEGAL

ARDNAMONA
Lough Eske

Tel 00 353 74 97 22650 **Fax** 00 353 74 97 22819
www.ardnamona.com
Location On Lough Eske, 8km north-east of Donegal
Opening hours 10am to 5pm, daily, all year
Admission fee Adults €5; children free

Ⓟ

Ardnamona is a masterpiece of huge arborescent rhododendrons, some as much as 20m (66ft) high, like a Himalayan forest on the lower slopes of the Blue Stack Mountains. A few date back to the introductions of Sir Joseph Hooker in the 1860s. Others were brought by Sir Arthur Wallace as seeds or cuttings from the imperial gardens in Peking and the palace gardens in Kathmandu. All are covered in moss and ferns that revel in the soft climate. Rocky outcrops add to the sense of awesome wilderness, but reclamation and replanting are well underway: the owners have made a big impact on the 40 acres of *Rhododendron ponticum*.
woodland garden; mature conifers; ancient rhododendrons; B&B offered

Owned by Mr and Mrs Kieran Clarke
Number of gardeners 1
Size 16ha (40 acres)

GLENVEAGH CASTLE
Churchill, Letterkenny

Tel 00 353 74 9137090 **Fax** 00 353 74 9137072
www.heritageireland.ie
Location 22km north-west of Letterkenny on R251
Opening hours 10am to 6.30pm, daily, February to early November
Admission fee Free; shuttle bus to garden €2

Ⓟ

Glenveagh was built for its view down the rocky slopes of Lough Veagh: nowhere in Ireland can boast such a contrast between the wild and rugged landscape of a National Park and its carefully nurtured gardens. Part of the gardens is known as the View Garden. Elsewhere is a series of outdoor rooms, each with a different character. The two-acre lawn in the Pleasure Grounds is fringed with rhododendron shrubberies, tree ferns and eucryphias, with massed underplantings of hostas, rodgersias and astilbes. Within the oak woods grow scented rhododendrons, rare trees and tender shrubs: Jim Russell advised on the planting. Paths lead to terraced enclosures furnished with Italian statuary and massive terracotta pots. The unusual shrubs are magnificent: tree-like griselinias and *Michelia doltsopa*, for instance. The *Jardin Potager* is bounded by herbaceous borders and planted with heritage vegetables, Irish apple cultivars and the rare *Dahlia* 'Matt Armour'. Prepare for a long and fascinating visit.
subtropical plants; roses (mainly old-fashioned); plantsman's collection of plants; Italianate features; fine collection of trees; restaurant at visitor centre; tea room at castle

Owned by The Heritage Service
Number of gardeners 4
Size 11ha (27 acres)

DUBLIN

ARDGILLAN PARK
Balbriggan

Tel 00 353 1 890 5629 **Fax** 00 353 1 890 5649
www.fingalcoco.ie/LeisureandTourism
Location Off coast road between Skerries and Balbriggan in Co. Dublin; signed from N1/M1
Opening hours 10am to dusk, daily, all year; guided tours of the walled garden: Thursdays at 3pm (€4); groups by appointment only
Admission fee Free

Ardgillan is a large country house with castellated embellishments, first built in 1738. The original gardens were almost lost, but restored by the council and opened to the public as a Regional Park in 1985. To the west of the house are the formal rose gardens, where modern roses are planted in the traditional way with one cultivar per bed. Climbing roses on rope swags run down the central avenue. The Victorian conservatory at the end has also been restored: it was originally constructed at Malahide in the 1880s by the Scottish firm McKenzie & Moncur. Nearby, the shrubby *Potentilla* collection is beautifully displayed for learning. The formal walled garden has been restored to its layout on the Ordnance Survey map of 1865. Four demonstration areas are devoted to herbs, vegetables, fruit (trained trees and soft fruit) and flowers. Along the walls are many interesting tender shrubs – crinodendrons, clianthus and huge echiums. And everywhere at Ardgillan you will find very high levels of horticultural interest and a good standard of maintenance.
roses (ancient and modern); potentillas (nearly 200 cvs.); walled garden; herb garden; *potager*; good herbaceous borders; ice house; 200-year-old yew walk; Victorian conservatory; tea rooms (closed on Mondays)

Owned by Fingal County Council
Number of gardeners 1
Size 1.6ha (4 acres)
NCCPG National Collections *Potentilla* (shrubby)

THE DILLON GARDEN
Ranelagh, Dublin 6

Tel/fax 00 353 1 4971308
www.dillongarden.com
Location 45 Sandford Road (behind trees, near junction of Sandford Road and Marlborough Road)
Opening hours 2pm to 6pm, daily, March, July and August; 2pm to 6pm, Sundays, April to June, and September; groups by appointment
Admission fee Adults €5

This much acclaimed plantsman's garden offers a fantastic range of rarities, from snowdrops and hellebores in spring, to tropaeolums in autumn. Unlike some collectors' gardens, Helen Dillon's is immaculately maintained, strictly planted according to colour and beautifully designed as a series of garden rooms whose design and decoration are constantly changing. In 2000, she replaced the main lawn with a canal with formal beds and small cascades set in limestone paving. In 2003, she took out the second lawn. In 2005, the front garden was completely renewed. Last year, after 25 years, she 'sent the red border to the great compost heap in the sky'; expect something new for 2007. This must be the most intensively gardened garden in the British Isles – a source of constant admiration and inspiration.
plantsman's collection of plants; excellent design; good herbaceous borders

Owned by Helen and Val Dillon
Number of gardeners 1
Size 0.2ha (1/2 acre)

FERNHILL
Sandyford, Dublin 18

Location 10km south of central Dublin on R117 Enniskerry road, between Lambs Cross and Stepaside
Opening hours 11am to 5pm (2pm to 5pm on Sundays), Tuesday to Sunday, and Bank Holidays, all year
Admission fee Adults €5; OAPs €4; children €2; RHS members €4

P 👪 ❁

This popular garden on the outskirts of Dublin has a good collection of rhododendrons and other woodland plants, and some magnificent trees 150 years old. There are steep woodland walks, an enclosed 19th-century garden.
woodland garden; rock garden; good herbaceous borders; fine collection of trees; sculpture exhibitions; rhododendrons; new fern plantings

Owned by Mrs Sally Walker
Number of gardeners 2
Size 16ha (40 acres)

NATIONAL BOTANIC GARDENS

Glasnevin, Dublin 9

Tel 00 353 1 804 0300 **Fax** 00 353 1 836 0080
www.botanicgardens.ie
Location 5km north of city centre between N1 and N2: from M 50 at Jct X or Y
Opening hours 9am to 6pm (10am to 4.30pm from 28 October to 3 February 2008); daily, except 25 December; open at 10am on Sundays
Admission fee Free

P 👪 ♿

Glasnevin was founded in 1795 to promote a scientific approach to the practice of agriculture: education remains a priority at the gardens which have a flourishing school of horticulture. The design of the botanic gardens is classically Victorian, laid out as a beautiful public park in undulating ground on the south bank of the River Tolka: plants are comprehensively documented, labelled and classified. Notable trees include a magnificent *Zelkova carpinifolia* near the new Herbarium building, good specimens of *Tetradium daniellii*, *Gymnocladus dioica* and *Davidia involucrata* and notable plants of a prostrate form of maidenhair tree (*Ginkgo biloba*) and the weeping Atlantic cedar (*Cedrus atlantica* 'Pendula'). Recent years have seen a dramatic programme of restoration and renewal. The elegant curvilinear range of glasshouses, built by Richard Turner between 1843 and 1868, has been magnificently restored. It has – among many tropical plants – a good collection of cycads. The great palm house (1882) has just been restored, too; its collection is very strong on tropical plants from Central America. The borders around the cactus and fern houses are planted with arum lilies and white watsonias – each have extensive collections, including a 400-year-old tree fern presented by the Melbourne Botanic Garden in the 1890s. The gardens are a focal point for horticulture and plant conservation in Ireland. New education and visitor facilities have recently been added and it remains the finest collection of plants in Ireland. Allow a full day to do justice to the garden and its attractions.
large collection of trees including conifers; plant families collection; rock garden and alpine yard; rose garden; vegetable garden; native plants; arboretum; herbaceous borders; seasonal bedding and displays; serpentine pond and heather garden; four ranges of public glasshouses; tropical water lilies; succulents; tender conifers and cycads; Vireya rhododendrons; house plants; palms; orchids; tallest variegated Plane tree *Platanus*; *hispanica* 'Suttneri' (21m; 69ft) in the British Isles, plus 25 other tree records; tea rooms

Owned by Office of Public Works
Number of gardeners 40
Size 20ha (50 acres)
NCCPG National Collections *Garrya*

PRIMROSE HILL

Primrose Lane, Lucan

Tel 00 353 1 6280373
Location Lucan village, at top of Primrose Lane, through black iron gates
Opening hours 2pm to 6pm, daily, February, then June to the beginning of August; and by appointment
Admission fee Adults €5; children €2

P 👪 ❁

Primrose Hill is a plantsman's garden, particularly interesting for its rare forms of herbaceous plants and its snowdrops. The planting continues, and includes a small arboretum, but this is a garden which gets better every year.
snowdrops; plantsman's collection of plants; good herbaceous borders

Owned by Robin Hall
Number of gardeners owner only
Size 2.4ha (6 acres)

TALBOT BOTANIC GARDENS
Malahide Castle, Malahide

Tel 00 353 1 8462456 **Fax** 00 353 1 8463620
www.fingalcoco.ie/LeisureandTourism
Location 16km north of Dublin off R107 Malahide road
Opening hours 2pm to 5pm (or by appointment), daily, May to September; groups by arrangement only
Admission fee Adults €4.50; groups €4

The Talbot Botanic Gardens at Malahide Demesne were the work of Milo Talbot, a passionate amateur botanist with a particular interest in southern hemisphere plants, notably the flora of Tasmania and Chile. He built up a collection of 5,000 different taxa and, since the soil is limey, they are mostly calcicole plants. The gardens consist of an 18-acre woodland garden and a four-acre walled garden, divided into seven distinct areas which gives the impression of a series of secret gardens, each with its own particular range of plants. It is in this walled garden that the rarer and tender species will be found. There are seven small glasshouses including a Victorian conservatory at the end of the central path – a prominent focal point. Each house is very different in its style and in its plantings. The smallest has a collection of *Primula auricula* cultivars, while the Victorian house has a collection of Australasian plants. There are extensive collections of escallonias, *Syringa*, philadelphus, nothofagus and pittosporum as well as the National Collection of *Olearia*. Malahide is best visited at 2pm on Wednesday afternoons when guided tours are offered of the walled garden (not otherwise open).

woodland garden; plantsman's collection of plants; mature conifers; fine collection of trees; alpine plants; Tasmanian plants; restaurant

Owned by Fingal County Council
Size 8.7ha (22 acres)
NCCPG National Collections *Olearia*

TRINITY COLLEGE BOTANIC GARDEN
Palmerston Park, Dartry, Dublin 6

Tel 00 353 1 497 2070 **Fax** 00 353 1 608 1147
Location 5km south of city centre, near Ranelagh, opposite Municipal Park
Opening hours 9am to 5pm, Monday to Friday, by prior arrangement only
Admission fee Free

This is essentially a teaching garden, with an emphasis upon conservation biology, taxonomy, physiological ecology and plant response to climate change. It also has a good collection of plants, including a systematic garden, an arboretum, seven greenhouses and the Irish Rare and Threatened Plant Genebank. It has acquired a considerable patina of horticultural charm since moving here from central Dublin in 1967.

Owned by Trinity College

GALWAY

ARDCARRAIG
Oranswell, Bushypark

Tel 00 353 91 524336
Location 5km from Galway, off road to Clifden
Opening hours 2pm to 6pm, 20 and 27 May, 3 June; and by appointment
Admission fee €5 for charity

Lorna McMahon started to make this garden in 1971, but the pace of her gardening has accelerated in recent years. The entire garden is won from a barren, peaty, granite wasteland and has now emerged as one of the best modern plantsman's gardens in Ireland. Trees as exotic as metasequoias and ginkgos give shelter to cyclamen, hellebores and small bulbs, but the best part is laid out around a series of small lakes or large ponds, edged with candelabra primulas, meconopsis and lobelias. Many of the trees and shrubs are tender: they include callistemons, acacias and the rare *Eucryphia lucida* 'Pink Cloud'. Parts of the garden have a distinct Japanese overlay – there is even a moss garden.
first-rate plantsman's garden

Owned by Lorna MacMahon
Number of gardeners owner only
Size 1.6ha (4 acres)

KERRY

DERREEN
Lauragh, Killarney

Tel 00 353 64 83588
Location 25km from Kenmare on the Castletown road
Opening hours 10am to 6pm, daily, April to October; closed from Monday to Wednesday in August
Admission fee Adults €6; children €3

Derreen is quite extraordinary. The rocky outcrops come right to the front door, but the fast, lush growth of its trees and shrubs is boundless. Tree ferns *Dicksonia antarctica* and myrtles *Luma apiculata* have gone native, and seed themselves everywhere. Moss, lichen and ferns abound. Large-leaved rhododendrons grow to great heights. It is a place of wonder on a sunny day in late April. Great for children, too.
woodland garden; subtropical plants; tree ferns; rhododendrons; tea room

Owned by Charlie Bigham
Number of gardeners 2
Size 24ha (60 acres)

MUCKROSS HOUSE & GARDENS
Muckross, Killarney

Tel 00 353 64 31440 **Fax** 00 353 64 33926
www.muckross-house.ie
Location 61/2 km south of Killarney on N71
Opening hours Dawn to dusk, daily, all year, except one week at Christmas
Admission fee Free

Killarney National Park provides a most beautiful setting for the gardens and ancient parkland of Muckross House. The walled garden has recently been restored, as has the range of Richardson greenhouses. There is a young arboretum (now fully open to visitors) and some enormous old rhododendrons, but the woodland is of oak, yew, Scots pines and arbutus trees and, even more exciting for a garden visitor, the rock garden is a natural one, of carboniferous limestone. Well maintained.
woodland garden; rock garden; mature conifers; fine collection of trees; rhododendrons; azaleas; greenhouse collection; extensive young conifer plantings in arboretum; craft shop; lunches, hot and cold snacks daily

Owned by Dept of Environment, Heritage and Local Government
Size 6ha (15 acres), plus 10-ha (25-acre) arboretum

KILDARE

JAPANESE GARDENS & ST FIACRA'S GARDEN

Tully, Kildare Town

Tel 00 353 45 521617 **Fax** 00 353 45 522964
www.irish-national-stud.ie
Location Signed in Kildare

Opening hours 9.30am to 6pm, daily, 12 February to 12 November
Admission fee Adults €10; OAPs €8; Children €5

The Japanese garden is a sequence which symbolises man's journey through life. It was made for Lord Wavertree by Japanese gardeners in the early years of the 20th century and contains some handsome old bonsai and cloud-clipped trees. That said, the garden is planted and maintained in a very Irish style – especially pretty in late spring when the wisteria and water irises are in flower. The standard of maintenance is excellent. Elsewhere on the estate is a very substantial new garden, dedicated to St Fiacre, the patron saint of gardeners, which provides a grand contrast. It has little of horticultural interest, but is very evocative of the Irish landscape as it developed in the 6th and 7th centuries. The unusual design, with its strange pseudo-outcrops of weathered limestone, has a strong spiritual quality which perfectly complements the oriental intellectualism of the Japanese garden.
Japanese garden; souvenir shop; light refreshments

Owned by Irish National Stud
Number of gardeners 3
Size 1.6ha (4 acres) in all

LODGE PARK WALLED GARDEN
Straffan

Tel 00 353 1 628 8412 **Fax** 00 353 1 627 3477
www.steam-museum.ie
Location Follow signs to Steam Museum Straffan from Maynooth and Kill
Opening hours 2pm to 6pm, Wednesday to Sunday and Bank Holidays, June to August; visits in May and September by appointment
Admission fee €7.50; price includes museum; groups (20+) €5 each

As it did in the 18th century, the walled garden at Lodge Park continues to produce fruit and vegetables with much more besides. The edible crops grow alongside an ever-increasing collection of lesser-known ornamental plants. Coloured borders of white, blue and yellow greet the visitor and a pink border begins the main walk of the garden, near a collection of peonies. Behind a new classical entrance, the original cold greenhouse allows semi-tender plants to be displayed. A more modern heated greenhouse gives protection for such plants as cymbidiums and brugmansias. The main walk of the garden is lined with box hedges, interrupted by topiary yews: behind the box lies a south-facing border of shrubs and perennials. In the centre is a new area of lawn and wide flower borders, with vegetables planted decoratively behind. The main herbaceous border has a backdrop of roses and is spectacular in July. The rose garden includes a circular iron structure clad in climbing roses topped by a copper rosebud. The north-facing border allows for a collection of shade-loving plants, especially hellebores and pulmonarias.
roses; good herbaceous borders; gift shop at museum; tea room

Owned by Mr and Mrs Robert Guinness
Number of gardeners 1½
Size 0.8ha (2 acres)

KILKENNY

KILFANE GLEN & WATERFALL
Thomastown

Tel 00 353 5677 24558 **Fax** 00 353 5677 27491
Location Off N9, 3km north of Thomastown
Opening hours 11am to 6pm, daily, July and August
Admission fee Adults €6; OAPs €5.50; children €5

A romantic landscape garden laid out in the 1790s and vigorously restored by the present owners. Sit in the tiny *cottage ornée*, admire the exquisite form of the waterfall across the ravine, and dream of Rousseau.
woodland garden; bluebells; excellent modern art pieces; teas by arrangement

Owned by Nicholas and Susan Mosse
Size 8ha (20 acres)

LAOIS

GASH GARDENS

Gash, Castletown, Portlaoise

Tel 00 353 57 8732247
Location 1km from N7 at Castletown
Opening hours 10am to 5pm, Monday to Saturday, May to September; at other times by appointment
Admission fee €5; group rates by appointment; not suitable for children

Nothing outside the garden gates suggests the length, extent or beauty of this extraordinary garden, tucked in along the edges of a dairy farm. It was initially laid out and developed by Noël Keenan in 1984 as a complement to his nursery business: his daughter Mary (who trained at UCD and taught at Glasnevin) is continuing to develop and maintain it. You open the high gates, and walk straight into a vast rock garden stuffed with interesting alpines and well-grown rhododendrons, where great artistry is shown in the choice and positioning of plants. Next comes a long narrow garden like a grassy glade with specimen trees and flowing island beds on either side, a bog garden with an island in the middle, foliage borders with phormiums, gunneras and brilliant contrasts of colour and shape, and a laburnum tunnel at the end. Every part is full of unusual plants and maintained to a very high standard. Open a small gate beyond the laburnum tunnel, and a long, narrow walk, sometimes in shade, sometimes in the open, runs down alongside a planted stream until finally you reach the River Nore right at the bottom. Here is a long, looped river walk, planted with poplars and larches, beautiful, simple and ingenious. The beauty, the ingenuity and the horticultural interest of the gardens at Gash are incomparable.
herbaceous perennials; rock garden; rhododendrons; plantsman's collection of plants; nursery at entrance, open all year

Owned by Mary Keenan and Ross Doyle
Number of gardeners owner, plus part-time help
Size 1.6ha (4 acres)

HEYWOOD GARDENS

Ballinakill

Tel 00 353 57 8733563
Location In grounds of Ballinakill Community School
Opening hours 8am to 7pm, daily, all year; closes at 5.30pm from October to March and 9pm from May to August; guided tours by arrangement
Admission fee Free

Heywood House disappeared in the Troubles (its place is taken by a hideous modern Salesian college) but fragments remain of the formal gardens designed by Lutyens in 1912 for Sir Hutcheson Poë. Three small terraced gardens enclosed by yew hedges – one is a herb garden – lead down to the magnificent, spacious oval garden with ragstone walls and oval portholes. It was boldly replanted in the 1990s with advice from Graham Stuart Thomas. A short formal lime avenue leads towards the other end of the terrace where a classical, arcaded pergola looks down a steep slope to a long lake full of water lilies and up across the countryside to the distant hills. Here, too, the stonework is impressive; in its heyday it must have been stunning. Go now, and imagine what an Edwardian garden looked like when newly made.
Lutyens garden; Graham Thomas plantings; woodland garden

Owned by Office of Public Works

LIMERICK

BALLYNACOURTY
Ballysteen

Tel 00 353 61 396409 **Fax** 00 353 61 396733
Location 5km from Askeaton, on River Shannon
Opening hours By appointment
Admission fee €5

Ballynacourty is a fine modern family garden: six densely planted acres won from open farmland. It is interesting for its selection of lime-tolerant trees and shrubs and to see how a garden of this size may be maintained with a minimum amount of help.
shrub roses (mainly old-fashioned); herbaceous borders

Owned by George and Michelina Stacpoole
Number of gardeners 1 part-time
Size 2.4ha (6 acres)

GLIN CASTLE
Glin

Tel 00 353 68 34173 **Fax** 00 353 68 34364
www.glincastle.com
Location On N69, 52km west of Limerick
Opening hours By appointment
Admission fee Adults €7

Simple formal gardens run down towards the park and merge with the surrounding woodland. The walled kitchen garden has recently received a makeover: cutting borders, herbs, herbaceous borders and such vegetables as sea-kale and asparagus. In the pleasure gardens are some fine ornamental trees – dogwoods, magnolias, cherries and parrotias, as well as rhododendrons and camellias. Taken with the Gothicised castle and its magnificent position on the Shannon estuary, Glin is a place of rare enchantment.
vegetables; subtropical plants; rhododendrons and azaleas; daffodils; camellias; bluebells

Owned by Desmond Fitzgerald, Knight of Glin
Number of gardeners 2
Size 2ha (5 acres)

OFFALY

BIRR CASTLE DEMESNE
Birr

Tel 00 353 5791 20336 **Fax** 00 353 5791 21583
www.birrcastle.com
Location Rosse Row in Birr, Co. Offaly
Opening hours 9am to 6pm or dusk, if earlier, daily, all year
Admission fee Adults €9; OAPs €7; children €5

The best garden in the Irish Midlands, Birr has a huge collection of trees and shrubs, a spacious river walk, a large park with wildflowers, a reedy lake and a good woodland garden. Many of the plants were grown from original collectors' material: some were collected in the wild by the owner's parents, Michael and Anne Rosse. The best bit is the formal garden designed by Anne Rosse in 1935 within the old walled garden. Here is a cloister of arched hornbeams, a lilac avenue, crinums, peonies, Irish yews, two rose gardens (*Rosa roxburghii* 5m – 16ft – high), and the tallest box hedges in the world, extraordinarily slender. Good plants are everywhere and the garden merits a long visit, though there are fewer gardeners now than there used to be and parts are now somewhat overrun by Irish melancholy and neglect.
roses (mainly old-fashioned); plantsman's collection of plants; fine collection of trees; *Paeonia* 'Anne Rosse'; *Magnolia* 'Anne Rosse'; tallest *Acer monspessulanum* (15m; 49ft) and boxwood *Buxus sempervirens* (12m; 39ft) in the British Isles, plus 49 other record species; gift shop; tea room

Owned by The Earl of Rosse
Number of gardeners 3
Size 48ha (120 acres)

ROSCOMMON

STROKESTOWN PARK
Strokestown

Tel 00 353 71 96 33013 **Fax** 00 353 71 96 33712
www.strokestownpark.ie
Location 23km from Longford on the N5
Opening hours 10am to 5.30pm, daily, 17 March to 31 October
Admission fee Adults €13

Strokestown's gardens were one of Ireland's first and (most successful) restoration projects. Even the symbols of Anglo-Irish hegemony have been faithfully restored, including the croquet lawn, the grass tennis court and the gazebo. Others are new interpretations of old features – the rose garden, the pergola, a wildflower garden, a fernery and longest herbaceous border in Britain and Ireland, planted in rainbow colours. In the grounds are many fine trees, including a vast tulip tree (*Liriodendron tulipifera*) and tall *Trachycarpus fortunei* palms. The latest addition has been the walled garden, where heritage fruit and vegetables are cultivated. It is dominated by a glasshouse range that dates back to 1780 – Ireland's oldest, still in use.
café

Owned by Westwood Holdings Ltd
Number of gardeners 3
Size 2.4ha (6 acres)

WATERFORD

CURRAGHMORE
Portlaw

Tel 00 353 51 387102 **Fax** 00 353 51 387481
Location 22km west of Waterford: enter by Portlaw gate
Opening hours 2pm to 5pm, Thursdays and Bank Holidays, Easter to mid-October; also, jointly with the house: 9am to 1pm, Monday to Friday, January, May and June; other times by prior appointment
Admission fee Garden & Shell House: €4; house €6; combined ticket €10

Lord Waterford's family has lived at Curraghmore since 1170, which is a long time even by Irish standards. It has fine terraced gardens with balustrades and an excellent collection of trees and shrubs, dating mainly from the 19th and early 20th centuries. The outstanding feature is the Shell Grotto which was built in 1754 by the heiress to the property, Catherine Poer, Countess of Tyrone. She personally decorated the interior walls with shells which were collected from all round the world. Curraghmore is a magnificent estate which deserves to be better known. The best time for a visit is from early May to mid-June, but there is much to enjoy at every season.
fine collection of trees; landscaped park

Owned by The Marquess of Waterford

LISMORE CASTLE
Lismore

Tel 00 353 58 54424 **Fax** 00 353 58 54896
www.lismorecastle.com
Location Centre of Lismore
Opening hours 1.45pm to 4.45pm, daily, 7 April to 30 September; opens at 11am in high season
Admission fee Adults €7; children €3.50

Lismore is best for the castellated house: the gardens are interesting rather than exceptional, but there is a pretty grove of camellias and a double yew walk planted in 1707. The upper enclosure is even older, a Jacobean survivor. The herbaceous border aligned on the cathedral spire has recently been replanted to give colour throughout the summer. Contemporary sculptures include one by Anthony Gormley. Visit the walled garden for some fine traditional kitchen gardening: the vinery was designed by Paxton – this is the Irish Chatsworth.
woodland garden; roses (mainly old-fashioned); magnolias; spring bulbs; interesting modern sculptures (including Anthony Gormley)

Owned by Lismore Estates
Number of gardeners 4
Size 2.8ha (7 acres)

MOUNT CONGREVE

Kilmeaden

Tel 00 353 51 384115 **Fax** 00 353 51 384576
Location 8km from Waterford on the Cork Road (N35)
Opening hours 9am to 4.30pm, Thursdays, March to September
Admission fee Free

Mount Congreve is the largest horticultural garden in Europe and the lifetime achievement of Ambrose Congreve, who celebrates his centenary this year (2007). He started gardening around his Georgian ancestral home when he was 11 years old. His garden's statistics today are: 9,000 different rare trees and shrubs, 3,500 cultivars of rhododendrons, 650 named camellias, 350 different cultivars of Japanese maples, 25 gardeners and 16 miles of paths, including half a mile of hostas. But even more impressive is Congreve's style of planting in large quantities – as many as 25 or 50 of each variety 'to make the proper statement when the garden matures'. A whole hillside is planted with scarlet embothriums. A 1km walk down to the River Suir is lined on one side with 100 *Magnolia campbellii* at 10m (33ft) intervals and on the other with 100 *Magnolia sargentiana* var. *robusta*. One of the walled gardens has four double herbaceous borders arranged month by month, one each for May, June, July and August. The vast glasshouses have huge collections of orchids, bromeliads, fuchsias, cyclamen, begonias and house plants. In the oak woodlands are near-complete collections of prunus, acers, azaras, eucryphias, michelias, pittosporums, pieris, berberis, viburnums, cornus and ericas. All will be willed to the Irish State and be more regularly open to the public one day in future.
magnolias; rhododendrons; plants of every sort

Owned by Ambrose Congreve
Number of gardeners 25
Size 28ha (70 acres)

WESTMEATH

TULLYNALLY CASTLE
Castlepollard

Tel 00 353 44 9661159 **Fax** 00 353 44 9661856
www.tullynallycastle.com
Location Signposted from Castlepollard; 20km from Mullingar
Opening hours Noon to 6pm, Saturdays and Sundays, May and June; daily, 1 July to 3 September; groups at other times by arrangement
Admission fee Adults €6; children €3

Tullynally has a romantic Loudonesque garden for a rambling Gothic Revival castle. Formal terraces overlook the park and lead to the woodland gardens, enriched with recent plantings of maples and magnolias. A fine avenue of Irish yews is the centrepiece of the walled garden: they are thought to be about 200 years old and thus among the oldest in existence. The owner, Thomas Pakenham, has followed up his acclaimed *Meetings with Remarkable Trees*, some of whose photographs were taken at Tullynally, with *Remarkable Trees of the World* (Weidenfeld, 2002). And he has introduced some interesting exotics to Tullynally from his travels abroad, notably from China and Tibet.
woodland garden; grotto; lake; new Chinese and Tibetan gardens; plants collected by owners; several of the largest beech trees *Fagus sylvatica* in the British Isles; shop; coffee shop; light lunches

Owned by Mr and Mrs Thomas Pakenham
Number of gardeners 3
Size 10ha (25 acres)

WEXFORD

JOHN F. KENNEDY ARBORETUM
New Ross

Tel 00 353 51 388171 **Fax** 00 353 51 388172
Location 13km south of New Ross off R733
Opening hours 10am to 8pm, May to August; 10am to 6.30pm, April and September; 10am to 5pm, October to March; closed Good Friday and Christmas Day
Admission fee Adults €2.90; OAPs €2.10; children and students €1.30; families €7.40

This is a memorial arboretum founded in 1968 (with financial help from Irish/American citizens) on 623 acres near the Kennedy homestead. Nearly 40 years on, the statistics are impressive: 4,500 types of trees and shrubs arranged taxonomically, and 200 plots laid out by geographical distribution. All are meticulously labelled, and planted with artistry. There is one circuit for broadleaves and another for conifers, interwoven at times to improve the overall appearance of the collection. Special features include an 'ericaceous garden' with 500 different rhododendrons, and many varieties of azaleas and heathers. There is also a slow-growing conifer collection, a hedge collection, a display of groundcover plants and a selection of climbing plants on a series of stone and timber shelters. In summer a miniature railway runs through plantings that represent each continent.
mature conifers; fine collection of trees; eight different tree records for the British Isles; souvenirs; café for teas/refreshments in summer

Owned by Office of Public Works
Number of gardeners 14
Size 252ha (623 acres)

JOHNSTOWN CASTLE GARDENS
Wexford

Tel 00 353 53 9171247 **Fax** 00 353 53 9142213
Location 6½ km south-west of Wexford
Opening hours 9am to 5pm, daily, all year, except Christmas day
Admission fee €5 car and passengers

Johnstown Castle has 50 acres of ornamental grounds with good trees, tall cordylines, three lakes and the Irish Agricultural Museum. There is a section in the museum devoted to old lawn mowers and antique garden equipment. The collection of 19th-century conifers in the park is exceptional, as is a huge *Rhododendron arboreum* nearby.
woodland garden; mature conifers; walled gardens; ornamental lakes; tallest *Cupressus macrocarpa* (40m; 131ft) in the British Isles; coffee shop with snacks (July and August only)

Owned by TEAGASC (Irish Agriculture and Food Development Authority)
Number of gardeners 5
Size 20ha (50 acres)

WICKLOW

KILLRUDDERY HOUSE
Southern Cross, Bray

Tel/fax 00 353 404 46024
www.killruddery.com
Location 23km south of Dublin, signed from N11
Opening hours 1pm to 5pm, weekends in April, then daily, April to September
Admission fee Adults €6; concession €5; children €2

P 🚻

Killruddery's formal garden escaped the 18th-century passion for landscaping. They were first laid out by a pupil of Le Nôtre's in the 1680s and added to in the 19th century. Two long stretches of water run away from the house towards a fountain with cascades. A large formal garden called The Angles lies to one side; its paths radiate out as *patte d'oie* when seen from halfway along the pools. Elsewhere are further pool, ponds and formal gardens, decorated with urns and statues. Killruddery will take you straight back to the 17th century in a way that no other garden in Ireland can.
historic formal layout

Owned by The Earl of Meath
Number of gardeners 2
Size 16ha (40 acres)

MOUNT USHER GARDENS
Ashford

Tel 00 353 404 40116 **Fax** 00 353 404 40205
www.mountushergardens.ie
Location Ashford, 50km south of Dublin off N11
Opening hours 10.30am to 6pm, daily, 9 March to 31 October
Admission fee Adults €7; OAPs and children €6; guided tours for pre-booked groups available (€40 extra)

P 🚻 ♿

These 20 acres of garden have the River Vartry running through their middle: both sides of the river are crowded with unusual trees and shrubs – 5,000 different species and cultivars, some of them *very* rare. The self-sown *Pinus montezumae* are justly famous. The collection of 100ft eucalyptus trees growing from a sea of bluebells is breathtaking. The *Nothofagus dombeyi* is the largest in Ireland. There are good herbaceous plants, too, and lilies in July. It is a truly remarkable plantsman's garden made in the Robinsonian style by four generations of Walpoles from 1868 to 1980 and extensively restored by the present owner.
woodland garden; subtropical plants; plantsman's collection of plants; mature conifers; fine trees; spring bulbs; pretty bridges across the river; tallest *Cornus capitata* (18m; 59ft) in the British Isles, plus 28 other record tree species; shopping courtyard; tea room with home-baked food

Owned by Mrs Madelaine Jay
Number of gardeners 5
Size 8ha (20 acres)

NATIONAL GARDEN EXHIBITION CENTRE
Kilquade, Kilpedder

Tel 00 353 1 2819890 **Fax** 00 353 1 2810359
www.gardenexhibition.ie
Location Signed from N11, 11km south of Bray
Opening hours 10am (1pm on Sundays) to 5.30pm (dusk in winter), daily, all year
Admission fee Adults €4.50; OAPs €3.50; groups (10+) €5 (with guided tour) or €3.50 (without guided tour)

P 🚻 ♿ ●

This is a permanent exhibition of contemporary style attached to a garden centre. It has 20 linked but distinct gardens: the Herb Garden; 'Oriental Reflections'; 'Shady Secrets'; the Contemplative Garden; the Celtic Garden; the 'Sensory Garden', and so on. Each was made by a different designer and construction team. It all adds up to the best of modern Irish design for small gardens: a shop window for ideas on style, plants and materials.
model gardens; garden centre; restaurant

Owned by Niall Power

POWERSCOURT GARDENS

Powerscourt Estate, Enniskerry

Tel 00 353 1 204 6000 **Fax** 00 353 1 204 6900
www.powerscourt.ie
Location 20km south of Dublin off N11
Opening hours 9.30am to 5.30pm (dusk in winter), daily, except 25 and 26 December, all year
Admission fee Gardens only: adults €7.50; OAPs €6.50; children €4.50

Powerscourt is a wonderful mixture of awesome grandeur and sheer fun. It is also extremely well organised for visitors. The main Italianate garden, dominated by a stately 1860s staircase down to a lake, has the Great Sugarloaf Mountain as an off-centre backdrop. It is lined with bedding plants, statues and urns (look out for the sulky cherubs). The life-sized winged horses guarding the lake, part of the Powerscourt family's coat of arms, were made in Berlin in 1861. To one side is the Japanese garden more Edwardian than Japanese – but full of twists and hummocks and with a series of concentric paths that lead the visitor round. In the arboretum are many rare trees, including a fine *Pinus torreyana* and *P. montezumae*. The walled garden, one of the oldest features at Powerscourt, has grand wrought-iron gates, lots of cheerful roses and a double herbaceous border. Powerscourt is busy in summer, but you can escape into solitude along the avenue of monkey puzzles. The magnificent house is now open to visitors again.

woodland garden; mature conifers; fine collection of trees; much recent restoration, including the Bamberg gates, and a remodelling of the Japanese garden; tallest *Abies spectabilis* (32m; 105ft) in the British Isles, plus 10 other record tree specimens; garden centre; terrace café with lunches

Owned by Powerscourt Estate
Number of gardeners 6
Size 19ha (47 acres)

PLANT-LOVER'S GUIDE

NCCPG NATIONAL COLLECTIONS

ACACIA
Tresco Abbey
Cornwall, England

ACANTHUS
Hillview Hardy Plants
Shropshire, England

ACER
Hergest Croft Gardens
Herefordshire, England

ACER **(Japanese cvs.)**
Westonbirt The National Arboretum
Gloucestershire, England

ACHILLEA
Capel Manor
London, England

ADIANTUM
Tatton Park
Cheshire, England

AESCULUS
West Dean Gardens
West Sussex, England

ALCHEMILLA
Cambridge University Botanic Garden
Cambridgeshire, England

AMORPHOPHALLUS
Royal Botanic Gardens, Kew
London, England

ANEMONE **(Japanese)**
Broadview Gardens
Kent, England

ANEMONE NEMOROSA
Kingston Lacy
Dorset, England

ANTHEMIS
Winterbourne Botanic Garden, University of Birmingham
West Midlands, England

AQUILEGIA
Hardwicke House
Cambridgeshire, England

ARALIA
Powis Castle & Garden
Powys, Wales

ARALIACEAE
Meon Orchard
Hampshire, England

ARBUTUS
Barton House
Warwickshire, England

ARTEMISIA
Elsworth Herbs
Cambridgeshire, England

ASPLENIUM SCOLOPENDRIUM
Sizergh Castle
Cumbria, England

ASTER
Temple Newsam Park
West Yorkshire, England

ASTER
(autumn-flowering)
The Picton Garden
Herefordshire, England

ASTILBE
Marwood Hill Gardens
Devon, England

ASTRANTIA
Warren Hills Cottage
Leicestershire, England

AUBRIETA
University of Leicester Botanic Garden
Leicestershire, England

AZARA
Exeter University Gardens
Devon, England

BEGONIA
Glasgow Botanic Garden
Strathclyde, Scotland

BERBERIS
Mill Hill Plants
Nottinghamshire, England

BERGENIA
Greenbank Garden
Strathclyde, Scotland

BERGENIA
(species & primary hybrids)
Cambridge University Botanic Garden
Cambridgeshire, England

BETULA
Wakehurst Place
West Sussex, England

BONSAI
Birmingham Botanical Gardens & Glasshouses
West Midlands, England

BRACHYGLOTTIS
Inverewe
Highland, Scotland

BUDDLEJA
Longstock Water Gardens
Hampshire, England

BUXUS
Ickworth
Suffolk, England

CALLUNA VULGARIS
RHS Garden Wisley
Surrey, England

CALTHA
Rowden Gardens
Devon, England

CAMELLIA
Mount Edgcumbe Gardens
Cornwall, England

CAMELLIA JAPONICA
Antony Woodland Garden
Cornwall, England

CAMELLIA x *WILLIAMSII*
Wentworth Castle Gardens
South Yorkshire, England

CAMPANULA
Lingen Nursery and Gardens
Shropshire, England

CARPINUS
The Sir Harold Hillier Gardens
Hampshire, England

CARPINUS BETULUS **(cvs.)**
Beale Arboretum
London, England

CASSIOPE
Branklyn Garden
Tayside, Scotland

CATALPA
Cliveden
Buckinghamshire, England

CEANOTHUS (DECIDUOUS)
Knoll Gardens
Dorset, England

CELMISIA
St Luke's Cottage
Northumberland and Tyne & Wear, England

CENTAUREA
Bide-a-Wee Cottage
Northumberland and Tyne & Wear, England

CHAMAECYPARIS LAWSONIANA
University of Leicester Botanic Garden
Leicestershire, England

CHAMAECYPARIS LAWSONIANA **(cvs.)**
Bedgebury National Pinetum
Kent, England

CHRYSANTHEMUM
(Charms & Cascade)
Temple Newsam Park
West Yorkshire, England

CITRUS
Hales Hall Gardens & Reads Nursery
Norfolk, England

CLEMATIS
Burford House Gardens
Shropshire, England

CLEMATIS VITICELLA
Longstock Water Gardens
Hampshire, England

CLEMATIS VITICELLA **(cvs.)**
Roseland House
Cornwall, England

COLCHICUM
Felbrigg Hall
Norfolk, England

CONOPHYTUM
Abbey Brook Cactus Nursery
Derbyshire, England

CONVALLARIA
Kingston Lacy
Dorset, England

COPROSMA
County Park Nursery
Essex, England

CORIARIA
Crûg Farm Plants
Gwynedd, Wales

CORNUS
RHS Garden Rosemoor
Devon, England

CORNUS **(excluding C. florida cvs.)**
Newby Hall
North Yorkshire, England

CORNUS;CORYLUS
The Sir Harold Hillier Gardens
Hampshire, England

CORYLUS (COBNUTS & FILBERTS)
Brogdale
Kent, England

COTINUS
Thorp Perrow Arboretum & Woodland Garden
North Yorkshire, England

COTONEASTER
The Sir Harold Hillier Gardens
Hampshire, England

CROCUS
RHS Garden Wisley
Surrey, England

x *CUPRESSOCYPARIS*
Bedgebury National Pinetum
Kent, England

CYDONIA OBLONGA
Norton Priory Museum & Gardens
Cheshire, England

CYSTOPTERIS
Sizergh Castle
Cumbria, England

DABOECIA
RHS Garden Wisley
Surrey, England

DAPHNE
Brandy Mount House
Hampshire, England

DELPHINIUM
Temple Newsam Park
West Yorkshire, England

DENDROBIUM
Glasgow Botanic Garden
Strathclyde, Scotland

DEUTZIA
The Hollies Park
West Yorkshire, England

DIANELLA
Mount Stewart
Co. Down, Northern Ireland

DIANTHUS
Kingstone Cottage Plants
Herefordshire, England

DIANTHUS (MALMAISON CARNATIONS)
Crathes Castle
Grampian, Scotland

DICKSONIACEAE
Glasgow Botanic Garden
Strathclyde, Scotland

DIERVILLA
Sheffield Botanical Gardens
South Yorkshire, England

DIGITALIS
The Botanic Nursery
Wiltshire, England

DRYOPTERIS
RHS Garden Harlow Carr
North Yorkshire, England

DWARF & SLOW-GROWING CONIFERS
Valley Gardens
Surrey, England

ECHINOPSIS HYBRIDS
Abbey Brook Cactus Nursery
Derbyshire, England

ELAEAGNUS
Beale Arboretum
London, England

EMBOTHRIUM
Bodnant Gardens
Clwyd, Wales

ENCEPHALARTOS
Royal Botanic Gardens, Kew
London, England

ENKIANTHUS
Clyne Gardens
Glamorgan, Wales

EPIMEDIUM
RHS Garden Wisley
Surrey, England

ERICA
Bell's Cherrybank Centre
Tayside, Scotland

ERYTHRONIUM
Greencombe Gardens
Somerset, England

EUCALYPTUS
Meon Orchard
Hampshire, England

EUCRYPHIA
Seaforde Gardens
Co. Down, Northern Ireland

EUONYMUS (DECIDUOUS)
East Bergholt Place
Suffolk, England

EUPHORBIA
Oxford Botanic Garden
Oxfordshire, England

FAGUS
Kirkley Hall Gardens
Northumberland and Tyne & Wear, England

FERNS
Valley Gardens
Surrey, England

FICUS
Hales Hall Gardens & Reads Nursery
Norfolk, England

FRAXINUS
Thorp Perrow Arboretum & Woodland Garden
North Yorkshire, England

FRITILLARIA
(European species)
Cambridge University Botanic Garden
Cambridgeshire, England

FUCHSIA
University of Leicester Botanic Garden
Leicestershire, England

FUCHSIA **(hardy)**
Kathleen Muncaster Fuchsias
Lincolnshire, England

FUCHSIA SECTION QUELUSIA
RHS Garden Harlow Carr
North Yorkshire, England

GALANTHUS
RHS Garden Wisley
Surrey, England

GARRYA
National Botanic Gardens
Co. Dublin, Republic of Ireland

GAULTHERIA
Greencombe Gardens
Somerset, England

GENTIANA
Christie's Nursery
Tayside, Scotland

GERANIUM
(species & primary hybrids)
Cambridge University Botanic Garden
Cambridgeshire, England

GREVILLEA
Pine Lodge Gardens & Nursery
Cornwall, England

GYMNOCALYCIUM
Abbey Brook Cactus Nursery
Derbyshire, England

HAMAMELIS
Swallow Hayes
Shropshire, England

HAWORTHIA
Abbey Brook Cactus Nursery
Derbyshire, England

HEDERA
Fibrex Nurseries Ltd
Warwickshire, England

HELENIUM
Holbrook Garden
Devon, England

HELICONIA
Royal Botanic Gardens, Kew
London, England

HELIOTROPIUM
Hampton Court Palace
London, England

HELLEBORUS
Broadview Gardens
Kent, England

HEMEROCALLIS
Antony
Cornwall, England

HEMEROCALLIS **(Coe hybrids)**
The Hollies Park
West Yorkshire, England

HEMEROCALLIS
(cvs. post-1970)
Rosewood Daylilies
Kent, England

'HILLIER' PLANTS
The Sir Harold Hillier Gardens
Hampshire, England

HOHERIA
Abbotsbury Sub-Tropical Gardens
Dorset, England

HOSTA **(large-leaved)**
The Hollies Park
West Yorkshire, England

HOSTA **(modern hybrids)**
Ann & Roger Bowden
Devon, England

HYACINTHUS ORIENTALIS
Ripley Castle Gardens
North Yorkshire, England

HYDRANGEA
Holehird Gardens
Cumbria, England

HYPERICUM
Wakehurst Place
West Sussex, England

ILEX
Valley Gardens
Surrey, England

IRIS
Myddelton House
London, England

IRIS
(fulva, pseudacorus, versicolor, virginica & laevigata cvs.)
Rowden Gardens
Devon, England

IRIS **(species)**
The Harris Garden
Berkshire, England

IRIS **(subgenus Scorpiris)**
Royal Botanic Gardens, Kew
London, England

IRIS ENSATA
Marwood Hill Gardens
Devon, England

IRIS SIBIRICA
Lingen Nursery and Gardens
Shropshire, England

IRIS SPURIA
Belsay Hall
Northumberland and Tyne & Wear, England

IRIS UNGUICULARIS
(provisional)
Winterbourne Botanic Garden, University of Birmingham
West Midlands, England

JUGLANS
Thorp Perrow Arboretum & Woodland Garden
North Yorkshire, England

JUNIPERUS
Bedgebury National Pinetum
Kent, England

LABURNUM
Powis Castle & Garden
Powys, Wales

LAPAGERIA
Roseland House
Cornwall, England

LAVANDULA
Downderry Nursery
Kent, England

LEWISIA
Ashwood Nurseries Ltd
Staffordshire, England

LIBERTIA
Mount Stewart
Co. Down, Northern Ireland

LIGUSTRUM
The Sir Harold Hillier Gardens
Hampshire, England

LILIUM
Branklyn Garden
Tayside, Scotland

LIRIODENDRON
West Dean Gardens
West Sussex, England

LITHOCARPUS
The Sir Harold Hillier Gardens
Hampshire, England

LITHOPS
Abbey Brook Cactus Nursery
Derbyshire, England

LONICERA **(shrubby species & primary hybrids)**
Cambridge University Botanic Garden
Cambridgeshire, England

LUPINUS **(Russell strains)**
Swallow Hayes
Shropshire, England

LYSIMACHIA
Cotswold Garden Flowers
Worcestershire, England

MAGNOLIA
Valley Gardens
Surrey, England

MAGNOLIA **(species)**
Wentworth Castle Gardens
South Yorkshire, England

MAGNOLIA **(spp.)**
Bodnant Gardens
Clwyd, Wales

MAHONIA
Valley Gardens
Surrey, England

MALUS
Granada Arboretum
Cheshire, England

MALUS **(apples, ornamental cvs. & cider apples)**
Brogdale
Kent, England

MAMMILLARIA
Abbey Brook Cactus Nursery
Derbyshire, England

MENTHA
Iden Croft Herbs
Kent, England

MISCANTHUS
Bressingham Gardens
Norfolk, England

MONARDA
Leeds Castle
Kent, England

MUSA
"Royal Botanic Gardens, Kew"
London, England

NARCISSUS
Brodie Castle
Grampian, Scotland

NARCISSUS **(miniature)**
Broadleigh Gardens
Somerset, England

NEPETA
Iden Croft Herbs
Kent, England

NERIUM OLEANDER
Elsworth Herbs
Cambridgeshire, England

NOTHOFAGUS
Wakehurst Place
West Sussex, England

NYMPHAEA
Kenchester Water Gardens
Herefordshire, England

OENOTHERA
Old Vicarage
Wiltshire, England

OLEARIA
Inverewe
Highland, Scotland

ORIGANUM
Chesters Walled Garden
Northumberland and Tyne & Wear, England

OSMUNDA
Sizergh Castle
Cumbria, England

PAEONIA LACTIFLORA
Kelways Ltd
Somerset, England

PAPAVER ORIENTALE
Water Meadow Nursery and Herb Farm
Hampshire, England

PARIS
Crûg Farm Plants
Gwynedd, Wales

PELARGONIUM
Fibrex Nurseries Ltd
Warwickshire, England

PENNISETUM
Knoll Gardens
Dorset, England

PENSTEMON
Pershore College
Worcestershire, England

PERNETTYA
Valley Gardens
Surrey, England

PHILADELPHUS
Pershore College
Worcestershire, England

PHLOX PANICULATA
Temple Newsam Park
West Yorkshire, England

PHORMIUM
Mount Stewart
Co. Down, Northern Ireland

PHOTINIA
The Sir Harold Hillier Gardens
Hampshire, England

PHYGELIUS
Knoll Gardens
Dorset, England

PIERIS
Clyne Gardens
Glamorgan, Wales

PINUS
The Quinta
Cheshire, England

PINUS **(excl. dwarf cvs.)**
The Sir Harold Hillier Gardens
Hampshire, England

PLANTS COLLECTED BY JOHN BARTRAM
Painshill Park
Surrey, England

PLANTS INTRODUCED BY SIR FREDERICK STERN
Highdown
West Sussex, England

PLATANUS
Mottisfont Abbey
Hampshire, England

PODOCARPACEAE
Meon Orchard
Hampshire, England

POLYGONATUM
Crûg Farm Plants
Gwynedd, Wales

POLYPODIUM
RHS Garden Harlow Carr
North Yorkshire, England

POLYSTICHUM
Greencombe Gardens
Somerset, England

POPULUS
Lackham Country Park
Wiltshire, England

POTENTILLA **(shrubby)**
Ardgillan Park
Co. Dublin, Republic of Ireland

POTENTILLA FRUTICOSA **(cvs.)**
Webbs
Worcestershire, England

PRIMULA **(Cortusoides section)**
Plant World Botanic Gardens
Devon, England

PRIMULA AURICULA
Golden Acre Park
West Yorkshire, England

PRUNUS **(cherries)**
Brogdale
Kent, England

PRUNUS **(plums)**
Brogdale
Kent, England

PRUNUS **(sato-sakura group)**
Batsford Arboretum
Gloucestershire, England

PULMONARIA
Stillingfleet Lodge Nurseries
North Yorkshire, England

PYRUS
Brogdale
Kent, England

QUERCUS
The Sir Harold Hillier Gardens
Hampshire, England

RHEUM **(culinary)**
RHS Garden Wisley
Surrey, England

RHEUM **(viewable on request)**
RHS Garden Harlow Carr
North Yorkshire, England

RHODODENDRON **(Barbatum, Glischra & Maculifera sections)**
Inverewe
Highland, Scotland

RHODODENDRON **(Ghent azaleas)**
Sheffield Park Garden
East Sussex, England

RHODODENDRON **(Knap Hill azaleas)**
Sherwood
Devon, England

RHODODENDRON **(Kurume azaleas, the Wilson 50)**
Isabella Plantation
London, England

RHODODENDRON **(part)**
Singleton Park & Swansea Botanical Gardens
Glamorgan, Wales

RHODODENDRON **(section Pogonanthum, subsections Campylogyna, Glauca & Uniflora, & Cox hybrids)**
Glendoick Gardens
Tayside, Scotland

RHODODENDRON **(species & Glenn Dale azaleas)**
Valley Gardens
Surrey, England

RHODODENDRON **(subsections Falconera, Grandia and Maddenia)**
Brodick Castle
Strathclyde, Scotland

RHODODENDRON **(subsections Triflora & Falconera)**
Clyne Gardens
Glamorgan, Wales

RHODODENDRON FORRESTII
Bodnant Gardens
Clwyd, Wales

RHODODENDRON **(species)**
Wentworth Castle Gardens
South Yorkshire, England

RIBES **(species & primary hybrids)**
Cambridge University Botanic Garden
Cambridgeshire, England

RIBES GROSSULARIA **(gooseberries)**
Rougham Hall Nurseries
Suffolk, England

RIBES NIGRUM **(blackcurrants)**
Brogdale
Kent, England

RIBES SATIVUM **(currants other than blackcurrants)**
Brogdale
Kent, England

ROSA
Mottisfont Abbey
Hampshire, England

ROSA **(19th-century shrubs)**
Malleny House Garden
Lothian, Scotland

ROSA **(David Austin 'English Rose' cultivars)**
David Austin Roses
Shropshire, England

ROSA **(History of European roses)**
"Winterbourne Botanic Garden, University of Birmingham"
West Midlands, England

ROSA **(species & cultivars)**
The Gardens of the Rose
Hertfordshire, England

ROSA **(species)**
Peter Beales Roses
Norfolk, England

ROSA RUGOSA
Ladyburn
Strathclyde, Scotland

ROSA SPINOSISSIMA
Ladyburn
Strathclyde, Scotland

ROSMARINUS
Downderry Nursery
Kent, England

RUSCUS
Cambridge University Botanic Garden
Cambridgeshire, England

SALIX
Westonbirt The National Arboretum
Gloucestershire, England

SALVIA
Kingston Maurward Gardens
Dorset, England

SAMBUCUS
Wallington
Northumberland and Tyne & Wear, England

SANGUISORBA
Chesters Walled Garden
Northumberland and Tyne & Wear, England

SARCOCOCCA
Capel Manor
London, England

SAXIFRAGA **(European species)**
Cambridge University Botanic Garden
Cambridgeshire, England

SAXIFRAGA **(Kabschia)**
Waterperry Gardens
Oxfordshire, England

SKIMMIA
Wakehurst Place
West Sussex, England

SOLENOSTEMON
Temple Newsam Park
West Yorkshire, England

SORBUS
East Durham & Houghall Community College
Co. Durham, England

SORBUS **(Aria & Micromeles groups)**
Winkworth Arboretum
Surrey, England

STEWARTIA
High Beeches
West Sussex, England

STREPTOCARPUS
Dibleys Nurseries
Clwyd, Wales

STYRACACEAE **(incl. Halesia, Pterostyrax, Styrax, Sinojackia)**
Holker Hall
Cumbria, England

SYRINGA
The Hollies Park
West Yorkshire, England

TAXUS
Bedgebury National Pinetum
Kent, England

THUJA
Bedgebury National Pinetum
Kent, England

THYMUS
Chesters Walled Garden
Northumberland and Tyne & Wear, England

TILIA
Thorp Perrow Arboretum & Woodland Garden
North Yorkshire, England

TRADESCANTIA
(Andersoniana Group)
Kayes Garden Nursery
Leicestershire, England

TROPAEOLUM **(species)**
Inveresk Lodge
Lothian, Scotland

TULBAGHIA
Marwood Hill Gardens
Devon, England

TULIPA **(species & primary hybrids)**
Cambridge University Botanic Garden
Cambridgeshire, England

VACCINIUM
Greencombe Gardens
Somerset, England

VIBURNUM
RHS Garden Hyde Hall
Essex, England

VIOLA ODORATA **(cvs.)**
C.W. Groves & Son Ltd.
Dorset, England

VITIS VINIFERA
(grapes)
Hales Hall Gardens & Reads Nursery
Norfolk, England

WEIGELA
Sheffield Botanical Gardens
South Yorkshire, England

YUCCA
Renishaw Hall
Derbyshire, England

ZELKOVA
Hergest Croft Gardens
Herefordshire, England

WHERE TO SEE...

ALPINES

Brandy Mount House
Hampshire, England
Cambridge University Botanic Garden
Cambridgeshire, England
Copt House Garden
Cumbria, England
Glen Chantry
Essex, England
Hillside
Co. Cork, Republic of Ireland
W.E.Th. Ingwersen Ltd
West Sussex, England
Jack Drake
Highland, Scotland
National Botanic Gardens
Co. Dublin, Republic of Ireland
Pershore College
Worcestershire, England
Pottertons Nursery
Lincolnshire, England
RHS Garden Wisley
Surrey, England
Royal Botanic Garden Edinburgh
Lothian, Scotland
Royal Botanic Gardens, Kew
London, England
St Luke's Cottage
Northumberland and Tyne & Wear, England
University of Leicester Botanic Garden
Leicestershire, England

ARBORETA

Abbotsbury Sub-Tropical Gardens
Dorset, England
Antony
Cornwall, England
Arley Arboretum
Worcestershire, England
Bath Botanic Gardens
Somerset, England
Batsford Arboretum
Gloucestershire, England
Bicton Park Gardens
Devon, England
Bluebell Arboretum & Nursery
Derbyshire, England
Bodenham Arboretum
Worcestershire, England
Caerhays Castle Gardens
Cornwall, England
Cambridge University Botanic Garden
Cambridgeshire, England
Chatsworth
Derbyshire, England
Chyverton
Cornwall, England
Cowdray Park
West Sussex, England
Cruickshank Botanic Garden
Grampian, Scotland
Dawyck Botanic Garden
Borders, Scotland
East Bergholt Place
Suffolk, England
Exbury Gardens
Hampshire, England
Exeter University Gardens
Devon, England
Fota Arboretum & Garden
Co. Cork, Republic of Ireland
Golden Acre Park
West Yorkshire, England
Granada Arboretum
Cheshire, England
Hergest Croft Gardens
Herefordshire, England
Highclere Castle
Hampshire, England
Landford Trees
Wiltshire, England
Lynford Arboretum
Norfolk, England
Marwood Hill Gardens
Devon, England
National Botanic Gardens
Co. Dublin, Republic of Ireland
Nymans
West Sussex, England
Pencarrow
Cornwall, England
Pershore College
Worcestershire, England
RHS Garden Hyde Hall
Essex, England
RHS Garden Rosemoor
Devon, England
RHS Garden Wisley
Surrey, England
Rowallane Garden
Co. Down, Northern Ireland
Royal Botanic Garden Edinburgh
Lothian, Scotland
Royal Botanic Gardens, Kew
London, England
Saling Hall
Essex, England
Seaforde Gardens
Co. Down, Northern Ireland
Sheffield Park Garden
East Sussex, England
Talbot Botanic Gardens
Co. Dublin, Republic of Ireland
Tatton Park
Cheshire, England
Thorp Perrow Arboretum & Woodland Garden
North Yorkshire, England
Torosay Castle & Gardens
Strathclyde, Scotland
Westonbirt The National Arboretum
Gloucestershire, England
Whitfield
Herefordshire, England
Winkworth Arboretum
Surrey, England
Woburn Abbey
Bedfordshire, England

BEGONIA

Blackmore & Langdon
Somerset, England
Glasgow Botanic Garden
Strathclyde, Scotland

Bluebells

Ardkinglas Woodland Garden
Strathclyde, Scotland
Blakenham Woodland Garden
Suffolk, England
Emmetts Garden
Kent, England
Fairhaven Woodland & Water Garden
Norfolk, England
Furzey Gardens
Hampshire, England
Galloway House Gardens
Dumfries & Galloway, Scotland
Haughley Park
Suffolk, England
High Beeches
West Sussex, England
Hole Park
Kent, England
Killerton
Devon, England
Lanhydrock
Cornwall, England
Leonardslee Lakes & Gardens
West Sussex, England
Lydney Park Gardens
Gloucestershire, England
Royal Botanic Gardens, Kew
London, England
Sheffield Park Garden
East Sussex, England
Stourhead
Wiltshire, England
Thorp Perrow Arboretum & Woodland Garden
North Yorkshire, England
Wakehurst Place
West Sussex, England
Winkworth Arboretum
Surrey, England

Border and Herbaceous Plants

Arley Hall
Cheshire, England
Barrington Court
Somerset, England
Beningbrough Hall & Gardens
North Yorkshire, England
Beth Chatto Gardens
Essex, England
Bressingham Gardens
Norfolk, England
Buscot Park
Oxfordshire, England
Castle Drogo
Devon, England
Clare College Fellows' Garden
Cambridgeshire, England
Cottesbrooke Hall
Northamptonshire, England
The Courts Garden
Wiltshire, England
East Ruston Old Vicarage
Norfolk, England
Felley Priory
Nottinghamshire, England
Forde Abbey
Dorset, England
Garsington Manor
Oxfordshire, England
Goodnestone Park
Kent, England
Great Dixter
East Sussex, England
Hatfield House
Hertfordshire, England
Helmingham Hall
Suffolk, England
Hestercombe Gardens
Somerset, England
Hinton Ampner
Hampshire, England
Hoveton Hall
Norfolk, England
Kingston Maurward Gardens
Dorset, England
Leeds Castle
Kent, England
The National Botanic Garden of Wales
Dyfed, Wales
National Botanic Gardens
Co. Dublin, Republic of Ireland
Ness Botanic Gardens
Cheshire, England
Newby Hall
North Yorkshire, England
Nymans
West Sussex, England
Packwood House
Warwickshire, England
Parham
West Sussex, England
Pashley Manor Gardens
East Sussex, England
Pershore College
Worcestershire, England
RHS Garden Hyde Hall
Essex, England
RHS Garden Wisley
Surrey, England
Rodmarton Manor
Gloucestershire, England
Royal Botanic Gardens, Kew
London, England
Sandringham House
Norfolk, England
Savill Garden
Surrey, England
Stourhead
Wiltshire, England
Tintinhull House
Somerset, England
Upton House & Gardens
Warwickshire, England
Wallington
Northumberland and Tyne & Wear, England

Cacti

Abbey Brook Cactus Nursery
Derbyshire, England
Birmingham Botanical Gardens & Glasshouses
West Midlands, England
Cambridge University Botanic Garden
Cambridgeshire, England
Holly Gate Cactus Nursery
West Sussex, England
National Botanic Gardens
Co. Dublin, Republic of Ireland
RHS Garden Wisley
Surrey, England
Royal Botanic Garden Edinburgh
Lothian, Scotland
Royal Botanic Gardens, Kew
London, England
University of Durham Botanic Garden
Co. Durham, England

CAMELLIAS

Bodnant Gardens
Clwyd, Wales
Burncoose Gardens & Nurseries
Cornwall, England
Coleton Fishacre Garden
Devon, England
Galloway House Gardens
Dumfries & Galloway, Scotland
Glendurgan
Cornwall, England
Greenway
Devon, England
Lydney Park Gardens
Gloucestershire, England
Marwood Hill Gardens
Devon, England
Mount Edgcumbe Gardens
Cornwall, England
RHS Garden Wisley
Surrey, England
Savill Garden
Surrey, England
Trewidden Gardens
Cornwall, England
Wentworth Castle Gardens
South Yorkshire, England

CARNATIONS

Crathes Castle
Grampian, Scotland
RHS Garden Wisley
Surrey, England

CHRYSANTHEMUMS

Halls of Heddon
Northumberland and Tyne & Wear, England
RHS Garden Wisley
Surrey, England

CLEMATIS

Burford House Gardens
Shropshire, England
Elworthy Cottage Plants
Somerset, England
Helmsley Walled Garden
North Yorkshire, England
Kelmscott Manor
Oxfordshire, England

CONIFERS

Ardkinglas Woodland Garden
Strathclyde, Scotland
Ascott
Buckinghamshire, England
Batsford Arboretum
Gloucestershire, England
Benmore Botanic Garden
Strathclyde, Scotland
Bressingham Gardens
Norfolk, England
Brodsworth Hall & Gardens
South Yorkshire, England
Chatsworth
Derbyshire, England
Clumber Park
Nottinghamshire, England
Cragside
Northumberland and Tyne & Wear, England
Dawyck Botanic Garden
Borders, Scotland
Eastnor Castle
Herefordshire, England
Elvaston Castle
Derbyshire, England
Fota Arboretum & Garden
Co. Cork, Republic of Ireland
Great Comp
Kent, England
Hergest Croft Gardens
Herefordshire, England
Kingston Lacy
Dorset, England
Mount Stuart
Strathclyde, Scotland
National Botanic Gardens
Co. Dublin, Republic of Ireland
Nymans
West Sussex, England
Pencarrow
Cornwall, England
RHS Garden Wisley
Surrey, England
Royal Botanic Gardens, Kew
London, England
Scone Palace
Tayside, Scotland
Sheffield Park Garden
East Sussex, England
Thorp Perrow Arboretum & Woodland Garden
North Yorkshire, England
Trelissick Garden
Cornwall, England
Wakehurst Place
West Sussex, England
Westonbirt The National Arboretum
Gloucestershire, England
Winkworth Arboretum
Surrey, England

CYCLAMEN

Ashwood Nurseries Ltd
Staffordshire, England
Cadenza
Surrey, England
Foxgrove
Berkshire, England
RHS Garden Wisley
Surrey, England
Tile Barn Nursery
Kent, England

DAFFODILS

Acorn Bank Garden
Cumbria, England
Broadleigh Gardens
Somerset, England
Brodie Castle
Grampian, Scotland
Chenies Manor
Buckinghamshire, England
Clandon Park
Surrey, England
Docton Mill
Devon, England
Erddig
Clwyd, Wales
Escot
Devon, England
Felley Priory
Nottinghamshire, England
Fota Arboretum & Garden
Co. Cork, Republic of Ireland
Guy Wilson Daffodil Garden
Co. Derry, Northern Ireland
Hever Castle
Kent, England
Overbury Court
Worcestershire, England

Petworth House
West Sussex, England
RHS Garden Wisley
Surrey, England
Springfields Festival Gardens
Lincolnshire, England
Stourhead
Wiltshire, England
Thorp Perrow Arboretum & Woodland Garden
North Yorkshire, England
Threave Garden
Dumfries & Galloway, Scotland

DAHLIAS

Anglesey Abbey
Cambridgeshire, England
Biddulph Grange Gardens
Staffordshire, England
Halls of Heddon
Northumberland and Tyne & Wear, England
Hever Castle
Kent, England
Orchid Paradise
Devon, England
Port Lympne
Kent, England
Savill Garden
Surrey, England
Valley Gardens
North Yorkshire, England

DELPHINIUM

Blackmore & Langdon
Somerset, England
Cambridge University Botanic Garden
Cambridgeshire, England
Falkland Palace
Fife, Scotland
Godinton House & Gardens
Kent, England
Haddon Hall
Derbyshire, England
RHS Garden Wisley
Surrey, England
Rougham Hall Nurseries
Suffolk, England

FERNS

Abbey Cottage
Hampshire, England
The Abbey House
Wiltshire, England
Brodsworth Hall & Gardens
South Yorkshire, England
Fibrex Nurseries Ltd
Warwickshire, England
Glasgow Botanic Garden
Strathclyde, Scotland
National Botanic Gardens
Co. Dublin, Republic of Ireland
RHS Garden Harlow Carr
North Yorkshire, England
RHS Garden Wisley
Surrey, England
Royal Botanic Garden Edinburgh
Lothian, Scotland
Royal Botanic Gardens, Kew
London, England
Sherborne Garden
Somerset, England
Sizergh Castle
Cumbria, England

FRUIT

Beningbrough Hall & Gardens
North Yorkshire, England
Berrington Hall
Herefordshire, England
Blackthorn Nursery
Hampshire, England
Brogdale
Kent, England
Broughton House Gardens
Dumfries & Galloway, Scotland
Croxteth Hall & Country Park
"Lancashire, Merseyside & Greater Manchester", England
Deacon's Nursery
Isle of Wight, England
Erddig
Clwyd, Wales
Felbrigg Hall
Norfolk, England
Garden Organic Ryton
Warwickshire, England
Hales Hall Gardens & Reads Nursery
Norfolk, England
Heligan Gardens
Cornwall, England
Highnam Court
Gloucestershire, England
Osborne House
Isle of Wight, England
Pershore College
Worcestershire, England
RHS Garden Wisley
Surrey, England
Reaseheath College
Cheshire, England
Rougham Hall Nurseries
Suffolk, England
Thornhayes Nursery Ltd
Devon, England
Upton House & Gardens
Warwickshire, England
West Dean Gardens
West Sussex, England
Westbury Court
Gloucestershire, England

FUCHSIAS

Green Island
Essex, England
Margam Country Park
Glamorgan, Wales
The Vernon Geranium Nursery
Surrey, England

GLADIOLI

RHS Garden Wisley
Surrey, England

GLASSHOUSES

Bicton Park Gardens
Devon, England
Birmingham Botanical Gardens & Glasshouses
West Midlands, England
Cambridge University Botanic Garden
Cambridgeshire, England
Duthie Park
Grampian, Scotland
The Eden Project
Cornwall, England
Houghton Lodge
Hampshire, England
The Living Rainforest
Berkshire, England

The National Botanic Garden of Wales
Dyfed, Wales
National Botanic Gardens
Co. Dublin, Republic of Ireland
Ness Botanic Gardens
Cheshire, England
Oxford Botanic Garden
Oxfordshire, England
Plantasia
Glamorgan, Wales
RHS Garden Wisley
Surrey, England
Roundhay Park & Tropical World
West Yorkshire, England
Royal Botanic Garden Edinburgh
Lothian, Scotland
Royal Botanic Gardens, Kew
London, England
Singleton Park & Swansea Botanical Gardens
Glamorgan, Wales
Sir George Staunton Country Park
Hampshire, England
Stapeley Water Gardens
Cheshire, England
Stowell Park
Gloucestershire, England
University of Durham Botanic Garden
Co. Durham, England
University of Leicester Botanic Garden
Leicestershire, England
Wentworth Castle Gardens
South Yorkshire, England

HEATHERS

The Abbey House
Wiltshire, England
The Bannut
Herefordshire, England
Bell's Cherrybank Centre
Tayside, Scotland
Champs Hill
West Sussex, England
Exeter University Gardens
Devon, England
Furzey Gardens
Hampshire, England
Jack Drake
Highland, Scotland
National Botanic Gardens
Co. Dublin, Republic of Ireland
Ness Botanic Gardens
Cheshire, England
RHS Garden Wisley
Surrey, England
Roundhay Park & Tropical World
West Yorkshire, England
Royal Botanic Garden Edinburgh
Lothian, Scotland
Royal Botanic Gardens, Kew
London, England
Threave Garden
Dumfries & Galloway, Scotland
Valley Gardens
Surrey, England

HEBES

University of Bristol Botanic Garden
Gloucestershire, England

HEMEROCALLIS

Ann & Roger Bowden
Devon, England
Apple Court
Hampshire, England
Rosewood Daylilies
Kent, England

HERBS

The Abbey House
Wiltshire, England
Acorn Bank Garden
Cumbria, England
Buckland Abbey
Devon, England
Chesters Walled Garden
Northumberland and Tyne & Wear, England
Downderry Nursery
Kent, England
Garden Organic Ryton
Warwickshire, England
Iden Croft Herbs
Kent, England
The National Botanic Garden of Wales
Dyfed, Wales
RHS Garden Rosemoor
Devon, England
RHS Garden Wisley
Surrey, England
Rosewood Daylilies
Kent, England
Royal Botanic Gardens, Kew
London, England
Salley Gardens
Nottinghamshire, England
University of Leicester Botanic Garden
Leicestershire, England
The Walled Garden
Worcestershire, England
York Gate
West Yorkshire, England

HOSTAS

Ann & Roger Bowden
Devon, England
Apple Court
Hampshire, England
Mill Hill Plants
Nottinghamshire, England
Park Green Nurseries
Suffolk, England

IRISES

The Abbey House
Wiltshire, England
Aulden Farm
Herefordshire, England
Broadleigh Gardens
Somerset, England
Kelways Ltd
Somerset, England
Lingen Nursery and Gardens
Shropshire, England
Marwood Hill Gardens
Devon, England
Mill Hill Plants
Nottinghamshire, England
Myddelton House
London, England
Park Green Nurseries
Suffolk, England
Rowden Gardens
Devon, England

Wakehurst Place
West Sussex, England

Lilies

Wakehurst Place
West Sussex, England

Magnolias

Batsford Arboretum
Gloucestershire, England
Bodnant Gardens
Clwyd, Wales
Caerhays Castle Gardens
Cornwall, England
Chyverton
Cornwall, England
Glendurgan
Cornwall, England
Lanhydrock
Cornwall, England
Marwood Hill Gardens
Devon, England
Millais Nurseries
Surrey, England
Mount Congreve
Co. Waterford, Republic of Ireland
RHS Garden Wisley
Surrey, England
Savill Garden
Surrey, England
Sherwood
Devon, England
Trewidden Gardens
Cornwall, England
Trewithen
Cornwall, England
Valley Gardens
Surrey, England
Wentworth Castle Gardens
South Yorkshire, England

Orchids

Eric Young Orchid Foundation
Jersey, Channel Islands
Glasgow Botanic Garden
Strathclyde, Scotland
Kelways Ltd
Somerset, England
RHS Garden Wisley
Surrey, England
Royal Botanic Garden Edinburgh
Lothian, Scotland
Royal Botanic Gardens, Kew
London, England
Scone Palace
Tayside, Scotland

Plantsman's Gardens

Angel Gardens
Shropshire, England
Antony
Cornwall, England
Ardcarraig
Co. Galway, Republic of Ireland
Beth Chatto Gardens
Essex, England
Biddulph Grange Gardens
Staffordshire, England
Birkheads Secret Gardens & Nursery
Northumberland and Tyne & Wear, England
Bishop Burton Botanic Garden
East Yorkshire, England
Bluebell Cottage Gardens & Lodge Lane Nursery
Cheshire, England
The Botanic Nursery
Wiltshire, England
Bressingham Gardens
Norfolk, England
Brook Cottage
Oxfordshire, England
Cally Gardens
Dumfries & Galloway, Scotland
Cambridge University Botanic Garden
Cambridgeshire, England
Capel Manor
London, England
Castle Howard
North Yorkshire, England
Chelsea Physic Garden
London, England
Chyverton
Cornwall, England
Coleton Fishacre Garden
Devon, England
Copt House Garden
Cumbria, England
Copton Ash Gardens
Kent, England
Cotswold Garden Flowers
Worcestershire, England
The Courts Garden
Wiltshire, England
Cruickshank Botanic Garden
Grampian, Scotland
Crûg Farm Plants
Gwynedd, Wales
The Dillon Garden
Co. Dublin, Republic of Ireland
Dundee Botanic Garden
Tayside, Scotland
East Ruston Old Vicarage
Norfolk, England
The Garden House
Devon, England
Glen Chantry
Essex, England
Gravetye Manor Hotel
West Sussex, England
Great Dixter
East Sussex, England
Greencombe Gardens
Somerset, England
The Harris Garden
Berkshire, England
Heathlands
Hampshire, England
Herterton House Gardens & Nursery
Northumberland and Tyne & Wear, England
Hidcote Manor Garden
Gloucestershire, England
High Beeches
West Sussex, England
Highdown
West Sussex, England
Hinton Ampner
Hampshire, England
Hodnet Hall Gardens
Shropshire, England
Holbrook Garden
Devon, England
Holehird Gardens
Cumbria, England
Home Covert Garden & Arboretum
Wiltshire, England

Howick Hall Gardens
Northumberland and Tyne & Wear, England
Hunt's Court
Gloucestershire, England
W.E.Th. Ingwersen Ltd
West Sussex, England
Kiftsgate Court
Gloucestershire, England
Killerton
Devon, England
Lackham Country Park
Wiltshire, England
Lamorran House
Cornwall, England
Leonardslee Lakes & Gardens
West Sussex, England
Longstock Water Gardens
Hampshire, England
Marwood Hill Gardens
Devon, England
Meon Orchard
Hampshire, England
Mount Congreve
Co. Waterford, Republic of Ireland
Myddelton House
London, England
National Botanic Gardens
Co. Dublin, Republic of Ireland
Newby Hall
North Yorkshire, England
North Court
Isle of Wight, England
Nymans
West Sussex, England
Old Vicarage
Wiltshire, England
Oxford Botanic Garden
Oxfordshire, England
Plant World Botanic Gardens
Devon, England
Ramster
Surrey, England
RHS Garden Harlow Carr
North Yorkshire, England
RHS Garden Hyde Hall
Essex, England
RHS Garden Rosemoor
Devon, England
RHS Garden Wisley
Surrey, England
Rock Farm
Kent, England
Rowallane Garden
Co. Down, Northern Ireland
Royal Botanic Garden Edinburgh
Lothian, Scotland
Royal Botanic Gardens, Kew
London, England
Saling Hall
Essex, England
Sausmarez Manor
Guernsey, Channel Islands
Savill Garden
Surrey, England
Scotney Castle Garden
Kent, England
Sheffield Park Garden
East Sussex, England
Sherborne Garden
Somerset, England
Snape Cottage
Dorset, England
Spetchley Park
Worcestershire, England
Spinners
Hampshire, England
St Andrews Botanic Garden
Fife, Scotland
Sticky Wicket
Dorset, England
Stillingfleet Lodge Nurseries
North Yorkshire, England
Stockton Bury
Hereford, England
Stone House Cottage Garden
Worcestershire, England
Talbot Botanic Gardens
Co. Dublin, Republic of Ireland
Tradewinds
Dyfed, Wales
Trebah Garden Trust
Cornwall, England
Tregrehan
Cornwall, England
Trelissick Garden
Cornwall, England
Trengwainton Garden
Cornwall, England
Tresco Abbey
Cornwall, England
Trewithen
Cornwall, England
University of Durham Botanic Garden
Co. Durham, England
University of Leicester Botanic Garden
Leicestershire, England
Valley Gardens
Surrey, England
Ventnor Botanic Garden
Isle of Wight, England
Wakehurst Place
West Sussex, England
Waterperry Gardens
Oxfordshire, England
West Dean Gardens
West Sussex, England
White Hall Plants
Suffolk, England
"Winterbourne Botanic Garden, University of Birmingham"
West Midlands, England
Woodpeckers
Warwickshire, England

PRIMROSES

Edrom Nurseries
Borders, Scotland

RHODODENRONS AND AZALEAS

Achamore Gardens
Strathclyde, Scotland
Angus Garden
Strathclyde, Scotland
Benmore Botanic Garden
Strathclyde, Scotland
Blackhills
Grampian, Scotland
Blakenham Woodland Garden
Suffolk, England
Bodnant Gardens
Clwyd, Wales
Borde Hill Garden
West Sussex, England
Bosahan
Cornwall, England
Brodick Castle
Strathclyde, Scotland
Cannizaro Park
London, England

Charts Edge
Kent, England
Chyverton
Cornwall, England
Clyne Gardens
Glamorgan, Wales
Cragside
Northumberland and Tyne & Wear, England
Crarae Gardens
Strathclyde, Scotland
Dawyck Botanic Garden
Borders, Scotland
Dorothy Clive Garden
Staffordshire, England
Exbury Gardens
Hampshire, England
Furzey Gardens
Hampshire, England
Glenarn
Strathclyde, Scotland
Glendoick Gardens
Tayside, Scotland
Glendurgan
Cornwall, England
Glenveagh Castle
Co. Donegal, Republic of Ireland
Gresgarth Hall
"Lancashire, Merseyside & Greater Manchester", England
Hergest Croft Gardens
Herefordshire, England
High Beeches
West Sussex, England
Highclere Castle
Hampshire, England
Higher Knowle
Devon, England
Hodnet Hall Gardens
Shropshire, England
Hydon Nurseries
Surrey, England
Isabella Plantation
London, England
Lanhydrock
Cornwall, England
Lea Gardens
Derbyshire, England
Leonardslee Lakes & Gardens
West Sussex, England
Logan House
Dumfries & Galloway, Scotland
Lukesland
Devon, England
Lydney Park Gardens
Gloucestershire, England
Marwood Hill Gardens
Devon, England
Millais Nurseries
Surrey, England
Minterne
Dorset, England
Mount Congreve
Co. Waterford, Republic of Ireland
Mount Stewart
Co. Down, Northern Ireland
Muncaster Castle
Cumbria, England
National Botanic Gardens
Co. Dublin, Republic of Ireland
Ness Botanic Gardens
Cheshire, England
Nymans
West Sussex, England
The Old Glebe
Devon, England
Plas Newydd
Gwynedd, Wales
Ramster
Surrey, England
RHS Garden Wisley
Surrey, England
Rowallane Garden
Co. Down, Northern Ireland
Royal Botanic Gardens, Kew
London, England
Savill Garden
Surrey, England
Scotney Castle Garden
Kent, England
Sheffield Park Garden
East Sussex, England
Sheringham Park
Norfolk, England
Sherwood
Devon, England
Singleton Park & Swansea Botanical Gardens
Glamorgan, Wales
Stody Lodge
Norfolk, England
Stourhead
Wiltshire, England
Trengwainton Garden
Cornwall, England
Trewithen
Cornwall, England
Tylney Hall
Hampshire, England
Valley Gardens
Surrey, England
Wakehurst Place
West Sussex, England
Wentworth Castle Gardens
South Yorkshire, England

Rock Gardens

Cambridge University Botanic Garden
Cambridgeshire, England
Cruickshank Botanic Garden
Grampian, Scotland
Dorothy Clive Garden
Staffordshire, England
Mount Ephraim
Kent, England
Mount Stuart
Strathclyde, Scotland
National Botanic Gardens
Co. Dublin, Republic of Ireland
Ness Botanic Gardens
Cheshire, England
RHS Garden Wisley
Surrey, England
Royal Botanic Garden Edinburgh
Lothian, Scotland
Royal Botanic Gardens, Kew
London, England

Roses, Modern

The Abbey House
Wiltshire, England
The Alnwick Garden
Northumberland and Tyne & Wear, England
Benvarden Garden & Grounds
Co. Antrim, Northern Ireland
Chartwell
Kent, England
David Austin Roses
Shropshire, England
The Gardens of the Rose
Hertfordshire, England

Hever Castle
Kent, England
Longleat House
Wiltshire, England
Mattocks Roses
Oxfordshire, England
Nunwell House
Isle of Wight, England
Polesden Lacey
Surrey, England
Queen Mary's Gardens
London, England
Ragley Hall
Warwickshire, England
RHS Garden Hyde Hall
Essex, England
RHS Garden Rosemoor
Devon, England
RHS Garden Wisley
Surrey, England
Royal Botanic Gardens, Kew
London, England
Savill Garden
Surrey, England
Sledmere House
East Yorkshire, England
"Winterbourne Botanic Garden, University of Birmingham"
West Midlands, England

Roses, Old

Arley Hall
Cheshire, England
Castle Howard
North Yorkshire, England
Coton Manor
Northamptonshire, England
Cruickshank Botanic Garden
Grampian, Scotland
David Austin Roses
Shropshire, England
Drum Castle
Grampian, Scotland
Felley Priory
Nottinghamshire, England
The Gardens of the Rose
Hertfordshire, England
Hardwick Hall
Derbyshire, England
Helmingham Hall
Suffolk, England
Highnam Court
Gloucestershire, England
The Hiller Garden
Warwickshire, England
Hunt's Court
Gloucestershire, England
Kiftsgate Court
Gloucestershire, England
Lackham Country Park
Wiltshire, England
Longleat House
Wiltshire, England
Mannington Gardens
Norfolk, England
Mariners
Berkshire, England
Mottisfont Abbey
Hampshire, England
Myddelton House
London, England
Nymans
West Sussex, England
Peter Beales Roses
Norfolk, England
RHS Garden Rosemoor
Devon, England
Royal Botanic Gardens, Kew
London, England
Rymans
West Sussex, England
Westbury Court
Gloucestershire, England
"Winterbourne Botanic Garden, University of Birmingham"
West Midlands, England

Snowdrops

Anglesey Abbey
Cambridgeshire, England
Attingham Park
Shropshire, England
Benington Lordship
Hertfordshire, England
Berrington Hall
Herefordshire, England
Birr Castle Demesne
Co. Offaly, Republic of Ireland
Brandy Mount House
Hampshire, England
Cambo Gardens
Fife, Scotland
Colesbourne Park
Gloucestershire, England
Colzium Walled Garden
Strathclyde, Scotland
East Lambrook Manor
Somerset, England
Easton Walled Gardens
Lincolnshire, England
Fairhaven Woodland & Water Garden
Norfolk, England
Foxgrove
Berkshire, England
Galloway House Gardens
Dumfries & Galloway, Scotland
Heale House Garden
Wiltshire, England
Heddon Hall
Devon, England
Hever Castle
Kent, England
Hodsock Priory
Nottinghamshire, England
Hopton Hall
Derbyshire, England
Kailzie Gardens
Borders, Scotland
Lacock Abbey
Wiltshire, England
Monksilver Nursery
Cambridgeshire, England
Myddelton House
London, England
Painswick Rococo Garden
Gloucestershire, England
Penrhyn Castle
Gwynedd, Wales
Plas-yn-Rhiw
Gwynedd, Wales
Polesden Lacey
Surrey, England
Rode Hall
Cheshire, England
Rodmarton Manor
Gloucestershire, England
Snape Cottage
Dorset, England
Studley Royal Water Gardens
North Yorkshire, England
Woodpeckers
Warwickshire, England

Sub-Tropical Plants

Abbotsbury Sub-Tropical Gardens
Dorset, England
Achamore Gardens
Strathclyde, Scotland
Antony
Cornwall, England
Blackpool Gardens
Devon, England
Bosahan
Cornwall, England
Coleton Fishacre Garden
Devon, England
Derreen
Co. Kerry, Republic of Ireland
Dunster Castle
Somerset, England
East Ruston Old Vicarage
Norfolk, England
The Eden Project
Cornwall, England
Exeter University Gardens
Devon, England
Fota Arboretum & Garden
Co. Cork, Republic of Ireland
Glendurgan
Cornwall, England
Greenway
Devon, England
Greenways
Oxfordshire, England
Knoll Gardens
Dorset, England
Lamorran House
Cornwall, England
Logan Botanic Garden
Dumfries & Galloway, Scotland
Meon Orchard
Hampshire, England
Mount Stewart
Co. Down, Northern Ireland
Mount Stuart
Strathclyde, Scotland
North Court
Isle of Wight, England
Overbeck's Museum & Garden
Devon, England
The Palm Centre
London, England
Penrhyn Castle
Gwynedd, Wales
Rowallane Garden
Co. Down, Northern Ireland
Royal Botanic Gardens, Kew
London, England
Sausmarez Manor
Guernsey, Channel Islands
Talbot Botanic Gardens
Co. Dublin, Republic of Ireland
Torosay Castle & Gardens
Strathclyde, Scotland
Trebah Garden Trust
Cornwall, England
Trelissick Garden
Cornwall, England
Trengwainton Garden
Cornwall, England
Tresco Abbey
Cornwall, England
University of Bristol Botanic Garden
Gloucestershire, England
Ventnor Botanic Garden
Isle of Wight, England

Topiary

Abbotsford
Borders, Scotland
Athelhampton
Dorset, England
Avebury Manor Garden
Wiltshire, England
Brodsworth Hall & Gardens
South Yorkshire, England
Burton Agnes Hall Gardens
East Yorkshire, England
Chirk Castle
Clwyd, Wales
Cliveden
Buckinghamshire, England
Drummond Gardens
Tayside, Scotland
Elvaston Castle
Derbyshire, England
Garsington Manor
Oxfordshire, England
Graythwaite Hall
Cumbria, England
Hatfield House
Hertfordshire, England
Herterton House Gardens & Nursery
Northumberland and Tyne & Wear, England
Hutton-in-the-Forest
Cumbria, England
Langley Boxwood Nursery
Hampshire, England
Levens Hall
Cumbria, England
"The Manor, Hemingford Grey"
Cambridgeshire, England
Mount Ephraim
Kent, England
Packwood House
Warwickshire, England
Pitmedden
Grampian, Scotland
Renishaw Hall
Derbyshire, England
St Mary's House
West Sussex, England
Torosay Castle & Gardens
Strathclyde, Scotland

Vegetables

Beningbrough Hall & Gardens
North Yorkshire, England
Croxteth Hall & Country Park
"Lancashire, Merseyside & Greater Manchester", England
Felbrigg Hall
Norfolk, England
Garden Organic Ryton
Warwickshire, England
Heligan Gardens
Cornwall, England
Le Manoir aux Quat'Saisons
Oxfordshire, England
Mertoun Gardens
Borders, Scotland
Pershore College
Worcestershire, England
Reaseheath College
Cheshire, England
RHS Garden Rosemoor
Devon, England
RHS Garden Wisley
Surrey, England
Upton House & Gardens
Warwickshire, England

West Dean Gardens
West Sussex, England
West Green House
Hampshire, England

VIOLAS

Elizabeth MacGregor
Dumfries & Galloway, Scotland
C.W. Groves & Son Ltd.
Dorset, England

WILDFLOWERS

The Garden House
Devon, England
Naturescape
Nottinghamshire, England

WOODLAND GARDENS

Broadleas
Wiltshire, England
Heligan Gardens
Cornwall, England
High Beeches
West Sussex, England
Hodnet Hall Gardens
Shropshire, England
Home Covert Garden & Arboretum
Wiltshire, England
Leonardslee Lakes & Gardens
West Sussex, England
Mount Stewart
Co. Down, Northern Ireland
Muncaster Castle
Cumbria, England
RHS Garden Wisley
Surrey, England
Rowallane Garden
Co. Down, Northern Ireland
Savill Garden
Surrey, England
Trebah Garden Trust
Cornwall, England
Trelissick Garden
Cornwall, England
Trengwainton Garden
Cornwall, England
Trewithen
Cornwall, England
Valley Gardens
Surrey, England
Wakehurst Place
West Sussex, England
Westonbirt The National Arboretum
Gloucestershire, England

UNITED KINGDOM & REPUBLIC OF IRELAND

Key To Garden Location Maps

Coastline
International border
Regional border
County border
M5 Motorway
A30 Dual carriageway
A39 Main road
Urban area
Garden location

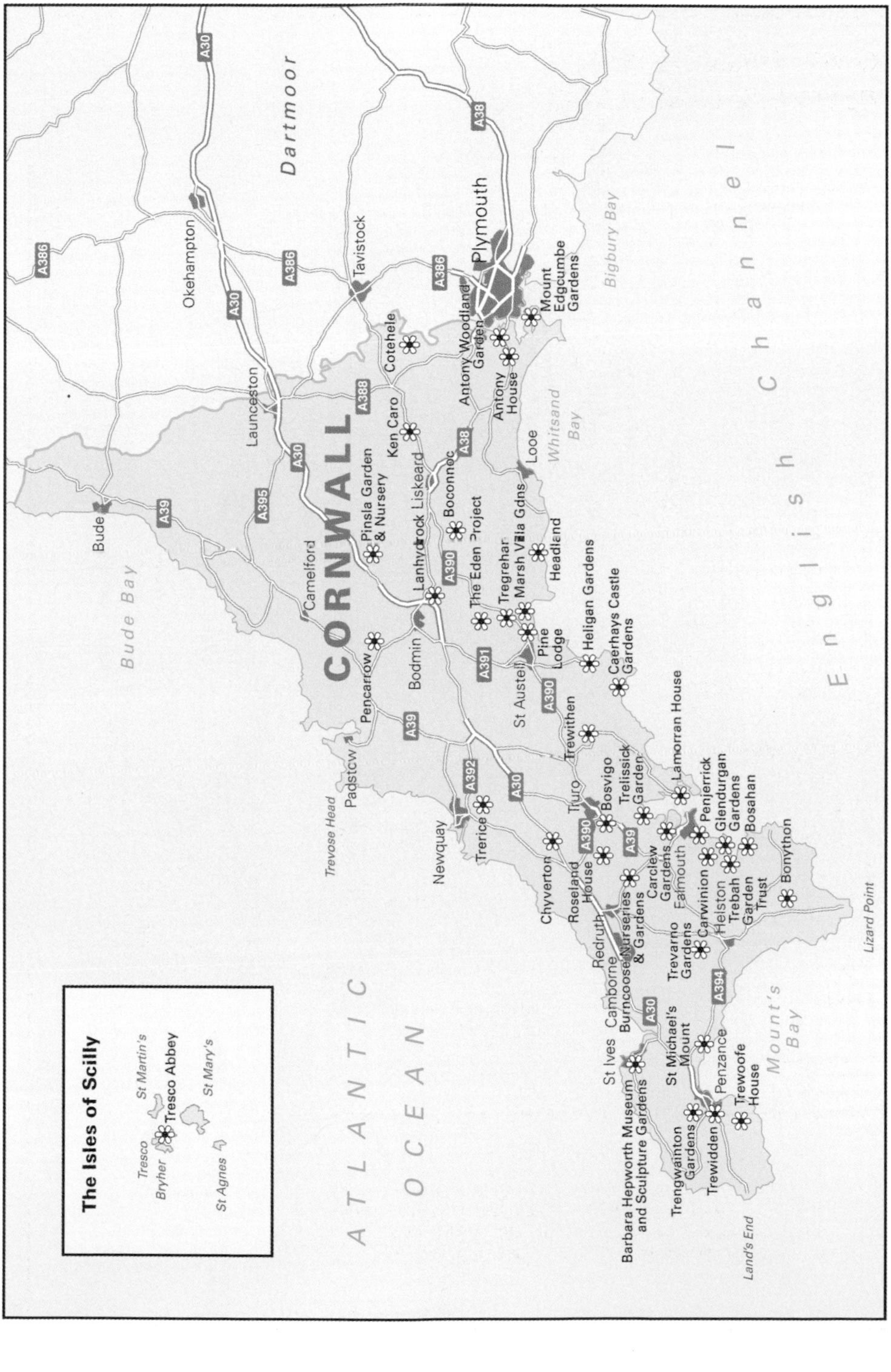

The Isles of Scilly
Tresco
Bryher
St Martin's
Tresco Abbey
St Mary's
St Agnes
Dartmoor
Okehampton
Tavistock
Plymouth
Launceston
Bude
Bude Bay
Camelford
CORNWALL
Pinsla Garden & Nursery
Ken Caro
Cotehele
Liskeard
Boconnoc
Lanhydrock
The Eden Project
Tregrehan
Marsh Villa Gdns
Headland
Pencarrow
Bodmin
Pine Lodge
Heligan Gardens
Caerhays Castle Gardens
St Austell
Trewithen
Lamorran House
Padstow
Trevose Head
Newquay
Trerice
Truro
Bosvigo
Trelissick Garden
Chyverton
Roseland House
Carclew Gardens
Falmouth
Penjerrick
Glendurgan Gardens
Bosahan
Trebah Garden Trust
Bonython
Carwinion
Helston
Redruth
Camborne
Burncoose Nurseries & Gardens
Trevarno Gardens
St Ives
Barbara Hepworth Museum and Sculpture Gardens
St Michael's Mount
Penzance
Trewoofe House
Trengwainton Gardens
Trewidden
Land's End
Lizard Point
Mount's Bay
Looe
Whitsand Bay
Antony House
Antony Woodland Garden
Mount Edgcumbe Gardens
Bigbury Bay
ATLANTIC OCEAN
English Channel
A30
A38
A386
A388
A395
A39
A390
A391
A392
A394

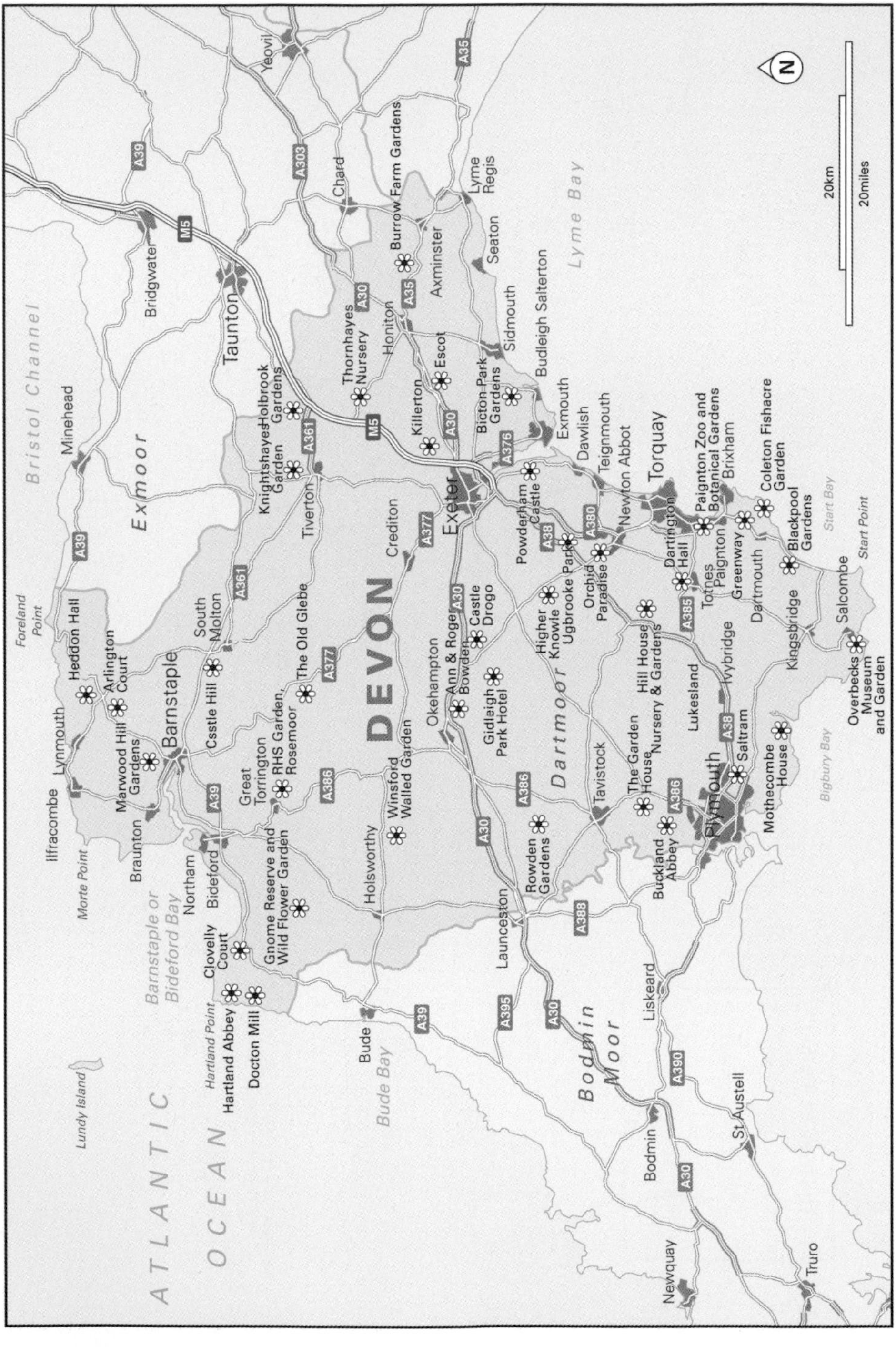
Bristol Channel
Exmoor
Minehead
Bridgwater
Taunton
Yeovil
Chard
M5
A39
A303
A35
Lyme Regis
Lyme Bay
Seaton
Axminster
Burrow Farm Gardens
Honiton
A30
Thornhayes Nursery
Escot
Killerton
Sidmouth
Budleigh Salterton
Bicton Park Gardens
Exmouth
A376
Dawlish
Teignmouth
Newton Abbot
Torquay
A380
Powderham Castle
Exeter
A377
Crediton
Tiverton
A361
Holbrook Gardens
Knightshayes Garden
Ugbrooke Park
Orchid Paradise
A38
Higher Knowle
Paignton Zoo and Botanical Gardens
Brixham
Coleton Fishacre Garden
Greenway
Paignton
Dartington Hall
Totnes
A385
Dartmouth
Blackpool Gardens
Start Bay
Start Point
Salcombe
Kingsbridge
Overbecks Museum and Garden
Ivybridge
Lukesland
Hill House Nursery & Gardens
Saltram
Plymouth
Mothecombe House
Bigbury Bay
The Garden House
Buckland Abbey
A386
Tavistock
Dartmoor
Castle Drogo
Ann & Roger Bowden
Gidleigh Park Hotel
Okehampton
DEVON
The Old Glebe
South Molton
Csstle Hill
Barnstaple
Arlington Court
Heddon Hall
Foreland Point
Lynmouth
Marwood Hill Gardens
Ilfracombe
Braunton
Morte Point
Barnstaple or Bideford Bay
Northam
Bideford
Great Torrington
RHS Garden, Rosemoor
Gnome Reserve and Wild Flower Garden
Winsford Walled Garden
Holsworthy
Rowden Gardens
Launceston
A388
Clovelly Court
Hartland Point
Hartland Abbey
Docton Mill
Bude
Bude Bay
A395
Bodmin Moor
Liskeard
A390
Lundy Island
ATLANTIC OCEAN
Bodmin
St Austell
Newquay
Truro
20km
20miles
N

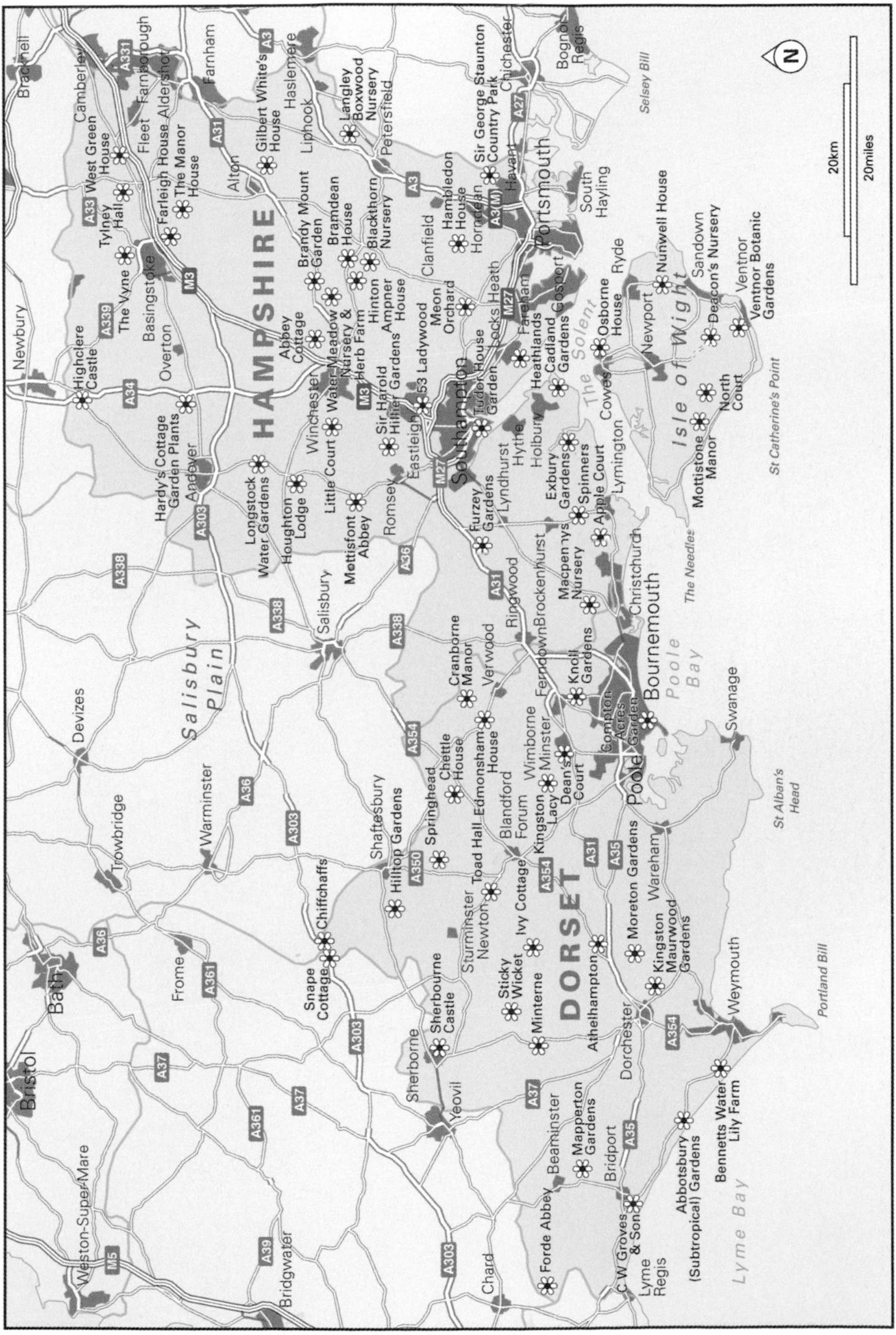
HAMPSHIRE
DORSET
Isle of Wight
The Solent
Salisbury Plain
Poole Bay
Lyme Bay
Selsey Bill
St Catherine's Point
The Needles
St Alban's Head
Portland Bill
Bracknell
Camberley
Farnborough
Fleet
Aldershot
Farnham
Haslemere
Liphook
Petersfield
Chichester
Bognor Regis
Havant
Portsmouth
South Hayling
Newbury
Basingstoke
Overton
Andover
Alton
Winchester
Eastleigh
Romsey
Southampton
Hythe
Holbury
Lyndhurst
Fareham
Gosport
Locks Heath
Horndean
Clanfield
Salisbury
Ringwood
Verwood
Ferndown
Brockenhurst
Christchurch
Bournemouth
Poole
Wimborne Minster
Blandford Forum
Swanage
Wareham
Weymouth
Dorchester
Bridport
Beaminster
Lyme Regis
Chard
Yeovil
Sherborne
Sturminster Newton
Shaftesbury
Warminster
Trowbridge
Devizes
Frome
Bath
Bristol
Weston-Super-Mare
Bridgwater
Lymington
Cowes
Newport
Ryde
Sandown
Ventnor
Highclere Castle
The Vyne
Tylney Hall
West Green House
Farleigh House
The Manor House
Gilbert White's House
Langley Boxwood Nursery
Sir George Staunton Country Park
Hambledon House
Blackthorn Nursery
Bramdean House
Brandy Mount Garden
Hinton Ampner House
Meon Orchard
Abbey Cottage
Water Meadow Nursery & Herb Farm
Sir Harold Hillier Gardens
53 Ladywood
Tudor House Garden
Little Court
Hardy's Cottage Garden Plants
Longstock Water Gardens
Houghton Lodge
Mottisfont Abbey
Furzey Gardens
Exbury Gardens
Spinners
Apple Court
Heathlands
Cadland Gardens
Osborne House
Nunwell House
Deacon's Nursery
Ventnor Botanic Gardens
North Court
Mottistone Manor
Macpenny's Nursery
Knoll Gardens
Cranborne Manor
Compton Acres Garden
Edmonsham House
Chettle House
Dean's Court
Kingston Lacy
Springhead
Toad Hall
Hilltop Gardens
Ivy Cottage
Sticky Wicket
Chiffchaffs
Snape Cottage
Sherbourne Castle
Minterne
Athelhampton
Moreton Gardens
Kingston Maurwood Gardens
Mapperton Gardens
Forde Abbey
C W Groves & Son
Abbotsbury (Subtropical) Gardens
Bennetts Water Lily Farm
20km
20miles
N
M3
M27
M5
A3
A3(M)
A27
A31
A33
A34
A35
A36
A37
A303
A331
A338
A339
A350
A354
A361
A39

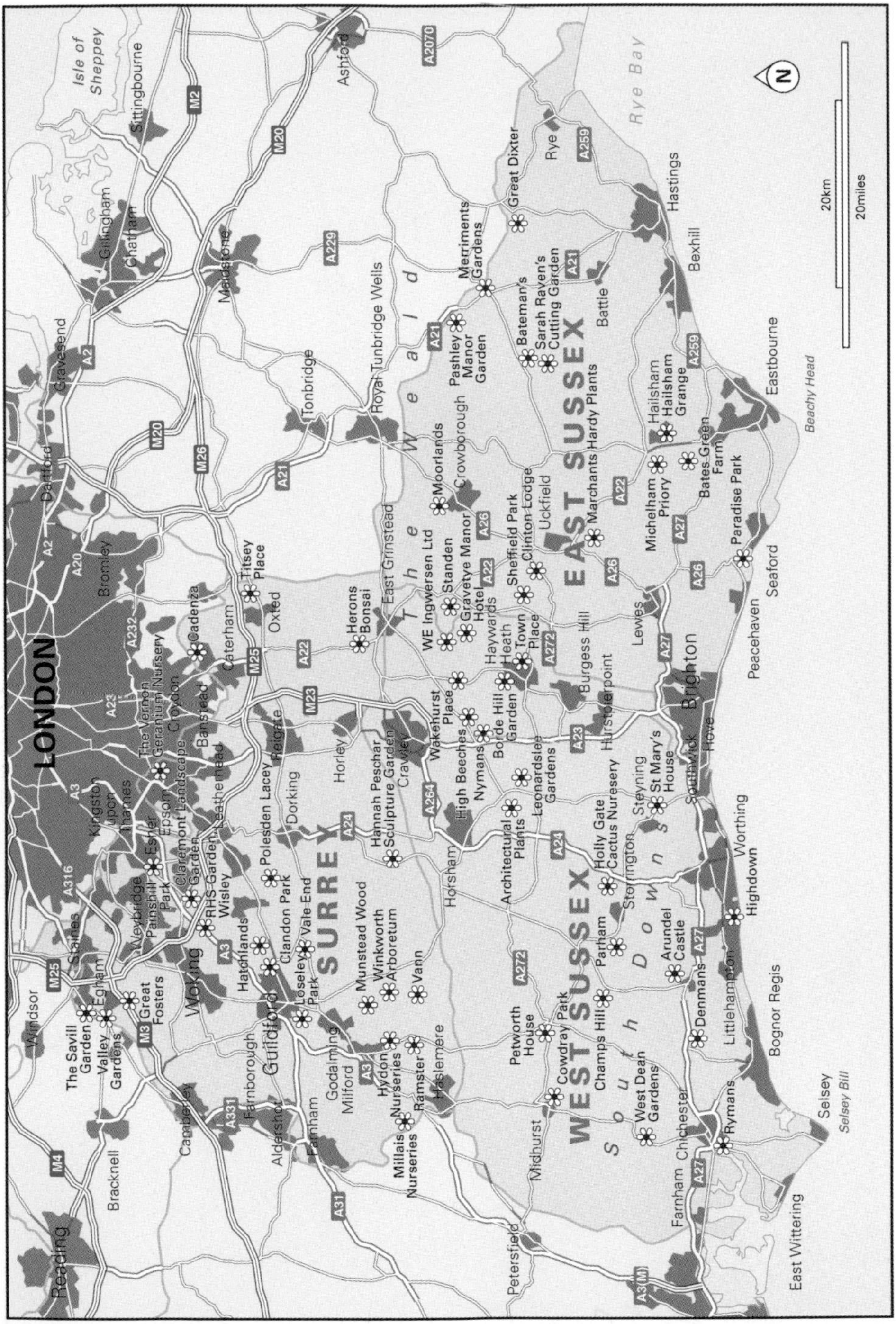
LONDON
SURREY
WEST SUSSEX
EAST SUSSEX
The Weald
South Downs
Isle of Sheppey
Rye Bay
Beachy Head
Selsey Bill
Reading
Bracknell
Windsor
Staines
Egham
Weybridge
Woking
Camberley
Farnborough
Aldershot
Farnham
Guildford
Godalming
Milford
Haslemere
Kingston upon Thames
Esher
Epsom
Leatherhead
Banstead
Croydon
Caterham
Oxted
Reigate
Dorking
Horley
Crawley
Horsham
East Grinstead
Bromley
Dartford
Gravesend
Gillingham
Chatham
Sittingbourne
Maidstone
Ashford
Tonbridge
Royal Tunbridge Wells
Crowborough
Uckfield
Haywards Heath
Burgess Hill
Hurstpierpoint
Lewes
Hailsham
Battle
Rye
Hastings
Bexhill
Eastbourne
Seaford
Peacehaven
Brighton
Hove
Southwick
Steyning
Storrington
Worthing
Highdown
Arundel Castle
Littlehampton
Bognor Regis
Chichester
Selsey
East Wittering
Farnham
Midhurst
Petersfield
The Savill Garden
Valley Gardens
Great Fosters
Painshill Park
Claremont Landscape Garden
RHS Garden Wisley
Hatchlands
Clandon Park
Polesden Lacey
Loseley Park
Vale End
Munstead Wood
Winkworth Arboretum
Vann
Hydon Nurseries
Ramster
Millais Nurseries
The Vernon Geranium Nursery
Cadenza
Titsey Place
Herons Bonsai
Hannah Peschar Sculpture Garden
Wakehurst Place
High Beeches
Nymans
Borde Hill Garden
Leonardslee Gardens
Architectural Plants
Holly Gate Cactus Nursery
St Mary's House
Parham
Denmans
Petworth House
Cowdray Park
Champs Hill
West Dean Gardens
Rymans
WE Ingwersen Ltd
Standen
Gravetye Manor Hotel
Town Place
Sheffield Park
Clinton Lodge
Moorlands
Marchants Hardy Plants
Michelham Priory
Bates Green Farm
Paradise Park
Hailsham Grange
Pashley Manor Garden
Bateman's
Sarah Raven's Cutting Garden
Merriments Gardens
Great Dixter
M25
M4
M3
M23
M20
M26
M2
A3
A3(M)
A31
A331
A316
A23
A232
A2
A20
A22
A21
A24
A264
A272
A27
A26
A259
A229
A2070
20km
20miles
N

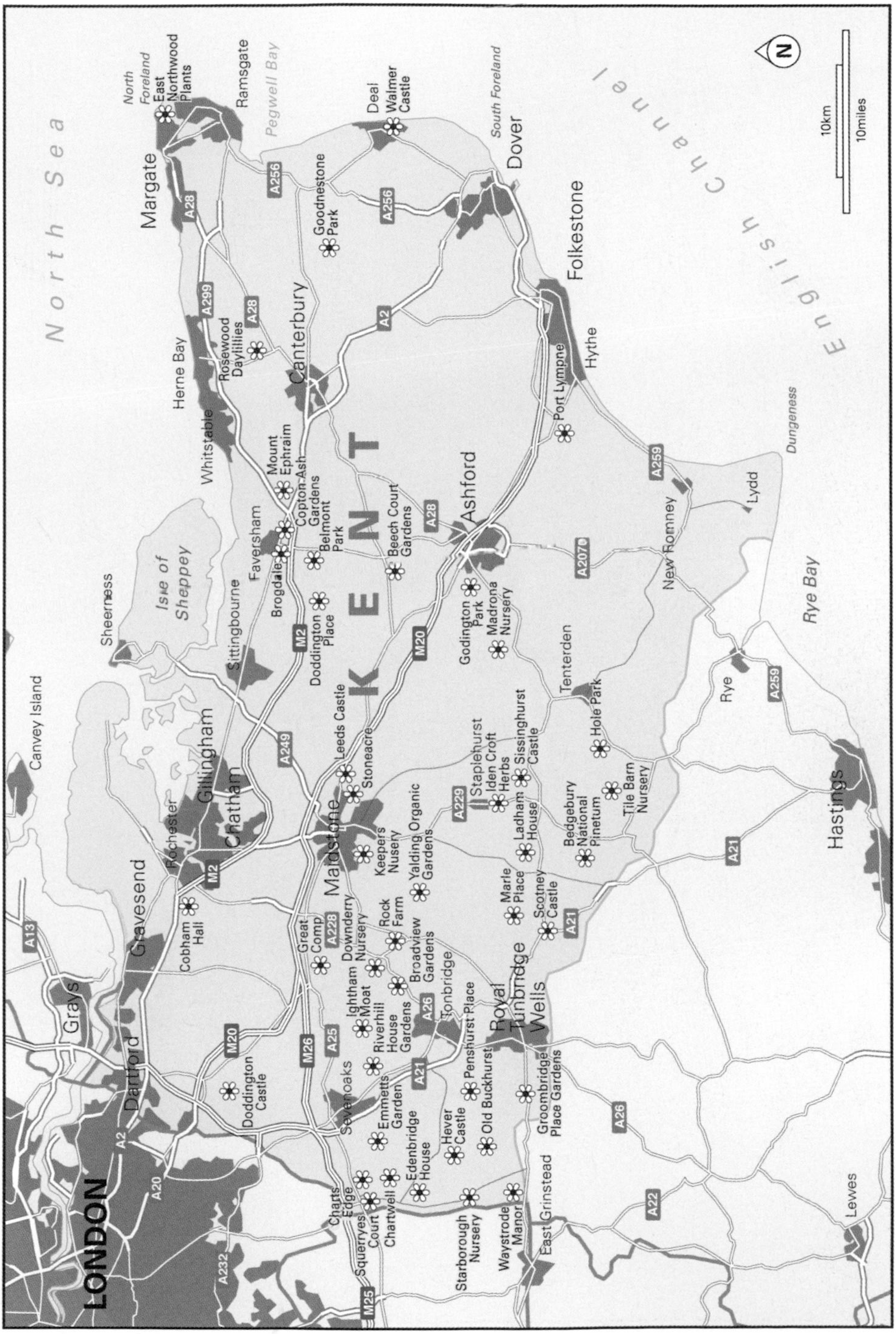
North Sea
North Foreland
East Northwood Plants
Ramsgate
Pegwell Bay
Margate
Herne Bay
Rosewood Daylillies
Canterbury
Goodnestone Park
Deal
Walmer Castle
South Foreland
Dover
Folkestone
Hythe
Port Lympne
English Channel
Whitstable
Mount Ephraim
Copton Ash
Gardens
Faversham
Belmont Park
Brogdale
Beech Court Gardens
Ashford
Isle of Sheppey
Sheerness
Sittingbourne
Doddington Place
Godington Park
Madrona Nursery
KENT
Lydd
Dungeness
New Romney
Rye Bay
Rye
Tenterden
Hole Park
Canvey Island
Gillingham
Chatham
Rochester
Gravesend
Leeds Castle
Stoneacre
Maidstone
Staplehurst
Iden Croft Herbs
Sissinghurst Castle
Ladham House
Bedgebury National Pinetum
Tile Barn Nursery
Hastings
Keepers Nusery
Yalding Organic Gardens
Marle Place
Scotney Castle
Cobham Hall
Great Comp
Downderry Nursery
Rock Farm
Broadview Gardens
Tonbridge
Royal Tunbridge Wells
Ightham Moat
Riverhill House Gardens
Penshurst Place
Old Buckhurst
Groombridge Place Gardens
Grays
Dartford
Doddington Castle
Sevenoaks
Emmetts Garden
Edenbridge House
Hever Castle
Chartwell
Squerryes Court
Charts Edge
Starborough Nursery
Waystrode Manor
East Grinstead
Lewes
LONDON
A2
A20
A232
M25
M20
M26
A25
A21
A26
A22
A13
M2
A228
A229
A249
M20
A20
A28
A299
A256
A259
A2070
10km
10miles
N

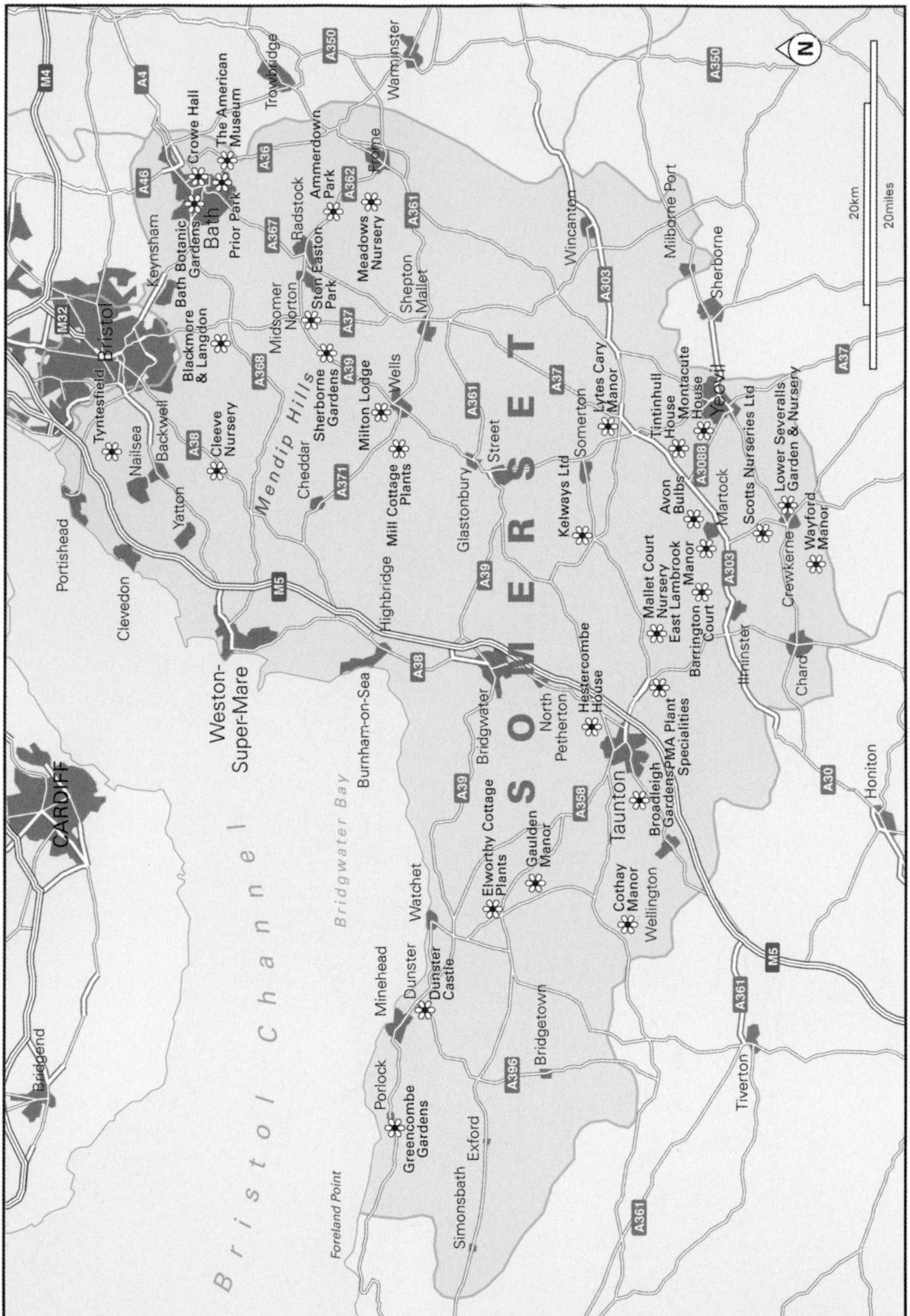
SOMERSET
Bristol Channel
Bridgwater Bay
Mendip Hills
Foreland Point
CARDIFF
Bridgend
Bristol
Bath
Weston-Super-Mare
Portishead
Clevedon
Nailsea
Backwell
Yatton
Tyntesfield
Keynsham
Bath Botanic Gardens
Crowe Hall
The American Museum
Prior Park
Trowbridge
Warminster
Frome
Radstock
Ammerdown Park
Ston Easton Park
Meadows Nursery
Midsomer Norton
Blackmore & Langdon
Cleeve Nursery
Cheddar
Sherborne Gardens
Milton Lodge
Wells
Mill Cottage Plants
Shepton Mallet
Glastonbury
Street
Highbridge
Burnham-on-Sea
Bridgwater
North Petherton
Hestercombe House
Kelways Ltd
Somerton
Lytes Cary Manor
Wincanton
Milborne Port
Sherborne
Tintinhull House
Montacute House
Yeovil
Avon Bulbs
Martock
East Lambrook Manor
Mallet Court Nursery
Barrington Court
Scotts Nurseries Ltd
Lower Severalls Garden & Nursery
Crewkerne
Wayford Manor
Ilminster
Chard
Honiton
PMA Plant Specialities
Taunton
Broadleigh Gardens
Wellington
Cothay Manor
Gaulden Manor
Elworthy Cottage Plants
Watchet
Minehead
Dunster
Dunster Castle
Bridgetown
Porlock
Greencombe Gardens
Exford
Simonsbath
Tiverton
M4
M32
M5
A4
A46
A36
A350
A367
A362
A361
A37
A368
A39
A38
A371
A303
A3088
A358
A396
A30
20km
20miles
N

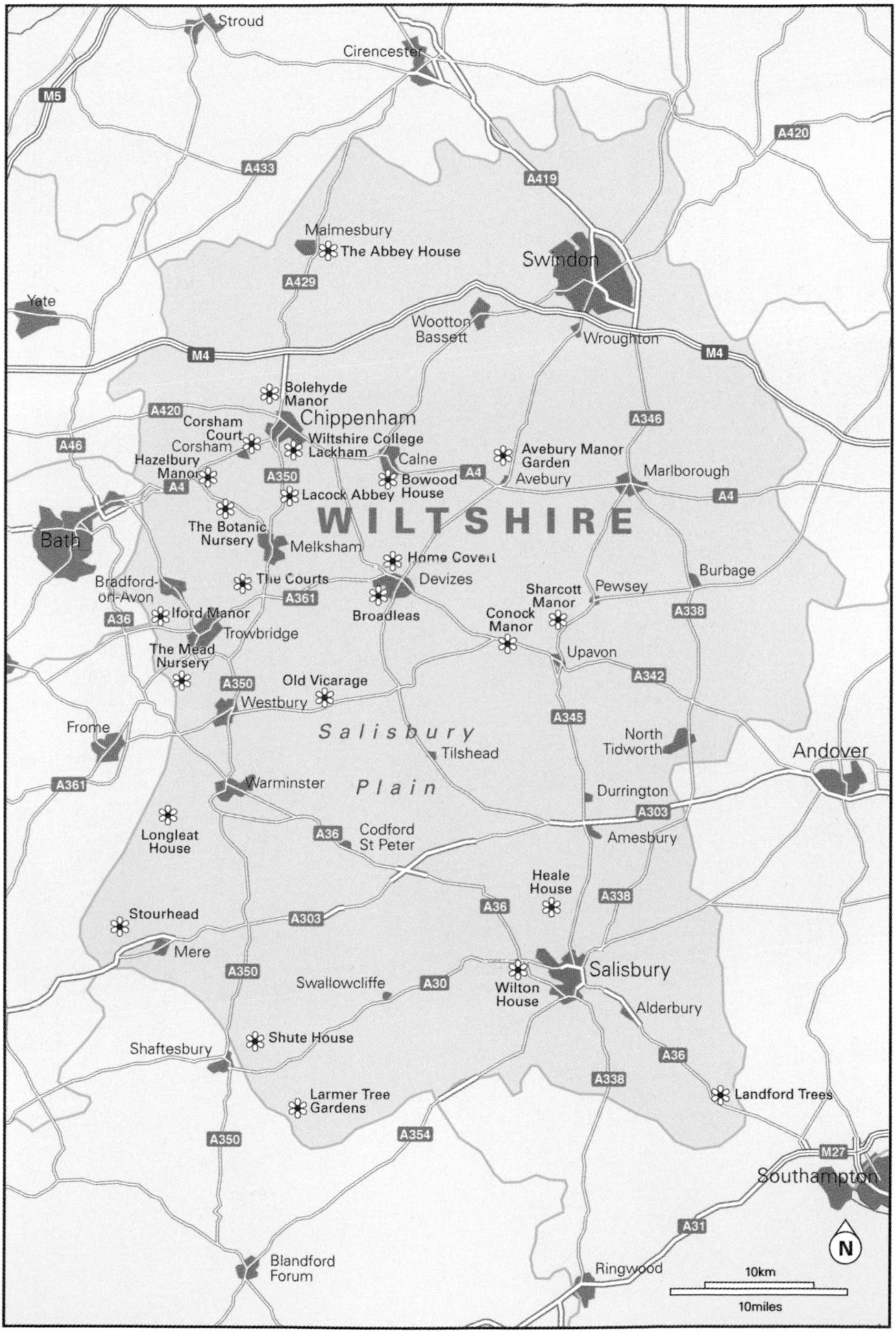
Stroud
Cirencester
M5
A420
A433
A419
Malmesbury
The Abbey House
Swindon
A429
Yate
Wootton Bassett
Wroughton
M4
M4
Bolehyde Manor
A420
Chippenham
A346
Corsham Court
Corsham
Wiltshire College Lackham
Calne
Avebury Manor Garden
A46
Hazelbury Manor
A350
A4
Avebury
Marlborough
A4
Bowood House
Lacock Abbey
A4
WILTSHIRE
Bath
The Botanic Nursery
Melksham
Home Covert
Bradford-on-Avon
The Courts
Devizes
Burbage
Sharcott Manor
Pewsey
A361
A36
Iford Manor
Broadleas
Conock Manor
A338
Trowbridge
The Mead Nursery
Upavon
A350
Old Vicarage
A342
Westbury
A345
Frome
Salisbury
North Tidworth
Tilshead
Andover
A361
Warminster
Plain
Durrington
A303
Longleat House
A36
Codford St Peter
Amesbury
Heale House
A338
A36
Stourhead
A303
Mere
A350
Swallowcliffe
A30
Wilton House
Salisbury
Alderbury
Shute House
Shaftesbury
A36
A338
Larmer Tree Gardens
Landford Trees
A350
A354
M27
Southampton
A31
N
Blandford Forum
Ringwood
10km
10miles

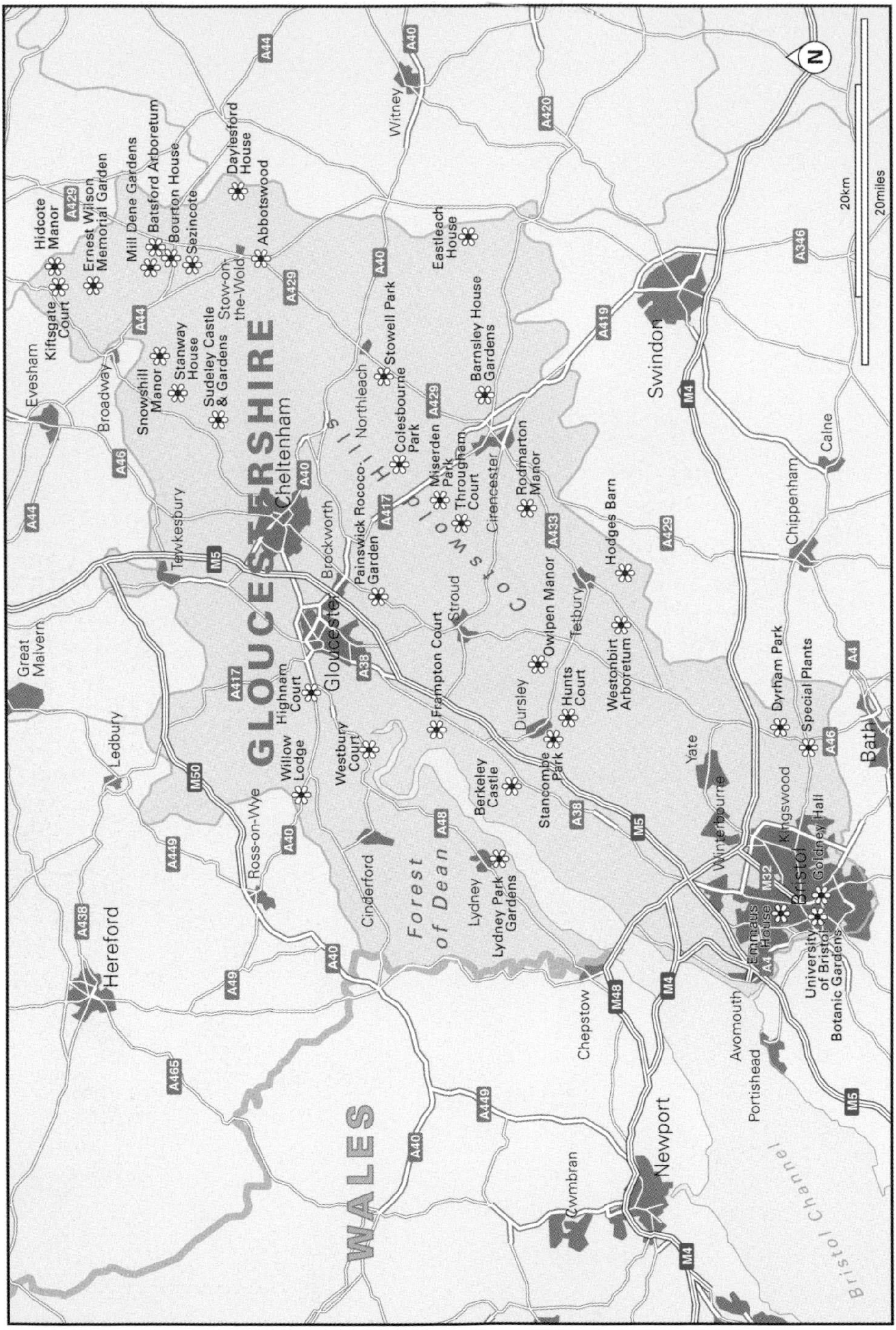
GLOUCESTERSHIRE
WALES
Cotswold Hills
Forest of Dean
Bristol Channel
Hidcote Manor
Kiftsgate Court
Ernest Wilson Memorial Garden
Mill Dene Gardens
Batsford Arboretum
Bourton House
Sezincote
Daylesford House
Abbotswood
Stow-on-the-Wold
Evesham
Broadway
Snowshill Manor
Stanway House
Sudeley Castle & Gardens
Cheltenham
Tewkesbury
Northleach
Stowell Park
Colesbourne Park
Eastleach House
Barnsley House Gardens
Brockworth
Painswick Rococo Garden
Miserden Park
Througham Court
Cirencester
Rodmarton Manor
Hodges Barn
Gloucester
Highnam Court
Willow Lodge
Westbury Court
Frampton Court
Stroud
Owlpen Manor
Tetbury
Westonbirt Arboretum
Hunts Court
Dursley
Stancombe Park
Berkeley Castle
Lydney
Lydney Park Gardens
Cinderford
Great Malvern
Ledbury
Ross-on-Wye
Hereford
Witney
Swindon
Calne
Chippenham
Dyrham Park
Special Plants
Bath
Yate
Winterbourne
Kingswood
Goldney Hall
Bristol
Emmaus House
University of Bristol Botanic Gardens
Avonmouth
Portishead
Chepstow
Newport
Cwmbran
A44
A40
A420
A429
A46
A417
A38
A433
A419
A346
A4
A48
A449
A438
A49
A465
M5
M50
M4
M48
M32
N
20km
20miles

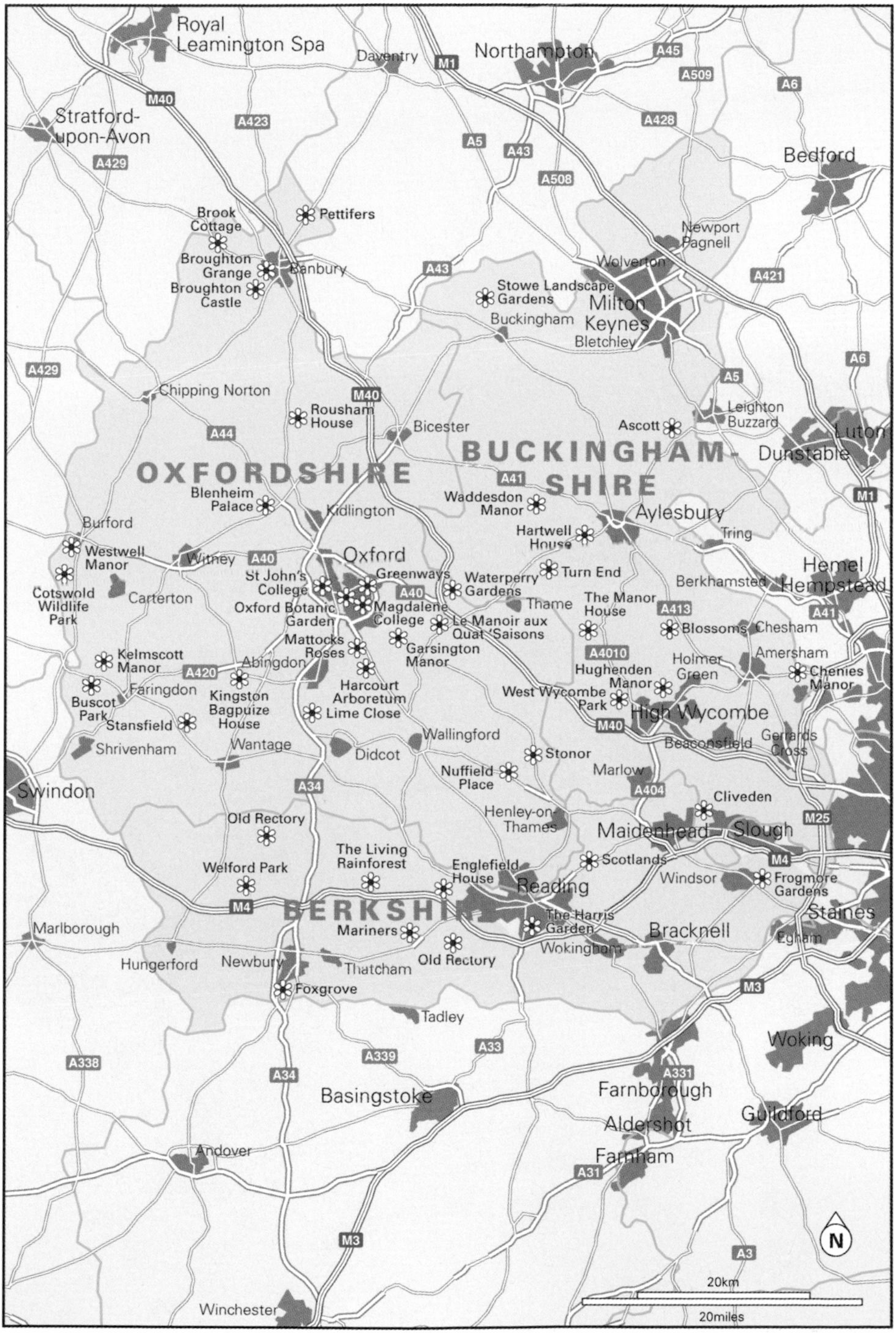
Royal Leamington Spa
Daventry
M1
Northampton
A45
A509
A6
M40
Stratford-upon-Avon
A423
A428
A5
A43
Bedford
A429
A508
Pettifers
Brook Cottage
Newport Pagnell
Broughton Grange
Banbury
Broughton Castle
A43
Wolverton
A421
Stowe Landscape Gardens
Milton Keynes
Buckingham
Bletchley
A429
A6
A5
Chipping Norton
M40
Rousham House
Leighton Buzzard
Bicester
Ascott
A44
Luton
BUCKINGHAMSHIRE
Dunstable
OXFORDSHIRE
A41
Blenheim Palace
Waddesdon Manor
Kidlington
Aylesbury
M1
Burford
Hartwell House
Tring
Westwell Manor
Witney
A40
Oxford
Hemel Hempstead
St John's College
Greenways
Waterperry Gardens
Turn End
Berkhamsted
Cotswold Wildlife Park
Carterton
A40
Thame
The Manor House
Oxford Botanic Garden
Magdalene College
A413
A41
Le Manoir aux Quat' Saisons
Blossoms
Chesham
Mattocks Roses
Garsington Manor
Amersham
A4010
Holmer Green
Kelmscott Manor
Abingdon
Hughenden Manor
Chenies Manor
A420
Faringdon
Harcourt Arboretum
Buscot Park
Kingston Bagpuize House
West Wycombe Park
Lime Close
High Wycombe
Stansfield
M40
Beaconsfield
Gerrards Cross
Wallingford
Shrivenham
Wantage
Didcot
Stonor
Nuffield Place
Marlow
Swindon
A34
A404
Cliveden
Henley-on-Thames
Old Rectory
Maidenhead
Slough
M25
M4
Scotlands
The Living Rainforest
Welford Park
Englefield House
Windsor
Frogmore Gardens
Reading
M4
BERKSHIRE
Staines
Marlborough
Mariners
The Harris Garden
Bracknell
Egham
Old Rectory
Wokingham
Hungerford
Newbury
Thatcham
M3
Foxgrove
Tadley
Woking
A33
A338
A339
A331
A34
Farnborough
Basingstoke
Guildford
Aldershot
Andover
Farnham
A31
N
M3
A3
20km
20miles
Winchester

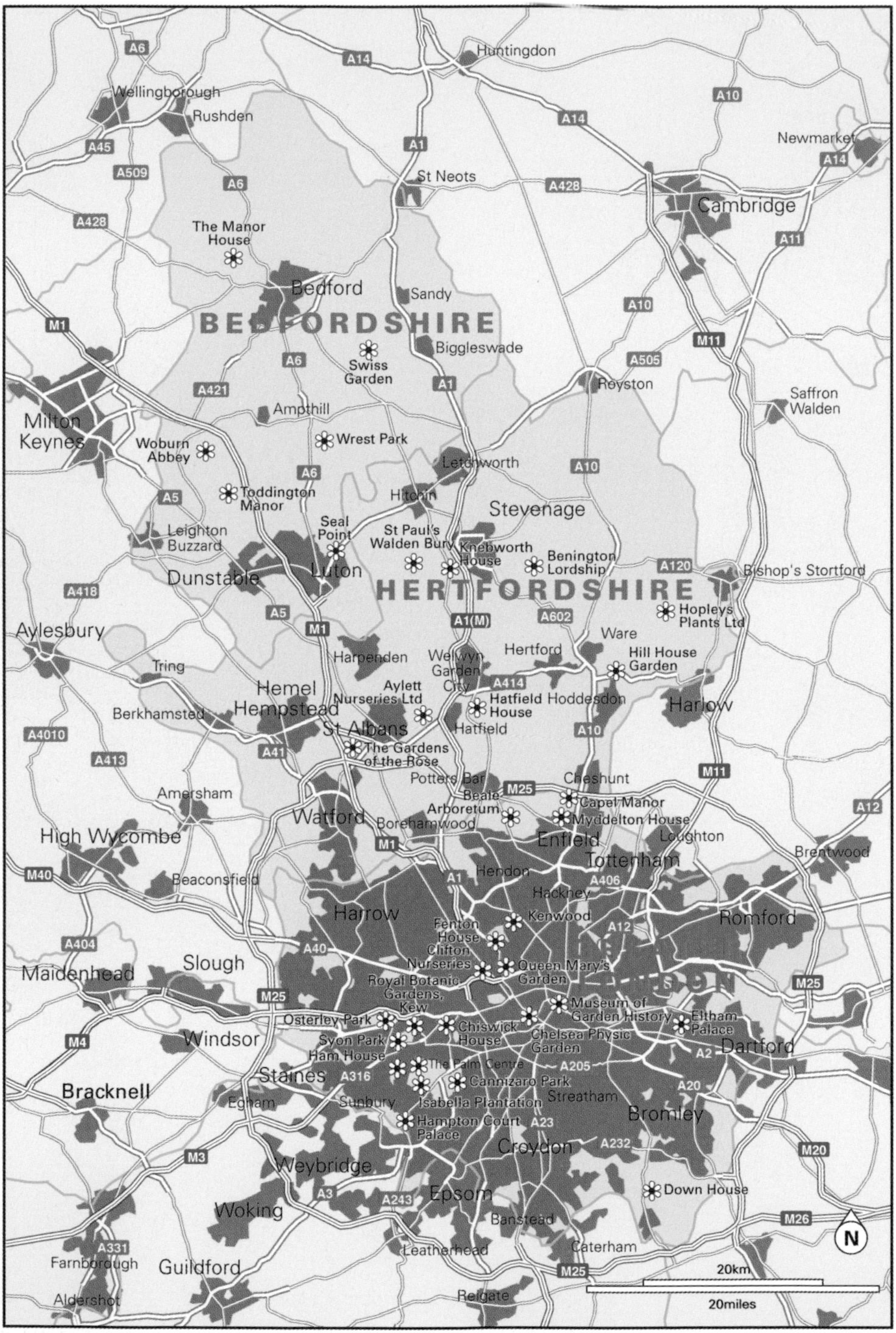
Huntingdon
Wellingborough
Rushden
Newmarket
St Neots
Cambridge
The Manor House
Bedford
Sandy
BEDFORDSHIRE
Biggleswade
Swiss Garden
Royston
Saffron Walden
Milton Keynes
Ampthill
Wrest Park
Woburn Abbey
Letchworth
Toddington Manor
Hitchin
Stevenage
Leighton Buzzard
Seal Point
St Paul's Walden Bury
Knebworth House
Benington Lordship
Dunstable
Luton
Bishop's Stortford
HERTFORDSHIRE
Hopleys Plants Ltd
Aylesbury
Ware
Tring
Harpenden
Welwyn Garden City
Hertford
Hill House Garden
Hemel Hempstead
Aylett Nurseries Ltd
Hatfield House
Hoddesdon
Harlow
Berkhamsted
St Albans
Hatfield
The Gardens of the Rose
Potters Bar
Cheshunt
Amersham
Beale Arboretum
Capel Manor
Myddelton House
Watford
Borehamwood
Enfield
Loughton
High Wycombe
Tottenham
Brentwood
Beaconsfield
Hendon
Hackney
Harrow
Kenwood
Romford
Fenton House
Clifton Nurseries
Queen Mary's Garden
Maidenhead
Slough
Royal Botanic Gardens, Kew
Museum of Garden History
Osterley Park
Chiswick House
Eltham Palace
Windsor
Syon Park
Chelsea Physic Garden
Ham House
Dartford
The Palm Centre
Staines
Cannizaro Park
Bracknell
Streatham
Egham
Sunbury
Isabella Plantation
Bromley
Hampton Court Palace
Croydon
Weybridge
Down House
Epsom
Woking
Banstead
Leatherhead
Caterham
Farnborough
Guildford
Aldershot
Reigate
20km
20miles
N
A6
A14
A10
A1
A45
A509
A428
M1
A421
A505
M11
A11
A5
A418
A120
A1(M)
A602
A414
A4010
A413
A41
M25
A12
M40
A406
A404
A40
M4
A316
A205
A2
A20
A23
A232
M3
A3
A243
A331
M20
M26

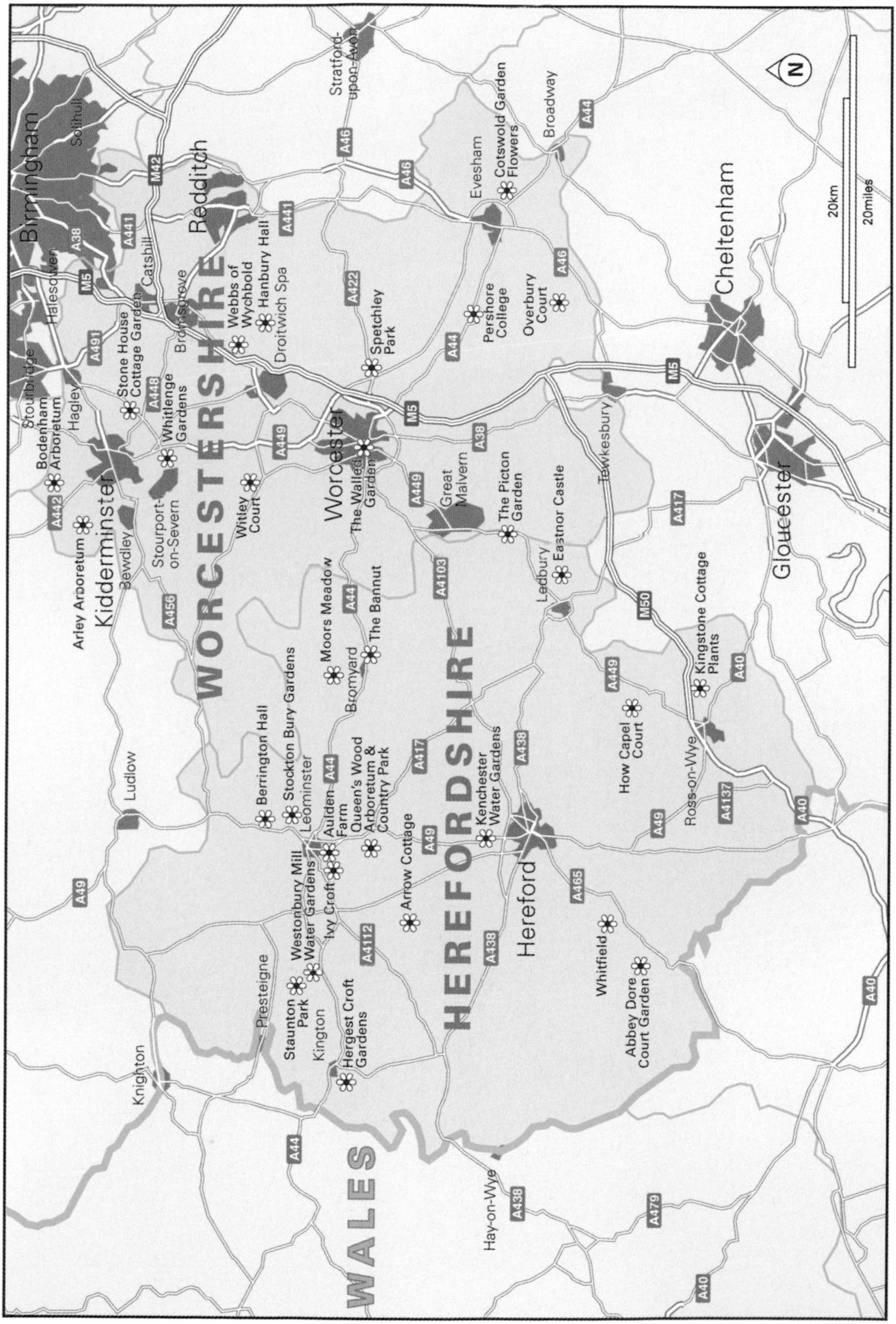
WORCESTERSHIRE
HEREFORDSHIRE
WALES
Birmingham
Solihull
Redditch
Stratford-upon-Avon
Stourbridge
Halesowen
Hagley
Bodenham Arboretum
Catshill
Bromsgrove
Stone House Cottage Garden
Whitlenge Gardens
Kidderminster
Arley Arboretum
Bewdley
Stourport-on-Severn
Webbs of Wychbold
Hanbury Hall
Droitwich Spa
Witley Court
Worcester
The Walled Garden
Spetchley Park
Evesham
Cotswold Garden Flowers
Broadway
Pershore College
Overbury Court
Great Malvern
The Picton Garden
Eastnor Castle
Tewkesbury
Cheltenham
Gloucester
Ledbury
Kingstone Cottage Plants
Moors Meadow
The Bannut
Bromyard
Berrington Hall
Stockton Bury Gardens
Leominster
Aulden Farm
Queen's Wood Arboretum & Country Park
Ludlow
Westonbury Mill Water Gardens
Ivy Croft
Arrow Cottage
Kenchester Water Gardens
Hereford
How Capel Court
Ross-on-Wye
Whitfield
Abbey Dore Court Garden
Presteigne
Staunton Park
Kington
Hergest Croft Gardens
Knighton
Hay-on-Wye
M5
M42
M50
A38
A441
A491
A448
A449
A442
A456
A44
A46
A422
A4103
A417
A49
A4112
A438
A465
A4137
A40
A479
20km
20miles
N

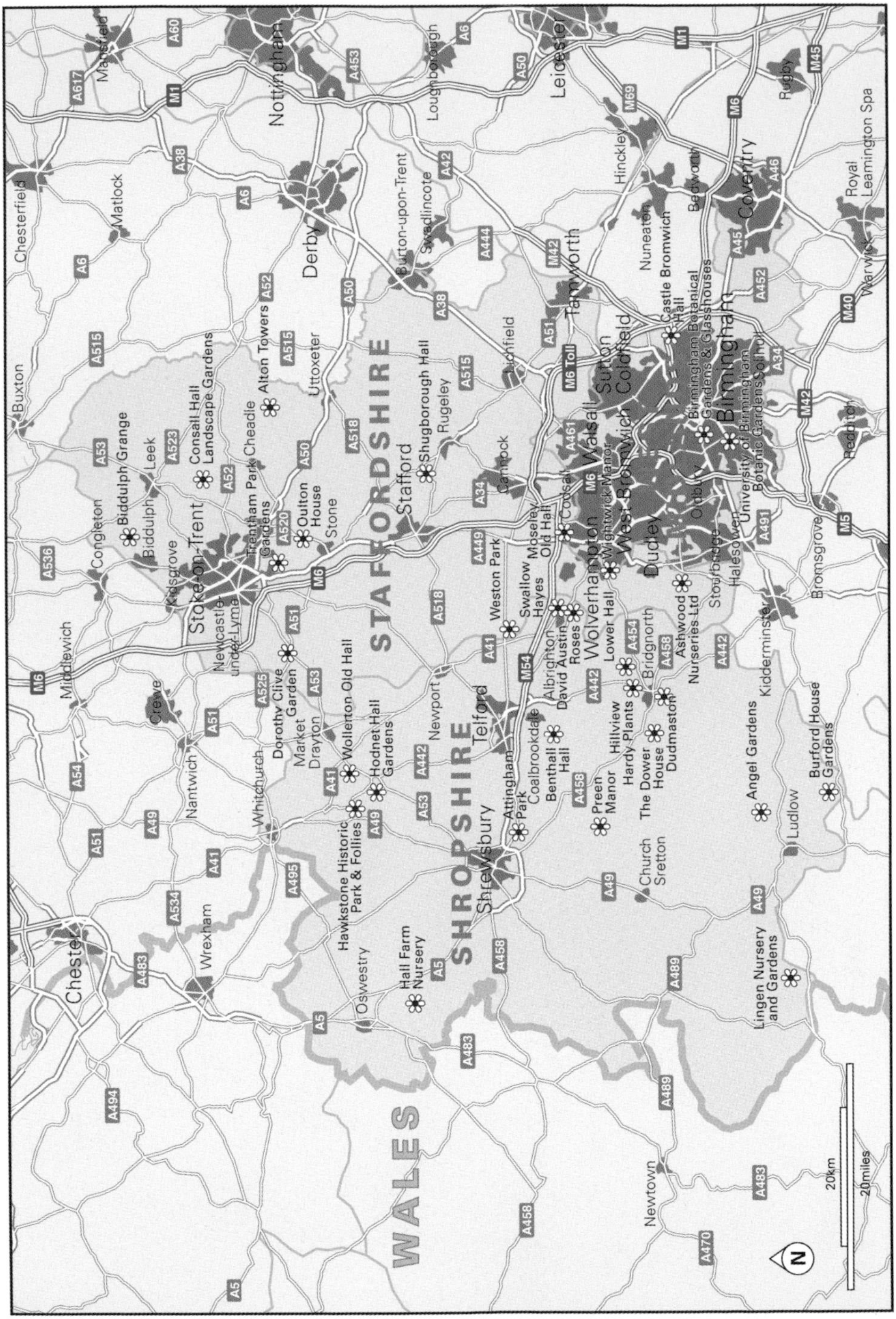
STAFFORDSHIRE
SHROPSHIRE
WALES
Chesterfield
Mansfield
Nottingham
Leicester
Loughborough
Matlock
Derby
Burton-upon-Trent
Swadlincote
Hinckley
Nuneaton
Bedworth
Coventry
Rugby
Royal Leamington Spa
Warwick
Tamworth
Buxton
Alton Towers
Consall Hall Landscape Gardens
Cheadle
Leek
Biddulph Grange
Biddulph
Congleton
Uttoxeter
Lichfield
Sutton Coldfield
Castle Bromwich Hall
Birmingham Botanical Gardens & Glasshouses
Birmingham
University of Birmingham Botanic Gardens
Solihull
Shugborough Hall
Rugeley
Stafford
Stone
Oulton House
Trentham Park Gardens
Stoke-on-Trent
Kidsgrove
Newcastle-under-Lyme
Cannock
Walsall
West Bromwich
Wightwick Manor
Oldbury
Redditch
Moseley Old Hall
Coseley
Wolverhampton
Dudley
Halesowen
Stourbridge
Bromsgrove
Swallow Hayes
Weston Park
Albrighton
David Austin Roses
Lower Hall
Ashwood Nurseries Ltd
Kidderminster
Bridgnorth
Dudmaston
The Dower House
Hillview Hardy Plants
Preen Manor
Benthall Hall
Coalbrookdale
Telford
Newport
Attingham Park
Middlewich
Crewe
Nantwich
Dorothy Clive Garden
Market Drayton
Wollerton Old Hall
Hodnet Hall Gardens
Whitchurch
Hawkstone Historic Park & Follies
Shrewsbury
Church Stretton
Angel Gardens
Ludlow
Burford House Gardens
Lingen Nursery and Gardens
Chester
Wrexham
Oswestry
Hall Farm Nursery
Newtown
20km
20miles
N

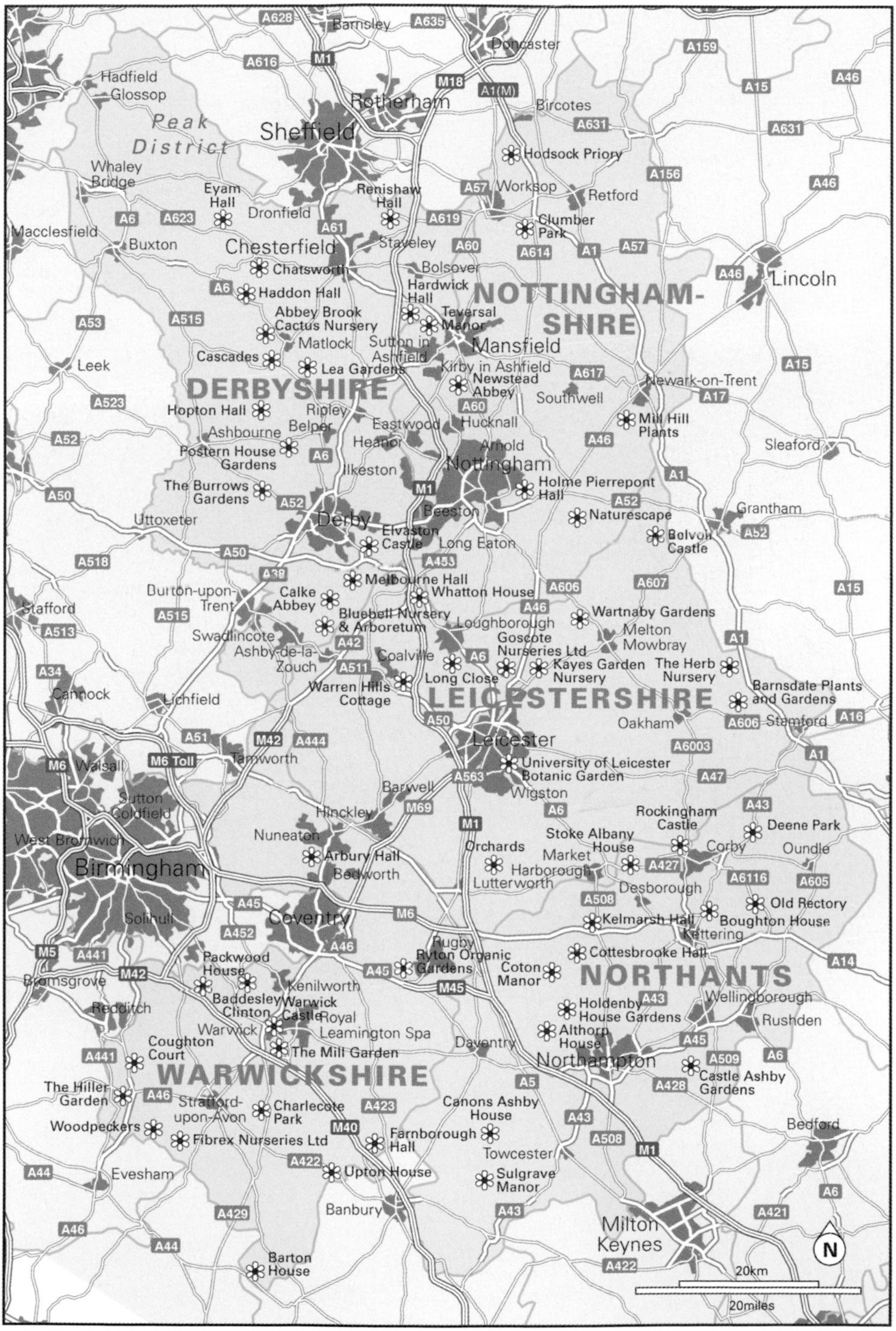
Barnsley
Doncaster
Hadfield
Glossop
Peak District
Rotherham
Sheffield
Bircotes
Hodsock Priory
Whaley Bridge
Eyam Hall
Renishaw Hall
Worksop
Retford
Dronfield
Clumber Park
Macclesfield
Buxton
Chesterfield
Staveley
Chatsworth
Bolsover
Lincoln
Haddon Hall
Hardwick Hall
NOTTINGHAMSHIRE
Abbey Brook Cactus Nursery
Teversal Manor
Matlock
Sutton in Ashfield
Mansfield
Leek
Cascades
Lea Gardens
Kirby in Ashfield
Newstead Abbey
Newark-on-Trent
DERBYSHIRE
Southwell
Hopton Hall
Ripley
Belper
Mill Hill Plants
Ashbourne
Eastwood
Hucknall
Heanor
Arnold
Sleaford
Postern House Gardens
Nottingham
Ilkeston
Holme Pierrepont Hall
The Burrows Gardens
Beeston
Grantham
Naturescape
Uttoxeter
Derby
Elvaston Castle
Long Eaton
Belvoir Castle
Melbourne Hall
Burton-upon-Trent
Calke Abbey
Whatton House
Stafford
Wartnaby Gardens
Bluebell Nursery & Arboretum
Loughborough
Melton Mowbray
Swadlincote
Goscote Nurseries Ltd
Ashby-de-la-Zouch
Coalville
Kayes Garden Nursery
The Herb Nursery
Warren Hills Cottage
Long Close
Barnsdale Plants and Gardens
Cannock
Lichfield
LEICESTERSHIRE
Oakham
Stamford
Leicester
Walsall
Tamworth
University of Leicester Botanic Garden
Sutton Coldfield
Barwell
Wigston
West Bromwich
Hinckley
Rockingham Castle
Nuneaton
Stoke Albany House
Deene Park
Orchards
Corby
Oundle
Birmingham
Arbury Hall
Market Harborough
Bedworth
Lutterworth
Desborough
Solihull
Coventry
Old Rectory
Kelmarsh Hall
Boughton House
Kettering
Rugby
Cottesbrooke Hall
Packwood House
Ryton Organic Gardens
Coton Manor
NORTHANTS
Bromsgrove
Kenilworth
Baddesley Clinton
Warwick Castle
Wellingborough
Holdenby House Gardens
Redditch
Royal Leamington Spa
Rushden
Warwick
Althorp House
Coughton Court
Daventry
The Mill Garden
Northampton
WARWICKSHIRE
Castle Ashby Gardens
The Hiller Garden
Stratford-upon-Avon
Charlecote Park
Canons Ashby House
Woodpeckers
Bedford
Farnborough Hall
Fibrex Nurseries Ltd
Towcester
Evesham
Upton House
Sulgrave Manor
Banbury
Milton Keynes
Barton House
N
20km
20miles

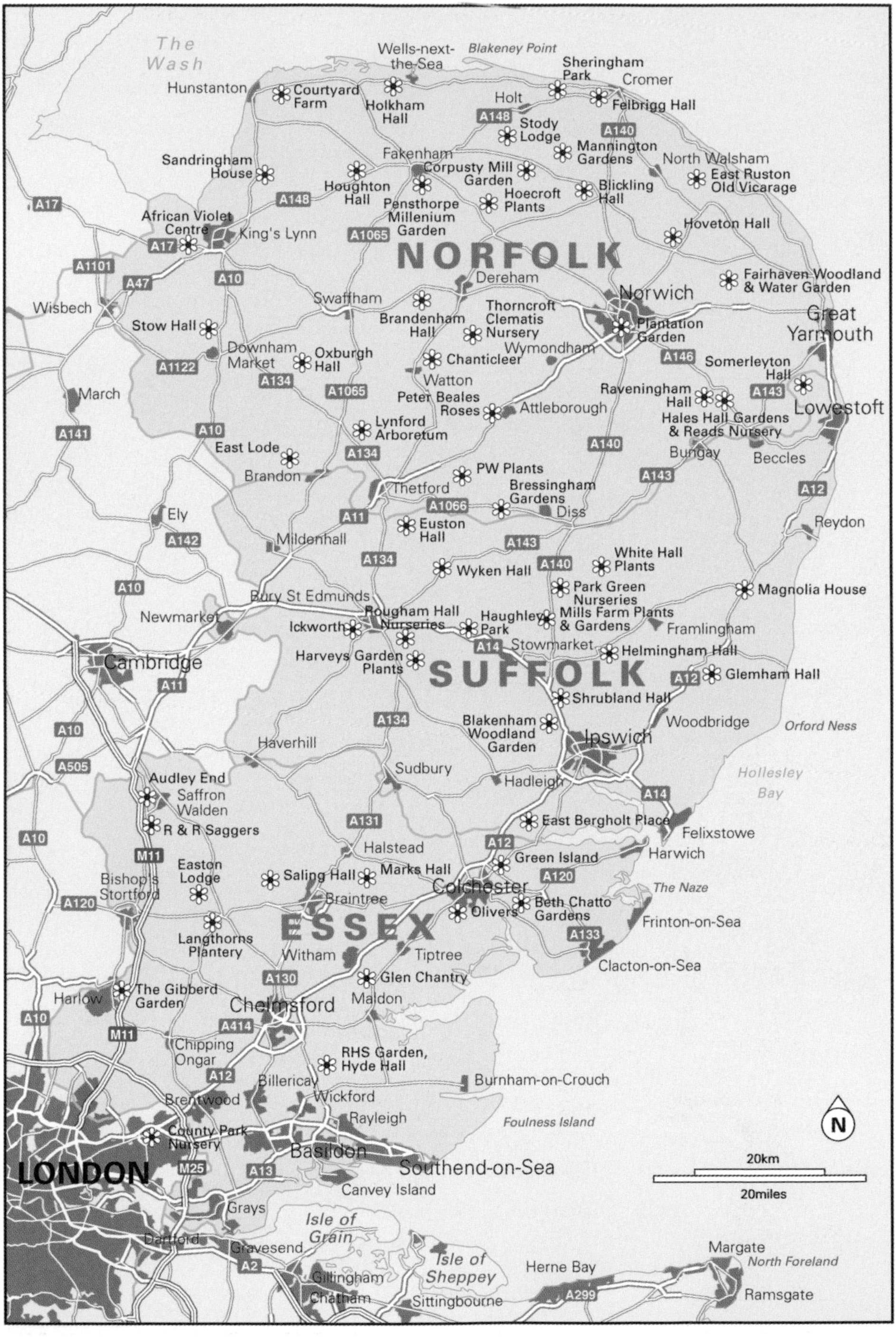
The Wash
Wells-next-the-Sea
Blakeney Point
Sheringham Park
Cromer
Hunstanton
Courtyard Farm
Holkham Hall
Holt
Felbrigg Hall
A148
Stody Lodge
A140
Mannington Gardens
Sandringham House
Fakenham
Corpusty Mill Garden
North Walsham
East Ruston Old Vicarage
Houghton Hall
Blickling Hall
A17
A148
Pensthorpe Millenium Garden
Hoecroft Plants
African Violet Centre
King's Lynn
A1065
Hoveton Hall
NORFOLK
A1101
A47
A10
Dereham
Fairhaven Woodland & Water Garden
Wisbech
Swaffham
Norwich
Great Yarmouth
Brandenham Hall
Thorncroft Clematis Nursery
Plantation Garden
Stow Hall
Downham Market
Oxburgh Hall
Wymondham
A1122
A134
Chanticleer
A146
Somerleyton Hall
Watton
Raveningham Hall
A143
March
A1065
Peter Beales Roses
Attleborough
Lowestoft
Hales Hall Gardens & Reads Nursery
A141
A10
Lynford Arboretum
East Lode
A140
Bungay
Beccles
A134
Brandon
PW Plants
A143
Thetford
Bressingham Gardens
A12
A1066
Diss
Ely
A11
Euston Hall
Reydon
A142
Mildenhall
A143
A134
White Hall Plants
A140
Wyken Hall
A10
Park Green Nurseries
Magnolia House
Bury St Edmunds
Newmarket
Rougham Hall Nurseries
Haughley Park
Mills Farm Plants & Gardens
Ickworth
Framlingham
Stowmarket
A14
Helmingham Hall
Harveys Garden Plants
Cambridge
SUFFOLK
A12
Glemham Hall
A11
Shrubland Hall
A134
Blakenham Woodland Garden
Woodbridge
Orford Ness
A10
Ipswich
Haverhill
A505
Sudbury
Hollesley Bay
Audley End
Hadleigh
Saffron Walden
A14
R & R Saggers
A10
A131
East Bergholt Place
Felixstowe
Halstead
A12
M11
Green Island
Harwich
Easton Lodge
Marks Hall
Bishop's Stortford
Saling Hall
A120
Colchester
The Naze
A120
Braintree
Beth Chatto Gardens
Olivers
ESSEX
Frinton-on-Sea
A133
Langthorns Plantery
Tiptree
Witham
Clacton-on-Sea
A130
Glen Chantry
The Gibberd Garden
Harlow
Maldon
Chelmsford
A10
A414
M11
Chipping Ongar
RHS Garden, Hyde Hall
A12
Billericay
Burnham-on-Crouch
Brentwood
Wickford
N
Rayleigh
Foulness Island
County Park Nursery
Basildon
20km
LONDON
M25
A13
Southend-on-Sea
20miles
Canvey Island
Grays
Isle of Grain
Dartford
Gravesend
Margate
Isle of Sheppey
Herne Bay
North Foreland
A2
Gillingham
A299
Chatham
Sittingbourne
Ramsgate

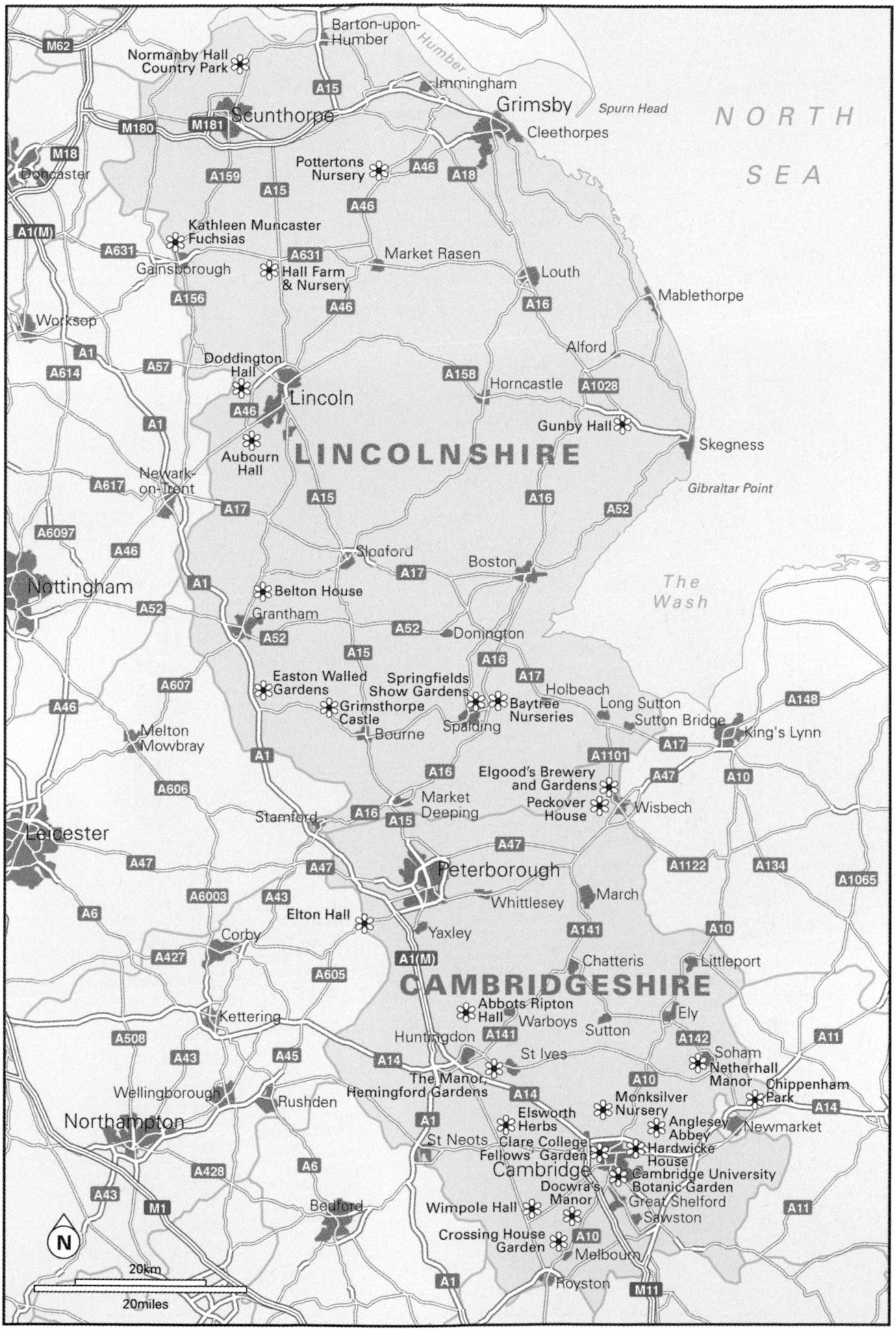
Barton-upon-Humber
Humber
M62
Normanby Hall Country Park
A15
Immingham
Grimsby
Spurn Head
NORTH SEA
Scunthorpe
M180
M181
Cleethorpes
M18
Doncaster
Pottertons Nursery
A46
A18
A159
A15
A46
A1(M)
Kathleen Muncaster Fuchsias
A631
A631
Market Rasen
Gainsborough
Hall Farm & Nursery
Louth
A156
A46
A16
Mablethorpe
Worksop
Alford
A1
A57
Doddington Hall
A614
A158
Horncastle
A1028
Lincoln
A46
Gunby Hall
A1
Aubourn Hall
LINCOLNSHIRE
Skegness
Newark-on-Trent
A617
A15
A16
Gibraltar Point
A17
A52
A6097
A46
Sleaford
Boston
A17
Nottingham
A1
Belton House
The Wash
A52
Grantham
A52
A52
Donington
A15
A16
A17
Easton Walled Gardens
Springfields Show Gardens
Holbeach
A607
Baytree Nurseries
Long Sutton
A148
A46
Grimsthorpe Castle
Spalding
Sutton Bridge
Melton Mowbray
Bourne
King's Lynn
A17
A1
A1101
A16
Elgood's Brewery and Gardens
A47
A10
A606
Market Deeping
Peckover House
Wisbech
Stamford
A16
A15
Leicester
A47
A47
Peterborough
A1122
A134
A1065
A47
A6003
A43
Whittlesey
March
A6
Elton Hall
Yaxley
A141
A10
Corby
A427
A1(M)
Chatteris
Littleport
A605
CAMBRIDGESHIRE
Abbots Ripton Hall
Ely
Kettering
Warboys
Sutton
A508
Huntingdon
A141
A142
A11
A43
A45
St Ives
Soham
A14
Netherhall Manor
The Manor, Hemingford Gardens
A10
Chippenham Park
Wellingborough
A14
Monksilver Nursery
Rushden
A14
Elsworth Herbs
Anglesey Abbey
Northampton
A1
Newmarket
St Neots
Clare College Fellows' Garden
Hardwicke House
Cambridge
A428
A6
Cambridge University Botanic Garden
Docwra's Manor
A43
M1
Bedford
Wimpole Hall
Great Shelford
A11
Sawston
N
Crossing House Garden
A10
Melbourn
20km
A1
Royston
M11
20miles

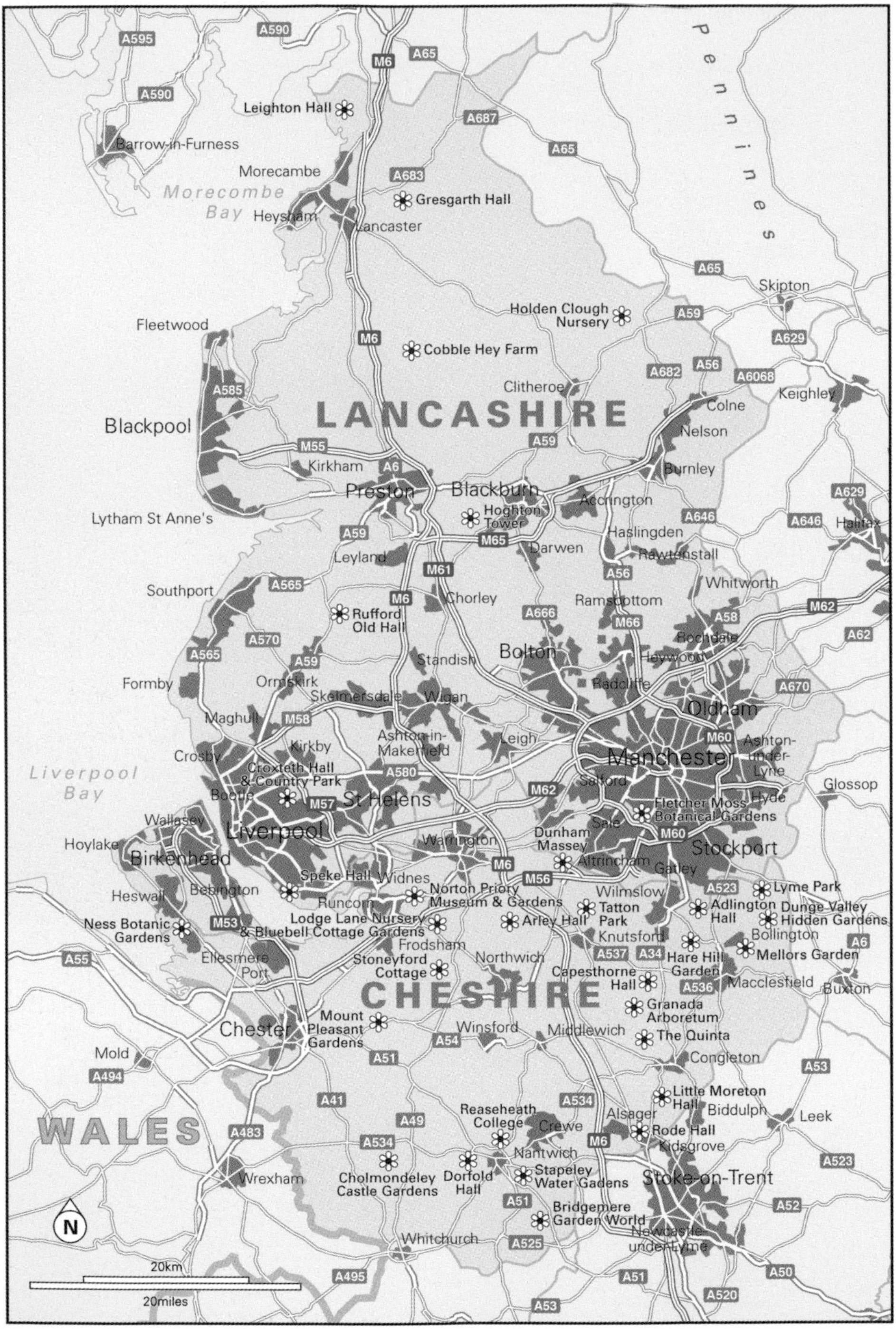
LANCASHIRE
CHESHIRE
WALES
Pennines
Morecombe Bay
Liverpool Bay
Leighton Hall
Barrow-in-Furness
Morecambe
Heysham
Lancaster
Gresgarth Hall
Holden Clough Nursery
Skipton
Fleetwood
Cobble Hey Farm
Clitheroe
Keighley
Colne
Nelson
Blackpool
Kirkham
Preston
Blackburn
Burnley
Hoghton Tower
Accrington
Lytham St Anne's
Haslingden
Halifax
Leyland
Darwen
Rawtenstall
Whitworth
Southport
Chorley
Ramsbottom
Rufford Old Hall
Rochdale
Heywood
Standish
Bolton
Formby
Ormskirk
Skelmersdale
Wigan
Radcliffe
Oldham
Maghull
Ashton-in-Makerfield
Leigh
Kirkby
Crosby
Croxteth Hall & Country Park
Manchester
Ashton-under-Lyne
Glossop
Bootle
St Helens
Salford
Hyde
Wallasey
Fletcher Moss Botanical Gardens
Liverpool
Sale
Hoylake
Birkenhead
Warrington
Dunham Massey
Stockport
Altrincham
Gatley
Speke Hall
Widnes
Heswall
Bebington
Norton Priory Museum & Gardens
Wilmslow
Lyme Park
Runcorn
Tatton Park
Adlington Hall
Dunge Valley Hidden Gardens
Ness Botanic Gardens
Lodge Lane Nursery & Bluebell Cottage Gardens
Arley Hall
Knutsford
Bollington
Frodsham
Mellors Garden
Ellesmere Port
Stoneyford Cottage
Northwich
Hare Hill Garden
Capesthorne Hall
Macclesfield
Buxton
Granada Arboretum
Mount Pleasant Gardens
Chester
Winsford
Middlewich
The Quinta
Mold
Congleton
Little Moreton Hall
Biddulph
Leek
Reaseheath College
Crewe
Alsager
Rode Hall
Kidsgrove
Cholmondeley Castle Gardens
Dorfold Hall
Nantwich
Stapeley Water Gadens
Stoke-on-Trent
Wrexham
Bridgemere Garden World
Newcastle-under-Lyme
Whitchurch
N
20km
20miles
A595
A590
A65
M6
A687
A683
A59
A629
A682
A56
A6068
M55
A6
A646
M65
M61
A565
A666
M66
A58
M62
A570
A62
A670
M58
M60
A580
M57
M56
A523
M53
A537
A34
A536
A55
A54
A51
A494
A53
A41
A534
A49
A483
A52
A525
A495
A50
A520

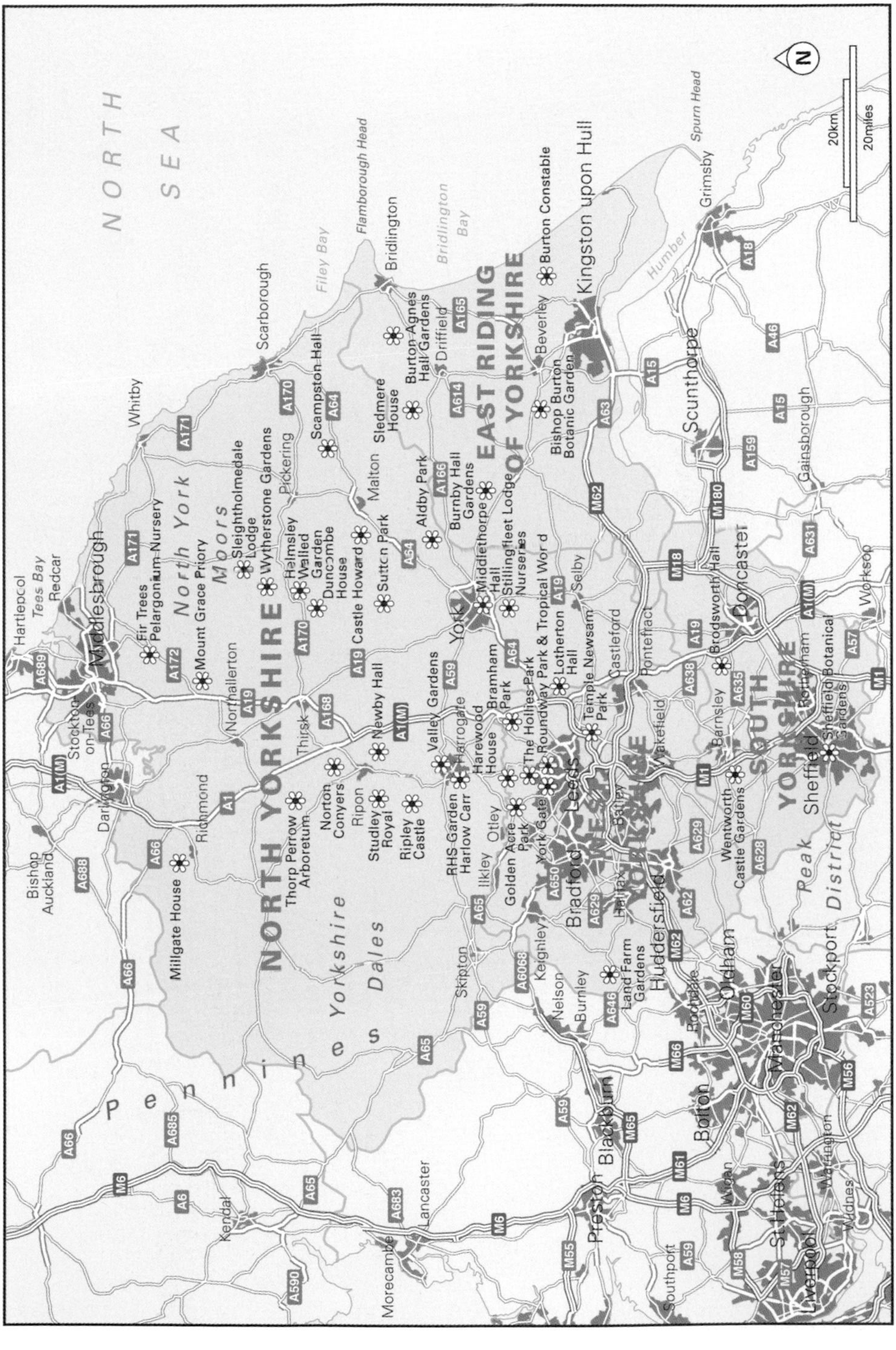
NORTH SEA
NORTH YORKSHIRE
EAST RIDING OF YORKSHIRE
WEST YORKSHIRE
SOUTH YORKSHIRE
North York Moors
Yorkshire Dales
Pennines
Peak District
Millgate House
Thorp Perrow Arboretum
Norton Conyers
Studley Royal
Ripley Castle
Newby Hall
Valley Gardens
RHS Garden Harlow Carr
Harewood House
Golden Acre Park
York Gate
The Hollies Park
Roundway Park & Tropical World
Bramham Park
Temple Newsam Park
Lotherton Hall
Stillingfleet Lodge Nurseries
Middlethorpe Hall
Burnby Hall Gardens
Aldby Park
Sutton Park
Castle Howard
Duncombe House
Helmsley Walled Garden
Wytherstone Gardens
Sleightholmedale Lodge
Mount Grace Priory
Fir Trees Pelargonium Nursery
Scampston Hall
Sledmere House
Burton Agnes Hall Gardens
Bishop Burton Botanic Garden
Burton Constable
Brodsworth Hall
Wentworth Castle Gardens
Sheffield Botanical Gardens
Land Farm Gardens
Hartlepool
Tees Bay
Redcar
Middlesbrough
Stockton-on-Tees
Darlington
Bishop Auckland
Richmond
Northallerton
Thirsk
Ripon
Harrogate
Whitby
Scarborough
Filey Bay
Flamborough Head
Bridlington
Bridlington Bay
Pickering
Malton
Driffield
Beverley
Kingston upon Hull
Humber
Spurn Head
Grimsby
Scunthorpe
Gainsborough
York
Selby
Castleford
Pontefract
Leeds
Bradford
Otley
Ilkley
Skipton
Keighley
Halifax
Batley
Wakefield
Huddersfield
Barnsley
Doncaster
Rotherham
Sheffield
Worksop
Oldham
Rochdale
Manchester
Stockport
Bolton
Blackburn
Burnley
Nelson
Preston
Lancaster
Morecambe
Kendal
Southport
Wigan
St Helens
Liverpool
Warrington
Widnes
A1(M)
A1
A19
A64
A66
A170
A171
A172
A59
M1
M62
M18
M180
A63
A15
A18
A46
A614
A165
A166
A65
M6
M61
M65
M66
M60
M56
M55
M57
M58
A6
A683
A590
20km
20miles
N

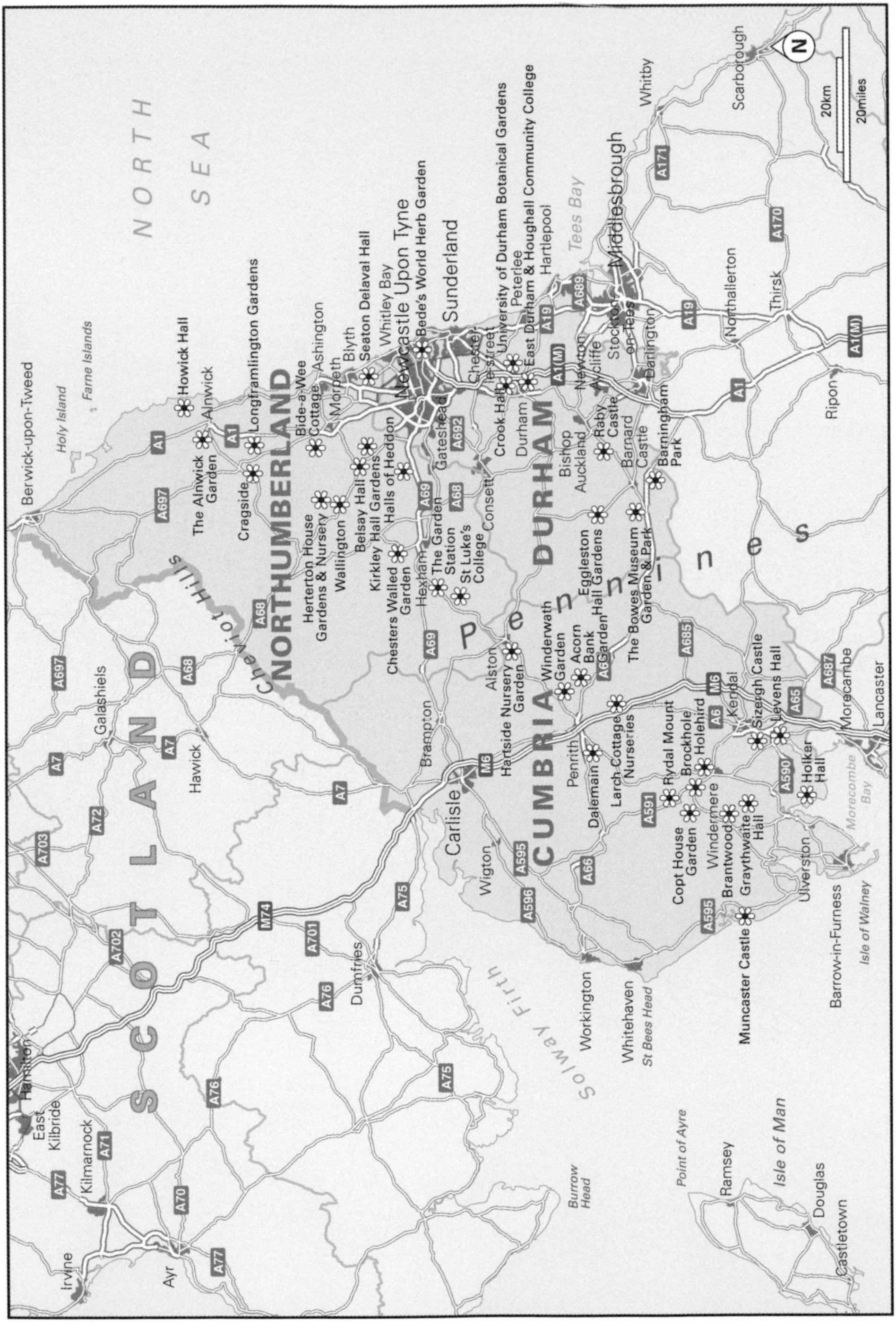
NORTH SEA
SCOTLAND
NORTHUMBERLAND
DURHAM
CUMBRIA
Pennines
Cheviot Hills
Solway Firth
Isle of Man
Tees Bay
Morecambe Bay
Berwick-upon-Tweed
Holy Island
Farne Islands
Howick Hall
Alnwick
The Alnwick Garden
Longframlington Gardens
Cragside
Bide-a-Wee Cottage
Ashington
Morpeth
Blyth
Seaton Delaval Hall
Whitley Bay
Newcastle Upon Tyne
Bede's World Herb Garden
Sunderland
University of Durham Botanical Gardens
Peterlee
East Durham & Houghall Community College
Hartlepool
Middlesbrough
Whitby
Scarborough
Herterton House Gardens & Nursery
Wallington
Belsay Hall
Kirkley Hall Gardens
Halls of Heddon
Gateshead
Chester-le-street
Crook Hall
Durham
Chesters Walled Garden
Hexham
The Garden Station
St Luke's College
Consett
Bishop Auckland
Raby Castle
Newton Aycliffe
Stockton-on-Tees
Darlington
Barnard Castle
Barningham Park
Eggleston Hall Gardens
The Bowes Museum Garden & Park
Northallerton
Thirsk
Ripon
Alston
Hartside Nursery Garden
Winderwath Garden
Acorn Bank Garden
Brampton
Carlisle
Penrith
Dalemain
Larch Cottage Nurseries
Rydal Mount
Brockhole
Holehird
Kendal
Sizergh Castle
Levens Hall
Morecambe
Lancaster
Holker Hall
Copt House Garden
Windermere
Brantwood
Graythwaite Hall
Muncaster Castle
Ulverston
Barrow-in-Furness
Isle of Walney
Wigton
Workington
Whitehaven
St Bees Head
Galashiels
Hawick
Dumfries
Hamilton
East Kilbride
Kilmarnock
Irvine
Ayr
Burrow Head
Point of Ayre
Ramsey
Douglas
Castletown
A1
A1(M)
A19
A689
A171
A170
A697
A68
A69
A692
A66
A685
A6
A65
A687
A590
A591
A595
A596
M6
M74
A7
A72
A703
A702
A701
A75
A76
A71
A77
A70
20km
20miles
N

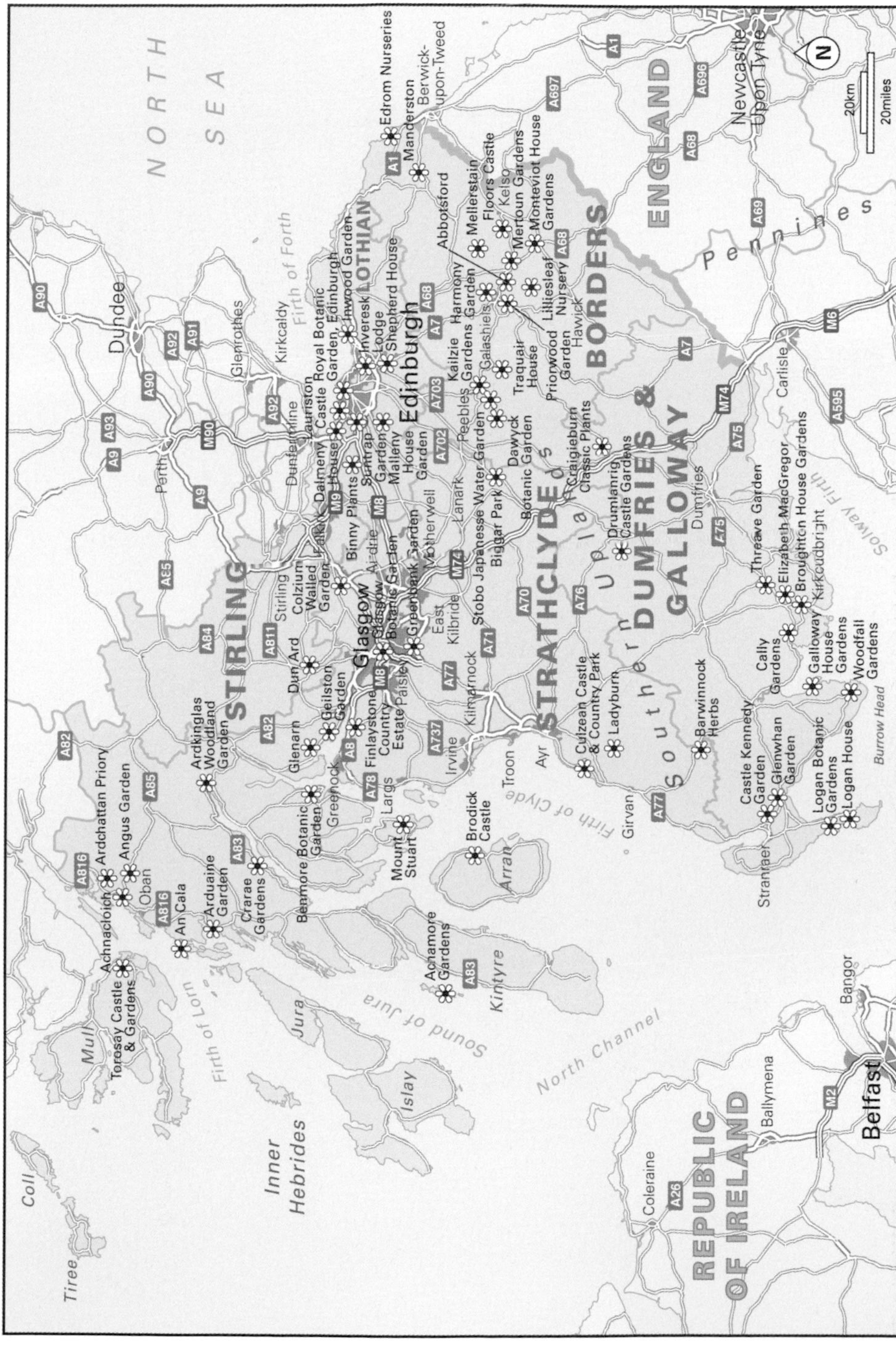
NORTH SEA
Dundee
Perth
Glenrothes
Kirkcaldy
Firth of Forth
Dunfermline
Stirling
STIRLING
Glasgow
Edinburgh
LOTHIAN
Edrom Nurseries
Manderston
Berwick-upon-Tweed
Newcastle upon Tyne
ENGLAND
Pennines
20km
20miles
Abbotsford
Mellerstain
Floors Castle
Kelso
Mertoun Gardens
Monteviot House Gardens
Harmony Garden
Galashiels
Lilliesleaf Nursery
Hawick
Priorwood Garden
Traquair House
Kailzie Gardens
Peebles
BORDERS
Carlisle
Royal Botanic Garden, Edinburgh
Inwood Garden
Inveresk Lodge
Shepherd House
Lauriston Castle
Dalmeny House
Suntrap Garden
Malleny House Garden
Binny Plants
Falkirk
Airdrie
Motherwell
Lanark
Colzium Walled Garden
Glasgow Botanic Garden
Greenbank Garden
East Kilbride
Stobo Japanese Water Garden
Biggar Park
Dawyck Botanic Garden
Craigieburn Classic Plants
Drumlanrig Castle Gardens
STRATHCLYDE
Southern Uplands
DUMFRIES & GALLOWAY
Dumfries
Solway Firth
Threave Garden
Elizabeth MacGregor
Broughton House Gardens
Kirkcudbright
Galloway House Gardens
Woodfall Gardens
Cally Gardens
Barwinnock Herbs
Castle Kennedy Garden
Glenwhan Garden
Logan Botanic Gardens
Logan House
Burrow Head
Stranraer
Girvan
Ayr
Troon
Culzean Castle & Country Park
Ladyburn
Kilmarnock
Irvine
Paisley
Finlaystone Country Estate
Geilston Garden
Dun Ard
Glenarn
Greenock
Largs
Firth of Clyde
Brodick Castle
Arran
Mount Stuart
Benmore Botanic Garden
Ardkinglas Woodland Garden
Crarae Gardens
Arduaine Garden
An Cala
Oban
Ardchattan Priory
Angus Garden
Achnacloich
Torosay Castle & Gardens
Mull
Firth of Lorn
Achamore Gardens
Kintyre
Jura
Sound of Jura
Islay
Inner Hebrides
Coll
Tiree
North Channel
Bangor
Belfast
Ballymena
Coleraine
REPUBLIC OF IRELAND
A1
A68
A696
A697
A69
A7
M6
A595
M74
A75
A76
A70
A71
A77
M8
M9
A702
A703
A8
A78
A737
A82
A811
A84
A85
A816
A83
A9
A90
A92
A91
A93
M90
A5
A26
M2

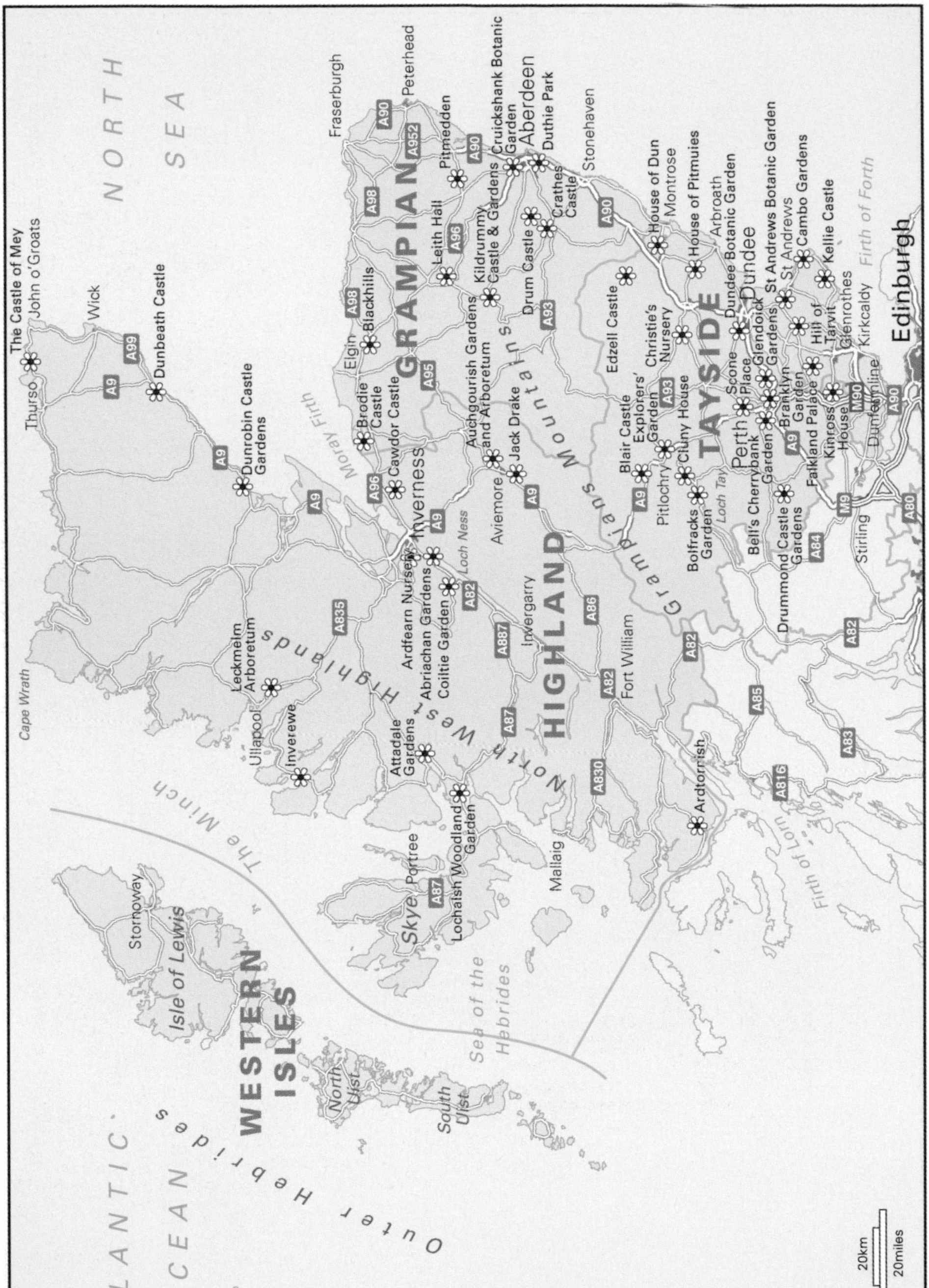

NORTH SEA
ATLANTIC OCEAN
Outer Hebrides
The Minch
Sea of the Hebrides
Moray Firth
Firth of Forth
Firth of Lorn
WESTERN ISLES
Isle of Lewis
Stornoway
North Uist
South Uist
Skye
Portree
Cape Wrath
Thurso
The Castle of Mey
John o'Groats
Wick
Dunbeath Castle
Dunrobin Castle Gardens
Leckmelm Arboretum
Ullapool
Inverewe
Attadale Gardens
Lochalsh Woodland Garden
Mallaig
North West Highlands
HIGHLAND
Ardfearn Nursery
Abriachan Gardens
Coiltie Garden
Loch Ness
Invergarry
Fort William
Ardtornish
Inverness
Cawdor Castle
Brodie Castle
Elgin
Blackhills
GRAMPIAN
Fraserburgh
Peterhead
Pitmedden
Leith Hall
Kildrummy Castle & Gardens
Cruickshank Botanic Garden
Aberdeen
Duthie Park
Crathes Castle
Drum Castle
Stonehaven
Auchgourish Gardens and Arboretum
Aviemore
Jack Drake
Grampian Mountains
Blair Castle
Pitlochry
Explorers' Garden
Cluny House
Bolfracks Garden
Loch Tay
Christie's Nursery
Edzell Castle
House of Dun
Montrose
House of Pitmuies
Arbroath
Dundee Botanic Garden
Dundee
TAYSIDE
Perth
Scone Place
Glendoick Gardens
Branklyn Garden
Bell's Cherrybank Garden
St Andrews Botanic Garden
St Andrews
Cambo Gardens
Kellie Castle
Hill of Tarvit
Falkland Palace
Kinross House
Glenrothes
Kirkcaldy
Dunfermline
Drummond Castle Gardens
Stirling
Edinburgh
A9
A99
A835
A96
A82
A887
A87
A86
A830
A95
A98
A90
A952
A93
M90
M9
A80
A84
A85
A83
A816
20km
20miles
N

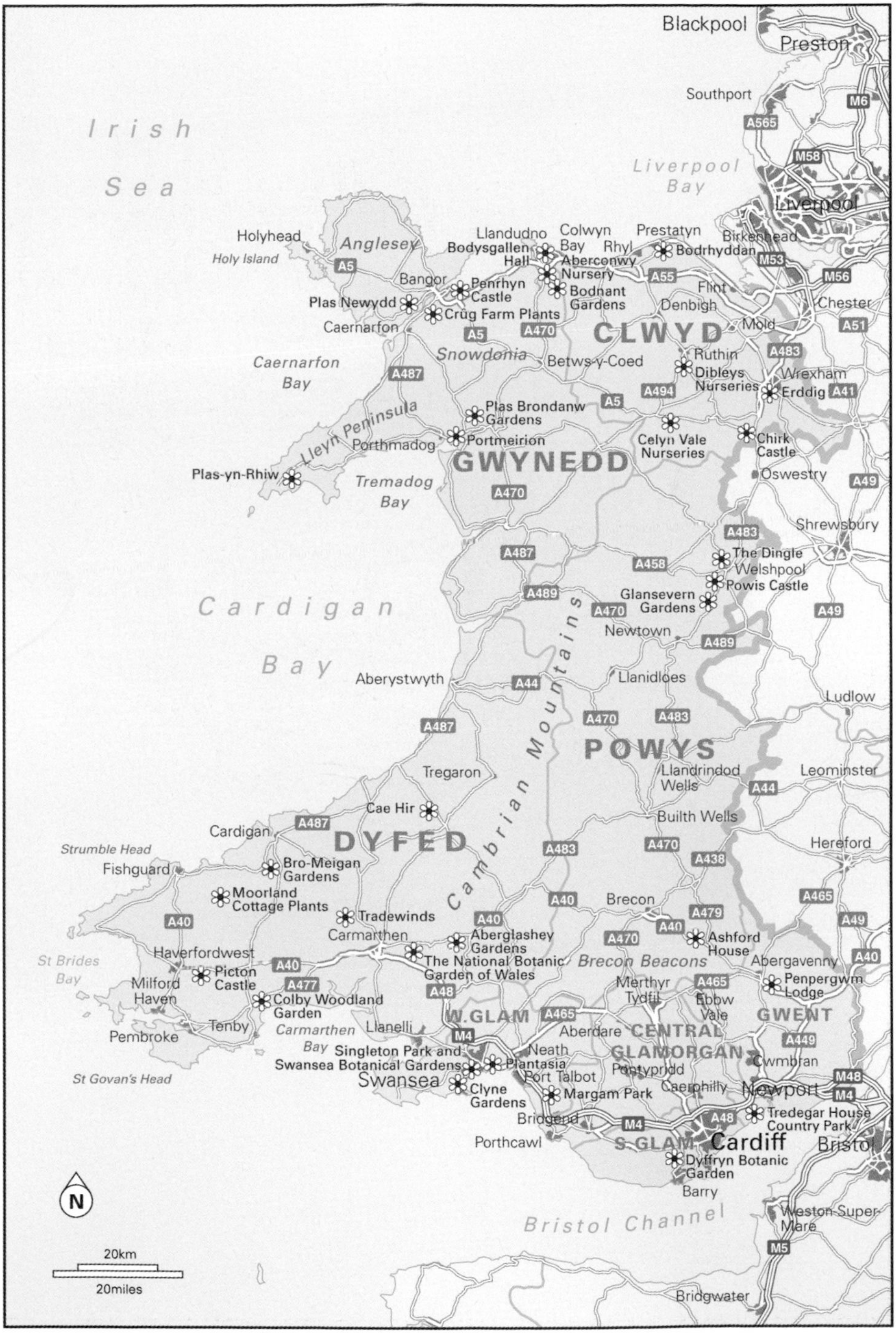
Blackpool
Preston
Southport
M6
A565
Irish
Sea
M58
Liverpool
Bay
Liverpool
Holyhead
Anglesey
Holy Island
A5
Llandudno
Bodysgallen
Hall
Colwyn
Bay
Rhyl
Prestatyn
Bodrhyddan
Birkenhead
Aberconwy
Nursery
M53
A55
Flint
M56
Bangor
Penrhyn
Castle
Bodnant
Gardens
Denbigh
Chester
Plas Newydd
Crûg Farm Plants
Caernarfon
A5
A470
CLWYD
Mold
A51
Caernarfon
Bay
Snowdonia
Betws-y-Coed
Ruthin
A483
A487
Dibleys
Nurseries
Wrexham
Erddig
A494
A41
Lleyn Peninsula
Plas Brondanw
Gardens
A5
Porthmadog
Portmeirion
Celyn Vale
Nurseries
Chirk
Castle
GWYNEDD
Plas-yn-Rhiw
Oswestry
Tremadog
Bay
A470
A49
Shrewsbury
A483
A487
The Dingle
Welshpool
A458
Powis Castle
A489
Glansevern
Gardens
Cardigan
A470
A49
Newtown
A489
Bay
Llanidloes
Aberystwyth
A44
Ludlow
A487
A470
A483
Cambrian Mountains
POWYS
Llandrindod
Wells
Leominster
Tregaron
A44
Cae Hir
Builth Wells
Cardigan
A487
DYFED
Strumble Head
A483
A470
Hereford
Fishguard
Bro-Meigan
Gardens
A438
Moorland
Cottage Plants
A465
Tradewinds
A40
Brecon
A40
A40
A479
A49
Carmarthen
Aberglashey
Gardens
A470
A40
Ashford
House
St Brides
Bay
Haverfordwest
The National Botanic
Garden of Wales
Brecon Beacons
Abergavenny
A40
Milford
Haven
Picton
Castle
A40
A477
Merthyr
Tydfil
A465
Penpergwm
Lodge
Colby Woodland
Garden
A48
Ebbw
Vale
W.GLAM
A465
GWENT
Pembroke
Tenby
Carmarthen
Bay
Llanelli
M4
Aberdare
CENTRAL
GLAMORGAN
A449
Singleton Park and
Swansea Botanical Gardens
Neath
Plantasia
Cwmbran
St Govan's Head
Swansea
Port Talbot
Pontypridd
Clyne
Gardens
Margam Park
Caerphilly
Newport
M48
M4
Bridgend
A48
Tredegar House
Country Park
M4
Porthcawl
S.GLAM
Cardiff
Bristol
Dyffryn Botanic
Garden
Barry
N
Bristol Channel
Weston-Super-
Mare
20km
20miles
M5
Bridgwater

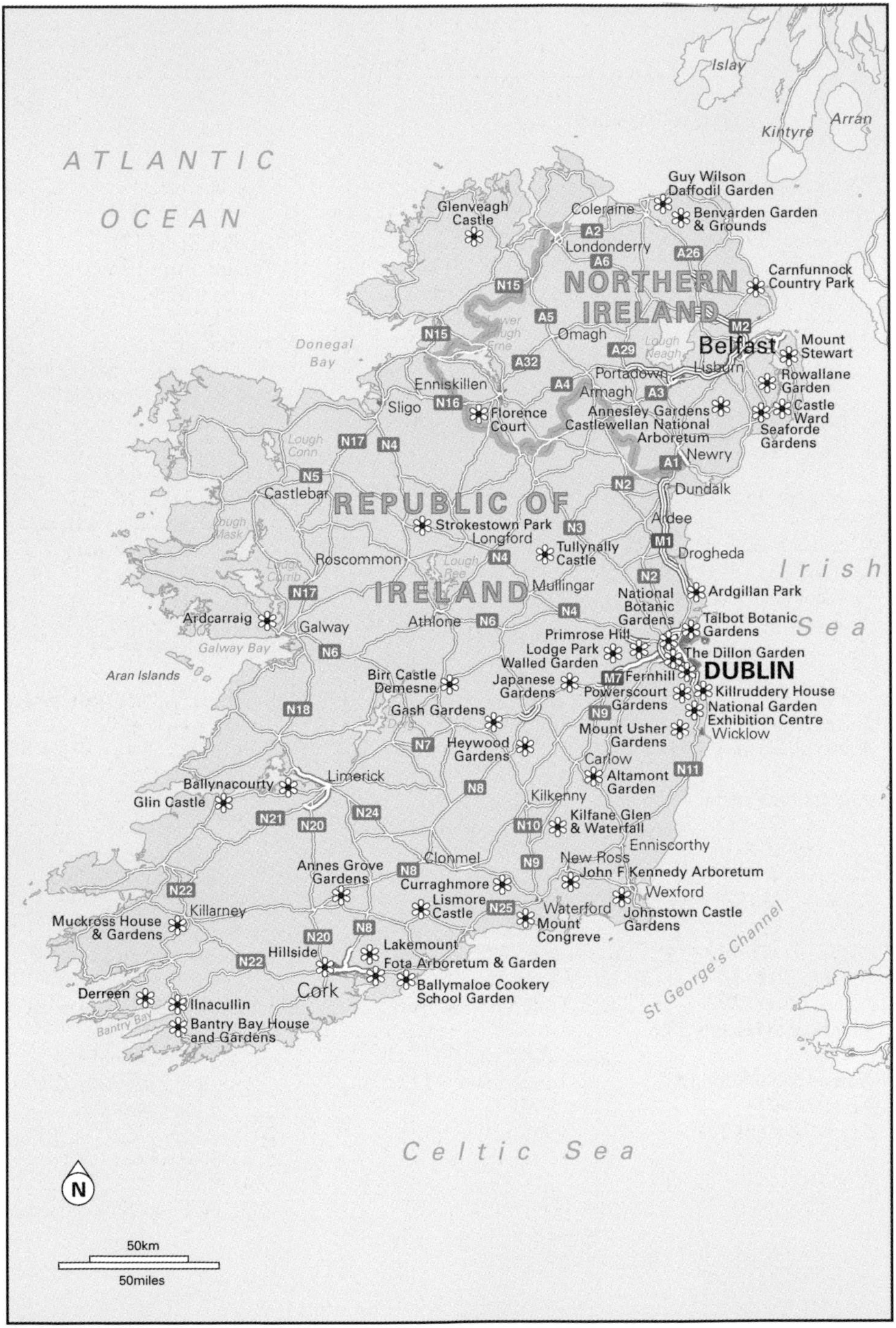

ATLANTIC OCEAN
Islay
Kintyre
Arran
NORTHERN IRELAND
REPUBLIC OF IRELAND
Irish Sea
Celtic Sea
St George's Channel
Guy Wilson Daffodil Garden
Benvarden Garden & Grounds
Coleraine
Londonderry
Glenveagh Castle
Carnfunnock Country Park
Omagh
Belfast
Mount Stewart
Lisburn
Portadown
Rowallane Garden
Enniskillen
Armagh
Sligo
Florence Court
Annesley Gardens
Castlewellan National Arboretum
Castle Ward
Seaforde Gardens
Newry
Donegal Bay
Lough Conn
Castlebar
Dundalk
Strokestown Park
Longford
Ardee
Tullynally Castle
Drogheda
Roscommon
Mullingar
Ardgillan Park
National Botanic Gardens
Talbot Botanic Gardens
Ardcarraig
Galway
Athlone
Galway Bay
Aran Islands
Primrose Hill
Lodge Park Walled Garden
The Dillon Garden
DUBLIN
Fernhill
Birr Castle Demesne
Japanese Gardens
Powerscourt Gardens
Killruddery House
National Garden Exhibition Centre
Gash Gardens
Mount Usher Gardens
Wicklow
Heywood Gardens
Carlow
Altamont Garden
Limerick
Ballynacourty
Glin Castle
Kilkenny
Kilfane Glen & Waterfall
Enniscorthy
Clonmel
New Ross
John F Kennedy Arboretum
Annes Grove Gardens
Curraghmore
Wexford
Lismore Castle
Waterford
Johnstown Castle Gardens
Mount Congreve
Killarney
Muckross House & Gardens
Lakemount
Hillside
Fota Arboretum & Garden
Ballymaloe Cookery School Garden
Cork
Derreen
Ilnacullin
Bantry Bay
Bantry Bay House and Gardens
A2
A6
A26
N15
A5
M2
A29
A32
A4
A3
N16
N17
N4
A1
N5
N2
N3
M1
N2
N17
N4
N6
N6
N4
M7
N9
N18
N7
N8
N11
N21
N20
N24
N10
N9
N8
N22
N25
N20
N8
N22
N
50km
50miles

INDEX

The entries in **bold** refer to main entries

YOUR COMPLETE GUIDE TO GARDENING TOOLS & SUPPLIES

THE Gardener's COMPANION

INDEX

Able Gardener
...bringing comfort to gardening
Garden Accessories
Garden Tools
Children's Gardening
Gardening Gifts
Watering the Garden
Gardening Wear
Visit our web site to view over 300 products
www.ablegardener.co.uk
Phone for a brochure : +44(0)1738 639222
Able Products Ltd, Kilda Way, Perth PH1 3XS
Fax +44(0)1738 621177 sales@ablegardener.co.uk

Ask for a
FREE
NO-OBLIGATION
DEMONSTRATION

Centre for Alternative Technology
Buy Green By Mail
☎ 01654 705959
mail.order@cat.org.uk
www.cat.org.uk
Fast and friendly mail order service
Extensive range of Organic Growing and Gardening books and products to help you live a more environmentally friendly, sustainable lifestyle
Please phone for a free catalogue quoting RHS06

www.gardenitems.co.uk
Design, Style, and Innovation to your door

www.
Wildforms
.co.uk
Gardening for Wildlife
Large range of products designed to attract wildlife to your garden
• Bird feeders
• Nest boxes
• Feeding Stations
• Hedgehog homes
• Squirrel feeders
• Insect boxes
• Frog homes
• Bat boxes
• Field Guides
• Wildlife Gifts
email: pete@wildforms.co.uk
tel: 01776 870453

Centre Sales Ltd are proud to launch the Showa Floreo range of gardening gloves, which includes the Floreo 265, Ultra light supple and comfortable, these gloves are ideal for fruit picking and handling young, fragile plants. Coated with nitrile to resist abrasion and tearing, the joints are left uncoated for greater dexterity. There are seamless elasticated cuffs and the back of the hand is ventilated to limit perspiration. Available in sizes 6,7,8 and 9.

Also included in the range are the Floreo 310 Grip glove, which is knitted from natural cotton and polyester, for lightness and suppleness, these gloves excel when it comes to outdoor work, gardening, pruning and horticulture.

Available in sizes 7,8,9 and 10. To view our full range of gloves, including the Rostaing and CSM brands, together with Joseph Bentley stainless steel garden tools, visit our website **www.centresalesgloves.co.uk** or telephone us on **01527 832092** for a colour catalogue. Alternatively, visit us at one of the RHS garden shows.

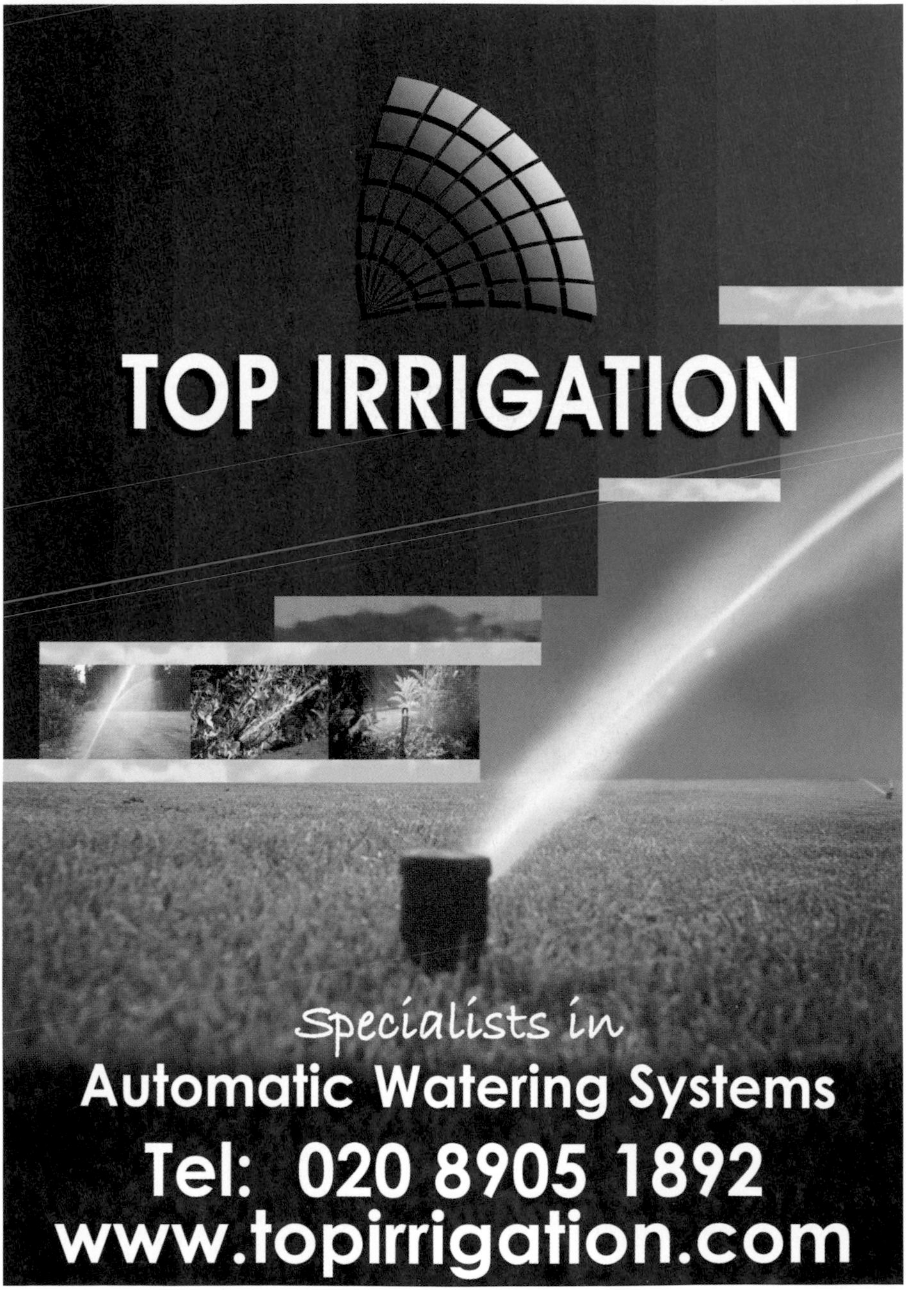
TOP IRRIGATION
Specialists in
Automatic Watering Systems
Tel: 020 8905 1892
www.topirrigation.com

Photo credits

Abbey Dore Court Gardens: Simon Ward
Abbey House: Ian & Barbara Pollard
Abbots Ripton Hall: Gavin Smith
American Museum: American Museum in Britain
Arley Hall: Jerry Davis
Belmont House and Gardens: David Archer, owner Belmont (Harris) Charity
Birr Castle Demesne: Birr Scientific & Heritage Foundation
Bressingham Gardens: Adrian Bloom/ Bloom Pictures
Brodsworth Hall and Gardens: Dan Booth/David Avery
Burton Agnes Hall: Burton Agnes Hall Gardens
Capel Manor: Capel Manor College and Gardens
Castle Howard: Castle Howard
Castlewellan Arboretum: Northern Ireland Forest Service
Cawdor Castle: Cawdor Castle Ltd
Chatto Gardens: Steven Wooster
Chenies Manor House: Mark Garton
Cothay Manor: Andrew Lawson
Cottesbrooke Hall and Gardens: Cottesbrooke Hall and Gardens
Denmans Garden: John Brookes
Docton Mills: Oscha Productions and Joe Bradford
Dyffryn Gardens: Vale of Glamorgan Council
East Ruston: East Ruston
Groombridge Place Gardens: Groombridge Place Gardens
Great Dixter House and Gardens: Jonathan Buckle/Perry Rodriguez
Haddon Hall: Nick McCann
Harewood House: The Harewood House Trust
Hestercombe Gardens: Andrew Lawson/ Jason Ingram
High Beeches Gardens: Susannah Bray, Edward Boscawen
Iford Manor: Chloe Hignett
Irish National Stud: Tim Hannan/ Martin Hickey
Kiftsgate: Andrew Lawson
Knoll Gardens: Dianna Jazwinski
Larch Cottage Nurseries: Joy Batey, Larch Cottage Nurseries
Leeds Castle: Leeds Castle Foundation
Levens Hall: Hal Bagot
Longstock Nursery Gardens: Peter Moore
Lydney: Derek Asken
Marwood Hill: Evanda Hill
Mill Gardens: Diana Levett
Mount Edgcumbe: Mount Edgcumbe
NTS Pics: Reproduced by kind permission of the National Trust for Scotland
Plant World Botanic Gardens: Plant World Devon Ltd
Powerscourt Gardens: Suzanne Clarke
RHS Garden Wisley: Clay Perry
Royal Botanic Gardens Edinburgh: RBGE
Stone House Cottage: Louisa Arbuthnott
Trebah Gardens: Trebah Garden Trust
Trewithen: Gary Long/Rupert Tenison
West Dean Gardens: West Dean Gardens, Steve Speller; Apple Store, Simon Ward
Winterbourne Botanic Gardens: Lee Hale
York Gate: John Whitaker